Understanding corporate reports:

A guide to financial statement analysis

Understanding corporate reports:
A guide to financial statement analysis

Leopold A. Bernstein

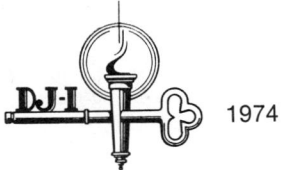

1974

Dow Jones-Irwin, Inc.   Homewood, Illinois   60430

© RICHARD D. IRWIN, INC., 1974

All rights reserved. No part of this publication may be reproduced, stored in a retrieval system, or transmitted, in any form or by any means, electronic, mechanical, photocopying, recording, or otherwise, without the prior written permission of the publisher.

A classroom edition of this book is published by Richard D. Irwin, Inc. under the title *Financial Statement Analysis: Theory, Application, and Interpretation* with additional chapters and problems.

This publication is designed to provide accurate and authoritative information in regard to the subject matter covered. It is sold with the understanding that the publisher is not engaged in rendering legal, accounting, or other professional service. If legal advice or other expert assistance is required, the services of a competent professional person should be sought.
From a Declaration of Principles jointly adopted by a Committee of the American Bar Association and a Committee of Publishers.

First Printing, September 1974
Second Printing, August 1975

ISBN 0-87094-084-8
Library of Congress Catalog Card No. 74–7869
Printed in the United States of America

To
University Distinguished Professor
Emanuel Saxe
Teacher, Colleague, and Friend

Preface

THIS BOOK aims to impart to the reader a comprehensive understanding of financial statements and of the tools and methods employed in their analysis. This book should prove of value to all those who need a thorough understanding of the uses to which financial statements are put as well as to those who must know how to use them intelligently and effectively. This encompasses *accountants, investors, security analysts, lending officers, credit analysts, managers,* and all others who must make decisions on the basis of financial data.

Investors, security analysts, lending officers, and *credit analysts, as well as others with financial responsibilities* will find in this work a discussion of accounting concepts and measurements undertaken from their point of view as users of such data. They will learn, in Part III, how such knowledge of the accounting framework is integrated with the best tools and techniques that are available for the analysis and interpretations of financial statements.

Accountants should benefit from this book in two major ways: (1) By obtaining a full appreciation of the uses to which the end-product of their work is put, they will be in a better position to improve upon it and to make it more responsive to the needs of users of financial statements. (2) Primarily because the analysis of financial statements demands a thorough understanding of how and on what bases financial statements are constructed, accountants have often been called upon to aid in their analysis and interpretation. The study of the tools and techniques of financial statement analysis will open to the accountant important opportunities for the creative extension of his basic services into areas which are often as intellectually satisfying as they are financially rewarding.

Investing, lending, and other financial decisions require the ability to forecast—to foresee. Alfred North Whitehead assured us that foresight can be taught when he wrote: "Foresight depends upon understanding. In practical affairs it is a habit. But the habit of foreseeing is elicited by the habit of understanding. To a large extent, understanding can now be acquired by a conscious effort and it can be taught. Thus the training of foresight is by the medium of understanding."

The keynote of this work, thus, is understanding. It focuses on understanding the data which are analyzed as well as the methods by which they are analyzed and interpreted.

August 1974   LEOPOLD A. BERNSTEIN

Contents

Part I
FINANCIAL STATEMENT ANALYSIS AND THE ACCOUNTING FRAMEWORK

1. Financial statement analysis and accounting   3

    The function of financial statement analysis. The raw material of analysis. Importance of accounting data. Limitations of accounting data: *Monetary expression. Simplifications and rigidities inherent in the accounting framework. Interim nature. Cost balances. Unstable monetary unit.* The function of accounting: *The recording function. Financial statements.*

2. Tools and techniques of financial statement analysis— an overview   16

    Basic approaches to financial statement analysis. The principal tools of analysis: *Comparative financial statements. Index-number trend series. Common-size financial statements. Ratio analysis. Specialized analysis.* Building blocks of financial statement analysis. Analytical review of accounting principles—Purposes and focus: *Example of importance of accounting assumptions, principles, and determinations: Illustration of a simple investment decision.*

Part II
FINANCIAL STATEMENTS—THE RAW MATERIAL OF ANALYSIS

3. Analysis of current assets   49

    Cash. Marketable securities: *Implications for analysis.* Receivables: *APB Opinion No. 21—"Interest on receivables and payables." Implications for*

x   Contents

financial analysis. Inventories: *Asset valuation. Cost accounting. Inventory cost flows. Inventory valuation at "market." Inventories under long-term contracts. Classification of inventories.* Implications for financial analysis.

4. **Analysis of noncurrent assets**   **72**

Long-term investments: *Investments in common stock. Implications for analysis.* Tangible fixed assets: *Asset valuation. Wasting assets. Method of acquisition. Implications for analysis.* Intangible assets: *Identifiable intangibles. Unidentifiable intangibles. Amortization of intangibles. Other considerations regarding the accounting for intangibles. Implication for analysis.* Prepaid expenses and deferred charges: *Prepaid expenses and deferred charges distinguished. Why costs are deferred. Research and development costs. Other types of deferred charges. Implications for analysis.* Unrecorded intangible or contingent assets.

5. **Analysis of liabilities**   **97**

Current liabilities. Long-term liabilities. Implications for analysis: *Assessing uncertainties. Evaluation of terms of indebtedness.* Obligations under leases: *Implications for analysis.* Commitments. Contingent liabilities. Deferred credits (income): *Deferred taxes. Deferred investment tax credit. Implications for analysis.* Reserves and provisions: *Implications for analysis.*

6. **Analysis of stockholders' equity**   **120**

Classification of capital stock: *Disclosure regarding capital stock. Additional capital. Treasury stock.* Retained earnings: *Dividends. Prior period adjustments. Appropriations of retained earnings. Restrictions on retained earnings.* Book value per share: *Significance of book value.* Implications for analysis.

7. **Intercorporate investments, business combinations and foreign operations**   **136**

Intercorporate investments: *Consolidated financial statements. The equity method. The cost method. Example of difference in income recognition—equity versus cost method. Intercorporate investments—less than majority ownership. Implications for analysis.* Accounting for business combinations: *Reasons for mergers. Distortions in accounting for mergers.* Accounting for business combinations: *Two methods.* Revised opinions on accounting for business combinations: *Pooling of interests and purchase accounting compared. Illustration of accounting mechanics: Purchase versus pooling of interest accounting. Pooling accounting. Purchase accounting. Implications for analysis. Pooling versus purchase accounting. Purchase accounting.* Accounting for foreign operations: *Foreign accounting practices and auditing standards. Translation of foreign currencies. Implications for analysis.*

8. **Analysis of the income statement—I**   **175**

A simple illustration. A variety of concepts of income. The accrual of revenue: *Conditions for revenue realization. Uncertainty as to collection*

Contents   xi

of receivables. Timing of revenue recognition. Contract accounting. Finance company accounting. Accounting for lease income. "Sales" to leasing subsidiaries. Additional examples of income recognition problems. Income of subsidiaries and affiliates. Implications for analysis. Cost and expense accrual: *Depreciation and depletion. Implication for analysis.*

9. **Analysis of the income statement—II**   **207**

   Pension costs and other supplementary employee benefits: *Pension costs. Other supplementary employee benefits. Implications for analysis.* Research, exploration, and development expenditures: *Types of research and development. The accounting problem. Exploration and development in extractive industries. Implications for analysis.* Goodwill: *Implications for analysis.* Interest costs: *Implications for analysis.* Income taxes: *Treatment of tax loss carry-backs and carry-forwards. Tax allocation. Investment tax credit. Implications for analysis.* Extraordinary gains and losses: *Implications for analysis.* The income statement—implications for analysis, an overview. Accounting changes: *Change in accounting principle. Change in accounting estimate. Change in reporting entity. Correction of an error. Materiality. Historical summaries of financial information. Implications for analysis.*

10. **Earnings per share—computation and evaluation**   **246**

    Major provisions of APB *Opinion No. 15: Simple capital structure. Computation of weighted average of common shares outstanding.* Complex capital structure: *Primary EPS. Fully diluted EPS. Requirements for additional disclosures in conjunction with the presentation of EPS data. Elections at the time EPS opinion became effective.* Comprehensive illustration of computation of EPS: *Facts and data.* Implications for analysis: *Statement accounting for changes in earnings per share.*

11. **Statements of changes in financial position— funds and cash**   **269**

    Significance and purpose. Two major concepts of liquidity. Statement of changes in financial position—a broader concept: *Basis of preparation. Analysis of fixed assets accounts. Additional data. Arriving at "source of funds form operation." The statement of sources and applications of funds. Illustration of "T-account" technique. Fixed assets. Accumulated depreciation. Goodwill. Bonds payable. Deferred income taxes. Capital stock and paid-in capital. Retained earnings. Analysis of changes in each element of working capital. Abbreviated method.* Statement of sources and applications of cash: *Technique of preparation. Additional provisions of APB Opinion No. 19. Implications for analysis.* Cash flow. Depreciation—A source of funds?

12. **Effects of price level changes on financial statements**   **295**

    Depreciation. Inventories. The need for comprehensive restatement of financial statements. Research and professional pronouncement. Principles underlying the preparation of price level adjusted financial statements. Extended illustration of statement restatement—illustration 4: *What the restated figures mean.* Implications for analysis. Limitations of restatement technique. Interpretation of effects of price level changes.

13. The auditor's opinion—meaning and significance 315

What the analyst needs to know: *Knowing the auditor. What the auditor's opinion means.* The auditor's report: *The scope of the audit. The opinion section.* Conditions giving rise to qualifications, disclaimers, or adverse opinions. Categories of qualified opinions: *Qualification—"except-for" type. Disclaimer of opinion. Adverse opinions. Limitations in the scope of the audit. Failure of financial statements to conform to generally accepted accounting principles. Financial statements subject to unresolved known uncertainties. Exceptions as to consistency. Long-form report. Special reports. Unaudited reports.* Implications for analysis: *Implications inherent in the audit process. Implications stemming from the standards which govern the auditor's opinion. Qualification, disclaimers, and adverse opinions.*

Part III
FINANCIAL STATEMENT ANALYSIS— THE MAIN AREAS OF EMPHASIS

14. Analysis of short-term liquidity 339

Significance of short-term liquidity. Working capital: *Current assets. Current liabilities. Other problem areas in definition of current assets and liabilities.* Working capital as a measure of liquidity. Current ratio: *Limitations of the current ratio. Implications of the limitations to which the current ratio is subject. The current ratio as a valid tool of analysis.* Measures which supplement the current ratio. Measures of accounts receivable liquidity. Average accounts receivable turnover ratio: *Collection period for accounts receivable. Evaluation.* Measures of inventory turnover: *Inventory turnover ratio. Days to sell inventory. The effect of alternative methods of inventory measurement.* Current liabilities: *Differences in the "nature" of current liabilities. Days purchases in accounts payable ratio.* Interpretation of the current ratio: *Examination of trend. Interpretation of changes over time. Possibilities of manipulation. The use of "rules of thumb" standards. The net trade cycle. Valid working capital standards. The importance of sales. Common-size analysis of current assets composition. The liquidity index.* Acid-test ratio. Other measures of short-term liquidity: *Cash flow ratios.*

15. Funds flow analysis and financial forecasts 374

Overview of cash flow and funds flow patterns. Short-term cash forecasts: *Importance of sales estimates. Pro forma financial statements as an aid to forecasting. Illustration of techniques of short-term cash forecasting.* Differences between short-term and long-term forecasts. Analysis of statements of changes in financial position: *First illustration of statement of changes in financial position analysis. Second illustration of statement of changes in financial position analysis. Third illustration of statement of changes in financial position analysis.* Evaluation of the statement of changes in financial position. Projection of statements of changes in financial position: *The impact of adversity.* Inclusion of "funds flow" and earnings forecasts in prospectuses.

Contents   xiii

16. Analysis of capital structure and long-term solvency   396

Importance of capital structure. Accounting principles: *Deferred credits. Long-term leases. Provisions and reserves. Commitments and contingent liabilities. Effect of intangible assets.* The significance of capital structure. Reasons for employment of debt: *The concept of financial leverage. The effect of tax deductibility of interest. Other advantages of leverage. Measuring the effect of financial leverage. Financial leverage index. Measuring the effect of capital structure on long-term solvency. Long-term projections—usefulness and limitations.* Capital structure analysis—common-size statements. Capital structure ratios: *Equity capital/total liabilities. Equity capital/long-term debt. Equity capital at market value.* Interpretation of capital structure measures. Measures of assets distribution. Measures of earnings coverage. Earnings available to meet fixed charges. Fixed charges to be included: *1. Interest on long-term debt. 2. Interest implicit in lease obligations. 3. Capitalized interest. 4. Other elements to be included in fixed charges.* Principal repayment requirements: *5. Other fixed charges. 6. Guarantees to pay fixed charges.* Illustration of earnings-coverage ratio calculations. Times-interest-earned ratio: *Computation of coverage ratio for an individual bond issue.* Ratios of earnings to fixed charges: *Fixed-charges-coverage ratio—the SEC standard. Fixed-charges-coverage ratios—expanded concept of fixed charges.* Recognition of benefits stemming from fixed charges. Computation of coverage ratio—expanded concept of fixed charges. Pro forma computations of coverage ratio. Cash flow coverage of fixed charges. Stability of "flow of funds from operations." Earnings coverage of preferred dividends. Evaluation of earnings-coverage ratios: *Importance of earnings variability. Importance of method of computation and of underlying assumptions. Examples of minimum standard of coverage.* Key elements in the evaluation of long-term solvency. Ratios as predictors of failure: *Empirical studies.* Conclusions.

17. Analysis of return on investment and of asset utilization   434

Diverse views of performance. Criteria of performance evaluation. Importance of return on investment (ROI). Major objectives in the use of ROI: *An indicator of managerial effectiveness. A method of projecting earnings. Internal decision and control tool.* Basic elements of ROI: *Defining the investment base. Difference between investor's cost and enterprise investment base. Averaging the investment base. Relating income to the investment base. Illustration of ROI computations.* Analysis and interpretation of ROI. Analysis of asset utilization: *Evaluation of individual turnover ratios. Use of averages. Other factors to be considered in return of asset evaluation.* Equity growth rate. Return on shareholders' equity. Equity turnover. Measuring the financial leverage index. Analysis of financial leverage effects.

18. Analysis of results of operation—I   458

The significance of income statement analysis. The major objectives of income analysis: *What is the income of the enterprise? What elements in the income statement can be used in forecasts? Determining the trend of income over the years.* Analysis of components of the income statement: *Accounting principles used and their implication. Tools of income statement analysis.* The analysis of sales and revenues: *Major sources of revenue.* Financial reporting by diversified enterprises: *Reasons for the need for data by significant enterprise segments. Disclosure of "line of business" data. Income statement data. Balance sheet data. Ratios, trend indices, and other measures of activity. Recommendations by the APB. Recommendations of research studies. SEC reporting requirements. Implications for analysis. Stability and trend of revenues. Methods of revenue determination.*

19. Analysis of results of operations—II   478

Analysis of cost of sales. Gross profit: *Factors in the analysis of gross profit.* Analysis of changes in gross margin. Examples of analysis of change in gross margin: *Interpretation of changes in gross margin.* Break-even analysis: *Concepts underlying break-even analysis. Equation approach. Graphic presentation. Steps in preparation. Contribution margin approach. Slide rule problem—additional considerations. Break-even technique—problem areas and limitations. Break-even analysis—uses and their implications. Analytical implications of break-even analysis. The significance of the variable cost percentage. The significance of the fixed cost level. The importance of the contribution margin.* Additional considerations in the analysis of cost of sales. Depreciation. Amortization of special tools and similar costs. Maintenance and repairs costs. Other costs and expenses—general: *Selling expenses. Future directed marketing costs.* General, administration, financial, and other expenses: *Financial costs. "Other" expenses.* Other income. Income taxes. The operating ratio. Net income ratio: *Statement accounting for variation in net income.*

20. The evaluation and projection of earnings   511

Objectives of earnings evaluation: *Evaluation of earnings level. The projection of earnings.* Evaluation of discretionary and future-directed costs: *Maintenance and repairs. Advertising. Research and development costs. Other future-directed costs.* Extraordinary gains and losses: *Significance of accounting treatment and presentation. Analysis and evaluation.* Balance sheet analysis as a check on the validity and quality of reported earnings: *Importance of carrying amounts of assets. Importance of provisions and liabilities. Balance sheet analysis and the quality of earnings. Effect of valuation of specific assets on the validity and quality of reported income.* Monitoring earnings trend: *Methods of earnings averaging and trend determination.* The evaluation of earnings trends. Interim earnings: *Year-end adjustments. Seasonality. APB Opinion No. 28. Revised SEC reporting requirements. Implications for analysis.*

21. Comprehensive analysis of financial statements   542

The methodology of financial statement analysis. Significance of the "building block" approach to financial analysis. The earmarks of good financial analysis. Special industry or environmental characteristics. Illustration of a comprehensive analysis of financial statements—Marine Supply Corporation: *Introduction. Financial statements. Additional information. Analysis of short-term liquidity. Analysis of funds flow. Analysis of capital structure and long-term solvency. Analysis of return on investment.*

Analysis of asset utilization. Analysis of operating performance. Summary and conclusions. Uses of the financial statement analysis. Computer assisted financial analysis: *1. Data storage and retrieval. 2. Specialized financial analysis.*

Index 579

part I
FINANCIAL STATEMENT ANALYSIS AND THE ACCOUNTING FRAMEWORK

1

Financial statement analysis and accounting

THE FUNCTION OF FINANCIAL STATEMENT ANALYSIS

FINANCIAL STATEMENT ANALYSIS is the judgmental process which aims to evaluate the current and past financial positions and the results of operations of an enterprise, with the primary objective of determining the best possible estimates and predictions about future conditions and performance.

Financial statement analysis may be undertaken for many purposes. The security analyst is interested in future earnings estimates and in financial strength as an important element in the determination of security values. The credit analyst wants to determine future funds flows and the resulting financial condition as a means of assessing the risks inherent in a particular credit extension. Present owners of securities analyze current financial statements to decide on whether to hold, enlarge, or sell their positions. Merger and acquisition analysts study and analyze financial statements as an essential part of their decision processes leading to recommendations regarding the merger and acquisition of business enterprises. These are examples of situations involving outsiders—external analysts—trying to reach conclusions principally on the basis of published financial data.

Internal financial analysts, on the other hand, utilize an even larger and more detailed pool of financial data to assess, for internal management and control purposes, the current financial condition and results of operations of an enterprise.

THE RAW MATERIAL OF ANALYSIS

The analytical processes which underlie the conclusions of security analysts, credit analysts, and other external analysts, as well as internal analysts, make use of a vast array of facts, information, and data—economic, social, political, and other. However, the most important quantitative data utilized by these analysts are the financial data which are the output of an enterprise's accounting system. Presented for external use, principally in the form of formal financial statements, these data are among the most important quantified elements in the entire mix of inputs utilized by the decision maker. Since financial accounting data are the product of a whole range of conventions, measurements, and judgments, their apparent precision and exactness can be misleading. Such data cannot be intelligently used in financial analysis without a thorough understanding of the accounting framework of which they are the end product, as well as of the conventions which govern the measurement of resources, liabilities, equities, and operating results of an enterprise. This text examines the accounting framework which underlies financial accounting data as well as the tools of analysis which have been found useful in the analysis and interpretation of such data.

IMPORTANCE OF ACCOUNTING DATA

Decision processes, such as those relating to the choice of equity investments or the extension of credit, require a great variety of data possessing a wide range of reliability and relevance to the decision at hand. The information used includes data on general economic conditions and on industry trends, as well as data on intangibles such as the character and the motivation of the management group. Financial statements and other data emanating from the accounting process represent measurable indicia of performance already achieved and of financial conditions presently prevailing.

In any given decision situation, the relative importance of unquantifiable intangibles, as against quantified actual experience reflected in financial statements, will, of course, vary. Nevertheless, in most cases no intelligent, well-grounded decision can be made without an analysis of the quantifiable data found in financial accounting reports.

In the realm of data available for meaningful analysis, financial statements are important because they are objective in that they portray actual events which already happened; they are concrete in that they can be quantified; and being quantifiable they can, perhaps most importantly, be measured. This attribute of measurability endows financial statement data with another important characteristic: since they are expressed in the common denominator of money, this enables us to add and combine the data, to relate them to other data, and to otherwise manipulate them arithmetically. The above attributes contribute to the great importance of financial accounting data, both historical or projected, to the decision-making process.

LIMITATIONS OF ACCOUNTING DATA

Recognition of the importance of financial accounting data should be tempered by a realization of the limitations to which they are subject. The following sections discuss some of the more important limitations.

Monetary expression

The first and most obvious limitation is that financial statements can only present information that lends itself to quantification in terms of the monetary unit; some significant facts about the enterprise do not lend themselves to such measurement. For example, the financial statements, as such, contain very little direct information about the character, motivation, experience, or age of the human resources. They do not contain, except in terms of aggregate final results, information about the quality of the research and development effort or the breadth of the marketing organization. Nor can we expect to find in the financial statements any detailed information on product lines, machinery efficiency, or advance planning. Equally absent will be information on organization structure and on such behavioral problems as the fact that the marketing manager is not on speaking terms with the controller, or that the entire success of the enterprise hinges on the talents of a single man. Nevertheless, without a uniform unit of measurement, financial statements, as we know them, would not be possible.

Simplifications and rigidities inherent in the accounting framework

The portrayal by means of accounting statements of highly complex and diverse economic activities involves the need for simplification, summarization, and the use of judgments and estimates.

The simplification process is necessary in order to classify the great variety of economic events into a manageable number of categories. Inevitably, this simplification can be achieved only at the expense of clarity and detail which, in some instances, may be useful to the user of financial data.

The need to keep the size of and detail in the financial statements within reasonable bounds requires a high degree of summarization of economic events both in the initial recording of these events in the accounting records and subsequently in the preparation of the financial statements. Inevitably, in the process of such summarization, financial statements lose, perhaps more often than they should, comprehensiveness of description and clarity.

The use of estimation and judgment in financial statements is inevitable. The limitation to be recognized here is the resulting variety in the quality and reliability of financial statement presentations. Financial statements may not be of uniform quality and reliability because of differences in the character and the quality of judgments exercised by accountants in their preparation.

Present-day financial statements are historical in nature, and their use for predictive purposes calls for the application of informed judgment by the user. Moreover, financial statements are general-purpose presentations; the extent of detail reflected therein is determined by the accounting profession's current view of the "average reader's" requirements and expectations. Such envisioned requirements do not necessarily coincide with those of a user with a specific purpose in mind.

Interim nature

A further limitation of financial statements stems from the need to report for relatively short periods of the total life-span of an enterprise To be useful, accounting information must be timely; and therefore determinations of financial condition and results of operations must be made frequently. But such frequency of reporting, particularly on the results of operations, requires a great deal of calculation based on judgments; and the greater the degree of such estimation required, the greater the amount of uncertainty that is inevitably introduced into the financial statements.

It is important to clarify the connection between the length of a period reported on and the degree of accounting uncertainty introduced. Many business transactions and operations require a long period of time for final completion and determination of results. For example, fixed assets are acquired for a long period of usefulness. The longer such period of use, the more tentative must be the estimates of their ultimate useful life-span. Similarly, the value, if any, of investments in research and development may not become apparent until many accounting periods after the one in which they are incurred. Long-term contracts are another example in which the greater the length of time involved, the more tentative the estimation process must be.

Cost balances

It is a basic convention of accounting that accounting determinations be subject to objective ascertainment. Since the cost of an asset arrived at by arm's-length bargaining may generally be objectively determined by inspection, it is claimed that the cost figure enjoys an objectivity surpassing any subsequent unrealized appraisal of value. Primarily for this reason accounting adheres, with few exceptions, to the cost concept. The price we pay for this objectivity in accounting adds up to yet another important limitation upon the usefulness of accounting statements. Cost balances do not, in most cases, represent current market values. Yet the user of financial statements usually looks for an assessment of value, and to him, historical cost balances are of very limited usefulness. Moreover, the analyst must be aware of valuation bases other than cost which are used in financial statements.

Unstable monetary unit

The first accounting limitation which we discussed above identified accounting expressions as being limited to those which could be expressed in monetary terms. The advantage of the monetary expression is, of course, that it provides a common denominator and enables us to add up the cost aggregates of such diverse assets as, say, shares of stock, tons of lead, and store furniture.

Over the years, however, the value of money in terms of general purchasing power has undergone significant fluctuations and generally has had a pronounced downward trend. The monetary unit has not retained its quality as a "standard of value" and, consequently, adding up the money cost of goods purchased in year 19x1 with those bought in 19x8 may result in serious distortions.

While the accounting profession has recognized that "the assumption that fluctuations in the value of money can be ignored is unrealistic," not much has been done in practice to issue supplementary statements which would shed light on the effect of price level changes on the conventional financial statements. Thus, the financial presentations found today remain subject to this serious limitation. The effect of price level changes on accounting determinations is examined in Chapter 12.

Having explored the relationship of financial statement analysis to the decision-making process and to the accounting framework on which it relies, we turn next to a more comprehensive consideration of the accounting process.

THE FUNCTION OF ACCOUNTING

Accounting is concerned with the quantitative expression of economic phenomena. As a discipline, it evolved from a need for a framework for recording, classifying, and communicating economic data. In the basic form existing today, it reflects the constant change and modification which it has undergone since its inception, in response to changing social and economic needs.

One of the best and most succinct definitions of the functions of accounting is found in *Accounting Research Study No. 1*, entitled "The Basic Postulate of Accounting,"[1] which had as its aim the identification of the postulates or conventions of the discipline. According to this study,

The function of accounting is:

(1) to measure the resources held by specific entities;
(2) to reflect the claims against and the interests in those entities;
(3) to measure the changes in those resources, claims and interests;
(4) to assign the changes to specifiable period of time; and
(5) to express the foregoing in terms of money as a common denominator.

The function and purposes of accounting are accomplished at two levels. One is the recording function which is that part of the discipline which governs the mechanics of recording and summarizing the multitude of transactions and economic events which occur in an enterprise and which can be quantified in terms of money. The other level, a more complex one and more subject to individual judgment and opinion, governs the methods, procedures, and principles by which accounting data are measured and presented. This chapter will concern itself with an examination of the recording level of the accounting discipline, while subsequent chapters will take up the conventions and principles which govern accounting measurements and their presentation.

The recording function

The recording function in accounting is governed by the principle of double-entry bookkeeping, an ingenious system of accounting which has stood the test of time since its description by an Italian mathematician in 1494.

The study of the theory of double-entry bookkeeping is an integral part of the study of accountancy. Users of accounting statements, as opposed to professional accountants, need have no detailed knowledge of the mechanical aspects of the subject. They will find, however, that a general understanding of the double-entry system will aid them significantly in the analysis of financial statements, which are an end product of this system.

The basic concept of the double-entry system is based on the duality of every business transaction. For example, if a business borrows $1,000,

---

[1] Maurice Moonitz, "The Basic Postulate of Accounting," *Accounting Research Study No. 1*. (New York: American Institute of Certified Public Accountants, 1961).

it acquires an asset (cash), and counterbalancing this is a claim against the enterprise (a liability) in an equal amount. Regardless of how many transactions an enterprise engages in, this duality and balance prevails at all times and provides the advantages of order, consistency, and control enjoyed under the system.

Continuing with a more generalized example, when an entity acquires an asset the counterbalancing effect results in one or a number of the following:

1. The incurrence of a liability.
2. The enlargement of the ownership's claim (capital funds).
3. The disposal of another asset.

Similarly, a liability is extinguished by:

1. The disposal of an asset, or
2. The enlargement of the ownership claim, or
3. Incurrence of another liability.

At all times the assets of an enterprise equal the outsider's claims against these assets (i.e., liabilities) and the equity of the ownership (i.e., capital). Thus, the basic equation prevailing under the double-entry system is:

$$\text{Assets} = \text{Liabilities} + \text{Capital}$$

An expense or a cost incurred in the operations of the enterprise is accompanied by one, or a combination of, the following:

1. Reduction of assets, or
2. Increase in liabilities, or
3. Increase in the ownership's claim.

Conversely, revenue received by the enterprise—

1. Increases assets, or
2. Decreases liabilities, or
3. Decreases the ownership's claim or affects a combination of the above.

Under the double-entry system, all transactions are recorded and classified and then summarized under appropriate account designations. Financial statements are formal, condensed presentations of the data derived from these accounts.

One of the best ways of visualizing the basic system of record-keeping and the principal interrelationships within it is by means of a diagram which portrays the major classes of accounts as well as the typical relationships among them.

Exhibit 1–1 is a graphic portrayal of the accounting cycle. A careful study of the illustration and the main movements reflected therein will

EXHIBIT 1-1
The accounting cycle

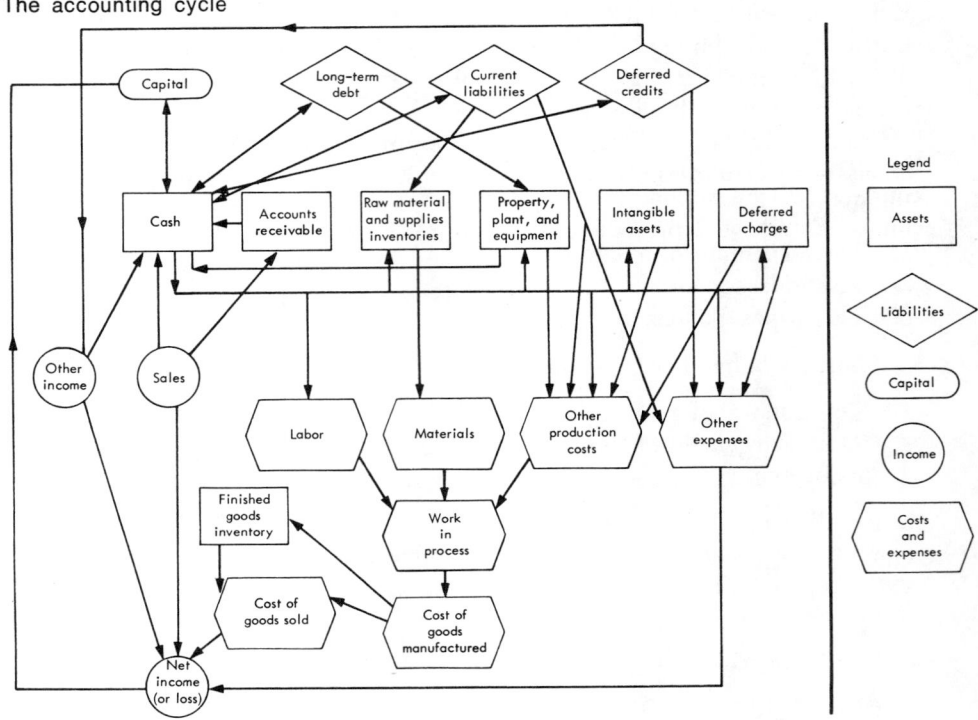

enable the reader to follow the principal basic financial relationships and flows within a manufacturing enterprise. For the sake of clarity, infrequent or unusual flows and relationships have not been included.

The arrows connecting the principal asset, liability, capital, income, cost, and expense accounts indicate the direction of the usual flows. They do not, of course, indicate the relative size of the flows, which vary considerably from business to business and from one set of circumstances to another. The reader will notice that no account is dead-ended, that is, there are flows in and out of all accounts. This simply emphasizes the dynamic aspects of business and the accounting system which portrays its financial flows. As management invests, buys, makes, incurs costs, and sells, the quantity of money represented in each account is changing while the system as a whole remains in balance, its debit accounts (generally assets, costs, and expenses) always equaling its credit accounts (generally capital, liabilities, and income).

The flows into and out of each account shown in Exhibit 1–1 can be clearly traced in the diagram, and the chapters which follow—on the measurement of assets, liabilities, capital, and income—should increase and sharpen the reader's understanding of these flows as well as the principles governing their measurement.

The flows shown in the diagram of Exhibit 1–1, while always expressed in dollars, can be in many forms, such as cash, costs, etc. Thus, for example, if we trace the inflows and outflows affecting the Property, Plant, and Equipment account in Exhibit 1–1, we can learn a great deal about the interrelationships among the various accounts. The reader can, of course, focus in similar fashion on any account or constellation of accounts. Exhibit 1–2 presents those accounts appearing in the accounting

EXHIBIT 1–2
Typical flows to and from the Property, Plant, and Equipment account

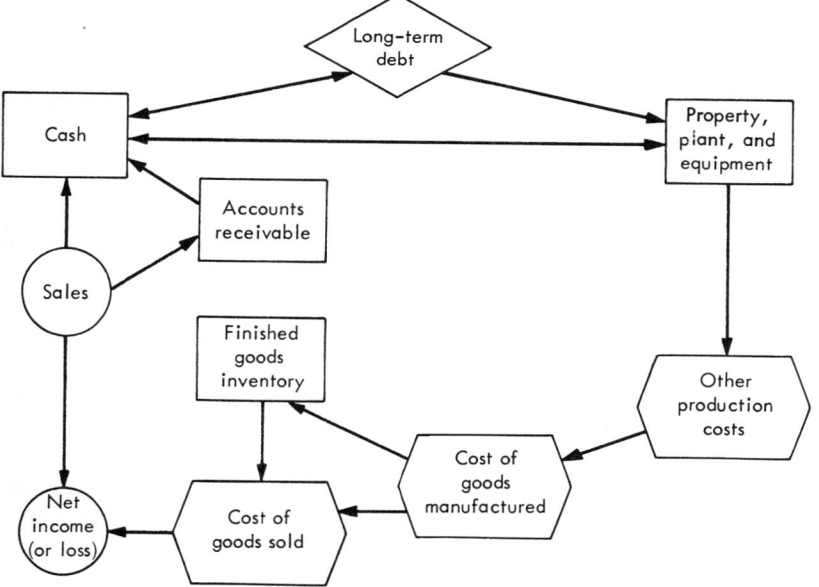

cycle diagram (Exhibit 1–1), which relate to the Property, Plant, and Equipment account and the flows into and out of it.

Three distinct phases can be discerned here:

1. The accounting for the acquisition and disposition of property, plant, and equipment (PPE).
2. The accounting for the use of PPE (depreciation).
3. Accounting for the recovery, out of revenue, of amounts invested in PPE.

Acquisition and disposition of PPE. The acquisition of PPE can be made by payment of cash or the incurrence of debt or both. Hence, the arrows in Exhibit 1–2 point to a flow from cash and/or long-term debt. Ultimately the debt is paid back by cash, and this accounts for the flow from cash toward long-term debt. The flow from PPE to cash represents instances where PPE is sold for cash at any stage of its use. In all cases the flows are equal, for example, an increase in PPE will result in an equal decrease in cash or a commensurate increase in long-term debt.

Use of PPE. PPE is acquired mostly for productive use. Consequently, its cost is allocated by means of the depreciation process (see Chapter 7) to "cost of goods manufactured." The flows shown in Exhibit 1–2 are from PPE to the "Other Production Costs" account from where they are charged to the "Costs of Goods Manufactured" account. The cost of goods manufactured which are sold is charged to the "Cost of Goods Sold" account which, in turn, flows into the Net Income (or Profit and Loss) account, where all cost and revenues of the period are accumulated. The unsold goods manufactured remain in the Finished Goods Inventory, which is an asset account to be carried over to the next period. Ultimately, when the finished goods are sold they find their way into the "Cost of Goods Sold" account.

Recovery of cost of PPE. To complete the cycle, we observe in Exhibit 1–2 that the sales of finished goods, which normally are made at amounts designed to recover all costs and earn a profit, generate sales which are either for cash or result in claims, such as accounts receivable which are subsequently collected in cash. It is through these sales that the outlay for PPE is ultimately recovered by the enterprise.

This completes our tracing of the Exhibit 1–2 subcycle of the accounting system where cash was used to buy PPE and was finally collected from the sale of the products in whose production the PPE was used. Examination of Exhibit 1–1 will reveal the existence of numerous other subcycles which make up the integrated whole.

Financial statements

The accounting system which we examined above continually collects, summarizes, and updates data on assets, liabilities, capital, revenues, costs, and expenses. Periodically it is necessary to take stock in order to ascertain the financial condition and the results of operations of the enterprise. This is done by presenting in summary form the details contained in the accounts. Based on the accounts included in the diagram of the accounting cycle (Exhibit 1–1) we can illustrate the composition of two major financial statements as follows:

Balance sheet (statement of financial condition). Exhibit 1–3 shows all assets, liabilities, and capital accounts extracted from Exhibit 1–1 and presented in conventional balance sheet format. This presentation

EXHIBIT 1–3
Statement of financial condition (balance sheet)

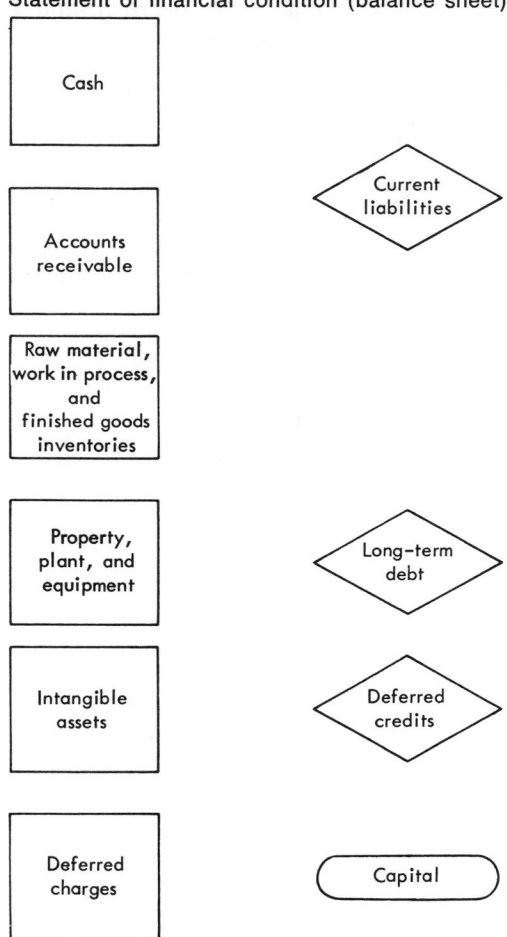

reveals a number of basic relationships worth noting. On the left side are all the assets and unexpired costs in which the resources of the enterprise are invested at a specific point in time. On the right side of the statement are the sources from which these invested funds were financed, that is, the liabilities and the equity (capital) accounts. Since the *current liabilities* represent a short-term claim against the enterprise, the balance sheet shows the *current assets* generally available to meet these claims, principally cash, accounts receivable, and inventories. The difference between current assets and current liabilities is the working capital.

14   Understanding corporate reports

Income statement (results of operations). The second major financial statement differs in some important respects from the balance sheet. The income statement format shown in Exhibit 1–4 does not show the

EXHIBIT 1–4
Income statement

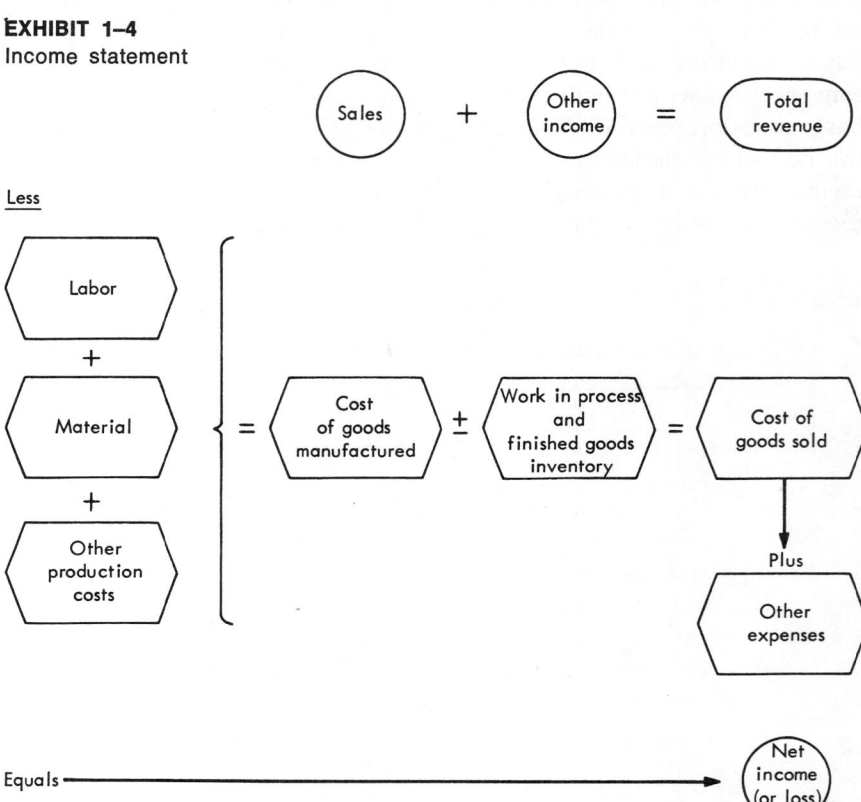

account balances as of a certain date, as is the case with the balance sheet, but rather shows the cumulative activity in the revenue, cost, and expense accounts for the period reported upon. This is a report on the dynamic aspects of the enterprise—its results of operations. The final net income (or loss) is added to or deducted from capital through the Retained Earnings account. Thus, the capital accounts link the net results of operations with the statement of financial condition.

Other financial statements explain other aspects of change. Thus, changes in the Retained Earnings account are detailed in financial statements. The statement of changes in financial position explains over a period of time changes in the net current funds available to the enterprise. It is examined more fully in Chapter 9.

Ingenious as the recording framework of accounting is, it represents only the mechanical aspects of the discipline. Controlling the method of recording of assets, liabilities, and capital, as well as the size and the timing of cost and revenue flows, is an elaborate and pervasive set of principles. These principles in turn reflect the application of the basic objectives and conventions of accountancy. Since this body of conventions and principles determines the methodology involved in the basic measurements in financial statements, as well as their form and the degree of disclosure therein, the intelligent analysis of these statements requires a thorough familiarity with, and an understanding of, these conventions and principles.

QUESTIONS

1. What is financial statement analysis?
2. Why are financial statements important to the decision process in financial analysis?
3. List some of the more important limitations to which accounting data are subject.
4. What are some of the simplifications and the rigidities inherent in the accounting framework?
5. Define briefly the function of accounting.
6. The functions and purposes of accounting are accomplished at two levels; describe them.
7. What is the basic equation prevailing under the double-entry system of bookkeeping?

2

Tools and techniques of financial statement analysis— an overview

Basic approaches to financial statement analysis

NOT EVERYONE who analyzes financial statements will want the same information from the same statement. Objectives differ from one group of analysts to another. The equity investor may want to know:

1. What has the company's operating performance been over the longer term and over the recent past? What does this record hold for future earnings prospects?
2. Has the company's earnings record been one of growth, stability, or decline? Does it display significant variability?
3. What is the company's current financial condition? What factors are likely to affect it in the near future?
4. What is the company's capital structure? What risks and rewards does it hold for the investor?
5. How does this company compare on the above counts with other companies in its industry?

The banker who is approached with a short-term loan request may look to the financial statements for answers to questions such as the following:

1. What are the underlying reasons for the company's needs for funds? Are these needs truly short term, and if so, will they be self-liquidating?
2. From what sources is the company likely to get funds for the payment of interest and the repayment of principal?
3. How has management handled its needs for short-term and long-term funds in the past? What does this portend for the future?

An important first step in any decision-making process is to identify the most significant, pertinent, and critical questions which have a bearing on the decision. Financial statement analysis does not, of course, provide answers to all such questions. However, each of the questions exemplified above can, to a significant extent, be answered by such analysis. Financial statement analysis utilizes a variety of approaches and techniques among which are the following:

Direct measurements. Some factors and relationships can be measured directly. For example, the relationship between the debt and the equity of an entity is a direct measurement. Both the amount of debt and that of equity can be measured in absolute terms (i.e., in dollars) and their relationship computed therefrom.

Indirect evidence. Financial statement analysis can provide indirect evidence bearing on important questions. Thus, the analysis of past statements of sources and applications of funds can offer evidence as to the financial habits of a management team. Moreover, the analysis of operating statements will yield evidence regarding management's ability to cope with fluctuations in the level of the firm's business activity. While such indirect evidence and evaluation are often not precise or quantifiable, the data derived therefore nevertheless possess importance because almost all managerial decisions, or the lack of them, are reflected in the entity's financial statements.

Predictive functions. Almost all decision questions, including those in the examples above, are oriented towards the future. Thus, an important measure of the usefulness of financial statement analysis tools and techniques is their ability to assist in the prediction of expected future conditions and results.

Comparison. This is a very important analytical process. It is based on the elementary proposition that in financial analysis no number standing by itself can be meaningful, and that it gains meaning only when related to some other comparable quantity. By means of comparison, financial analysis performs an important evaluative, as well as attention-directing and control, function. Thus, it focuses on exceptions and variations, and saves the analyst the need to evaluate the normal and the expected. Moreover, by means of comparison, selection among alternative choices is accomplished.

Comparison may be performed by using:

1. A company's own experience over the years (i.e., internally derived data);
2. External data, such as industry statistics; or
3. Compiled yardsticks, including standards, budgets, and forecasts.

Historical company data can usually be readily obtained and most readily adjusted for inconsistencies.

Useful comparison may also be made with external data. The advantages of external data are: (1) they have an objective and independent character to them; (2) they have been derived from similar operations, thus performing the function of a standard of comparison; and (3) if current, they reflect events occurring during an identical period having as a consequence similar business and economic conditions in common.

External information must, however, be used with great care and discrimination. Knowledge of the basis and method of compilation, the period covered, and the source of the information will facilitate a decision of whether the information is at all comparable. At times, sufficient detail may be available to adjust data so as to render them comparable. In any event, a decision on a proper standard of comparison must be made by choosing from those available. Differences between situations compared must be noted. Such differences may be in accounting practices or specific company policies. It must also be borne in mind that the past is seldom an unqualified guide to the future.

THE PRINCIPAL TOOLS OF ANALYSIS

In the analysis of financial statements, the analyst has available a variety of tools from which he can choose those best suited to his specific purpose. The following principal tools of analysis will be discussed in this chapter:

1. Comparative financial statements
    a) Year-to-year changes
2. Index-number trend series
3. Common-size financial statements
    a) Structural analysis
4. Ratio analysis
5. Specialized analyses
    a) Cash forecasts
    b) Analysis of changes in financial position
    c) Statement of variation in gross margin
    d) Break-even analysis

The application of these tools in this, as well as in the following, chapters will be illustrated by means of the financial statements of the hypothetical Finefood Corporation, a food wholesaler serving a large number of small independent grocers. The following are the basic financial statements whose analysis will be illustrated:

Exhibit

2–1 Comparative balance sheets, 19x1–x6
2–2 Income statement, years ending December 31, 19x3–x6
2–3 Condensed income statements, 19x1–x6

Comparative financial statements

The comparison of financial statements is accomplished by setting up balance sheets, income statements, or statements of changes in financial position, side by side and reviewing the changes which have occurred in individual categories therein from year to year and over the years.

The most important factor revealed by comparative financial statements is *trend*. The comparison of financial statements over a number of years will also reveal the direction, velocity, and the amplitude of trend. Further analysis can be undertaken to compare the trends in related items. For example, a year-to-year increase in sales of 10 percent accompanied by an increase in freight-out costs of 20 percent requires an investigation and explanation of the reasons for the difference. Similarly, an increase of accounts receivable of 15 percent during the same period would also warrant an investigation into the reasons for the difference in the rate of increase of sales as against that of receivables.

Year-to-year change. A comparison of financial statements over two to three years can be undertaken by computing the *year-to-year change* in absolute amounts and in terms of percentage changes. Longer term comparisons are best undertaken by means of *index-number trend series*.

Year-to-year comparisons of financial statements are illustrated in Exhibits 2–4 and 2–5. When a two- or three-year comparison is attempted, such presentations are manageable and can be understood by the reader. They have the advantage of presenting changes in terms of absolute dollar amounts as well as in percentages. Both have to be considered because the dollar size of the different bases on which percentage changes are computed may yield large percentage changes which are out of proportion to their real significance. For example, in the same financial statements, a 50 percent change from a base figure of $1,000 is far less significant than the same percentage change from a base of $100,000. Thus, reference to the dollar amounts involved is always necessary in order to retain the proper perspective and to reach valid

EXHIBIT 2–1

FINEFOOD CORPORATION
Comparative Balance Sheets, 19x1-x6

December 31

Assets	19x6	19x5	19x4	19x3	19x2	19x1
Current Assets:						
Cash on hand and on deposit	$ 24,659	$ 27,923	$ 18,240	$ 26,906	$ 11,818	$ 6,030
Accounts receivable, trade	136,875	73,436	53,550	62,813	37,506	50,028
Accounts and claims receivable, nontrade	174	4,095	395	388	1,402	1,105
Inventories:						
Groceries	$261,954*	$176,180*	$179,599*	$200,251*	$116,021*	$128,777
Frozen foods	60,027*	13,777	6,679	10,751	14,485	29,381
Total Inventories	$321,981	$189,957	$186,278	$211,002	$130,506	$158,158
Total Current Assets	$483,689	$295,411	$258,463	$301,109	$181,232	$215,321
Cash surrender value, life insurance	$ 2,180	$ 1,563	$ 1,020	$ 276	$ 20	
Land	$ 1,500	$ 1,500	$ 1,500	$ 1,500	$ 1,500	$ 1,500
Buildings	15,437	16,150	16,863	17,575	18,288	19,000
Improvements	5,105	4,525	3,201	3,783	4,365	4,948
Total Real Estate	$ 22,042	$ 22,175	$ 21,564	$ 22,858	$ 24,153	$ 25,448
Furniture and equipment	2,643	3,291	2,901	2,763	3,217	7,833
Delivery truck	100	320	699	1,937	2,970	3,734
Automobiles	2,886	3,174	4,242	1,521	1,117	1,866
Total Fixed Assets	$ 27,671	$ 28,960	$ 29,406	$ 29,079	$ 31,457	$ 38,881
Miscellaneous receivables			$ 310	$ 612		
Deposit premiums and unexpired insurance	$ 2,734	$ 1,743	2,080	2,393	$ 1,261	$ 1,648
Other deferred charges	199	199	341	106	104	240
Officers' and employees' accounts	22,064	1,696			978	
Total Other Assets	$ 24,997	$ 3,638	$ 2,731	$ 3,111	$ 2,343	$ 1,888
Total Assets	$538,537	$329,572	$291,620	$333,575	$215,052	$256,090

Liabilities and Capital

Current Liabilities:

Notes payable, bank (secured by inventory)	$220,000*	$ 90,000*	$ 90,000*	$100,000*	$ 73,500*
Notes payable, secured by equipment	310	400	...	...	256
Notes payable, unsecured	...	...	...	...	4,000
Notes payable, autos	...	...	1,215	...	...
Accounts payable, trade	190,871	113,880	77,684	113,810	37,970
Due officers	...	...	715	461	...
Provision for taxes	6,342	6,621	4,261	7,150	6,739
Accrued expenses and other liabilities	4,032	1,953	3,340	3,353	980
Amortization of mortgage payable	1,500	1,500	1,500	1,350	1,500
Total Current Liabilities	$423,055	$214,354	$178,715	$226,124	$124,945
Mortgage payable, real estate	$ 24,000	$ 25,500	$ 27,000	$ 28,650	$ 23,625
Capital stock	$ 75,300	$ 74,200	$ 70,000	$ 63,800	$ 53,000
Retained earnings	16,182	15,518	15,905	15,001	13,482
Total Capital	$ 91,482	$ 89,718	$ 85,905	$ 78,801	$ 66,482
Total Liabilities and Capital	$538,537	$329,572	$291,620	$333,575	$215,052

	$106,479
	13,000
	55,897
	7,830
	1,590
	1,500
	$186,296
	$ 25,125
	$ 32,500
	12,169
	$ 44,669
	$256,090

*Inventory of $116,021 pledged to secure note of $73,500 on December 31, 19x2.
Inventory of $194,834 pledged to secure note of $100,000 on December 31, 19x3.
Inventory of $173,388 pledged to secure note of $90,000 on December 31, 19x4.
Inventory of $169,829 pledged to secure note of $90,000 on December 31, 19x5.
Inventory of $285,000 pledged to secure note of $220,000 on December 31, 19x6.

EXHIBIT 2-2

FINEFOOD CORPORATION
Income Statement
Years Ending December 31, 19x3-x6

	19x6 $	19x6 %	19x5 $	19x5 %	19x4 $	19x4 %	19x3 $	19x3 %
Sales	2,394,326	101.06	1,899,760	101.34	1,655,196	101.31	1,531,189	101.35
Returns and allowances	25,063	1.06	25,182	1.34	21,348	1.31	20,392	1.35
Net sales	2,369,263	100.00	1,874,578	100.00	1,633,848	100.00	1,510,797	100.00
Cost of goods sold:								
Opening inventory	189,957	...	186,279	...	211,002	...	130,506	...
Net purchases*	2,370,991	...	1,712,742	...	1,449,650	...	1,446,945	...
Freight	12,604	...	4,723	...	4,539	...	7,548	...
	2,573,552		1,903,744		1,665,191		1,584,999	
Closing inventory	321,981	...	189,957	...	186,279	...	211,002	...
	2,251,571	95.04	1,713,787	91.42	1,478,912	90.52	1,373,997	90.95
Gross profit	117,692	4.96	160,791	8.58	154,936	9.48	136,800	9.05
Selling expenses:								
Advertising	1,813	.07	4,602	.25	5,195	.32	5,408	.36
Payroll, sales	20,741	.87	37,607	2.01	26,405	1.61	36,165	2.39
Sales promotion	5,412	.23	1,225	.06	1,060	.06	1,160	.08
Payroll expense	1,591	.07	1,680	.09	1,552	.10	1,258	.08
Total selling expense	29,557	1.24	45,114	2.41	34,212	2.09	43,991	2.91
Warehouse and handling	16,876	.72	26,774	1.43	26,046	1.60	29,641	1.96
Delivery expense	20,509	.86	41,573	2.22	34,975	2.14	22,374	1.48
Administrative expense†	43,185	1.82	42,583	2.27	53,784	3.29	35,153	2.33
Total operating expenses	110,127	4.64	156,044	8.33	149,017	9.12	131,159	8.68
Income before income taxes	7,565	.32	4,747	.25	5,919	.36	5,641	.37
Federal and state income taxes	3,945	.17	2,508	.13	2,765	.17	2,596	.17
Net income	3,620	.15	2,239	.12	3,154	.19	3,045	.20
*After deduction of cash discounts of	16,650		29,502		24,134		28,060	
†Includes interest expenses	12,400		5,800		5,800		6,400	

EXHIBIT 2-3

FINEFOOD CORPORATION
Condensed Income Statements, 19x1–x6

	19x6 $	%	19x5 $	%	19x4 $	%	19x3 $	%	19x2 $	%	19x1 $	%
Net sales	2,369,263	100.00	1,874,578	100.00	1,633,848	100.00	1,510,797	100.00	1,140,752	100.00	1,216,110	100.00
Cost of goods sold	2,251,571	95.04	1,713,787	91.42	1,478,912	90.52	1,373,997	90.95	1,038,473	91.03	1,109,612	91.24
Gross profit	117,692	4.96	160,791	8.58	154,936	9.48	136,800	9.05	102,279	8.97	106,498	8.76
Total operating expenses*	110,127	4.64	156,044	8.33	149,017	9.12	131,159	8.68	101,199	8.87	100,297	8.25
Income before income taxes	7,565	.32	4,747	.25	5,919	.36	5,641	.37	1,080	.10	6,201	.51
Net income	3,620	.15	2,239	.12	3,154	.19	3,045	.20	1,801	.16	3,199	.26
*Includes interest expense of	12,400		5,800		5,800		6,400		5,100		7,200	

EXHIBIT 2–4

FINEFOOD CORPORATION
Comparative Balance Sheets, 19x4–x6

	December 31			Increase (decrease)			
				Amount		Percent	
Assets	19x6	19x5	19x4	19x6 / 19x5	19x5 / 19x4	19x6 / 19x5	19x5 / 19x4
Current Assets:							
Cash on hand and on deposit	$ 24,659	$ 27,923	$ 18,240	$ (3,264)	$ 9,683	(11.7)	53.0
Accounts receivable, trade	136,875	73,436	53,550	63,439	19,886	86.4	37.1
Accounts and claims receivable, nontrade	174	4,095	395	(3,921)	3,700	(95.8)	936.7
Inventories:							
Groceries	261,954	176,180	179,599	85,774	(3,419)	48.7	(1.9)
Frozen foods	60,027	13,777	6,679	46,250	7,098	335.7	106.3
Total Inventories	$321,981	$189,957	$186,278	$132,024	$ 3,679	69.5	2.0
Total Current Assets	$483,689	$295,411	$258,463	$188,278	$36,948	63.7	14.3
Cash surrender value, life insurance	$ 2,180	$ 1,563	$ 1,020	$ 617	$ 543	39.5	53.2
Land	$ 1,500	$ 1,500	$ 1,500				
Buildings	15,437	16,150	16,863	(713)	(713)	(4.4)	(4.2)
Improvements	5,105	4,525	3,201	580	1,324	12.8	41.4
Total Real Estate	$ 22,042	$ 22,175	$ 21,564	$ (133)	$ 611	(.6)	2.8
Furniture and equipment	2,643	3,291	2,901	(648)	390	(19.7)	13.4
Delivery truck	100	320	699	(220)	(379)	(68.8)	(54.2)
Automobiles	2,886	3,174	4,242	(288)	(1,068)	(9.1)	(25.2)
Total Fixed Assets	$ 27,671	$ 28,960	$ 29,406	$ (1,289)	$ (446)	(4.5)	(1.5)
Miscellaneous receivables			$ 310		$ (310)		(100.0)
Deposit premiums and unexpired insurance	$ 2,734	$ 1,743	2,080	$ 991	(337)	56.9	(16.2)
Other deferred charges	199	199	341		(142)		(41.6)
Officers' and employees' accounts	22,064	1,696		20,368	1,696	1,201.0%	100.0
Total Other Assets	$ 24,997	$ 3,638	$ 2,731	$ 21,359	$ 907	587.1	33.2
Total Assets	$538,537	$329,572	$291,620	$208,965	$37,952	63.4	13.0

Liabilities and Capital

Current Liabilities:					
Notes payable, autos............	...		$ 1,215	$(1,215)	(100.0)
Due officers...................	...		715	(715)	(100.0)
Accounts payable, trade.........	$113,880		77,684	36,196	46.6
Notes payable, bank (secured by inventory).....	90,000		90,000	...	...
Notes payable, secured by equipment.....	400		...	400	...
Provision for taxes.............	6,621		4,261	2,360	55.4
Accrued Expenses and other liabilities.......	1,953		3,340	(1,387)	(41.5)
Amortization of mortgage payable......	1,500		1,500	...	...
Total Current Liabilities........	$214,354		$178,715	$35,639	19.9
Mortgage payable, real estate......	$ 25,500	$ 27,000		$(1,500)	(5.6)
Capital stock....................	$ 74,200	$ 70,000		$ 4,200	6.0
Retained earnings................	15,518	15,905		(387)	(2.4)
Total Capital....................	$ 89,718	$ 85,905		$ 3,813	4.4
Total Liabilities and Capital...	$329,572	$291,620		$37,952	13.0

	$190,871				
	220,000		$ 76,991		67.6
	310		130,000		144.4
	6,342		(90)		(22.5)
	4,032		(279)		(4.2)
	1,500		2,079		106.5
	$423,055		$208,701		97.4
	$ 24,000		$ (1,500)		
	$ 75,300		$ 1,100		1.5
	16,182		664		4.3
	$ 91,482		$ 1,764		2.0
	$538,537		$208,965		63.4

EXHIBIT 2-5

FINEFOOD CORPORATION
Comparative Income Statements, 19x4-x6

	December 31			Increase (decrease)		Percent	
	19x6	19x5	19x4	19x6 / 19x5	19x5 / 19x4	19x6 / 19x5	19x5 / 19x4
Sales	$2,394,326	$1,899,760	$1,655,196	$494,566	$244,564	26.0	14.7
Returns and allowances	25,063	25,182	21,348	(119)	3,834	(.04)	18.0
Net sales	$2,369,263	$1,874,578	$1,633,848	$494,685	$240,730	26.4	14.7
Cost of goods sold:							
Opening inventory	$ 189,957	$ 186,279	$ 211,002	$ 3,678	$ (24,723)	2.0	(11.7)
Net purchases*	2,370,991	1,712,742	1,449,650	658,249	263,092	38.4	18.1
Freight	12,604	4,723	4,539	7,881	184	166.9	4.1
	$2,573,552	$1,903,744	$1,665,191	$669,808	$238,553	35.2	14.3
Closing inventory	321,981	189,957	186,279	132,024	3,678	69.5	2.0
	$2,251,571	$1,713,787	$1,478,912	$537,784	$234,875	31.4	15.9
Gross profit	$ 117,692	$ 160,791	$ 154,936	$ (43,099)	$ 5,855	(26.8)	3.8
Selling expenses:							
Advertising	$ 1,813	$ 4,602	$ 5,195	$ (2,789)	$ (593)	(60.6)	(11.4)
Payroll, sales	20,741	37,607	26,405	16,866	11,202	44.8	42.4
Sales promotion	5,412	1,225	1,060	4,187	165	341.8	15.6
Payroll expense	1,591	1,680	1,552	(89)	128	(5.3)	8.2
Total selling expense	$ 29,557	$ 45,114	$ 34,212	$ (15,557)	$ 10,902	(34.5)	31.9
Warehouse and handling	16,876	26,774	26,046	(9,898)	728	(37.0)	2.8
Delivery expense	20,509	41,573	34,975	(21,064)	6,598	(50.7)	18.9
Administrative expense	43,185	42,583	53,784	602	(11,201)	1.4	(20.8)
Total operating expenses	$ 110,127	$ 156,044	$ 149,017	$ (45,917)	$ 7,027	(29.4)	4.7
Income before income taxes	$ 7,565	$ 4,747	$ 5,919	$ 2,818	$ (1,172)	59.4	(19.8)
Federal and state income taxes	3,945	2,508	2,765	1,437	(257)	57.3	(9.3)
Net income	$ 3,620	$ 2,239	$ 3,154	$ 1,381	$ (915)	61.7	(29.0)
*After deduction of cash discounts of	$ 16,650	$ 29,502	$ 24,134	$ (12,852)	$ 5,368	(43.6)	22.2

conclusions regarding the relative significance of the changes disclosed by this type of analysis.

The computation of year-to-year changes is a simple matter. However, a few clarifying rules should be borne in mind. When a negative amount appears in the base year and a positive amount in the following year, or vice versa, no percentage change can be meaningfully computed. When an item has a value in a base year and none in the following period, the decrease is 100 percent. Where there is no figure for the base year, no percentage change can be computed. The following summary will illustrate this:

Item	19x1 $	19x2 $	Change increase (decrease) Amount $	%
Net income (loss)	(4,500)	1,500	6,000	...
Tax expense	2,000	(1,000)	(3,000)	...
Notes payable	...	8,000	8,000	...
Notes receivable	10,000	...	(10,000)	(100)

Comparative financial statements can also be presented in such a way that the cumulative total for the period for each item under study and the average for that period are shown. Exhibit 2–6 presents such a comparative statement using the condensed income statements of the Finefood Corporation for the years 19x4 to 19x6.

The value of comparing yearly amounts with an average covering a number of years is that unusual factors in any one year are highlighted. Averages smooth out erratic or unusual fluctuations in data.

Index-number trend series

When a comparison of financial statements covering more than three years is undertaken, the year-to-year method of comparison described above (and illustrated in Exhibits 2–4 and 2–5) becomes too cumbersome. The best way to effect such longer term trend comparisons is by means of index numbers. Such a comparative statement for the Finefood Corporation is illustrated in Exhibits 2–7 and 2–8.

The computation of a series of index numbers requires the choice of a base year which will, for all items, have an index amount of 100. Since such a base year represents a frame of reference for all comparisons, it is best to choose a year which, in a business conditions sense, is as typical or normal as possible. If the earliest year in the series compared cannot fulfill this function, another year is chosen. In our

EXHIBIT 2–6

FINEFOOD CORPORATION
Condensed Income Statements, 19x4–x6
(with cumulative amounts and annual average amounts)

	19x6	19x5	19x4	Cumulative amount	Annual average amount
Net sales	$2,369,263	$1,874,578	$1,633,848	$5,877,689	$1,959,230
Cost of goods sold	2,251,571	1,713,787	1,478,912	5,444,270	1,814,757
Gross profit	$ 117,692	$ 160,791	$ 154,936	$ 433,419	$ 144,473
Total operating expenses	110,127	156,044	149,017	415,188	138,396
Income before income taxes	$ 7,565	$ 4,747	$ 5,919	$ 18,231	$ 6,077
Net income	$ 3,620	$ 2,239	$ 3,154	$ 9,013	$ 3,004

example of the Finefood Corporation comparative statements, the year 19x3, rather than the first year in the series, was chosen.

As is the case with the computation of year-to-year percentage changes, certain changes, such as those from negative to positive amounts, cannot be expressed by means of index numbers. All index numbers are computed by reference to the base year.

ILLUSTRATION. Assume that in the base year 19xA cash has a balance of $12,000. Based on an index number of 100 for 19xA, if the cash balance in the following year (19xB) is $18,000, then the index number will be

$$\frac{18,000}{12,000} \times 100 = 150$$

In 19xC if the cash balance is $9,000, the index will stand at 75 arrived at as follows:

$$\frac{9,000}{12,000} \times 100 \left(\frac{\text{Balance in current year}}{\text{Balance in base year}} \times 100 \right)$$

It should be noted that when using index numbers, percentage changes cannot be read off directly except by reference to the base year. Thus, the change of the cash balance between 19xA and 19xB is 50 percent (index 150 − index 100), and this can be read off directly from the index numbers. The change from 19xB to 19xC, however, is not 75 percent (150−75), as a direct comparison may suggest, but rather 50 percent (i.e., 9,000/18,000), which involves computing the 19xB to 19xC change by reference to the amount at 19xB. The percentage change can, however, be computed by use of the index numbers only, for example, 75/150 = .5 or a change of 50 percent.

In planning an index-number trend comparison, it is not necessary to include in it all the items in the financial statements. Only the most significant items need be included in such a comparison.

Care should be exercised in the use of index-number trend comparisons because such comparisons have weaknesses as well as strengths. Thus, in trying to assess changes in the current financial condition, the analyst may use to advantage comparative statements of changes in financial position. On the other hand, the index-number trend comparison is very well suited to a comparison of the changes in the *composition* of working capital items over the years.

The interpretation of percentage changes as well as those of index-number trend series must be made with a full awareness of the effect which the inconsistent application of accounting principles over the years can have on such comparisons. Thus, where possible, such inconsistencies must be adjusted. In addition, the longer the period covered by the

EXHIBIT 2-7

FINEFOOD CORPORATION
Balance Sheet Analysis—Index Numbers
Base Year, 19x3

Assets	19x6	19x5	19x4	19x3	19x2	19x1
Current Assets:						
Cash on hand and on deposit	95.0	103.8	67.8	100.0	43.9	22.4
Accounts receivable, trade	218.0	116.9	85.3	100.0	59.7	79.6
Accounts and claims receivable, nontrade	44.8	1,055.4	101.8	100.0	361.3	284.8
Inventories:						
Groceries	131.0	88.0	89.7	100.0	57.9	64.3
Frozen foods	560.0	128.1	62.1	100.0	134.7	273.3
Total Inventories	152.0	90.0	88.3	100.0	61.9	75.0
Total Current Assets	160.0	98.1	85.8	100.0	60.2	71.5
Cash surrender value, life insurance	789.9	566.3	369.6	100.0	7.2	
Land	100.0	100.0	100.0	100.0	100.0	100.0
Buildings	87.8	91.9	95.9	100.0	104.1	108.1
Improvements	134.9	119.6	84.6	100.0	115.4	130.8
Total Real Estate	96.4	97.0	94.3	100.0	105.7	111.3
Furniture and equipment	95.7	119.1	105.0	100.0	116.4	283.5
Delivery truck	5.2	16.5	36.1	100.0	153.3	192.8
Automobiles	189.7	208.7	278.9	100.0	73.4	122.7
Total Fixed Assets	95.2	99.6	101.1	100.0	108.2	133.7
Miscellaneous receivables			50.7	100.0		
Deposit premiums and unexpired insurance	114.2	72.8	86.9	100.0	52.7	68.9
Other deferred charges	187.7	187.7	321.7	100.0	98.1	226.4
Officers' and employees' accounts*						
Total Other Assets	805.0	116.9	87.8	100.0	75.3	60.7
Total Assets	162.0	98.8	87.4	100.0	64.5	76.8

Liabilities and Capital

Current Liabilities:					
Notes payable, unsecured*	...	...	...	...	...
Notes payable, autos*	...	...	...	...	...
Due officers	...	...	...	...	...
Accounts payable, trade	178.0	100.1	155.1	100.0	33.4	49.1
Notes payable, bank (secured by inventory)	220.0	90.0	68.3	100.0	33.4	49.1
Notes payable, secured by equipment*			90.0	100.0	73.5	106.5
Provision for taxes	88.7	92.6	59.6	100.0	94.3	109.5
Accrued expenses and other liabilities	120.3	58.2	99.6	100.0	29.2	47.4
Amortization of mortgage payable	111.1	111.1	111.1	100.0	111.1	111.1
Total Current Liabilities	187.0	94.8	79.0	100.0	55.3	82.4
Mortgage payable, real estate	83.8	89.0	94.2	100.0	82.5	87.7
Capital stock	118.0	116.3	109.7	100.0	83.1	50.9
Retained earnings	107.9	103.4	106.0	100.0	89.9	81.1
Total Capital	116.1	113.9	109.0	100.0	84.4	56.7
Total Liabilities and Capital	162.0	98.8	87.4	100.0	64.5	76.8

*No base year figure.

EXHIBIT 2-8

FINEFOOD CORPORATION
Condensed Income Statement Analysis—Index Numbers
Base Year 19x3

	19x6	19x5	19x4	19x3	19x2	19x1
Net sales	156.8	124.1	108.1	100.0	75.5	80.5
Cost of goods sold	163.9	124.7	107.6	100.0	75.6	80.8
Gross profit	86.0	117.5	113.3	100.0	74.8	77.8
Total operating expenses	84.0	119.0	113.6	100.0	77.2	76.5
Income before income taxes	134.1	84.2	104.9	100.0	19.1	109.9
Net income	118.9	73.5	103.6	100.0	59.1	105.1

comparison, the more distortive are the effects of price level changes on such comparisons likely to be, and the analyst must be aware of such effects (see Chapter 12).

One important value of trend analysis is that it can convey to the analyst a better understanding of management's philosophies, policies, and motivations, conscious or otherwise, which have brought about the changes revealed over the years. The more diverse the economic environments covering the periods compared are, the better a picture can be obtained by the analyst of the ways in which the enterprise has weathered its adversities and taken advantage of its opportunities.

Common-size financial statements

In the analysis of financial statements it is often instructive to find out the proportion of a total group or subgroup which a single item within them represents. In a balance sheet, the assets as well as the liabilities and capital are each expressed as 100 percent and each item in these categories is expressed as a percentage of the respective totals. Similarly, in the income statement net sales are set at 100 percent, and every other item in the statement is expressed as a percent of net sales. Since the totals always add up to 100 percent, this community of size has resulted in these statements being referred to as "common size." Similarly, following the eye as it reviews the common-size statement, this analysis is referred to as "vertical" for the same reason that the trend analysis is often referred to as "horizontal" analysis.

The comparative common-size balance sheet analysis of the Finefood Corporation over the years is presented in Exhibit 2-9, and the income statement in Exhibit 2-2 presents common-size percentages for components of that statement.

Structural analysis. The analysis of common-size financial statements may best be described as an analysis of the internal structure of the

EXHIBIT 2-9

FINEFOOD CORPORATION
Balance Sheet Analysis—Common-Size Percentages

	19x6	19x5	19x4	19x3	19x2	19x1
Assets						
Current Assets:						
Cash on hand and on deposit	4.6	8.5	6.2	8.1	5.5	2.4
Accounts receivable, trade	25.4	22.3	18.4	18.8	17.4	19.5
Accounts and claims receivable, nontrade	.0	1.2	.1	.1	.7	.4
Inventories:						
Groceries	48.8	53.4	61.6	60.1	54.0	50.3
Frozen foods	11.2	4.2	2.3	3.2	6.7	11.5
Total Inventories	60.0	57.6	63.9	63.3	60.7	61.8
Total Current Assets	90.0	89.6	88.6	90.3	84.3	84.1
Cash surrender value, life insurance	.4	.5	.4	.1	.0	
Land	.3	.4	.5	.4	.7	.6
Buildings	2.8	4.9	5.8	5.3	8.5	7.4
Improvements	.9	1.4	1.1	1.1	2.0	1.9
Total Real Estate	4.0	6.7	7.4	6.8	11.2	9.9
Furniture and equipment	.5	1.0	1.1	.8	1.5	3.1
Delivery truck	.0	.1	.2	.6	1.4	1.5
Automobiles	.5	1.0	1.4	.5	.5	.7
Total Fixed Assets	5.0	8.8	10.1	8.7	14.6	15.2
Miscellaneous receivables	...	...	.1	.2	...	...
Deposit premiums and unexpired insurance	.5	.5	.7	.7	.6	.6
Other deferred charges	.0	.1	.1	.0	.0	.1
Officers' and employees' accounts	4.1	.5			.5	
Total Other Assets	4.6	1.1	.9	.9	1.1	.7
Total Assets	100.0	100.0	100.0	100.0	100.0	100.0
Liabilities and Capital						
Current Liabilities:						
Notes payable, unsecured	...	...	...	...	1.9	5.1
Notes payable, autos	...	...	.4	...	...	...
Due officers	...	...	.2	.1	...	...
Accounts payable, trade	35.4	34.6	26.6	34.1	17.6	21.8
Notes payable, bank (secured by inventory)	41.0	27.3	30.9	30.0	34.2	41.6
Notes payable, secured by equipment	.0	.1	...	...	.1	...
Provision for taxes	1.2	2.0	1.5	2.2	3.1	3.1
Accrued expenses and other liabilities	.7	.6	1.2	1.0	.5	.6
Amortization of mortgage payable	.3	.5	.5	.4	.7	.6
Total Current Liabilities	78.6	65.1	61.3	67.8	58.1	72.8
Mortgage payable, real estate	4.4	7.7	9.2	8.6	11.0	9.8
Capital stock	14.0	22.5	24.0	19.1	24.6	12.7
Retained earnings	3.0	4.7	5.5	4.5	6.3	4.7
Total Capital	17.0	27.2	29.5	23.6	30.9	17.4
Total Liabilities and Capital	100.0	100.0	100.0	100.0	100.0	100.0

financial statements. In the analysis of a balance sheet this structural analysis focuses on two major aspects:

1. What are the sources of capital of the enterprise, that is, what is the distribution of equities as between current liabilities, long-term liabilities, and equity capital?
2. Given the amount of capital from all sources, what is the distribution of assets (current, fixed, and other) in which it is invested? Stated differently, what is the mix of assets with which the enterprise has chosen to conduct its operations.

The common-size balance sheet analysis can, of course, be carried further and extended to an examination of what proportion of a subgroup, rather than the total, an item is. Thus, in assessing the liquidity of current assets, it may be of interest to know not only what proportion of total assets is invested in inventories but also what proportion of current assets is represented by this asset.

In the case of the income statement, common-size statement analysis is a very useful tool transcending perhaps in importance the analysis of the balance sheet by such means. This is so because the income statement lends itself very well to an analysis whereby each item in it is related to a central quantum, that is, sales. With some exceptions the level of each expense item is affected to some extent by the level of sales, and thus it is instructive to know what proportion of the sales dollar is absorbed by the various costs and expenses incurred by the enterprise.

Comparisons of common-size statements of a single enterprise over the years are valuable in that they show the changing proportions of components within groups of assets, liabilities, costs, and other financial statement categories. However, care must be exercised in interpreting such changes and the trend which they disclose. For example, the table below shows the amount of patents and total assets of an enterprise over three years:

	19x3	19x2	19x1
Patents	50,000	50,000	50,000
Total assets	1,000,000	750,000	500,000
Patents as a percentage of total assets	5%	6.67%	10%

While the amount of patents remained unchanged, the increase in total assets made this item a progressively smaller proportion of total assets. Since this proportion can change with either a change in the absolute amount of the item or a change in the total of the group of which it is a part, the interpretation of a common-size statement comparison requires an examination of the actual figures and the basis on which they are computed.

Common-size statements are very well suited to intercompany comparison because the financial statements of a variety of companies can be recast into the uniform common-size format regardless of the size of individual accounts. While common-size statements do not reflect the relative sizes of the individual companies which are compared, the problem of actual comparability between them is a matter to be resolved by the analyst's judgment.

Comparison of the common-size statements of companies within an industry or with common-size composite statistics of that industry can alert the analyst's attention to variations in account structure or distribution, the reasons for which should be explored and understood. A comparison of selected common-size statement items of the Finefood Corporation with similar industry statistics is presented in Exhibit 4–10.

Ratio analysis

Ratios are among the best known and most widely used tools of financial analysis. At the same time their function is often misunderstood, and consequently their significance may easily be overrated.

A ratio expresses the mathematical relationship between one quantity and another. The ratio of 200 to 100 is expressed as 2:1 or as 2. While the computation of a ratio involves a simple arithmetical operation, its interpretation is a far more complex matter.

To begin with, to be significant the ratio must express a relationship that has significance. Thus, there is a clear, direct, and understandable relatonship between the sales price of an item on one hand and its cost on the other. As a result, the ratio of cost of goods sold to sales is a significant one. On the other hand, there is no a priori or understandable relationship between freight costs incurred and the marketable securities held by an enterprise; and hence, a ratio of one to the other must be deemed to be of no significance.

Ratios are tools of analysis which, in most cases, provide the analyst with clues and symptoms of underlying conditions. Ratios, properly interpreted, can also point the way to areas requiring further investigation and inquiry. The analysis of a ratio can disclose relationships as well as bases of comparison which reveal conditions and trends that cannot be detected by an inspection of the individual components of the ratio.

Since ratios, like other tools of analysis, are future oriented, the analyst must be able to adjust the factors present in a relationship to their probable shape and size in the future. He must also understand the factors which will influence such ratios in the future. Thus, in the final analysis, the usefulness of ratios is wholly dependent on their intelligent

EXHIBIT 2-10

FINEFOOD CORPORATION
Financial Data for Finefood Corporation and the Wholesale Grocery Trade
Grocery Wholesalers with Asset Size $250,000 to $1,000,000

	Finefood 19x6	Industry 19x6	Industry 19x5	Industry 19x4
No. of statements analyzed		93	80	79
	%	%	%	%
Assets				
Current Assets:				
Cash	4.6	5.25	5.45	4.22
Marketable securities	...	.42	.56	1.48
Receivables (net of doubtful accounts provision)	25.4	21.13	20.05	21.16
Merchandise	60.0	51.92	53.32	52.02
All other	...	1.33	1.18	.90
Total Current Assets	90.0	80.05	80.56	79.78
Plant and equipment	5.0	14.23	13.05	13.45
All other	5.0	5.72	6.39	6.77
Total Noncurrent Assets	10.0	19.95	19.44	20.22
Total Assets	100.0	100.00	100.00	100.00
Liabilities				
Current Liabilities:				
Due to banks	41.0	12.45	12.34	13.68
Due to trade creditors	35.4	17.10	13.96	15.44
Federal income taxes	1.2	1.80	2.33	1.80
All other	1.0	7.05	7.93	5.42
Total Current Liabilities	78.6	38.40	36.56	36.34
Due to banks (long-term)	...	1.39	1.81	1.10
Other long-term debt	4.4	3.71	3.98	4.54
Total debt	83.0	43.50	42.35	41.98
Reserves	...	.48	.52	.78
Net worth	17.0	56.02	57.13	57.24
Total Liabilities	100.0	100.00	100.00	100.00
Income Data				
Net sales	100.00	100.00	100.00	100.00
Cost of sales	95.04	92.24	91.51	91.42
Gross profit	4.96	7.76	8.49	8.58
All other expense (net)	4.64	7.02	7.24	7.42
Income before taxes	.32	.74	1.25	1.16
Federal income taxes	.17	.34	.54	.39
Net income	.15	.40	.71	.77
Ratios:				
Current	1.14	2.09	2.20	2.20
Net worth/total noncurrent assets	1.74	2.81	2.94	2.83
Net worth/total debt	.22	1.29	1.35	1.36
Sales/receivables	17.2	26.13	24.93	21.88
Receivables turnover (days)	21	14	14	16
Sales/merchandise	7.40	10.64	9.38	8.90
Merchandise turnover (days)	41	34	38	40
Sales/total noncurrent assets	45.00	27.69	25.72	22.89
Sales/net worth	26.00	9.86	8.75	8.09
Profits/net worth	3.98	4.00	6.24	6.21
Sales/total assets	4.40	5.52	5.00	4.63
Profits/total assets	.67	2.24	3.57	3.55

Source: Adjusted data from Robert Morris Associates Statement Studies.

and skillful interpretation. This is, by far, the most difficult aspect of ratio analysis. Let us, by way of example, consider the interpretation of a ratio derived from an area outside that of the business world: In comparing the ratio of gas consumption to mileage driven, A claims to have a superior performance, that is, 28 M.P.G. compared to B's 20 M.P.G. Assuming that they drove identical cars, the following are factors which affect gas consumption and which will have to be considered before one can properly interpret the ratios and judge whose performance is better:

1. Weight of load driven.
2. Type of terrain (flat versus hilly).
3. City or country driving.
4. Kind of gasoline used.
5. Speed at which cars were driven.

Numerous as the factors which influence gas consumption are, the evaluation of the gas consumption ratio is, nevertheless, a simpler process than the evaluation of most ratios derived from business variables. The reason for this is that the interrelationships of business variables and the factors which affect them are multifaceted and very complex. In addition to the internal operating conditions which affect the ratios of an enterprise, the analyst must be aware of the factors, such as general business conditions, industry position, management policies, as well as accounting principles, which can affect them. As far as the latter are concerned, the discussion of accounting principles in Part II of this text points up their influence on the measurements on which ratios are based.

Ratios, like most other relationships in financial analysis, are not significant in themselves and can be interpreted only by comparison with (1) past ratios of the same enterprise, or (2) some predetermined standard, or (3) ratios of other companies in the industry. The range of a ratio over time is also significant as is the trend of a given ratio over time.

A great many ratios can be developed from the multitude of items included in an enterprises' financial statements. Some ratios have general application in financial analysis, while others have specific uses in certain circumstances or in specific industries. Listed below are some of the most significant ratios which have general applicability to most business situations. They are grouped by major objectives of financial analysis:

Each of the above five major objectives of financial statement analysis will be examined in subsequent chapters; and therein the computation, use, and interpretation of the ratios listed under each category as well as other ratios will be examined in detail and thoroughly discussed.

Understanding corporate reports

Major categories of ratios	Method of computation
Short-term liquidity ratios:	
Current ratio................	$\dfrac{\text{Current assets}}{\text{Current liabilities}}$
Acid test...................	$\dfrac{\text{Cash + Cash equivalents + Receivables}}{\text{Current liabilities}}$
Days sales in receivables (collection period)............	$\dfrac{\text{Accounts receivables}}{\text{Credit sales} \div 360}$
Inventory turnover...........	$\dfrac{\text{Cost of goods sold}}{\text{Average inventory during period}}$
Capital structure and long-term solvency ratios:	
Net worth to total debt........	$\dfrac{\text{Net worth}}{\text{Total debt}}$
Net worth to long-term debt....	$\dfrac{\text{Net worth}}{\text{Long-term debt}}$
Net worth to fixed assets......	$\dfrac{\text{Net worth}}{\text{Fixed assets}}$
Times interest earned.........	$\dfrac{\text{Income before interest and taxes}}{\text{Interest expenses}}$
Return on investment ratios:	
Return on total assets.........	$\dfrac{\text{Net income + Interest expense}}{\text{Total assets}}$
Return on equity capital.......	$\dfrac{\text{Net income}}{\text{Equity capital}}$
Operating performance ratios:	
Gross margin ratio............	$\dfrac{\text{Gross profit (margin)}}{\text{Sales}}$
Operating profits to sales......	$\dfrac{\text{Operating profit}}{\text{Sales}}$
Pretax income to sales........	$\dfrac{\text{Pretax income}}{\text{Sales}}$
Net income to sales...........	$\dfrac{\text{Net income}}{\text{Sales}}$
Asset-utilization ratios:	
Sales to cash................	$\dfrac{\text{Sales}}{\text{Cash}}$
Sales to accounts receivables...	$\dfrac{\text{Sales}}{\text{Accounts receivable}}$
Sales to inventories..........	$\dfrac{\text{Sales}}{\text{Inventories}}$
Sales to working capital.......	$\dfrac{\text{Sales}}{\text{Working capital}}$
Sales to fixed assets..........	$\dfrac{\text{Sales}}{\text{Fixed assets}}$
Sales to other assets..........	$\dfrac{\text{Sales}}{\text{Other assets}}$
Sales to total assets..........	$\dfrac{\text{Sales}}{\text{Total assets}}$

EXHIBIT 2-11

FINEFOOD CORPORATION
Selected Ratios for the Years 19x1–x6

	19x6	19x5	19x4	19x3	19x2	19x1
Short-term liquidity ratios:						
Current ratio	1.1	1.4	1.5	1.3	1.5	1.2
Acid test	.38	.49	.40	.40	.41	.31
Days sales in receivables (collection period: 360-day basis)	21	14	12	15	12	15
Inventory turnover	8.8	9.1	7.4	8.0	7.2	7.0*
Capital structure and long-term solvency ratios:						
Net worth to total debt	.20	.37	.42	.31	.45	.21
Net worth to long-term debt	3.8	3.5	3.2	2.8	2.8	1.8
Net worth to fixed assets	3.3	3.1	2.9	2.7	2.1	1.2
Times interest earned	1.6	1.8	2.0	1.9	1.2	1.9
Return on investment ratios:						
Return on total assets	3.0%	2.4%	3.1%	2.8%	3.2%	4.1%
Return on equity capital	4.0%	2.5%	3.7%	3.9%	2.7%	7.2%
Operating performance ratios:						
Gross margin ratio	5.0%	8.6%	9.5%	9.1%	9.0%	8.8%
Operating profits to sales	.32%	.25%	.36%	.37%	.10%	.51%
Pretax income to sales	.32%	.25%	.36%	.37%	.10%	.51%
Net income to sales	.15%	.12%	.19%	.20%	.16%	.26%
Capital utilization ratios:						
Sales to cash	96	67	90	56	97	202
Sales to accounts receivable	17.3	25.5	30.5	24.1	30.4	24.3
Sales to inventories	7.4	9.9	8.8	7.2	8.7	7.7
Sales to working capital	39.1	23.1	20.5	20.1	20.3	41.9
Sales to fixed assets	85.6	64.7	55.6	52.0	36.3	31.3
Sales to other assets	95	515	598	486	487	644
Sales to total assets	4.4	5.7	5.6	4.5	5.3	4.7

*Based on ending inventory only.

Exhibit 2–11 presents the above-listed ratios of the Finefood Corporation for the years 19x1 to 19x6.

Specialized analysis

In addition to the multipurpose tools of financial statement analysis which we discussed above, such as trend indices, common-size statements, and ratios, the analyst has at his disposal a variety of special-purpose tools. These tools focus on specific financial statements or segments of such statements or they can address themselves specifically to the operating conditions of a particular industry, for example, occupancy-capacity analysis in the hotel industry.

The special-purpose tools which will be briefly reviewed here are:

1. Cash forecasts.
2. Analysis of changes in financial position.

3. Statements of variation in gross margin.
4. Break-even analysis.

Cash forecasts. Supplementing and reinforcing the analysis of liquidity, by means of ratios and other tools, is the cash forecast. This is a dynamic analysis which projects the future cash resources of an enterprise over time and the demands which are expected to be made against them. This analysis is helpful in analyzing short-term and long-term debt repayment capacity, as well as future cash and financing requirements.

Analysis of changes in financial position. An analysis of past statements of changes in financial position of an enterprise can supply important information regarding the uses of funds, such as for expansion or acquisitions, as well as data on the sources of funds used and the financing habits of management. A projection of sources and uses of funds into the future will focus on the needs for future funds and the sources from which they are likely to become available.

Statement of variation in gross margin. The gross margin, or gross profit, of an enterprise is a very important element of operating performance. It is from the gross margin that all indirect costs and expenses as well as discretionary expenses must be covered if the enterprise is to operate at a profit.

The statement of variation in gross margin analyzes changes in all the important elements which enter the determination of gross margin. In this way the most important factors responsible for changes can be identified and singled out for further analysis.

Break-even analysis. Another important tool in the analysis of operating performance is break-even analysis. This analysis is based on the observed behavior pattern of costs and expenses and is an important factor in the estimation of operating results which are likely to be achieved under differing levels of sales.

BUILDING BLOCKS OF FINANCIAL STATEMENT ANALYSIS

Whatever approach to financial statement analysis the analyst takes and whatever methods he uses he will always have to examine one or more of the important aspects of an enterprise's financial condition and results of its operations. All such aspects, with perhaps the exception of the most specialized ones, can be found in one of the following six categories:

1. Short-term liquidity.
2. Funds flow.
3. Capital structure and long-term solvency.

4. Return on investment.
5. Operating performance.
6. Assets utilization.

Each of the above categories and the tools used in measuring them will be discussed in greater depth in later chapters. In this way the financial analysis required by any conceivable set of objectives may be structured by examining any or all of the above areas in any sequence and with any degree of relative emphasis called for by circumstances. Thus these six areas of inquiry and investigation can be considered as building blocks of financial statement analysis.

ANALYTICAL REVIEW OF ACCOUNTING PRINCIPLES—PURPOSES AND FOCUS

In the chapters which follow we shall present a review of accounting principles used in the preparation of financial statements. The purpose of this review is to examine the variety of principles which can be applied to similar transactions and circumstances, as well as the latitude which is possible in the interpretation and application of these principles in practice. Thus, the focus is on an understanding of accounting principles as well as on an appreciation of the impact which the application of these principles may have on the reported financial condition and results of operations of an enterprise. Such possible impact must be appreciated and understood before any intelligent analysis can be undertaken or any useful and meaningful comparison is made.

Example of importance of accounting assumptions, principles, and determinations: Illustration of a simple investment decision

The importance of principles and assumptions in accounting determinations can perhaps be best illustrated and understood within the framework of an exceedingly simple example of a business situation. Let us assume that the owner of an apartment building has found an interested buyer. How should the price be set? How should the buyer gain confidence in the soundness and profitability of such investment at a given price?

The first question is the method to be followed in arriving at a fair value of the building. While many approaches are possible, such as comparable current values, reproduction costs, etc., let us settle here on the most widely accepted method for the valuation of income-producing properties as well as other investments: the capitalization of earnings. If earning power is the major consideration, then the focus must be on the income statement. The prospective buyer is given the following income statement:

184 EAGLE STREET APARTMENT HOUSE
Income Statement for the Year
Ending December 31, 19x9

Rental revenue		$46,000
Garage rentals		1,440
Other income from washer and dryer concession		300
Total revenue		$48,740
Expenses:		
Real estate taxes	$4,900	
Mortgage interest	2,100	
Electricity and gas	840	
Water	720	
Superintendent's salary	1,600	
Insurance	680	
Repairs and maintenance	2,400	13,240
Income before depreciation		$35,500
Depreciation		9,000
Net income		$26,500

The first questions the prospective buyer will want to ask himself about the foregoing income statement are these:

1. Can I rely on the fairness of presentation of the income statement?
2. What adjustments have to be made so as to obtain a net income figure which can be used with confidence in arriving at a proper purchase price?

In our society the most common way of gaining assurance about the fairness of presentation of financial statements is to rely on the opinion of an independent certified public accountant. This professional is assumed to perform a skilful audit and to satisfy himself that the financial statements do accurately portray the results of operations and the financial position, in accordance with principles which are generally accepted as proper and useful in the particular context in which they are applied. Such an auditor is also presumed to understand that someone like our prospective buyer will rely on his opinion in reaching a decision on whether to buy and at what price. In Chapter 13 we will explore in more detail the function of the auditor and what his opinion means to the user of financial statements.

Our prospective buyer's second question is far more complex. The auditor's opinion relates to the income statement as representing fairly the net income for the year ended December 31, 19x9. That in no way means that this is *the* relevant figure to use in arriving at a valuation of the apartment building. Nor would an auditor ever claim that his opinion is directed at the relevance of financial statement figures to any particular decision. Let us then examine what information our buyer will need and what assumptions he will have to make in order that he may arrive at a figure of net income which can be used in setting the value of the apartment building.

Rental income. Does the $46,000 figure represent 100 percent occupancy during the year? If so, should an allowance be made for possible vacancies? What are rental trends in the area? What would rents be in five years? In 10 years? Are demand factors for apartments in the area going to stay stable, improve, or deteriorate? The aim, of course, is to come nearest to that figure of yearly rental income which approximates a level which, on the average, can be expected to prevail over the forseeable future. Prior years' data will be useful in judging this.

Real estate taxes. Here the trend of taxes over the years is an important factor. That in turn depends on the character of the taxing community and revenue and expense trends within it.

Mortgage interest. This expense is relevant to the buyer only if he assumes the existing mortgage. Otherwise the interest cost which will be incurred as a result of new financing will have to be substituted.

Utilities. These expenses must be scrutinized with a view to ascertaining whether they are at a representative level of what can be expected to prevail.

Superintendent's salary. Is the pay adequate to secure acceptable services? Can the services of superintendent be retained?

Insurance. Are all forseeable risks insured for? Is the coverage adequate?

Repairs and maintenance. These expenses must be examined over a number of years in order to determine an average or representative level. Is the level of expenses such that it affords proper maintenance of the property or is the expense account "starved" so as to show a higher net income?

Depreciation. This figure is not likely to be relevant to the buyer's decision unless his cost approximates that of the seller. If the cost to the buyer differs, then depreciation will have to be computed on that cost using a proper method of depreciation over the useful life of the building, so as to recover the buyer's original cost.

The buyer must also ascertain whether any expenses which he will be properly expected to incur are omitted from the above income statement. Additional considerations concern the method of financing this acquisition and other costs related thereto.

It should be understood that most of the above questions will have to be asked and properly answered even if the auditor issues an unqualified opinion on the financial statements. Thus, for example, while "generally accepted accounting principles" require that insurance expense include accruals for the full year, they are not concerned with the adequacy of insurance coverage or of the maintenance policy, or the superintendent's pay, or with expected, as opposed to actual, revenues or expense levels.

If one views the many complex questions and problems that arise in the attempt to analyze this very simple income statement for decision-making purposes, one can begin to grasp the complexities involved in the analysis of the financial statements of a sizable, modern business corporation.

It is clear that essential to an intelligent analysis of such statements is an appreciation of what financial statements do portray as well as what they do not or cannot portray. As we have seen, there are items which properly belong in such statements and there are items which, because of an inability to quantify them or to determine them objectively, cannot be included.

Those items which properly belong in the financial statements should be presented therein in accordance with principles of accounting which enjoy general acceptance. The wide variety of principles which are "acceptable" as well as the even greater variety in the ways in which they can be applied in practice make it imperative that the user of financial statements be fully aware of these possibilities and their implications. The following chapters will explore this important area.

The example of the apartment house buyer illustrates the obvious fact that despite their limitations, financial statements and presentations are indispensible to the decision-making process. While the potential buyer could not use the income statement without obtaining more information and making further assumptions and adjustments, he would not have had any basis for his decision without it. Had he not received one, he would have had to make one up without utilization of the objectivity and the benefit of the experience of actual transactions over a period of time. Thus, in most cases, the interpretation of historical financial statements represents the essential first step in the decision-making process.

QUESTIONS

1. As a potential investor in a common stock, what information would you seek? How do you get such information?
2. The president of your client company approached you, the financial officer of a local bank, for a substantial loan. What could you do?
3. What, in broad categories, are some of the approaches utilized by the financial analyst in diagnosing the financial health of a business?
4. How useful is a comparative financial analysis? How do you make useful comparison?

2. Tools and techniques of financial statement analysis

5. What are some of the precautions required of a financial analyst in his comparative analytical work?
6. Give four broad categories of analysis tools.
7. Is the trend of the past a good predicator of the future? Give reasons for your argument.
8. Which is the better indicator of significant change—the absolute amount of change or the change in percentage? Why?
9. What conditions would prevent the computation of a valid percentage change? Give an example.
10. What are some of the criteria to be used in picking out a base year in an index number comparative analysis?
11. What information can be obtained from trend analysis?
12. What is a common-size financial statement? How do you prepare one?
13. What does a common-size financial statement tell about an enterprise?
14. Do all ratios have significance? Explain.
15. What are some of the limitations of ratio analysis?
16. Give five ratios that can be prepared by use of balance sheet figures only.
17. Give five ratios that can be prepared by use of income statement data only.
18. Give seven ratios that require data from both the balance sheet and the income statement.
19. Give four examples of special-purpose analytical tools commonly utilized by the financial analyst.
20. What are the steps generally taken by the financial analyst in his work? What do these steps achieve?
21. Identify and explain two significant limitations associated with ratio analysis of financial statements. (C.F.A.)

part II

FINANCIAL STATEMENTS—THE RAW MATERIAL OF ANALYSIS

3

Analysis of current assets

IN CONSIDERING the variety of principles which govern accounting transactions, determinations, and financial presentations, we shall be primarily concerned here with an examination of their significance to the intelligent user and analyst of financial statements. In this chapter we shall deal with the principles which underly the measurement and presentation of current assets.

CASH

Cash is considered the most liquid of assets. In fact, it represents the starting point, as well as the finish line, of what is known as the "accounting cycle." This cycle encompasses the purchase and manufacture of goods and services as well as their sale and the collection of the proceeds. The realization of a transaction is measured by sale and later by the ultimate conversion of the consideration received into cash. Disregarding fixed commitments to the satisfaction of which cash must be applied, cash represents that point in the accounting cycle at which management has the maximum discretion with regard to the deployment and use of the resources.

By the very nature of its inherent liquidity, cash does not present serious valuation problems even though this characteristic requires special precautions against theft and defalcation. Care should be taken in the classification of cash items when restrictions have been placed on its disposition. For example, in the case of a segregation for plant expansion or for some other type of specific restriction, the cash balance involved should be separately shown. It may not, of course, be properly includible among current assets, which heading denotes liquidity and availability for the payment of current obligations. However, accountants do not regard compensating balances maintained under a loan agreement as a restriction on cash because banks would generally honor checks drawn against such a balance. However, in assessing the current ratio the analyst must consider the repercussions which may follow from the breaking of a tacit agreement with the bank. This may involve the loss of a credit source, and thus have an effect on a company's liquidity and access to ready funds.

MARKETABLE SECURITIES

Marketable securities represent in most instances temporary repositories of excess cash. They are usually shown among current assets. However, marketable securities which are temporary investments of cash designated for special purposes such as plant expansion or the meeting of requirements under sinking fund provisions should be shown among long-term investments.

The accounting for marketable securities has been a matter of considerable controversy, and recently an APB *Draft Opinion* has been circulated suggesting that investments in *equity* securities be accounted for at fair value. This point of view has, so far, not been adopted.

Present accounting practice is to carry marketable securities at cost. They must, however, be written down when there is evidence of a permanent decline in value. There is no authoritative pronouncement on how a "permanent" decline in value is to be determined.

An exception to the general practice of valuing marketable securities at cost can be found in the stock brokerage industry where traditional thinking of necessity gave way to operating realities and needs. In this industry it was agreed that it was appropriate to carry marketable securities, including those held as investments, at market quotations and that it was also appropriate in this industry to carry securities which are not readily marketable at fair values.

The Prospectus dated April 9, 1970 of Donaldson, Lufkin & Jenrette, Inc. illustrates the accounting for this securities house. It states: "For financial statement purposes all marketable securities held in dealer inventory accounts and in investment accounts are valued at market with resultant changes reflected in net income for the period."

Implications for analysis

The carrying of marketable securities at cost is not useful accounting from the analyst's point of view. The analyst should be alert for supplementary disclosure of the market value of such securities so that he can evaluate their overvaluation or undervaluation in the balance sheet. The analyst should recognize that present accounting principles call for "evidence of a permanent decline in market value" before the carrying value of such investments has to be written down from cost to market. This is obviously not an objective test since few things in the market are "permanent."

The current market value of investments is always relevant to an assessment of management performance. The argument that unrealized gains are only "paper profits" which could melt away before the investments are actually sold or otherwise disposed of does not recognize the fact that management makes the decision to hold or sell. Thus, a reduction in unrealized appreciation of an investment is as much a loss as would be a similar size loss on inventories or on equipment which became prematurely obsolete.

The analyst should treat with suspicion the amortization of bond discount (i.e., write-up of bond by crediting income) of an issue which from all available evidence sells at a discount because of doubt as to the ultimate collectibility of the principal amount.

The analyst, aware of accounting principles governing the presentation of investments, must pay particular attention to their valuation. On the one hand they can be grossly undervalued on the balance sheet because of the convention prohibiting their write-up to market value no matter how obvious and soundly based such value may be.

On the other hand the analyst must be alert to impairment of market value which because of loose standards in practice may not be fully reflected on the financial statements. If separately disclosed, the income generated by the investment may, at times, provide a clue to its fair value.

While the recognition of profits in nonequity securities must, according to present theory, await realization (i.e., in most cases sale), losses must be taken when they are deemed to be permanent in nature. However, the criteria for determining when a loss is "permanent" in nature are indefinite and allow for much leeway. With hope springing eternal, such write-downs occur in practice only when the evidence of loss in value is overwhelming. Since proper disclosure requires that the market value of securities be indicated, the alert analyst will be on the lookout for this information so that he can exercise his own judgment regarding the proper value to assign to these securities for the purpose of his analysis.

RECEIVABLES

Receivables are amounts due arising generally from the sale of goods or services. They may also represent accrued amounts due, such as rents, interest, etc. Notes receivable represent a more formal evidence of indebtedness due, but this characteristic does not make them more readily collectible than accounts receivable. Generally speaking, notes receivable are more easily negotiable and pledged for loans than are accounts receivable and, consequently, are considered the more liquid of the two. As a practical matter this is, however, a superficial distinction.

Receivables classified as current assets should be reasonably expected to be realized or collected within a year or within the normal operating cycle of a business. *The normal operating cycle* is a concept which is important in the classification of items as current or noncurrent. The operating cycle generally encompasses the full circle of time from the commitment of cash for purchases until the collection of receivables resulting from the sale of goods or services. Exhibit 3–1 illustrates the concept.

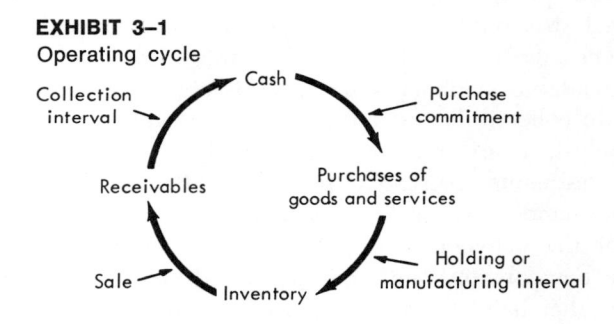

EXHIBIT 3–1
Operating cycle

Cash
Collection interval
Purchase commitment
Receivables
Purchases of goods and services
Sale
Inventory
Holding or manufacturing interval

If the normal collection interval of receivables is longer than a year (e.g., longer term installment receivables), then their inclusion as current assets is proper provided the collection interval is normal and expected for the type of business the enterprise is engaged in. Because of their nature, certain types of receivables require separate disclosure. Examples are: receivables from affiliated companies, officers, or employees.

Certain types of receivables are established without formal billing of the debtor. Thus, costs accumulated under a cost-plus-fixed-fee contract or some other types of government contracts are recorded as receivables as they accumulate. Similarly, claims for tax refunds from the government are usually classified as receivables if no substantial question of technical compliance is involved.

To the financial analyst the valuation of receivables is important from two main points of view:

1. The realization value of the assets.
2. The impact on income.

These two aspects are, of course, interrelated. It is a fact supported by experience that not all receivables will be collected nor will they all necessarily be collected in their entirety.

While a judgment about the collectibility of any one account can be made at any appropriate time, the collectibility of receivables as a group is best estimated on the basis of past experience with due allowance for current conditions. The "accounting risk" here is that the past experience may not be an adequate measure of future loss or that current developments may not have been fully taken into account. The resulting loss can be substantial and will affect both the current asset position as well as the net income for the period under review.

ILLUSTRATION. Brunswick Corporation, in 1963, made a "special provision for possible losses on receivables" of $15,000,000 *after* taxes. The assumption is that factors which became clear in 1963 were not "visible" or obvious to the auditor at the end of 1962 when a substantial amount of the receivables provided for was outstanding. Management explained the write-off as follows:

"Delinquencies in bowling installment payments, primarily related to some of the large chain accounts, *continued* at an unsatisfactory level. Nonchain accounts, which comprise about 80% of installment receivables, are generally better paying accounts.

"In the last quarter of 1963, average bowling lineage per establishment fell short of the relatively low lineage of the comparable period of 1962, resulting in an aggravation of collection problems on certain accounts. The bowling business may have felt the competition of outdoor activities associated with the unseasonably warm weather during the latter part of 1963. Some improvement in bowling lineage was noted in the early months of 1964 which tends to confirm this view. However, the fact that collections were lower in late 1963 contributed to management's decision to increase reserves. After the additional provision of $15,000,000, total reserves for possible future losses on all receivables amounted to $66,197,000, including *$30,000,000 transferred from deferred income taxes.*

"This transfer was made because the installment basis of reporting income from bowling equipment installment sales is followed for income tax purposes. Income taxes applicable to these sales are payable over the terms of installment notes receivable as payments are received from customers. To the extent that such installment notes receivable are not collected, the related deferred income taxes previously provided will not be payable and consequently, are available to cover losses, if any, on such installment notes." [Author's emphasis.]

While it may be impossible to define the precise moment when the collection of a receivable is doubtful enough to require provision, the question may be properly asked whether the analyst could not, in 1962, have made an independent judgment on the adequacy of the bad debt provision in the light of developments in the bowling industry with which he should have been thoroughly familiar. It should be noted that Brunswick's earnings peaked out in early 1962.

54 Understanding corporate reports

Another aspect of receivable valuation relates to long-term receivables which are noninterest bearing or which bear unrealistically low rates of interest.

APB *Opinion No. 21*—"Interest on receivables and payables"

Objective. The primary objective of this Opinion is to refine the manner of applying existing accounting principles when the face amount of a note (as defined below) does not reasonably represent the present value of the consideration given or received in an exchange.

The Opinion covers receivables and payables which represent contractual rights to receive or pay money on fixed or determinable dates. These are collectively referred to as "notes."

The Opinion does not apply to trade receivables and payables due within one year, progress payments, deposits, retainages, customary activities of lending institutions, notes which bear interest at rates prescribed by governmental agencies, or intercompany transactions.

Significant provisions. A note may be issued for cash or for property, goods, or services.

When issued for cash, a note is presumed to have a present value at issuance measured by the cash proceeds exchanged, unless other rights or privileges (stated or unstated) are included (such as the issuance of a noninterest bearing loan to a supplier who, in turn, charges less than the prevailing market price for products purchased by the lender under a contractual agreement).

When issued in a noncash transaction, the stated face amount of the note is generally presumed to represent the fair value of the consideration exchanged unless:

1. Interest is not stated,
2. The stated interest rate is unreasonable, or
3. The stated face amount of the note is materially different from the current sales price for the same or similar items or from the market value of the note at the date of the transaction.

When the stated face amount of the note does not represent the fair value of the consideration exchanged, the present value of the note must be established, taking into consideration:

1. The fair value of the consideration exchanged,
2. The market value of the note, or
3. The present value of all future payments.

The imputed rate of interest used for valuation purposes will normally be at least equal to the rate at which the debtor can obtain financing of a similar nature from other sources at the date of the transaction and may be influenced by:

1. An approximation of the prevailing market rates for the sources of credit that would provide a market for sale or assignment of the note;
2. The prime or higher rate for notes which are discounted with banks, giving due weight to the credit standing of the maker;
3. Published market rates for similar quality bonds;
4. Current rates for debentures with substantially identical terms and risks that are traded in open markets; or
5. The current rate charged by investors for first or second mortgage loans on similar property.

The difference between the present value and the face amount of the note should be treated as discount or premium and amortized as interest expense or income over the life of the note in such a way as to result in a constant rate of interest when applied to the amount outstanding at the beginning of any period (interest method).

The discount or premium should be reported in the balance sheet as a direct deduction from or addition to the face amount of the note.

Example of application of imputation of interest. The XYZ Corporation issued a noninterest bearing note (face amount $5,180) to Toro Machinery Company for purchase of machinery on August 17, 19x1. The face amount of the note is to be paid on July 31, 19x8. It is felt that for a similar type note an interest rate of 8 percent is applicable.

Toro Machinery Company will record as sales and as the receivable from XYZ, $3,032, representing the present value of $5,180 to be received on July 31, 19x8. Over the intervening periods, Toro Machinery will pick up as interest income the increases in the present value of the receivable from XYZ. If we assume that Toro's fiscal year-end is September 30, the pattern of interest income pickup on a yearly basis, and the carrying amounts of the receivable will be as follows:

Year	Month end	Face amount	Imputed interest income	Unamortized discount	Discounted value of receivable (rounded)
19x1	8	$5,180.00	...	$2,147.54	$3,032.00
19x1	9	5,180.00	$ 29.65	2,117.89	3,062.00
19x2	9	5,180.00	245.69	1,872.20	3,307.00
19x3	9	5,180.00	264.62	1,607.58	3,572.00
19x4	9	5,180.00	285.79	1,321.79	3,858.00
19x5	9	5,180.00	308.66	1,013.13	4,166.00
19x6	9	5,180.00	333.35	679.78	4,500.00
19x7	9	5,180.00	360.02	319.76	4,860.00
19x8	7	...	319.76	...	...
Total			$2,147.54		

Implications for financial analysis

The two most important questions facing the financial analyst with respect to receivables are:

1. Is the receivable genuine, due, and enforceable?
2. Has the probability of collection been properly assessed?

While the unqualified opinion of an independent auditor should lend assurance with regard to an affirmative answer to these questions, the financial analyst must recognize the possibility of an error of judgment as well as the lack of it.

1. The description of the receivables or the notes to the financial statement will usually not contain sufficient clues to permit an informed judgment as to whether a receivable is genuine, due, and enforceable. Consequently, a knowledge of industry practices and supplementary sources of information must be used for additional assurance.

In some industries, such as the phonograph record, toy, or bakery business, customers enjoy a substantial right of merchandise return, and allowance must be made for this.

The following note to the financial statements appearing in the 1964 annual report of the O. M. Scott & Sons Company exemplifies the type of disclosure which does shed additional light on the contingencies to which receivables are subject:

Accounts receivable: Accounts receivable are stated net after allowances for returns, allowances, and doubtful accounts of $472,000 at September 30, 1964 ($640,000 at September 30, 1963).

Accounts receivable at September 30, 1964 include approximately $4,785,000 ($7,090,000 at September 30, 1963) for shipments made under a deferred payment plan whereby title to the merchandise is transferred to the dealer when shipped; however, the Company retains a security interest in such merchandise until sold by the dealer. Payment to the Company is due from the dealer as the merchandise is sold at retail. The amount of receivables of this type shall at no time exceed $11,000,000 under terms of the loan and security agreement. . . .

In some instances a receivable may not represent a true sale but rather a merchandise or service advance; they cannot be considered in the same light as regular receivables.

2. Most provisions for uncollectible accounts are based on past experience, although they should also make allowance for current and emerging industry conditions. In actual practice the accountant is likely to attach more importance to the former than to the latter. In such cases the analyst must use his own judgment and knowledge of industry

conditions to assess the adequacy of the provision for uncollectible accounts (see example of the Brunswick Corporation earlier in this chapter).

Unfortunately, information that would be helpful in assessing the general level of collection risks in the receivables is not usually found in published financial statements. Such information can, of course, be sought from other sources or from the company directly. Examples of such information are:

1. What is the customer concentration? What percentage of total receivables is due from one or a few major customers? Would failure of any one customer have a material impact on the company's financial condition?
2. What is the age pattern of the receivables?
3. What proportion of notes receivable represent renewals of old notes?
4. Have allowances been made for trade discounts, returns, or other credits to which customers are entitled?

The financial analyst, in assessing the current financial position and a company's ability to meet its obligations currently, as expressed by such measures as the current ratio (discussed in Chapter 14), must recognize the full import of those accounting conventions which relate to the classification of receivables as "current." Thus, the operating cycle theory allows the inclusion of installment receivables which may not be fully collectible for years. In balancing these against current obligations, allowance for these differences in timing should be made.

INVENTORIES

With the possible exception of some service organizations, in most businesses inventories represent assets of great importance. From the point of view of the analyst of financial statements, inventories are significant for two main reasons:

1. They represent a significant, major component of the assets devoted to the conduct of the business.
2. They enter importantly in the determination of net income.

Asset valuation

Inventories are goods which are acquired for resale or which enter into goods produced for resale. In nonmanufacturing enterprises, such as retail establishments, purchased merchandise requires little or no additional work before resale. In manufacturing organizations we classify three main types of inventories:

1. Raw materials,
2. Goods in process, and
3. Finished goods,

depending on their stage of completion in the production process.

The importance attached to methods of inventory valuation and the controversies surrounding them is due primarily to the fact that they enter into the determination of the cost of goods sold and thus into the determination of net income. It is easy to understand why this is so. All material or goods purchased by an enterprise for resale are either sold or carried in inventory for use and sale at some future time. Thus, excluding material written off as worthless or missing, whatever is not on hand in the ending inventory must have been disposed of and, therefore, be part of the cost of goods sold and vice versa.

A most important factor to be recognized about accounting principles which govern the valuation of inventories is that they are primarily aimed at obtaining the best matching of cost and revenues. As a result of this orientation towards the income statement, the resulting, or residual, balance sheet inventory figure may be rendered inaccurate or even meaningless. This, as we shall see, can often be the case.

The basic principle of inventory valuation is that it be valued at "the lower of cost or market." This simple phrase belies the complexities and the variety of alternatives to which it is subject. This variety can, in turn, lead to significantly different figures of periodic income all "in accordance with generally accepted accounting principles."

What is cost? The complexities of cost determination are caused by a diversity of assumptions and of practice in two main areas:

1. What is includable cost?
2. What assumptions do we make about the flow of inventory costs through an enterprise?

What is includable cost? Let us start with a simple example. An office supply store buys a desk for resale. The invoice cost of the desk is obviously the basic cost. To that may properly be added the cost of freight-in as well as the costs of assembling the desk if that is the form in which it is kept in inventory. If the desk was imported, duty and other direct costs of clearing the desk through customs may properly be added. Suppose the president and others expend a great deal of time and effort in purchasing the desks. Should any part of the cost of their time be allocated to it, that is, inventoried if the desk is unsold at year-end? Here the answer is not so clear. Accounting principles would sanction allocation of such costs to inventories, but they would also sanction the current expensing of such costs. This will, of course, make a difference in the reported results for the year. Should expenses incurred in selling desks be added to their cost? Here there is more unanimity of view that such costs do not belong in inventory.

In spite of its importance, the matter of what costs are included in inventory or, conversely, excluded therefrom, is only rarely discussed or disclosed in published financial statements. The following example of disclosure, appearing in the 1967 annual report of the Eckmar Corporation, is an exception:

Note—inventories. The carrying amounts of inventories as of December 31, 1967, include estimated amounts of costs, aggregating approximately $270,000, incurred for purchasing, freight, receiving, material handling, and warehousing applicable to materials and merchandise and for certain administrative functions considered to relate to manufacturing operations. Such costs previously had been charged to income when incurred. Inventories at December 31, 1967, also include certain items of supplies, amounting to approximately $30,000, not previously inventoried. The inclusion of these amounts in inventories as of December 31, 1967, had the effect of reducing cost of products and merchandise sold by approximately $150,000 and selling, administrative, and general expenses by approximately $150,000, and the net loss of the Corporation and subsidiaries for the year by approximately $300,000.

The need for this disclosure becomes clearer when we find that the auditor's opinion includes the following statement: "As explained in Note B to the financial statements, the Corporation revised as of December 31, 1967, its inventory policies to include in inventory additional amounts of overhead and supplies; our approval of these changes is conditioned upon the ability of the Corporation to recover such amounts in subsequent operations. In our opinion, subject (1) realization of the carrying amounts of inventories. . . ."

Consider the following note on inventories appearing in the 1970 financial statements of Celanese Corporation:

Inventories. Inventories, generally, are valued at standard costs that approximate current production costs and are not valued in excess of market. Inventory values are stated after deducting an allowance for obsolesence and do not include depreciation of property, plant and equipment.

The exclusion of depreciation from inventories did not result in any comment on the part of the independent auditors.

It is important to understand the difference between the current expensing of a cost and its inclusion in inventory. The current expensing of a cost converts it into what is known as a "period cost," that is, a cost deemed to expire during the fiscal period in which it is incurred, rather than its continuance by virtue of its conversion into an asset. Conversely, a cost which is inventoried does not become a charge against current income and remains, instead as an asset to be charged against future operations which are presumed to benefit from it. It can be readily seen that a decision to inventory a cost rather than expense it *shifts* a charge to income from the present to the future.

Cost accounting

The foregoing desk inventory example was relatively simple because the inventory problem was that of a retailer. If we consider the cost problem of the desk manufacturer, additional complexities are introduced.

In producing the desk from its basic components, the manufacturer will incur three main types of cost:

1. Raw materials going into the desk.
2. Labor to produce and assemble the desk.
3. Indirect expenses such as wear and tear of machinery, auxiliary supplies, heat, light and power, various factory occupancy costs, supervisory costs, etc.

While the first two categories of expense may present some problems of classification, it is in the third group that we will find the greatest variety of treatments and the most problems. This category is also known as indirect expenses or overhead costs.

Overhead costs. While it may be reasonably feasible to maintain control over the direct material and direct labor costs that go into the making of a desk, it is not practicable, if not impossible, to trace the specific overhead costs to the desk. This requires *allocation* of an entire pool of costs to the many products (e.g., desks, chairs, shelves, bookcases, etc.) which the manufacturer produces. This allocation requires a number of assumptions and decisions such as:

1. What items should be includable in overhead costs?
2. Over how many units (e.g., desks) do we allocate the overhead costs?

Includable costs in overhead. When we examine the costs which the retailer could include in the "cost per desk," we see that certain costs were generally accepted as includable while others were not clearly includable. In the area of manufacturing overheads, differences between theory and practice are even more prevalent because of the far greater variety of expenses involved and because of the wide variety of acceptable methods or because of practice which is not subject to meaningful restraints. In the matter of includable expenses, consider, for example, the following questions:

a) Should costs of developing and testing new designs and materials of a desk be charged to inventories? If so, on what basis and over how many units?

b) Should general and administrative costs be included in inventory?

As of now there may be general acceptance of a number of ways in which to answer these questions. But there is by no means a single answer that is accepted more than all others.

Assumptions of activity. The allocation of overhead costs to all the desks, chairs, and other items produced must, of course, be done on a rational basis designed to get the best approximation of actual cost. However, this is far from an easy matter. The greatest difficulty stems from the fact that a good part of overhead represents "fixed costs," that is, costs which do not vary with production but vary mostly with the passage of time. Examples are rent payments and the factory manager's salary. Thus, assuming for a moment that only desks are produced, if the fixed costs are $100,000 and 10,000 desks are produced, each desk will absorb $10 of fixed costs. However, if only 5,000 desks are produced, each desk will have to absorb $20 of fixed costs. Clearly then, the level of activity itself is an important determinant of unit cost. In other words, wide fluctuations in output can result in wide fluctuations in unit cost.

Since the allocation of overhead depends also on an accurate estimate of total overhead costs which will be incurred during the period, variations between estimated and actual costs can also result in overabsorbed or underabsorbed overhead.

In order to allocate fixed costs over output, an assumption must be made at the outset of the fiscal period as to how many units (desks) the company expects to produce and that in turn will determine over how many units the overhead costs will be allocated. This procedure entails estimates of sales and related production. To the extent that the actual production differs from estimated production, the overhead will be either overabsorbed or underabsorbed. That means that production and inventory are charged with more than total overhead costs or with an insufficient amount of overhead costs.

A cost system which charges cost of goods sold and inventories with predetermined estimated costs is called a *standard cost* system. Variations between the estimates or standards and actual costs are called cost accounting variances. Generally speaking when an inventory is described as being valued at standard cost, that should mean that variances are insignificant or have been allocated or otherwise adjusted; in other words, standard costs would approximate actual costs. It is not permissible to carry inventories at only direct costs with the current expensing of all fixed overheads.

The next area of inventory cost determination which we will examine relates to assumptions regarding the *flow* of goods and their costs. While the methods used in this connection (Lifo, Fifo, average cost) are the most controversial methods associated with inventory accounting, it should be clear from the foregoing discussion that the problems of cost accounting and overhead allocations may produce even more variation in reported results than can the assumptions about cost flows.

Inventory cost flows

In order to keep the discussion simple let us return to our example of the office furniture retailer and assume that in the fiscal year ended December 31, 19x2, the inventory record of desks showed the following details:

Inventory on January 1, 19x2	100 desks @ $40	$ 4,000
First purchase in 19x2	200 desks @ $50	10,000
Second purchase in 19x2	100 desks @ $50	5,000
Third purchase in 19x2	200 desks @ $60	12,000
Total available for sale	600 desks	$31,000

Assuming that 50 desks are in inventory as at December 31, 19x2, how should they be valued?

There are a number of methods, all enjoying the "generally accepted" label, of which the three most common are discussed in the sections that follow.

First-in, first-out (Fifo). This method assumes what is probably the most common and justified assumption about the flow of goods in a business, that is, that those units bought first are sold (or used) first. This is also in accordance with best inventory management practice. Under this method the 50 desks will be valued at $60 each, the unit cost of the last purchase, or $3,000. The resulting cost of goods sold is $28,000 ($31,000 representing the cost of all goods available for sale less $3,000 the value assigned to the ending inventory).

Last-in, first-out (Lifo). The assumption that the earliest purchases are the ones in inventory has been likened to the pile "flow" of inventory. If an inventory consists of a pile of salt, or crushed rock or coal, then the last quantity bought is likely to be the first removed and sold. But this concern with a parallel to physical movement of inventories misses the real intention in inventory valuation. That relates primarily to an assumption about the flow of *costs* rather than of physical units, and the flow of costs is chosen not because it parallels the physical goods movement but rather because it achieves certain objectives of inventory valuation. The major objective of the Lifo method is to charge cost of goods sold with the most recent costs incurred. Quite obviously where the price level remains stable the results under either the Fifo or the Lifo method will be much the same; but under a changing price level, as the advancing one in our example, the results in the use of these methods will differ significantly. The use of the Lifo method has increased greatly due to its acceptance for tax purposes. Our tax law stipulates that its use for tax purposes makes mandatory its adoption for financial reporting. The aim is to obtain a better matching of current revenues with current costs in times of inflation. As will be seen in the discussion of the effects of price level changes, this objective is not always achieved.

In our example the inventory of 50 desks under the Lifo method will be valued at $40 each or $2,000. The cost of goods sold is $29,000 ($31,000 − $2,000). The inventory figure of $2,000 on the balance sheet will be one third below current market (or at least one third below the latest cost), but the income statement will be more realistically presented in terms of matching current costs with current revenues.

Average cost. The average cost method smoothes out cost fluctuation by using a moving-average cost in valuing inventories and in pricing out the cost of goods sold. While the moving-average cost of goods sold will depend on the timing of sales, we can, in this example, consider the average cost of all purchases during the year and the opening inventory. On that basis the average price per desk is $51.67 ($31,000 ÷ 600), and the 50 desks will be valued at $2,583.50. The cost of goods sold would be $28,416.50 ($31,000 − $2,583.50).

To summarize, under the three methods the following results are obtained:

	Fifo	Lifo	Average
Ending inventory	$ 3,000.00	$ 2,000.00	$ 2,583.50
Cost of goods sold	28,000.00	29,000.00	28,416.50

Assuming that the sales of desks for the period amounted to $35,000, the gross profit under each method would be as follows:

	Fifo	Lifo	Average
Sales	$35,000.00	$35,000.00	$35,000.00
Cost of goods sold	28,000.00	29,000.00	28,416.50
Gross profit	$ 7,000.00	$ 6,000.00	$ 6,583.50

It is clear that the choice of method (i.e., the assumption about cost flows) can make a significant difference in the determination of cost of goods sold and the valuation of inventories. Generally, the Fifo method provides a "good" inventory figure because it reflects the latest costs. The Lifo method, on the other hand, produces a better matching of costs and revenues. In times of changing prices, both virtues cannot be achieved simultaneously under the cost method.

A method of inventory valuation in use especially for interim statement results is the gross profit method. This method derives the inventory figure by estimating the cost of goods sold on the basis of a normal gross profit ratio experienced in practice. This method is accurate only if the gross profit ratio has in fact not changed and if there are no unusual inventory shortages or spoilage.

The retail method of inventory estimation is an extension of the gross profit method. It uses sophisticated techniques which involve physical inventory taking, priced first at retail, and the reduction of this inventory to cost by means of gross profit ratios.

Inventory valuation at "market"

With the exception of Lifo cost, the inventory at cost must be compared with inventory at market and the lower of the two used.

"Market value" is defined as current replacement cost except that market shall not be higher than net realizable value nor should it be less than net realizable value reduced by the normal profit margin.

The upper limit of market value in effect considers the costs associated with sale or other disposition costs. The lower limit means that if the inventory is written down from cost to market it be written down to a figure that will in sure the realization of a "normal" gross profit on its sale in a subsequent period.

Inventories under long-term contracts

The accumulation of costs under long-term contracts, reduced by progress billings, are in the nature of inventories. Two methods of accounting are acceptable here, but it is intended that their use should be dictated by surrounding circumstances.

1. Where estimates of the final outcome or results of the contracts are difficult or impossible to make and are too speculative to be reliable, the *completed contract* method should be used. Under this method all costs of the contract, including related general and administrative costs, are accumulated and carried as assets (inventories) until completion of the contract when final net profit or loss is determined.
2. Where estimates of cost and related incomes at each stage of completion of the contract can be made, the *percentage-of-completion* method of long-term contract accounting should be used. Under

this method the estimated proportionate profit earned up to any particular point in time may be credited to income and correspondingly included in accumulated costs (inventories).

Under either method, losses that are ascertainable at any point in time should be recognized and accounted for when first determined.

Classification of inventories

Generally, inventories are classified as current assets. Indeed they represent in most cases a very important part of the current asset group, although, ordinarily, they are considered less liquid than cash or receivables.

Under the "normal operating cycle" concept, inventories which would be kept beyond a year because of the requirements typical of an industry would nevertheless be classified as current. Thus, inventories in the tobacco industry or the liquor industry, which go through prolonged aging cycles, are nevertheless classified as current.

Inventories in excess of current requirements should not be classified as current.

ILLUSTRATION. Molybdenum Corporation of America (prospectus dated November 24, 1964) had a note to financial statements which read in part:
"The December 31, 1963 and June 30, 1964 inventories include $758,725 and $706,586 respectively of rare earth inventories considered necessary for current requirements. Additional rare earth inventories considered in excess of current requirements and valued at lower of cost or market in amount of $1,213,298 at December 31, 1963 and June 30, 1964 are classified in the balance sheets immediately following current assets."

IMPLICATIONS FOR FINANCIAL ANALYSIS

It is obvious that to the extent to which alternative choices of accounting principles, and the methods of their application, proliferate, the wider is management's flexibility in reporting results and in presenting the enterprise's financial condition. In the area of inventory accounting, where the impact of differing methods on income can be substantial, this flexibility is all the more likely to be availed of by management.

The auditor's opinion should provide assurance that certain minimum standards were upheld in the exercise of discretion with which such principles are applied. However, in some areas of inventory accounting the permitted leeway is so considerable that management can exercise a great deal of discretion in its choices. Thus, as a minimum, the financial analyst must understand what these choices are, and he must judge them in the light of conditions which apply to each specific situation.

With regard to inventories, the financial analyst will expect information and assurance as to the following:

1. Is the inventory physically in existence and is it fairly valued?
2. Has the accounting for inventories been consistent?
3. Can the effect of the different accounting methods used be measured?

Audit procedures designed to give assurance about the physical existence of inventories have been improving over the years and have been especially tightened up since the 1938 SEC hearings in the matter of McKesson & Robbins, Inc. In this case, large-scale fraud which resulted in a substantial overstatement of inventories was not uncovered by the audit primarily because no attempt was made by the auditors to establish physical contact with the inventories. The SEC stated:

> In our opinion, the time has come when auditors must, as part of their examination whenever reasonable and practicable, make physical contact with the inventory and assume reasonable responsibility therefor as had already become the practice in many cases before the present hearings. By this we do not mean that auditors should be, or by making such tests become, the guarantors of inventories any more than of any of the other items in the financial statements but we do mean that they should make all reasonable tests and inquiries, and not merely those limited to the books, in order to state their professional opinion, as auditors, as to the truthfulness of that item in the same way as they do for the other items in the statements.

The accounting profession responded by adopting the requirement that auditors observe the taking of physical inventories whenever it was reasonable and practicable to do so. This requirement, as well as the refinement of audit techniques, has brought about great improvements in the reliability of inventory audits. Nevertheless, exceptional cases still arise. For example, in 1967 Medco Inc., an operator of leased jewelry departments in discount stores, had to revise previously results substantially because an audit disclosed overstatements of inventory. The significance of this lies not only in the possibility that such inventory overstatements had occurred but also in the very substantial impact (35 percent in 1967) which they had on reported earnings.

The fair statement of inventories is, of course, not dependent merely on a proper accounting for physical inventories but also on their proper pricing and summarization.

While under the going-concern convention accountants are not concerned with the sale of inventories other than in the normal course of business, the analyst, and especially the credit analyst concerned with current values, may be interested in the composition of inventories. Thus, raw material may be much more readily salable than work in process since once raw material is converted into parts of certain specifications, it rapidly loses its value in case it then has to be liquidated.

Accepted reporting standards (which are part of generally accepted auditing standards) require that changes in the application of accounting principles be noted and the impact of the change reported. Thus, in audited financial statements the analyst will expect to be alerted to changes in principles of inventory accounting, such as, for example, from Lifo to Fifo. However, the analyst must be aware of the fact that only changes in accounting principles call for a consistency exception, whereas other changes affecting comparability do not necessarily call for disclosure in the auditor's report. (In SEC filings, all changes affecting comparability must be so disclosed.) As was seen in the discussion on the accounting for inventories, in many areas freedom of choice may result in change such as in the definition of costs properly includable in inventory.

It is a fact that in most published reports insufficient information is given to allow the analyst to convert inventories accounted for under one method to a figure reflecting a different method of inventory accounting. Most analysts would want such information in order to be able to better compare the financial statements of companies which use different inventory accounting methods.

Converting an inventory figure from one method to another is made even more difficult by the use of different methods for various components of inventory. Thus, for example, in its 1970 annual report, Graniteville Company presented inventory information as follows:

Current Assets:
  Inventories (Note 2)
    Raw materials............ $ 2,428,394
    Stock in process 1,963,531
    Finished goods 16,583,153
    Dyes, chemicals, etc........ 1,160,776
      Total Inventories....... $22,135,854

Note 2: Inventories Inventory items of raw materials, stock in process and finished goods are principally valued on the Lifo basis with additions computed at first quarter average cost, except for the synthetic fiber content of these inventories, which is valued on the basis of the lower of average cost or market. At January 2, 1971, the carrying value of Lifo inventories was less than market.

Inventories of dyes, chemicals, etc., are valued on the basis of moving-average cost. Certain supplies, repair parts, maintenance materials, and similar items are charged as operating expenses when purchased in accord with the company's accounting policy, followed on a consistent basis.

The lack of information necessary to adjust for different inventory methods is not necessarily due to a desire on the part of management to be secretive. In most cases it is not readily available, and obtaining it would require laborious calculations and record keeping. Thus, in most cases financial analysts will have to make an overall assessment of the impact of differing inventory methods on the comparability of inventory figures. Such an assessment should be based on a thorough understanding of the inventory methods in use and the effect they are likely to have on inventory values. The differences between such informed approximations and the exact figures that can be arrived at only with use of additional data will in most cases not be material from the analyst's point of view.

A study[1] of the impact of the Lifo method on financial ratios revealed the following interesting conclusions:

> . . . regardless of the reason given, the information necessary to analyze the effects of differing inventory valuation methods is rarely available. . . .
> An examination of the influence of the last-in, first-out inventory on current ratios reveals that for the most part, the effect is comparatively small. . . .
> . . . It appears that the inventory turnover ratio cannot be reliably used as a measure of comparability between commercial or industrial firms unless they employ similar methods of inventory valuation, and even then, the reliability of the comparison is questionable if LIFO valuation is in use.
> *The exact influence of LIFO inventory valuation on financial ratios can be discerned only if one has information regarding the difference between the inventory valuation under LIFO and* what it would have been under some other method. The average financial analyst does not have this information and, in nearly all cases, will be unable to obtain it. Very few companies include this information in their annual reports and those which do not will normally refuse, for various reasons, to divulge it. *It is, therefore, fortunate that the effect of LIFO inventories on ratios does prove to be a rather* insignificant variation in most instances.

Very few useful generalizations about the effect of differing methods of inventory valuation on financial analysis can be made. We know, for instance, that under conditions of fluctuating price levels the Lifo inventory method will have a smoothing effect on income. Moreover, this method results, in times of price inflation, in an unrealistically low book inventory figure. This in turn will lower the current ratio of a company and at the same time tend to increase its inventory turnover ratio. We also know that the Lifo method affords management an opportunity to manipulate profits by allowing inventory to be depleted in poor years, thus drawing on the low-cost base pool. A judgment on all these effects can only be made on the basis of an assessment of all surrounding circumstances. Thus, for example, a slight change in a current ratio of 4:1 may be of no significance, whereas the same change in a ratio of 1.5:1 may be of far greater importance.

The "lower-of-cost-or-market" principle of inventory accounting has additional implications for the analyst. In times of rising prices it tends

---

[1] George C. Holdren, "LIFO and Ratio Analysis," *The Accounting Review,* January 1964.

to undervalue inventories regardless of the cost method used. This in turn will depress the current ratio below its real level since the other current assets (as well as the current liabilities) are not valued on a consistent basis with the methods used in valuing inventories.

To illustrate the effect which the use of a variety of inventory methods can have on reported net income or financial ratios, let us examine the case of a retailer who deals in only one product. We assume here no opening inventory, operating expenses of $5 million, and 2 million shares outstanding. The following purchases are made during the year:

	Units	Per unit	
January	100,000	$10	$ 1,000,000
March	300,000	11	3,300,000
June	600,000	12	7,200,000
October	300,000	14	4,200,000
December	500,000	15	7,500,000
Total	1,800,000		$23,200,000

Ending inventory at December 31 was 800,000 units. Assets, excluding inventories, amounted to $75 million, of which $50 million were current. Current liabilities amounted to $25 million, and long-term liabilities came to $10 million.

The tabulation which follows shows the net income arrived at by applying the Fifo, Lifo, and average cost method respectively. Sales are at $25 per unit, and taxes are ignored.

Computation of net income

	Fifo method	Lifo method	Average costs
Sales:			
1 million units @ 25	$25,000,000	$25,000,000	$25,000,000
Cost of sales:			
Beginning inventory	...	...	...
Purchases	$23,200,000	$23,200,000	$23,200,000
Cost of goods available for sale	$23,200,000	$23,200,000	$23,200,000
Less: Ending inventory	11,700,000	9,100,000	10,312,000
Cost of sales	$11,500,000	$14,100,000	$12,888,000
Gross profit	$13,500,000	$10,900,000	$12,112,000
Operating expenses	5,000,000	5,000,000	5,000,000
Net income	$ 8,500,000	$ 5,900,000	$ 7,112,000
Net income per share	$4.25	$2.95	$3.56

The Fifo inventory computation was based upon 500,000 units at $15 and 300,000 at $14 which yields a total of $11,700,000. The Lifo inventory cost was obtained following the assumption that the units purchased last were the first sold. Therefore, the 800,000 units are priced as 100,000 units at $10, 300,000 units at $11, and 400,000 units at $12, totaling $9,100,000. The average cost was obtained by dividing $23,200,000 by 1,800,000 units purchased, yielding an average unit price of $12.89. The $12.89 unit price multiplied by 800,000 ending inventory units gives a total inventory cost of $10,312,000.

The table below shows the effect of the three inventory methods on a number of selected ratios:

	Fifo method	Lifo method	Average costs
Current ratio	2.47:1	2.36:1	2.41:1
Debt equity ratio	1:5.17	1:4.91	1:5.03
Inventory turnover	2:1	3:1	2.5:1
Return on total assets	9.8%	7.0%	8.3%
Gross margin	54%	44%	49%
Net profit as % of sales	34%	24%	29%

As the above discussion and examples clearly show, the analysis of financial statements where inventories are important requires that the analyst bring to bear a full understanding of inventory accounting methods and their impact on results.

QUESTIONS

1. Under presently accepted but changing practice, compensating balances under a bank loan agreement are considered as unrestricted cash and are classified as current assets.
    a) From the point of view of the analyst of financial statements, is this a useful classification?
    b) Give reasons for your conclusion and state how you would evaluate such balances.
2. Outline briefly the accounting for marketable securities. Is this accounting useful to the user of the financial statements? Support your views with adequate reasoning.
3. a) What is meant by the "operating cycle"?
    b) What is the significance of the operating cycle concept to the classification of current versus noncurrent items in the balance sheet?
    c) Is this concept useful to those concerned with measuring the current debt-paying ability of an enterprise and the liquidity of its working capital components?
    d) Give the effect of the operating cycle concept on the classification of selected current assets in the following industries:
        (1) Tobacco.
        (2) Liquor.
        (3) Retailing.

4. *a)* What are the financial analyst's primary concerns when it comes to the evaluation of accounts receivable?
   b) What information, not usually found in published financial statements, should the analyst obtain in order to assess the overall risk of noncollectibility of the receivables?
5. Why do financial analysts generally attach such great importance to inventories?
6. Comment on the effect which the variety of accounting methods for determining the cost of inventories have on the determination of an enterprise income. As to the inclusion of which costs in inventories, is there considerable variation in practice? Give examples of three types of such cost elements.
7. Of what significance is the *level* of activity on the unit cost of goods produced by a manufacturer? The allocation of overhead costs requires the making of certain assumptions. Explain and illustrate by means of an example.
8. What is the major objective of Lifo inventory accounting? What are the effects of this method on the measurement of income and of inventories particularly from the point of view of the user of the financial statements?
9. Comment on the disclosure with respect to inventory valuation methods which is practiced today. In what way is such disclosure useful to the analyst? What type of disclosure is relatively useful to the reader?
10. Accountants generally follow "the lower-of-cost-or-market" basis of inventory valuations.
    a) Define "cost" as applied to the valuation of inventories.
    b) Define "market" as applied to the valuation of inventories.
    c) Why are inventories valued at the lower of cost or market? Discuss.
    d) List the arguments against the use of the lower of cost or market method of valuing inventories. (AICPA)
11. Compare and contrast effects of the Lifo and Fifo inventory cost methods on earnings during a period of inflation. (C.F.A.)
12. Discuss the ways and conditions under which the Fifo and Lifo inventory costing methods produce different inventory valuations. Do not discuss procedures for computing inventory cost.

4

Analysis of noncurrent assets

IN THIS CHAPTER we conclude our examination of the measurement of assets by a discussion of the analysis of noncurrent assets.

LONG-TERM INVESTMENTS

Long-term investments are usually investments in assets such as debt instruments, equity securities, real estate, mineral deposits, or joint ventures acquired with longer term objectives in mind. Such objectives may include the ultimate acquisition of control or affiliation with other companies, investment in suppliers, securing of assured sources of supply, etc.

With the exception of the accounting for investments in common stock of certain sizes, which is discussed below, long-term investments are generally carried at cost, and temporary downward fluctuations in market value are usually ignored. However, when there is evidence of a loss of value of a permanent nature, it should be written down.

Investments in common stock

Investments in common stock representing less than 20 percent of the equity securities of the investee continue to be accounted for at cost. For certain exceptions please refer to the discussion under "marketable securities" in the preceding chapter.

Companies 20 percent to 50 percent owned. APB *Opinion No. 18* concluded that even a position of less than 50 percent of the voting stock may give the investor the ability to exercise significant influence over the operating and financial policies of the investee. When such an ability to exercise influence is evident, the investment should be accounted for under the "equity method." Basically this means at cost plus the equity in the earnings or losses of the investee since acquisition, with the addition of certain other adjustments. The mechanics of the equity method are discussed in Chapter 6.

Evidence of the investor's ability to exercise significant influence over operating and financial policies of the investee may be indicated in several ways, such as management representation and participation, but in the interest of uniformity of application the APB concluded that in the absence of evidence to the contrary, an investment (direct or indirect) of 20 percent or more in the voting stock of an investee should lead to the presumption of an ability to exercise significant influence over the investee. Conversely, an investment in less than 20 percent of the voting stock of the investee leads to the presumption of a lack of such influence unless the ability to influence can be demonstrated.

It should be noted that while the eligibility to use the equity method is based on the percentage of voting stock outstanding, which may include, for example, convertible preferred stock, the percentage of earnings which may be picked up under the equity method depends on ownership of *common stock* only.

ILLUSTRATION. Company A owns 15 percent of the common stock of Company B. By virtue of additional holdings of convertible preferred stock, the total percentage of voting power held is 20 percent. While the total holdings entitle Company A to account for its investment in Company B at equity, it can only pick up 15 percent of Company B net results because that is the percentage of ownership of *common* stock that it holds.

The above principle of picking up income under the equity method is not consistent with the concept of "common stock equivalents" used in the computation of earnings per share (see Chapter 10). The effect of possible conversions, etc. must, however, be disclosed.

Corporate joint ventures. Joint ventures represent investments by two or more entities in an enterprise with the objective of sharing sources of supply, the development of markets, or other types of risk. A common form of joint venture is a 50–50 percent sharing of ownership, although other divisions of interest are also found. An investment in a *corporate* joint venture should, according to APB *Opinion No. 18,* be accounted for by the equity method. An investment in a joint venture not evidenced by common stock ownership may presumably be accounted for at cost.

EXHIBIT 4–1
Summary of accounting treatments by investor for investments in common stocks

Size of investment in a given investee

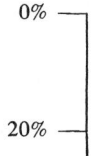

0% — Investors should, with certain exceptions, account for investments in common stock at cost.

20% — Ownership of 20 percent or more of voting stock leads to the presumption that investor has the ability to influence operating and financial policies of the investee. In such cases the equity method should be used (APB *Opinion No. 18*). Otherwise the accounting for investment positions of less than 20 percent is indicated (see above).

50% — Corporate joint ventures should be accounted for under the equity method (APB *Opinion No. 18*).

Subsidiaries (i.e., companies over 50 percent owned) should be consolidated. In certain cases use of the "equity method" may be appropriate. In case of serious doubt regarding the ultimate transferability or realization of subsidiary earnings, the "cost method" may be used (see discussion in Chapter 9).

100% —

Overview of how investments in common stock are accounted for. Exhibit 4–1 presents a summary indicating how investments in common stock of different sizes are accounted for under APB *Opinion No. 18* and other pronouncements governing the principles of consolidation accounting.

Implications for analysis

The analyst, aware of accounting principles governing the presentation of investments, must pay particular attention to their valuation. On the one hand they can be grossly undervalued on the balance sheet because of the convention prohibiting their write-up to market value, no matter how obvious and soundly based such value may be.

On the other hand the analyst must be alert to impairment of market value which, because of loose standards in practice, may not be fully reflected on the financial statements. If separately disclosed, the income generated by the investment may, at times, provide a clue to its fair value.

The accounting for investments in *common stock* has undergone significant improvement. The carrying of investments representing control of 20 percent or over at equity is an improvement over the practice which prevailed prior to the issuance of APB *Opinion No. 18*—that of carrying such investments at cost. While the equity method is more realistic than cost, it must be borne in mind that it is not the equivalent of fair market value which, depending on circumstances, may be significantly larger or lower than the carrying amount at equity.

The analyst must remember that the assumption that an investment in 20 percent or more of the voting securities of an investee results in significant influence over that investee is an arbitrary one which had to be made in the interest of accounting uniformity. If such influence is indeed absent, then there may be some question regarding the investor's ability to realize the amount stated at equity. The marketplace does not necessarily pay close attention to book values. An improvement brought about by APB *Opinion No. 18* is the requirement that where available, the market value of investments in common stock (other than in subsidiaries) be disclosed.

APB *Opinion No. 18* states that "a loss in value of an investment which is other than a temporary decline should be recognized the same as a loss in value of other long-term assets." This leaves a great deal to judgment and interpretation, and in the past this approach has resulted in companies being very slow to recognize losses in their investments. Since the Opinion does not consider a decline in market value to be conclusive evidence of such a loss, the analyst must be alert to detect situations where hope rather than reason supports the carrying amount of an investment. It must be recognized that the equity method reflects only current operating losses rather than the capital losses which occur when the earning power of an investment deteriorates or disappears.

Another area where assumptions and management discretion influences accounting is that regarding the provision for taxes to be paid at some future time when earnings recognized under the equity method are distributed in the form of dividends by the investee to the investor. APB *Opinion No. 23*, "Accounting for Income Taxes—Special Areas," held that the nature of an investor's influence over an investee is significantly different from the influence exercised by a parent over a subsidiary and, consequently, the investor should provide for taxes that will be payable when the earnings of the investee are received or otherwise realized by the investor. Thus, whether taxes at regular or capital-gains rates are provided for remains a matter of judgment by management and the independent auditors.

In the case of joint ventures, APB *Opinion No. 23*, held that unless there are indications of a limited life for the joint venture, the same tax treatment as is applicable to subsidiaries should apply, that is, provision or nonprovision of taxes on unremitted earnings depends basically on management's judgment of whether these earnings are, or are not, to be permanently invested in the subsidiary or joint venture. Since the Opinion calls for disclosure of the tax provision which would have been made had permanent investment of earnings not been assumed, the analyst is not only able to form his own opinion regarding such probabilities but is also in a position to adjust for such taxes should his views of future probabilities differ from those of the reporting entity.

The accounting for common stock positions of less than 20 percent of the equity securities of an investee as well as that for other long-term investments is presently not helpful to the analyst since historical cost is in most cases not relevant to decisions affecting the evaluation of profitability or of managerial performance. Moreover, the analyst must be alert to the overvaluation of longer term investment under the present theory of lack of "permanent" impairment in value. Managements, as is well known, often take a very optimistic view of the final workout of their investment which has temporarily fallen in market value.

The lack of definite standards of valuation of marketable securities can also result in the undervaluation of securities and, what is more significant, the manipulation of reported periodic income.

ILLUSTRATION. National General Corporation had the following note in its financial statements included in a prospectus dated 7/7/71:

"*Marketable securities.* At December 31, 1970, marketable securities acquired in 1969 and prior years are carried at market value at December 31, 1969 and securities acquired subsequent to that date are carried at cost, plus or minus amortization of bond discount or premium.

"At December 31, 1969, in the absence of any indication that the 1969 decline in the securities market was temporary, the companies reduced the carrying amounts of such investments to market value at that date.

"Gains and losses on marketable securities realized in 1970 resulted in a net gain of $3,047,000. At December 31, 1970 net unrealized losses on marketable securities were in excess of this gain, and therefore it has been deferred."

The company chose 1969, a year which resulted in the first operating loss in many years, to write down its marketable securities by over $70 million. It has not changed this valuation since even though market declines more severe than those of 1969 occurred subsequently. Elsewhere in the prospectus the company stated: "National does not adjust investments to reflect increases in market value, or to reflect declines considered of uncertain duration."

TANGIBLE FIXED ASSETS

Assets that have an expected useful life of over a year and are used in operations and not acquired for sale in the ordinary course of business comprise this category. Property, plant, and equipment is the most important asset group included in it. They consist of those tangible assets used by business enterprises for the purpose of producing and distributing its goods and services.

Asset valuation

Currently the only permissible basis of accounting for fixed assets in this country is historical cost. Historical cost means the amount of dollars paid for the asset at the date of acquisition plus any other costs properly includable, such as freight, installation, setup costs, etc.

The primary reasons advanced for retention of the historical cost basis are that it is conservative in that it does not anticipate replacement costs; it is the amount for which management is accountable; and, above all, it is the only objectively determinable cost available. Moreover, after many years of acceptance as the basis at which fixed assets are stated, historical costs are recognized as not representing value but rather original costs which have not yet been charged to operations. Some even question the usefulness of costs based on some concept of current value which would change from year to year.

To the analyst of financial statements the concept of fixed assets at (historical) cost is not a complicated one. The distinction between a current expenditure and an outlay which results in an asset which will be allocated to future operations is a well-established one which depends primarily on the purpose of the outlay, the expected life of the asset, and for internal accounting expediency, on the amount involved. Accounting principles in this area, if consistently applied, do not lend themselves to serious distortion. Such, of course, is not the case with the determination of depreciation which is another matter to be discussed later.

One type of expense, sometimes included in the cost of fixed assets and which is subject to some debate, is interest cost during construction. This represents the cost of funds tied up while the property is being constructed and before it becomes productively utilized. This cost of funds committed to construction becomes part of the cost of the plant and equipment and is allocated to future operations along with all other costs. The inclusion of this cost in the cost of fixed assets is customary, primarily in the case of public utilities, where they are thus also included in the utility's rate base.

Another area of controversy relates to costs included in fixed assets constructed in a company's own facilities. While most direct costs are includable without question, one problem area is the allocation of variable overhead and particularly fixed overhead cost to such assets. Where idle capacity has been utilized to construct capital assets, the inclusion of fixed overhead may be debatable. However, if usable production was foregone to build such assets, there is full justification for the inclusion of all proportionate overhead in the cost of the fixed assets.

One serious problem which confronts the analyst of financial statements which include fixed assets stated at historical cost is that these long-lived assets are not expressed in terms of a stable measuring unit. The accumulation of costs of assets purchased in different years represents the aggregation of units of differing purchasing power. Since depreciation—that is, the currently expired portion of the cost of these assets—is based on this original cost, the distortion is carried into the income statement. Thus, repeatedly the case has been made for adjusting original cost for changes in the price level—not as an attempt to arrive at some kind of current market value but rather to adjust the original cost for changes in the size of the dollar. This, it is argued, will not only result in more valid income statements and in a proper distinction between income and "real" capital, but will also present a fairer measure of how responsibly management has dealt with invested capital in terms of the purchasing power which has been entrusted to it.

The above discussion has pointed out the possible distortions to which historical cost accounting for long-lived assets may be subject. Further discussion of this broad subject will be found in Chapter 12 dealing with the problem of accounting under changing price levels.

The Property, Plant, and Equipment account is assumed to include assets in active or productive use. If such assets are temporarily idle, disclosure of this fact will usually be made in notes or comments in order to explain the resulting excess cost and lower profit margins.

Should a substantial segment of assets be idle for a longer period of time and without definite prospects of use, they should no longer be included in the property, plant, and equipment designation where their inclusion would distort such relationships as that of sales to plant or the return on fixed assets. Instead, they should be segregated from other assets pending their reactivation, sale, or other disposition. Such idle assets represent not only an investment on which no return is earned but they often involve expenses of upkeep and maintenance.

While the write-up of assets to current market or appraised values is not an accepted accounting procedure in the United States, the convention of conservatism requires that a permanent impairment of value and/or loss of utility of fixed assets be reflected in the accounts by a write-down. This is needed not only to reflect a loss of value and utility but also in order to relieve future periods of charges which the usefulness and productivity of the assets can no longer support and justify. Thus, for example, Cudahy Packing Company, after many years of unsatisfactory operating results, decided in 1965 to write down some of its facilities and had the following explanation in its annual report:

Operating income at the Company's four mid-western meat packing plants (Omaha, Wichita, Denver and Salt Lake City) has been generally unsatisfactory in recent years, and management studies give no assurance that significant long-term improvement can be expected. Earnings of these plants have not been sufficient to cover applicable depreciation, general office administrative and interest costs. In recognition of the loss in value of these plants as measured by their demonstrated lack of earning power, the Board of Directors determined that a special reserve should be provided equal to the net book value of the property and equipment at the four plants. No salvage values were reflected in view of the substantial contingent liabilities under the labor contract covering employees at these plants. . . . This action was taken upon the recommendation of Arthur Andersen & Co., the Company's auditors. The special property reserve ($13,789,617) and the elimination of related deferred charges ($1,087,694) have been reflected as a special charge in the accompanying statements of income and earned surplus.

Depreciation expense for these plants has been provided for 1965 and 1964, and has been shown separately on the statement of income. Such depreciation provisions will no longer be required; however, property renewals, replacements and additions at these plants (which amounted to $175,000 in 1965 and $160,000 in 1964) will be charged directly to expense in future years.

The accompanying statement of income has been prepared to show the operations of the midwestern meat packing plants separately from other operations of the Company and its subsidiaries.

The significance of Cudahy Packing Company's action should not be lost to the financial analyst. The cost of plant and equipment is an outlay of capital which must be recovered through revenues generated by operations before net income can be recognized. The process by means of which the cost of productive assets is allocated to operations is called depreciation. Depreciation covers not only deterioration due to physical wear and tear but also loss of value due to obsolescence which is caused by technical innovation and other economic factors. Prior to 1960 Cudahy reported net income, and in retrospect it appears that the depreciation provision was inadequate in that it did not allow for the obsolescence of the company's plant. Losses in the years 1960 to 1965 convinced the management of the need to relieve future operations of heavy depreciation charges, and the write-off has achieved just that.

It is interesting to note that in 1967, after what management described as further "study and analysis" of the situation, management reversed itself and reestablished part of the 1965 write-down of plant and equipment. Thus, depreciation on the book values was resumed and retroactively restated. Possibly some of the impetus for this action may have had its origin outside the company. Such vacillating accounting is, to say the least, confusing to the analyst and completely baffling to the average reader. It destroys continuity and introduces confusion into the reporting of operating results.

Riegel Paper Corporation presents an example where facilities have been retired and the assets invested therein have been "redeployed." In addition the company established concurrently reserves for future costs and losses associated with this program. (Chapter 9 contains a further discussion of the implication of such reserves to the analysis of financial statements.) The pertinent excerpts from the 1970 annual report of the company follow:

Fixed Assets, at Cost:
Property, plant, and equipment:
Land	$ 1,049,000
Buildings	41,900,000
Machinery and equipment	133,078,000
Construction in progress	4,684,000
	$180,711,000
Less accumulated depreciation and allowance for estimated losses for facilities retirement and disposition and asset redeployment (Note 7)	95,164,000
Property, plant, and equipment, net	$ 85,547,000
Timberlands	$ 13,527,000
Less accumulated depletion	4,532,000
Timberlands, net	$ 8,995,000
Fixed assets, net	$ 94,542,000

Note 7: Plan for facilities retirement and disposition and asset redeployment. On October 23, 1970, the Board of Directors approved a plan for facilities retirement and disposition and asset redeployment with respect to certain principal **facilities of the Paper Division's New Jersey** operations. The aggregate losses and costs expected to be incurred in connection with the plan, less the related current and deferred tax benefits of $3,000,000 and $6,550,000, respectively, are shown as an extraordinary charge in the accompanying statement of consolidated income. The charge takes into effect the estimated proceeds (fair market or salvage value) to be received upon the retirement and disposition of the affected facilities and the estimated time considered necessary to effect an orderly execution of the plan. While it is not presently possible to determine the actual losses and costs to be incurred in connection with the plan, it is the opinion of management of the Company that adequate provision has been made in the accompanying **financial statements** for all amounts which may be reasonably anticipated at the present time.

The reserves created by the extraordinary charge, less actual costs incurred ($234,000) and losses on fixed asset retirements ($3,039,000) through January 3, 1971, are included in the accompanying consolidated balance sheet as a reduction of property, plant and equipment.

The subject of depreciation, an important cost factor in most companies, is complex and subject to controversy. Its importance to the analyst cannot be overrated. It will be considered in Chapter 8 dealing with income determination.

Wasting assets

A category of assets which requires separate treatment is natural resources. With the exception of resources such as timber, which can be replenished by planned cutting and reseeding, most of such assets once exhausted cannot be used and lose most of their value. Examples of such resources are oil, gas, coal, iron ore, and sulphur.

Generally accepted accounting principles require that such assets be stated at original cost plus costs of discovery, exploration, and development. That means that the very significant value increment which occurs following the discovery of natural resources is not given immediate accounting recognition but shows up through the income stream when and as the resource is exploited.

The total cost of a wasting asset is generally allocated over the total units of estimated reserves available. This allocation process is known as depletion. Some companies in the mining field do not charge depletion to the income statement primarily because they believe the related assets to be grossly understated in terms of current and potential value. The subject of depletion will be discussed in Chapter 8.

Method of acquisition

Generally speaking, the method of acquiring assets or the use of assets should have no bearing on the basis on which they are carried in the accounting records. One method of acquisition which deserves separate mention, however, is leasing. Where leasing is short term, where it covers a period shorter than the asset's useful life, and where no property rights are acquired, no asset accounting is called for. In recent years, the practice of acquiring assets by means of leases which are in essence a financing method of purchases has grown and proliferated. Such leases should be accounted for as purchases, thus calling for the setting up of an asset at an amount equal to the present value of future rental payments. Since the outstanding characteristic of this transaction is the *method* of financing, this topic will be considered in the chapter devoted to the measurement of liabilities.

Implication for analysis

In valuing property, plant, and equipment and in presenting it in conventional financial statements, accountants are concerned with a number of the objectives and conventions. They are concerned with the objectivity of original cost and the conservatism implicit therein, and with an accounting for the number of dollars originally invested in such assets. Judging from the resulting figures, they are quite clearly not overly concerned with the objectives of those who analyze financial statements. They are content to proclaim that "a balance sheet does not purport to reflect and could not usefully reflect the value of the enterprise." Not that the accountant is necessarily unmindful of the interests of those who use his statements; it is rather that his overwhelming concern lies in the real or imagined problems of his own art.

While clearly in the minority, some managements are concerned about the disparity between the original cost figures presented in their reports and the market values of assets which are potentially much more useful to the reader. Thus, the management of Utilities and Industries Corporation inserted the following footnote in their 1967 annual report:

1. The Board of Directors of the Corporation believes that the Corporation's properties have a present value materially in excess of the "original cost" basis at which its properties are carried on its books by reason of the requirements of the Uniform System of Accounts prescribed by the Public Service Commission; and also that the reserve for depreciation, accrued at straight-line rates approved by the Commission, is in excess of the depreciation as demonstrated by the actual condition of the property. Pertinent to the Board's conclusion is the Corporation's experience in property condemnations (or sales in lieu thereof) since 1951. In these property dispositions, the Corporation and subsidiaries received awards or equivalent aggregating $48,637,000 for properties with a rate base carrying value of $23,869,000 on the several corresponding dates, as recorded on the books in conformity with Commission requirements.

In addition, there is included in other assets a parcel consisting of 66 acres of land in the Massapequa section of Nassau County, which land is not used in the utility operations of the Corporation and is being held for development, possibly by The South Bay Corporation, a subsidiary of the Corporation, or by others. This land is recorded in the above accounts at "original cost" to predecessors, which, in the judgment of the Board of Directors, is materially less than the value of said property.

In the context of the company's annual report, this disclosure merely hints at present market value and does not give the analyst the figure he may want, that is, what, in management's and other experts' opinions, the properties may really be worth. However, it does show a recognition of the problem faced by those who want to derive meaningful conclusions from financial statements.

Only by sheer coincidence can historical costs be useful to analysts. They are not relevant to questions of current replacement or of future needs. They are not directly comparable to similar data in other companies' reports. They do not enable us to measure the opportunity cost of disposal and alternative use of funds, nor do they provide a valid yardstick against which to measure return. Moreover, in times of changing price levels they represent an odd conglomeration of a variety of purchasing power disbursements.

It may be claimed that the value of assets is derived from their ability to earn a return and that consequently the key to their value lies in the income statement. While this is true in a significant number of cases, it does not provide the only avenue to an evaluation of an asset's worth. Thus, the earning of a return on an investment is dependent on managerial skill, and assets have a value tied to their capacity to produce. But in recognizing the importance of net income in the assessment of an asset's worth, the analyst must be aware of the problem which the method of depreciation has on the determination of net income. This aspect of the valuation of fixed assets and its effect on income is discussed fully in Chapter 8 on the analysis of income.

The effect of price level changes on fixed asset valuation will be explored more fully in Chapter 12 dealing with this general topic.

In utilizing the published figures of an enterprise's *gross* cost of property, plant, and equipment, the analyst must be aware of the fact that they are *undepreciated* balances of original cost. Thus, the first determination which he must make is whether such figures can be used for the purpose which he has in mind and, if not, what adjustments are necessary to make them more relevant.

INTANGIBLE ASSETS

Intangible assets represent rights to future benefits. One distinguishing characteristic of these assets, which is not, however, unique to them, is that they have no physical existence and depend on such expected future benefits for most of their value. In many cases, the value of these benefits is inextricably tied to the continuity of the enterprise.

Some important categories of intangibles are:

1. Goodwill.
2. Patents, copyrights, and trademarks.
3. Leases, leaseholds, and leasehold improvements.
4. Exploration rights and cost of development of natural resources.
5. Formulae, processes, and designs.
6. Licenses, franchises, and memberships.

The basic rule in accounting for purchased intangibles is that they be carried at cost. If property other than cash is given in exchange for the intangible, it must be recorded at the fair market value of the consideration given. If liabilities are assumed, the intangible is valued by taking into consideration the present value of the future obligations.

There are some paradoxes in the valuation of intangibles which should be understood by the analyst. If a company spends material and labor in the construction of a "tangible" asset, such as a machine, these costs are capitalized and recorded as an asset which is depreciated over its estimated useful life. On the other hand, a company which spends a great amount of resources advertising a product or training a sales force to sell and service it, which, as we shall see, is a process of creating internally developed "goodwill," cannot usually capitalize such costs even though they may be as, or more, beneficial to the company's future operations than is the "tangible" machine. The reason for this inconsistency in accounting for the two assets is steeped in such basic accounting conventions as conservatism, which casts greater doubt on the future realization of unidentifiable intangible costs (such as advertising or training which create "goodwill") than costs sunk into tangible "hard" and visible goods.

APB *Opinion No. 17* distinguishes between identifiable and unidentifiable intangible assets.

Identifiable intangibles

Identifiable intangibles can be separately identified and given reasonably descriptive names such as patents, trademarks, franchises, and the like. Identifiable intangibles can be developed internally, acquired singly or as part of a group of assets. In either case, they should be recorded at cost and amortized over their useful lives. Write-down or complete write-off at date of acquisition is not permitted.

Unidentifiable intangibles

Unidentifiable intangibles can be developed internally or purchased from others. They cannot, however, be acquired singly but form part of a group of assets or part of an entire enterprise. The excess of cost of an acquired company over the sum total of identifiable net assets is the most common unidentifiable intangible asset. APB *Opinion No. 17* refers to this unidentifiable mass of assets as "goodwill," and this is actually a residual amount in an acquisition after the amount of tangible and identifiable intangibles have been determined. It represents an expansion of the goodwill concept from what has obtained before this Opinion was issued.

The costs of developing, maintaining, or restoring intangibles which are unidentifiable, have indeterminate lives, or are inherent in a continuing enterprise should be expensed as incurred. By contrast, such intangible assets which are purchased must be carried at cost and amortized over their useful lives and cannot be written down or written off at date of acquisition.

Amortization of intangibles

Both types of intangibles, those identifiable as well as those unidentifiable, are believed to have limited useful lives and must be amortized accordingly. Depending on the type of intangible asset, its useful life may be limited by such factors as legal, contractual, or regulatory provisions; demand and competition; life expectancies of employees; and economic factors.

The cost of each intangible should be amortized over its individual useful life taking into account all factors which determine its length. The period of amortization cannot, however, exceed 40 years.

Other considerations regarding the accounting for intangibles

Goodwill is often a sizable asset. Since it can only be recorded on acquisition from a third party, it can be recorded only upon the purchase of an on-going business enterprise. The description of what is being paid for varies greatly, and the variety of views add to the confusion surrounding this subject. Some refer to the ability to attract and keep satisfied customers, while others point to qualities inherent in an enterprise that is well organized and is efficient in production, service, and sales. This distinction can also be seen in the difference that obviously exists between a business that is just starting and one that is successful and well established in its industry and which has spent a great deal on training and research to get there. Thus, what is obviously being paid for here is earning power, and since any given amount of invested capital should expect a minimum return depending on risk, most accountants agree that goodwill is associated with a level of earnings over and above that minimum. These are otherwise referred to as "super-earnings." Thus goodwill implies exceptional profitability, and that should normally be evident when goodwill is being purchased, except in those cases where there is obvious mismanagement and the potential is evident and awaits to be tapped by good management.

National Can Corporation described its goodwill accounts as follows:

Acquisition of companies. In 1969, the Corporation purchased the net assets and business pertaining to the manufacture of glass containers for $9,100,000. In August 1970, the Corporation purchased the net assets and business of two companies engaged in the sale of glass, metal and plastic containers for 78,466 shares of Common Stock and under certain conditions the Corporation may be required to deliver up to 63,282 additional shares of Common Stock. These acquisitions have been accounted for as purchases. The Corporation believes that the excess of cost over the fair value of net assets acquired in these transactions in 1969 and 1970 (approximately $3,240,000) is of such nature that no diminution in value is expected in the foreseeable future, and accordingly, the Corporation does not intend to amortize this intangible.

General Motors, on the other hand, reported as follows:

Goodwill. Goodwill represents the difference between the purchase price and the value ascribed to net tangible assets of businesses acquired in 1943 and prior years and, beginning in 1970, is being amortized in accordance with the recommendation of the Accounting Principles Board. The period of amortization will be ten years.

When a business is being acquired, the book values, that is, the amounts at which its net assets are carried in accordance with accounting principles discussed in this book, are quite obviously not relevant in arriving at a purchase price, if only because they represent unamortized cost balances rather than values. Thus, the first requirement in purchase accounting is that the amount paid for the entity as a whole be allocated to all identifiable assets in accordance with their fair market values. If an excess remains after such allocation is made, it may be ascribed to the intangible "goodwill." If the fair market value of assets acquired exceeds the purchase price, a "bargain purchase credit" results and it can be amortized to income over a reasonable number of years. A detailed examination of the accounting for business combinations will be found in Chapter 7.

Most other intangible assets have a useful life which is limited by law, regulation, or agreement. Thus, *patents* are rights conveyed by government authority to the inventor giving him the exclusive right to his invention for a term of years. Registered copyrights and trademarks also convey exclusive rights for specified periods of time. The cost of these assets should be written off against the revenues they help create over the maximum period coinciding with their legal life or over the minimum period of their estimated economic life.

The cost of franchises, licenses, or other such benefits must be written off over the period during which they are deemed to be economically productive. The cost of leaseholds and leasehold improvements are benefits of occupancy which are contractually limited. Thus, their cost must be amortized over the period of the lease contract.

As is true with all assets, accounting principles require that if it is evident that an intangible has lost all or most of its value or utility, it should be written down to its net realizable value measured by either future estimated utility or selling price, whichever is more appropriate in the circumstances.

Implication for analysis

Because of their very nature, intangibles have often been treated with suspicion by financial analysts. Quite obviously caution and clear understanding of the nature of these assets is required in the evaluation of their worth to the enterprise. However, since these assets may, in many instances, be the most valuable asset an enterprise owns and since they can be undervalued as well as, as is often the case, carried at inflated amounts, it is inadvisable to remove them from all consideration in financial analysis.

Goodwill is a case in point. Having understood the accounting conventions governing the recording of goodwill, the analyst realizes that only purchased goodwill will be found among the recorded assets and that more "goodwill" may exist off the balance sheet than on it.

Another key point here is that if there is value in goodwill it must be reflected in earnings. True, if a mismanaged situation with great potential was purchased, the profits may not become visible immediately; but if there is value to goodwill, then such an asset should give rise to superior earnings within a reasonably short time after acquisition. If those earnings are not in evidence, it is a fair assumption that the investment in goodwill is of no value regardless of whether it is found on the balance sheet or not.

Another important factor of which the analyst must be aware is that in practice, the accounting for goodwill is far from faithful to the theory. Due to the beneficial effect that an absence of write-off of assets has on the results of operations, goodwill and other intangibles may not be written off as speedily as a realistic assessment of their useful life may require. While the overall limitation of 40 years on the assumed useful life of intangibles is arbitrary and may, in some instances, result in excessive amortization, it is safe to assume that in most cases the bias will be in the direction of too slow a rate of amortization. The analyst must be alert to this possibility.

Regardless of the amount of outlays incurred in the acquisition or in the internal development of an intangible, the rule applicable to the carrying amount of any asset is that it be carried at an amount not in excess of realizable value in terms of sales price or future utility. That, at least, is the intention and the theory. But, as in most other categories of accounting theory, actual implementation in practice is another matter, and the analyst must be prepared to form his own judgment on the amounts at which intangible assets are carried. The analyst must also bear in mind that goodwill recorded as a result of business combinations initiated before November 1, 1970 does not have to be amortized at all and that at the cutoff date there were billions of dollars of unamortized goodwill on corporate balance sheets in this country.

The analyst must also be alert to the consideration with which the enterprise has parted in the acquisition of goodwill, for this may affect the amount of the intangible recorded. Payments in promoter stock should be thoroughly scrutinized. Also of concern to the analyst is the rate at which goodwill is amortized. The 40-year maximum, after all, is a long period exceeding a generation. The assumption of useful life should be realistic and should reflect the proper allocation of costs to revenues. A lump-sum write-off of an intangible may bring the asset down to its proper realizable value but by no means does it make up for the implicit overstatement of earnings of prior years.

PREPAID EXPENSES AND DEFERRED CHARGES

Prepaid expenses and deferred charges distinguished

Prepaid expenses represent advance payments for services yet to be received. Examples are advance payments for rent or prepaid insurance on a longer term policy. Small supplies of stationery or stamps are often included in prepaid expenses. Prepaid expenses are generally classified among current assets because the services-due which they represent would otherwise require the use of current resources during the following operating cycle. For reasons of expediency and lack of materiality, services due beyond one year are usually included among prepaid expenses classified as current.

Unlike prepaid expenses which represent advance payments for services yet to be received, *deferred charges* represent charges already incurred which are deferred to the future either because they are expected to benefit future revenues or because they represent a proper allocation of costs to future operations.

Over the years the complexities of business operations as well as custom have sanctioned an ever increasing number and types of deferred charges.

Why costs are deferred

The basic theory behind the deferral of expenses and costs is relatively simple. If a cost incurred in one period is going to benefit a future period or periods by a contribution to revenues or reduction in costs, then such a cost should be deferred to such future period. The basic accounting convention involved here is that of matching costs and revenues. Thus, if a 20-year bond of $1,000 face value is issued for $950, the $50 discount (plus expenses of issue) is properly allocated to the

20 years which benefit from the use of the borrowed money. Looked at another way, the discount reflects an interest cost effectively higher than the coupon rate of the bond and should be treated as such.

While the future benefit, in terms of use of money which the bond discount affords, is pretty clear and obvious, such is not the case with many other kinds of deferred charges.

Research and development costs

Research and development costs is one category of costs where there are often doubts as to future relevance and benefits. In the absence of major investment in research for a new product, most big companies which have a permanent research organization and staff consider research expenses as period costs and hence expense rather than defer them. It is the smaller and financially weaker organization which usually defers these expenses, and in cases of serious doubt the auditors will pass on to the reader their uncertainty about future recoverability and with it the task of reaching a conclusion about such deferred costs.

Thus, for example, the Farrington Manufacturing Company had the following note to its financial statements:

Deferred research and development. As of December 31, 1967 the Company has deferred a net amount of $1,869,797 of which $863,564 represents the cost of uncompleted projects. The recoverability of these deferred costs is dependent upon successful completion of these projects and future profitable sales of the equipment being developed. In the opinion of management, these costs are fully recoverable. The Company has adopted the policy of amortizing these costs by charges to earnings over the first three years of commercial production or writing them off entirely at the time the projects are determined to be valueless.

The auditors qualified their opinion on the Farrington Manufacturing Company's statements as "subject to the recoverability of the deferred research and development costs." Practice shows, however, that a lack of such a qualification is no real assurance about the validity of a deferral. There are numerous examples where after years of deferral, companies subsequently write the asset off as unrecoverable. Such subsequent action does not mitigate the fact that prior year operating results were overstated.

For example, the Signal Companies, Inc., described as follows their treatment of development costs:

Development costs. Development costs, $6,407,000 at December 31, 1970, represent the remaining costs of large development programs, principally aircraft turbine engines, with a relatively long-term development period which The Garrett Corporation (a wholly-owned subsidiary) commenced deferring in 1969. Such remaining deferred costs, and additional costs expected to be incurred in the future, are to be amortized on a unit basis at the time products are sold.

Under present economic conditions, which have resulted in a stretch-out in the estimated demand for products being developed, and because of increasing costs of development, management deemed it appropriate as of December 31, 1970 to reduce costs accumulated on such programs by $51,255,000 (before related income tax credits of $18,834,000) and to defer only $6,407,000 at that date.

A change in economic conditions and resulting stretch-outs in demand provided the reason for a write-off of costs which had been defended over a number of years.

APB *Opinion No. 17*, which deals with the accounting for intangible assets, states that the subject of research and development costs and preoperating costs require separate study and, hence, is not covered by this Opinion. Practice in this area, as a consequence, remains "wide-open." The Financial Accounting Standards Board, in 1973, selected the subject of accounting for research and development costs as one of seven key areas to which it will devote particular attention.

Other types of deferred charges

Another category of deferred charges which borders on a deferral of costs of dubious future benefit is that of moving expenses and to a lesser degree, start-up costs. Thus, Willcox & Gibbs, Inc., had the following note in its annual report:

The Company has deferred approximately $782,000 related to moving expenses and start-up costs associated with new facilities placed into operation during 1968. It is the Company's intention to amortize these costs over a five year period beginning in 1969.

The auditors expressed no doubt about this item but did qualify their opinion with respect to the deferral of development costs.

As indicated before, the variety of deferred costs has been growing constantly over the years due to new complexities in both technology and in business practice. Since deferred charges represent future intangible benefits, they are sometimes very close in nature to intangible assets. Regardless of terminology, the following list should give the reader an indication of the variety of deferred charges now found in financial statements:

1. Product research and development costs.
2. Business development, expansion, merger, and relocation costs.
    a) Preoperating expenses, initial start-up costs, and tooling costs.
    b) Initial operating losses or preoperating expenses of subsidiaries.

  c) Moving, plant rearrangement, and reinstallation costs.
  d) Merger or acquisition expenses.
  e) Purchased customer accounts.
  f) Noncompete agreements.
3. Deferred expenses.
  a) Advertising and promotional expenses.
  b) Imputed interest.
  c) Selling, general, and administrative expenses.
  d) Pension plan costs.
  e) Property and other taxes.
  f) Rental and leasing costs.
  g) Vacation pay.
  h) Seasonal growing and packing expenses.
4. Intangible costs.
  a) Intangible drilling and development costs.
  b) Contracts, films, copyright materials, art rights, etc.
5. Debt discount and expenses.
6. Future income tax benefits.
7. Organization costs.
8. Advance royalties.
9. Property losses and conversions.

While we are here focusing on the validity of the assets represented by deferred charges, we must always bear in mind that each of these assets has "another side of the coin," that is, the deferral of a cost which would otherwise have been charged to results from operations. The impact of this aspect will be more fully discussed in Chapter 9, which is devoted to principles of income measurement.

Implications for analysis

While prepaid expenses are usually neither of the size or the significance sufficient to be of real concern to the analyst, deferred charges can be both sizable and significant and, hence, can present real challenges of understanding and interpretation.

Certain types of deferred charges, such as bond discount, can be easily understood and defended. Moreover, the period of their amortization is clearly dictated by the circumstances which gave rise to them. Deferred charges, such as organization costs, on the other hand, while clearly designated to benefit an organization in the future cannot be amortized on a logical or obvious basis. Thus while an indefinite life may be inferred from the going-concern or continuity convention of accounting, organization costs are nevertheless usually amortized over an arbitrarily determined period of time.

However, the validity of deferring many other charges, such as research and development costs, moving and start-up costs, promotional costs, or initial operating losses of, say, loan offices, is subject to many imponderables and estimates. Similarly, the period over which they should properly be amortized is often subject to serious doubt. The analyst must be alert to the situation where the deferred charge is not really an asset representing a future benefit but is rather a deferred loss which is being carried forward for no better reason than the desire of management not to burden current operating results. While the auditor's opinion or mention of such assets can be helpful to the analyst, he must be prepared to evaluate on his own the evidence and information regarding such deferrals. The other and perhaps even more significant implication which deferred charges carry is their effect on proper income determination, and this aspect will be examined in Chapter 9, which is devoted to this subject.

In conclusion, the case of Computer Sciences will provide an illustration, albeit not a unique one, of the problems faced by the analyst in this area of accounting.

A case of deferral and write-off. Computer Sciences Corporation had a practice of deferring development and other costs on proprietary programs and systems in progress. At March 28, 1969, the company had deferred costs on two programs as follows:

                COMPUTICKET $4,266,000
                INFONET 2,849,000

By March 27, 1970, the company wrote off the entire investment in COMPUTICKET, which by that time had grown to about $6 million. On that date, the deferred costs of INFONET had grown to $15.6 million. By April 2, 1971, the deferrals of costs on INFONET mushroomed to $39.6 million, which at that time represented about 86 percent of the company's entire equity capital. The auditors did not even mention this intangible in their opinion on the financial statements ending on that date. The financial statements contained the following note:

Investments and other assets. It is the Company's policy to accumulate all direct, indirect, technical and marketing costs (less any revenue received) during the development period of each proprietary program or system and thereafter to amortize these costs on the basis of estimated domestic revenues or over the anticipated life, which provides the earlier amortization.

The Company is developing a network information service (INFONET) utilizing large-scale computers at various locations in the United States. At April 2, 1971, the investment (net of total revenues of approximately $3,300,000) in INFONET amounted to $39,606,000 in development and $15,032,000 in computers and related equipment used in the system. By September 30, 1972, investments of approximately $18,000,000 (net of anticipated revenues) for development and $3,000,000 for computers and related equipment are contemplated. The development phase of the program is presently scheduled to be completed as of September 30, 1972 and amortization of deferred costs over an eight-year period is scheduled to commence.

On February 16, 1972, the *Wall Street Journal* reported that Computer Sciences decided to "adopt a new policy eliminating the deferral of all development costs," and that this will result in a write-down of about $59 million of INFONET System development costs. A company spokesman said that "the policy change is undertaken in an effort to clarify and reduce to the simplest terms the company's financial status, objectives and prospects." He added that the policy of eliminating deferral of all development costs doesn't "indicate a reevaluation of INFONET's prospects, but rather arises out of recognition by the company of financial reporting practices which have become increasingly favored by the financial community."

To the analyst this case holds the following significant implications:

1. The auditor's opinion provided no clue of the imminent write-down even though the company had been unsuccessful in the development of such programs in the past and the amount at stake was equal to 86 percent of the company's equity. Thus, the financial analyst who evaluated Computer Science's position at April 2, 1971, would have been better off relying on his own evaluation of the company's record and prospects with regard to the INFONET deferred costs than he would have fared by relying on the auditor's "clean" opinion.
2. The company, and presumably its auditors as well as others, regards the matter of expensing or deferring of development costs a mere choice among acceptable alternatives. Based on such an attitude and such views the accounting for research and development costs is of very limited usefulness to the intelligent user of financial statements.
3. Computer Sciences' spokesman indicated that the write-off did not indicate a "reevaluation of INFONET's prospects." The suggestion that the write-down of the bulk of a company's assets, when their utility and prospects were not being downgraded, represents a proper and "favored" practice indicates that the accounting in this area is much too loose to be useful to the analyst. The abuses which can result from the wholesale write-off of "future costs" are discussed further in Chapter 8.

It is clear that until the accounting for research and development costs, as well as for other intangibles, becomes better defined, more meaningful, and more realistic, the analyst will have to use all the information on deferred cost which he can obtain and arrive at his own evaluation of the utility and significance of these deferred items.

UNRECORDED INTANGIBLE OR CONTINGENT ASSETS

A discussion of principles of asset measurement would not be complete without an examination of that category of assets which under generally accepted accounting principles would not be recorded in a statement of financial condition.

One category of assets which are not recordable has already been mentioned in the discussion of goodwill. In this case if the intangible is internally developed rather than purchased from an outside party, it cannot normally be capitalized and results instead in a charge to current operations. Thus, to the extent that a valuable asset has been created, one that can be either sold or which possesses earning power, the income charged with the expense of its development has been understated. This the analyst must realize and, if significant, take into account.

Another type of unrecorded asset is a tax loss carry-forward benefit which has a high probability of being realized in future years. Present accounting theory sanctions the recording of such a benefit only in those rare cases where its realization is "assured beyond any reasonable doubt." Thus, the analyst must look for evidence of such assets in the footnotes to the financial statements and other material containing comments about the company's financial condition.

Struther Wells Corporation presents the following disclosure of net operating loss carry-overs as well as the dates of expiration of such benefits:

Tax carryovers. At November 30, 1970 the Company had a consolidated net operating loss carryover subject to final determination by the Internal Revenue Service of $6,900,000 which expires as follows

November 30,	
1971	$ 620,000
1972	430,000
1973	2,800,000
1974	50,000
1975	3,000,000
	$6,900,000

In addition, the Company has approximately $285,000 of investment tax credits available to reduce Federal income taxes. These credits expire in varying amounts during the next seven years.

A contingent asset in the form of claims for damages is disclosed by Garlock, Inc., as follows:

Note 7: There are no suits pending against the Company. In 1967, Company brought an action against other parties alleging misappropriations of its trade secrets and other acts injurious to the Company. Any damages awarded in this suit would be for the Company's benefit and are indeterminable at this time.

Future contingent benefits are disclosed by Masonite Corporation as follows:

Timber contract. The company has a 10-year contract to supply St. Regis Paper Company with timber cut from a substantial portion of the company's timberlands. Cutting under the contract commenced in 1968. Income under the contract of $5,464,000 in 1970 and $3,725,000 in 1969 has been reflected in the accompanying income statements. Also reflected as a cost in the income statements is the acquisition of a portion of this timber from St. Regis Paper Company by Hood Industries Division acquired in 1970 and accounted for as a pooling-of-interests.

QUESTIONS

1. What accounting principles govern the valuation and presentation of long-term investments? Distinguish between the accounting for investments in the common stock in an investee of (*a*) less than 20 percent of the shares outstanding, and (*b*) 20 percent or more of the shares outstanding.
2. *a*) Evaluate the accounting for investments in between 20 percent to 50 percent of the common stock of an investee from the point of view of an analyst of the financial statements.
   b) When are losses in long-term investments recognized? Evaluate the accounting which governs the recognition of such losses.
3. How should idle plant and equipment be presented in the balance sheet. Explain the reasons for the presentation you describe.
4. The income of an enterprise from the exploration of wasting assets often bears no logical relation to the amount at which such investment is shown on the balance sheet.
   a) Why is this so?
   b) Under what circumstances would a more logical relationship be more likely to exist?
5. From the point of view of the user of financial statements, what are the objections to the use of original cost as the basis of carrying fixed assets?
6. *a*) What are the basic principles governing the valuation of intangible assets?
   b) Distinguish between the accounting for internally developed versus purchased intangibles.
   c) Of what significance is the distinction between (1) identifiable intangibles and (2) unidentifiable intangibles?
   d) What principles and guidelines underlie the amortization of intangible assets?
7. What are the implications for analysis of the accounting for goodwill?

8. Describe present-day accounting for research and development costs and its implication to the analyst.
9. List five categories of deferred charges and describe the rationale which is usually given for this deferral.
10. *a)* Give examples of two or more types of assets which are not recorded on the balance sheet.
    b) How should such assets be evaluated by the analyst?

5

Analysis of liabilities

LIABILITIES are obligations to pay money, render future services, or convey specified assets. They are claims against the company's present and future assets and resources. Such claims are usually senior to those of the ownership as evidenced by equity securities. This discussion will be broadly construed to include current liabilities, long-term liabilities, and deferred credits which, as shall be seen, can vary significantly from conventional liabilities.

CURRENT LIABILITIES

Current liabilities are usually obligations for goods and services acquired, taxes owed, and any other accruals of expenses. They include deposits received, advance payments, trade acceptances, notes payable, short-term bank loans, as well as the current portion of long-term debt.

To be properly classified as current, a liability should require the use of current resources (assets) or the incurrence of another current liability for its discharge. As in the case of current assets the period over which such liabilities are expected to be retired is one year or the current operating cycle, whichever is longer.

As a general principle, the offsetting of assets against liabilities is permissible only where such a right specifically exists. Thus the availability of cash for the payment of a liability does not justify the offset of one against the other. In practice the only instances where offset is permissible is where government securities specifically designated as acceptable for the payment of taxes are acquired for that purpose.

LONG-TERM LIABILITIES

Long-term liabilities may either represent bank term loans or more formal issuances of bonds, debentures, or notes. They represent obligations payable beyond the period of one year or beyond that encompassed by the operating cycle. Debt obligations may assume many and varied forms, and their full assessment and measurement requires disclosure of all significant conditions and covenants attached to them. Such information should include the interest rate, maturities, conversion privileges, call features, subordination provisions, and restrictions under the indenture. In addition, disclosure of collateral pledged (with indication of book and possible market values), sinking fund provisions subordination, revolving credit provisions, and sinking fund commitments should be disclosed. Any defaults in adherence to loan provisions, including defaults of interest and principal repayments, must also be disclosed.

Since the exact interest rate which will prevail in the bond market at the time of issuance of bonds can never be predetermined, bonds are sold in excess of par, or at a premium, or below par, that is, at a discount. The premium or discount represents in effect an adjustment of the effective interest rate. The premium received is amortized over the life of the issue, thus reducing the coupon rate of interest to the effective interest rate incurred. Conversely, the discount allowed is similarly amortized, thus increasing the effective interest rate paid by the borrower.

A variety of incentives are offered in order to promote the sale of bonds and to reduce the interest rates which would otherwise be required. They may take the form of convertibility features, attachments of warrants to purchase the issuer's common stock, or even warrants to purchase the stock of another company. It requires no great persuasion to understand that to the extent that these incentives are valuable they carry a cost to the issuing company. Whether the cost represents dilution of the equity or a fixed price call on an investment, these costs should be recognized. Although slow in doing so, accountants have recognized such costs and given expression to them as follows:

1. In the case of convertible features—through their effect on the computation of earnings per share (see the discussion of earnings per share in Chapter 20 for further details).
2. In the case of warrants—by assigning a discount factor at the time of debt issuance which charge is amortized to income. In addition, the dilutive effects of warrants are given recognition in earnings per share computations. (Further discussion can be found under the topics of "equities" and "earnings per share.")

Generally the prohibitions against offsetting of assets against liabilities apply to the offsetting of debt against related assets. However, if a real estate company buys property subject to a mortgage which it does not assume, it may properly deduct the amount of the mortgage from the asset, thus showing it net.

When debt is not interest bearing, it is appropriate to show it at the present value of the amount that will be payable in the future discounted at the rate at which the company would otherwise borrow money. This not only shows debt as a proper amount, comparable to other interest bearing debt obligations, but it also provides for the computation of the interest charge which reflects the use of these funds. Moreover, if the debt is the result of the acquisition of an asset, this treatment insures that its cost is not overstated through the overstatement of the amount of debt incurred.

Reference to the discussion on the imputation of interest in the "receivables" section of Chapter 3 will show that under the provisions of APB *Opinion No. 21*, noninterest bearing obligations, or those bearing unreasonable rates of interest, must, under certain conditions, be shown at an amount which reflects the imputation of a reasonable discount rate.

Valuable disclosure, from the analyst's point of view, is the yearly loan payment requirement for at least the next five years.

Georgia-Pacific Corporation presents an example of detailed disclosure of terms and conditions to which its debt obligations are subject, including details of future maturities:

Long-term debt

	December 31, 1971	*June 30, 1972*
Banks—		
Principally 5% to 5¾% term loans (varies with changes in the prime rate) payable annually in varying amounts through 1976	$250,640	$223,260
Insurance companies—		
Principally 5¼% to 5¾% term loans payable annually in varying amounts through 1989	179,190	176,480
Revolving credit financing	29,880	76,100
Purchase contracts covering land, timber and equipment, payable annually in varying amounts through 1992	34,150	32,700
Industrial revenue bonds principally 4⅛% to 6%, with varying annual payments to 1992	133,350	133,400
5% subordinated debentures payable $770 annually, with final payment of $8,460 in 1976 (less treasury debentures of $2,420 and $1,660 at December 31, 1971, and June 30, 1972, respectively)	9,120	9,110
	$636,330	$651,050

100   Understanding corporate reports

Repayment of principal through 1977 on debt outstanding is as follows:

	December 31, 1971	June 30, 1972
1973	$104,390	$ 71,590 (six months)
1974	99,860	100,290
1975	94,300	94,730
1976	90,010	100,580
1977	21,350	57,910

Property totalling approximately $235,000 is subject to mortgages securing industrial revenue bonds and $35,750 of insurance company debt at June 30, 1972.

In January 1972, Georgia-Pacific secured a $120,000 loan commitment from banks. Until December 31, 1974, this commitment will be a revolving credit with interest at ¼ of 1% over prime interest for any portion of the credit borrowed with a commitment fee of ½ of 1% on the unused portion. Georgia-Pacific intends to utilize commercial paper during this period. On or before January 1, 1975, the commitment can be converted to a term loan with interest at ½ of 1% over prime interest and with repayment from 1975 through 1978.

It has been the policy of Georgia-Pacific to capitalize interest on borrowed funds during construction periods. Accordingly, the interest capitalized on projects under construction was $4,820, $4,600, $10,890, $15,720 and $7,520 in 1967 through 1971, respectively, and $2,500 for the six months ended June 30, 1972.

Convertible subordinated debentures. The 5¾% and 5¼% debentures due 1994 and 1996 were convertible into common stock at $53.10 and $64.54 per share, respectively, at June 30, 1972, adjusted for declaration of stock dividends through August 7, 1972. The conversion prices are subject to adjustment under certain conditions including common stock dividends and distributions of property other than cash that is distributed to common stockholders.

IMPLICATIONS FOR ANALYSIS

Liabilities are prior claims against a company's assets and resources; and the analyst needs assurance that they are fully stated with proper descriptions as to their amount, due dates, and the conditions, encumbrances, and limitations to which they subject the company.

The means by which auditors satisfy themselves that all liabilities have been properly recorded are such procedures as scrutiny of board of director meeting minutes, the reading of contracts and agreements, and inquiry of those who may have knowledge of company obligations and liabilities. Since the nature of double-entry bookkeeping requires that for every asset, resource, or cost, a counterbalancing obligation, or investment must be booked, the areas subject to considerable difficulty are those relating to commitments and contingent liabilities because they do not involve the commensurate recording of assets or costs. Here, the analyst must rely on the information which is provided in the notes to financial statements and in the general management commentary found in the text of the annual report and elsewhere.

Assessing uncertainties

Due to the uncertainties involved, the descriptions of commitments and especially of contingent liabilities in footnotes are often vague and indeterminate. In effect, that means that the burden of assessing the possible impact of the contingencies as well as the probabilities of their occurrence is passed on to the reader. The analyst should always determine whether the auditors feel that a contingency is serious enough and material enough to call for a qualification in their report. This was the case in the financial statements of Berry Petroleum Company where the opinion was made subject to the effect on the financial statement of the determination of the company's ultimate liability in respect to alleged price discrimination as explained in Note 6. That note reads in part:

During the year ended October 31, 1967 the state of Arkansas filed suits against the Company for alleged price discrimination in sales of asphalt. At the present time, counsel for the Company have been unable to make an evaluation of the claim: however, management of the Company denies that it has discriminated against the state. While the possibility exists that the Company's financial condition could be materially and adversely affected by the outcome of this litigation, counsel for the Company are of the opinion that these actions are not likely to have that result.

A situation such as Berry Petroleum's poses difficult problems of analysis. However, the auditor has at least unequivocally declared that not only is he unable to assess the ultimate impact of the contingency upon the company's financial position, but that the impact could be material enough to require him to qualify his opinion on the financial statement as a whole.

While utilizing all the information available, the analyst must nevertheless bring his own critical evaluation to bear on the assessment of all the contingencies to which the company may be subject. This process must draw not only on available disclosures and information but also on an understanding of industry conditions and practices.

Evaluation of terms of indebtedness

The disclosure of the terms and conditions of regular recorded indebtedness and liabilities is another area deserving the analyst's careful attention. Here, the analyst must examine critically the description of debt, its terms, conditions, and encumbrances with a view to satisfying himself as to the term's feasibility and completeness. Important in the evaluation of a liability's total impact are such features as:

1. The terms of the debt.
2. Restrictions on deployment of resources and freedom of action.
3. Ability to engage in further financing.
4. Requirements such as relating to maintenance of ratios of working capital, debt to equity, etc.
5. Dilutive conversion features to which the debt is subject.

Minimum disclosure requirements as to debt provisions vary somewhat, but auditors are bound by reporting standards to disclose any breaches in loan provisions which may restrict a company's freedom of action or set it on the road to insolvency. Thus, the analyst should be alert to any explanations or qualifications in the notes or in the auditor's opinion such as the following which appeared in the annual report of Lionel Corporation:

Reference is made to Note G to the financial statements relating to a provision of the indenture covering the 5½% Convertible Subordinated Debentures due in 1980 and to information contained therein as to the failure of the Company to maintain the net working capital required thereunder and to the possible failure to observe other indenture covenants. The management has represented to us that it is actively negotiating certain arrangements and planning certain actions, which, it believes, will have the ultimate effect of remedying any breaches of covenants that may exist under the indentures as referred to in Note G.

In view of the possible material effect which the final resolution of the matters referred to above could have on the consolidated financial position of the companies, and in view of the lack of knowledge at this time of the ultimate effect which the aforementioned negotiations and plans may have in finally disposing of the matters, we are precluded from expressing an opinion as to the fair presentation of the consolidated balance sheet and related consolidated statement of earned surplus of the companies.

Naturally, an analyst would like to be able to foresee developments such as those described in the Lionel situation. One of the most effective ways of doing this is by means of financial analysis that compares the terms of debt with the margin of safety by which existing compliance exceeds the requirements under those terms.

OBLIGATIONS UNDER LEASES

Leasing, as a means of acquiring assets and the services and use of assets, has been known for a long time, but in recent decades its use has grown considerably. Our consideration of lease obligations at this point is due to their similarity to debt. Lease terms usually oblige

5. Analysis of liabilities

companies to make a series of payments over a future period of time, and it is well known that in many cases such payments are determined by financial tables and contain elements of interest and principal amortization. The debate over which features of a lease agreement clinch it as a purchase (i.e., as a financing method) and which characteristics cause it to retain the nature of a rental contract has been going on for a long time and is by no means settled. The basic question is when and which leases are to be considered, in effect, installment purchases and should, consequently, be capitalized at the present value of the future rental obligations. *Accounting Research Study No. 4* commissioned by the American Institute of Certified Public Accountants concluded that, "To the extent, then, that the rental payments represent a means of financing the acquisition of property rights which the lessee has in his possession and under his control, the transaction constitutes the acquisition of an asset with a related obligation to pay for it." Under this concept, virtually all material leases would be capitalized since almost all leases involve some property rights.

However, APB *Opinion No. 5* summarily dismissed the concept of recording "property rights" and concluded that leases should be capitalized only if they are "clearly in substance installment purchases" and "the terms of the lease create a material equity in the property."

Thus, the Opinion regarded a lease arrangement as being essentially an installment purchase of property if the lease terms resulted in the creation of a material equity in the property for the benefit of the lessee. In discussing this point, *Opinion No. 5* stated that

either of the two following conditions will usually establish that a lease should be considered to be in substance a purchase:

(a) The initial term is materially less than the useful life of the property, and the lessee has the option to renew the lease for the remaining useful life of the property at substantially less than the fair rental value; or

(b) The lessee has the right, during or at the expiration of the lease, to acquire the property at a price which at the inception of the lease appears to be substantially less than the probable fair value of the property at the time or times of permitted acquisition by the lessee.

It stated that in these cases the fact that rents usually run well ahead of any reasonable measure of service life expiration coupled with bargain renewal or purchase options constituted convincing evidence that an equity in the property was being built up through the rental payments.

Opinion No. 5 did not, however, furnish any guidance as to how the equity buildup to which it referred should be measured, nor did it indicate any basis for deciding when such an equity should be considered as material.

Paragraph 11 of APB *Opinion No. 5* lists four circumstances which tend to indicate that a lease arrangement is in substance a purchase and which, the Opinion says, should be considered unless it is clear that the lease payments do not result in the creation of a material equity in the leased property:

(a) The lessor is an unconsolidated subsidiary of the lessee, or lessee and the lessor are subsidiaries of the same parent and either is unconsolidated.
(b) The lessee and the lessor have common officers, directors, or shareholders to a significant degree.
(c) The lessor has been created, directly or indirectly, by the lessee and is substantially dependent on the lessee for its operations.
(d) The lessee (or its parent) has the right, through options or otherwise, to acquire control of the lessor.

It appears that these circumstances are relevant only where there may be uncertainty as to whether or not lease arrangements result in the creation of equity in the leased property.

Paragraph 12 of APB *Opinion No. 5* states that where "the lessee and lessor are related, leases should often be treated as purchases even though they do not meet the criteria set forth in paragraph 10 and 11 [relating to creation of equity through rental payments] i.e., even though no direct equity is being built-up by the lessee."

It is quite clear that this, as well as the other major provision of the Opinion, leaves a lot of leeway to interpretation.

Real estate subsidiaries whose principal purpose is to lease properties to the parent (directly or indirectly) should, according to paragraph 3 of APB *Opinion No. 10*, be consolidated with such parent. This has been reiterated by APB *Opinion No. 18*.

A variation of leasing arrangements is found in the sale-and-leaseback arrangement whereby the ultimate user of property has it custom-built to its specifications and then sells it to a third party from which it is subsequently leased back. The need to capitalize leases under this type of arrangement must be judged on the basis of the criteria considered above.

On the matter of accounting for profits on sales of leased-back property, APB *Opinion No. 5* states: "Neither the sale price nor the annual rental can be objectively evaluated independently of the other. Consequently, material gains or losses resulting from the sale of properties which are the subject of sale and leaseback transactions, together with the related tax effect, should be amortized over the life of the lease as an adjustment of the rental cost (or, if the leased property is capitalized as an adjustment of depreciation)."

The APB has thus concluded that a profit from a sale and leaseback should not be considered as realized separately and distinct from the entire transaction.

Responding to demands by users of financial statements for better and more relevant informaton on lease commitments of lessees, the APB, after some hesitation, issued as its last pronouncement, *Opinion No. 31* "Disclosure of Lease Commitments by Lessees." This Opinion, expands the disclosure requirements of APB *Opinion No. 5* by requiring the following disclosures:

1. Total rental expense (reduced by rentals from subleases, with disclosure of such amounts) entering into the determination of results of operations for each period for which an income statement is presented
2. The minimum rental commitments under all noncancelable leases should be disclosed, as of the date of the latest balance sheet presented, in aggregate and by major categories of properties, such as real estate, aircraft, truck fleets, and other equipment, for:
   a) Each of the five succeeding fiscal years,
   b) Each of the next three five-year periods, and
   c) The remainder as a single amount.

The Opinion also states that information concerning the present values of the commitments may be helpful in evaluating the credit capacity of the lessee and in comparing the lessee's financial position with that of other entities using other means of financing to obtain the use of property. Such disclosures, which are voluntary, should include, as of the date of the latest balance sheet presented:

a) The present values of the net fixed minimum lease commitments (based on the interest rates implicit in the terms of the leases at the times of entering into the leases) in the aggregate and by major categories of properties.
b) Either the weighted average interest rate (based on the present values) and range of rates, or specific interest rates, for all lease commitments included in the amounts disclosed under (*a*) above.
c) The present value of rentals to be received from existing noncancelable subleases of property included in (*a*) above (based on the interest rates implicit in the terms of the subleases at the times of entering into the subleases).

Additional disclosures relating to rental payments, terms of renewal, restrictions, etc., are also required.

These disclosure requirements are a welcome addition to the provisions of APB *Opinion No. 5* at least until the Financial Accounting Standards Board, which has designated this area as one of seven enjoying top priority, will get around to make the accounting for leases more responsive to the needs of users of financial statements.

In addition, the SEC, in what is an apparent display of impatience with the APB's hesitation in this area, has proposed its own disclosure rules which will create another example of divergence in requirements between the SEC's rules of practice and generally accepted accounting principles.

The SEC's required disclosure would include the following: (1) total lease rental expense for all years for which income statements are presented; (2) lease rentals payable for each of the next five-years and for the next three subsequent five-year periods; (3) the capitalized present value of financing leases in the aggregate and by major category of assets; and (4) the impact on net income had financing leases been capitalized.

Financing leases are defined as leases which extend for 75 percent or more of an asset's life or which result in the recovery of the lessor's capital plus a reasonable return. The Financial Accounting Standards Board has designated the area of lease accounting as one of seven enjoying top priority.

APB *Opinion No. 27*, "Accounting for Lease Transactions by Manufacturer or Dealer Lessors," establishes more specific criteria (than were contained in APB *Opinion No. 7*) to determine when a manufacturer or dealer lessor should recognize a lease transaction with an independent lessee as if it were a sale. It concludes that a manufacturer or dealer lessor can so recognize a lease transaction when collectibility of the payments required from the lessee is reasonably assured, no important uncertainty remains regarding costs yet to be incurred under the lease, and one of a number of other specified conditions is present. Only when such conditions exist is it appropriate to conclude that the manufacturer or dealer lessor has transfered the risks and rewards of ownership to an independent third party.

Implications for analysis

Leasing as a means of financing is another area deserving the analyst's particular scrutiny. The major objective here is to make sure that accounting form is not permitted to mask the economic substance of debt and its effect on capital structure, as well as exposure to fixed charges and the effects of leverage.

It is quite obvious that many long-term leases have all or most of the earmarks of debt. They create an obligation for payments under an agreement which is not cancellable. This represents a commitment to fixed payments which is what a debt obligation amounts to. The adverse effects of debt are also present in the case of a lease, that is, an inability to pay may result in insolvency. The fact that statutory limitations on lease obligations in case of bankruptcy limit the obligation to pay rent to one or a number of years is not a mitigating factor of substance because the process of financial analysis is usually designed to evaluate the probability of bankruptcy and the attendant adverse effects on asset values and credit standing, rather than an evaluator of the amount and standing of the obligations after insolvency proceedings have been started. The importance of the leased property to company operations is also a factor, since it may be so vital as to preclude the company's abandonment of the lease in reorganization proceedings.

It is very difficult, if not impossible, to compare the financial position of companies which use different methods of financing, including installment purchase in the form of a lease, for the financing of different assets. That is also true of comparisons of income, since under the leasing method of financing, the early years of income are increased artificially because aggregate interest expense is combined with depreciation and charged to income on a level (straight-line) basis rather than starting at higher amounts and declining as the outstanding obligations are reduced.

We have seen from the discussion in this chapter that the accounting profession has moved in the direction of recognizing that many leases represent methods of financing the acquisition of property and that they should be so accounted for. The problem facing the analyst, however, is that he is not justified in assuming that all lease arrangements which were intended as financing devices or which have all the earmarks of debt will in fact be accounted for as purchases of property. The reason for this is that the criteria of APB *Opinion No. 5*, which require the capitalization of leases, are loose and undefined.

The primary requirement for lease capitalization under APB *Opinion No. 5* is that the terms of the lease result in the creation of a material equity in the property. However, the method of measuring the equity buildup is far from clear, nor is the concept of materiality clarified in the Opinion or elsewhere. Thus, in practice, the auditor and the company have a great deal of leeway in the interpretation of the Opinion, and often the company's desire to give itself the benefit of the doubt may prevail.

While the most obvious examples of financing by lease, such as exemplified in the note by Atcoa reproduced below, result in treatment as purchases, other situations may not be accorded such treatment:

Property, plant and equipment, at cost. In accordance with *Opinion 5* of the Accounting Principles Board of the American Institute of Certified Public Accountants, land and buildings leased from the President of the Company, Joseph P. Bruno and his wife, Dolores D. Bruno, have been capitalized and the buildings are being depreciated over their estimated useful lives. The lease agreements dated May 31, 1969 and December 31, 1969 respectively, provide purchase options at the option exercise price of $201,000 until May 31, 1971 and with slight increases until May 31, 1973 to $213,060. The Company intends to exercise the option before May 31, 1973.

With regard to those leases which for one reason or another a company chooses not to capitalize, the information provided is often inadequate, although as a minimum the analyst should have the following details:

1. Number of leases.
2. Types of assets covered.
3. Terms of remaining leases.
4. Other terms such as purchase and renewal options, services included, variable rentals, residual values, etc.
5. Minimum annual rentals payable over the next 5 to 10 years.
6. The interest rate implicit in the lease agreements.
7. Total rentals charged against operations.

This information, if provided in sufficient detail, can facilitate assessment and analysis but cannot completely compensate for an absence of capitalization of the obligation and the corresponding property rights and their inclusion on the balance sheet. The accountants, with their complete knowledge of all attendant circumstances, rather than the analysts, are in the best position to apply the proper discount factor to the capitalization of the lease obligations. Total lease payments in the future will exceed the value of the leased asset by the amount of the interest factor built into the lease contract. Thus, the capitalization of a lease, using an appropriate interest rate in computing the present value of future payments, allows the analyst to compare the obligation with other forms of debt. While the company most likely knows the rate of interest implicit in the lease, the analyst can, at best, only guess it. However, in the absence of capitalization, an informed guess is superior to ignoring the impact of the financial lease. When financial leases are not capitalized, the assumption is implicitly made that the asset value and the debt are zero, and that, in turn, leads to distortions in important ratios using fixed assets and long-term debt as factors.

In the income statement, lease rentals are often lumped with cost of goods sold. However, proper disclosure, particularly in SEC filings, requires the separate disclosure of rentals. Using these, an attempt can be made to break lease rentals down into:

1. Operating expenses—fixed charges for a variety of services which go with the lease.
2. Interest portion—which is really part of financial fixed charges.
3. Debt repayments. It is interesting to note that in outlining the computation of "fixed charge coverage" the SEC defines fixed charges as including in addition to interest "an appropriate portion of rentals under long-term leases." This is intended to exclude from rentals that portion which is attributable to debt amortization.

In a study of the effect of capitalizing leases on some commonly used financial ratios, Professor A. Tom Nelson[1] found that many such ratios are importantly affected by the capitalization process. Ratios, such as the current ratio, debt to equity, debt to total capital, times interest charges earned, and fixed assets to net worth, among others, are affected negatively by capitalization. The author concluded that "other things remaining equal, the financial analyst could easily have made faulty decisions . . . if he had based his analysis on ratios which were computed from conventional financial statements."

A major write-off by General Foods Corporation, in fiscal 1971, of its investment in a fast-food chain demonstrated anew that long-term lease commitments can be very much like debt. This is particularly true when, as was the case here, the leases are for special-purpose facilities such as specialized food-stands. A good part of the loss General Foods had to recognize stemmed from such long-term leases.

The analyst should be aware of the important difference between the two methods of accounting for leases entered into by lessors: (1) the *financing* method, which essentially recognizes a lease as the equivalent of a loan or a sale; and (2) the *operating* method, which recognizes a lease as only a rental agreement. Although many leases can be clearly identified as being either "financing" or "operating" leases, other leases are difficult to classify. For example, a lessor may sell or assign a lease to an independent financing institution or similar entity with certain guarantees, raising questions as to the accounting for the sale or assignment. Likewise, a manufacturer or dealer may sell property to an independent financing entity which leases the property under certain guarantees by the manufacturer or dealer, creating complications in accounting for the "sale." Additional complications are created if these transactions are with an affiliated entity rather than with an independent entity.

A lease which transfers title to the property without cost or at nominal cost to the lessee by the end of its fixed, noncancellable term is clearly a financing lease if it has predictable credit risks and predictable future costs. If a lease does not contain these provisions, the other major aspects of the transfer of the risks and rewards of ownership during the noncancellable term must be assessed. When there are no significant uncertainties, the lessor should account for the lease under the financing method if the present value of the lease payments (excluding residual or salvage value) during the fixed, noncancellable term (excluding renewal and purchase options) is equal to or greater than the selling price for an outright sale or the fair value (either of which may be less than cost) of the property. When the selling price or the fair value of the property cannot be satisfactorily determined, the financing method

[1] A. T. Nelson, "Capitalizing Leases—the Effect on Financial Ratios," *The Journal of Accountancy*, July 1963, pp. 49–53.

may be followed only if the fixed, noncancellable term of the lease (excluding renewal and purchase options) is substantially equal to the estimated useful life of the property.

When a leasing transaction is accounted for by the financing method and a sale is recorded, the cost of the property and the estimated future costs should be charged against income in the period of the sale. In some cases, this will result in a loss on the sale. The analyst should recognize that a lessor usually uses the financing method because it will tend to maximize earnings in earlier years. A lessee uses the operating method of accounting because it decreases the liabilities shown on his balance sheet.

COMMITMENTS

Commitments are claims which may occur upon the future performance under a contract. They are not given expression in accounting records since the mere signing of an executory contract or the issuance of a purchase order does not result in a completed transaction.

Examples of commitments are long-term noncancellable contracts to purchase goods or services at specified prices or purchase contracts for fixed assets which call for payments during construction. In a sense, a lease agreement is also regarded by some as a form of commitment.

Commitments call for disclosure of all the factors surrounding the obligation, including amount, conditions, timing, and other facts of importance.

For example, Storer Broadcasting Company revealed the following commitment in its annual report:

The Company has entered into contracts, covering rentals of television films, under which it is obligated to make payments totaling approximately $7,000,000 during the next six years. Payments under these contracts are recorded as deferred film rentals which are charged to expense as the films are used by the Company.

Cenco Instruments Corporation disclosed the following in a prospectus issued in 1971:

Other Commitments and Contingent Liabilities—included the following:
  (a) Guarantee of indebtedness of unconsolidated foreign subsidiary in an amount of up to approximately $280,000.
  (b) Long-term leases expiring 1974–2063 under which the total annual rentals are approximately $1,350,000 to 1975 and substantially less thereafter.
  (c) During the years 1966–1971 the companies made sales to the United States Government which are subject to review under the provisions of the Renegotiation Act. The Renegotiation Board has determined that an adjustment of approximately $70,000 (before federal income

(d) tax effect) should be made for the 1966 year. The company is contesting the proposed determination. Management is of the opinion that there will not be any material adjustments as a result reviews for the 1967–1971 years.
(d) Employment contracts expiring 1974 through 1979 under which the maximum aggregate annual basic compensation amounts to approximately $901,000.
(e) Construction commitments for new medical complexes (under contracts to sell) amounted to approximately $7,250,000. Other commitments for land acquisition and construction amounted to approximately $1,300,000.
(f) The company may be required to issue additional shares of its common stock in connection with the acquisition of companies and businesses as follows:

	Number of shares
Prior year acquisitions:	
Hospital Planning and Engineering	8,000
Calumet Coach	10,000
Superior Sleeprite	35,835
Maple Manor and Pine Manor	6,779
Current year acquisitions:	
Medical Enterprises Diversified, Inc.	10,000
Liberty-Tomlen Companies	20,000

Issuances of the shares are based on earnings and other factors through various years ending up to 1973.

The company may also be required to issue up to an additional 30,000 shares of Series B $3 cumulative convertible preferred stock in connection with the Eye Gate House, Inc. acquisition based on the earnings by that company through April 30, 1972.

CONTINGENT LIABILITIES

Business enterprise is subject to constant and all-pervading uncertainty. It is assumed that the informed reader of the financial statements is aware of this. However, certain events may point to specific probabilities and contingencies in the future and should be disclosed as such. *Accounting Research Bulletin No. 50* states that "in accounting, a contingency is an existing condition, situation, or set of circumstances, involving a considerable degree of uncertainty, which may, through a related future event, result in the acquisition or loss of an asset, or the incurrence or avoidance of a liability, usually with the concurrence of gain or loss."

The basic nature of a contingency is its dependence on a future development or intervening factor or decision by an outside factor. Usually the contingency is uncertain as to probability of occurrence, timing, and amount. The financial statements must disclose the degree of probability of occurrence and, if possible, the best estimate of financial impact.

Examples of contingent liabilities are those which could arise from litigation, from guarantees of performance, from agreements and contracts, such as purchase or repurchase agreements, and from tax assessments or renegotiation claims.

The note of Cenco Instruments in the preceding section provides one example of disclosure of contingent liabilities. Control Data Corporation provides another such example:

The Company has been named defendent in three patent infringement suits whereunder the plaintiffs allege that certain of the computers or peripheral equipment manufactured infringe patents held by them and request injunctive relief and damages. Should the plaintiffs prevail, the effect of such litigation could be material. However, based on the advice of its counsel, the Company believes that no infringement liability exists and has filed answers denying liability in each case. The Company has no other material litigation pending.

DEFERRED CREDITS (INCOME)

An ever-increasing variety of items and descriptions is included in this group of accounts. In many cases these items are akin to liabilities; in others, they represent deferred income yet to be earned, while in a number of cases, they serve as income-smoothing devices. The confusion confronting the analyst is compounded by a lack of agreement among accountants as to the exact nature of these items or the proper manner of their presentation. Thus, regardless of category or presentation, the key to their analysis lies in an understanding of the circumstances and the financial transactions which brought them about.

At one end of this group's spectrum we find those items which have the characteristics of liabilities. Here we may find included such items as advances or billings on uncompleted contracts, unearned royalties and deposits, and customer service prepayments. Quite clearly, the outstanding characteristic of these items is their liability aspects, even though, as in the case of advances of royalties, they may, after certain conditions are fulfilled, find their way into the company's income stream. Advances on uncompleted contracts represent primarily methods of financing the work in process, while deposits of rent received represent, as do customer service prepayments, security for performance of an agreement. Even though found sometimes among "deferred credits," such items are more properly classified as liabilities, or current liabilities if due within the company's operating cycle.

Next, we consider deferred income items which represent income or revenue received in advance and which will be earned over future periods through the passage of time, the performance of services, or the delivery of goods. Examples of deferred income items are: magazine subscription income, representing the receipts by magazine publishers of advance payment for long-term subscriptions; and unearned rental income, which represents receipt of advance payment for rent. Other examples are unearned finance charges, deferred profit on installment sales, deferred gain on sales-and-leaseback arrangements, and unrealized profit on layaway sales.

It should be noted that this category includes a liability for future performance as well as a possible profit component in such income items received but not yet earned as, for example, subscription income, the future earning of which is dependent on the delivery of magazines. It also includes unearned finance charges which have already been deducted but which are allocated to the future on the assumption that they are earned with the mere passage of time. Still further along the "earned" scale are profits on installment sales which are deferred, not because they have not been earned but rather because the collection of the receivable resulting from such sales is going to occur over a period of time in the future. The preferred accounting treatment is not to defer such gains on installment sales but rather to give expression to any doubts about future collectibility of receivables by establishing a provision for doubtful accounts for that purpose.

Further on the other extreme of the deferred credit spectrum are so-called "bargain purchase credits" which arise in cases where the fair value of certain assets of an acquired company exceeds the consideration given. (Purchase accounting which is governed by APB *Opinion No. 16* is discussed in Chapter 7.) In such cases the resulting credit is amortized to income over what is usually an arbitrarily determined number of years. What we have here is a benefit derived from what is presumably an advantageous acquisition. The reason for the deferral of this benefit and its taking up in income over a number of years is not necessarily that this benefit has not been realized, but because of a desire to spread it out, or smooth its effect over a number of years.

One of the most complicated and controversial, as well as the most substantial, of deferred credits are deferred income taxes.

Deferred taxes

Tax allocation which is the accounting process giving rise to deferred tax credits (or debits in reverse circumstances) is primarily a device for matching the applicable tax expense with corresponding pretax income. A more comprehensive analysis of this accounting technique and its implications will be undertaken in Chapter 9 on the measurement of income. Here we will examine primarily the nature of the deferred credit to which it gives rise.

For purposes of understanding how this deferred tax credit arises, let us consider the example of the depreciation deducted under circumstances where a company may elect an accelerated-depreciation method for tax purposes while using the straight-line method for book purposes. Since more depreciation is deducted for tax purposes in the early years, two things are evident: (1) there is a tax deferral in the early years and (2) that will have to be made up in the later years since in no event can depreciation for tax purposes exceed the total original cost. Thus, in theory, the tax savings are temporary; and under tax allocation these savings are not used to reduce the tax expense but are rather accumulated as a deferred tax credit.

In practice, as a study by the accounting firm of Price Waterhouse and Company shows, this "deferred tax liability" is rarely paid in full. The reason for this is that most companies keep expanding their plant so that every year there is new accelerated depreciation on new facilities to balance—and usually outweigh—the reduced depreciation on facilities that got the accelerated treatment earlier.

The accounting profession which, in APB *Opinion No. 11,* adopted the concept of comprehensive tax allocation, states that it does not regard deferred taxes as a liability but considers them rather a deferred credit account which must be established for the proper matching of costs and revenues. Be that as it may, the analyst must understand what this account represents when he finds it included within the deferred credits category. While we used depreciation as an example here, deferred taxes may arise in any instance where expense or income items are treated one way for tax purposes and another for book purposes.

Deferred investment tax credit

Frequently included among deferred income taxes is the deferred investment credit. While also a tax benefit, the similarity between the deferred income taxes, discussed above, and the deferred investment credit is more apparent than real.

Under various revenue acts, as amended, up to 7 percent of the cost of certain depreciable assets purchased and put into service during the year has been allowed as a credit against federal income taxes. Unlike deferred income taxes, which represent a postponement of tax liability, the investment credit is an effective reduction of taxes in the years in which it is earned. Under one alternative treatment, it is taken into income by means of a reduction of tax expenses in the year in which it is taken on the tax return, while under another alternative, it is taken into income over the productive lives of the assets whose acquisition gave rise to it. It is in the latter case that the deferred investment credit account is found on the balance sheet; and what it represents is, in essence, a device for spreading a benefit already earned over a number of years, in order to achieve a more fair determination of income. The income aspect of the investment credit will be considered more fully in the chapter devoted to this subject.

Now that we have covered the entire spectrum of that family of accounts designated as deferred credits, we can clearly see that each must be examined and understood on its own merits if its significance to the analyst is to be properly assessed.

Found among liabilities, and sometimes in the equity section, but not really representing an immediate claim on company resources, are the minority interests in consolidated entities. These represent the proportionate interest of minority stockholders in a majority-owned subsidiary which is consolidated. Since all the net assets (i.e., assets less liabilities) of the subsidiary are included in the consolidated statements, the minority's portion is shown as a liability in the consolidated balance sheet.

Implications for analysis

The key to the proper analysis of deferred credits is a clear understanding of what has brought them about. In the discussion concerning the accounting principles involved, we have pointed out that they encompass a wide variety of dissimilar items.

Those items which represent prepayments on services yet to be performed or goods yet to be delivered must be regarded as temporary sources of funds. In fact, often advances on contracts yet to be executed serve exactly the purpose of affording temporary financing to the supplier.

Deferred reserves may be viewed by the analyst as items which are on their way to the income stream of a company. What should not be lost sight of is the fact that many such items do not represent pure income elements as may be the case with interest on deferred installment sale profit which are deemed to be earned by the mere passage of time without the incurrence of additional expense. Thus, deferred subscription income represents the amount received in advance for magazines yet to be delivered. In spite of the fact that the earning of such subscription revenue will require paper, printing, editorial, and postage expense, such costs are usually not provided for when the revenue is deferred. Thus, while such items do represent temporary sources of funds, they are not sources of net profit and may, in fact, ultimately result in a net loss.

Certain deferred income items are clearly created, not for the purposes of fair presentation of financial positions but rather for purposes of income smoothing or equalization. Thus the "bargain purchase credit" discussed earlier has as its main purpose and justification the smoothing of income over a period of years and must be regarded as such. Similarly the ratable taking up of installment sales profit is designed to provide for the contingency of possible noncollection of the sales price.

Perhaps the most confusing deferred credit to many analysts is the deferred tax credit. Because of its size, it is, by far, the most important item in this category. Its location in the twilight zone between liabilities and equity indicates that it is neither, but that in itself does not shed light on its true nature.

The reason that the deferred tax credit is not a liability is that it lacks some of the more important characteristics of debt. The government has no present claim for taxes nor is there a timetable for repayment. While the deferred tax account represents the loss of future deductibility of assets for tax purposes, the drawing down of this account to reduce tax expenses depends on future developments, such as asset acquisition and depreciation policies which are not predictable with certainty.

This kind of uncertainty attests to the fact that the deferred tax credit is also not in the nature of equity capital because it represents a tax benefit in the nature of a postponement of taxes rather than a savings of taxes.

The most meaningful thing that can be said about this account from the point of view of financial analysis is that it represents a temporary source of funds derived from the postponement of taxes and that the duration of the overall postponement depends on factors such as the future growth or stability of the company's depreciable assets pool. It is the assessment of such factors and their future likelihood that will be helpful to the analysis of the deferred tax account.

RESERVES AND PROVISIONS

Another group of accounts, found between long-term liabilities and the stockholders' equity section, is that of reserves and provisions. These accounts are often lumped together or even found among current liabilities or as deductions from related asset accounts; consequently it is most useful to classify them broadly so as to facilitate an understanding of their true nature.

The first category is most correctly described as comprising provisions for liabilities and obligations which have a higher probability of occurrence, but which are in dispute or are uncertain in amount. As is the case with many financial statement descriptions, neither the title nor the location in the financial statement can be relied upon as a rule of thumb guide to the nature of an account. Thus, the best key to analysis is a thorough understanding of the business and financial transactions which give rise to the account. The following are representative items in this group: provisions for product guarantees, service guarantees, and warranties, which are established in recognition of the fact that these undertakings involve future costs which are certain to arise though presently impossible to measure exactly. Consequently, the provision is established by a charge to income at the time products covered by guarantees are sold, in an amount estimated on the basis of experience or on the basis of any other reliable factor.

Another type of obligation which must be provided for on the best basis available is the liability for unredeemed trading stamps issued. To the company issuing the trading stamps, there is no doubt about the liability to redeem the stamps for merchandise. The only uncertainty concerns the number of stamps which will be presented for redemption.

Another important group of future costs which must be provided for is that of employee compensation. These, in turn, give rise to compensation reserves.

Contractual or other arrangements call for the funding of employee retirement and pension plans. Regardless of how these plans are *funded,* they must be accrued by charges to income in accordance with the provisions of APB *Opinion No. 8.* These accruals are computed on an actuarial basis and based on the assumptions of the pension or retirement plans.

In addition to pensions we find provisions for deferred compensation, incentive compensation, supplemental unemployment benefits, bonus plans, welfare plans, and severance pay.

Finally the category of estimated liabilities includes provisions for claims arising out of pending or existing litigation.

The second category comprises reserves for expenses and losses, which by experience or estimate are very likely to occur in the future and which should properly be provided for by current charges to operations.

One group within this category comprises reserves for operating costs such as maintenance, repairs, painting, or furnace relining. Thus, for example, since furnace relining jobs may be expected to be required at regularly recurring intervals, they are provided for rateably by charges to operations in order to avoid charging the entire cost to the year in which the actual relining takes place.

Another group comprises provisions for future losses stemming from decisions or actions already taken. Included in this group are reserves for relocation, replacement, modernization, and discontinued operations.

Reserves for contingencies comprise the third group in the reserves category.

Reserves for self-insurance are designed to provide an accumulation against which specific types of losses not covered by insurance may be charged. Although the term self-insurance contradicts the very concept of insurance, which is based on the spreading of risks among many business units, it nevertheless is a practice which has a good number of adherents.

Other contingencies provided against by means of reserves are those arising from foreign operations and exchange losses due to official or de facto devaluations.

Over the years, fewer and fewer companies have established reserves against general or unspecified contingencies, and this trend has much to commend it.

This last category of reserves is the one which the accounting profession has recommended that the term "reserve" be restricted to. It does not, however, belong in our discussion of reserves "above the equity section" in that it is properly shown as an appropriation of retained earnings. This subject will be discussed in Chapter 6 devoted to the equity section.

Implications for analysis

Provisions, such as for service guarantees and warranties, represent, in effect, revenue received for services yet to be performed. Of importance to the analyst is the adequacy of the provision which is often established on the basis of prior experience or, absent that, on the basis of other estimates. Concern with adequacy of amount is a prime factor in the analysis of all other reserves, whatever their purpose. Reserves and provisions appearing above the equity section should almost invariably be created by means of charges to income. They are designed to relieve the income statement of charges which, while belonging to the present, will be incurred in the future.

Reserves for future losses represent a category of accounts which require particular scrutiny. While conservatism in accounting calls for recognition of losses as they can be determined or clearly foreseen, companies tend, particularly in loss years, to overprovide for losses yet to be incurred such as a disposal of assets, relocation, or plant closings. Overprovision does, of course, shift expected future losses to a present period which already shows adverse results. (A more extended discussion of such practices will be found in Chapter 9.) The problem with such reserves is that once established there is no further accounting for the expenses and losses which are charged against them. Only in certain financial statements required to be filed with the SEC (such as Form 10k) are details of changes in reserves required, and even here there is no requirement for detailed disclosure of the nature of the changes. Normally no information is given, and the analyst must adopt a critical attitude towards the establishment of such reserves and the means of their disposition.

A basic reason why we have overprovisions of reserves is that the income statement effects are accorded much more importance than the residual balance sheet effects. While a provision for future expenses and losses establishes a reserve account which is analytically in the never-neverland between liabilities and the ownership (equity) accounts, it serves the important purpose of creating a cushion which can absorb future expenses and losses, thus shielding the all-important income statement from them. The analyst should endeavor to ascertain, as best he can, that provisions for future losses reflect losses which can reasonably be expected to have already occurred rather than be used as a means of artificially benefiting future income by adding excessive provisions to present adverse results.

QUESTIONS

1. How do bond discounts and premiums usually arise? How are they accounted for?
2. Both the conversion feature of debt as well as warrants attached to debt instruments aim at increasing the attractiveness of debt securities and at lowering their interest cost. Describe how the costs of these two similar features are accounted for.
3. How does the analyst of financial statements evaluate an enterprise's liabilities—both present and contingent?
4. What are some of the most important criteria which presently determine, for accounting purposes, that a lease commitment is in effect a purchase requiring capitalization?
5. If a lease is properly capitalizable, should all rental payments in a leasing arrangement be capitalized?
6. Is it true that any lease which is not capitalized needn't show up in the financial statements of the lessee except as an expense in the income statement?
7. What is APB *Opinion No. 7* concerned with?
   a) Contrast the financing method of allocating rental revenue and expenses over the lease period with the operating method.
   b) On what basis is a selection between these two methods made?
   c) What is the proper financial presentation under each method?
8. In what respects have the professional pronouncements relating to the accounting for leases left problem areas for the financial analyst?
9. Distinguish between different kinds of "deferred credits" appearing on a balance sheet. How should those be analyzed?
10. Describe the nature of deferred tax credits. How should the analyst interpret this account?
11. Into what types should reserves and provisions be subdivided for purposes of financial statement analysis?
12. Why must the analyst be particularly alert to the accounting for reserves for future costs and losses?

6

Analysis of stockholders' equity

THE STOCKHOLDERS' EQUITY section of the balance sheet represents the investment of the ownership in the assets of a business entity. While the claims of the ownership are junior to those in the current and long-term liability sections of the balance sheet, they represent, on the other hand, residual claims to all assets, once the claims of creditors have been satisfied. Thus, while being exposed to the maximum risk associated with the enterprise, the ownership is entitled to all the residual rewards that are associated with it.

The accounting for the equity section as well as the presentation, classification, and footnote disclosure associated therewith have certain basic objectives, the most important among which are:

1. To classify and distinguish the major sources of capital contributed to the entity.
2. To set forth the rights and priorities of the various classes of stockholders and the manner in which they rank in partial or final liquidation.
3. To set forth the legal restrictions to which the distribution of capital funds may be subject for whatever reason.
4. To disclose the contractual, legal, managerial, or financial restrictions to which the distribution of current or retained earnings may be subject.
5. To disclose the terms and provisions of convertible securities, of stock options, and of other arrangements involving the future issuance of stock, contingent and otherwise.

CLASSIFICATION OF CAPITAL STOCK

There are two basic kinds of capital stock—preferred and common. There are a number of different varieties within each category, and these, too, have basic differences worth noting.

The preferred stock is usually preferred in liquidation and preferred as to dividends. It may be entitled to par value in liquidation or it may be entitled to a premium. On the other hand its rights to dividends are generally fixed, although they may be cumulative, which means that preferred shareholders are entitled to arrearages of dividends before the common stockholders may receive any dividends. The preferred features, as well as the fixed nature of the dividend, give the preferred stock some of the earmarks of debt with the important difference that preferred stockholders are not generally entitled to demand redemption of their shares. Nevertheless, there are preferred stock issues which have set redemption dates and which may require sinking funds to be established for that purpose.

Characteristics of preferred stock which may make them more akin to common stock are divided participation rights, voting rights, and rights of conversion into common stock.

Within the preferred stock classes we may find a variety of orders of priority and preference relating to dividends and liquidation rights.

The common stock is the basic ownership equity of a company having no preference but reaping all residual rewards as well as being subject to all losses. Occasionally there is more than one class of common stock. In such cases the distinctions between one class and the other express themselves in dividend, voting, or other rights.

The preferred stock generally has a par value which may or may not be the amount at which it was originally sold. Common stock may have a par value, and if not, it is usually assigned a stated value. The par value of the common stock has no substantive significance for analytical purposes.

Disclosure regarding capital stock

Proper disclosure requires that an analysis and explanation of changes in the number of shares of capital stock be given in the financial statements or in the notes related thereto. Such changes may be due to a variety of reasons including the following:

1. *Increases in capital stock outstanding:*
    a) Sale of stock.
    b) Conversion of debentures or preferred stock.

c) Issuance pursuant to stock dividends or stock splits.
d) Issuance of stock in acquisitions or mergers.
e) Issuance of stock pursuant to stock options granted or warrants exercised.

2. *Decreases in capital stock outstanding:*
   a) Purchase and retirement of stock.
   b) Purchase of treasury stock.
   c) Reverse stock splits.

Another important aspect of disclosure with regard to the various classes of capital stock is the various options held by others which, when exercised, would cause the number of shares outstanding to be increased. Such options include:

1. Conversion rights of debenture or preferred stock into common.
2. Warrants outstanding for a specified period entitling the holder to exchange them for stock under specified conditions.
3. Stock options under supplementary compensation and bonus plans which call for the issuance of capital stock over a period of time at prices fixed in advance, such as qualified stock option plans and "employee stock purchase plans."
4. Commitments to issue capital stock, such as under merger agreements which call for additional consideration contingent on the happening of an event such as the reaching of certain earning levels by the acquired company, etc.

The importance of such disclosures lies in the need to alert all interested parties to the potential increase in the number of shares outstanding. The degree of the resultant dilution in earnings and book value per share depends, of course, on such factors as the amount to be paid in per share and other rights given up when conversions of securities are effected.

Up to the mid-1960s the accounting profession has almost completely ignored the effect that potential dilution has on such basic valuation yardsticks as earnings per share and, to a lesser extent, book value per share. More recently, alerted by the use of even more complex securities, the profession has finally recognized that dilution represents a very real cost to a company, a cost which had been given little if any formal recognition in financial statements. The impact of dilution on earnings per share will be examined in Chapter 10. Problems in the computation of book value are examined at the end of this chapter.

Disclosure must be made of a variety of terms to which preferred stock may be subject, including:

1. *Dividend rights,* including participating and cumulative features.
2. *Liquidation rights.* In APB *Opinion No. 10* the Board stated:

> Companies at times issue preferred (or other senior) stock which has a preference in involuntary liquidation considerably in excess of the par or stated value of the shares. The relationship between this preference in liquidation and the par or stated value of the shares may be of major significance to the users of the financial statements of those companies and the Board believes it highly desirable that it be prominently disclosed. Accordingly, the Board recommends that in these cases, the liquidation preference of the stock be disclosed in the equity section of the balance sheet in the aggregate, either parenthetically or "in short" rather than on a per share basis or by disclosure in notes.

Such disclosure is particularly important since the discrepancy between the par and liquidation value of preferred stock can be very significant as is the case, for example, in General Aniline & Film Corporation where at one point in time the par value was $3.9 million as against a liquidation value of $85.7 million!

3. *Voting rights,* which may change with conditions such as arrearages in dividends.
4. *Conversion rights.*
5. *Sinking fund provisions,* which are not too common.
6. *Call provisions,* which usually protect the preferred stockholder against premature redemption. Call premiums often decrease over time.

In addition to a description of terms, disclosure must be made of any conditions affecting the relative standing of the various classes of stock such as, for example, dividend arrearages on preferred stock, which must generally be paid before the common stock can get any distribution at all.

An example of such disclosure is provided by American Saint Gobain Corporation:

(a) 5% Cumulative Preferred Stock:
The 5% Cumulative Preferred Stock is redeemable, through operation of a sinking fund, at par value plus accrued and unpaid dividends. The sinking fund provides for contributions based on annual earnings with a maximum limit of $175,000 per year. However, under the restrictions contained in the indenture agreements covering the Company's long-term debt, no payments may be made in 1968 to the sinking fund without prior consent of the holders of at least two-thirds of the debt. At December 31, 1967, cumulative payments to the sinking fund amounting to $350,000 were omitted due to the long-term debt restrictions. The stock is callable at the option of the Corporation at $25.25 per share, plus accrued and unpaid dividends. As of December 31,

1967, twenty-seven quarterly dividend payments amounting to approximately $8.44 per share or $1,340,800 in the aggregate were unpaid. The holders of this Preferred Stock presently have the right to elect two directors in addition to the directors elected by the holders of Common Stock.

(b) 6% Cumulative Preference Stock:

The 6% Cumulative Preference Stock is callable at the option of the Corporation at prices ranging downward from $102.00 per share, plus accrued and unpaid dividends. As of December 31, 1967, twenty-four quarterly dividend payments amounting to approximately $35.27 per share or $1,058,000 in the aggregate were unpaid. The stock has no voting rights.

Additional capital

Amounts paid in for capital stock are usually divided into two parts. One part is assigned to the par or stated value of capital shares, and the rest is shown in the capital surplus section. The term "surplus" is actually falling into disuse so that the additional capital section contains accounts having such descriptive titles as "capital in excess of par or stated value," "additional capital," "additional paid-in capital," and "paid-in capital." No matter what the title, these accounts signify the amounts paid in for capital stock in excess of par or stated value.

The additional accounts in the "capital" group do not result only from amounts paid in excess of par but include also charges or credits from a variety of other capital transactions, examples of which are:

1. Gains or losses from sale of treasury stock.
2. Capital changes arising from business combinations.
3. Capital donations, usually shown separately as donated capital.
4. Capital stock expenses, merger expenses, and other costs of a capital nature.
5. Capitalization of retained earnings by means of stock dividends.

Informative financial statements must contain a reconciliation of all capital surplus accounts so as to explain the changes which have occurred therein.

Treasury stock

Treasury stock is stock which has once been issued and was outstanding and which has been subsequently reacquired by the company. Treasury stock is generally carried at cost, and the most common method of presentation is to deduct such cost from the total equity section. Some companies which reserve their own treasury stock for such purposes as profit sharing, contingent compensation, deferred compensation, or other compensation plans, or for purposes of acquisitions of other companies do sometimes present such stock among assets.

RETAINED EARNINGS

While the capital stock and capital surplus accounts show primarily the capital contribution by various classes of stock, the Retained Earnings account represents generally the accumulation of undistributed earnings since inception. Conversely, a deficit account represents the accumulated net losses of the corporation.

Although some states permit distributions to shareholders from capital surplus accounts such distributions represent, in effect, capital distributions. Thus, the Retained Earnings account is the prime source of dividend distributions to shareholders, and amounts distributed by charge to other accounts do not, strictly speaking, deserve the label "dividend."

Dividends

The most common form of dividend is the cash dividend which, once declared, becomes a liability of the company. A second form of dividend is the dividend in kind, such as dividends in goods (e.g., cases of liquor) or dividends in the stock of another corporation. Such dividends should be valued at the fair market value of the assets distributed.

A third form of dividend is the stock dividend which, in effect, represents the permanent capitalization of company earnings. As evidence of such a shift from retained earnings to the permanent capital accounts, shareholders receive additional shares. Generally accepted accounting principles require that the stock dividends be valued at the fair market value of the shares to be issued as determined at the date of declaration. This principle is designed to put a realistic limit to the number of shares that can be issued as stock dividends. A stock distribution exceeding 20–25 percent is no longer to be accounted as a stock dividend and should instead be accounted for as a stock split. The latter represents, in essence, the subdivision of the net corporate pie into smaller shares.

Prior period adjustments

APB *Opinion No. 9* had defined the relatively rare instances which justify other charges or credits to the Retained Earnings account. These are limited primarily to material prior period adjustments which:

(a) can be specifically identified with, and directly related to, the business activities of prior periods;
(b) are not attributable to economic events occurring subsequent to the date of the financial statements for the period;
(c) depend primarily on determination by persons other than management; and
(d) were not susceptible of reasonable estimation prior to such determination.

Prior year adjustments, examples of which are material nonrecurring litigation settlements and income tax adjustments, are now the only items of gain or loss permitted to be included in the Retained Earnings account. This contrasts with the practice prior to issuance of APB *Opinion No. 9* when the inclusion in the retained earnings of a wide variety of extraordinary gains and losses was sanctioned.

In addition to dividends and prior year adjustments, changes in retained earnings may include adjustments due to business combinations and other capital adjustments such as premiums on redemption of preferred stock, losses on sales of treasury stock, etc.

Appropriations of retained earnings

By managerial action, or in compliance with legal requirements, retained earnings are often appropriated or reserved.

Appropriated retained earnings, also known as reserves, established by managerial action include reserves for general contingencies, plant expansion, self-insurance, and other business contingencies. The basic idea here is to preserve a specific amount of capital which is available for absorption of possible losses or is frozen to provide permanent funds, such as for expansion. Thus, such appropriations should never be used to relieve the income statement of charges which are properly chargeable against it. After having served their purpose, such appropriations should be restored to unappropriated retained earnings.

Appropriations of retained earnings in an amount equal to the cost of treasury stock purchased is an example of appropriations established under the legal requirements of certain states. Such appropriations are restored to retained earnings after the treasury stock is sold, retired, or otherwise disposed of.

The equity section of American Bakeries Company, represents an example of presentation in the financial statements:

Stockholders' Equity

Cumulative prior preferred stock:	
$1.80 series, 87,512 shares, stated at liquidating value of $35 per share	$ 3,062,920
$1.80 convertible series, 100,000 shares, stated at par value of $25 per share	2,500,000
5% cumulative convertible preferred stock, $100 par value; outstanding 83,855 shares in 1970 and 83,939 shares in 1969	8,385,500
Common stock, no par value: authorized 5,000,000 shares; issued 2,038,455 shares in 1970 and 2,038,058 shares in 1969	8,096,524
Retained earnings	29,747,936
	$51,792,880

Less capital stock held in treasury, at cost:
Common (7,237 shares) . . . . $ 213,856
$1.80 cumulative prior preferred
 (2,261 shares).   39,225
5% cumulative convertible preferred
 (2,033 shares).   130,906
$ 383,987
$51,408,893

Restrictions on retained earnings

An important aspect of disclosure relating to retained earnings involves restrictions imposed on its distribution as dividends. This is, obviously, information of importance to potential investors and others. Examples of such restrictions which stem from debt indentures are:

FEDDERS CORPORATION

Notes to consolidated financial statements

Long-term debt and surplus restriction. The most restrictive agreement covering the Company's long-term debt provides, among other things, that the Company may not (1) declare or pay any dividends on its capital stock (other than dividends in capital stock of the Company), (2) expend for acquisition of its capital stock more than the net proceeds from sale of capital stock or (3) make any restricted payment, as defined, on the subordinated indebtedness unless, immediately after giving effect to such transaction, its net current assets will not be less than $60,000,000 and the sum of such transactions from August 31, 1968 will not exceed $4,000,000 plus 75% of net income of the Company, as defined, from August 31, 1968. Under this restriction, $24,731,000 of earned surplus was not available for cash dividends at August 31, 1970.

THE GRAND UNION COMPANY

Notes to financial statements

Restrictions on dividends. The note agreements and the 4⅛% debenture indenture contain provisions as to the maintenance of working capital and payment of cash dividends. The most restrictive of these provides that consolidated working capital may not be less than $14,500,000, and that payments for net acquisitions of the company's stocks and for cash dividends will be limited in the aggregate to 75% of the consolidated net earnings after March 2, 1957. At February 28, 1970, 75% of such consolidated net earnings exceeded such payments by approximately $42,000,000 and, accordingly, none of the balance of retained earnings is so restricted.

An example of restrictions on retained earnings stemming from preferred stock provisions is provided by a note in the financial statements of Colgate Palmolive Company:

Dividend restrictions. The preferred stock provisions of the Certificate of Incorporation contain restrictions on the payment of cash dividends to common shareholders. At December 31, 1970, domestic retained earnings were free of such restrictions to the extent of $120,383,000.

BOOK VALUE PER SHARE

The term "book value" is conventional terminology referring to net asset value, that is, total assets reduced by the senior claims against them. Thus, the book value of the common stock equity is equal to the total assets less liabilities and claims of securities senior to the common stock, such as preferred stock, mostly at amounts at which they are carried on the financial statements. We consider this computation here because an alternative and simpler way of computing book value is to add up the common stock equity accounts and reduce the total by any senior claims not reflected in the financial statements such as preferred stock dividend arrearages, liquidation premiums, etc.

Book value is almost always presented on a per share basis (the significance of this figure will be considered later in the chapter). Once the underlying principles of computation are understood, the calculation of book value is relatively simple.

ILLUSTRATION 1. The following is the equity section of the Zero Corporation for years ended in 19x4 and 19x5:

	19x5	*19x4*
Preferred stock, 7% cumulative, par value $100 (authorized 4,000,000 shares; outstanding 3,602,811 shares)	$ 360,281,100	$ 360,281,100
Common stock (authorized 90,000,000 shares; outstanding 54,138,137 shares at December 31, 19x5 and 54,129,987 shares at December 31, 19x4)	3,264,581,527	3,122,464,738
Par value $16²/₃ per share. . . . . $ 902,302,283		
Income reinvested in business 2,362,279,244		
Total	$3,624,862,627	$3,482,745,838

The preferred shares are nonparticipating but are callable at 105. Dividends for 19x5 are in arrears.

Required:

Calculate the book value per share of both the common and preferred stock as of December 31, 19x5.

6. Analysis of stockholders' equity

Computations

	Preferred	+	Common	=	Total
Preferred stock* (@ $100)	$360,281,100				$ 360,281,100
Dividends in arrears (7%)	25,219,677				25,219,677
Common stock			$ 902,302,283		902,302,283
Retained earnings (net of amount attributed to dividends in arrears)			2,337,059,567		2,337,059,567
Total	$385,500,777		$3,239,361,850		$3,624,862,627
Divided by number of shares outstanding	3,602,811		54,138,137		
Book value per share	$107.00		$59.84		

*The call premium does not normally enter into the computation of book value per share because the call provision is at the option of company.

ILLUSTRATION 2. The following is the stockholders' equity section of the balance sheet of the XYZ Company on June 30, 19x1:

Preferred stock—authorized 200,000 shares, issued and outstanding 100,000 shares, par value $100, 6% cumulative, nonparticipating	$10,000,000
Common stock—authorized 375,000 shares, issued and outstanding 200,000 shares, par value $100	20,000,000
Capital contributed in excess of par value	5,000,000
Retained earnings (deficit)	(7,000,000)
Total Stockholders' Equity	$28,000,000

The preferred shares have a liquidation value of $105 and are callable at $110. No dividends have been declared or paid by the company for either the preferred or common shares for two years. Assume that the preferred stock has a preference on assets in liquidation.

Required:

Compute the book value (equity) per share for all classes of stock as of June 30, 19x1.

Computations

	Preferred	Common
Par value	$10,500,000	$20,000,000
Dividends in arrears	1,200,000	
Net deficit (all applicable to common stock)		(3,700,000)
Total	$11,700,000	$16,300,000
Divided by number of shares outstanding	100,000	200,000
Book value (equity) per share	$117.00	$81.50

Explanations:
1. Liquidation value for preferred shares ($105) is used; call value does not enter into the computation of book value per share.
2. Preferred shares are entitled to two years' dividends (12% of $10,000,000 = $1,200,000).
3. Preference of assets for preferred shares means that the deficit is wholly applicable to the common.
4. Computation of net deficit:

Retained earnings (deficit)	$(7,000,000)
Paid-in capital	5,000,000
Dividends in arrears	(1,200,000)
Preferred liquidation premium	(500,000)
Net deficit	$(3,700,000)

As can be seen from the above illustrations, the major adjustments in book value per share computations arise from rights and priorities of securities which are senior to the common. In most cases these are premiums, and liquidation priority rights of a variety of classes of preferred stock.

Care must be taken to determine the liquidation value of preferred stock. Some companies have preferred stock issues outstanding which give the right to very substantial liquidation premiums which are far above the par value of such shares. The effect of such liquidation premiums on the book value of the common and other junior equities can be substantial.

ILLUSTRATION. In a listing application (A-25189) of Glen Alden Corporation appear the following details of book value computation:

Equity per Share:

Equity per share of Glen Alden, Warner and the Surviving Corporation, based on the initial redemption values of the preferred stocks and on the consolidated balance sheets of Glen Alden and Warner at December 31 and August 27, 1966, respectively, and the pro forma combined balance sheet follows:

Initial redemption per share values	Preferred stocks	Glen Alden, December 31, 1966	Warner, August 27, 1966	Pro forma surviving corporation
$ 52.50	Senior stock	$52.50		$ 52.50
$107.00	Class B senior stock			$100.70
$110.00	Preferred stock	$88.89		None
$ 90.00	Class C stock	$72.73		None
None	Common stock	None	$19.51	None

Based on the pro forma combined balance sheet there would be no book value attributable to the preferred stock, class C stock and common stock of the Surviving Corporation when the equity applicable to the senior stock and the class B senior stock is considered at aggregate initial redemption value. The aggregate initial redemption value of the senior stock and class B senior stock exceeds total pro forma stockholders' equity by approximately $141,816,000.

The pro forma initial redemption and liquidation prices of the preferred stocks in the aggregate ($343,821,848) exceed their stated values by $296,179,211, and such excess exceeds the aggregate amount of common stock and surplus by approximately $141,816,000. Upon liquidation the senior stock is first in order of preference, followed by the class B senior stock. The preferred stock and class C stock are junior to the class B senior stock, but rank on a parity with each other. There are no restrictions upon surplus arising out of such excess.

As the above example shows, the liquidation premium of the senior stocks is of such magnitude as to wipe out the entire residual book value of the junior preferred and common stock issues.

The accounting profession has, in APB *Opinion No. 10*, recognized the problem posed by preference rights in involuntary liquidation which are substantially in excess of stated par values. Thus, the Opinion recommends that the aggregate liquidation preference be prominently disclosed in the equity section of the balance sheet. The Opinion also calls for disclosure of call prices and dividend arrearages.

Judging by actual practice, the rules involving "common stock equivalents" which govern the computation of earnings per share (see Chapter 10) do not seem to apply to the computation of book value per share. Nevertheless, a case can be made for extending the earnings per share rules to book value computations. The recent merger movement has given rise to increasingly complex securities, and there is not much justification for ignoring these in book value computations.

ILLUSTRATION. Kinney National Service Company proxy dated May 16, 1969 reveals an interesting type of preferred stock issued in connection with the company's merger with Warner Bros.–Seven Arts, Ltd. Thus the series C preferred:
1. Has an annual cumulative dividend rate of only 5 cents.
2. Will be convertible commencing six months after closing date into one share of Kinney common stock either by payment of $37 (for a period ending 10 years and six months after such closing date) or by surrender of 15 additional series C preferred shares.
3. Will be entitled to one-half vote.
4. May not be redeemed by Kinney before 10 years after closing date and at $2.50 thereafter.

It appears that this preferred issue has most of the characteristics of a common stock warrant and few of the characteristics of a true preferred stock. Convertible debentures and convertible preferred stock issues can, of course, also affect significantly the book value per share computations if their conversion features are given effect.

ILLUSTRATION. Company A has the following simplified balance sheet:

Assets less current liabilities	$1,000,000
Convertible debentures	100,000
Net assets	$ 900,000
Common shares.	100,000

The debentures are convertible into 20,000 shares of common stock.
The company also has warrants outstanding entitling the holder to buy 10,000 shares at $6 per share. Stock options to buy 10,000 shares at an average price of $8 per share are also outstanding.
The conventional method of book value calculation would yield a book value per share of $9 (net assets/common shares = $900,000/100,000).

Giving effect to possible conversions, the book value computation will look as follows:

Net assets (as above)	$ 900,000
Add convertible debentures	100,000
Proceeds from exercise of warrants (10,000 × $6)	60,000
Proceeds from exercise of stock options (10,000 × $8)	80,000
Adjusted net asset value	$1,140,000
Common shares outstanding	100,000
Add:	
Conversion of debentures	20,000
Exercise of warrants	10,000
Exercise of options	10,000
Adjusted number of common shares	140,000
Book value per share ($1,140,000/140,000)	$8.14

Clearly, the effect of conversions of debentures, options, etc., on book value depends on the conversion terms. If stock is converted at prices below conventional book value per share, the effect is, as in the above example, dilutive. Conversely, if the conversion is at prices above conventional book value, the effect will be antidilutive. Applying the conservative principles which have been devised by the accounting profession for the computation of earnings per share (see Chapter 10), antidilutive effects (i.e., those which enhance book value per share) would not be allowed to enter the computations.

Significance of book value

Once an important variable in investment decision making, book value has gradually dwindled in importance. The basic reason for this is that investment analysis generally emphasizes earning power and not asset size. Thus, the value of a company's securities is based primarily on the earning capacity of its asset base rather than on its size.

There are, of course, exceptions to this generalization, and they account for the continued use of the book value per share statistic:

1. Book value, properly adjusted, is often used in an assessment of merger terms.
2. Due to the fact that the rate base of public utilities often approximates its book value, this measure is important in this industry.
3. The analysis of companies which have mostly liquid assets such as those in the finance, investment, insurance, and banking fields, rightfully affords greater than usual importance to book values.
4. The analyst of high-grade bonds and preferred stock usually attaches considerable importance to asset coverage in addition to earning capacity.

There are, of course, other factors which make net assets a measure of some importance in financial analysis. A company's earnings growth is sooner or later dependent on growth in assets and, consequently, on a choice of how to finance them. A large asset base has, depending on its composition, a certain potential of profitable utilization.

The accounting considerations that enter into computation of book value should be thoroughly understood by any user of this statistic:

1. The carrying values of assets, particularly long-lived assets such as plant and equipment, long-term investments, and some inventories, is usually at cost and may differ significantly from current market values. Moreover, such carrying values will, as was seen in the preceding chapters, vary according to the accounting principles selected. Thus, for instance, in times of rising prices the carrying value of inventories under the Lifo method of inventory accounting will be lower than under the Fifo method.
2. Intangible assets of great value may not be reflected in book value nor are contingent liabilities, which may have a high probability of occurrence, usually so reflected.

The decline in the use of book value may be due to a lack of usefulness of this measure. It is, undoubtedly also due to the very crude approaches taken in its reporting and application. Thus, for example, the blanket exclusion from book value of goodwill, patents, franchises, and other intangibles cannot make up for the lack of the analysis required to adopt this measure to the particular objective it is designed to meet. Either book value is computed on a "current value" basis or on a cost basis. In the latter case, the arbitrary exclusion of intangible assets makes no sense. If, for example, book value is to be used in comparing the relative value of two companies engaged in merger negotiations, adjustments, such as the following, may be required so that an intelligent comparison can be made:

1. The carrying value of assets should be adjusted to current market values.
2. Differences in the application of accounting principles should be adjusted for.
3. Unrecorded intangibles should be given recognition.
4. Contingent liabilities should be assessed and given appropriate recognition.
5. Accounting and other errors should be adjusted on the books of both companies.

Other adjustments may also be called for. Thus, if the preferred stock has the characteristics of debt, it may be appropriate to capitalize it at the prevailing interest rate, thus reflecting the benefit or disadvantage of it to the company.

The emphasis of earning power has, as was discussed above, resulted in a deemphasis of asset size. Sterile or unproductive assets are worse than worthless. They are often a drag on earnings because they require a minimum of upkeep and management expenses. Like any other analytical tools, book value is a measure which can be useful for certain purposes provided it is used with discrimination and understanding.

IMPLICATIONS FOR ANALYSIS

The accounting principles which apply to the equity section do not have a marked effect on income determination and, as a consequence, do not hold many pitfalls for the analyst. From the analysis point of view, the most significant information here relates to the composition of the capital accounts and to the restrictions to which they may be subject.

The composition of the equity capital is important because of provisions affecting the residual rights of the common equity. Such provisions include dividend participation rights, conversion rights, and the great variety of options and conditions which are characteristic of the complex securities frequently issued under merger agreements, most of which tend to dilute the common equity.

An analysis of restrictions imposed on the distribution of retained earnings by loan or other agreements will usually shed light on a company's freedom of action in such areas as dividend distributions, required levels of working capital. Such restrictions also shed light on the company's bargaining strength and standing in credit markets. Moreover, a careful reading of restrictive covenants will also enable the analyst to assess how far a company is from being in default of these provisions.

QUESTIONS

1. What are the objectives of the classifications and the footnote disclosure associated with the equity section of the corporate balance sheet? Of what significance are such disclosures to readers of financial statements?
2. What features of a preferred stock issue make it akin to debt? What features make it more like common stock?
3. Why is it important from the point of view of the analyst of financial statements that the liquidation value of preferred stock, if different from par or stated value, be clearly disclosed?
4. Presidential Realty Corporation reported as follows on distributions paid on common stock:

6. Analysis of stockholders' equity   135

"The cash distributions on common stock were charged to paid-in surplus because the parent company has accumulated no earnings (other than its equity in undistributed earnings of certain subsidiaries) since its formation. . . ."

a) Are these cash distributions dividends?

b) Why do you suppose did this realty company make such distributions?

5. Why does the proper accounting for stock dividends require that the fair market value, rather than the par value, of the shares distributed be charged against retained earnings?

6. What conditions must a gain or loss conform to before it may be treated as a prior period adjustment?

7. Some companies present "minority interests in subsidiary companies" between the long-term debt and the equity sections of the consolidated balance sheet; others present them as part of equity capital.

a) What is a "minority interest"? (Refer to Chapter 7.)

b) Where on the consolidated balance sheet does it belong? What different points of view do these differing presentations represent?

8. What is book value per share? How is it computed? What is its significance? (C.F.A.)

9. Why has the use of the "book value per share" declined in relative importance over the past decades? What valid uses of book value are still made today?

10. What are some of the accounting considerations which enter into the computation of book value and about which the analyst should be aware?

11. What adjustments may be necessary to render the book value per share measure comparable as between two enterprises?

7

Intercorporate investments, business combinations, and foreign operations

IN THIS CHAPTER we shall examine the analytical implications of a number of specialized topics in accounting, most of which straddle the areas of asset, liability, and income measurements and are thus discussed best in their entirety and in a separate and distinct fashion.

INTERCORPORATE INVESTMENTS

When one corporation owns all or a majority of the voting equity securities of another corporation, a parent-subsidiary relationship is said to exist. The reasons why one company may form or buy control of another entity are many and include sources of supply, enlargement of market coverage, entrance into new lines of business, taxes, reduction of risk because of limited liability, and the requirements of government regulation.

There are three basic methods by which a parent company can account for its ownership in a subsidiary. These are:

1. Consolidated financial statements.
2. Equity method.
3. Cost method.

We shall examine these hereunder in this order, which is the order of their preference from an accounting theory standpoint. This order

7. Intercorporate investments, combinations, & foreign operations   137

of preference coincides also with that from the point of view of the financial analyst since, as we will see from the discussion which follows, the methods differ significantly in the amount of information they provide the analyst about the financial condition and results of operations of the combined parent-subsidiary entity.

Consolidated financial statements

On the parent company's financial statements the ownership of stock in a subsidiary is evidenced by an investment account. From a legal point of view the parent company owns the stock of its subsidiary; it does not own the subsidiary's assets nor is it normally responsible for the subsidiary's debts, although it frequently guarantees them. Consolidated financial statements disregard the legality of this situation in favor of its business substance and reflect the economic reality of a business entity under centralized control. There is a presumption that in most cases, consolidated financial statements are more meaningful than separate financial statements and that they are required for fair presentation of financial conditions and results of operations.

Basic technique of consolidation. Consolidated financial statements combine the assets, liabilities, revenues, and expenses of subsidiaries with the corresponding items in the financial statements of the parent company. To the extent that the parent does not own 100 percent of a subsidiary's equity securities, the minority interest of outsiders is recognized in the consolidation. Intercompany items are eliminated in order to avoid double counting and the premature recognition of income.

ILLUSTRATION. Exhibit 7–1 presents the simplified balance sheet of Company P (the parent) at the time of its acquisition of Company S (the subsidiary). The assets and liabilities included in the balance sheet of Company S are already stated in terms of their fair market values at the time of acquisition. Company P paid $78,000 for 90 percent of Company S's common stock. Accounts receivable of Company P include $4,000 owed it by Company S.

The adjustments in the work sheet which combine the two companies are as follows:

a) The investment at acquisition is eliminated against 90 percent of the equity (capital stock plus retained earnings) of Company S. The remaining 10 percent of Company S's equity belongs to outside stockholders and is shown as "minority interest" in the consolidated balance sheet. The amount of $6,000 which Company P paid in excess of the fair value of 90 percent of the tangible net assets of Company S is carried as "goodwill" in the consolidated balance sheet. The method of determination of goodwill will be discussed later in this chapter under "purchase" accounting.

EXHIBIT 7–1

COMPANY P AND COMPANY S
Consolidated Balance Sheet Worksheet
Date of Acquisition

Assets	Company P	Company S	Adjustments and eliminations	Minority interest	Consolidated
Cash	16,000	11,000			27,000
Accounts receivable	32,000	19,000	(b) 4,000		47,000
Inventories	42,000	18,000			60,000
Fixed assets	64,000	42,000			106,000
Investment in Company S:					
Fair value at acquisition	72,000	...	(a) 72,000		...
Excess of cost over fair value (goodwill)	6,000	...			6,000
Total Assets	232,000	90,000			246,000
Liabilities and Equity					
Accounts payable	12,000	10,000	(b) 4,000		18,000
Capital stock:					
Company P	120,000				120,000
Company S		50,000	(a) 45,000	5,000	
Retained earnings:					
Company P	100,000				100,000
Company S		30,000	(a) 27,000	3,000	
Minority interest					8,000
Total Liabilities and Equity	232,000	90,000			246,000

b) The accounts receivable of Company P and the corresponding payable of Company S are eliminated in consolidation.

Under the consolidation method the income statement of Company S will be combined with that of Company P, and the 10 percent share of the minority interest in the net income or loss of Company S for the period will be deducted from the consolidated income (or loss) in order to show the consolidated net results of operations of the group.

In consolidating the income statement of subsidiary Company S with parent Company P, intercompany profits on sales of inventories which remain within the consolidated group at year-end and intercompany profits on other assets, such as fixed assets, must be eliminated. This is so because the equity interest in the earnings of a consolidated entity relate to earnings with parties *outside* the group. Transactions among members within the group are viewed as incomplete, and the profit as unrealized.

Principles governing consolidation policy. There is a general presumption that consolidated statements are more meaningful than separate parent and subsidiary statements. Consequently, consolidation is the preferred method of presenting the financial statements of a parent and its subsidiaries. There are, however, a number of valid reasons why a subsidiary should not be consolidated. They are as follows:

1. *Incomplete or temporary control.* In general, in order to consolidate a subsidiary, a parent should have ownership or effective management control over the subsidiary. Thus, ownership of over 50 percent of the voting stock is generally required for consolidation, and consolidation is inappropriate where the control is temporary or where it will be disposed of or otherwise lost in the near future.

2. *Lack of homogeneity.* The concept of what constitutes a homogenous unit has undergone considerable change over the years. More recently, corporate diversification has led to the creation of conglomerates which have interests in many different types of industries and activities. Generally speaking, a mere difference in the nature of business is not sufficient reason to bar consolidation. Nevertheless, certain businesses are so different in nature that consolidation can become not only meaningless but also misleading. Thus, banking and insurance subsidiaries of industrial parents have types and proportions of assets, liabilities, and income statement items so different from those of the parent that their commingling would be more confusing than revealing.

3. *Uncertainty as to income.* Where there is reason for serious doubt whether an increase in equity in a subsidiary has really accrued to the parent, consolidation is not appropriate. Such doubt can occur particularly in the case of foreign subsidiaries when there are restrictions on the conversion of foreign currencies or on the remittance of foreign earnings.

The need to consolidate leasing subsidiaries. APB *Opinion No. 18* reaffirms the requirement that subsidiaries whose principal business activity consists of leasing property or facilities to their parents or other affiliates be consolidated with such parents. The reason for this requirement is the significance of the assets and liabilities of such subsidiaries to the consolidated financial position of the entire group.

The equity method

The equity method should be used in both parent company and consolidated financial statements for investments in common stock of all unconsolidated subsidiaries (foreign or domestic) where for reasons, such as those discussed above, consolidation is not appropriate. Such reasons would include, for example, the ownership of an insurance subsidiary by an industrial group. Under APB *Opinion No. 18* the equity method is not a valid substitute for consolidation and should not be used to justify exclusion of a subsidiary when consolidation is otherwise appropriate.

The difference between consolidation and the equity method lies in the details reported in the financial statements. Under the equity method the parent's share of the subsidiary results are presented in its income statement as a line item, and this has resulted in the equity method being also referred to as "one line consolidation."

As we saw in the discussion of the accounting for intercorporate investments in Chapter 6, the equity method of accounting should, generally, be used for investments in common stock which represent interests 20 percent or over in the voting stock of a company's equity securities, and it may be appropriate in some cases even for investments representing an interest of less than 20 percent.

Recognizing the wide application of the equity methods to investments in subsidiaries, to investments in corporate joint ventures, as well as to investments in less than majority owned investees, APB *Opinion No. 18* listed a number of procedures which should be followed in applying this method:

1. Intercompany profits and losses should be eliminated until realized by the investor or investee as if a subsidiary, corporate joint venture, or investee company were consolidated.
2. A difference between the cost of an investment and the amount of underlying equity in net assets of an investee should be accounted for as if the investee were a consolidated subsidiary. (APB *Opinion No. 17* requires amortization of goodwill over a term not exceeding 40 years.)
3. The investment(s) in common stock should be shown in the balance sheet of an investor as a single amount, and the investor's share of earnings or losses of an investee(s) should ordinarily be shown in the income statement as a single amount except for the extraordinary items and prior period adjustments which should be separately classified in the income statement of the investor.
4. A transaction of an investee of a capital nature that affects the investor's share of stockholders' equity of the investee should be accounted for as if the investee were a consolidated subsidiary.
5. Sales of stock of an investee by an investor should be accounted for as gains or losses equal to the difference at the time of sale between selling price and carrying amount of the stock sold.
6. If financial statements of an investee are not sufficiently timely for an investor to apply the equity method currently, the investor ordinarily should record its share of the earnings or losses of an investee from the most recent available financial statements. A lag in reporting should be consistent from period to period.

7. A loss in value of an investment which is other than a temporary decline should be recognized the same as a loss in value of other long-term assets. Evidence of a loss in value might include, inability to recover the carrying amount of investment, decline in market value, etc. All relevant factors must be evaluated.
8. The investor ordinarily should discontinue applying the equity method when the investment (and net advances) is reduced to zero and should not provide for additional losses unless the investor has guaranteed obligations of the investee or is otherwise committed to provide further financial support for the investee. If the investee subsequently reports net income, the investor should resume applying the equity method only after its share of that net income equals the share of net losses not recognized during the period the equity method was suspended.
9. When an investee has outstanding cumulative preferred stock, an investor should compute its share of earnings (losses) after deducting the investee's preferred dividends, whether or not such dividends are declared.
10. The carrying amount of an investment in common stock of an investee that qualifies for the equity method of accounting as described above may differ from the underlying equity in net assets of the investee. The difference should affect the determination of the amount of the investor's share of earnings or losses of an investee as if the investee were a consolidated subsidiary. However, if the investor is unable to relate the difference to specific accounts of the investee, the difference should be considered to be goodwill and amortized over a period not to exceed 40 years, in accordance with APB *Opinion No. 17*.

The cost method

The cost method is, under the prevailing system of accrual accounting, the method least preferred among the three alternative ways of presenting investments in subsidiaries. Under this method the investment in a subsidiary is recorded at cost and income is recognized only as it is received in the form of dividend distributions. A permanent impairment in the value of the investment, due to losses or other causes, should be recognized by a write-down of the investment.

The use of the cost method is now restricted to cases where there is considerable doubt that the equity in the earning of a subsidiary is effectively accruing to the benefit of the parent. Such cases include foreign subsidiaries which operate under conditions of exchange restrictions, controls, or other uncertainties of a type that casts doubt on the parent's ability to achieve an ultimate realization of these earnings.

Example of difference in income recognition—equity versus cost method

On 1/1/x1 Company P acquired 80 percent of Company S for $900,000. The net assets of Company S at date of acquisition were $1,000,000.

During 19x1 Company S earned $100,000 and paid $40,000 in dividends, while in 19x2 it lost $20,000 and paid a dividend of $30,000. Exhibit 7-2 contrasts the accounting by Company P for the investment in Company S and the income derived from it under (1) the cost method and (2) the equity method:

EXHIBIT 7-2
Cost and equity methods of accounting for investment in subsidiary

	Cost method		Equity method	
	Investment	Income (loss)	Investment	Income (loss)
Cost at acquisition..........	$900,000		$900,000	
Earnings for 19x1......			80,000	$ 80,000 (1)
Amortization of goodwill..........			(2,500)	(2,500) (2)
Dividends—19x1		$32,000 (3)	(32,000)	
Earnings pickup—19x1.............		$32,000		$ 77,500
Loss for 19x2.........			(16,000)	$(16,000) (4)
Amortization of goodwill..........			(2,500)	(2,500) (2)
Dividends—19x2		$24,000 (5)	(24,000)	
Earnings (loss) pickup—19x2.......		$24,000		$(18,500)
Investment at 12/31/x2..........	$900,000		$903,000	

(1) 80% equity in earnings of $100,000.
(2) Cost of 80% interest in Company S..................... $900,000
    80% of net assets ($1,000,000—assumed to represent fair market value).. 800,000
    Excess of cost over net assets (goodwill).................. $100,000
    Yearly amortization (40-year basis)...................... $ 2,500
(3) 80% of $40,000.
(4) 80% of $20,000.
(5) 80% of $30,000.

The disparity in the amount of income reported by the parent under the two methods is readily apparent. Under the cost method the income pickup bears no relationship to actual results achieved during the period but is, instead, dependent on the amount of dividend distributions.

The amount at which the investment is carried on the books of the parent company also varies considerably among these two methods. Under the cost method the investment account remains unchanged (except in the case of losses which lead to a permanent impairment in value), while under the equity method the investment account reflects the parent company's equity in the underlying net assets of the subsidiary. Goodwill should, however, be amortized also under the cost method.

Intercorporate investments—less than majority ownership

Investments by one company in less than the majority of the voting security of another enterprise and investments in joint ventures are discussed in Chapter 4.

Implications for analysis

From the analyst's point of view the financial reporting of intercorporate investments has recently undergone substantial improvement. This improvement is due in large measure to the sharp restrictions which are now placed on the use of the cost method of accounting.

Under the cost method, dividends remitted, rather than income earned, are the basis on which a parent company recognizes the earnings accruing from an investment in a subsidiary. The obvious disadvantage of the cost method is that the cost basis does not reflect the results of operations of the subsidiary and lends itself to income manipulation. Thus, dividends included in the parent company's income may be unrelated to the subsidiary's earnings, and losses of the subsidiary may go unreported for a number of periods. The trend in earnings can be completely distorted by use of the cost method.

Validity of taking up earnings. Consolidation and the equity method are based on the assumption that a dollar earned by a subsidiary is at least equal to a dollar's worth of parent company earnings. Even disregarding the possible tax liability which the parent company may incur on the remittance of earnings by the subsidiary, this dollar-for-dollar equivalence in earnings cannot be taken for granted. The following are some possible reasons for this:

1. The subsidiary may be under the supervision of a regulatory authority which can intervene in dividend policy.
2. The subsidiary may operate in a foreign country where there exist restrictions on the remittance of earnings abroad and/or where the value of the currency can deteriorate rapidly. Furthermore, changes in political climate may result in hampering the subsidiary's operations.
3. Dividend restrictions in loan agreements may become effective.
4. The presence of a stable or powerful minority interest may reduce the parent's discretion in setting dividend and other policy.

While considerations such as the above should govern the independent accountant's decision on whether or not to use the cost method, the analyst should, as a check on that judgment, form his own opinion in each given situation on whether a dollar earned by a subsidiary can indeed be considered the equivalent of a dollar earned by the parent company.

There are other problems in the analysis of consolidated financial statements or investments in subsidiaries carried at equity which the financial analyst must consider carefully.

Provision for taxes on undistributed earnings of subsidiaries. APB *Opinion No. 23*, "Accounting for Income Taxes—Special Areas," concluded that including undistributed earnings of a subsidiary in the pretax accounting income of a parent company, either through consolidation or accounting for the investment by the equity method, may or may not require a concurrent provision for taxes depending on the actions and intent of the parent company.

The Board believes that it should be presumed that all undistributed earnings will be transferred to the parent and that a provision for taxes should be made by assuming that the unremitted earnings were distributed to the parent in the current period and that the taxes provision is based on a computation benefiting from all the tax-planning alternatives to which the company may be entitled.

The foregoing presumption can be overcome if persuasive evidence exists that the subsidiary has or will invest the undistributed earnings permanently or that the earning will be remitted in a tax-free liquidation.

The analyst should be aware that the decision of whether taxes on undistributed earnings should or should not be provided is, in effect, left largely to management. However, following an innovative trend in the latest APB Opinions, management will not only have to disclose its reasoning behind a decision not to provide for such taxes but also disclose the amount of undistributed earnings on which the parent company has not recognized income taxes.

Debt shown in consolidated financial statements. Liabilities shown in the consolidated financial statements do not operate as a lien upon a common pool of assets. The creditors, be they secured or unsecured, have recourse in the event of default only to assets owned by the individual corporation which incurred this liability. If, on the other hand, a parent company guarantees a specific liability of a subsidiary, then the creditor would, of course, have the guarantee as additional security.

The consolidated balance sheet obscures rather than clarifies the margin of safety enjoyed by specific creditors. To gain full comprehension of the financial position of each part of the consolidated group, the analyst needs also examine the individual financial statements of each subsidiary.

Additional limitations of consolidated financial statements. Consolidated financial statements generally represent the most meaningful presentation of the financial condition and the results of operations of a group. However, they do have limitations in addition to those discussed above:

1. The financial statement of the individual companies in the group may not be prepared on a comparable basis. Accounting principles applied and valuation bases and amortization rates used may differ, thus destroying homogeneity and the validity of ratios, trends, and relationships. Year-end dates of individual members of a group can vary by as much as 90 days.
2. Companies in relatively poor financial condition may be combined with sound companies, thus obscuring information necessary for analysis.
3. The extent of intercompany transactions is unknown unless *consolidating* financial statements are presented. The latter generally reveal the adjustments involved in the consolidation process.
4. Unless specifically disclosed, it may be difficult to establish how much of the consolidated Retained Earnings account is actually available for payment of dividends.
5. The composition of the minority interest, for example, as between common and preferred, cannot be determined because the minority interest is generally shown as a combined amount in the consolidated balance sheet.

ACCOUNTING FOR BUSINESS COMBINATIONS

The combination of business entities by merger or acquisition is not a new phenomenon on the business scene. What is relatively new is the utilization of the merger technique as an instrument for the creation of "glamour" or of an image of growth, and as a means of increasing reported earnings.

Reasons for mergers

There are, of course, many legitimate reasons for *external* business expansion, that is, expansion by means of business combinations under which two or more entities are brought under common control. These reasons include: (1) acquisition of sources of new materials, productive facilities, production know-how, marketing organizations, and established shares of a market; (2) the acquisition of financial resources; (3) the acquisition of competent management; (4) savings of time in entering new markets; and (5) achieving economics of scale and acquiring tax advantages such as those relating to tax-loss carry-overs.

Distortions in accounting for mergers

In addition to the above legitimate reasons for entering into business combinations, financial "architects" and operators of the 1960s have utilized merger techniques and loose merger accounting to serve up to a stock market obsessed with "earnings growth" a picture of such growth which was, in large part, illusory.

The means by which such illusions of earnings growth were achieved were many. Briefly, some were as follows:

1. A great variety of convertible securities were issued without any recognition being given to their future potential dilutive effects on the common stockholder's equity. This phenomenon reached such heights of abuse that it was finally remedied by the issuance of APB *Opinion No. 15*. Chapter 20 contains an extended discussion of this subject.
2. The merger of growing companies which have earned a high price-earnings ratio in the marketplace with companies of lesser growth prospects was achieved by payment in high price-earnings ratio stock. This contributed to further earnings per share growth, thus reinforcing and even increasing the acquiring company's high price-earnings ratio. However, in many cases the market failed to take into account the lower quality of the *acquired* earnings. This is a problem inherent in the market evaluation mechanism and is not readily subject to remedy by external factors.

ILLUSTRATION. An excellent illustration of the dynamics of this problem is given by May:[1]

> "Company A stock is selling at a price-earnings ratio of 30 because of expected growth of 33% per year in its earnings per share. Company B is not expected to have any growth and its stock is selling at a price-earnings ratio of 10. Both firms are earning $1.00 per share and both have 1,000,000 shares outstanding. The price of Company A stock is $30.00 per share and the price of Company B stock is $10.00 per share. Company A offers to acquire all of the stock of Company B by exchanging stock on the basis of one-half share ($15.00's worth) of Company A stock for each share of Company B stock. This is 50% over market for Company B stock and the offer is accepted.
>
> "The transaction is completed. No changes in operating earnings occur during the next period, and the combined earnings remain at $2,000,000. At this point Company A has 1,500,000 shares outstanding, the 1,000,000

---

[1] Marvin M. May, "The Earnings per Share Trap," *Financial Analysts Journal*, May–June 1968, pp. 113–17.

which were out before the acquisition plus 500,000 new shares issued to acquire Company B. Earnings per share of Company A stock thus rise to $1.33, a growth of 33% as expected. The price-earnings ratio remains at 30 and the stock price rises to $40.00 per share. Company A stockholders are, of course, very pleased. The entire $1.33 in earnings is available for dividends, and the price of their stock has risen 33% in addition. Former Company B stockholders are equally pleased. Not only did they receive 50% more for their stock than the market price, but that one-half of Company A stock they received has already gone up in value from $15.00 to $20.00. They have doubled their net worth, at market prices, in less than one year.

"The following year Company A acquires Company C and Company D. Both companies have the same earnings and number of shares outstanding as Company B had. Company A again pays $15.00 per share in new Company A stock, issuing 375,000 shares for each of the two new acquisitions raising the total of outstanding shares to 2,250,000. The earnings of Company C and Company D bring total earnings up to $4,000,000 and per share earnings again rise 33% to $1.77, and the market price of the stock rises to $53.33.

"To keep the system in motion it is necessary for Company A to double the number of firms it acquires each year. This isn't too difficult. . . ."
As May explains it, this is no trick with numbers.
"The explanation is that the rate of growth in earnings per share is not an appropriate benchmark of growth for valuation purposes when mergers or acquisitions are involved."

3. The utilization of loose accounting rules governing merger accounting in order to create the illusion of earnings growth where, in fact, there is none. This is to be distinguished from the genuine economies and advantages which can accrue from business combinations. This problem area will be discussed below in our consideration of alternative accounting methods for business combinations.

Accounting for business combinations: Two methods

Prior to World War II the accounting for business combinations was governed by the legal form which it assumed and that resulted in a majority of acquisitions by one company of another being treated as purchases. To businessmen, the one immediate disadvantage of purchase accounting was the creation of "goodwill" as an asset representing usually the excess of cost of acquisition over the amounts at which the acquired company's net assets were recorded on the acquiring company's books. Not only was goodwill a nontax deductible item which, if amortized, would have resulted in a reduction of earnings, but it was also an asset which bankers and other lenders considered of dubious value.

Pooling of interests. For this and other reasons, the search for an alternative method of accounting for business combinations led to the pooling of interests method. The rationale behind this method is that instead of an acquisition of one company by another, a pooling of interests reflects the merging of two stockholder groups which share in future risks and opportunities.

This accounting convention, which has gained wide acceptance in the post-1945 period, is based on the following assumptions about the two corporations combining—

1. That they would exchange voting securities; essentially, ownership would be continuing.
2. That the two corporations would be roughly comparable in size.
3. That management personnel would continue with the merged corporation.

The great attraction of the pooling method along with the vague criteria which were promulgated to govern its accounting led to a significant deterioration in actual practice. The criterion of relative size erroded, all manner of equity securities became acceptable, various means of circumventing the continuity of ownership provisions were devised, and where it was clearly impossible to justify the use of a full pooling, a part-pooling part-purchase method was devised.

With the growth in these abuses the chorus of criticism grew, and this resulted in a call by many for the abolition of pooling of interests accounting. Instead, members of the APB compromised and issued *Opinion No. 16* which, as we shall see, established stricter and more specific conditions for use of this method of accounting in the future.

Purchase accounting. In the permissive atmosphere of the 1960s, accounting under the "purchase" convention also deteriorated in relation to its original intent. Abuses occurred in two major areas:

1. Assets and liabilities of purchased entities were not revalued at fair value before being included in the accounts of the acquiring company.
2. The resulting "goodwill" represented merely the excess of amounts paid over the carrying amounts of assets and liabilities assumed without even the pretense that such assets and liabilities were fairly valued. This resulting "goodwill" was very rarely amortized. It thus became a repository for all kinds of costs incurred in acquiring the company, costs which were thus kept out of present and future income statements. The curt note found in the Gould Inc. prospectus dated 2/17/70 was characteristic of this kind of treatment: "The cost of acquired businesses in excess of recorded net assets at dates of acquisition are considered to be attributable to intangible assets which will not be amortized."

While, in theory, a purchase is in substance, quite a different business combination from a pooling of interests, by the late 1960s the accounting for them became *in effect* quite similar. Under the pooling method the understatement of assets took the form of carrying forward the merged company's assets at book value, while under the "polluted purchase"[2] method the assets were similarly understated and the excess of cost over these understated assets was merely carried as a nondescript composite intangible which was rarely amortized. Thus, under either method substantial costs were kept out of the income statement.

REVISED OPINIONS ON ACCOUNTING FOR BUSINESS COMBINATIONS

In an attempt to improve the accounting for business combinations, the APB issued in 1970 *Opinions No. 16* and *No. 17*.

We shall first consider the accounting required under these new Opinions. Following this consideration we shall consider the implications which this new accounting holds for the analyst.

Pooling of interests and purchase accounting compared

Pooling of interests accounting is based on the assumption that the combination is a uniting of ownership interests achieved by means of an exchange of equity securities. Under this method the former ownership interests continue and the recorded assets and liabilities of the constituents are carried forward to the combined entity at their recorded amounts. Since this is a combining of interests, income of the combined corporation includes income of the constituents for the entire fiscal period in which the combination occurs. Prior periods are also restated to show the combined companies as merged since their respective inceptions.

The purchase method of accounting views the business combination as the acquisition of one entity by another. The acquiring entity records the acquired assets, including goodwill, and liabilities at its cost which is based on fair values at date of acquisition. The acquiring entity picks up the income of the acquired entity, based on its cost, only from date of acquisition.

APB *Opinion No. 16* concluded that if a business combination meets the 12 specific criteria enumerated in it, it must be accounted for as a pooling of interests. Otherwise it must be accounted for as a purchase.

---

[2] This term was coined by Professor Abraham J. Briloff who has done more than anyone else to expose the abuses under both pooling and purchase accounting. Starting in 1967 his incisive and analytical articles, appearing mostly in the *Financial Analysts Journal* and *Barron's*, contributed greatly to a wider understanding of the distortions for which this type of accounting was responsible.

150   Understanding corporate reports

Conditions for the pooling of interests method. There are 12 conditions which must be met under the provision of APB *Opinion No. 16* before a business combination may be accounted for as a pooling of interests. These can be grouped under three main categories:

I. Attributes of the combining companies.
II. Manner of combining interests.
III. Absence of planned transactions.

I. Attributes of the combining companies
1. Each of the combining companies should be autonomous and not have operated as a subsidiary or division of another company within two years before the plan of combination is initiated. An exception to this condition concerns the divestiture of assets which was ordered by a governmental or judicial body. A subsidiary which is divested under an order or a new company which acquires assets disposed of under such an order is considered autonomous for this condition.
2. Each of the combining companies must be independent of each other. That means that no combining company or group of combining companies can hold as an intercompany investment more than 10 percent of the outstanding voting common stock of any other combining company. To illustrate the 10 percent requirement, let's assume that Company A plans to issue its voting common stock to acquire the voting common stock of Companies B and C. If Companies A and B each own 7 percent of Company C's outstanding common stock, A can pool with B, but the combined entity cannot subsequently pool with C since more than 10 percent of Company C's outstanding stock would have been held by the other combining companies.

II. Manner of combining interests
3. The combination should be effected in a single transaction or should be completed in accordance with a specific plan within one year after the plan is initiated. The Opinion provides an exception to this one year rule when the delay is beyond the control of the combining companies because of proceedings of a governmental authority or pending litigation.
4. The combination should involve the issuance of voting common stock only in exchange for substantially all of the voting common stock interest of the company being combined. "Substantially all" in this context means at least 90 percent of the voting common stock interest of the company being combined. Thus, the issuer may purchase for cash or other nonvoting

7. Intercorporate investments, combinations, & foreign operations 151

    common stock consideration up to 10 percent of the voting common shares of the company to be pooled. Such a cash outlay may be necessary to eliminate fractional shares or to pay dissenting stockholders. The rationale of this criterion is that substantially all of the voting common stock interest in each party to a pooling should be carried forward as a voting common stock interest in the issuer in the pooling. The payment of cash, debt, or an equity instrument which does not satisfy this test destroys the most fundamental basis of a pooling. If the company being combined has securities other than voting stock, such securities may be exchanged for common stock of the issuing corporation or may be exchanged for substantially identical securities of the issuing corporation.

5. None of the combining companies should change the equity interest of their voting common stock in contemplation of effecting the combination. This restriction applies during the period from two years preceding the date the plan is initiated through the date the plan is consummated. Changes in the equity interest of the voting common stock which may violate this condition include distributions to shareholders, additional issuance or exchange of securities, and the retirement of securities. The purpose of this rule is to disallow changes in equity interests prior to a combination because such changes indicate a sale rather than a combining and sharing of risks.
6. Each combining company may reacquire shares of voting common stock only for purposes other than business combinations, and no company may reacquire more than a normal number of shares between the date the plan of combination is initiated and consummated.
7. The ratio of the interest of an individual common stockholder to those of other common stockholders in a combining company should remain the same as a result of the exchange of stock to effect the combination. This condition insures that no common stockholder is denied his potential share of a voting common stock interest in a combined corporation.
8. The stockholders of the resulting combined corporation cannot be derived of, nor restricted in, their ability to exercise their voting rights on common stock of the combined corporation. For example, establishing a voting trust to hold some of the shares issued in the combination disqualifies the combination as a pooling of interests.
9. The combination must be resolved at the date the plan is consummated, and there must be no contingent arrangements for the issuance of additional securities or other consideration.

All consideration to be given to effect the combination of the companies must be determinable as of the date the plan of combination is consummated. The only exception to this would be a provision to adjust the exchange ratio as a result of a subsequent settlement of a contingency such as an existing lawsuit.

III. Absence of planned transactions
  10. The combined corporation should not agree directly or indirectly to retire or reacquire any of the common stock issued to effect the combination.
  11. The combined corporation cannot enter into other financial arrangements for the benefit of the former stockholders of a combining company, such as a guarantee of loans secured by stock issued in the combination. This financial arrangement may require the payment of cash in the future which would negate the exchange of equity securities, and thus the combination would not qualify for pooling of interests treatment.
  12. The combined corporation may not intend to plan to dispose of a significant part of the assets of the combining companies within two years after the combination. Some disposal of assets may be effected within the two-year period provided the disposals would have been in the ordinary course of business of the formerly separate companies or if the disposals were to eliminate duplicate facilities or excess capacity.

If a combining company remains a subsidiary of the issuing corporation after the combination is consummated, the combination could still be accounted for as a pooling of interests, as long as all the conditions for a pooling are met. Any business combination which meets all of the above conditions *must* be accounted for under the pooling of interests method.

Application of the purchase method. As we have seen in the foregoing discussion, under purchase accounting the business combination is viewed as the acquisition of one entity by another.

Problem of valuation of the consideration. One of the major problems in accounting for a purchase is to determine the total cost of an acquired entity. The same accounting principles apply whether determining the cost of assets acquired individually, in a group, or in a business combination. It is the nature of the transaction which determines which accounting principles apply in arriving at the total cost of assets acquired.

There usually is no problem in determining the total cost of assets acquired for cash, since the amount of cash disbursed is the total cost of the acquired assets. The difficulty is, however, in the proper allocation of the total cost to the individual assets acquired.

7. Intercorporate investments, combinations, & foreign operations

If assets are acquired by incurring liabilities, total cost of the assets is the present value of the amounts to be paid in the future. The present value of a debt security is the fair value of the liability. If the debt security has been issued at an interest rate which is substantially above or below the present effective rate for a similar security, the appropriate amount of premium or discount should be recorded. In some cases the characteristics of a preferred stock may be so similar to a debt security that it should be valued in the same manner.

If assets are acquired in exchange for stock, the general rule for determining the total cost of the assets acquired would be that it is the fair value of the stock given or the fair value of the assets received, whichever is more clearly evident.

The fair value of securities traded in the market is normally more clearly evident than is the fair value of the acquired company. Quoted market price should serve as a guide in determining total cost of an acquired company after considering market fluctuations, the quantities traded, issue costs, and so forth.

If the quoted market price is not a reliable indicator of the value of stock issued, it is still necessary to determine the fair value of the assets received, including goodwill, even though this valuation is difficult.

In these cases the best means of estimation should be used, including a detailed review of the negotiations leading up to the purchase and the use of independent appraisals.

Contingent additional consideration. The amount of any additional contingent consideration payable in accordance with the purchase agreement is usually recorded when the contingency is resolved and the consideration is to be issued or becomes issuable. Two of the most common types of contingencies are based on either earnings or security prices.

The following guides to the accounting for such contingent additional consideration are contained in APB *Opinion No. 16:*

1. A contingent issuance of additional consideration should be disclosed but should not be recorded as a liability or shown as outstanding securities unless the outcome of the contingency is determinable beyond a reasonable doubt.
2. A contingent issuance of additional consideration based on future earnings should be recorded as an additional cost of the acquisition when the contingency is resolved. In this case the total amount of consideration representing cost was not determinable at the date of acquisition.
3. A contingent issuance of additional consideration which is based on future security prices should be considered as an adjustment of the amount originally recorded for the securities at the date of acquisition.

Allocation of total cost. Once the total cost of an acquired entity is determined, it is then necessary to allocate this total cost to the individual assets received. All identifiable assets acquired and liabilities assumed in a business combination should be assigned a portion of the total cost, normally equal to their fair value at date of acquisition. The excess of the total cost over the amounts assigned to identifiable assets acquired, less liabilities assumed, should be recorded as goodwill. Such goodwill must be amortized over a period not to exceed 40 years.

It may be possible in some cases that the market or appraisal values of identifiable assets acquired less liabilities assumed, exceeds the cost of the acquired company. In those cases, the values otherwise assignable to noncurrent assets acquired (except long-term investments in marketable securities) should be reduced by a proportionate part of the excess. Negative goodwill should not be recorded unless the value assigned to such long-term assets is first reduced to zero. If such allocation results in an excess of assets over cost, it should be classified as a deferred credit and should be amortized systematically to income over the period estimated to be benefited but not in excess of 40 years.

Guidelines for valuation of assets and liabilities. APB *Opinion No. 16* established general guides for assigning amounts to individual assets and liabilities assumed, except goodwill, as follows:

1. Marketable securities should be recorded at current net realizable values.
2. Receivables should be recorded at the present values of amounts to be received, determined at appropriate current interest rates, less allowances for uncollectibility and collection costs, if necessary.
3. Inventories:
    a) Finished goods should be recorded at selling prices less cost of disposal and reasonable profit allowance.
    b) Work in process inventories should be stated at estimated selling prices of finished goods less the sum of the costs to complete, costs of disposal, and a reasonable profit allowance for the completing and selling effort of the acquired corporation.
    c) Raw materials should be recorded at current replacement costs.
4. Plant and equipment to be used in the business should be stated at current replacement costs for similar capacity unless the expected future use of the assets indicates a lower value to the acquirer. Replacement cost may be determined directly if a used asset market exists for the assets acquired. Otherwise, replacement cost should be approximated from replacement cost new, less estimated accumulated depreciation.
5. Indentifiable intangible assets should be valued at appraised values.
6. Other assets, such as land, natural resources, and marketable securities, should be recorded at appraised values.

7. Accounts and notes payable, long-term debt, and other claims payable should be stated at present values of amounts to be paid, determined at appropriate current interest rates.

An acquiring corporation should not record as a separate asset goodwill previously recorded by an acquired company, and it should not record deferred income taxes previously recorded by an acquired company. Amounts assigned to identifiable assets and liabilities should recognize that their value may be less, if part or all of the assigned value is not deductible for income taxes. However, the acquiring corporation should not record deferred tax accounts for the tax effect of these differences at the date of acquisition.

Treatment of goodwill. APB *Opinion No. 17* provides that for the intangible assets acquired in a business combination, the method of allocating the total cost of the acquired company depends on whether or not the asset is identifiable, such as a patent, or unidentifiable, such as goodwill. The cost of an identifiable intangible asset should be based on the fair value of the asset. The cost of an unidentifiable intangible asset is measured by the difference between total cost and the amount assigned to other assets acquired and liabilities assumed.

The cost of an intangible asset should not be written off in the period of acquisition but instead should be amortized based on the estimated life of that specific asset; the period of amortization, however, should not exceed 40 years. The straight-line method of amortization should be used unless the company can demonstrate that another systematic method is more appropriate. The method and period of amortization should be disclosed in the financial statements.

Pro forma supplementary disclosure. Under the purchase method, notes to the financial statements of the acquiring corporation for the period in which a business combination occurs should include as supplemental information the following results of operations on a pro forma basis:

1. Combined results of operations for the current period as though the companies has combined at the beginning of the period unless the acquisition was at or near the beginning of the period.
2. If comparative financial statements are presented, combined results of operations for the immediately preceding period should be reported as though the companies had combined at the beginning of that period.

This supplemental pro forma information should, as a minimum, show revenue, income before extraordinary items, net income, and earnings per share.

Illustration of accounting mechanics: Purchase versus pooling of interest accounting

Company Buy has agreed to acquire Company Sell in a transaction under which it will issue 1,200,000 of $1 par value common shares for all the common shares of Company Sell. The transaction qualifies as a pooling of interests, and consequently the fair market value of Sell's assets and liabilities at date of the merger do not enter into the accounting for it. Exhibit 7–3 presents in columnar fashion the balance sheets

EXHIBIT 7–3
Merger of Company Sell into Company Buy
Summary of Pro Forma Condensed Combining Balance Sheet
(in thousands of dollars)

	Company Buy	Company Sell	Combining adjustments Debit	Combining adjustments Credit	Combined
Assets.	157,934	28,013	. . .	. . .	185,947
Liabilities	42,591	11,218	. . .	. . .	53,809
Stockholders' equity:					
Company Buy:					
Preferred stock	810	. . .	. . .	. . .	810
Common stock	7,572	. . .	. . .	1,200	8,772
Company Sell:					
Common stock	. . .	1,285	1,285	. . .	. . .
Additional paid-in capital	31,146	137	. . .	85	31,368
Retained earnings	75,815	15,373	. . .	. . .	91,188
Total Stockholders' Equity.	115,343	16,795	1,285	1,285	132,138
	157,934	28,013	1,285	1,285	185,947

of Company Buy and Company Sell as well as the adjustments needed to effect the combination under pooling of interests accounting.

Pooling accounting

Briefly, the pooling method requires taking up Sell's assets and liabilities at recorded amounts and carrying forward the equity account balances, subject to adjustments required by differences in the par values of the securities exchanged.

Since the amount of the par value of the common stock of Company Buy ($1,200,000) is smaller than the amount of the par value of the stock of Company Sell which is exchanged ($1,285,000), the difference

7. Intercorporate investments, combinations, & foreign operations 157

is credited to "Additional Paid-In Capital." In a pooling where the reverse to the above situation prevails, additional par value is taken out first of the existing "paid-in capital" accounts of the constituents and, if insufficient, from retained earnings. The balance in the retained earnings accounts is carried forward.

The entry on Company Buy's books of the pooling with Company Sell will be as follows:

	Debit	Credit
	(in thousands of dollars)	
Assets..	28,013	
Liabilities...		11,218
Common stock.......................................		1,200
Additional paid-in capital...........................		222
Retained earnings....................................		15,373

To record the issuance of 1,200,000 shares of $1 par value common stock for the merged net assets of Sell and to credit to Retained Earnings the balance of retained earnings of Sell at date of acquisition.

Exhibit 7–3 reflected the pooling as a "statutory merger," that is, the assets and liabilities of the two companies were combined and Company Sell ceased its separate existence. If we assume that Company Sell was to continue as a wholly owned subsidiary of Company Buy, the pooling would be recorded as shown in Exhibit 7–4.

EXHIBIT 7–4
Merger of Company Buy and Company Sell (Company Sell remains as a fully owned subsidiary of Company Buy)

Summary of Pro Forma Condensed Balance Sheet
(in thousands of dollars)

	Company Buy Before pooling	Parent company only		
		Adjustments		After pooling
		Debit	Credit	
Assets.....................	157,934	...	...	157,934
Investment in Sell.............		16,795	...	16,795
	157,934	16,795	...	174,729
Liabilities	42,591	...	...	42,591
Stockholders' equity:				
Company Buy:				
Preferred stock	810	...	...	810
Common stock	7,572	...	1,200	8,772
Company Sell: Common stock	...	...	...	...
Additional paid-in capital	31,146	...	222	31,368
Retained earnings...........	75,815	...	...	75,815
Retained earnings from pooled company.................	...	...	15,373	15,373
Total Stockholders' Equity	115,343	...	16,795	132,138
	157,934	...	16,795	174,729

The accounting entries made on the parent company's books are as follows:

	Debit	Credit
Investment in Company Sell.............................	16,795	
Common stock..		1,200
Additional paid-in capital............................		222
Retained earnings from pooled company...............		15,373

To record the issuance of 1,200,000 shares of $1 par value common stock for the common stock of Sell and to credit to Retained Earnings the balance of retained earnings of Sell at date of acquisition.

The investment in Company Sell will continue to be carried on an equity basis by Company Buy, the parent. In consolidation the investment account in Company Sell will be eliminated against subsidiary Company Sell's common stock, additional paid-in capital, and the parent company's retained earnings from the pooled company, all in accordance with normal consolidation procedure.

Purchase accounting

Let us now assume that instead of acquiring Company Sell in an exchange of common stock, Company Buy acquires Company Sell for $25,000,000 in cash. Since this acquisition must be accounted for as a purchase, it is necessary to determine the fair values of Company Sell's assets and liabilities. The following tabulation compares Company Sell's recorded asset and liability amounts with indicated fair values at date of acquisition:

	Amounts on Company Sell books	Fair values determined at date of acquisition
	(in thousands of dollars)	
Assets.......................	28,013	34,000
Liabilities	11,218	13,000
Net assets	16,795	21,000
Cost to Company Buy	...	25,000
Amount assigned to goodwill	...	4,000

Assets and liabilities are valued in accordance with the valuation principles outlined in APB *Opinion No. 16*. The excess of purchase price over the fair value of net assets acquired assigned to goodwill must be amortized over its useful value not to exceed 40 years.

Exhibit 7–5 presents the consolidated balance sheet of Company Buy right after the purchase of Company Sell so as to enable a contrast

EXHIBIT 7–5
Purchase of Company Sell by Company Buy

Summary of Pro Forma Condensed Consolidated Balance Sheet
(in thousands of dollars)

	Company Buy	Company Sell (at fair values on date of acquisition)	Combining and consolidating adjustments Debit	Combining and consolidating adjustments Credit	After purchase
Assets					
Assets (exclusive of goodwill)	157,934	34,000		25,000	166,934
Goodwill			4,000		4,000
Total Assets	157,934	34,000			170,934
Liabilities and Stockholder's Equity					
Liabilities	42,591	13,000			55,591
Stockholder's Equity:					
Company Buy:					
Preferred stock	810				810
Common stock	7,572				7,572
Additional paid-in capital	31,146				31,146
Retained earnings	75,815				75,815
Net assets at fair value of company sell		21,000	21,000		
Total Stockholder's Equity	115,343	21,000			115,343
Total Liabilities and Stockholder's Equity	157,934	34,000	25,000	25,000	170,934

with the balance sheet obtained right after the pooling accounting presented in Exhibit 7–3 above.

A cash acquisition is, of course, not the only method requiring purchase accounting. As described earlier, under a great number of conditions involving an acquisition for stock purchase accounting would be required.

The following difference between the pooling and the purchase accounting should be noted. In the purchase—

1. The assets and liabilities are recorded at fair value. Goodwill is recognized. These will result in higher charges to income reflecting the higher net asset values acquired.
2. The total stockholder equity remains unchanged. There has been an exchange of resources, that is, Company Sell's net assets of $25,000,000 for Company Buy's cash.

Implications for analysis

An examination of the revised guidelines and principles governing the accounting for mergers and acquisitions reveals a serious attempt by the accounting profession to improve the accounting in this area and to prevent some of the glaring distortions and abuses of the past, as they perceived them, from recurring.

The new rules which govern the accounting for pooling of interests and for purchases are the result of a lengthy process of compromise; another important objective was the elimination of *specific* abuses of practice. The analyst must recognize this as well as the fact that the rationale which accountants use in distinguishing pooling of interests from purchases combinations are not necessarily relevant to his attempt to measure and analyse the economic consequences of business combinations.

Thus, in determining the implications which the new accounting rules on business combinations hold for the analyst of financial statements, we must examine the impact which these rules have on the realistic portrayal of the results of mergers and acquisition.

Pooling versus purchase accounting

Before we examine the effect of pooling accounting on the financial statements of a combined entity, let us summarize the main arguments which have been advanced in defense of this method:

1. If cash is given as consideration in a business acquisition, the acquirer parts with a resource. But if a company's own unissued stock is given in exchange, no resource is given; instead the equity is increased.
2. In exchange of common stock, the "seller" is getting back a part of itself as well as part of the buyer. Since he does not part with ownership in his own company, there is no valid basis for establishing new values.
3. In a combination of equals, which results from an exchange of stock, it is hard to determine who acquired whom.

It is not at all clear that cash is a resource while unissued stock is not. After all, if stock is an acceptable consideration to a seller, it should also command a price on the market. The valuation of noncash consideration is a problem which accountants have to face frequently. Moreover, if a combination fails as a pooling on any one of the technical conditions enumerated in APB *Opinion No. 16*, a valuation of the stock issued will become necessary in order to account for the combination as a purchase.

7. Intercorporate investments, combinations, & foreign operations

There is some validity to the second argument above, but in most business combinations the relative size of the pooled-in company to the surviving entity is small indeed.

The third argument is rarely relevant today because the size-test of poolings has been abandoned and consequently a large company can acquire a very small enterprise and still account for the combination as a pooling.

Aside from the above considerations, from the point of view of the analyst it is the results of pooling accounting which really matter. These can be best illustrated by means of a simplified example.

Assume that Company B which wants to acquire Company S earns $1,000 of net income and has 500 shares outstanding. Company S's condensed balance sheet is as follows:

Fixed assets*.........	$ 400	Liabilities	$ 200
Other assets	600	Capital accounts......	800
	$1,000		$1,000
*Current value.	$ 600		

Company S has a net income of $200 after deduction of $40 for depreciation (10 percent of $400 in fixed assets).

Let us now consider the operating results of Company B one year after the acquisition of Company S for a price of $1,400 paid in (1) cash or (2) stock. Let us assume that the earnings of both companies remain unchanged and that the $1,400 purchase price (of Company S) is arrived at as follows:

Fixed assets (current value)	$ 600
Other assets	600
Goodwill...................	400
	$1,600
Less liabilities assumed..........	200
Purchase consideration..........	$1,400

Payment in cash. If the purchase price was in cash, the combined company's income statement would be accounted for on a purchase basis as follows:

Income of B........................			$1,000
Income of S (before depreciation)		$240	
Depreciation (10% of $600).............	$60*		
Goodwill amortization (2½% of 400†).......	10	70	170
Net income of the combined enterprise			$1,170

*Before tax.
†Assuming amortization over 40 years.

Payment in stock. If, however, the purchase price was in stock, under the pooling method of accounting the income statement of the enterprise would be as follows:

Income of B	$1,000
Income of S	200
Net income of the combined enterprise	$1,200

The difference in the net income is due to the inclusion, under the pooling method, of fixed assets at $400, the original cost on the books of Company S, and the complete omission of the goodwill which Company B paid in the acquisition of Company S.

Whether the reported income of the combined company is $1,200 or $1,170 depends in this case on how the purchase price was paid. Moreover, if the purchase price is paid in common stock and *any* of the other 11 conditions of a pooling are not met, the acquisition would have to be accounted for as a purchase and the reported income would be $1,170 instead of $1,200.

This, then, is the basic difference between pooling and purchase accounting. The nonrecording or suppression of asset values for which the acquiring company paid generally results in an understatement of assets and an overstatement of income. This is the primary reason why earnings which are the result of pooling combinations are viewed as being overstated in comparison with similar earnings resulting from purchase accounting.

APB *Opinion No. 16* has done nothing to remove this problem which is inherent in the pooling of interests method. It has removed some of the abuses of the original criteria of the pooling of interests concept such as part pooling-part purchase, issuance of complex securities other than common stock in a pooling, retroactive pooling, and contingent additional consideration. But these features, while enabling the application of pooling accounting to many mergers, are not in themselves responsible for the suppression of asset values. This suppression is *inherent* in the pooling of interests concept, and all that APB *Opinion No. 16* achieved in this regard is to limit significantly the application of the concept by making it more difficult for companies to meet the criteria of a pooling. But once having met these criteria, many of the old problems and distortions remain.

Let us now summarize the most important features of pooling of interests accounting which, from the point of view of the analyst, differentiate it from purchase accounting:

1. Assets acquired are carried at "book value" rather than at the current fair values reflected in the consideration given. To the extent that "goodwill" is paid for, the amount is not shown on the acquiring company's balance sheet.

2. The understatement of assets leads to an understatement of capital employed by the enterprise.
3. The understatement of assets such as inventory, property, plant, and equipment, as well as goodwill and other intangibles, will lead to an understatement of expenses such as cost of goods sold, depreciation, and amortization of goodwill and intangibles. In turn, this will lead to an overstatement of income.
4. The understatement of assets can lead not only to an understatement of expenses but can also result in an overstatement of gains realized on their disposition. Thus, the acquiring corporation can claim as part of its results of operations gains on the sale of assets which at the time of their acquisition were carried forward at unrealistically low amounts, amounts which are actually far below the amount which, in the negotiations preceding the merger, was the agreed fair value of these assets. In these cases income is overstated and management performance is overrated. What we have here is clearly a recovery of cost rather than a profit.
5. Both the understatement of invested capital and the overstatement of income will lead to an overstatement of the return on investment.
6. The retained earnings of the acquired enterprise can be carried forward to the surviving company.
7. The income statements and the balance sheets of the combined enterprise are restated for all periods presented. Under purchase accounting they are combined only since the date of acquisition, although pro forma statements showing preacquisition combined results are also furnished.

A crude way of adjusting for omitted values in a pooling is to determine the difference between the fair or market value of assets acquired. This difference can then be amortized against reported income on some reasonable basis in order to arrive at results which would be comparable to those achieved under purchase accounting.

Purchase accounting

Since purchase accounting is designed to recognize the acquisition values on which the buyer and seller of a business entity bargained, it is a more meaningful method of accounting from the analyst's point of view. Purchase accounting is more relevant to the analyst's needs because he is interested in values which were exchanged in a business combination rather than in amounts which represent original costs to the seller.

As we have noted earlier in this chapter, the abuses in purchase accounting which preceded the issuance of APB *Opinions No. 16* and

No. 17 centered on attempts by acquiring companies to suppress the fair values of net assets acquired and paid for and to transplant the values paid for to a nondescript intangible asset account which was not amortized.

The Effect of APB Opinions No. 16 and No. 17. APB *Opinions No. 16* and *No. 17* have directly and forthrightly addressed themselves to the problem and have as their primary objective the elimination of these abuses. However, the analyst must not confuse theory with practice. He must realize that the objectives of many merger and acquisition-minded managements with respect to the accounting for these business combinations were in the past and are now likely to remain—

1. To reduce as much as possible the impact on present and future income of charges arising from assets acquired in the purchase.
2. To increase the post-acquisition income by understating assets acquired or by overproviding for future costs and contingencies.

Remaining room for distortions. While APB *Opinion No. 16* contains specific provisions on the valuation of assets and liabilities, room for abuses and loose interpretations remains. In addition to the leeway which inevitably exists when broad rules of valuation and appraisal are applied, the analyst must be particularly alert to understatements of assets and overstatement of liabilities which result from provisions for future costs and losses. A profession which tolerates the provision of such indeterminate reserves in the normal process of income determination (see discussion in Chapter 8) cannot be expected to forbid their use in the general process of realignment of values which occurs in purchase accounting. Two examples of such kind of provisions and adjustments will illustrate what we have in mind:

1. City Investing Company in its prospectus dated August 12, 1971 disclosed the following:

Certain Accounting Adjustments made in connection with the Acquisition of The Home Insurance Company. City accounted for its acquisition of The Home Insurance Company on August 31, 1968 as a "purchase of assets" rather than as a "pooling of interests." As a result, City was required, in accordance with generally accepted accounting principles, to establish a new cost basis of Home's net assets at the date of acquisition based upon the fair values of Home's assets and liabilities in the light of conditions then prevailing. In arriving at such fair values, it was determined that the reserves for underwriting losses and loss expenses on Home's books at the date of acquisition did not adequately reflect the amounts that could reasonably be expected to be paid in respect of casualty losses which actually occurred prior to the acquisition. Accordingly, such reserves were increased by $43,181,000 through a charge to the income of Home for the eight-month period ended August 31, 1968, the period prior to the acquisition of Home by City. As a result of this adjustment, payments by Home in respect of

7. Intercorporate investments, combinations, & foreign operations

casualty losses which occurred prior to the acquisition will not be deducted from City's income unless they exceed by $43,181,000 the reserves on Home's books for such losses prior to such adjustment. In addition, in determining the estimated realizable value of Home's investment portfolio as of the date of acquisition, it was considered appropriate, in the opinion of Lehman Brothers, to recognize a discount from quoted market of 15%, or $65,709,000, in the case of equity securities and 5%, or $14,074,000 in the case of debt instruments so as to reflect liquidation factors such as block transaction discounts, type of market, trading volume and similar factors. As a result of this adjustment, the aggregate amount of gains ultimately recognized in City's income from the sale of all portfolio securities held by Home at the date of acquisition (when and if all such securities are sold) will exceed by $79,783,000 the amount that would have been recognized if such adjustments had not been made. Net pre-tax gains on the sale of investments include approximately $13,000,000 and $25,000,000 during the years ended April 30, 1969 and 1970, respectively, and $1,356,000 and $15,661,000 during the eight months and year ended December 31, 1970, respectively, attributable to such portfolio adjustment.

Here are substantial provisions for costs and expenses which are not normally provided for and which, apparently, the auditors of the Home Insurance Company did not insist on in prior years.

2. General Leisure Products Corporation in its prospectus dated July 27, 1971 disclosed the following:

Effective January 31, 1971, the company was acquired by Arctic Enterprises, Inc. in a transaction which was accounted for as a purchase. As a result, management of Arctic Enterprises, Inc. decided not to proceed with previous management's policies with regard to inventories. . . . Based on the change in management policies and the physical inventory taken as of January 31, 1971, an inventory reserve of $1,139,000 was recorded and has been included in cost of sales in the unaudited statement of operations for the six months ended January 31, 1971. Based on decisions of new management, the inventory reserve was established to provide for quantities which are in excess of current sales requirements, parts related to discontinued models and defective and obsolete parts.
In addition, new management wrote-off the unamortized deferred product line development costs . . . to conform with the accounting practices followed by Arctic Enterprises, Inc. Accordingly, $78,363 of such unamortized deferred product line development costs have been expensed and included in cost of sales in the unaudited statement of operations for the six months ended January 31, 1971.

Here too we have substantial provisions for expected losses which are charged by the acquiring management to preacquisition results in order to achieve management decisions and conformance with stated accounting policies.

In assessing the effect of a business combination accounted for as a purchase, the analyst must evaluate in detail the disclosures which he finds regarding the process of valuation applied by the acquiring company. On the basis of such information he must reach his own conclusions on the fairness of presentation of the acquired companies assets and liabilities.

Acquisitions for equity securities. When an acquisition accounted for as a purchase is effected for stock or other equity securities, the analyst must be alert to the valuation of the net assets acquired in the combination. In periods of high market price levels, purchase accounting may tend to introduce inflated values when net assets, and particularly the intangibles assets, of acquired companies are valued on the basis of market prices of the stock issued. Such values, while determined on the basis of temporarily inflated stock prices, remain on a company's balance sheet and affect its operating results on a long-term basis.

The effect of goodwill amortization. APB *Opinion No. 17* recognized that a payment made in anticipation of future earnings should be recovered from those earnings over the period of those excess earnings. The mandatory amortization of goodwill is, from the point of view of realistic income determination, a step in the right direction. The analyst must, however, remain alert to the possibility that many companies will use the maximum period of 40 years for amortization purposes rather than the "reasonable" estimate of useful life which APB *Opinion No. 17* calls for.

ACCOUNTING FOR FOREIGN OPERATIONS

When the user of financial statements attempts to analyze an entity which has investments and operations in a foreign country, he must add to the problems which are discussed throughout this book those which are peculiar to foreign operations. These subdivide, broadly speaking, into two major categories:

1. Problems related to differences in accounting principles and practices which are peculiar to the foreign country in which the operations are conducted.
2. Problems which arise from the translation of foreign assets, liabilities, equities, and results of operations into the U.S. dollar.

Foreign accounting practices and auditing standards

While there has been some movement in the direction of greater uniformity in international accounting procedures and auditing standards, significant differences remain in these areas between practices in the United States and those in foreign countries.

Differences in auditing standards. In the area of auditing, which is discussed in Chapter 13 and is concerned with the function of attesting to the reliability of financial statements, a wide variety of standards in international practice exist. In some countries, such as the United Kingdom and Canada for example, the auditing profession is strong and well regarded, while in others its standing may be weak and, consequently, the reliability of financial statements may be subject to considerable doubt. Nevertheless, an auditing firm of international repute can enhance the credibility of a company's financial statements regardless of the location of the company's home base. Thus, the analyst must assess the reliability of the financial statements which he uses on the basis of the individual circumstances surrounding their preparation and attestation.

Peculiarities of foreign accounting practices. One of the central theses of this text is that no intelligent analysis of financial statements is possible without a thorough understanding of the assumptions and principles on the basis of which such statements were prepared. It follows that in the case of foreign companies the analyst must at least obtain a working familiarity with such assumptions and principles.

While the differences in accounting practice between those obtaining in the United States and those in other countries vary significantly from country to country, they can be substantial. The following are merely indicative of the nature and extent of such differences. Thus, in some countries—

1. Inventory reserves and other secret reserves may be sanctioned.
2. Excessive depreciation may be recorded.
3. Because of substantial price level changes, restatements of property accounts may be effected based on coefficients established by, and frequently revised by, the local government.
4. "Legal reserves" amounting to a fixed percentage of net income may be established.
5. Tax allocation may not be practiced.
6. Stock dividends may be recorded only on the basis of the par value of the stock issued.
7. Pooling of interests accounting may not be sanctioned.
8. Consolidation of parent and subsidiary financial statements may not be required.

A recitation of the differences in accounting as practiced in the United States and in other countries is beyond the scope of this text. The analyst must consult up-to-date sources of information[3] which are relevant to the proper understanding and analysis of financial statements.

In consolidating their foreign subsidiaries, U.S.-based multinational companies will usually conform their subsidiaries' accounting to those principles generally accepted in this country.

Translation of foreign currencies

In the discussion of intercorporate investments earlier in this chapter, it was emphasized that the consolidation of majority-owned subsidiaries is now a generally accepted procedure and the reasons for nonconsolidation are few and well defined. With respect to subsidiaries of U.S.-based multinational companies, the most common reason for nonconsolidation would be substantial uncertainty regarding the ultimate realization or transferability of foreign earnings.

In addition to the above provisions, APB *Opinion No. 18*, issued in 1971, requires a parent company to recognize in its financial statements the equity in earnings or losses of (1) unconsolidated foreign subsidiaries, (2) corporate joint ventures, and (3) other companies, less than 50 percent owned, over which the investor company exerts a significant influence.

The translation process. The consolidation of, as well as equity accounting for, foreign subsidiaries and affiliates requires that their financial statements be translated into U.S.-dollar equivalents. This is, of course, necessary before the accounts of such foreign subsidiaries or affiliates can be combined with those of the U.S.-based company.

The practical effect of the translation into dollars of an asset or a liability expressed in terms of a foreign currency can be best visualized by focusing on a few concrete examples:

1. If a foreign subsidiary holds an amount of foreign currency, then the value of that currency to the U.S. parent is the amount of U.S. dollars it will buy. That calls for translation at the current (balance sheet date) rate. If the value of the foreign currency falls in relation to the dollar, then the parent will experience a loss on conversion. Should the dollar decline in relation to that foreign currency, the parent company will sustain a gain on translation.
2. When the foreign subsidiary incurs a debt payable in the currency of the country in which it conducts its operations, then a decline of that currency in terms of dollars will result in a translation gain,

---

[3] See for example, *Professional Accounting in 25 Countries* (New York: AICPA, 1964); and Gerhard G. Muller, *International Accounting* (New York: MacMillan Co., 1967).

that is, fewer dollars will be needed to obtain the amount of foreign currency in order to repay the loan. But suppose that the subsidiary took out a long-term loan and the value of the dollar declined in relation to the foreign currency. The dollar equivalent of the liability has now increased. While it can be argued that the parent has incurred a loss, there are those who feel that because of the long-term nature of the obligation, only a contingent loss has been incurred or that an additional borrowing cost exists which should be charged off over the term of the loan.

3. When the foreign subsidiary acquires property, plant, and equipment with foreign currency, should it be translated at the current exchange rate, that is, should the translated dollar equivalent vary with fluctuations in the exchange rates? Up to now the general view has been that it should not because such assets are "nonmonetary," that is, in this case the subsidiary is not holding assets expressed in fixed amounts of the foreign currency. Thus, translation into dollars continues at the rate at which these assets were acquired, that is, the "historical rate," on the assumption that foreign-currency selling prices will increase under inflationary condition and that this will prevent deterioration in the economic value of assets such as property, plant, and equipment.

The current generally accepted methods of translation of foreign-currency financial statements are found in Chapter 12 of the AICPA's *Accounting Research Bulletin No. 43* (*ARB No. 43*) and were most recently revised by APB *Opinion No. 6*.

In practice to date, companies translate foreign-currency financial data into U.S. dollars using either the current/noncurrent approach or the monetary/nonmonetary approach.

The current/noncurrent approach. Under the current/noncurrent approach, net current assets, with the possible exception of inventories, are translated into U.S. dollars using the current rate (the rate of exchange at the balance sheet date). Other net assets are translated at the historical rate (the rate of exchange prevailing when the assets were acquired or capital stock issued). Exceptions to these general rules are permitted as to both inventory which, under certain circumstances, may be stated at the rate prevailing at the acquisition date, and long-term debt issued in connection with the acquisition of long-term assets shortly before a substantial and presumably permanent change in the exchange rate. In the latter case, the long-term debt may be restated at the new rate, with an equivalent adjustment of the long-term assets.

Income statement items, exclusive of amortization of long-term assets based on the historical rate cost, are translated at the rates prevailing during the year.

The monetary/nonmonetary approach. Under the monetary/nonmonetary approach, assets and liabilities are considered "monetary" if their amounts are fixed by contract or otherwise in terms of foreign currency (such as cash and accounts and notes receivable or payable in cash). Monetary items are translated at the current rate; nonmonetary items at the historical rate.

Treatment of translation gains and losses. Translation losses under either approach ordinarily are charged against operations; translation gains should preferably be deferred except to the extent that they offset prior provisions for translation losses. Most recently, some adjustments resulting from translation of long-term foreign currency receivables and liabilities at the current rate have been deferred for amortization over future periods, thus deriving somewhat the same effect as that obtained where similar receivables and liabilities are translated at the historical rate.

Translation devaluation gains should be applied to similar devaluation losses. Devaluation gains should preferably be deferred as recommended in paragraph 11 of Chapter 12 of *ARB No. 43*.

As will be seen from the discussion of the criteria for determining extraordinary gains and losses (Chapter 8), only a gain or loss resulting from a major devaluation or upward revaluation of a foreign currency can be considered "extraordinary." How the analyst should evaluate "extraordinary items" is discussed in Chapter 19.

The following note found in a prospectus of Johnson & Johnson is an example of disclosure related to accounting practices regarding foreign subsidiaries:

The Consolidated Financial Statements include the accounts of Johnson & Johnson and subsidiaries. All material intercompany accounts have been eliminated.

In 1970, the Company adopted the policy of consolidating all majority owned subsidiaries. In prior years all foreign subsidiaries were excluded from the consolidation and income was recognized only as received in the United States. Accordingly, all financial data contained in this Prospectus has been restated to reflect this change. Retained earnings at December 31, 1966 have also been increased by $44,177,000 to reflect the change relative to consolidation of foreign results. The effect on Sales, Net Earnings and Earnings per Share for the years ended December 28, 1969 and prior periods is shown in Note (a) to the Consolidated Statement of Earnings included elsewhere in this Prospectus.

The Company's equity in net assets of consolidated subsidiaries at January 2, 1972 exceeded the carrying value of its investment by $192,381,000. Of such amount $194,205,000 has been credited to Retained Earnings and $1,824,000 has been charged to Additional Capital.

7. Intercorporate investments, combinations, & foreign operations 171

Operating accounts, except for depreciation, are translated at approximate average rates of exchange for the respective years. In 1971, foreign sales and earnings reflect $9,177,000 and $1,276,000 ($.02 per share), respectively, arising out of the upward adjustment of certain world currencies against the United States dollar.

Assets and liabilities are translated at the approximate year-end rates of exchange except for property, plant and equipment accounts which are translated at the approximate rates of exchange at dates of acquisition. Losses ($1,649,000 in 1971), and gains to the extent offset by such losses, resulting from translating asset and liability accounts are reflected in net earnings. Translation gains ($2,301,000 in 1971, equivalent to $.04 per share) not offset by losses are deferred and included in the Reserve for Foreign Exchange Losses.

After translation of foreign currencies into United States dollar equivalents and elimination of intercompany profits and loans and accounts, the following amounts are included in the consolidated financial statements for subsidiaries located outside of the United States:

	January 2, 1972
Current assets	$151,038,000
Current liabilities	83,923,000
Net property, plant and equipment	81,869,000
Parent company equity in net assets	129,385,000
Excess of equity of parent company over investment	102,811,000
Sales to customers	355,013,000
Net earnings (after elimination of minority interest)	39,200,000

Implications for analysis

The principles of accounting which govern the translation of foreign accounts were originally developed in times of deteriorating foreign currencies and a relatively stable U.S. dollar. More recently there has occurred a fundamental change in these relationships.

After issuing an exposure draft of a proposed Opinion entitled "Translating Foreign Operations" and considering comments received during the exposure process, the APB deferred action on the proposed Opinion pending completion of a research study and further analysis of problems caused by the U.S. dollar devaluation.

The analyst must realize that presently existing alternative methods of translation can result in substantial differences in reported income. Thus, under the current/noncurrent approach to foreign currency transaction, inventories are usually considered current and are translated at the current rate of exchange, while under the monetary/nonmonetary approach inventories, being nonmonetary, would be translated at the rate prevailing when they were acquired. This can have a substantial effect on reported income, current assets, the current ratio, etc. These two approaches can similarly result in different translations for long-term debt which in turn will affect net income as well as various balance sheet ratios.

QUESTIONS

1. *a)* List and explain three main reasons why a parent company may not choose to include certain subsidiaries in its consolidated financial statements.
    b) What significant information may be disclosed by inspection of individual parent company and subsidiary statements in addition to the consolidated statements? (C.F.A.)
2. "A parent company is not responsible for the liabilities of its subsidiaries nor does it own the assets of the subsidiaries. Therefore, consolidated financial statements distort legal realities." Evaluate this statement from the financial analyst's viewpoint.
3. Which of the following cases would require consolidated financial statements?
    a) The parent company has a two-fifths ownership of the subsidiary.
    b) The parent company has temporary but absolute control over the subsidiary.
    c) The parent company has a controlling interest in the subsidiary but plans to dispose of it.
    d) Control of the subsidiary is to be relinquished in the near future as a result of a minority shareholder's derivative suit.
    e) A conglomerate parent company has a majority interest in diversified subsidiaries.
    f) The parent company has a 100 percent interest in a foreign subsidiary in a country where the conversion of currencies and the transfer of funds is severely restricted by the governmental authorities.
    g) The parent company has a 100 percent interest in a subsidiary whose principal business is the leasing of properties to the parent company and its affiliates.
4. Why is the cost method of accounting for investments in subsidiaries regarded as the least desirable?
5. Give some examples of situations in which the use of the cost method, rather than the equity method, is more appropriate.
6. What are some of the important limitations to which consolidated financial statements are subject?
7. The following note appeared in the financial statements of the Best Company for the period ending December 31, 19x1:
    "*Event subsequent to December 31, 19x1:* In January 19x2 the Company acquired Good Products, Inc. and its affiliates by the issuance of 48,063 shares of common stock. Net assets of the combined companies amounted to $1,016,198 and net income for 19x1 approximated $150,000.

7. Intercorporate investments, combinations, & foreign operations

To the extent that the acquired companies earn in excess of $1,000,000 over the next five years, the Company will be required to issue additional shares not exceeding 151,500, limited, however, to a market value of $2,000,000."
- a) Is the disclosure necessary and adequate?
- b) If the Good Products, Inc. was acquired in December 19x1, at what price should the Best Company have recorded the acquisition, assuming the Best Company's shares are traded at $22 on that day?
- c) On what is the additional consideration contingent?
- d) If the contingency materializes to the maximum limit, how should Best Company record the investment?

8. How would you determine the valuation of assets acquired in a purchase in the following cases?
   - a) Assets acquired by incurring liabilities.
   - b) Assets acquired in exchange of common stock.

9. Assuming the total cost of a purchased entity is appropriately determined, how should the total cost be allocated to the following assets?
   - a) Goodwill.
   - b) Negative goodwill (bargain purchase).
   - c) Marketable securities.
   - d) Receivables.
   - e) Finished goods.
   - f) Work in process.
   - g) Raw materials.
   - h) Plant and equipment.
   - i) Land and mineral reserves.
   - j) Payables.
   - k) Goodwill recorded in the book of the acquired company.

10. One of the arguments for pooling of interests is that in pooling no resource is given in exchange for the acquisition: since the acquiring company gives its unissued stock, the acquisition cannot be regarded as purchase. Do you agree?

11. Company A accounts as a pooling of interests the acquisition of Company B, the market value of whose net assets is much higher than their book value. What will be the effect of the pooling of interests method on Company A's income statement? On its balance sheet? What significance does APB *Opinion No. 16* have on such effects?

12. How is "goodwill" treated in an acquisition accounted for as a pooling of interests?

13. If assets are understated as a result of a pooling of interests, what effect(s) would the understatement have on the following:
    - a) Capital account.
    - b) Various expenses.
    - c) Disposition of assets acquired.

14. Is there any way an analyst can adjust the income statement under the pooling of interests method so that it can be comparable to a purchase method income statement?

174   Understanding corporate reports

15. From the analyst's point of view, which method of accounting for a business combination is preferable and why?
16. When an acquisition accounted for as a purchase is effected for stock or other equity securities, what should the analyst be alerted to?
17. When the balance sheet shows a substantial amount of goodwill, to what should the analyst be alert?
18. A current accounting controversy concerns the widespread use of pooling in mergers. Opponents of the use of pooling believe that the surviving company often uses pooling (rather than purchase) to hide the "true" effects of the merger. What may be "hidden" and how is the analysis of a company's securities affected by pooling practices? (C.F.A.)
19. Company X has engaged in an aggressive program of acquiring other companies through exchange of common stock.
    a) Explain briefly how an acquisition program might contribute to the rate of growth in earnings per share of Company X.
    b) Explain briefly how the income statements of prior years might be adjusted to reflect the potential future earnings trend of the combined companies. (C.F.A.)
20. What are some factors which could change management's original estimates of the useful life of intangible assets?
21. What are some significant problem areas in accounting for foreign operations?
22. When a consolidated financial statement includes foreign operations, to what must the financial analyst be particularly alert?
23. Although cash generally is regarded as the simplest of all assets to account for, certain complexities can arise for both domestic and multinational companies.
    a) What are the normal components of cash?
    b) Under what circumstances, if any, do valuation problems arise in connection with cash?
    c) Unrealized and/or realized gains or losses can arise in connection with cash. Excluding consideration of price level changes, indicate the nature of such gains or losses and the context in which they can arise in relation to cash. (AICPA)
24. For the fiscal year ended December 31, 1970, International Business Machines Corporation reported record earnings per share of $8.92, up 9 percent from earnings per share of $8.21 in 1969. "For the first time, net earnings of IBM World Trade Corp., the foreign subsidiary, accounted for more than half of the huge computer maker's total annual—50.27%."

    In what ways does the growing importance of international operations such as World Trade make more difficult the analysis of the income statements of multinational corporations? (C.F.A.)

# 8

Analysis of the income statement—I

THE INCOME STATEMENT portrays the net results of operations of an enterprise. Since results are what enterprises are supposed to achieve and since their value is, in large measure, determined by the size and quality of these results, it follows quite logically that the analyst attaches great importance to the income statement.

This chapter and the one that follows will examine the principles which underlie the preparation and presentation of the income statement. The analysis and interpretation of this important financial statement is discussed in Chapters 18 and 19. Such analysis can be intelligently undertaken only after the principles outlined in this chapter are fully understood.

What is income? An examination of this subject will reveal that significant differences of opinion exist among thoughtful and competent accountants, economists, and financial analysts on what income is and on how the net income of an enterprise for a given period should be measured.

A simple illustration

Take, for example, the very simple case of a business unit which has only $1,000 in cash, with which it buys, at the beginning of the year, a bond priced at par, and carrying a 6 percent coupon. While we may readily agree that the gross income is $60 (the interest), the determination of net income depends, among other factors, on the value of the bond at year-end. Thus, if the market price at year-end is $950, the $50 loss would be recognized by the economist while the accountant may or may not recognize it, depending on a judgment of whether there has been a permanent impairment in the value of the bond and, also, on whether the loss must be recognized if it is the present intention of the enterprise to hold it to a not too distant maturity date. The economist would claim that it is not right to recognize the income of $60 without the offsetting shrinkage in capital in the amount of $50. The essence of this argument is that the enterprise was not as well off at the end of the period as it was at the beginning if the $60 is all recognized as income and so distributed.

If, instead, the bond had a market quotation at year-end of $1,100, then some economists would consider the $100 accretion as a gain to be added to the $60 in interest earned. This the accountant would not do, because the gain is not realized and the market value of the bond could fluctuate in either direction before it is finally sold. Other theoreticians would not rely on the current market price of the bond but, taking the going interest rate into account, would value the bond at the present value of future interest receipts ($60 a year) plus the present value of the bond principal at maturity discounted at the appropriate rate and would use such value in the determination of net income for the period. There again, accountants have, so far, shied away from such approaches mostly because the variables which make up the bond value can change very frequently before final realization through sale or redemption of the bond. They consider such realization as the necessary objective evidence needed to warrant recording of the gain. To complicate matters even further, consider the effect on income of holding the bond during a period when the price level has risen by 10 percent. Clearly there has been a loss of purchasing power, but so far conventional accounting statements give no recognition of this. The problem of measuring the gain or loss in purchasing power will be more fully considered in Chapter 12.

If such a simple income-producing asset as the bond, which involves no complexities on the expense side, can give rise to so many possible interpretations of what the amount of the net income it produced is, it is obvious that the determination of the amount of net income of a full-fledged business enterprise is far more complex. It is in this light that one can, at least, understand, even if not fully agree with, the principles of income determination which accountants have established over the years.

A variety of concepts of income

Going from our simple specific example to generalizations, we see that the economist's concept of income is the amount that could be consumed or distributed by an entity during a period and still leave it as "well-off" at the end of the period as it was at the beginning.

It is in the area of measuring the degree of "well-offness" of an enterprise that the gap between the economist's view and that of the accountant is widest. The economist maintains that capital value can be measured by the present value of future net receipts. But such receipts are based on highly subjective and constantly shifting estimates of future probabilities applying to both the *size* of the net receipts and the discount factors to be applied to them. The degree of uncertainty present here dwarfs that involved in estimating, for example, the future useful life of plant and equipment or the probability of debt collection, which are estimates of a kind which accountants now make. Thus, while the economist, cognizant of the uncertainty pervading all of business life, is impatient with the accountant's great concern for objectivity, verifiability, and conservatism, the latter believes that the very utility of his professional service to the community is dependent upon his upholding these qualities and characteristics.

Because of the divergencies in viewpoint such as those discussed above, the differences in the concepts of income of economists and accountants have not been appreciably narrowed. This is, in large measure, also due to difficulties which a practicing profession found in implementing in practice the theoretical concepts of economic thought.

One way in which income can be measured is by comparing the capital balances at the beginning and end of a period. Since capital is the excess of assets over liabilities, the problem of income determination is thus inseparable from the problem of asset and liability measurement. While, as we have seen, the economist focuses on a comparison of capital balances at successive points in time, in modern accounting the income determination process centers around the matching of current costs and revenues within a specific span of time. To the analyst who is interested in using the income statement as a means of predicting future streams of income and expense, this is a much more useful approach, because he is very much interested in all the elements which make up the final net income figure.

The process of income determination thus involves two basic steps: (1) identification of the revenues properly attributable to the period reported upon and (2) the matching of the corresponding costs with the revenues of this period either through direct association with the cost of the products sold therein or by assignment as expenses properly applicable as period costs.

THE ACCRUAL OF REVENUE

For every profit-seeking enterprise the first step in the process of profit recognition is the accrual of revenue. Thus, the very important question arises when, that is, at what point in the entire sequence of revenue-earning activities in which an enterprise is engaged, is it proper to recognize revenue as earned? The improper accrual of revenue can have one of two undesirable effects:

1. Revenue may be recorded prematurely or belatedly, that is, it may be assigned to the wrong fiscal period.
2. Revenue may be recorded before there is a reasonable certainty that it will actually be realized. This in turn can lead to reporting of gain derived from such revenue in one period and the cancellation or reversal of such profit, with a resultant loss, in a subsequent period. The effect of this is to overstate net income in one period and to understate it in a subsequent period.

Conditions for revenue realization

These two effects are, of course, highly undesirable and misleading, and in order to minimize such possibilities accountants have adopted strict and conservative rules regarding the recognition or realization of revenues. The following criteria exemplify the rules which have been established to prevent the premature anticipation of revenues. Thus, realization is deemed to take place only after the following conditions have been met:

1. The earning activities undertaken to create revenue have been substantially completed, for example, no significant effort is necessary to complete the transaction.
2. In case of sale, the risk of ownership has been effectively passed on to the buyer.
3. The revenue, as well as the associated expenses, can be measured or estimated with substantial accuracy.
4. The revenue recognized should normally result in an increase in cash, receivables, or marketable securities, and under certain conditions in an increase in inventories or other assets.
5. The business transactions giving rise to the income should be at arm's length with independent parties (i.e., not with controlled parties).
6. The transactions should not be subject to revocation, for example, carrying the right of return of merchandise sold.

While the above criteria may appear to be pretty straightforward, they are, in fact, subject to a number of exceptions and have, in practice, been interpreted in a variety of ways. The best way to understand these variations is to examine the application of these concepts in a variety of circumstances.

Uncertainty as to collection of receivables

In normal circumstances, doubts about the collectibility of receivables resulting from a sale should be reflected in a provision for doubtful accounts. APB *Opinion No. 10* affirms this when it states that "profit is deemed to be realized when a sale in the ordinary course of business is effected, unless the circumstances are such that the collection of the sales price is not reasonably assured." At what point the collection of a receivable is no longer reasonably assured is, of course, a matter of judgment based on all the surrounding circumstances. Moreover, such judgment may be conservative or it may be based on liberal or optimistic assumptions.

Installment sales. Installment sales normally result in a receivable which is collectible over a period of many months or even many years. Time is an important dimension in the assessment of risk, for the more distant the time of the collection of the proceeds of the sale, the more uncertain the final collection of the receivable. Conceivably, then, the length of time of collection is an important factor in assessing the probability of ultimate collection. Except in situations where the doubt about the collection of installment receivables is such as to make a reasonable estimate impossible, profit on installment sales is properly recognized at the time of sales.

Real estate accounting. The sale of real estate is often characterized by payment terms stretching over long time periods. A long-delayed collection period increases uncertainty, and thus the recognition of profit on such sales is dependent on an ability to assess the probability of collection of the full sales price. For this reason, real estate companies have frequently taken up the profit on sale of real estate on an installment basis, that is, on a basis which takes up profit only in proportion to the actual cash collection of the sales price.

Accountants feel that theoretically there should be no connection between recognizing the profit on a sale and the time it takes to collect the ensuing receivable. APB *Opinion No. 10*, as indicated above, gives expression to this principle, and companies have recently been adopting it. Thus, Tishman Realty and Construction Company disclosed the switch in accounting as follows:

During the year ended September 30, 1968, in order to conform to the provisions of Opinion No. 10 of the Accounting Principles Board of the American Institute of Certified Public Accountants, the Company adopted the policy for financial reporting purposes of recording the entire profit on dispositions of real estate in the year of sale, except in those instances where collection of the proceeds of sale is uncertain. Had the Company continued its policy of reporting profits on sales of real estate on the installment basis, net income for the year ended September 30, 1968 would have been approximately $1,950,000 less.

The circumstances attending the sale of real estate continue, however, to raise questions of when the profit can properly be recorded.

The SEC has expressed reservations about certain types of attending circumstances by issuing *Accounting Series Release No. 95* which stated that—

circumstances such as the following tend to raise a question as to the propriety of current recognition of profit:
1. Evidence of financial weakness of the purchaser.
2. Substantial uncertainty as to amount of costs and expenses to be incurred.
3. Substantial uncertainty as to amount of proceeds to be realized because of form of consideration or method of settlement; e.g., nonrecourse notes, non-interest-bearing notes, purchaser's stock, and notes with optional settlement provisions, all of indeterminable value.
4. Retention of effective control of the property by the seller.
5. Limitations and restrictions on the purchaser's profits and on the development or disposition of the property.
6. Simultaneous sale and repurchase by the same or affiliated interests.
7. Concurrent loans to purchasers.
8. Small or no down payment.
9. Simultaneous sale and leaseback of property.

Any such circumstance, taken alone, might not preclude the recognition of profit in appropriate amount. However, the degree of uncertainty may be accentuated by the presence of a combination of the foregoing factors.

While this release is concerned with sales of real estate in particular, these principles may be applied, of course, to other sales as well, and that adds to their overall significance.

Finally, we find examples of sales by companies which retail building lots and account therefor by taking up profit on a transaction where the buyer has made only a very nominal commitment or down payment, and where the payment period is long. Moreover, adding to the uncertainties, such sales involve promises of land improvements to be performed in the future, the cost of which must be estimated at the time the sale and cost of the sale are recorded.

The following disclosure of real estate accounting procedures is taken from notes to the financial statements of the General Development Corporation:

Accounting procedures. The Company records the full sales price of a homesite sold under an installment contract at the time the purchaser makes his first monthly installment payment, substantially all contracts require payments over an average period of 10 years. Interest on the contract balance is recorded as income as monthly payments on the homesite sales contract are received.

Expenses related to a homesite sale are charged against income at the time of sale. Such expenses comprise average cost of unimproved land by development area, capitalized mortgage interest and real estate taxes, sales commissions and estimated cost of required improvements, such as grading, roads and canals.

Sales of homesites are generally made in advance of the completion of land improvements and the cost of such development work to be completed in the future is recorded as an estimated liability.

There are, of course, many other variations of the problem of sales recognition when substantial doubt about the possibilities of collection exists. The field of *franchising* provides an additional example. The buyer of a franchise undertakes, among many other obligations, to pay a franchise fee. However, only a minor portion is usually paid in cash to the franchise issuer, the balance being evidenced by a note payable over a period of years. The problem involved in recognizing the entire franchise fee at the time the agreement is signed revolves around the value of the note received for a substantial portion of the fee. Since many franchise buyers are inexperienced and undercapitalized and operate under severe competitive conditions, the doubts involved in the collection of the note may be strong enough to warrant taking up the franchise fee only in proportion to actual cash collections.

Timing of revenue recognition

Another major problem area in revenue recognition is the matter of *timing*. It is a basic principle of accounting that gains accrue only at the time of sale and that gains may not be anticipated by reflecting assets at their current sales prices. There are some exceptions to the rule such as in the case of gold and silver production, where a government controlled fixed price market exists, or as in the case of some agricultural, mineral, or other fungible products which enjoy immediate marketability at quoted market prices. After completion, such products may be recorded at market price less costs of disposal. Another area of seeming exception is contract accounting where, in effect, the sale normally precedes production or construction and where profit may, under certain conditions, be taken up in proportion to activity.

Contract accounting

The basis of recording income on short-term construction or production contracts poses no special problems. Profit is ordinarily recognized when the end product is completed and has been accepted by the owner.

Long-term construction contracts, be they for buildings, battleships, or complex machinery, present a more difficult accounting problem. Here the construction cycle may extend over a number of accounting periods while substantial costs accumulate, financed in part by progress billings. Two generally accepted methods of accounting are in use!

1. The *percentage-of-completion* method is preferred when estimates of costs to complete and estimates of progress towards completion of the contract can be made with reasonable dependability. A common basis of profit estimation is to record that part of the estimated total profit which corresponds to the ratio that costs incurred to date bear to expected total costs. Other methods of estimation of completion can be based on units completed or on qualified engineering estimates.
2. The *completed-contract* method of accounting is preferable where the conditions inherent in the contracts present risks and uncertainties which result in an inability to make reasonable estimates of costs and completion time. Problems under this method concern the point at which completion of the contract is deemed to have occurred as well as the kind of expenses to be deferred. Thus, some companies defer all costs to the completion date, including general and administrative overhead, while others consider such costs as period costs to be expensed as they are incurred.

Under either of the two contract accounting methods, losses, present or anticipated, must be fully provided for in the period in which the loss first becomes apparent.

Finance company accounting

Generally the accrual of interest is a function of time. The income on a bond or a loan to others depends on principal outstanding, time elapsed, and rate.

Finance companies, such as in the consumer or sales finance fields, make loans under which a finance charge is added on to the face amount of the rate, that is, discount and add-on loans.

A number of alternative methods of taking up this discount exist. Thus, if the face of the note is $2,400 and the cash advanced is $2,160, the $240 unearned finance charge can be taken up over, say, 12 months, in a number of ways:

1. Under the *straight-line method,* one twelfth or $20 would be taken up each month as an installment is collected.
2. Under the *sum-of-the-years'-digits* method, larger amounts of income

are recognized in the early part of the loan contract than in its latter period. In the case of a 12-month loan, the sum of the digits is 78. In the first month of the contract, 12/78th of the finance charge ($36.92) is taken into income; and in the last month, 1/78th ($3.14) is taken up. Under this method the interest earned bears a closer relationship to funds out at risk than it does under the straight-line method. That is also true of other methods which take up income in proportion to the decreasing balance of the loan outstanding.

3. A variation of either of the above methods involves taking into income, immediately on granting of the loan, an amount, also called "acquisition factor," which is designed to offset the initial loan acquisition expenses incurred by the company. The balance of the unearned finance charge is then taken into income by means of one of alternative methods.

Accounting for lease income

Another special branch of revenue accounting is found in the case of companies leasing property to others; and here too, the timing and method of taking up income can have an important effect on timing in the reporting of periodic results.

There are two basic kinds of leases:

1. The *operating lease* which usually covers a period shorter than the useful life of the item leased and under which the lessor performs most of the functions associated with property ownership. Short-term car rentals is one example, and computer leasing by the manufacturer is another.
2. *Finance leases* under which the lessor recovers the invoice cost of the item leased over the initial term of the lease. The lease is usually noncancellable and may give the lessee an option to buy or lease the equipment at a nominal price at the termination of the original term of the lease. This method of leasing is in effect a method by which the user finances the acquisition of an item for substantially all of its service or useful life.

The accounting for lease income by the lessor seeks, in effect, to recognize the substance of the transaction rather than its form.

Thus, APB *Opinion No. 7* sets forth the methods as follows:

Operating lease rentals. These are taken into income in accordance with the lease contract unless the rent receipt pattern departs radically from the straight-line basis in which case it should be taken into income in a manner that reflects economic usefulness. Upkeep, depreciation, and maintenance expenses related to the leased equipment are accrued in the same way as any other revenue earning property.

ILLUSTRATION. Saunders Leasing System discloses the accounting for truck leases as follows:

"The companies follow the operating method of accounting for vehicles purchased for rental to customers, recording the vehicles as fixed assets, and rentals only as they become receivable.

"Interest included in the face amount of the equipment obligations is recorded as prepaid interest and amortized ratably to income over the life of the obligation."

Finance leases. In the case of these leases, the aggregate rentals receivable over the term of the lease less cost of the equipment leased (minus residual value) is in the nature of interest on loan and is recorded as unearned income. This interest is then taken up into income over the life of the lease in decreasing amounts related to the declining balance of the unrecovered loan outstanding.

ILLUSTRATION. American Financial Corporation disclosed its accounting for leases in the following note:

"The Corporation has adopted the "finance method" of accounting for income under substantially all its lease contracts. Under this method, the aggregate lease revenue is recorded as a lease receivable and the excess of that amount over the cost (less estimated residual value) of the related rental assets represents income to be recognized over the life of the lease. Ten percent of the income (approximately equal to cost of completing a lease transaction) is taken into operating income at the time a lease is executed. The remaining 90% is taken into operating income monthly over the term of the lease substantially in proportion to the balance of rents receivable at the beginning of each month. For federal income tax purposes, advance and monthly rental payments are recognized as income when received and rental assets are depreciated."

ILLUSTRATION. United States Leasing International commented as follows on its method of accounting:

"*Bases of recognizing income.* At the time a lease is executed a portion of lease income that approximately offsets the expenses incurred in consummating the lease, including a provision for doubtful accounts, is taken into income. The remainder of the lease income is taken into income over the life of the lease on a declining basis in proportion to the related receivables outstanding or at the time a lease contract is terminated.

"Income from Lease Underwriting comprises lease placement fees received at the time leases are executed and participations in the residual proceeds of the leased equipment at lease termination. Lease placement fees are recorded as income on the lease commencement date. Participations in residuals are recorded as income at their discounted value on the lease commencement date and the remainder is taken into income over the lives of the related leases.

. . . .

"With regard to our residual income, we estimate the equipment's residual value at the commencement of a lease. This estimated value is spread over the life of the lease, and a portion is taken into income each year.

. . . .

"Our accounting methods are conservative and essentially risk free. Where residuals are concerned, we follow a policy of assigning a residual value that is well below the residual proceeds we are actually realizing."

"Sales" to leasing subsidiaries

Before revenue under a sale can be considered as realized there must be a genuine transfer of risk from seller to buyer. An interesting example of the importance of this principle is provided by the furor caused by a recent attempt by Memorex Corporation to treat as an immediate sale the transfer of the equipment to the company's leasing subsidiary.

The basic flaw in this proposed accounting was (1) that the subsidiary had not been capitalized by the infusion of third-party capital and could, as a consequence, not pay Memorex for the equipment; and (2) that Memorex had agreed to protect the subsidiary against losses. In short, these conditions clearly demonstrated that there was no transfer of the risk of ownership from Memorex to third parties, and consequently there was no genuine sale. Thus, the company had to agree to treat the transfer of the leased equipment as a lease rather than as an outright sale.

Additional examples of income recognition problems

Additional examples of problems regarding the timing of revenue recognition can be found in a number of industries.

Thus, Time, Inc. reports as follows on the accounting for unearned subscription income:

Unearned portion of paid subscriptions. Sales of Subscriptions to magazines are credited to deferred income (unearned portion of paid subscriptions) at the gross subscription price at the time of sale. Accounts receivable resulting from charge sales have been deducted from deferred income. As magazines are delivered to subscribers, proportionate shares of the gross subscription price are credited to revenues. All costs in connection with the procurement of subscriptions are expensed as incurred; agents' commissions are deducted from subscription revenues and other procurement costs are charged to selling expenses.

In the liquor industry, Schenley Industries, Inc., reported on a timing aspect of income recognition as follows:

The company sells certain whiskey in barrels in bond under agreements which provide for future bottling. In prior years, profits on such transactions were reflected as of the date of sale. The present company policy, effective as of September 1, 19x9, is to treat such profits as deferred income until the whiskey is bottled and shipped.

Finally, let us consider the accounting of O. M. Scott & Sons which, while unusual, does provide an additional insight into the motivations of managements in the area of revenue timing. The following note appeared in the annual report for 1961:

Sales. In the financial statements for the year ended September 30, 1960, attention was directed to the Company's policy of including in the operating statement firm orders received, billed, and costed out in late September which were shipped early in the immediately following October. During 1961, this policy was discontinued.

The auditors took exception to the above policy prior to its discontinuance.

In its 1968 annual report, management explained as follows the inauguration of a "revenue reserve."

On the basis of the information obtained as of June 30, management decided to report the company's nine months earnings after setting up a revenue reserve against the possibility that dealer inventories might curb their buying in future periods.

At year end, inventories of Scotts products in the hands of our retailers were likely lower in relation to consumer purchases than any time in our history. Despite this lower ratio, total dealer inventories increased during the year. When such increases occur, management feels that reported earnings should be adjusted to more nearly reflect consumer purchases during the year.

Accordingly, the revenue reserve established at year end and shown in this report defers earnings on the difference between our reported net sales (adjusted for increase in retail outlets) and the total of products actually purchased by consumers during the year, calculated at Scotts billing prices. The effect was to reduce earnings 14¢ per share.

In the future, the revenue reserve will be adjusted upward or downward, at nine months and year end, to reflect the relationship between consumer purchases and the company's net sales.

Neither the auditors nor the Internal Revenue Service accept this particular method of accounting at this time. This is not surprising since adjusting earnings in this conservative fashion is an unusual accounting treatment. Nevertheless, management believes it is in keeping with the economic realities of the company's unique business endeavor and that it is sound, valid and proper for Scotts business.

Income of subsidiaries and affiliates

When a company owns a part or the whole of another entity, the interest of the company in the subsidiary's income may be accounted for in a number of ways.

1. Consolidated financial statements may be prepared, thus including the subsidiary's income in the consolidated income statement while excluding any minority interest in that income. While generally accepted accounting principles do not expressly require the presentation of consolidated financial statements, it is generally recognized that they do in most cases represent the best and more meaningful presentation of the financial position and results of operations. Subsidiaries may be excluded from consolidation because their businesses do not lend themselves to meaningful consolidation with the group, because their physical location represents special risks, because of lack of effective control, or because of temporary control.

2. If a subsidiary is not consolidated, two methods of reporting the parent company's investment in it are possible:

a) *The cost method* under which only dividends received are recorded as income by the parent. Because the latter has the power to control the amount and timing of dividend declarations by the subsidiary, the dividends may not reflect the actual earnings performance of the subsidiary and thus may lead to income distortion or manipulation.

ILLUSTRATION. In 1967, Newmont Mining Corporation which presents parent company statement only reported an increase in earnings at a time when its major subsidiaries showed year-to-year earnings declines. Newmont was able to do this by ordering the subsidiaries to increase their dividend payout. The company has since changed its reporting method.

Because of the above-mentioned possible distortions, APB *Opinion No. 18* now requires that if consolidation is not appropriate, for whatever reason, the investments in subsidiaries be carried "at equity."

b) *The equity method* takes up the parent company's proportionate part of a subsidiary's profits and losses, thus reflecting best the parent company's share of the subsidiary's results. The equity method is, thus, appropriate in all cases except those where there are serious limitations or restrictions on remittance of dividends, or where control is likely to be temporary or where it is not adequate.

When the parent company and its subsidiary are consolidated or when the parent picks up the equity with earnings of the subsidiary, intercompany sales and profits must be eliminated.

Jointly owned companies. Frequently two corporations join in forming a new corporation which, in effect, represents a joint venture in which each owns a 50 percent interest and has a voice in management. APB *Opinion No. 18* concluded that the equity method reflects best the underlying nature of investments in such ventures and calls for accounting for the investment at equity, thus recording a proportionate share of the results as they are earned. This method may be used even when the ownership is less than 50 percent where circumstances are such that owners exercise control in concert or at least each retains a "veto right" with respect to management decisions.

The accounting for intercorporate investments is discussed in Chapter 7.

Implications for analysis

The income statement, presenting as it does, the results achieved by an enterprise and the return achieved on invested capital is of great importance to the analyst in his evaluation of the worth of the enterprise. For exactly this reason and for such reasons as pride, bonuses based on income, and the value of stock options, management is greatly interested in the results it reports. Consequently, the analyst can expect managements to choose those accounting principles and procedures which come closest to achieving their purposes.

The objectives of income reporting which management is desirous of achieving do not always result in the fairest or most proper measurement of results, and consequently the analyst must be aware of management's propensities as well as the choices available to it.

Since the recording of revenue is the first step in the process of income recognition and on which the recognition of any and all profit depends, the analyst should be particularly inquisitive about the accounting methods chosen.

Problem of collectibility. One element which casts doubt on the recording of revenue is *uncertainty about the collectibility* of the resulting receivable. We have examined the special problems relating to installment sales, real estate sales, and franchise sales. Problems of collection exist, however, in the case of all sales, and the analyst must be alert to them.

Let us conclude the consideration of the collection problem by an example from the bowling equipment manufacturing industry. The early 1960s witnessed a bowling boom which was attended by the building of a large number of bowling alleys which competed for a limited amount of business in restricted territories. The two major manufacturers of bowling equipment sold it to inexperienced and poorly financed operators against notes and receivables, mostly secured by the equipment itself. The full profit on this equipment was immediately taken up while the provision for bad debts concurrently established underestimated the special risks involved by a wide mark. Brunswick Corporation wrote off very substantial amounts of accounts receivable in 1963, while American Machine & Foundry made similarly substantial write-offs of receivables only five years later. Long before the write-offs were announced, the alert analyst could have taken his cue from the deteriorating business conditions in the bowling industry. There was, however, little in the financial statements of the bowling manufacturers to forewarn him of the losses yet to come.

Timing of revenue. The analyst must also be alert to the problems related to the *timing of revenue recognition*. We have examined the accounting concept of realization and the reasons for the accountant's great preoccupation with objective and verifiable evidence in this area. While the justification for this position is the subject of much debate within and without the accounting profession, it behooves the analyst to understand the implications of present accounting in this area on his work.

The present rules of realization generally do not allow for recognition of profit in advance of sale. Thus, increases in market value of property such as land, equipment, or securities, the accretion of values in growing timber, or the increase in the value of inventories are not recognized in the accounts. As a consequence, income will not be recorded before sale, and the timing of sales is in turn a matter which lies importantly within the discretion of management. That, in turn, gives management a certain degree of discretion in the timing of profit recognition.

Contract accounting. In the area of contract accounting, the analyst should recognize that the use of the completed-contract method is justified only in cases where reasonable estimates of costs and the degree of completion are not possible. In fact, from the statement user's point of view it is a poor method. Yet, as the following footnote of Convalariums of America, Inc., indicates, some companies consider the choice of method a matter of discretion:

In 1968 the Company, through a subsidiary, began constructing health care facilities. The Company has elected to recognize profits on construction contracts under the completed contract method. Under this method, profits from contracts are reflected only in the periods in which the contracts are completed. Since none of the construction contracts were completed by December 31, 1968, no construction income has been included in the accompanying historical and pro forma consolidated statements of income and all other operating expenses of the construction company have been deferred. Use of the completed contract method may result in wide variances in income between accounting periods inasmuch as income from contracts is reflected only in the periods in which the contracts are completed.

As stated above, the Company is following the completed contract method of accounting for its construction contracts. In accordance with generally accepted accounting principles, the Company could have elected to report its income on construction contracts under the percentage of completion method. Under this method, that portion of the total contract price and that portion of the total estimated cost that corresponds to the physical percentage of completion of each project will be used in determining gross income from operations. If the Company had elected to follow the percentage of completion method for the nine (9) months ended December 31, 1968, total construction income would have been $405,765, construction gross profit $34,711, and construction net income $10,926. Pro forma net income per share would have been $.02 greater.

In addition to the basic choice of method, the matter of which costs are to be considered contract costs and which period costs remains, to a significant degree, an area of management discretion.

Other problem areas of revenue recognition. In finance company accounting, the analyst must be aware of the variety of methods, as outlined earlier in this chapter, available in the recognition of income as well as the option of taking into income at the inception of loan agreements of amounts designed to offset loans acquisition costs.

Other alternative methods of taking up revenue, as in the case of lessors, must be fully understood by the analyst before he attempts an evaluation of a company's earnings or a comparison among companies in the same industry.

The reporting of results of subsidiary and affiliated companies has been subject to considerable improvement, the trend being evidenced by the provisions of APB *Opinion No. 18*. Whenever the cost method of carrying the investment of subsidiaries or 50 percent owned affiliates is retained, the analyst should critically examine the reasons for the retention of the cost method and the validity of such given reasons. On the other hand, the recording of losses on investment in subsidiaries and affiliates is necessary under either the cost or the equity method. Thus, equity in losses should be recorded as they occur. The analyst should carefully examine cases such as that of Steward Warner Corporation which failed to recognize such losses and explained its procedures as follows:

Notes to the consolidated financial statements:
(1) During the early part of 1966, Stewart-Warner Corporation acquired an additional 41% stock interest in Thor Power Tool Company, resulting in its ownership of 62% of Thor's outstanding shares at the year end. Following are a Summary of Financial Position as of December 31, 1966, and a Summary of Income for the year then ended, for Thor Power Tool Company and subsidiary companies, as reported by Thor:

8. Analysis of the income statement—I

Summary of Financial Position

Current Assets	$15,605,227
Current Liabilities	4,957,534
Working Capital	$10,647,693
Property (net) and Other Assets	5,340,963
Total	$15,988,656
Long-term Debt	$ 6,200,000
Other Liabilities	1,570,365
Total Long-term Liabilities	$ 7,770,365
Shareholders' Equity	$ 8,218,291

Summary of Income

Net Sales	$27,915,435
Income before Taxes	647,723
Net Income for the Year	108,805

At the year end Stewart-Warner's investment (at cost) in Thor Power Tool Company amounted to $11,367,215, consisting of 452,333 shares of Thor's capital stock, $1,023,000 principal amount of Thor's 4⅞% convertible subordinated debentures purchased at discounts from face value and the Corporation's equity in Thor's undistributed earnings for 1966. The investment in Thor is included under Other Assets in Stewart-Warner's Consolidated Statement of Financial Position.

During 1965 two lawsuits were filed against Thor and several other defendants asserting claims based upon the conduct of the business by the previous management. Thor has been advised by legal counsel that it is not possible to forecast the outcome of this litigation or the ultimate effect on Thor's financial condition because of many unsettled legal issues and uncertainties about the facts. However, Thor has also been advised by counsel that Thor's cross-claim against its former independent public accountants has merit and that if Thor should be held liable in this litigation, it should prevail in its cross-claim for the amount of its liability.

It has been Thor's practice to evaluate inventories based on anticipated future requirements as reflected by its marketing plans. Following this policy, inventories of $8,123,378 at December 31, 1966, are stated net of reserves of $3,582,327 for excess, obsolete and damaged inventories. Thor's auditors have qualified their opinion on Thor's consolidated financial statements as being subject to the effect of the ultimate adjustment arising from the disposition of these inventories.

In the opinion of Stewart-Warner's management, the matters discussed above will not materially affect Stewart-Warner's consolidated financial statements.

In their report, the independent auditors included the following middle paragraph and dismissed the entire matter on the basis of lack of materiality.

We did not examine the consolidated financial statements of Thor Power Tool Company (summarized in Note 1), the investment in which represents approximately 11% of the assets of Stewart-Warner, but we were furnished with the report of other auditors thereon. The opinion of the other auditors was qualified as being subject to the final outcome of Thor's pending litigation and to the ultimate adjustments arising from disposition of Thor's inventories, discussed in Note 1. However, in our opinion, the effect of these matters is not material in relation to Stewart-Warner's consolidated financial statements.

Concept of materiality in income determination. The analyst must be aware of the fact that the concept of materiality remains undefined in accounting and is consequently subject to abuse and uncertainty. It is all too often employed by auditors in defense of the omission of disclosure when their clients are adamant in their resistance to certain disclosures. The analyst must also realize that the accountant's concept of materiality is presently a very narrow one indeed. It does not attempt to take into account the future implications of an emerging situation. All to often, what looks like a small problem area may be the beginning of a serious future problem. Recent examples of this were provided by Celanese Corporation; which lost heavily from what was initially a relatively small foreign venture, and American Express Company, which had to make good the losses of its relatively insignificant warehousing subsidiary when large-scale defalcations in the famous "salad oil swindle" were discovered.

COST AND EXPENSE ACCRUAL

Costs and expenses are resources (assets) and service potentials consumed, spent, or lost in the pursuit or production of revenues. The major problems of accounting for costs concern the measurement (size) of costs and the timing of their allocation to production time periods.

A basic objective of income accounting is to match costs to the revenues recognized during a period. This is far from easy to do. There are many kinds of costs, and they behave in a variety of ways. Some costs can be specifically identified with a given item of revenue. At the other end of the spectrum are costs which bear no identifiable relationship to specific elements of revenue at all and can be identified only with the time period during which they are incurred. This variation in behavior of costs has given rise to certain useful classifications which are helpful in understanding the matching and allocation problems:

Variable costs are those which vary in direct proportion to activity, whether the latter is measured by means of sales, production, or other gauges of activity. Thus, for example, in the manufacture of electric cable, the consumption of copper wire may be said to vary in direct proportion to a given unit of wire length. The higher the cable sales figure the higher the copper wire cost. In practice many costs, while varying somewhat in proportion to activity, do not vary in exact proportion to it and are usually referred to as semivariable costs.

Fixed costs are those which remain relatively constant over a considerable range of activity. Rent, property taxes, and insurance are examples of fixed costs. No category of cost can remain fixed indefinitely. For example, after reaching a certain level of activity an enterprise will have to rent additional space thus bringing the rent expense to a new and higher level.

Costs can be classified in many additional ways depending on the purpose. Focusing on the problem of matching costs with revenues, we have *product costs* which attach to a specified good or service from which revenue is derived. Costs which cannot be identified with a product or service are called *period costs* because they can be identified only with the period in which they occur. We have already touched on this distinction of costs in our examination of inventory and related cost of goods sold accounting in Chapter 3. The allocation of costs to products sold and particularly manufactured products gives rise to a distinction among three major classes of cost:

1. *Direct product costs* represent charges which can be identified specifically with a product. Thus, for example, in a retailing business it is the cost of the item sold as well as the direct freight and other acquisition cost incurred in obtaining it. In a manufacturing enterprise it represents the specific or direct cost of material and labor entering the production of the item. Direct product costs generally vary in amount in direct proportion to revenues, a characteristic which results in their being classified as variable costs. Direct product costs are among the easiest costs to match with specific revenue flows.

2. The cost of materials acquired for resale or manufacture should logically include in addition to invoice costs such additional costs as receiving, inspecting, purchasing, and storing. In reality most enterprises find it impractical to allocate such costs or costs such as indirect labor directly to specific products. Consequently such *indirect costs* are allocated to relate products on some reasonable bases. Most fixed costs, such as depreciation or supervision, are treated as indirect overhead costs and are allocated to products or services on bases which attempt to reflect consumption or benefits derived.

3. *Joint product costs* are costs which cannot be identified with any of a number of products which they jointly benefit as for example is the case in the meat-processing industry. Such costs are usually allocated on some reasonable basis which may include that based on the selling prices of end products.

Having outlined some basic aspects of cost behavior and the methods of cost allocation which have been devised in response to it, we shall now proceed to examine the accounting problems which are encountered in the measurement and allocation of major categories of costs and expenses. Generally, a cost is a measure of service potential or utility which may be utilized in one accounting period or another. Those costs which are to be matched with the revenue of future periods may be viewed as deferred costs and are shown as assets on the balance sheet. Major examples of such assets are inventories; property, plant, and equipment; intangibles; and deferred charges. The accounting problems of inventories are examined in Chapter 3. Property, plant, and equipment gives rise to allocations of costs in the form of depreciation and depletion, and they will be considered in this chapter. The allocation and amortization of intangibles and deferred charges have been examined in the chapter on asset measurement, and the income measurement aspects of these costs will be further considered in this chapter.

Generally, expenses are costs which are immediately chargeable to income. Most period costs become current expenses; and some categories of expense, such as selling and administrative, are not usually deferred to the future. The measurement of costs and expenses is complicated whenever a significant lapse of time occurs between the time of payment for or incurrence of the cost and the time of its utilization in the earning of revenues. The longer such lapse of time the more complicated and speculative such allocations and measurements become.

Let us now consider some important categories of costs and the principles governing their allocation to revenue.

Depreciation and depletion

The cost of assets which are in productive use, or otherwise income-producing, must be allocated or assigned to the time periods which comprise their useful life. It is a basic principle of income determination that income which benefits from the use of long-lived assets must bear a proportionate share of their cost. Thus, the cost of the long-lived assets should, at the end of their useful lives, have been charged to operations.

Depreciation is the process whereby the cost of property, plant, and equipment is allocated over its useful life. The purpose of depreciation is to recover from operations, by means of this allocation, the original cost of the asset. Consequently, if operations are not profitable, the depreciation becomes an unrecovered cost, that is, a loss. This is as true of depreciation as it is of any other cost which cannot be recovered because of inadequate revenues. The depreciation process in itself is not designed to provide funds for the replacement of an asset. That objective can only be achieved by means of a financial policy which accumulates funds for a specific purpose to be available at a given time.

The above principles of depreciation accounting are now so firmly established that there are no significant differences of opinion about them. Nevertheless, depreciation remains an expense item which is the subject of confusion and controversy among users of financial statements. The controversy and confusion stems from the methods and the assumptions on the basis of which the cost of assets is allocated to operations over their useful life.

Factors influencing the rate of depreciation

1. Useful life

Almost all assets are subject to physical deterioration. A major exception is land which is consequently not subject to depreciation. While the "indestructible powers of the earth" have an unlimited life-span, this quality does not insure a similar resistance to loss of economic value. Such loss is, however, not provided for by means of depreciation but is instead recognized as and when it occurs. The exhaustion of natural resources lodged in or above the earth is recognized by means of depletion accounting which will be discussed later.

Useful lives of assets can vary greatly. The *Depreciation Guidelines and Rules,* published by the Internal Revenue Service, list the useful life of warehouses as 60 years, while assets used in heavy construction are assumed to have a useful life of 5 years. The assumption as to the useful lives of assets should be based on economic and engineering studies, on experience, and on any other available information about an asset's physical and economic properties.

Physical deterioration is one important factor which limits the useful life of an asset. The frequency and quality of maintenance has a bearing on it. Maintenance can extend the useful life but cannot, of course, prolong it indefinitely.

Another limiting factor is obsolescence. Obsolescence is the impairment of the useful life of an asset due to progress or changes in technology, consumption patterns, and similar economic forces. Ordinary obsolescence occurs when technological improvements make an asset inefficient or uneconomical before its physical life is fully exhausted. Extraordinary obsolescence occurs when inventions of a revolutionary nature or radical shifts in demand take place. Electronic data processing equipment and propeller driven aircraft were subject to rapid obsolescence. The development of Xerography brought about extraordinary obsolescence in equipment using alternative methods of reproduction.

The integrity of the depreciation charge, and with it that of income determination, is dependent on a reasonably accurate estimate of useful life. That estimate should be determined solely by projections relating to physical life and economic usefulness and should not be influenced by management's desires with regard to the timing of income reporting.

2. Methods of allocation

Once the useful life of an asset has been determined, the amount of the periodic depreciation cost depends on the method used to allocate the asset's cost over its useful life. As will be seen hereunder, that cost can vary significantly depending on which method is chosen from the array of acceptable alternatives available:

Straight-line method. This method of depreciation assigns the cost of the asset over its useful life on the basis of equal periodic charges. Thus, in Table 8-1 we can see how an asset which cost $110,000, has

TABLE 8-1
Straight-line method of depreciation

Year	Depreciation	Accumulated depreciation	Undepreciated asset balance
			110,000
1	10,000	10,000	100,000
2	10,000	20,000	90,000
3	10,000	30,000	80,000
4	10,000	40,000	70,000
5	10,000	50,000	60,000
6	10,000	60,000	50,000
7	10,000	70,000	40,000
8	10,000	80,000	30,000
9	10,000	90,000	20,000
10	10,000	100,000	10,000

an estimated useful life of 10 years, and an estimated salvage value of $10,000 at the end of that period is depreciated. Every one of the 10 years is charged with an allocation of one tenth of the asset's cost less the estimated salvage value.

The basic rationale of the straight-line depreciation method is that the process of physical deterioration occurs uniformly over time. This is a more valid assumption with regard to fixed structures than with regard to, say, machinery where utilization or running time is a more important factor. Moreover, the other element of depreciation, that is, obsolescence, does not necessarily occur at a uniform rate over time. However, in the absence of concrete information on the probable rate of actual depreciation in the future, the straight-line method has the advantage of simplicity. This faculty, perhaps more than any other, accounts for the method's popularity and widespread adoption in practice.

There are other theoretical flaws in the straight-line depreciation method. If the service value of an asset is to be charged evenly over its useful life, then the loss of productivity and the increased maintenance costs should not be ignored. Under the straight-line method, however, the depreciation charges in the first years is the same as in the last years when the asset can be expected to be less efficient and to require higher cost of repairs and maintenance.

Another objection to the straight-line method, one which is of particular interest to the financial analyst, is that it results in a distortion in the rate of return on capital by introducing a built-in increase in this return over the years. Assuming that the asset depreciated in Table 8–1 is a heavy crane which yields a uniform return of $20,000 per year *before* depreciation, we can see that the return on investment will be as follows:

Year	Book value	Income before depreciation	Depreciation	Net income	Return on book value
1	$110,000	$20,000	$10,000	$10,000	9.1%
2	100,000	20,000	10,000	10,000	10.0
3	90,000	20,000	10,000	10,000	11.1
10	10,000	20,000	10,000	10,000	100.0

Increasing maintenance costs may render the constant "income before depreciation" assumption a bit too high but will not negate the overall effect of a constantly increasing return on investment. Obviously, this increasing return on the investment in an aging asset is not an entirely realistic portrayal of the economic realities of investments. Under accelerated methods of depreciation, this kind of distortion in the return on book value of the asset can be even more marked.

Decreasing charge method. The decreasing charge method of depreciation, also known as declining balance or accelerated depreciation, is a method whereby charges for depreciation decrease over the useful life of an asset.

The strongest support for this method arose from its approval by the Internal Revenue Code in 1954. Its value for tax purposes is obvious and relatively simple to understand. The earlier an asset is written off for tax purposes the larger amount of tax deferred to the future and the more funds are available for current operations.

The theoretical justification of the decreasing charge method of depreciation for financial accounting is not clear-cut. Arguments in its favor are that over the years an asset declines in operating efficiency and service value and that lower depreciation charges would offset the higher repair and maintenance costs which come with the older age of assets. Moreover, it is claimed that to compensate for the increasing uncertainty regarding the incidence of obsolescence in the future, the earlier years should bear a larger depreciation charge.

There are two principal methods of computing the decreasing charge to depreciation. One, the declining balance method applies a constant percentage to the declining asset balance. Given the salvage value (S), the original cost (C), and the number of periods over which the asset is to be depreciated (N), the rate (percentage) to be applied to the asset can be found by the following formula:

$$\text{Rate } (\%) = 1 - N\sqrt{\frac{S}{C}}.$$

In practice an approximation of the proper rate of declining charge depreciation is to take it at twice the straight-line rate. Thus an asset with an assumed 10-year useful life would be depreciated at a declining balance rate of 20 percent. This is referred to as the double-declining balance method.

The other method, involving simpler computations, is known as the sum-of-the-years'-digits method. Thus, the cost of an asset to be depreciated over a 5-year period is written off by applying a fraction whose denominator is the sum-of-the-years'-digits $(1 + 2 + 3 + 4 + 5)$, that is, 15 and whose numerator is the remaining life from the beginning of the period, that is, $5/15$ in the first year and $1/15$ in the last year of assumed useful life.

Table 8-2 illustrates the depreciation of an asset having a cost of

TABLE 8-2
Accelerated depreciation methods

	Depreciation		Cumulative amount	
Year	Double declining	Sum of the years' digits	Double declining	Sum of the years' digits
1	$22,000	$18,182	$22,000	$ 18,182
2	17,600	16,364	39,600	34,546
3	14,080	14,545	53,680	49,091
4	11,264	12,727	64,944	61,818
5	9,011	10,909	73,955	72,727
6	7,209	9,091	81,164	81,818
7	5,767	7,273	86,931	89,091
8	4,614	5,455	91,545	94,546
9	3,691	3,636	95,236	98,182
10	2,953	1,818	98,189	100,000

$110,000, a salvage value of $10,000, and an assumed useful life of 10 years under the double-declining balance method and the sum-of-the-years'-digits method. Since under the first method an asset can never be depreciated to a zero balance, salvage value is not deducted before applying the yearly rate (20 percent) to the original cost.

The main theoretical justifications for the decreasing charge method are that charges for depreciation should decrease over time so as to compensate for (1) increasing repair and maintenance charges; (2) decreasing revenues and operating efficiency; and, in addition, to give recognition to the uncertainty of revenues in the later years of assumed useful life.

Other methods of depreciation. A method of depreciation found in some industries, such as steel and heavy machinery, relates depreciation charges to activity or intensity of use. Thus, if a machine is assumed to have a useful life of 10,000 running hours, then the depreciation charge will vary with number of hours of running time rather than the lapse of time. In order to retain its validity it is particularly important that the initial assumption about useful life in terms of utilization be periodically reviewed in order to check its validity under changing conditions.

Another method of depreciation once advocated by some utilities but not now in general use is the compound interest method of depreciation. This method views an investment in property as the present value of anticipated earnings. Thus, the depreciation charge is the amount which, invested yearly at a capital cost rate, will equal the cost of the asset, less any salvage value, at the end of its useful life. The addition of this interest factor causes this method to result in systematically increasing depreciation over the years. One advantage claimed for it is that it will result in a more uniform rate of return on investment than is the case with the other methods.

Depletion. Depletion is the process by means of which the cost of natural resources is allocated on the basis of the rate of extraction and production. The essential difference between depreciation and depletion is that the former represents an allocation of the cost of a productive asset over time, and the latter represents the exploitation of valuable stocks such as coal deposits, oil pools, or stands of timber. Thus, in the case of depletion the proportionate allocation of cost is entirely dependent on production, that is, no production, no depletion.

The computation of depletion is easy to understand. If the cost of an ore body containing an estimated 10,000,000 recoverable tons is $5,000,000, then the depletion rate per ton of ore mined is $.50. A yearly production of 100,000 tons would result in a depletion charge of $50,000 and a cost balance in the asset account at the end of the year of $4,950,000. The analyst must be aware of the fact that here, as in the case of depreciation, a simple concept may nevertheless result in a multitude of complications. One is the reliability of the estimate of recoverable resources, and it should be periodically adjusted in accordance with experience and new information. Another is the definition of "cost," particularly in case of a property still in process of development. Also, in the case of oil fields, for example, the depletion expense will vary with the definition of what constitutes an "oil field," since the depletion computation is not based on individual wells but rather on entire fields. The depletion expense can vary with the definition of the boundaries of the field.

The argument, sometimes advanced, that the discovery value of a natural resource deposit is so great in relation to its cost that no depletion need be allowed for, is not a valid one nor is the argument that depletion should be ignored because of the very tenuous nature of the estimate of reserves.

Implication for analysis

Most companies utilize long-lived productive assets in their operations, and whenever this is the case, depreciation tends to become a significant cost of operations. If we add to this the fact, as we have seen in the foregoing discussion, that many subjective assumptions enter into the determination of useful lives of assets and that alternative methods of depreciation coexist and that these factors can result in widely differing depreciation charges, all "in accordance with generally accepted accounting principles," it is obvious that the financial analyst needs a thorough understanding of all the factors entering into the depreciation computation before he can assess a reported earnings figure or before he attempts to compare it with that reported by another company.

The information on depreciation methods presently available in corporate reports varies and, generally speaking, more is available in documents filed with the SEC than is available in annual reports. Thus, typically the more detailed information will contain the method or methods of depreciation in use as well as the range of useful lives assumptions which are applied to various categories of assets. Two things are obvious to the intelligent reader of this information. One is that it is practically useless for purposes of deriving any conclusion from it. After all, what can one conclude from a statement which talks about this or that method being used without a quantitative specification of the extent of its use and the assets to which it applies. The second is that this information is supplied because it is required and not because of the supplying company's conviction about its usefulness.

Giving the ranges of useful lives or depreciation rates looks more informative than it is. It actually contributes very little to the basic objectives of the analyst, that is, the ability to predict future depreciation charges or the ability to compare the depreciation charges of a number of companies in the same industry.

The typical information supplied appears something like this:

The annual rates of depreciation used were as follows:

Land improvements	2 –12½%
Buildings	2½–10
Machinery and equipment:	
Acquisitions prior to 1954	2 – 5
Acquisitions subsequent to 1953	5 –33⅓
Furniture and fixtures	6 –25

There is usually no identification of the relationship between the depreciation rates disclosed and the size of the asset pool to which such rates apply. Moreover, there is normally no identification between the rate used and the depreciation method applied, that is, which rates are used in conjunction with straight-line methods of depreciation and which with accelerated methods.

There are, of course, additional complications. While the straight-line method of depreciation enables the analyst to approximate future depreciation charges with some degree of accuracy, accelerated methods of depreciation make this task much more difficult unless the analyst is able to obtain from the company additional data not now disclosed in public reports.

Another problem area in depreciation accounting arises from differences in the methods used for book purposes and those used for tax purposes. Three possibilities exist here:

1. The use of straight-line depreciation methods for both book and tax purposes.
2. The use of straight-line depreciation for book purposes and accelerated methods for tax purposes. The favorable tax effect which results from the higher depreciation for tax purposes compared to that for book purposes is offset by the use of tax allocation which will be discussed later in this chapter. The advantage to the reporting company is the postponement of tax payments, that is, the cost-free use of funds.
3. The use of accelerated methods for both book and tax purposes. This method gives a higher depreciation charge than does method one in early years, and for an expanding company, even in subsequent years.

Unfortunately, the amount of disclosure about the impact of these differing methods is not always adequate. The best type of disclosure is the one which gives the amount of depreciation which would have been charged under a number of alternatives, such as, for example, what the difference in depreciation would have been under an accelerated method as opposed to a straight-line method. If a company gives the amount of deferred taxes which arose from accelerated depreciation for tax purposes, the analyst can get the approximate amount of extra depreciation due to acceleration by dividing the deferred tax amount by the current tax rate.

Analysts who have despaired of making meaning out of depreciation information have tended to ignore it altogether by looking at income before depreciation in comparing company results. As will be more thoroughly discussed in the chapter on fund flows, depreciation is an expense which derives from funds spent in the past and thus does not require the outlay of current funds. For this reason income before depreciation has also been called cash flow, an oversimplification for what is meant to be described as cash inflow from operations. This is, at best, a limited and superficial concept since it involves only selected inflows without considering a company's commitment to such outflows as plant replacement, investments, or dividends. Nor is this inflow strictly of a cash nature because funds provided by the recovery of depreciation charges from revenue are not necessarily kept as cash but may be invested in receivables, inventories, or other assets.

Another and even more dangerous misconception which derives from the cash flow concept, and against which the analyst must guard, is that depreciation is a kind of bookkeeping expense, somehow different from such expenses as labor or material and that it can be ignored or at least accorded less importance than is accorded to other expenses.

One reason for this thinking is the cash outlay aspect already mentioned above. This represents, of course, entirely fallacious thinking. The purchase of a machine with a useful life of, say, five years is, in effect, a prepayment for five years of services. Let us assume that the machine is a bottle-filling machine and that its task can be performed normally by a worker working eight hours a day. If, as is not common but quite feasible, we contract with the worker for his services for a five-year period and pay him for it in advance, we would obviously have to spread this payment over the five years of his work. Thus at the end of the first year, one fifth of the payment would be an expense and the remaining four-fifth prepayment would represent an asset in the form of a claim for future services. It requires little elaboration to see the essential similarity between the labor contract and the machine. In year 2 of the labor contract no cash is spent, but can there be any doubt about the validity of the bottle-filling labor cost? The depreciation of the machine is a cost of an essentially identical nature.

Another reason for doubts about the genuine nature of depreciation expense is related to doubts about the loss of value of the asset subject to depreciation. On further examination we can break these doubts into two major categories:

1. Doubts about the rate of loss in utility of productive equipment.
2. Doubts about loss in market value of assets such as real estate.

1. When we see one airline depreciating a jet plane over eight years and another airline spreading the depreciation of an identical aircraft over, say, 12 years, we realize that depreciation rates are matters of opinion. What is not a matter of opinion is that the effect on income of such differing assumptions can be significant and can distort comparisons. Thus, the effect must be assessed by the analyst as best as he can in the light of industry practice as well as the apparent reason-

ableness of the useful life assumption. While there may be some guidelines about useful lives of assets for tax purposes, there are practically none for financial accounting purposes. Auditors are not specialists in the longevity or useful life of equipment, and they will challenge management's estimates only when they are way out of line with industry practice or recorded experience. Where recorded experience is nonexistent, as in the case of a new industry such as computer leasing, the auditor's willingness to question management's estimate is further reduced. All this leaves a great deal of room for interpretation and income manipulation. While it does nothing to render depreciation as less of a genuine expense than any other, it does raise questions about the proper allocation of a productive asset's cost over time. Moreover, as between two estimates of useful life on similar equipment in an industry, there is obviously more risk to the longer life assumption than to the lower.

The rate of write-off is another aspect of depreciation the analyst must be alert to. When the tax laws first permitted a variety of accelerations in the computation of depreciation, many companies adopted the method for both book and tax purposes. Later, however, a number of companies, such as those in the steel and paper industries, wanted to soften the impact of depreciation on reported income and switched back to the straight-line method while retaining accelerated methods for tax purposes. Such switching back and forth can usually not be said to be made in the interest of better reporting. Thus, though mostly unjustified and contributing to a discontinuity in comparability, it is nevertheless accepted by the accounting profession whose limited self-imposed responsibility it is to highlight the change and report its effect in the year in which it occurs. This practice along with the leeway allowed in setting useful lives has contributed in good measure to the skepticism regarding the measurement of depreciation expenses. APB *Opinion No. 20*, "Accounting Changes," which is more fully considered below, is designed to remedy this obvious reporting deficiency by insisting that changes be made only in the direction of "preferable" accounting principles. Since the concept of "preferable" in relation to accounting principles remains undefined, the analyst must retain a vigilant and critical attitude towards this area of accounting practice.

2. In the case of assets such as real estate, the problem of depreciation is somewhat different. For one thing, constant maintenance can prolong its useful life considerably more than can maintenance of, say, machinery or automobiles. Moreover, those who look at loss of market value as a true index of depreciation, claim that in times of rising price levels buildings gain rather than lose in value.

These are, however, not arguments against depreciation as such but rather questions of useful economic life and the proper time period over which an asset's cost should be written off. There is not more justification to a depreciation rate which is excessive than there is to one that is insufficient. Possibly, those companies which depreciate buildings at a rate exceeding their physical and economic decline do so in order to justify the rates they use for tax purposes. This procedure does not, however, result in proper income determination and must be understood as such by the analyst.

Rising real estate values are, of course, no reason to discontinue providing for depreciation. The adequacy of depreciation is dependent on many factors both physical and economic. The process of depreciation can be retarded but never abolished or reversed. The following note to the financial statements of Louis Lesser Enterprises, Inc., covering the year ended June 30, 1967, a period of generally rising prices, makes this clear:

> As a result of the general decline in certain aspects of the real estate industry, accentuated by conditions in the money market and continuing vacancy factors in certain of the Company's rental properties, management is of the opinion that the full cost of certain properties and investments in and advances to companies not majority owned will not be recovered in the normal course of operations or through sale. Accordingly, the carrying values of such properties and investments and advances have been reduced to the amount of expected recovery.

The losses above provided for exceeded $4 million in a year when the company's total revenues were only about $6 million. In retrospect it is clear that management and its auditors underestimated the process of depreciation and value erosion of the company's income-producing properties. The values of such properties depend more on their income-generating capacity under a variety of economic conditions than on physical characteristics and maintenance levels.

As the above case illustrates, it is not prudent to rely on temporary economic conditions or market quotations to redress overoptimism which results in the willful underestimation of depreciation. After all, the depreciation concept encompasses a number of factors such as physical life, economic usefulness, and technological and economic factors which affect obsolescence.

Changing price levels also introduce many complexities to the depreciation problem. Particularly in industries which are based on holdings of real estate, the argument is often advanced that rising prices (due in great measure to the decline in the purchasing power of money) obviate or reduce the need for depreciation charges. These arguments confuse the problems resulting from price level changes, which affect all accounts rather than only the fixed assets, with the function of depreciation which is designed to allocate the cost of an asset over its useful life. Price level changes in themselves do not, of course, prolong the useful life of an asset. The problem of price level changes must be dealt with fully and separately from that of depreciation. Price level problems will be examined in Chapter 12.

The analyst should realize that the variety of depreciation methods in use will cause not only problems of comparisons with other companies but also internal measurement problems. This is particularly true with regard to the rate of return earned on the carrying value (book value) of an asset subject to different methods of depreciation. As the following example shows, only the "annuity" method of depreciation provides a level return on investment over the useful life of an asset. This method is, however, rarely found in practice.

ILLUSTRATION. Assume that a machine costing $300,000 and having a useful life of five years with no salvage value generates a yearly income before taxes of $100,000. According to the annuity method of depreciation, the cost of depreciable assets is the present value of an anticipated stream of future services, determined at some rate of discount. In our illustration the assumed rate of discount is 19.86 percent. The following are the rates of return realized annually under (a) straight-line, (b) sum-of-the-years'-digits, and (c) annuity depreciation methods (which is identical to the sinking fund depreciation method):

Year	Income before depreciation	Depreciation	Income after depreciation	Asset book value at beginning of year	Rate of return
		a) Straight-line depreciation			
1	$100,000	$ 60,000	$ 40,000	$300,000	13.3%
2	100,000	60,000	40,000	240,000	16.7
3	100,000	60,000	40,000	180,000	22.2
4	100,000	60,000	40,000	120,000	33.3
5	100,000	60,000	40,000	60,000	66.7
	$500,000	$300,000	$200,000		
		b) Accelerated depreciation (sum-of-years'-digits)			
1	$100,000	$100,000	$ ...	$300,000	.0
2	100,000	80,000	20,000	200,000	10.0
3	100,000	60,000	40,000	120,000	33.3
4	100,000	40,000	60,000	60,000	100.0
5	100,000	20,000	80,000	20,000	400.0
	$500,000	$300,000	$200,000		
		c) Annuity depreciation			
1	$100,000	$ 40,421	$ 59,579	$300,000	19.86
2	100,000	48,450	51,550	250,570	19.86
3	100,000	58,076	41,924	211,129	19.86
4	100,000	69,612	30,388	153,053	19.86
5	100,000	83,441	16,559	83,441	19.86
	$500,000	$300,000	$200,000		

From the foregoing discussion it is clear that the accounting for depreciation, which is a very real and significant cost of operation, contains many pitfalls for the analyst. Moreover, the information frequently supplied in published reports is mostly useless from the point of view of meaningful analysis. Thus, the analyst has to approach the evaluation of this cost with an understanding of the factors discussed above and with an attitude of questioning independence. In assessing the depreciation provision, he may have to evaluate its adequacy by such measures as the ratio of depreciation expense to total asset cost as well as its relationship to other factors which affect its size.

QUESTIONS

1. Why does the financial analyst attach great importance to the analysis of the income statement?
2. What conditions should usually be met before revenue is considered realized?
3. Distinguish between the two major methods used to account for revenue under long-term contracts.
4. What is the difference between the "financial method" and the "operating method" in recognizing lease rental income?
5. To what aspects of revenue recognition must the financial analyst be particularly alert?
6. Can the analyst place reliance on the auditor's judgment of what constitutes a "material" item in the income statement?
7. Distinguish between (a) variable, (b) semivariable, and (c) fixed costs.
8. Depreciation accounting leaves a lot to be desired; and no real progress, from the analyst's point of view, is imminent. Comment on the following observation:
   "The analyst of course cannot accept the depreciation figure unquestioningly. He must try to find out something about the age and efficiency of the plant. He can obtain some help by comparing depreciation, current and accrued, with gross plant, and by comparisons among similar companies. Obviously, he still cannot adjust earnings with the precision that the accountant needs to balance his books, but the security analyst doesn't need that much precision."
9. What means of adjusting for inconsistencies in depreciation methods are sometimes employed by analysts? Comment on their validity.
10. Which method of depreciation would result in a level return on asset book values? Why?

9

Analysis of the income statement—II

THIS CHAPTER continues and concludes the discussion of the analysis of the income statement which was begun in Chapter 8.

PENSION COSTS AND OTHER SUPPLEMENTARY EMPLOYEE BENEFITS

Pension costs

Pensions are a major employee-benefit cost designed to contribute to security after retirement. Pension commitments by companies are formalized in a variety of ways by means of pension plans. As pensions grew in importance and in size as a significant cost of operations, so did the accounting for such costs become a matter of great significance.

APB *Opinion No. 8*, issued after years of loose accounting practice in this area, represents a significant improvement in the prescribed accounting for pension costs. Basically, the Opinion views pension costs as long term in nature because they encompass the entire work-span of a group or groups of employees. Thus, such costs must be provided for on an accrual basis based on the actuarial assumptions which govern the pension plan. Limitations of legal liability to pay pensions should not normally affect accruals which are based on an assumption of indefinite continuance of benefits. Nor should the method used to fund the pension obligation affect the accrual of proper cost. Funding of pension obligations is essentially a matter of financial management, and it may or may not coincide with proper accrual for accounting purposes, which is a decision as to the appropriate charge of pension costs against the operations of a given period.

APB *Opinion No. 8* establishes both a floor and a ceiling for the annual accrual of pension costs. Under *either* the minimum or the maximum pension cost provision, the *normal accrual cost* must be provided for. This must be arrived at by use of an actuarial cost method which is rational, systematic, and consistently applied and which relates to years after adoption of the pension plan.

The minimum and maximum cost provision is as follows:

Minimum pension cost provision:
1. The normal cost.
2. A provision of interest on unfunded prior service cost.
3. A supplementary provision called for in cases where the value of vested benefits at the beginning of the year are not reduced by at least 5 percent in relation to the comparable amounts at the end of the year. Such comparison should be made exclusive of any net increase of vested benefits occurring during the year. If a supplementary provision for vested benefits is required, the total pension provision may be the lesser of the amount computed above or on amount sufficient to make the aggregate annual pension provision equal to:
    a) The normal cost.
    b) Amortization of prior service cost on 40-year basis (including interest).
    c) Interest equivalents on the difference between the provisions for pension costs accrued and the amount of such costs actually funded.

Maximum pension cost provision:
1. The normal cost.
2. Ten percent of past service cost at inception of plan and of increases and decreases in prior service cost arising from plan amendments. Since the 10 percent includes an interest factor, it will require, depending on interest rate assumed, more than 10 years for full amortization.
3. Interest equivalents on the difference between provision for pension costs and the amount of such costs actually funded.

In the above context "past service cost" refers to the portion of the total pension cost that under the actuarial cost method in use is identified with periods prior to the adoption of the pension plan. "Vested benefits" refers to benefits accrued which are not contingent on the employee's continuing in the service of the employer.

APB *Opinion No. 8* generally aims at avoiding wide year-to-year fluctuations in pension costs. Consequently it proscribed the averaging of actuarial gains and losses as well as of unrealized appreciation or depreciation of fund investments.

To the extent that actual experience subsequent to an actuarial valuation differs from the actuarial assumptions (e.g., those relating to employee turnover, mortality or income yield of investments), actuarial gains or losses will arise. Under the Opinion such losses or gains should be spread or averaged over a period from 10 to 20 years.

The Opinion calls for recognition of unrealized appreciation or depreciation of fund assets in the determination of pension cost on a rational and systematic basis that avoids giving undue weight to short-term market fluctuations. Thus, the Opinion recommends the averaging of such appreciation or depreciation or its recognition on the basis of expected long-term performance.

The following is designed to illustrate the actual workings of the minimum-maximum pension cost provision approach. For purposes of this illustration, we assume the following:

```
Normal pension cost for the year (i.e., the
    cost arrived by an acceptable
    actuarial method). . . . . . . . . . . . . . . . . . . . $   400,000
Prior service cost:
    Unfunded at beginning of year . . . . . . . . . . . . .    3,000,000
    Funded in prior years . . . . . . . . . . . . . . . . .    2,000,000
Amortization of actuarial gains . . . . . . . . . . . . . .        7,000
Amortization of unrealized appreciation. . . . . . . . .           3,000
Unfunded pension accruals . . . . . . . . . . . . . . .          100,000
Actuarial value of vested benefits:
    Beginning of year. . . . . . . . . . . . . . . . . . . .  10,000,000
    End of year . . . . . . . . . . . . . . . . . . . . . .   10,600,000
Fund assets:
    Beginning of year. . . . . . . . . . . . . . . . . . . .   4,000,000
    End of year . . . . . . . . . . . . . . . . . . . . . .    4,800,000
Assumed rate of interest . . . . . . . . . . . . . . . . .           4%
```

Under the above assumptions the computation of minimum and maximum allowable provisions for current pension costs would be as shown at top of page 210.

APB *Opinion No. 8* also specified a greater degree of disclosure than hitherto required. The following are considered by the Board to be appropriate disclosures on pension plans:

1. A statement that such plans exist, identifying or describing the employee groups covered.
2. A statement of the company's accounting and funding policies.
3. The provision for pension cost for the period.
4. The excess, if any, of the actuarially computed value of vested bene-

210 Understanding corporate reports

		Minimum		
		A	B	Maximum
1.	Normal cost	$400,000	$400,000	$400,000
2.	Interest on unfunded prior service cost	120,000		
3.	Provision for vested benefits (Note 1)	95,000		
4.	Amortization of prior service cost:			
	I on a 40-year basis, interest included (Note 2)		252,500	
	II at 10% per year			500,000
5.	Interest on excess of prior years' accounting provisions over amounts actually funded		4,000	4,000
6.	Amortization of actuarial gains	(7,000)	(7,000)	(7,000)
7.	Amortization of unrealized asset appreciation	(3,000)	(3,000)	(3,000)
	Total	$605,000	$646,500	$894,000

The pension expense for the year may not exceed the maximum amount and may not be less than the lesser of columns A or B under the minimum provision caption.

Note 1: The provision for vested benefits is arrived at as follows:

		This year's valuation	Preceding valuation
1.	Actuarial value of vested benefits	$10,600,000	$10,000,000
2.	Amount of pension fund	4,800,000	4,000,000
3.	Unfunded amount (1 − 2)	$ 5,800,000	$ 6,000,000
4.	Net amount of balance sheet pension accruals	100,000	100,000
5.	Actuarial value of unfunded (unprovided for) vested benefits (3 − 4)	$ 5,700,000	$ 5,900,000
6.	5% of item 5 for prior year	295,000	
7.	Year-to-year change in item 5	200,000	
8.	Excess of item 6 over item 7 which represents provision for vested benefits	$ 95,000	

Note 2: Level annual charge which will amortize total prior service cost of $5,000,000 (with interest) on a 40-year basis; amortization will cease when the unfunded component of $1,500,000 has been amortized.

fits over the total of the pension fund and any balance sheet pension accruals, less any pension prepayments or deferred charges.

5. Nature and effect of significant matters affecting comparability for all periods presented, such as changes in accounting methods (actuarial cost method, amortization of past and prior service cost, treatment of actuarial gains and losses, etc.), changes in circumstances (actuarial assumptions, etc.), or adoption of amendment of a plan.

The following is considered by the Board to be an example of appropriate disclosure regarding pension plans:

The company and its subsidiaries have several pension plans covering substantially all of their employees, including certain employees in foreign countries. The total pension expense for the year was $ . . . . , which includes, as to certain of the plans, amortization of prior service cost over periods ranging from 25 to 40 years. The company's policy is to fund pension cost accrued. The actuarially computed value of vested benefits for all plans as of December 31, 19 . . . , exceeded the total of the pension fund and balance-sheet accruals less pension prepayments and deferred charges by approximately $ . . . . A change during the year in the actuarial cost method used in computing pension cost had the effect of reducing net income for the year by approximately $ . . . .

Other supplementary employee benefits

Social pressures, competition, and the scarcity of executive talent have led to the proliferation of employee benefits which are supplementary to wages and salaries. Some fringe benefits, such as vacation pay, bonuses, current profit sharing, and paid health or life insurance are clearly identifiable with the period in which they are earned or granted and thus do not pose problems of accounting recognition and accrual.

Other supplementary compensation plans, because of the tentative or contingent nature of their benefits, have not been accorded full or timely accounting recognition, but accounting pronouncements have recently resulted in improvements in this area.

Deferred compensation contracts are usually awarded to executives with whom the company wants to develop lasting ties and who are interested in deferring income to their post retirement and lower tax-bracket years. Generally, provisions in such contracts which specify an employee's undertaking not to compete or which specify his availability for consulting services are not significant enough to justify deferring the current recognition of such costs. Thus, APB *Opinion No. 12* requires that at least the present value of deferred compensation to be paid in the future "be accrued in a systematic and rational manner over the period of active employment from the time the contract is entered into, unless it is evident that future services expected to be received by the employer are commensurate with the payments or a portion of the payments to be made." Similar accruals are called for in cases of contracts which guarantee minimum payments to the employee or his beneficiaries in case of death.

Stock options are incentive compensation devices under which an executive receives the right to buy a number of shares at a certain price over a number of years and subject to conditions designed to identify him with the employer's interests.

The usual rationale advanced in defense of stock options is that business will be run better by managers who are important share owners. Options allow executives to build an estate and offer significant tax advantages.

In theory the accounting for stock options defines the compensation to be recognized as the excess of the fair value of the optioned shares, at the dates the options are granted, over the option price. In practice, since the spread, if any, between the market price and the option price at the date of grant is negligible, the compensation inherent in stock options was generally not recorded on the basis of lack of materiality.

APB *Opinion No. 25,* issued in 1972, "Accounting for Stock Issued to Employees," specifies that when stock options are granted, the excess of the market price of the stock over the option/price should be accounted for as compensation over the periods benefited. In this computation the discounting of market value to allow for restrictions placed on the use or disposition of the stock by the employee is not permitted.

Implications for analysis

In 1958 U.S. Steel Corporation suffered an earnings decline, and consequently it decided to cut employee benefit and pension contribution from a pre-1958 yearly level of around $250 million to about $140 million. Such an arbitrary regulation of pension cost was one of the undesirable practices which preceded APB *Opinion No. 8.* Others were "pay-as-you-go" pension accounting which reflected only the pension payments to employees actually retired and the "terminal funding" method which charged expenses with the cost of providing pensions for employees at the time of their retirement.

By providing for full and systematic accrual of all pension costs, APB *Opinion No. 8* has narrowed the areas of differences in pension accounting and improved the underlying theory. The financial analyst is, however, not yet entitled to assume that the intent of the APB Opinions will be adhered to in all cases. There remains a great deal of room for maneuvering in this area.

The question of materiality is one aspect of the problem. Thus, the 1968 annual report of the Youngstown Sheet and Tube Company contains the following note on pensions:

The company has contributory and noncontributory retirement plans covering hourly and salaried employees. It is the policy to accrue and fund pension costs each year in an amount approximating current service costs and interest on unfunded past service costs, adjusted for estimated long-term appreciation of trust fund assets. In determining 1968 pension costs actuarial assumptions as to the interest rate and the rate of appreciation of trust assets were increased to reflect investment experience, thus reducing pension costs by $3,300,000. Trust funds at December 31, 1968 were sufficient to cover the estimated liability for pensions already granted as well as pensions for those employees eligible for retirement.

We know that APB *Opinion No. 8* requires the spreading of actuarial gains and losses such as the $3.3 million reduction in pension costs of Youngstown. The apparent reason the benefit was all taken into 1968 rather than spread over 10 to 20 years is the lack of materiality of the $3.3 million as against an income before taxes of $61 million. However, if such changes are made frequently and are all deemed "immaterial" in relation to the particular year in which they were made, the cumulative effect on earnings may, nevertheless, be considerable thus defeating the intent of the pension cost Opinion.

Consider, moreover, part of the note on pension plans inserted by North American Rockwell Corporation in its financial statements:

> In 1966, amendments to North American Rockwell's principal retirement plans became effective and the actuarial method for computing retirement costs for these plans was changed from the entry-age normal method to the aggregate cost method. In 1968, certain revisions were made in actuarial assumptions and methods used in calculating costs for certain of North American Rockwell's pension and retirement plans. Under provisions of sales contracts in existence, these changes in accounting methods and retirement plan amendments did not have a material effect on consolidated net income for these years.

The financial analyst is left wondering here what relevance, in the determination of materiality, provisions of sales contracts have and what the change in pension costs, as a result of the revisions in actuarial assumptions, really was.

The accounting problem regarding stock options is serious. Basically there is a failure to reflect in operating costs compensation granted to employees. No serious student of accounting and finance can deny the real cost to a company of selling its shares at prices below what it could get on the open market. The justification of the lack of accounting for the cost of stock option is a sort of "coin clipping" operation whereby the small annual dilution of stockholder equity is overlooked without an assessment of its more significant cumulative effect.

The plain fact is that the compensation inherent in stock options is unrecorded under present generally accepted accounting principles. The improvements brought about by APB *Opinion No. 25* are more apparent than real. This Opinion continues the accounting profession's long-standing reluctance to face up to the fact that an option to buy a share of stock for a number of months or years at the current market price is a valuable privilege. The prices at which puts and calls as well as longer term warrants sell in the marketplace is adequate testimony to this.

In 1972 the United States Pay Board faced the problem of valuing stock options and decided that their value is equivalent to 25 percent of the fair market value of the stock at the date of grant plus the excess of fair market value of the shares over the option price at the time of grant (Regulation 201.76). This rule is somewhat arbitrary in that it may fail to take into account restrictions to which a stock option is subject or the length of its duration. Nevertheless, it proves that stock options can be valued, and this valuation is a far more realistic approach than that adopted by the accounting profession in this matter. Financial analysts may well use the Pay Board's valuation rule as a rough guide whenever they want to estimate the unbooked compensation inherent in stock option plans.

One saving feature in the stock option accounting problem is a development brought about through "the back door" by APB *Opinion No. 15* on "Earnings per Share." Under this Opinion, stock options which have a dilutive effect on earnings per share must enter into the computation of that figure, thus showing in this statistic some of the effect which is missing in the reported "net income" figure. The computation and evaluation of earnings per share is discussed in Chapter 10.

RESEARCH, EXPLORATION, AND DEVELOPMENT EXPENDITURES

Research, exploration, and development efforts are undertaken by business enterprises for a variety of reasons, all aiming at either short-term improvements or longer term profit and improved market position. Some research efforts are directed towards maintaining existing product markets while others aim at the development of new products and processes.

Types of research and development

One type of research is *basic* or *pure research,* that is, directed towards the discovery of new facts, natural laws, or phenomena without regard to the immediate commercial application to which the results may be put. Benefits from such research programs are very uncertain, but if successful, they may be among the most rewarding of all.

Unlike pure research, *applied research* is directed towards more specific goals such as product improvement or the perfection and improvement of processes or techniques of production.

Exploration is the search for natural resources of all kinds. Exploration is always an "applied" kind of activity in that it has a definite and known objective.

Development begins where research and exploration end. It is the activity devoted to bringing the fruits of research or the resources discovered by exploration to a commercially useful and marketable stage. Thus development may involve efforts to exploit a new product invention or it may involve the exploitation of an oil well, a mineral deposit, or a tract of timber.

Research and development may be one part of many activities of an ongoing enterprise or it may be the almost sole activity of an enterprise in its formative stages.

The accounting problem

The problem of accounting for research and development costs is difficult and defies easy solutions. There are a number of reasons for this, among which the most important are:

1. The great uncertainty of ultimate results which pervades most research efforts. Generally, the outcome of a research project is more uncertain than that of an immediately productive operation.
2. In most cases there is a significant lapse of time between the initiation of a research project and the determination of its ultimate success or failure. This, in effect, is another dimension of uncertainty.
3. Often the results of research are intangible in form, a fact which contributes to the difficulty of evaluation.

It is this all-pervading uncertainty of ultimate results which causes the difficulty in accounting for research and development costs rather than the absence of logical reasoning or a lack of clear objectives of accounting. Such objectives are clear and well known:

1. Costs should be matched with the revenues to which they are related.
2. Costs should not be deferred unless there is a reasonably warranted expectation that they will be recovered out of future revenues or will benefit future operations.

Thus, to this day, the accounting profession has not come up with an authoritative pronouncement on this subject. This is not due to a lack of interest or consideration of the subject but rather to an inability to come up with an agreement on criteria which are going to provide an improvement over the present loose theory on the subject. While there may be said to be a presumption in favor of current expensing of research costs, present-day accounting can be any one of a number of alternatives such as the following:

1. Charge income as the research expenditures are incurred.
2. Defer all expenditures and amortize them over a number of years.
3. Defer all expenditures and amortize successful research while writing off unsuccessful research as soon as that becomes apparent.
4. Charge off pure research as incurred and defer and amortize applied research and development.

5. Charge off pure and applied research as incurred and defer and amortize development costs.
6. Defer only research and development costs related to new products.
7. Provide a reserve for research costs by charges to income; charge all expenditures to the reserve.

While all of the above practices are in use, those described in 1 through 4 above are in far greater use than the subsequent ones. Some of the practices are due to the degree of uncertainty attaching to specific activities. Thus, the future benefits of pure research are most difficult to estimate, benefits from new product or process research are easier to estimate, while benefits from product and process improvement costs are even more susceptible to estimation. In the absence of definite criteria, practices are often influenced by a desire for specific reported results, by notions of conservatism, or by other considerations.

Practice indicates that it is considered acceptable accounting to defer research and development costs of companies in the development stage.

While it is difficult to estimate the future benefits from research and development outlays, it is even more difficult and speculative to estimate the future benefits to be derived from costs of training programs, product promotions, and advertising. Consequently deferral of such costs is very difficult to justify.

Exploration and development in extractive industries

The search for new deposits of natural resources is the function of a very important industry segment encompassing the oil, natural gas, metals, coal, and nonmetallic minerals industries. While the unique accounting problems of these industries deserve separate consideration, it should be borne in mind that no new accounting principles are involved here but rather the application of such principles and concepts to special circumstances. Thus, while the search for and development of natural resources is characterized by exposure to high degrees of risk, so is, as we have seen, the search for new knowledge, new processes, and new products. Risk involves uncertainty; and within a framework of periodic income determinations, uncertainty always presents very serious problems of income and expense determination.

In extractive industries the major problems lie on the cost and expense side. Essentially, the problem is one of whether exploration and development costs which may reasonably be expected to be recoverable out of the future lifting of the natural resources should be charged in the period incurred or should be capitalized and amortized over future recovery and production.

While many companies charge off all exploration costs currently, some charge off only a portion and capitalize another portion. A few companies capitalize almost all development costs and amortize them over future periods.

The following note in Sun Oil Company's financial statements illustrates the variety of principles in use:

. . . Sunray has followed the generally accepted accounting principle prevalent throughout the industry of capitalizing intangible development costs and charging income for the amortization thereof over a period of years. Sun's method, which is also in accordance with generally accepted accounting principles, has been to charge these costs to expense as incurred. . . .

The accounting profession has recognized that the divergent practices create a need for reforms in this area. As a first step, *Accounting Research Study No. 11*, "Financial Reporting in the Extractive Industries," recommends, among others, that:

Expenditures for prospecting costs, indirect acquisition costs and most carrying costs should be charged to expense when incurred as part of the current cost of exploration.

Direct acquisition costs of unproved properties should be capitalized and the estimated loss portion should be amortized to expense on a systematic and rational basis as part of the current cost of exploration.

Unsuccessful exploration and development expenditures should be charged to operations even though incurred on property units where commercially recoverable reserves exist.

The adoption, in practice, of these as well as the other guidelines of the study, including rational bases of deferred cost amortization, will go a long way towards improving accounting in this important segment of industry.

In mid-1973 the Committee on Extractive Industries of the APB rendered its final report with the purpose of providing the FASB with a summary of the Committee's research in accounting for the oil and gas industry. The Committee stated:

Throughout the Committee's deliberations it became increasingly clear that there exists in practice two basic concepts or philosophies regarding accounting in the oil and gas industry; namely, full-cost accounting and successful efforts accounting. The basic concept of the full-cost method is that all costs, productive and non-productive, incurred in the search for oil and gas reserves should be capitalized and amortized to income as the total oil and gas reserves are produced and sold. The basic concept of the successful efforts method is that all costs which of themselves do not result directly in the discovery of oil and gas reserves have no future benefit in terms of future revenues and should be expensed as incurred. It was equally clear that the application of the two concepts in practice varies to such an extent that there are in fact numerous different methods of accounting.

The Committee then pointed out the dilemma which faces anybody charged with narrowing accounting alternatives in areas affected by strong industry interests:

All attempts by the Committee to find the one theoretically best method of accounting in the oil and gas industry met with vehement resistance from either one or both of the factions supporting the alternative methods of accounting. The results of the aborted attempts to find one method of accounting also make it clear that the major issue is whether or not the two basic methods of accounting for the oil and gas industry should be allowed as equally acceptable alternatives.

Implications for analysis

The evaluation of research and development expenditures poses serious problems to the analyst of financial statements. Often the size of these expenditures is such that they must be taken into account in any analysis of the income statement. Moreover, regardless of the variety of allowable methods of accounting for such costs, their impact on future earning power must be assessed. A number of difficulties should be noted here.

In order to assess on his own the importance and possible impact of research and development outlays, the analyst needs a great deal of information. Even today there are no minimum disclosure requirements with respect to this important cost, and we can find many cases where even the total amount remains undisclosed. The revised Regulations S-X promulgated by the SEC call for disclosure of research and development costs.

In order to form an opinion on the quality and potential of research outlays, the analyst needs to know, of course, far more than the total amount of research and development outlays. He needs information on the type of research performed, the areas covered, and the success experienced to date. Such information is rarely, if ever, publicly disclosed.

Accounting practices with regard to research and development costs may serve a number of objectives such as objectivity, consistency, conservatism, etc., but they do not serve the needs of the analyst. Thus, conservatism may call for the current expensing of costs which may hold significant benefits for the future. This in turn causes a mismatching of current costs and revenues and also causes assets to be understated. The concern with objectivity and verifiability causes purchased research in the form of a patent to be capitalized and amortized while leading to the write-off of equally valuable internally developed research.

The freedom of choice among the variety of methods of accounting for research and development is contributing to a situation where those companies which are successful and strong financially and where the probability of success is larger expense their research outlays, while small and speculative companies subject to high risk and uncertainty defer such costs because of inadequate revenues to charge them against. The analysts should in all cases consult the auditor's opinion for references to the future realizability of such costs. As is pointed out in the chapter on the auditor's opinion, the disclaimer which pleads inability to assess the future benefits from such outlays is often an evasion which is unfortunately of little help to the reader. Compounding the difficulty is a lack of disclosure of the data which served as a basis for the auditor's conclusions with regard to the future recoverability of deferred research and development costs.

It is obvious that no useful generalization about the impact on the analyst's work of the variety of accounting methods for research and development costs can be made. The degree of disclosure made and all the surrounding circumstances must be assessed. Thus, for instance, in companies having on-going research programs with permanent staffs and regular research budgets, the difference between current expensing and the deferral and amortization of research costs may not be very significant. On the other hand, in situations where research efforts and expenses vary significantly from period to period, the best accounting and analysis must be based on an estimate of what benefits present outlays hold for the future. With regard to exploration and development costs in the extractive industries, the analyst faces at present the problem of a variety of acceptable methods of treating such costs. This in turn hampers the comparison of results among companies in the same industry. Hopefully the profession is moving towards the establishment of more uniform rules for the treatment of such costs. Even the establishment of such uniform rules will not solve all of the analyst's problems in this area. The considerations entering into the measurement and allocations of these costs are so complex and varied (e.g., what constitutes a unit of production?) as to allow for a great deal of diversity of treatment. Moreover, in the quest for uniformity, accounting rules must inevitably be somewhat arbitrary. This may lead to the current expensing of costs holding benefits for future operations. The analyst must be aware of these possibilities and adjust for them on the basis of the information available to him.

GOODWILL

Finally in a consideration of intangible costs, we should add here to the discussion of goodwill which was begun in the chapter on asset measurement.

Goodwill is usually the measure of value assigned to a rate of earnings above the ordinary. It is, in some respects, similar to the premium paid for a bond because its coupon rate exceeds the going interest rate. That goodwill has value at the time it is purchased cannot be disputed. Otherwise corporations would be spending billions for assets devoid of value. The real problem with the accounting for purchased goodwill is that of measuring its expiration. There is no need to write off against earnings an asset whose value does not expire. Land is a prominent example of this. However, the difficulty of measuring the expiration of the continuing value of goodwill is not a valid reason for completely ignoring the problem. Goodwill can, at times, be the major part of the consideration paid for a going business. Thus, Standard & Poor's Corporation reported as follows:

. . . Standard & Poor's purchased all the stock of Trendline Corp. and O. T. C. Publications, Inc., for a price of approximately $2,425,000, which exceeded the net tangible assets of the acquired companies by $2,154,061. That amount was charged to goodwill.

The Company's policy as to goodwill is one of periodic review with a view to establishing an amortization program in the event that future results render it appropriate. At present an amortization program has not been established since the value is considered to be of a permanent nature.

As can be seen in the more comprehensive discussion of the subject in Chapters 4 and 6, APB *Opinion No. 17* requires that the excess paid over fair market value of net assets acquired in a purchase, that is, goodwill, be amortized to income over a period not to exceed 40 years.

Implications for analysis

One of the most common solutions applied by analysts to the complex problems of the analysis of goodwill is to simply ignore it. That is, they ignore the asset shown on the balance sheet. As for the income statement they have the assistance of accountants in trying to ignore its effect, that is, the amortization of goodwill has in the past been the exception rather than the rule. Moreover, even in those cases where amortization occurred, the expense is treated with a skepticism which implies a questioning of its real nature.

As was already noted in Chapter 4, by ignoring goodwill, analysts ignore investments of very substantial resources in what may often be a company's most important asset.

Ignoring the impact of goodwill on reported periodic income is, of course, also no solution to the analysis of this complex cost. Thus, even considering the limited amount of information available to the analyst, it is far better that he understand the effects of accounting practices in this area on reported income rather than dismiss them altogether.

Goodwill is measured by the excess of cost over the *fair market value* of tangible net assets acquired in a transaction accounted for as a purchase. It is the excess of the purchase price over the fair value of all the tangible assets acquired, arrived at by carefully ascertaining the value of such assets. That is the theory of it. At least up to 1970 when APB *Opinion No. 17* took effect, companies have failed to assign the full fair market value to tangible assets acquired and have, instead, preferred to relegate as much of the purchase price as possible to an account bearing the rather literally descriptive, but meaningless, title of "excess of cost over book value of assets acquired." The reasons for this tendency are simple to understand. Costs assigned to such assets as inventories, plant and equipment, patents, or future tax benefits must all ultimately be charged to income. Goodwill, prior to APB *Opinion No. 17*, had to be amortized only when its value was impaired or was expiring and such a judgment was difficult to prove let alone to audit or second-guess. Thus, many companies have included much of the cost of acquisition over the book value on the *seller's* books in the "excess of cost . . ." account and thereafter proceeded to claim that the amount is not amortized because its value to the enterprise is undiminished. We may add here that since the amortization of goodwill is not a tax-deductible expense, its deduction for financial reporting purposes has a magnified adverse impact which managements desire to avoid. The change in accounting requirements toward mandatory amortization will change the effects of the aforementioned practices over time. Financial analysts should, however, be aware of the large stagnant "pools" of goodwill which will remain on the books of many corporations.

Thus, the financial analyst must be alert to the makeup and the method of valuation of the Goodwill account as well as to the method of its ultimate disposition. One way of disposing of the Goodwill account, frequently chosen by management, is to write it off at a time when it would have the least serious impact on the market's judgment of the company's earnings, for example, a time of loss or reduced earnings. The write-off is usually shown as an extraordinary item, and a tax deduction may be available at that time. Thus, for example, Fred Mayer, Inc., reported this as follows:

During 1968 management determined that goodwill which arose in 1965 upon the purchase of certain stores had no material value to future years' operations. Five of the stores acquired in 1965 were sold in 1969 and the Company intends to sell the remaining store. The stores sold contributed approximately 5% of total 1968 consolidated sales. The Company does not expect to recover its cost of $495,175 for the goodwill. Therefore, the goodwill has been written off in 1968 as an extraordinary item of $225,175, after reduction of $270,000 for the related income tax effect.

Under normal circumstances goodwill is not indestructible but is rather an asset with a limited useful life. Whatever the advantages of location, of market dominance and competitive stance, of sales skill or product acceptance, or other benefits are, they cannot be unaffected by the passing of time and by changes in the business environment. Thus, the amortization of goodwill gives recognition to the expiration of a resource in which capital has been invested, a process which is similar to the depreciation of fixed assets. The analyst must recognize that a 40-year amortization period, while adhering to minimum accounting requirement, which represents a compromise position, may not be realistic in terms of the time expiration of economic values. Thus, he must assess the propriety of the amortization period by reference to such evidence of continuing value as the profitability of units for which the goodwill consideration was originally paid.

INTEREST COSTS

The interest cost to an entity is the nominal rate paid including, in the case of bonds, the amortization of bond discount or premium. A complication arises when companies issue convertible debt or debt with warrants, thus achieving a nominal debt coupon cost which is below the cost of similar debt not enjoying these added features.

After trial pronouncements on the subject and much controversy, APB *Opinion No. 14* has concluded that in the case of *convertible debt* the inseparability of the debt and equity features is such that no portion of the proceeds from the issuance should be accounted for as attributable to the conversion feature.

In the case of debt issued with stock warrants attached, the proceeds of the debt attributable to the warrants should be accounted for as paid-in capital. The corresponding charge is to a debt discount account which must be amortized over the life of the debt issue, thus increasing the effective interest cost.

Interest, being an expense that accrues with the lapse of time, is generally regarded as a period cost. In certain instances, however, such as in long-term capital projects which require financing during construction, interest may be deferred and included as part of the cost of the asset. This practice is particularly prevalent in public utility accounting. As an example of practice in industrial companies, Allan Wood Steel Company noted that: "Interest expense related to the financing of additional steel making facilities is being capitalized during the period of construction. The amount capitalized during 1967 was $1,363,991."

Implications for analysis

Financial analysts should realize that in spite of the position taken in APB *Opinion No. 14,* there are many who disagree with the Opinion's position on convertible debt. The dissenters, which include members of the APB, contend that by ignoring the value of the conversion privilege and instead using as a sole measure of interest cost the coupon rate of interest, the Opinion specifies an accounting treatment which ignores the true interest cost to the corporation.

It should be noted, however, that APB *Opinion No. 15* on "Earnings per Share" by requiring, in specified circumstances, the inclusion in the computation of earnings per share of the number of shares issuable in the event of conversion of convertible debt, in effect creates a cost additional to the coupon interest cost by thus diluting the reported earnings per share figure.

INCOME TAXES

Income taxes are a very substantial cost of doing business. In most cases they will amount to roughly half a corporation's pretax income. It follows that the accounting for income taxes is an important matter which should be clearly understood. This discussion is not concerned with matters of tax law but rather with the accounting principles which govern the proper computation of the periodic tax expense. APB *Opinion No. 11* is the accounting profession's authoritative pronouncement on this subject.

The current provision for taxes is governed by any number of tax regulations which may apply in a given situation. Regulations such as those concerning the depletion allowance or capital gains treatment can reduce the effective tax rate of a corporation below normal levels. Proper disclosure requires that information be given regarding the reasons for deviations from normal tax incidence.

Treatment of tax loss carry-backs and carry-forwards

A corporation incurring an operating loss may carry such loss *back;* and if it cannot be fully utilized in the preceding three years, it may be carried *forward* for five years. The status of a tax loss *carry-back* is usually simple to determine: either it is available or it is not. The value of a tax loss *carry-forward* depends on a company's ability to earn taxable income in the future, and that in most cases is not a certainty.

Thus, the tax effects of a tax loss carry-back should be recognized in the determination of the results of the loss period. The benefits of tax loss carry-forward should not normally be recognized until they are actually realized. The only exception to this rule occurs in unusual circumstances when realization of the tax loss carry-forward is assured "beyond any reasonable doubt."

Tax reductions resulting from tax loss carry-forwards are, if material, shown as extraordinary credits so as not to distort the normal relationship prevailing between a company's income and the tax to which it is subject.

Tax allocation

It is well known that financial accounting, which is governed by considerations of fair presentation of financial position and results of operations, does not share in all respects the principles which govern the computation of taxable income. Thus, there are a great many cases of difference between tax and "book" accounting. Some of the differences are permanent, that is, they are not equalized over time. For example, certain items of revenue, such as interest on municipal bonds, are excludable from taxable income, while certain expenses, such as premiums on officers' life insurance, are not deductible for tax purposes.

Another type of tax-book difference stems from the timing of the inclusion of such items for book purposes as opposed to tax purposes.

ILLUSTRATION. For financial accounting purposes a company depreciates a $1,000 asset over 10 years on a straight-line basis. To conserve its cash, the company elects for tax purposes to use the double declining-balance method of depreciation. In the first year the book depreciation is $100 while the tax depreciation is $200. In later years, the book depreciation will exceed the tax depreciation because under either method the total depreciation cannot exceed $1,000. Thus the difference is one of timing.

There are a variety of timing differences between tax and financial accounting. The following are some examples:

1. Revenue or income is deferred for tax reporting purposes but is recognized in the current period for financial reporting purposes.
    a) The installment method is used for tax purposes; the accrual method is used for financial reporting purposes.
    b) The completed-contract method is used for tax purposes; the percentage-of-completion method is used for financial reporting purposes.
2. Expenses deducted for tax purposes in the current period exceed expenses deducted for financial reporting purposes.
    a) Accelerated depreciation is taken for tax purposes; straight-line depreciation is used for financial reporting purposes.
    b) Pension costs are deducted earlier for tax purposes than for financial reporting purposes.
    c) Research and development, land reclamation, and similar costs are deducted for tax purposes; capitalization and amortization are utilized for financial reporting purposes.

3. Revenue or income is recognized for tax purposes in the current period, but all or part of the amount is deferred for financial reporting purposes.
   a) Rent income or other income received in advance is recognized for tax purposes.
   b) Unearned finance charges and other deferred credits are recognized for tax purposes but are taken into income over a number of years for financial reporting purposes.
4. Expenses deducted for financial reporting purposes in the current period exceed expenses deducted for tax purposes.
   a) Estimated expenses (repair and maintenance, warranty servicing costs, and vacation wages) are accrued for financial reporting purposes but not deducted for tax purposes.
   b) Estimated refunds due the government for price redetermination and renegotiation are accrued for financial reporting purposes.

The basic problem with these timing differences, from the accounting point of view, is that there will be differences between the income before tax shown in the income statement and the taxable income shown in the tax return. Thus, if the actual tax paid is considered as the period expense, it will not match the pretax income shown in the income statement. This would violate the basic accounting principle that there should be a matching of income and related costs and expenses. Interperiod tax allocation is designed to assure that in any one period income shown in the financial statements is charged with the tax applicable to it regardless of how such income is reported for tax purposes.

The following example will illustrate the principle of tax allocation:

A retailer sells air conditioners on the installment basis. On January 1, 19x1, he sells a unit for $720 payable at the rate of $20 a month for 36 months. For purposes of this illustration, we ignore finance charges and assume a gross profit to the retailer of 20 percent and a tax rate of 50 percent.

In accordance with proper accrual accounting, the retailer will recognize in the year of sale (19x1) a gross profit of $144 (20 percent of $720). For tax purposes he can recognize profit based on actual cash collections as follows:

	Cash collection	Taxable gross profit (20%)	Actual tax payable
19x1	$240	$ 48	$24
19x2	240	48	24
19x3	240	48	24
Total	$720	$144	$72

In the absence of tax allocation the results shown by the retailer on this transaction would be as follows:

	Pretax profit	Tax payable	Profit (loss)
19x1	$144	$24	$120
19x2	...	24	(24)
19x3	...	24	(24)
Total	$144	$72	$ 72

The flaws in this presentation are readily apparent. The book profit of 19x1 does not bear its proper share of tax, thus resulting in a profit overstatement of $48, which distortion is carried over to 19x2 and 19x3, whose profits will be understated by $24 each because they will bear a tax without inclusion of the revenues which gave rise to it. Moreover, this kind of accounting would appear to suggest that in 19x1 our retailer is more profitable than his competitor who may have sold the air conditioner for cash ($720), realized a gross profit of $144, and paid a tax of $72, thus realizing an after-tax profit of $72 (versus $120 on the installment sale).

Tax allocation is designed to remedy the above distortions by means of a deferred tax account, which results in the matching of tax with the corresponding revenue as follows:

		Taxes				
Year	Pretax profit	Actually payable	Deferred	Total	After-tax profit	Deferred tax account
19x1	$144	$24	$ 48	$72	$72	$48
19x2	...	24	(24)	...	...	24
19x3	...	24	(24)	...	...	...

APB *Opinion No. 11* has adopted the position that the deferred tax account (e.g., the $48 in 19x1) is not a liability but rather a deferred credit meaning an equalization account which is used to achieve a matching of income and expense. Such an equalization account would appear on the asset side as a deferred charge when, due to timing differences, the taxable income is higher than the book income. The present-day emphasis on the importance of the income statement has resulted in balance sheet items designed specifically to serve such expense and revenue allocation purpose. The deferred tax account may also be viewed as a source of funds, and this aspect will be discussed further in Chapter 11.

The above installment sale example is a simplification of a complex process. While the tax deferral pertaining to the *specific* air conditioner is, as shown in the example, completely extinguished at the end of the third year, the aggregate tax deferral account will usually not behave this way. Thus, if another air conditioner is sold in 19x2, the aggregate deferred tax account will stay the same; and if a growing number of air conditioners are sold, the deferred tax account will also grow. In the case of tax-book differences attributed to depreciation, where the assets are long lived, the deferred tax account may grow over the years or at least stabilize. A study by Price Waterhouse & Company of 100 major corporations concluded that the bulk of the deferred tax accounts were not likely to be "paid off" or drawn down. There are also those who claim that only taxes actually due should be accrued. While the matter of accepted accounting practice for taxes has been settled by APB *Opinion No. 11,* the controversy surrounding it has not ended.

Another form of tax allocation concerns the distribution of the tax effect within the various segments of the income statement and the retained earnings of a period. The basic principle here is that each major category should be shown net of its tax effect. Thus, for example, an extraordinary item should be shown net of its appropriate tax effect so that the tax related to operating results is properly stated. This is known as *intra*period allocation.

Investment tax credit

The investment tax credit has been used as an instrument of economic policy for the stimulation of capital investment when this is deemed a desirable objective. Thus, for example, the 7 percent investment credit was allowed in the year of an asset's acquisition. An industrial company acquiring an asset of $100,000 would have its tax bill for the year reduced by $7,000.

The APB has repeatedly tried to obtain acceptance of an accounting treatment whereby the investment credit benefit would be spread over the useful life of the asset acquired. The basic argument in favor of this method is that one does not enhance earnings by the act of buying assets but rather by using them. Under the deferral method, if the above-mentioned asset has a useful life of 10 years, the $7,000 investment credit would be taken into income (as a reduction of taxes) at the rate of $700 per year.

The APB has not been successful in obtaining acceptance of this view. The position of those who favor the immediate reflection of the investment credit in income (also known as the "flow-through" method) is that the investment credit is a selective reduction in taxes unrelated to the use of the asset. The "flow-through" method of taking the investment credit into income in the year of the asset purchase is in more widespread use than the deferral method. Both methods enjoy the label of "generally accepted accounting principles."

Implications for analysis

Taxes are almost always substantial expense items, and the analyst must be sure that he understands the relationship between pretax income and the income tax expense. Proper disclosure requires an explanation of any deviations from the expected or normal tax level, but this is unfortunately not always the case. Thus, the analyst must be prepared to supplement whatever disclosure he finds with an understanding of possible reasons for changes in the effective tax rate within an industry or due to special circumstances.

The analyst should note that the procedures applied to loss carry-forwards differ from those applied to carry-backs. While the tax loss carry-back represents a reduction of tax in the loss year and is recognized as such, a loss carry-forward which should have a similar impact is not so recognized because its realization is not usually "assured beyond any reasonable doubt." Thus, in this situation the "realization convention" in accounting takes precedence over the "matching concept." The subsequent actual realization of a tax loss carry-forward is designated as an extraordinary item so as to indicate that it has really nothing to do with the normal tax for the year.

In spite of all the heated arguments surrounding tax allocation, it is obvious that this accounting principle makes an important contribution to proper tax accrual and, hence, income reporting. It separates tax strategy from the reporting of results of operations, thus removing one possibility of management determining the size of results by means of bookkeeping techniques alone.

Another good argument for tax allocation, from an analytical point of view, is the fact that assets whose future tax deductibility is reduced cannot be worth as much as those which have a higher tax deductibility. Thus, for example, if two companies depreciate an identical asset costing $100,000 under different tax methods of depreciation which result in a first-year depreciation of $10,000 and $20,000 respectively, then it is obvious that at the end of that year, one company has an asset which it can still depreciate for tax purposes to the tune of $90,000 while the other can depreciate it only to the extent of $80,000. Obviously the two assets are not equally valuable, and the tax deferral adjustment recognizes this fact.

One of the flaws remaining in tax allocation procedures is that no recognition is given to the fact that the present value of a future obligation, or loss of benefits, should be discounted rather than shown at par as today's tax deferred accounts actually are. This was a question which was also debated within the APB, but the Board decided to postpone a decision on this matter.

An error sometimes committed by analysts is to assume that deferred tax accounting acts as a complete offset to differences between tax and financial accounting methods. Actually, if we assume that the accelerated depreciation method used for tax purposes is more realistic than the straight-line method used in reporting income, then the effect of deferred taxes is to remove only approximately *half* of the overstatement of income which results from the use, for book purposes, of the slower depreciation method.

Accounting for the investment credit is subject to two very different acceptable alternatives. In our example of the company which buys a 10-year life asset for $100,000, one allowable method is to take the $7,000 investment credit into income in the first year while under the alternative, and preferred method, only $700 is so taken into the first year income. It is obvious that the $6,300 tax difference on a $100,000 asset purchase may have a significant impact on results and on intercompany comparability. The fact is that the "flow-through" method enjoys substantial acceptance and the analyst must be aware of this in his evaluation of relative results.

EXTRAORDINARY GAINS AND LOSSES

Most items of revenue and cost discussed so far in this chapter are of the ordinary operating and recurring variety. Thus, it can be assumed that their inclusion in the income statement results in a figure which is a fair reflection of the period's operating results. Such reported results are a very important element in the valuation of securities, in the evaluation of managements, and in many other respects; and they are used as indicators of a company's earning power. Consequently, ever since the income statement became the important financial statement it is today, the treatment of unusual and extraordinary gains and losses and prior period adjustments has been a major problem area of income measurement and reporting.

Extraordinary items are distinguished by their unusual nature *and* by the infrequency of their occurrence. Examples of extraordinary items include substantial uninsured losses from a major casualty (such as an earthquake) or a loss from an expropriation.

Items affecting results of prior years are those representing adjustments of charges and credits incurred in prior years that have proved, in the light of subsequent experience or knowledge, to be either inadequate or excessive. The following are examples of situations that would produce such items:

1. Agreement is reached on settlement of a tax liability relating to a prior year.

2. A contract price adjustment for work performed in a prior year is collected.

In most cases there is no question about the propriety of including these items in the determination of net income. The only question is how to present them in a period subsequent to the one to which they belong.

There are two main schools of thought on how to handle extraordinary gains and losses. One is the "all-inclusive" concept, which gives recognition in determining net income to all items affecting the change in equity interests during the period except dividend payments and capital transactions. The other is the so-called "current-operating-performance" concept. This concept would exclude from net income any items which, if included, would impair the significance of the net income as a measure of current earning power. Much as the latter concept has to commend it, under this concept, prior to 1966, actual income reporting practice had deteriorated to such an extent that a complete reversal in philosophy and approach became necessary. APB *Opinion No. 9*, issued in 1966, instituted these changes to a considerable degree.

The Opinion adopted the following position:

17. The Board has considered various methods of reporting the effects of extraordinary events and transactions and of prior period adjustments which are recorded in the accounts during a particular accounting period. The Board has concluded that net income should reflect all items of profit and loss recognized during the period with the sole exception of the prior period adjustments described below. *Extraordinary items* should, however, be segregated from the results of ordinary operations and shown separately in the income statement, with disclosure of the nature and amounts thereof. . . .

18. With respect to *prior period adjustments*, the Board has concluded that those rare items which relate directly to the operations of a specific prior period or periods, which are material and which qualify under the criteria described in (the opinion) below should, in single period statements, be reflected as adjustment of the opening balance of retained earnings. When comparative statements are presented, corresponding adjustments should be made of the amounts of net income (and the components thereof) and retained earnings balances (as well as of other affected balances) for all of the periods reported therein, to reflect the retroactive application of the prior period adjustments. . . .

The criteria of APB *Opinion No. 9* proved much too vague and weak to withstand the pressure exerted by managements in their desire to use the extraordinary item category for purposes of explaining away loss or failure or of "managing" the reporting of periodic net income (see Chapter 20 for a further discussion of this problem). The accounting profession recognized this, and so the stage was set for a second improvement in this area. In 1973 APB *Opinion No. 30* restricted further the use of the extraordinary category by requiring that in order to qualify for this designation an item be *both* unusual in nature and infrequent of occurrence. It defined these terms thus:

(a) *Unusual nature*—the underlying event or transaction should possess a high degree of abnormality and be of a type clearly unrelated to, or only incidentally related to, the ordinary and typical activities of the entity, taking into account the environment in which the entity operates.
(b) *Infrequency of occurrence*—the underlying event or transaction should be of a type that would not reasonably be expected to recur in the foreseeable future, taking into account the environment in which the entity operates.

APB *Opinion No. 30* holds that certain gains and losses should not be reported as extraordinary items because they are usual in nature and may be expected to recur as a consequence of customary and continuing business activities. Examples include:

1. Write-down or write-off of receivables, inventories, equipment leased to others, deferred research and development costs, or other intangible assets.
2. Gains or losses from exchange or translation of foreign currencies, including those relating to major devaluations and revaluations.
3. Gains or losses on disposal of a segment of a business.
4. Other gains or losses from sale or abandonment of property, plant, or equipment used in the business.
5. Effects of a strike, including those against competitors and major suppliers.
6. Adjustment of accruals on long-term contracts.

The Opinion also calls for the separate disclosure in income before extraordinary items of unusual *or* nonrecurring events or transactions that are material but which do not meet both conditions for classification as extraordinary. In addition the Opinion deals with the reporting of discontinued operations and with the accounting for the disposal of a segment of a business.

Implications for analysis

To the intelligent analyst the single most desirable characteristic in the income statement is that of adequate disclosure. Most analyses of the income statement, except possibly for evaluation of the quality of management, are predictive in nature. Analysts rely on factors whose stability of relationship and recurrence facilitate the extrapolation and forecasting function. Similarly, adjustments must be made for the erratic, sporadic, and nonrecurring elements of reported income. For all this the analyst needs, above all, sufficient information about the nature of all the material elements entering the determination of the results of operations of a period. He needs such information presented in adequate detail so as to enable him to form an opinion as to its impact on his conclusions and projections, and he needs it presented without bias so that he can use it with confidence. This, then, is the reason for the need for the largest possible measure of fair and adequate disclosure.

While there is need for full details of all normal operating elements of revenue and expense, the need for information regarding the nature of extraordinary gains and losses is even more essential. This is true because of the material nature of such items as well as the need to form judgments and conclusions regarding how they should be treated in an assessment of the overall results of operations and what probability of recurrence should be assigned to them. It is this special nature of extraordinary items that has caused so much debate and controversy within the accounting profession as to their treatment.

The financial analyst should realize that one important aspect of that controversy is of no real concern to him. It focuses on the one figure of net income which many superficial users of financial data rely upon almost to the exclusion of all other factors. In such a context the matter of whether an extraordinary item is or is not included in the determination of net income is of great importance. To the analyst who most carefully analyzes all elements of the income statement, the exact positioning of the extraordinary item within the income statement is not of great import. He is much more concerned with the adequate description of the extraordinary item as well as the circumstances which gave rise to it.

Prior to APB *Opinion No. 9*, the accounting profession felt that it was its duty to give the reader a "sharply defined" figure of operating income. In other words, using his great familiarity with a company's operations and the circumstances surrounding them, the accountant felt that it was his function to designate an undistorted measure of current operating results which would then serve as nearly as possible as an index of earning power. Unfortunately, his self-assumed function of deciding which items to include in such a figure and which to exclude from it, on the basis that it might "distort" the operating results, has been misused by managements who, of course, exercise a great deal of influence and leverage on the professional auditor. Thus, in their desire to present results in a way that will show them up in the best light and will achieve their objectives in the timing and trend of income reporting, some managements have been able to prevail upon their auditors to use a constantly deteriorating set of flexible rules in order to serve their own purposes. Thus, for example, they have the auditors agree to put the "extraordinary" label on items which were simply the result of unfortunate normal business decisions and as such have them excluded from the determination of reported net income.

The multiplication of abuses in this area and the criticism which this evoked led ultimately to a sweeping reconsideration of the entire matter by the accounting profession and to the issuance of APB *Opinion No. 9*.

APB *Opinion No. 9* represents a reversal of attitude on the part of the accounting profession with regard to its responsibilities towards income reporting. Apparently discouraged by the abuses which resulted under the former approach, the profession has all but abandoned its professed intention to arrive at a meaningful or reliable measure of current operating performance. Instead, in order to insulate itself from the pressures of managements, the profession decided that with the exception of "rare" prior year adjustments, *all* items of income and expense shall be included in the determination of a "net income" figure which thus assumed a new and altogether different meaning.

While one may wonder whether those who rely on the sole "net income" statistic will be helped by this new approach, the analyst must clearly understand the implications which the reporting under APB *Opinions No. 9* and *No. 30* holds for him.

To begin with, the analyst should not assume that the accountant's designation of an item as "extraordinary" even under the stricter criteria set forth by *Opinion No. 30* renders it automatically excludable from the measure of periodic operating results. The best that can be expected here is that under the requirements of the Opinion, full disclosure will be made of all *material* credits and charges in the income statement regardless of their designation. However, despite the fact that "materiality" is an important criterion in determining whether an item is "extraordinary" or not, the profession has, so far, not developed a meaningful standard that would guide it in distinguishing between items which are material and those which are not. Consequently, practice enjoys an undue amount of flexibility in this area.

The analyst must also be aware that neither *Opinion No. 9* nor *Opinion No. 30* have eliminated many abuses of income reporting which existed prior to their promulgation. The discussion which follows will point out areas which are particularly vulnerable to manipulation.

An extraordinary item is one which is outside the context of a company's normal operations. It is, sometimes, the result of a freak or of an unexpected or unpredictable occurrence. However, this concept of normalcy is one which must not be taken too seriously. Business is always subject to contingencies and to the unexpected. This is the very essence of business risk. Moreover, variability is a fact of business life; and in spite of management's desire for stable growth trends, business results do not come in neat uniform installments. Thus, the "bunching up" of positive and negative factors which often causes items to become extraordinary should not lead to the conclusion that since they require adjustment of any one year's result they should be disregarded in an evaluation of an entity's long-term average performance.

Extraordinary items should never be completely disregarded. They often bear the mark of the particular type of risks to which an enterprise is subject. While they may not recur yearly, the fact of their occurrence attests to the possibility of their recurrence. In their final impact on a business entity, they are not different from operating items. After all, a loss on the sale of a building affects the entity's wealth every bit as much as does an equal loss on the sale of merchandise below cost. Moreover, the cumulative importance of extraordinary items can be considerable.

The analyst should always be aware of management's reporting propensities and the fact that often it is in its power to decide both the size and the *timing* of gains and losses. Thus, management can decide when to sell an asset, when to discontinue a product line, or when to provide for a future loss; and often the timing of such decision is affected by its probable impact on reported results. Since materiality is a consideration in the determination of whether an item is "extraordinary" or not, losses which are small and considered "operating" can be permitted to accumulate to the point where they are large enough to be labeled "extraordinary." In assessing extraordinary items, the analyst should be aware of the possibility that both their size and their timing can be "managed."

Chapter 20 contains a more thorough discussion of the significance of extraordinary and other unusual items to the financial analyst. What must be emphasized here is that regardless of the good intentions of those who promulgate official accounting policies, the analyst can never assume that the intent and spirit of these pronouncements will be implemented in practice. Instead he must pay close attention to actual practice. For example, the author has documented the serious abuses of practice which have occurred after the promulgation of APB *Opinion No. 9*.[1] Neither the new Opinion dealing with the subject nor any other changes, institutional or otherwise, that have occurred since then assure us that such abuses will not recur. Two particularly objectionable practices which undermine the very integrity of the periodic income reporting process will illustrate this problem.

The technique of offset. A particularly insidious method of "manag-

---

[1] See "Reserves for Future Costs and Losses—Threat to the Integrity of the Income Statement," *Financial Analysts Journal*, January–February 1970, pp. 45–48; and "Reporting the Results of Operations—A Reassessment of APB *Opinion No. 9*," *Journal of Accountancy*, July 1970, pp. 57–61.

ing" the impact of extraordinary items is the practice of "offset." Thus, for example, when a company realizes a substantial "extraordinary gain," it simultaneously establishes a provision for losses in the same amount, the effect being that the two cancel each other out.

The propensity of management to offset items of extraordinary gains with provisions for present and future losses is not difficult to understand. It accomplishes two objectives: (1) it removes from the income stream an unusual profit boost which an earnings-trend conscious company may find difficult to match in the following year and (2) it provides a discretionary "cushion" against which future losses and expenses can be charged so as to improve the earnings trend, or it provides for losses which up to now it did not find expedient to provide for. Thus the timing of income and loss recognition can be "managed."

ILLUSTRATION 1. Litton Industries provided in the 1969 fiscal year $23.2 million for nonrecurring estimated start-up costs on new shipbuilding facilities. This provision is interesting in that it incorporates two highly questionable practices of income reporting.

One practice is to charge, for whatever reason, future costs against present income. In Litton's case the justification is hard to understand. Litton is an example of a well-managed company, and hence it is hard to imagine that it would undertake a project, such as shipyards improvements, that would not justify its cost. If so, why the need to provide for such costs out of present revenues? Perhaps the answer here can be best found in Litton's senior vice president's own statement. Mr. J. T. Casey was quoted in the *New York Times* of June 28, 1969 as having said: "The setting up of this reserve will, in fact, enhance earnings in future years because there will be lower charges for depreciation and start-up costs over the next three years while our shipyards are under construction."

The second aspect of Litton's accounting is the arbitrary offsetting in the income statement of unrelated items of income and expense. Thus, Litton appears to have decided to provide the reserve for future costs because it reaped a nonrecurring gain of $23.2 million on the sale of an investment in stock. Since the provision for future losses is in the *exact* amount of that gain, one is justified in wondering whether, without the benefit of this gain, Litton would have made the provision for future costs at all. At any rate, it seems clear that there is absolutely no relationship between the gain on the sale of stock and the provision for future costs.

ILLUSTRATION 2. Deere & Company in its 1969 annual report had the following "neat" offset of extraordinary gains and losses:

"An opinion requiring the use of comprehensive interperiod income tax allocation procedures was issued by the American Institute of Certified Public Accountants. This opinion requires fiscal year companies to use these procedures no later than their 1969 fiscal year and has resulted in Deere & Company reporting an extraordinary income item of $16,700,000 in 1969.

This amount represents the net tax reduction that should be realized in the future on the portion of various provisions for losses and accruals, etc., that were made in the books prior to 31 October 1968, but had not yet been deducted for income tax purposes on that date. The credit is applicable to accounts as follows:

Reserves for returns and allowances and doubtful receivables	$ 8,733,000
Accrued volume discounts	2,745,000
Intercompany profit eliminations from inventories	2,092,000
Accrued sales bonuses to dealers	1,700,000
Other—net	1,430,000
Total	$16,700,000

"Offsetting the above amount was extraordinary expense of $16,700,000, which amount consists of the following:

Provision for major plant rearrangements, including transfers between plants, less related deferred income taxes	$11,933,000
Write-off unamortized excess of cost of investments in subsidiaries over equity acquired	4,316,000
Special provision for pensions, less related deferred income taxes	451,000
Total	$16,700,000

ILLUSTRATION 3. Finally, Amerada Hess Corporation in its 1971 annual report presented the following "zero sum" extraordinary items:

Sale of warrants to purchase the capital stock of The Louisiana Land and Exploration Company (less income tax of $11,776,695)	$12,758,086
Gain on sale of properties (less income tax of $12,951,781)	12,184,500
Provision for contingencies arising from economic and other factors in major operating areas (net of income tax effect of $11,978,200)	(14,630,800)
Charges associated with discontinued business activities and consolidation of certain operations (net of income tax effect of $7,735,616)	(8,966,531)
Currency revaluation losses (net of income tax effect of $77,459)	(1,345,255)
	$ ...

By what stretch of the imagination can one consider such exact netting out to be the result of pure coincidence?

Reserves for future costs and losses. The offsetting of extraordinary gains is one example of possible income shifting to which the analyst must be alert. The provision of large reserves for future costs and losses, which can be frequently found in practice, is another aspect of the same problem of potential income distortion. Although it is impossible, on the basis of the data usually supplied, to assess the justification for the establishment of reserves for future costs and losses, attending circumstances often make such provision highly suspect. Such attending circumstances include losses or comparative adverse results, when this bad news already had an impact, and changes of management and the attendant desire to make a "clean sweep." In cases such as Litton, as discussed above, the description of the provision itself may indicate its questionable propriety.

Allis Chalmers Manufacturing Company provides a reserve. Let us consider, for example, the provision for future costs and losses which Allis Chalmers Manufacturing Company established in the last quarter of 1968.

The company would have reported, before establishment of reserves, a profit of about $1 million for 1968, down from $5 million in 1967. Unquestionably, Allis Chalmers' fortunes were on the downgrade; and in 1968 the company got a new management. The management promptly effected "major surgery that is absolutely necessary to free us from past fiscal and operating problems." This included the income statement where the following charges brought the final loss for the year to $54 million *after* recording of estimated future tax benefits of $43 million.

Provision for anticipated costs and losses were established for:

1. Parts replacements, warranty costs, repossession losses, and price allowance, etc. (charged to sales, cost of sales, selling, general and administrative expenses). $40.2 million.
2. Provision for relocation and discontinuance of products and facilities (shown as an extraordinary charge—$13.4 million, net of tax). $28.5 million.

What makes this case somewhat unusual is that in spite of today's widespread use of such provisions, the auditors in this case felt that they could not estimate the proper amounts of reserves to be established. Thus, they passed the task of evaluation on to the reader by rendering their opinion "subject to" their inability "to determine at this time the amounts of costs and losses which ultimately will be charged against the reserves." Conceivably, the auditors were disturbed by the possibility of stockholders wondering why none of these substantial write-offs and provisions were required in 1967, prior to the change in top management.

Having provided for the absorption of such significant amounts of future expenses, management exuded confidence. It closed its report to stockholders by saying "We do not anticipate any lag time. As of today, we have the capability and confidence to produce a significant profit."

Threat to integrity of income statement. The growing use of reserves for future costs and losses impairs the significance of periodically reported income and should be viewed with skepticism by the analyst of financial statements. That is especially true in circumstances when the reserves are established in years of heavy losses and a concurrent desire for a fresh start, when they are established in an arbitrary amount designed to offset an extraordinary gain, or when they otherwise appear to have as their main purpose the relieving of future income of expenses properly chargeable to it.

SEC Accounting Series Release No. 138. In a partial response to this problem *Accounting Series Release No. 138* of the SEC contains requirements for rather detailed information relating to extraordinary items in Form 8-K. For example, there is a requirement for a statement setting forth the years in which costs being reflected in a charge were or are expected to be incurred and the amount of cost for each year by main components, reasons for the charges or credits, and a description and detailed schedule (with follow-up reconciliations) of provisions for future losses. Also required is a description of accounting principles followed in connection with the charge or credit and the estimated net cash outlays associated with a charge.

From the above discussion it is obvious that the financial analyst must adopt an independent and critical attitude towards items in the income statement classified as unusual or extraordinary. Only on the basis of a full understanding of the nature of such items can a conclusion be reached regarding their impact on the earnings performance of a business entity.

THE INCOME STATEMENT—IMPLICATIONS FOR ANALYSIS, AN OVERVIEW

The position of importance and predominance assumed by the income statement is due to a number of factors. For one, it is the financial statement which presents the dynamic aspects of an enterprise, the results of its operations, and the quality of its performance. Moreover, it is the basis on which extrapolations and projections of future performance are built. The income statement's importance is emphasized by the accounting process which favors it and focuses on it, often to the detriment of the balance sheet. The attempt to increase the significance of the income statement has often resulted in distortions in the balance sheet. Thus, for example, the use of the Lifo method of inventory accounting in times of rising price levels introduces current costs into the income statement but undermines the significance of the balance sheet where inventories are carried at unrealistically low amounts. The balance sheet is cast mostly in a supporting role, containing as it does residual balances of assets and deferred credits which will ultimately become costs and revenues, the investments and working funds necessary to conduct operations, and the various sources of assets such as the liability and capital accounts.

9. Analysis of the income statement—II

As we have seen throughout this and the preceding chapters, the accounting rules governing the determination and measurement of periodic income are far from uniform, and much leeway exists in their selection, interpretation, and application. It may be useful to conclude this discussion with an overview of the possibilities that exist in the distortion of reported income.

If we accept the proposition that there is such a thing as "true" or "real" income, that is, income that could be determined when all the facts are known and all the uncertainties are resolved, then it is obvious that most reported income must deviate somewhat from this ideal figure. We can never be sure about the useful life of an asset until it has actually come to an end; we cannot be certain about the value of a research project until it has seen its fruition, nor can we be certain about the revenue received from a transaction until the sales price is actually collected. There is nothing one can do about these uncertainties except to estimate their ultimate disposition on the basis of the best information and judgment available. Periodic income reporting requires that we do not wait for final disposition of uncertainties but that we estimate them as best as we can. Such a system is subject to many errors: errors of estimation, errors of omission, and errors of commission. The better and the more conscientious a company's management and the better its internal controls the less likely it is that such errors will substantially distort reported results.

The more serious and frequent cases of income distortion arise when managements set out to "manage" reported results in such a way that instead of portraying economic results as they are, they are presented as nearly as possible as management wants them presented.

We have seen that such distortions can be accomplished by means of the timing of transactions, the choice from a variety of generally accepted principles, the introduction of conservative or, alternatively, very optimistic estimates, and the arbitrary choice of methods by which elements of income and expenses are presented or their nature is disclosed.

Generally, an enterprise wishing to benefit current income at the expense of the future will engage in one or a number of practices such as the following:

1. It will choose inventory methods which allow for maximum inventory carrying values and minimum current charges to cost of goods or services sold.
2. It will choose depreciation methods and useful lives of property which will result in minimum current charges as depreciation expense.
3. It will defer all manner of costs to the future such as, for example;

a) Research and development costs.
b) Preoperating, moving, rearrangement, and start-up costs.
c) Marketing costs.
Such costs would be carried as deferred charges or included with the costs of other assets such as property, plant, and equipment.
4. It will amortize assets and defer costs over the longest possible period. Such assets include:
a) Goodwill.
b) Leasehold improvements.
c) Research and development costs.
d) Patents and copyrights.
5. It will elect the method requiring the lowest possible pension and other employment compensation cost accruals.
6. It will inventory rather than expense administrative costs, taxes, etc.
7. It will choose the most accelerated methods of income recognition such as in the areas of leasing, franchising, real estate sales, and contracting.
8. It will take into income right away, rather than defer, such benefits as investment tax credits.

Enterprises which wish to "manage" the size of reported income can resort to classification as "extraordinary" of items which arise from the normal and usual risks to which the business is subject or can regulate the flow of income and expense by means of reserves for future costs and losses.

Exhibit 9–1 illustrates the possible impact on reported income of some of the alternative accounting principles available to managements.

ACCOUNTING CHANGES

In an attempt to reduce the unwarranted switching by management from one accepted method of accounting to another, APB *Opinion No. 20* states that:

... in the preparation of financial statements there *is a presumption that an accounting principle once adopted should not be changed in accounting for events and transactions of a similar type.* Consistent use of accounting principles from one accounting period to another enhances the utility of financial statements to users by facilitating analysis and understanding of comparative accounting data.

. . . .

The presumption that an entity should not change an accounting principle *may be overcome* only if the enterprise justifies the use of an alternative acceptable accounting principle on the basis that *it is preferable.* . . . (Emphasis supplied.)

EXHIBIT 9-1

Example of the effect of the variety of accounting principles on reported income

RIVAL MANUFACTURING COMPANY
Consolidated Statement of Income
For Year Ended 19xx

	Method A	Method B
Net sales	$365,800,000	$365,800,000
Cost of goods sold (1) (2) (3) (4) (5)	(276,976,200)	(274,350,000)
	$ 88,823,800	$ 91,450,000
Research and development costs (6)	(7,326,000)	(7,000,000)
Selling, general, and administrative expenses (5) (7)	(44,600,000)	(35,700,000)
	$ 36,897,800	$ 48,750,000
Other income (expenses):		
Interest expenses	(3,085,000)	(3,095,000)
Net income—subsidiaries	1,538,000	1,460,000
Amortization of goodwill (8)	(390,000)	(170,000)
Miscellaneous expenses	(269,000)	(229,000)
Income before taxes	$ 34,691,800	$ 46,715,800
Taxes:		
Income taxes—deferred	(756,000)	(850,000)
Income taxes—current (9)	(16,716,900)	(22,397,900)
Reductions from investment tax credits (10)	10,400	758,400
Net income	$ 17,229,300	$ 24,226,300
Earnings per share	$5.74	$8.08

Explanations:
  (1) Inventories:
       A uses last-in, first-out
       B uses first-in, first-out
       Difference—$1,780,000
  (2) Administrative costs:
       A includes some administrative costs as period costs
       B includes some administrative costs as inventory costs
       Difference—$88,000
  (3) Depreciation:
       A uses sum-of-the-years'-digits method
       B uses straight-line method
       Difference—$384,200
  (4) Useful lives of assets:
       A uses conservative assumption—8 years (average)
       B uses liberal assumption—14 years (average)
       Difference—$346,000
  (5) Pension costs:
       A uses "maximum provision" under APB *Opinion No. 8*
       B uses "minimum provision" under APB *Opinion No. 8*
       Difference—$78,000
  (6) Research expenses:
       A charges as incurred
       B amortizes over 5 years
       Difference—$326,000
  (7) Executive compensations:
       A compensates executives with cash bonuses
       B compensates executives with stock options
       Difference—$840,000
  (8) Goodwill from acquisition:
       A amortizes over 10 years
       B amortizes over 40 years
       Difference—$220,000
  (9) Taxes on subsidiary profits:
       A makes provision as income earned
       B makes no provision until dividends received
       Difference—$67,000
  (10) Investment tax credits:
       A amortizes over useful lives of equipment
       B credits against current taxes
       Difference—$748,000

The Board distinguishes in this Opinion among three types of accounting changes, that is, a change in (1) an accounting principle, (2) an accounting estimate, and (3) the reporting entity.

Change in accounting principle

As a general rule (see exceptions below), the cumulative effect of the change (net of taxes) on the amount of retained earnings at the beginning of the period in which the change is made should be included in net income and shown in the statement of income between "extraordinary items" and "net income." This is the so-called "catch-up adjustment." Previously issued financial statements should *not* be adjusted.

A change in the method of allocating the cost of long-lived assets to various accounting periods, if adopted only for newly acquired assets, does not result in the "catch-up adjustment" described above.

Under this general rule the following disclosures are called for:

1. Nature of and justification for adopting the change.
2. Effect of the new principle on income before extraordinary items and net income for the period of change, including related earnings per share data.
3. Pro forma effects of retroactive application of the accounting change on income before extraordinary items and the net income (and related earnings per share data) should be shown on the face of the income statement for all periods presented.

When pro forma effects are not determinable, disclosure must be made as to why such effects are not shown.

There are three specific exceptions to the general rule that previously issued financial statements not be restated. In the case of the following accounting changes previously issued statements should be restated:

1. Change *from* Lifo to another inventory pricing method.
2. Change in accounting method for long-term construction type contracts.
3. Change *to* or *from* the "full cost" method used in extractive industries.

These exceptions were included presumably because these adjustments normally result in large credits to income.

Change in accounting estimate

In accounting, periodic income determination requires the estimation of future events such as inventory obsolescence, useful lives of property, or uncollectible receivables. These are known as accounting estimates.

The following provisions in APB *Opinion No. 20* apply to changes in accounting estimates:

1. Retroactive restatement is prohibited.
2. The change should be accounted for in the period of change and, if applicable, future periods.
3. A change in accounting estimate that is recognized by a change in accounting principle should be reported as a change in estimate.
4. Disclosure is required of the effect on income before extraordinary items and net income (including related earnings per share data) of the current period when a change in estimate affects future periods as well.

Change in reporting entity

A change in the reporting entity can occur in the following ways:

1. Initial presentation of consolidated financial statements.
2. Changing the consolidation policy with respect to specific subsidiaries.
3. Adopting the equity method for a subsidiary previously accounted for on the cost method.
4. A pooling of interests.

APB *Opinion No. 20* calls for restatement of all periods presented in the financial statements and for disclosure of the nature of the change and the reasons therefor.

Correction of an error

APB *Opinion No. 20* does not consider the correction of an error as being in the nature of an accounting change. Consequently, the connection of an error should be treated as a prior period adjustment and disclosure should include:

1. The nature of the error.
2. The effect on previously reported income before extraordinary items and net income (and related earnings per share data).

Materiality

The materiality of an accounting change for reporting and disclosure purposes should be considered in relation to current income on the following bases:

1. Each change separately.
2. The combined effect of all changes.

3. The effect of a change on the trend of earnings.
4. The effect of a change on future periods.

The APB, in what appears to be a reaction to the increasing dissatisfaction of financial statement users with the failure of the profession to promulgate criteria for judging materiality, has narrowed its interpretation of this concept as applied to *Opinion No. 20*. Particularly noteworthy is the recognition by the Board of the importance which the analyst and other users of financial statements accord to earnings *trends*.

Historical summaries of financial information

APB *Opinion No. 20* also applies to historical summaries of financial information which customarily appear in published financial statements or elsewhere. However, since these summaries are not normally covered by the auditor's opinion and their presentation is not mandatory, companies can avoid the need for restatement by merely shortening the period which they cover or by omitting them altogether.

Implications for analysis

The requirement that changes in accounting principles be undertaken only when the change is in the direction of preferable accounting is a significant development. Much depends on the judgment which independent accountants will use in deciding when a change is in the direction of preferable accounting and when it is not. The potential for improvements in financial reporting which APB *Opinion No. 20* holds is undeniably great.

The inclusion of the "catch-up" adjustment, which results from accounting changes, in the determination of the net income of the period in which the change takes place strengthens the need to deemphasize the net income of any one year and to focus instead on the average earnings achieved over a number of years.

The financial analyst, while welcoming improvements in the scope and quality of financial statements as well as in their integrity and reliability, must nevertheless be ever alert to the innumerable possibilities and avenues available for the distortion of reported results.

QUESTIONS

1. Name some key provisions of APB *Opinion No. 8* dealing with the accounting for pension costs.
2. Which are some of the important disclosure requirements of APB *Opinion No. 8?*

3. How is compensation granted by means of stock options measured? Does APB *Opinion No. 25* call for a realistic recognition of the compensation cost inherent in stock options granted?
4. Distinguish between the various types of research and development activities. Why is the accounting for such costs so difficult?
5. In what ways can the analyst evaluate an enterprise's accounting for research and development costs?
6. To what aspects of the valuation and the amortization of goodwill must the analyst be alert?
7. Contrast the computation of total interest costs of a bond issue with warrants attached with that of an issue of convertible debt.
8. Why is the potential benefit of an operating loss carry-forward so seldom recognized in the financial statements in the year of the loss?
9. List four circumstances giving rise to book-tax timing differences.
10. Describe "income tax normalizing." (C.F.A.)
11. Name one flaw to which tax allocation procedures are still subject.
12. How has the accounting profession defined an extraordinary item? Give three examples of such items.
13. What conditions are necessary before an item qualifies as a prior period adjustment?
14. In the never-ending debate on the proper treatment of extraordinary items, what should be the financial analyst's main interest?
15. Describe some of the abuses in the area or extraordinary item reporting which are found in practice and which have not been dealt with by recent APB pronouncements on this subject.
16. In what ways can the establishment of "reserves for future costs and losses" undermine the integrity and hence, the usefulness of periodic income reporting?
17. Why is it impossible to arrive at an absolutely "precise" measure of periodic net income?
18. What are some of the types of methods by means of which income can be distorted?
19. For each of the items below (1–4), explain:
    a) Two acceptable accounting methods for corporate reporting purposes.
    b) How each of these two acceptable accounting methods will affect the earnings of the current period.
    (1) Depreciation.
    (2) Research and development.
    (3) Inventory.
    (4) Installment sales. (C.F.A.)
20. What are the objectives of APB *Opinion No. 20?* It distinguishes among four types of accounting changes. Which are they?

10

Earnings per share— computation and evaluation

THE DETERMINATION of the earnings level of an enterprise which is relevant to the purposes of the analyst is a complex analytical process. This earnings figure can be converted into an earnings per share (EPS) amount which is useful in the evaluation of the price of the common stock, in the evaluation of dividend coverage and dividend paying ability, as well as for other purposes. The analyst must, consequently, have a thorough understanding of the principles which govern the computation of EPS.

The intelligent analyst will never overemphasize the importance of, or place exclusive reliance on, any one figure, be it the widely used and popular EPS figure or any other statistic. In using the EPS figure he should always be alert to the composition of the "net income" figure used in its computation.

In the mid-1960s, when a wave of mergers brought with it the widespread use of convertible securities as financing devices, the attention of analysts and of accountants turned also to the denominator of the EPS computation, that is, the number of shares of common stock by which the earnings should be divided. It became obvious that the prior practice of considering only the common shares actually outstanding without a consideration of the future potential dilution which is inherent in convertible securities, had often led to an overstatement of EPS.

The managements of merger-minded companies had discovered that it was possible to buy the earnings of a company by compensating its owners with low-yield convertible securities which in effect represented a deferred equity interest. Since the acquired earnings were immediately included in the combined income of the merged enterprise while the dilutive effect of the issuance of convertible securities was ignored, an illusory increase in EPS was thus achieved. Such growth in EPS increased the value of the securities, thus enabling the merger-minded company to carry this value enhancing process even further by using its attractive securities to effect business combination at increasingly advantageous terms for its existing stockholders.

ILLUSTRATION. Merging Company A, which pays no dividend and whose stock sells at $35, issued to merged Company B, which is earning $3 per share, $1 convertible preferred, on a share-for-share basis which allows for conversion into Company A's common at $40 per share. Because of the dividend advantage there is no prospect of an early conversion of the convertible preferred into common. Thus, prior to APB *Opinion No. 15,* Company A realized "instant earnings" by getting a $3 per share earnings boost in return for a $1 preferred dividend requirement. It is obvious that the $1 convertible preferred derives most of its value from the conversion feature rather than from its meager dividend provision.

MAJOR PROVISIONS OF APB *OPINION NO. 15*

APB *Opinion No. 15,* issued in 1969, put an end to this unrealistic disregard of the potential dilutive effect of securities convertible into common stock. The Opinion looks to the substance of a securities issue rather than merely to its legalistic form.

Simple capital structure

If a corporation has a simple capital structure which consists only of common stock and does not include potentially dilutive securities, then most of the provisions of the Opinion do not apply. In that case a single presentation of EPS is called for and is computed as follows:

$$\frac{\text{Net income less claims of senior securities}}{\text{Weighted average number of common shares outstanding during the period after adjustments for stock splits and dividends (including those effected after balance sheet date but before completion of financial statements)}}$$

In the above computation dividends of cumulative senior securities, whether earned or not, should be deducted from net income or added to net loss.

Computation of weighted average of common shares outstanding

The theoretically correct weighted average number of shares is the sum of shares outstanding each day divided by the number of days in the period. Less precise averaging methods, such as on a monthly or quarterly basis, where there is little change in the number of shares outstanding, is also permissible.

In the computation—

1. Reacquired shares should be excluded from date of acquisition.
2. Previously reported EPS data should be adjusted retroactively for changes in outstanding shares resulting from stock splits or stock dividends.

Example of computation of weighted average number of shares outstanding

19x1	Transactions in common stock	Number of shares
January 1	Outstanding	1,200
February 2	Stock options exercised	200
April 15	Issued as 5% stock dividend	70
August 16	Issued in pooling of interests	400
September 2	Sale for cash	300
October 18	Repurchase of treasury shares	(100)
		2,070

Computation of weighted average number of shares

		Shares outstanding		Product: Share–days
		Number	Days	
Date of change:				
January 1		1,200		
Retroactive adjustment:				
For stock dividend (5%)		60		
Issued in pooling		400		
January 1–adjusted		1,660	32	53,120
February 2–stock option	200			
+5% stock dividend	10	210		
		1,870	212	396,440
September 2–sale for cash		300		
		2,170	46	99,820
October 18–repurchase		(100)		
		2,070	75	155,250
			365	704,630

19x1 weighted average number of shares $\frac{704{,}630}{365}$ = 1,930 shares

As can be seen in the illustrations above, shares issued in a pooling of interests are included in the computation of EPS as of the beginning of all periods presented. This is so because under the pooling of interests concept the merged companies are assumed to have been combined since their respective inceptions. In the case of purchases the EPS reflect new shares issued only from date of acquisition.

Example of computation

Pooling of interests

Assumptions: On July 1, 19x2 Company A and B merged to form Company C. The transaction was accounted for as a *pooling of interests*.

	Company A	Company B
Net income January 1 to June 30, 19x2	$100,000	$150,000
Outstanding shares of common stock at June 30, 19x2	20,000	8,000
Shares sold to public April 1, 19x2	10,000	

	Company C
Net income July 1 to December 31, 19x2	$325,000
Common shares issued for acquisition of:	
Company A	200,000
Company B	400,000
Computation:	
Net income ($100,000 + $150,000 + $325,000)	575,000

Average shares outstanding during year, using equivalent shares for pooled companies:

Company A:		
100,000 × 3 months	300,000	
200,000 × 3 months	600,000	
Company B:		
400,000 × 6		2,400,000
Company C:		
600,000 × 6		3,600,000
		6,900,000
Average		575,000

Net income per weighted average number of shares of common stock outstanding during the year (equivalent shares used for pooled companies) $1.00

Purchase

Assumptions: Company X has outstanding at December 31, 19x2, 120,000 shares of common stock. During the year (October 1) Company X issued 30,000 shares of its own common stock for another company. This transaction was accounted for as purchase. Net income for 19x2 was $292,500.

Computation:
9 months × 90,000 shares outstanding.   810,000
3 months × 120,000 shares outstanding   360,000
                                                            1,170,000

$$\text{Average shares } \frac{1,170,000}{12} = 97,500$$

Net income per weighted average number of shares of common stock outstanding during the year $\frac{\$292,500}{97,500} = \$3.00$

COMPLEX CAPITAL STRUCTURE

A company is deemed to have a complex capital structure if it has outstanding potentially dilutive securities such as convertible securities, options, warrants, or other stock issue agreements.

By dilution is meant a reduction in EPS (or increase in net loss per share) resulting from the assumption that convertible securities have been converted into common stock, or that options and warrants have been exercised, or that shares have been issued in compliance with certain contracts.

A company having a complex capital structure has to give a dual presentation of EPS if the aggregate dilutive effect of convertible and other securities is more than 3 percent. Such dual presentation is to be effected with equal prominence on the income statement and show: (1) primary EPS and (2) fully diluted EPS.

Primary EPS

Primary EPS is the amount of earnings attributable to each share of common stock outstanding plus dilutive common stock equivalents.

Definition of common stock equivalents (CSE). The concept of CSE is basic to the approach adopted in the APB *Opinion No. 15*. It denotes a security which derives the major portion of its value from its common stock characteristics or conversion privileges. Thus, a CSE is a security which, because of its terms or the circumstances under which it was issued, is in substance equivalent to common stock. The following are examples of CSE.

1. *Convertible debt and convertible preferred stocks* are CSE only if at the time of issuance they have a cash yield (based on market price) of less than 66⅔ percent of the then current bank prime interest rate. If a convertible security is issued which is a CSE and that same security was previously issued when it was not a CSE at time of issuance, the earlier issued shares or debt should be considered a CSE *from the date of issuance of the later shares or debt.*

Prior periods EPS should not be restated. Similarly, any subsequent issuance of shares or debt with the same terms as previously issued shares or debt classified as a CSE should be classified as a CSE at its time of issuance even though the later issue of shares or debt would not be a CSE under the yield test at the later date of issue. This requirement can be overcome by a change in a term having economic significance which is expected to affect prices in the securities market.

2. *Stock options and warrants (including stock purchase contracts)* are always to be considered as CSE.
3. *Participating securities and two-class common stocks* are CSE if their participation features enable their holders to share in the earnings potential of the issuing corporation, on substantially the same basis as common stock, even though the securities may not give the holder the right to exchange his shares for common stock.
4. *Contingent shares*—if shares are to be issued in the future upon the mere passage of time, they should be considered as outstanding for purposes of computing EPS. If additional shares of stock are issuable for little or no consideration upon the satisfaction of certain conditions, they should be considered as outstanding when the conditions are met.
5. *Securities of subsidiaries* may be considered common stock equivalents and conversion or exercise assumed for computing consolidated or parent company EPS when—
   a) As to the subsidiary
      (1) Certain of the subsidiaries' securities are CSE in relation to its own common stock.
      (2) Other of the subsidiary's convertible securities, although not CSE in relation to its own common stock, would enter into the computation of its fully diluted earnings per share.
   b) As to the parent
      (1) The subsidiary's securities are convertible into the parent company's common stock.
      (2) The subsidiary issues options and warrants to purchase the parent company's common stock.

Computation of primary EPS. If CSE with a dilutive effect are present, then primary EPS should be based on the weighted average number of shares of common stock and CSE. The computation is also based on the assumption that convertible securities which are CSE were converted at the beginning of the period (or at time of issuance, if later), and that requires adding back to net income any deductions for interest or dividends, net of tax effect, related to such securities.

Use of treasury stock method for options, warrants, and other securities requiring "boot" for conversion. The *treasury stock* method recognizes the use of proceeds that would be obtained upon exercise of options and warrants in computing EPS. It assumes that any proceeds would be used to purchase common stock at current market prices. For options and warrants the treasury stock method of computing the dilution to be reflected in EPS should be used (except for two exceptions to be explained). Under the treasury stock method:

1. EPS data are computed as if the options and warrants were exercised at the beginning of the period (or at time of issuance, if later) and as if the funds obtained thereby were used to purchase common stock at the average market price during the period.
2. But the assumption of exercise is not reflected in EPS data until the market price of the common stock obtainable has been in excess of the exercise price for substantially all of three consecutive months ending with the last month of the period to which EPS relate.

> **Example of treasury stock method**
> *Assumptions:*
>   1,000,000 common shares outstanding (no change during year)
> $80 average market price for the common stock for the year
>   100,000 warrants outstanding exercisable at $48
> *Computation:*
>   Shares
>   100,000 shares issuable on exercise of warrants (proceeds $4,800,000)
>   (60,000) shares acquirable with $4,800,000 proceeds (at $80 per share)
>   40,000 CSE
>   1,000,000 common shares
>   1,040,000 shares used for computing primary EPS

First exception to treasury stock method. Warrants or debt indentures may permit or require certain uses of funds with exercise of warrants. Examples:

1. Debt is permitted or required to be tendered towards exercise price.
2. Proceeds of exercise are required to retire debt.
3. Convertible securities require cash payments upon conversion.

In these cases, an "if converted" method, which assumes conversion on exercise at the beginning of the period should be applied as if retirement or conversion of the securities had occurred and as if the excess proceeds, if any, had been applied to the purchase of common stock under the treasury stock method.

Second exception to treasury stock method. If the number of shares of common stock obtainable upon exercise of outstanding options and warrants in the aggregate exceeds 20 percent of the number of common shares outstanding at the end of the period for which the computation is being made, the treasury stock method should be modified. In these circumstances all the options and warrants should be assumed to have been exercised and the aggregate proceeds therefrom to have been applied in two steps:

1. As if the funds obtained were first applied to the repurchase of outstanding common shares at the average market price during the period (treasury stock method) but not to exceed 20 percent of the outstanding shares; and then
2. As if the balance of the funds were applied first to reduce any short-term or long-term borrowings and any remaining funds were invested in U.S. government securities or commercial paper, with appropriate recognition of any income tax effect.
3. The results of steps 1 and 2 of the computation (whether dilutive or antidilutive) should be aggregated, and if the net effect is dilutive, it should enter into the EPS computation.

Example of second exception of treasury stock method

	Case 1	Case 2
Assumptions:		
Net income for year	$ 4,000,000	$ 3,000,000
Common shares outstanding (no change during year)	3,000,000	3,000,000
Options and warrants outstanding to purchase equivalent shares	1,000,000	1,000,000
20% limitation on assumed repurchase	600,000	600,000
Exercise price per share	$15	$15
Average market value per common share to be used	$20	$14*
Interest rate on borrowings	6%	6%
Computations:		
Application of assumed proceeds ($15 × 1,000,000 shares) toward repurchase of outstanding common shares at applicable market value (600,000 × $20) and (600,000 × $14)	$12,000,000	$ 8,400,000
Reduction of debt	3,000,000	6,600,000
	$15,000,000	$15,000,000
Adjustment of net income:		
Actual net income	$ 4,000,000	$ 3,000,000
Interest reduction on debt (6%) less 50% tax effect	90,000	198,000
Adjusted net income (A)	$ 4,090,000	$ 3,198,000
Adjustment of shares outstanding:		
Actual number outstanding	3,000,000	3,000,000
Net additional shares issuable (1,000,000–600,000)	400,000	400,000
Adjusted shares outstanding (B)	3,400,000	3,400,000
Primary EPS:		
Before adjustment	$1.33	$1.00
After adjustment (A ÷ B)	$1.20	$ .94

*The three consecutive months test has previously been met.

Provisions concerning antidilution. Antidilution is an increase in EPS resulting from the assumption that convertible securities have been converted or that options and warrants have been exercised or other shares have been issued upon the fulfillment of certain conditions. For example, although stock options and warrants (and their equivalents) and stock purchase contracts should always be considered CSE, they should not enter into EPS calculations until the average market price of the common stock exceeds the exercise price of the option or warrant for preferably three consecutive months before the reporting period.

Computations of primary EPS should not give effect to CSE or other contingent issuance for any period in which their inclusion would have the effect of increasing the EPS amount or decreasing the loss per share amount otherwise computed.

Fully diluted EPS

Definition of fully diluted EPS. Fully diluted EPS is designed to show the maximum potential dilution of current EPS on a prospective basis. Fully diluted EPS is the amount of current EPS reflecting the maximum dilution that would have resulted from conversions, exercises, and other contingent issuances that individually would have decreased EPS and in the aggregate would have had a dilutive effect. All such issuances are assumed to have taken place at the beginning of the period (or at the time the event or contingency arose, if later).

When required. Fully diluted EPS data are required for each period presented if shares of common stock (1) were issued during the period on conversions, exercise, etc., or (2) were contingently issuable at the close of any period presented and if primary EPS for such period would have been affected (dilutively or incrementally) had such actual issuances taken place at the beginning of the period or would have been reduced had such contingent issuances taken place at the beginning of the period.

Computation of fully diluted EPS. The computation should be based on the assumption that all such issued and issuable shares were outstanding from the beginning of the period (or from the time the contingency arose, if after the beginning of the period). Interest charges applicable to convertible securities and nondiscretionary adjustments that would have been made to items based on net income or income before taxes—such as profit-sharing expense, certain royalties, and investment credit—or preferred dividends applicable to the convertible securities should be taken into account in determining the balance of income applicable to common stock.

Use ending market price for treasury stock method. The treasury stock method (with the two exceptions) should be used to compute fully diluted EPS if dilution results from outstanding options and warrants; however, in order to reflect maximum potential dilution, the market price at the close of the period reported upon should be used to determine the number of shares which would be assumed to be repurchased (under the treasury stock method) if such market price is higher than the average price used in computing primary EPS.

Example of computation of fully diluted EPS. Assume that there are 1,000,000 shares of Class A preferred stock and 1,500,000 shares of Class B preferred stock outstanding, both issues convertible into common on a share-for-share basis. Two million shares of common are outstanding. Class A preferred is a CSE with a $1.80 dividend; Class B is a nonCSE preferred with a $1 dividend. Net income before either preferred dividend was $7,300,000.

Computation

	Shares	Net income	EPS
Net income		$7,300,000	
Shares outstanding	2,000,000		
$1.80 preferred dividend.............		(1,800,000)	
$1.00 preferred dividend.............		(1,500,000)	
($2 per share).....................	2,000,000	4,000,000	
Assume conversion of CSE Class A preferred	1,000,000	1,800,000	
	3,000,000	5,800,000	
Primary EPS.........................			$1.93
Assume conversion of nonCSE Class B preferred ..	1,500,000	1,500,000	
	4,500,000	$7,300,000	
Fully diluted EPS (beginning with primary EPS) ..			$1.62

Since the intention in presenting fully diluted EPS is to show the *maximum* dilution possible, an alternative computation is possible in this case which would yield a lower figure of fully diluted EPS. This computation has as a starting point the outstanding common shares and income after preferred dividends rather than the primary EPS.

Computation

	Shares	Net income	EPS
Shares outstanding and income after dividends ...	2,000,000	$4,000,000	
Assume conversion of nonCSE Class B preferred ..	1,500,000	1,500,000	
	3,500,000	$5,500,000	
Fully diluted EPS—beginning with outstanding shares and income after preferred dividends....			$1.57

The reason why the alternative computation yields a lower fully diluted EPS is that while the $1.80 preferred issue is dilutive for purposes of computing primary EPS, it is antidilutive for purposes of computing the fully diluted EPS.

Provisions regarding antidilution. As with primary EPS, no antidilution should be recognized. Consequently, computations should exclude those securities whose conversion, exercise, or other contingent issuance would have the effect of increasing the EPS amount or decreasing the loss per share amount for each period.

Requirements for additional disclosures in conjunction with the presentation of EPS data

Complex capital structures require additional disclosures either on the balance sheet or in notes. Financial statements should include a description sufficient to explain the pertinent rights and privileges of the various securities outstanding.

With regard to EPS data, disclosure is required for—

1. The bases upon which both primary and fully diluted EPS are calculated, identifying the securities entering into computations.
2. All assumptions and any resulting adjustments used in computations.
3. The number of shares issued upon conversion, exercise, etc. during at least the most recent year.

Supplementary EPS data should be disclosed (preferably in a note) if—

1. Conversions during the period would have affected primary EPS (either dilutive or incremental effect) if they had taken place at the beginning of the period, or
2. Similar conversions occur after the close of the period but before completion of the financial report.

This supplementary information should show what primary EPS would have been if such conversions had taken place at the *beginning* of the period.

It should be understood that the designation of securities as CSE is done solely for the purpose of determining primary EPS. No changes from present practices in the accounting for such securities or in their presentation within the financial statements are required.

Elections at the time EPS opinion became effective

APB *Opinion No. 15* became effective for fiscal periods beginning after December 31, 1968, for *all* EPS data (primary, fully diluted, and supplementary) regardless of when the securities entering into computations of EPS were issued. In addition, an election was available as of May 31, 1969, for all securities whose time of issuance had been prior to June 1, 1969. This election is only for purposes of computing primary EPS. Under this election a computation is made by either:

1. Determining the classifications of all such securities under APB *Opinion No. 15* or,
2. Determining the classification under APB *Opinion No. 9* regardless of how they would be classified under APB *Opinion No. 15*. This election in effect "freezes" securities as previously classified.

10. Earnings per share—computation and evaluation   257

This means that in determining EPS for reporting after May 31, 1969, certain securities can be classified as CSE under either the old rules or the new. Regardless of the election made, computations of EPS should be based on the guidelines set forth in APB *Opinion No. 15*.

COMPREHENSIVE ILLUSTRATION OF COMPUTATION OF EPS

The following illustration of the computation of EPS shows the application of many of the provisions included in the foregoing discussion of APB *Opinion No. 15*. To facilitate comprehension the illustration is organized as follows:

Schedules

	Facts and data
I	EPS: Computation
II	EPS: Summary of share computations
A	Weighted average common shares outstanding
B	Share computations—5% subordinated debentures
C	Share computations—5% convertible preferred stock
D	Share computations—warrants
E	Share computations—options
F	Share computations—contingently issuable—purchase

Facts and data

The Multiplex Corporation has the following capital structure, with special factors as noted:

5% subordinated debentures, convertible into common stock at $50 per share:
Issued 4/1/x1	$1,000,000	Not a CSE at
Issued 4/1/x2	1,000,000	time of issue
Issued 8/1/x2 (bank prime rate 8½%)	1,000,000	
Converted 12/1/x2 into 30,000 shares of common.	(1,500,000)	
Outstanding 12/31/x2 convertible into 30,000 shares of common	1,500,000	

7% prior preference stock, authorized, issued, and outstanding:
December 31, 19x1 and 19x2.   100,000
Annual dividends . . . . $ 700,000

$5 convertible preferred stock, convertible into common stock at $50 (2 shares for 1), authorized 1,000,000 shares, issuable in series:
Series A—issued 2/1/x1 in a pooling of interests	100,000	A CSE since time of issue

Series B—issued 6/1/x2 in a purchase (bank prime rate,
    7½%; market value at issuance was $100)   100,000
Converted 11/1/x2 into 25,000 shares of common—
    Series A . . . .   (12,500)
Outstanding, 12/31/x2:
    Series A   87,500
    Series B   100,000
    Total (convertible into 375,000 shares of common) . . .   187,500

Warrants to purchase common stock at $50 per share—issued with Series A preferred:
Total number   100,000
Exercised 12/1/x2 . . . .   (20,000)
Outstanding 12/31/x2   80,000

Options granted under executives stock option plans at market value on date of grant:
Plan B—granted 3/1/x1 at $30 per share 8,000
Exercised 7/1/x2 . . . . (8,000)
Plan C—granted 12/1/x2 at $60 per share, none
exercised. 5,000

Shares contingently issuable in connection with 6/1/x2 purchase:
If acquired net earnings for the three years 19x2–19x4 are at least equal to certain amounts, a total number of additional shares will then be issued, as shown:

$1,500,000 . . . . 10,000 shares
2,250,000 20,000
3,000,000 40,000

Net earnings of the purchased company for 19x2 were $520,000.

Other relevant hypothetical facts about the hypothetical corporation are as follows:

1. On April 1, 19x2 the corporation completed a public offering of 200,000 common shares.
2. On October 1, 19x2 the corporation purchased 60,000 common shares for its treasury.
3. Market prices of the company's common stock during 19x2 were:

	First	Average	Quarterly	19x2 average
January.	40	34		
February.	30	30	32	
March.	30	32		
April	35	35		
May.	40	43	42	
June	45	48		
July.	50	47		
August	40	38	43	
September	35	44		
October.	55	51		
November	50	54	55	
December	60	60		43

The closing market price on December 31 was 65.

4. For the year 19x2, the corporation's earnings, in condensed form, were:

Income before extraordinary items $5,000,000
Extraordinary credits, net of taxes 1,000,000
Net income. $6,000,000

5. Included in the above is pretax interest on the subordinated debentures, as follows:

January 1–March 31 . . . . $12,500
April 1–July 31 33,333
August 1–December 1 50,000
December 1–December 31 6,250

6. Not included are total preferred dividends (paid quarterly, March 1, June 1, September 1, and December 1) as follows:

7% prior preference stock $700,000
Series A 484,375
Series B. 250,000

SCHEDULE I
EPS: Computations

	Income before extra-ordinary item	Extra-ordinary item	Net income
Amounts before adjustment	$5,000,000	$1,000,000	$6,000,000
Less: Dividend on 7% prior preference stock	(700,000)		(700,000)
Amounts after preferred dividends	$4,300,000	$1,000,000	$5,300,000
Adjustments for computing primary EPS:			
Interest on 5% convertible subordinated debentures, net of tax effect (assumed 50% rate).	28,125		28,125
Income for primary EPS	$4,328,125	$1,000,000	$5,328,125
Adjustments for computing fully diluted EPS:			
Interest on 5% convertible subordinated debentures, net of tax effect (assumed 50% rate)	$ 22,916		$ 22,916
Income for fully diluted EPS	$4,351,041	$1,000,000	$5,351,041
Adjustments for computing supplementary EPS:			
Income for primary EPS, as above	$4,328,125	$1,000,000	$5,328,125
Add: Additional interest on 5% convertible subordinated debentures (net of assumed 50% tax effect).	18,750		18,750
Income for supplementary EPS	$4,346,875	$1,000,000	$5,346,875

Note: Interest is eliminated (a) for primary EPS, for period after 8/1/x2 (date on which entire issue became a CSE), and (b) for fully diluted EPS, for all earlier months. For supplementary EPS, interest eliminated for primary EPS is increased to reflect the assumption that the actual conversion of debentures took place as of the beginning of the year (or date of issuance).

Weighted average common and common equivalent shares (from Schedule II) . . .	1,497,069	1,497,069	1,497,069
Related income, as above.	$4,328,125	$1,000,000	$5,328,125
Earnings per common share and common equivalent share	$2.89	$.67	$3.56
Weighted average shares adjusted for full dilution (from Schedule II)	1,529,649	1,529,649	1,529,649
Related income, as above.	$4,351,041	$1,000,000	$5,351,041
Earnings per common share, assuming full dilution	$2.84	$.66	$3.50

Note: Dilution is less than 3%, and could therefore be considered immaterial.

Supplementary data:

Weighted average common and common equivalent shares adjusted to give pro forma effect to actual conversions as though made at the beginning of the year (from Schedule II)	1,512,069	1,512,069	1,512,069
Related income, as above.	$4,346,875	$1,000,000	$5,346,875
Supplementary earnings per common and common equivalent share, giving pro forma effect to conversions. . . .	$2.87	$.66	$3.54

Note: Effect on primary EPS is clearly immaterial, and disclosure would probably be confined to noting that that is the case.

SCHEDULE II
EPS: Summary of share computations

	Shares
Weighted average common shares outstanding (Schedule A).......	1,147,333
Weighted average CSE:	
5% subordinated debentures (Schedule B)................	22,500
$5 convertible preferred (Schedule C)..................	312,500
Warrants (Schedule D)...............................	8,146
Options (Schedule E).................................	757
Contingently issuable—purchase (Schedule F)............	5,833
Weighted average common and common equivalent shares........	1,497,069 *(To Sch. I)*
(Used to compute primary EPS)	
Adjustments for full dilution:	
5% subordinated debentures (Schedule B)................	18,333
$5 convertible preferred (Schedule C)..................	...
Warrants (Schedule D)...............................	13,372
Options (Schedule E).................................	875
Contingently issuable—purchase (Schedule F)............	...
	32,580
Weighted average shares adjusted for full dilution............	1,529,649 *(To Sch. I)*
(Used to compute fully diluted EPS)	
Weighted average common and common equivalent shares, as above	1,497,069
Adjustment for supplementary purposes:	
5% subordinated debentures (Schedule B)................	15,000
Weighted average shares giving pro forma effect to conversions of debentures as though made at beginning of year (or date of issue)...	1,512,069 *(To Sch. I)*
(Used to compute supplementary EPS)	

SCHEDULE A
Weighted average common shares outstanding

		Number of shares			
Date	Source	Increase (decrease)	Total	Months	Weighted product
Jan. 1......	Balance		1,000,000	3	3,000,000
Apr. 1......	Public offering	200,000	1,200,000	3	3,600,000
July 1......	Stock options exercised	8,000	1,208,000	3	3,624,000
Oct. 1......	Treasury stock	(60,000)	1,148,000	1	1,148,000
Nov. 1	Conversion—Series A preferred	25,000	1,173,000	1	1,173,000
Dec. 1......	Conversion—debentures Exercise of warrants	30,000 20,000 }	1,223,000	1	1,223,000
				12	13,768,000
Weighted average common shares outstanding					1,147,333

SCHEDULE B
5% subordinated debentures

	Total shares	Weight	Weighted average shares
CSE for primary EPS:			
Equivalent shares—issue of 4/1/x1	20,000	5/12 ⎫	
Equivalent shares—issue of 4/1/x2	20,000	5/12 ⎬	25,000
Equivalent shares—issue of 8/1/x2	20,000	5/12 ⎭	
Less: Shares issued on conversion 12/1/x2 and included in shares outstanding	(30,000)	1/12	(2,500)
Weighted CSE—debentures—primary EPS			22,500

Note: Issue of 8/1/x2 was a CSE at time of issuance because cash yield was less than two thirds of the bank prime rate. Accordingly, earlier issues of this security with same terms acquired CSE status at that time.

Fully diluted EPS:			
Equivalent shares—issue of 4/1/x1	20,000	12/12	20,000
Equivalent shares—issue of 4/1/x2	20,000	9/12	15,000
Equivalent shares—issue of 8/1/x2	20,000	5/12	8,333
			43,333
Less: Shares issued on conversion 12/1/x2 and included in shares outstanding (as above)			(2,500)
Share equivalents included in CSE above.			(22,500)
Net additional shares—debentures—fully diluted EPS.			18,333

Note: For fully diluted EPS, convertibility before acquiring CSE status relates to entire period during which issues were outstanding.

Supplementary EPS:			
Equivalent shares—actual conversions as though made at beginning of year (or date of later issuance):			
Issue of 4/1/x1 (entire)	20,000	12/12	20,000
Issue of 4/1/x2 (part)	10,000	9/12	7,500
Equivalent shares—not converted:			
Issue of 4/1/x2 (remainder)	10,000	5/12	4,167
Issue of 8/1/x2	20,000	5/12	8,333
			40,000
Less: Shares and CSE reflected in primary EPS (as above)			(25,000)
Net additional shares—debentures—supplementary EPS			15,000

SCHEDULE C
$5 convertible preferred stock

	Total shares	Weight	Weighted average shares
CSE for primary EPS:			
Series A—equivalent shares	200,000	12/12	200,000
Less: Shares issued on conversion 11/1/x2 and included in shares outstanding	(25,000)	2/12	(4,167)
			195,833
Series B—equivalent shares—issue of 6/1/x2	200,000	7/12	116,667
Weighted CSE—preferred—primary EPS			312,500

Note: The cash yield of Series B at time of issuance was *not* less than two thirds the prime rate. This security, which thus would not have been a CSE, assumes that status because Series A—an outstanding security with the same terms—was a CSE. (Because the issuance involved a *purchase*, Series B is a CSE only from 6/1/x2.)

Fully diluted EPS:
No additional effect: convertible preferred was a CSE during entire period outstanding.

Supplementary EPS:
Had the conversion of Series A taken place at the beginning of the year, primary EPS would not have been affected, because the issue was a CSE during the entire period. Accordingly, this conversion does not call for supplementary EPS disclosure.

SCHEDULE D
Warrants

		Total shares	Weight	Weighted average shares
CSE for primary EPS:				
As to warrants exercised December 1:				
Number of shares.		20,000		
Exercise price—proceeds.	$1,000,000			
Average market price, 4th quarter, prior to exercise	$52.50			
Treasury stock shares		(19,048)		
Net shares added in respect of period before exercise		952	11/12	873
As to warrants outstanding December 31:				
Number of shares.		80,000		
Exercise price—proceeds.	$4,000,000			
Average market price, 4th quarter.	$55			
Treasury stock shares		(72,727)		
Net shares added in respect of outstanding		7,273	12/12	7,273
Weighted CSE—warrants— primary EPS.				8,146

Note: Average quarterly market prices were *antidilutive* during the 1st, 2d, and 3d quarters, and *dilutive* during the 4th quarter. Accordingly the first three quarters are ignored in the computation, which is based on the average market price during the 4th quarter. For warrants exercised, the average price used is that for the portion of the 4th quarter prior to exercise.

Fully diluted EPS:				
As to warrants exercised December 1:				
Number of shares.		20,000		
Exercise price—proceeds.	$1,000,000			
Market price at date of exercise	$60			
Treasury stock shares		(16,667)		
Shares added in respect of period before exercise		3,333	11/12	3,056
As to warrants outstanding December 31:				
Number of shares.		80,000		
Exercise price—proceeds.	$4,000,000			
Market price at December 31	$65			
Treasury stock shares.		(61,538)		
Shares added in respect of outstanding		18,462	12/12	18,462
Total shares added				21,518
Less: CSE added (as above)				8,146
Weighted average additional shares—warrants, for fully diluted EPS				13,372

Note: For fully diluted EPS, market prices at *date of exercise* and *year-end* as appropriate, are used rather than *averages*.

SCHEDULE E
Options

		Total shares	Weight	Weighted average shares
CSE for primary EPS:				
Plan B: Shares optioned at beginning of year............		8,000		
Exercise price—proceeds........	$240,000			
Average market price during the 6-month period before exercise...............	$37			
Treasury stock shares		(6,486)		
Shares added (to date of exercise)................		1,514	6/12	757
Plan C: Shares optioned December 1..............		5,000		
Exercise price............	$60			
Average market price, December..............	$60			
No effect				
Weighted CSE—options— primary EPS				757
Fully diluted EPS:				
Plan B: Prior to exercise		8,000		
Exercise price—proceeds.......	$240,000			
Market price at date of exercise...............	$50			
Treasury stock shares		(4,800)		
Shares added to date of exercise		3,200	6/12	1,600
Less: CSE added (as above)				(757)
Net shares added—Plan B				843
Plan C:		5,000		
Exercise price—proceeds.......	$300,000			
Market price at December 31	$65			
Treasury stock shares		(4,615)		
Shares added—Plan C		385	1/12	32
Weighted average shares—options— fully diluted EPS				875

Note: **For fully diluted EPS, market prices at** *date of exercise* **and** *year-end,* **as appropriate, are used rather than** *averages.*

SCHEDULE F
Contingently issuable—purchase

	Total shares	Weight	Weighted average shares

CSE for primary EPS:
If total earnings for 19x2-x4 of the acquired company are $1,500,000, an additional 10,000 shares will be issued. This is equivalent to annual earnings of $500,000 for each of these three years; since this level has been attained, the entire 10,000 shares are regarded *as though issued,* for primary EPS:
Shares (weighted from date of purchase) .... 10,000 $7/12$ 5,833

Fully diluted EPS:
Both of the other earnings levels (i.e., $750,000 and $1,000,000 average annual) specified as a basis for additional share issuances are above that currently attained. In no case would these enter primary EPS; they would, however, enter fully diluted EPS *if dilutive.* Neither of the increased-earnings contingencies is dilutive, and therefore neither enters the computation of fully diluted EPS. (The fact that neither is dilutive is readily seen by reference to the *incremental* factors: the *increment* of $250,000 in earnings will result in an *increment* of 10,000 shares—representing $25 per *incremental* share; *incremental* earnings of $500,000 will result in an *increment* of 30,000 shares—representing $16.67 per *incremental* share.)

IMPLICATIONS FOR ANALYSIS

APB *Opinion No. 15* has been criticized, particularly by accountants, because it covers areas outside the realm of accountancy, relies on pro forma presentations which are influenced in large measure by market fluctuations, and because it deals with areas properly belonging to financial analysis.

Whatever the merit of these criticisms, and they do have merit, the financial analyst must welcome this initiative by the accounting profession. It does provide specific and workable guidelines for a meaningful recognition of the dilutive effects, present and prospective, of securities which are the equivalents of common stock. The elements entering the consistent computation of primary EPS and fully diluted EPS are so many and varied and require so much internal data that it is best that the accounting profession has assumed the responsibility for their computation rather than choosing the alternative of disclosing the information on the basis of which outsiders can make their own computations. The financial analyst must, however, have a thorough understanding of the bases on which EPS are computed.

APB *Opinion No. 15* has a number of flaws and inconsistencies which the analyst must consider in his interpretations of EPS data:

1. There is a basic inconsistency in treating certain securities as the equivalent of common stock for purposes of computing EPS while not considering them as part of the stockholders equity in the balance sheet. Consequently the analyst will have difficulty in interrelating reported EPS with the debt-leverage position pertaining to the same earnings.
2. There are a number of arbitrary benchmarks in the Opinion, such as the 20 percent treasury stock repurchase assumption limitation and the 66⅔ percent of prime rate test. The latter is particularly vulnerable to criticism because it does not differentiate among the types of securities issued, their credit standing, or between short-term and long-term interest rates. The prime rate is basically a short-term rate, whereas an interest rate placed on convertibles is mostly a long-term rate. Normally short-term rates are lower than long-term rates. The effect of this is that many low coupon convertibles can be issued which would nevertheless not qualify as CSE under the Opinion.
3. Generally EPS are considered to be a factor influencing stock prices. The Opinion considers options and warrants to be CSE at all times, and whether they are dilutive or not depends on the price of the common stock. Thus, we can get a circular effect in that the reporting of EPS may influence the market price, which, in turn, influences EPS. Also, under these rules earnings may depend on market prices of the stock rather than only on economic factors within the enterprise.

Under these rules the projection of future EPS requires not only the projection of earnings levels but also the projection of future market prices.
4. Since the determination of whether a security is a CSE or not is made only at the time of issuance, it is quite possible that a security which was not originally a CSE is later so recognized in the marketplace. Nevertheless, the status of the security in the computation of EPS cannot be changed to recognize the new reality.

Despite these limitations, primary EPS and fully diluted EPS computed under the provisions of APB *Opinion No. 15* are more valid measurements of EPS than those which were obtained under the rules which were previously in effect.

Statement accounting for changes in earnings per share

When analyzing or projecting EPS the analyst can focus on changes in income on a per share basis. Table 10-1 presents an analysis of the changes in the EPS of a large chemical company for 19x4.

TABLE 10–1
Analysis of changes in earnings per share

		Earnings per share
Year 19x3 earnings		$2.77
Additional earnings resulting from:		
Higher sales volume	$1.20	
Manufacturing cost savings	.37	
Lower raw material prices	.06	
	$1.63	
Reductions in earnings caused by:		
Lower selling prices . . . . $ .25		
Higher selling, administrative, research,		
development, and other expenses 49	.74	
Increase in operating results		.89
		$3.66
Nonoperating items:		
Lower income taxes, due primarily to		
difference in tax rate	$ .12	
Higher investment tax credit on		
property additions	.12	
Other income and charges—net	.03	
Unusual write-offs:		
Obsolescence . . . . $(.06)		
Self-insurance reserve . . . . . (.07)		
Other 03	(.10)	
Effect on earnings of shares		
issued during the year	(.11)	.06
Year 19x4 earnings		$3.72
Increase in EPS		$ .95

This published analysis is noteworthy particularly because it contains details such as those pertaining to changes due to sales volume and selling prices, which are normally available only to those with access to internal management records. This information, whenever available, can be of great help to the analyst in the evaluation and prediction of earnings and EPS.

QUESTIONS

1. Why is a thorough understanding of the principles governing the computation of EPS important to the financial analyst?
2. What developments caused the accounting profession to issue an Opinion on the computation of EPS?
3. Discuss uses of EPS and reasons or objectives of the method of reporting EPS under APB *Opinion No. 15*.
4. What is the purpose in presenting fully diluted EPS?
5. How do cumulative dividends on preferred stock affect the computation EPS for a company with a loss?

6. What is the two-class method and when is it used?
7. At the end of the year a company has a simple capital structure consisting only of common stock, as all its preferred stock was converted into common shares during the year. Is a computation of fully diluted EPS required?
8. If a warrant is not exercisable until seven years after the end of the period presented, should it be excluded from the computation of fully diluted EPS?
9. Under APB *Opinion No. 15* how should dividends per share be presented?
10. How does the payment of dividends on preferred stock affect the computation of EPS?
11. When and why would the following securities be considered CSE:
    a) Convertible debentures?
    b) Shares issuable in the future upon satisfaction of certain conditions?
12. EPS can affect market prices. Can market prices affect EPS?
13. Can CSE enter into the determination of EPS in one period and not in another?
14. What is meant by the term *antidilution*? Give an example of this condition.
15. How do we include stock options and warrants as CSE? What is the treasury stock method?
16. Is the treasury stock method always used? Which are the exceptions?
17. What are supplementary EPS? How are they disclosed?
18. APB *Opinion No. 15* has a number of flaws and inconsistencies which the analyst must consider in his interpretation of EPS data. Discuss these.
19. In estimating the value of common stock, the amount of EPS is considered to be a very important element in the determination of such value.
    a) Explain why EPS are important in the valuation of common stock.
    b) Are EPS equally important in valuing a preferred stock? Why or why not? (C.F.A.)

11

Statements of changes in financial position—funds and cash

SIGNIFICANCE AND PURPOSE

THE CASH and working capital resources of a business entity represent important indicators of financial health. The ability of an enterprise to meet its obligations as they become due and its ability to expand and grow depend on adequate levels of liquid funds. The statements of changes in financial position provide information regarding the sources and uses of working capital or cash over a period of time as well as information about major financing and investment activities which do not involve sources and uses of working capital or cash.

While fragmentary information on sources and uses of funds can be obtained from comparative balance sheets and from the income statements, a comprehensive picture of this important area of activity can be gained only from a statement of changes in financial position. This fact accounts for the growing importance and use of such statements which can provide information on such questions as:

1. What utilization was made of funds provided by operations?
2. What was the source of funds invested in new plant and equipment?
3. What use was made of funds derived from a new bond issue or the sale of common stock?
4. How was it possible to continue payment of the regular dividend in the face of an operating loss?
5. How was the debt repayment achieved or what was the source of the funds used to redeem the preferred stock?
6. How was the increase in working capital financed?

7. Why, despite record profits, is the working capital position lower than last year?

TWO MAJOR CONCEPTS OF LIQUIDITY

There are a number of recognized indicators of liquidity, but the two most common are working capital and cash (including cash equivalents such as marketable securities). In the present context, the term "funds" is equivalent to "working capital," and these two terms are used interchangeably in practice. The statement of sources and applications of working capital (funds) explains the change in the level of working capital between two dates by listing the factors which contributed to its increase and those which brought about its decrease. Similarly, the statement of sources and applications of cash explains the reasons for increases and decreases of this asset over a given period of time.

STATEMENT OF CHANGES IN FINANCIAL POSITION— A BROADER CONCEPT

Recognizing that the statement of sources and applications of working capital as well as the statement of sources and applications of cash can omit important financing and investing transactions which do not involve either working capital or cash, APB *Opinion No. 19* called for a broadening of both statements to include such transactions and recommended that it be referred to as a "statement of changes in financial position."

In general, the statement of changes in financial position focuses on changes in working capital or, less frequently, on changes in cash. In addition, either statement includes major financing and investing transactions which do not involve funds or cash such as the following:

1. Issuance of securities to acquire property or other long-term assets.
2. Conversion of long-term debt or preferred stock into common stock.

The intelligent analysis and use of any financial statement requires a thorough understanding of the principles and methods which underlie its preparation. We shall examine below the principles underlying the preparation of the statement of source and application of funds. The principles governing the preparation of the statement of sources and applications of cash will be examined later in this chapter.

Basis of preparation

In order to focus on changes in working capital, let us visualize two highly condensed balance sheets which are divided into sections disclosing (1) current (or working capital) items and (2) all the other (noncurrent) accounts:

11. Statements of changes in financial position

	End of year 1	End of year 2
Current Items:		
Current assets	$12,000	$16,000
Current liabilities	8,000	10,000
Total Current Items (Net Working Capital)	$ 4,000	$ 6,000
Noncurrent Items:		
Noncurrent assets	$ (6,000)	$ (8,000)
Long-term liabilities	3,000	5,000
Equity (capital) accounts	7,000	9,000
Total Noncurrent Items	$ 4,000	$ 6,000

While the above is certainly not a conventional form of balance sheet presentation, it provides a very useful framework for understanding the interaction between changes in the current (i.e., working capital) section and changes in the noncurrent section. Thus, we can readily observe that the change in working capital from year-end 1 to year-end 2 ($2,000) is matched exactly, both in amount and direction, by the change in the net noncurrent items between these two year-ends ($2,000). This is, of course, true because assets always equal liabilities plus capital and, consequently, a change in one sector of the balance sheet must be matched by an equal change in the remaining accounts.

The above-described relationship between the current and noncurrent sectors of the balance sheet provides a useful means for understanding the basis underlying the preparation of the statement of sources and applications of working capital. Visualizing the two sections of the balance sheet as follows,

CURRENT SECTION	Current assets	Current liabilities
NONCURRENT SECTION	Fixed assets Other assets	Long-term liabilities Deferred credits Equity accounts

the following generalizations may be made:

1. Net changes in the current section can be explained in terms of changes in the accounts of the noncurrent section. These are the *only* changes with which the conventional statement of sources and applications of working capital is concerned.
2. Internal changes *within* the current section are not relevant here because the statement indicates the *net* change in working capital without regard to individual changes in the composition of the working capital accounts. Thus, for example, the purchase of inventory for cash or the payment of a current liability, while affecting the composition of the working capital, leaves no effect on its net amount. APB *Opinion No. 19* requires, however, a separate statement explaining the changes in working capital components.

272 Understanding corporate reports

3. Similarly, internal changes *within* the noncurrent section have no effect because the statement is not concerned with the composition of the noncurrent sector of the balance sheet. Thus, for example, such transactions as the conversion of debt into equity or the declaration of a stock dividend would not appear on the conventional statement of sources and applications of funds, even though they are significant financial transactions. As discussed earlier, the statement of changes in financial position would include some such transactions.

The best way for us to start the discussion of how the statement of sources and applications of funds is prepared is to examine a very simple illustration of the principles involved. The following is a pair of simplified and condensed comparative balance sheets as at two consecutive year-ends.

Condensed Balance Sheets
(000 omitted)

		December 31		Changes during 19x2	
		19x1	19x2	Use of funds	Source of funds
1.	Working capital.	$320	$ 290		$ 30
2.	Fixed assets (net).	460	630	$170	
3.	Intangible assets	150	100		50
	Total Assets	$930	$1,020		
4.	Long-term debt.	$420	$ 400	20	
5.	Capital stock and paid-in-capital.	250	300		50
6.	Retained earnings.	260	320		60
	Total Equities	$930	$1,020		
	Total			$190	$190

The extension columns showing the year-end to year-end changes in account balances do not represent a comprehensive statement of sources and applications of funds because they can hide a considerable amount of significant detail. The following analysis of each change will make this clear:

1. The $30,000 change in working capital should be viewed as the difference to be explained because it is the change in funds (i.e., working capital) on which the statement focuses. The decline is viewed as a source of funds because it generated a corresponding increase in the noncurrent section by either increasing assets or decreasing claims on the enterprise represented by liability or equity accounts.

2. The $170,000 increase of net fixed assets in most cases represents

a change composed of a number of elements. Thus, if depreciation of fixed assets during the year is given as $64,000 and the sale (at book value) of fixed assets was $80,000 (cost $100,000 and related accumulated depreciation $20,000), a reconstruction of the fixed asset and related depreciation accounts is needed in order to arrive at a complete picture of changes in these accounts.

Analysis of fixed assets accounts

Reconstructing the accounts, on the basis of the given supplementary information, we get (in thousands of dollars):

Fixed Assets

1/1/x2	Balance		660	During		
During				19x2	Sale of assets	100
19x2	Purchases		314	12/31/x2	Balance	874
			974			974

Accumulated Depreciation (Fixed Assets)

During	Accumulated depre-			1/1/x2	Balance	200
19x2	ciation on assets			12/31/x2	Depreciation charged	
	sold		20		during 19x2	64
12/21/x2	Balance		244			
			264			264

The 12/31/x1 fixed assets (net) balance (which corresponds, of course, to the 19x2 beginning balance) of $460,000 in the condensed balance sheet is composed of fixed assets of $660,000 less accumulated depreciation of $200,000. Similarly, the net balance of fixed assets at the end of 19x2 in the amount of $630,000 is the difference between the fixed asset balance of $874,000 less the accumulated depreciation of $244,000. From an analysis based on the additional information, it is obvious that the $170,000 net change shown in the comparative condensed balance sheet is a complex one composed of:

Purchases of fixed assets (a use of funds)............	$314,000
Proceeds from sale of fixed assets (a source of funds).............................	80,000
	$234,000
Depreciation charged to income in 19x2............	64,000
Increase in fixed assets (net)................	$170,000

Since sales of fixed assets and the depreciation charges for 19x2 were given, the purchases of fixed assets may be derived as a balancing figure.

The above clearly illustrates that conclusions regarding a net change figure, such as the $170,000 increase in fixed assets, can be misleading unless it is analyzed further with the help of additional data.

Additional data

3. In the absence of further data, the decline of $50,000 in the intangible assets can represent a sale of an intangible or the amortization of the intangible by a charge to income. Let us assume here that the latter is true.
4. The net reduction of $20,000 in the long-term debt represents a repayment of this amount. (Additional information could have revealed that the net change is the difference between assumption of new debt and a larger repayment of old debt.)
5. The increase in the capital stock and paid-in capital accounts is deemed to be due to the sale of stock by the company.
6. The change in the retained earnings balance almost always requires further data for proper analysis. The data provided here are as follows:

Balance of retained earnings, 1/1/x2	$260,000
Net income for 19x2	180,000
	$440,000
Less cash dividends paid	120,000
Balance of retained earnings, 12/31/x2	$320,000

From the above it is clear that the cash dividend represented a use of funds of $120,000 and that the net income of $180,000 provides the basis for computing the sources of funds from operations. The reason why the $180,000 cannot be taken to be a source of funds arising from operations is that the income statement includes items of income and expense which do not provide or use funds (working capital items). The net income figure must be adjusted for such items. Let us now see how this is done.

Arriving at "sources of funds from operations"

Normally, a detailed income statement is provided. In the present example the income statement is as follows:

Sales		$900,000
Cost of sales:		
Labor	$200,000	
Material	120,000	
Depreciation	64,000	
Other overhead	76,000	460,000
Gross margin		$440,000
Selling, general, and administrative expenses (including $50,000 of intangible amortization)		85,000
Income before taxes		$355,000
Income taxes—current		175,000
Net income		$180,000

11. Statements of changes in financial position

An examination of this income statement reveals that the individual items have the following usual (normal) effect on other balance sheet items:

Items affected

	Working capital	Other
Sales	Cash, accounts receivable	
Labor	Cash, accounts payable	
Material	Cash, accounts payable and inventories	
Depreciation		Fixed assets
Other overhead	Cash, accounts payable and prepaid expenses	
Selling, general, and administrative expenses	Cash, accounts payable and prepaid expenses	
Amortization of intangibles		Intangible assets
Income taxes (current)	Cash, accounts payable	

We see, thus, that in this example depreciation and amortization of intangibles are expenses which, unlike all others, do not require an outlay of current funds. In other words, they "feed" on the noncurrent section of the balance sheet and, since the income statement is included in the Retained Earnings account of the balance sheet, they are internal to the noncurrent section of the balance sheet and are of no concern in the preparation of the statement of sources and applications of funds.

The required adjustment in our case is to start with the net income of $180,000 and add back charges which did not require funds.

Net income		$180,000
Depreciation	$64,000	
Amortization of intangibles	50,000	114,000
Funds provided by operations		$294,000

We can readily see that this figure of $294,000 could also have been obtained by reconstructing the income statement so as to include only those items which either provide or require funds (working capital).

Sales		$900,000
Cost of sales:		
Labor	$200,000	
Material	120,000	
Other overhead	76,000	396,000
		$504,000
Selling, general, and administrative expenses		35,000
		$469,000
Income taxes		175,000
Funds provided by operations		$294,000

The reason the net-income-adjustment method is almost always used in practice to arrive at the "funds provided by operations" figure is that it makes unnecessary the reciting of all the above detail which is to be found in the income statement anyway. Thus, the point to understand here is that the "net income" figure is a convenient starting point for arriving at the adjusted "funds provided by operations" figure. Moreover, doing it this way provides a verifiable and reassuring link to the income statement.

In addition to depreciation and amortization of intangibles the following are further examples of items which may appear in the income statement and which have no effect on funds (working capital).

Income statement item	Drawn from the following noncurrent balance sheet item
Amortization of bond premium	Deferred bond premium
Amortization of bond discount	Deferred bond discount
Warranty expenses	Provision for warranty costs
Deferred income tax expense	Deferred taxes
Amortization of leasehold improvements	Leasehold improvements
Subscription income	Deferred subscription income (noncurrent portion)

The statement of sources and applications of funds

Returning to our example, we may now construct a statement of sources and applications of funds which is more detailed and more comprehensive than if based solely on the changes which we could have developed from the comparative balance sheets above.

Sources of funds:
Funds provided by operations:
  Net income $180,000
  Add back—charges not requiring funds in the current period:
    Depreciation $64,000
    Amortization of intangibles. 50,000   114,000 $294,000
Sale of fixed assets 80,000
Sale of capital stock 50,000
Decrease in working capital 30,000
    Total. $454,000

Uses of funds:
Purchases of fixed assets. $314,000
Payment of dividends 120,000
Repayment of long-term debt. 20,000
    Total. $454,000

Illustration of "T-account" technique

The simple illustration above indicated some of the more common problems involved in the preparation of the statement of sources and applications of funds. These, and others found in more complex examples, are:

1. The analysis of net changes based on further detail provided.
2. The reversal or elimination of transactions internal to the noncurrent accounts.
3. Regrouping and reconstruction of transactions in the noncurrent group which affect, and hence explain, the changes in the working capital sector.

The methods used to implement these adjustments vary from elaborate multicolumn work sheets to highly summarized adjustments which are performed mentally. One of the most direct and most flexible methods utilizes the reconstruction of summarized "T-accounts." This method, developed by Professor W. J. Vatter, will be illustrated here.

The basic objective of the T-account method is to reconstruct in summary fashion by means of T-accounts for the noncurrent accounts all the transactions which went through them during the period reported upon. If the reconstructed transaction reveals that it was a source or a use of funds, it is posted to a special Sources and Uses of Funds Summary account. If the transaction has no effect on funds, it is reversed among the applicable noncurrent T-accounts. The following is a summary of the steps involved in this method:

1. A T-account is set up for each noncurrent account appearing in the change column of the comparative balance sheet. The change in each item is posted to the T-account as it appears in the change column, and underlined thus:

	Fixed Assets	
Change	170	

2. Two additional T-accounts are established.
    a) Operations Summary
    b) Sources and Uses of Funds Summary
3. Based on information supplied and inferences drawn from the changes in the noncurrent account, the balance in the T-account is reconstructed by
    a) Debiting or crediting all income and expense items to the Operations Summary.
    b) Debiting or crediting all other items affecting working capital (funds) to the Sources and Uses of Funds Summary.

4. Finally the Operations Summary is closed out to the Sources and Uses of Funds Summary so that the latter is the only one left after the others have been balanced out.
5. The Sources and Uses of Funds Summary will contain the detail necessary to the preparation of a statement of Sources and Applications of Funds.

Illustration. The following are the comparative balance sheets of the Wilson Company, as at December 31, 19x1 and 19x2 and the changes during 19x2.

THE WILSON COMPANY
Comparative Balance Sheet as at December 31

	19x1	19x2	Increase (decrease)
Assets			
Current Assets:			
Cash	$ 240,000	$ 120,000	$ (120,000)
Receivables	360,000	450,000	90,000
Inventories	750,000	1,053,000	303,000
Total Current Assets	$1,350,000	$1,623,000	$ 273,000
Fixed assets	$4,500,000	$6,438,000	$1,938,000
Accumulated depreciation	(1,500,000)	(1,740,000)	(240,000)
Goodwill	1,950,000	1,980,000	30,000
Total Assets	$6,300,000	$8,301,000	$2,001,000
Liabilities and Capital			
Accounts payable	$ 360,000	$ 540,000	$ 180,000
Bonds payable	300,000	700,000	400,000
Deferred income taxes	240,000	260,000	20,000
Capital stock	2,400,000	3,200,000	800,000
Paid-in capital	900,000	1,300,000	400,000
Retained earnings	2,100,000	2,301,000	201,000
Total Liabilities and Capital	$6,300,000	$8,301,000	$2,001,000

The following additional information is available:

1. On May 1, 19x2, the company bought the assets of another business—$300,000 worth of equipment and $150,000 worth of inventory and accounts receivable. The amount paid was $510,000, the excess of $60,000 being considered as the cost of goodwill acquired. Of the $510,000 paid, $310,000 was in cash and $200,000 by issuing long-term bonds.
2. Old machinery was sold for $18,000; it originally cost $36,000, and $20,000 of depreciation had been accumulated to date of sale.
3. On February 1, 19x2, The Wilson Company received $1,000,000 in cash for a new issue of capital stock which had a par value of $600,000. $200,000 of convertible bonds were converted into capital stock, par value $200,000. Long-term bonds were also sold for $400,000 (at par).

11. Statements of changes in financial position

4. The Wilson Company had a net income of $951,000, after deductions of $260,000 for depreciation, $30,000 for amortization of goodwill, and $20,000 in deferred income taxes. Dividends paid amounted to $750,000.

Based on the above financial statements and the additional data, we are to prepare a statement of sources and applications of funds by means of the T-account method.

The first step is to set up T-accounts for:

1. All noncurrent accounts in order to reconstruct the transactions affecting working capital (funds).
2. The Operations Summary where the sources and uses of funds from operations are summarized.
3. The Sources and Uses of Funds Summary which will equal the change in working capital and which summarizes all sources and uses of funds.

T-Accounts
(in thousands of dollars)

Fixed Assets

Change	1,938			
(c)	1,974	(a)		36

Accumulated Depreciation

		Change		240
(a)	20	(d)		260

Goodwill

Change	30			
(e)	60	(f)		30

Bonds Payable

		Change		400
(h)	200	(b)		200
		(g)		400

Deferred Income Taxes

		Change		20
		(j)		20

Capital Stock

		Change		800
		(i)		200
		(k)		600

Paid-In Capital

		Change		400
		(k)		400

Retained Earnings

		Change		201
(m)	750	(l)		951

280   Understanding corporate reports

Sources and Uses of Funds Summary

Sources			Uses	
Change		93		
(a) Sale of fixed assets		18	(c) Purchase of fixed assets	1,974
(b) Exchange of long-term bonds			(e) Purchase of Goodwill	60
bonds for fixed assets		200	(h) Conversion of bond into	
(g) Sale of bonds		400	capital stock	200
(i) Conversion of bond into capi-			(m) Payment of dividend	750
tal stock		200		2,984
(k) Sale of capital stock		1,000	Increase in working capital	93
		1,818		3,077
Funds provided by operations		1,259		
		3,077		

Operations Summary

(d) Depreciation		260	(a) Gain on sale of fixed assets	2
(f) Goodwill amortization		30	Transfer to sources and uses of	
(j) Deferred income taxes		20	funds summary	1,259
(l) Net income		951		1,261
		1,261		

The following are the entries which record the changes:

Fixed assets

We know that equipment costing $36,000 and having accumulated depreciation of $20,000 was sold for $18,000. Entry (a) reconstructs the transactions in summary fashion.

(a)

Sources and Uses of Funds............................	18,000	
Accumulated Depreciation............................	20,000	
Fixed Assets..		36,000
Operations Summary.................................		2,000

Since the net change in the Fixed Asset account is $1,938,000, we know, by deduction, that the charges (debits) to the account must have amounted to $1,938,000 plus $36,000 (to offset the credit arising from the sale) or $1,974,000. In the absence of other information, the most logical assumption is that this amount represents purchases of fixed assets (including $300,000 included in the May 1, 19x2 purchase of equipment of a business), and we so treat it. In the purchase of the business, $200,000 in long-term bonds were issued in addition to the cash payment. Although this $200,000 issue of bonds is not a use of working capital, it represents a significant financing-investing transaction which should be reflected in a statement of changes in financial position.

(b)

Sources and Uses of Funds...	200,000	
Bonds Payable...		200,000

(c)

Fixed Assets...	1,974,000	
Sources and Uses of Funds...		1,974,000

At this point the explained changes in the Fixed Asset T-account (after entries (a), (b), and (c) are made) equal the change we set out to explain and which is entered at the top of the account and underlined, that is, $1,938 thousands.

Accumulated depreciation

The net change of $240,000 and the $20,000 charge for accumulated depreciation on fixed asset sold suggests that $260,000 must have been credited to Accumulated Depreciation for the year, and this is confirmed by the supplementary information given. Since net income was decreased by the amount of depreciation charged, we transfer it to the Operations Summary so as to cancel the charge which did not require funds (working capital).

(d)

Operations Summary...	260	
Accumulated Depreciation...		260

Goodwill

We know that goodwill in the amount of $60,000 was bought in 19x2. Hence, retracing the original entry, we get:

(e)

Goodwill...	60,000	
Sources and Uses of Funds...		60,000

The supplementary information tells us that $30,000 of Goodwill was amortized in 19x2. Since this charge to income did not require funds (i.e., it drew a "noncurrent" account), we increase the Operations Summary by this amount, thus:

(f)

Operations Summary...	30,000	
Goodwill...		30,000

Thus, the net change in the Goodwill account has been accounted for.

Bonds payable

The sale of bonds resulted in a source of funds which is reflected as follows:

(g)
Sources and Uses of Funds..........................	400,000	
Bonds Payable.................................		400,000

The conversion of bonds into capital stock is not a transaction affecting working capital. It is, nevertheless, a significant financing transaction resulting in a change in capital structure and, as such, should be reflected in a statement of changes in financial position. This is done as follows:

(h)
Bonds Payable.....................................	200,000	
Sources and Uses of Funds......................		200,000

(i)
Sources and Uses of Funds..........................	200,000	
Capital Stock..................................		200,000

Deferred income taxes

The charge for deferred income taxes increases a noncurrent deferred credit account and, like that for depreciation and goodwill amortization, does not require current funds, and thus the adjustment is carried to the Operations Summary.

(j)
Operations Summary...............................	20,000	
Deferred Income Taxes.........................		20,000

Capital stock and paid-in capital

The sale of stock is a source of funds and is reconstructed as follows:

(k)
Sources and Uses of Funds..........................	1,000,000	
Capital Stock..................................		600,000
Paid-In Capital................................		400,000

Retained earnings

Reconstruction of the Retained Earnings account change usually relies on supplementary detail provided. Thus net income amounted to $951,000, and this source of funds (*before* adjustment for nonfund items) is transferred to Operations Summary.

(l)

Operations Summary...............................	951,000	
Retained Earnings.............................		951,000

The cash dividends amounted to $750,000, and this is a use of funds.

(m)

Retained Earnings.................................	750,000	
Sources and Uses of Fund.......................		750,000

We have now accounted for the net changes in all the noncurrent T-accounts differences. The changes internal to the noncurrent group of T-accounts do not affect working capital. However, most of such changes, which represent significant financing and/or investing activities, must be included in the statement of changes of financial position which is more comprehensive than the statement of sources and uses of funds, the information of which it also includes.

The next step is to close out the Operations Summary, which contains the net income and adjustments for nonfund items, to the Sources and Uses of Funds Summary. The gain on sale of fixed assets, which is included in net income, is also removed from it because it was included with the sources of funds from sale of fixed assets. The net amount of $1,259,000 is transferred as a source of funds from operations.

Adding up the "sources" column of the Sources and Uses of Funds Summary, we find that it exceeds the "uses" column by $93,000 which corresponds to the increase in working capital. This is a "use" of funds, and with this addition, the uses and sources of funds are in balance as they always must be. From the Sources and Uses of Funds Summary, we can now proceed to prepare the statement of changes in financial position. The Operations Summary contains the necessary detail needed to reconcile the net income figure with the funds provided by operations figure, as is usually done in the body of the statement of changes in financial position.

The resulting statement of changes in financial position is shown in Exhibit 11–1.

Analysis of changes in each element of working capital

It will be noted that the above statement of changes in financial position includes an analysis of increases and decreases in the items comprising working capital. That is in accordance with requirements of APB *Opinion No. 19* which calls for an analysis of this nature even though the reader can prepare one if comparative balance sheets are furnished.

EXHIBIT 11-1

THE WILSON COMPANY
Statement of Changes in Financial Position
For the Year Ended December 31, 19x2

Financial resources were provided by:

Net income			$ 951,000
Add: Expenses not requiring outlay of working capital in the current period:			
Depreciation of fixed assets	$260,000		
Amortization of goodwill	30,000		
Deferred income taxes	20,000	310,000	
		$1,261,000	
Less: gain on sale of fixed assets (included in proceeds from sale)		2,000	
Working capital provided by operations for the period			$1,259,000
Sale of fixed assets		$ 18,000	
Net proceeds of sale of bonds		400,000	
Issuance of bonds in exchange of fixed assets		200,000	
Conversion of debentures into capital stock		200,000	
Sale of capital stock		1,000,000	1,818,000
			$3,077,000

Financial resources were used for:

Purchase of fixed assets*		$1,974,000	
Purchase of goodwill		60,000	
Retirement of debentures on conversion into capital stock		200,000	
Payment of dividends		750,000	$2,984,000
Increase in working capital			93,000
			$3,077,000

Analysis of increase (decrease) in working capital:

Cash		$ (120,000)	
Receivables		90,000	
Inventory		303,000	
Net increase in current assets			$ 273,000
Increase of accounts payable			(180,000)
Net increase in working capital			$ 93,000

*Includes $300,000 of fixed assets acquired as part of purchase of business.

Abbreviated method

Careful examination of The Wilson Company example above will reveal the nature of the flexibility of preparation of the statement of sources and applications of funds which the T-account method affords. Thus, given a little experience in the preparation of the statement by this method, we can omit the step of preparing T-accounts for most of the simple changes and, instead, post the changes directly to the

Operations Summary or the Sources and Uses of Funds Summary. T-accounts will then be necessary only for the reconstruction of the accounts containing the most complex entries. These will involve, in most cases, the fixed assets and retained earnings accounts. In this way the time of preparation of the statement of sources and applications of funds statement can be considerably shortened and the process simplified.

STATEMENT OF SOURCES AND APPLICATIONS OF CASH

Some companies, because of a belief that the changes in the most liquid of resources should be highlighted or because of the nature of their operations, present a statement of sources and applications of cash rather than a funds statement. Thus, for example, the General Development Company, which is in the business of development and installment selling of real estate, believes that a "summary of cash receipts and

EXHIBIT 11–2

GENERAL DEVELOPMENT COMPANY
Example of Comparative Statement

	19x2	19x1
Operating cash receipts:		
Collections on homesite contracts (principal and interest)	$44,589,000	$35,195,000
Proceeds from house sales and other receipts	17,720,000	14,553,000
	$62,309,000	$49,748,000
Operating cash expenditures:		
Land development	$10,044,000	$ 6,183,000
House construction	10,704,000	6,467,000
Commissions, advertising, and other selling expenses	23,250,000	19,387,000
General and administrative	6,554,000	5,706,000
Other	6,053,000	6,856,000
	$56,605,000	$44,599,000
Cash generated from operations	$ 5,704,000	$ 5,149,000
Other cash receipts and (expenditures):		
Increase (decrease) in mortgages and notes payable:		
Per balance sheets	$ 2,357,000	$ 2,483,000
Less, purchase money mortgages issued in connection with land acquisitions	990,000	174,000
	$ 1,367,000	$ 2,309,000
Proceeds from exercise of stock options and warrants	770,000	2,704,000
Purchases of property, plant and equipment	(9,923,000)	(6,471,000)
	$(7,786,000)	$(1,458,000)
Net increase (decrease) in cash and marketable securities	$(2,082,000)	$ 3,691,000

expenditures" is more meaningful to the readers of its annual report. Exhibit 11–2 is an example of a comparative statement presented by the company.

Under APB *Opinion No. 19*, if the statement focuses on the change in cash rather than on the changes in working capital, the statement of changes in financial position will have to include important financing and investment transactions which do not involve cash. In addition, changes in elements of working capital, other than cash, are disclosed in the statement.

Let us now turn to an examination of the technique of preparation of the statement of sources and applications of cash.

Technique of preparation

The method of preparing the statement of sources and applications of cash is similar to that preparing the funds statement except that the focus is on the Cash account rather than on working capital. Under the T-account method of preparation, the Cash account becomes the master T-account where all changes are explained in terms of changes in all other accounts. The preparation of the statement of sources and applications of cash requires that all cash transaction be reconstructed in the same way as the preparation of the funds statement required the reconstruction of transactions affecting the working capital group of accounts.

Additional provisions of APB *Opinion No. 19*

In addition to provisions of APB *Opinion No. 19*, mentioned earlier in this chapter, the following requirements included in it are noteworthy:

1. The statement of changes in financial position is now a basic financial statement required to be furnished whenever a profit-oriented business entity issues financial statements that present *both* financial position (balance sheet) *and* results of operations (statement of income and retained earnings).
2. The statement of changes should be based on a broad concept embracing all changes in financial position. The recommended title of the "funds statement" was changed to reflect this broad concept. Thus, all information concerning the financing and investing activities of a business enterprise should be included in the statement of changes, whether or not cash or working capital is affected by the transaction. Accordingly, transactions such as the following should be included:

a) Assets acquired in exchange for capital stock or for long-term debt.
   b) Exchanges of property.
   c) Capital donations affecting noncurrent items.
   d) Conversion of debt into equity.
   e) Refinancing of long-term debt.
   f) Issuance, redemption, or purchase of capital stock.
   g) Dividends in kind (except for stock dividends and stock splits).
3. Items such as the following should be shown broad and not netted against each other unless one item is immaterial:
   a) Acquisition and retirement of property, plant, and equipment.
   b) New long-term borrowings and repayment of long-term debt.
4. The statement should prominently disclose and appropriately describe working capital provided from or used in operations for the period:
   a) Effects of extraordinary items should be reported separately from the effects of normal items in arriving at working capital or cash provided from or used in operations.
   b) The statement should begin with income or loss before extraordinary items, if any, and add or deduct items recognized in that amount which did not use or provide working capital or cash during the period. As an acceptable alternative, the statement may begin with total revenue and deduct operating costs and expenses that required the outlay of working capital or cash. In either case, this subtotal should be followed immediately by the effect of extraordinary items on working capital or cash after being similarly adjusted for items recognized that did not provide or use working capital or cash during the period.

Implications for analysis

The balance sheet portrays the variety of assets held by an entity at a given moment in time and the manner in which those assets are currently financed. The income statement portrays the results of operations for a specific fiscal period. Income results in increases of a variety of kinds of assets. Expenses result in the consumption of many kinds of assets (or the incurrence of liabilities)—some current and some noncurrent. Thus, net income cannot be equated with an increment in liquid resources. It is quite conceivable that a very profitable enterprise may find it difficult to meet its current obligations and to lack funds for further expansion. The very fact that a business is successful in expanding sales may bring along with it a worsening of liquidity and the tying up of its funds in assets which cannot be liquidated in time to meet maturing obligations.

The statement of changes in financial position sheds light on changes in liquidity over a period of time, focuses on such matters as what became of net income during the period, and on what assets were acquired and how they were financed. It can highlight clearly the distinction between net income and funds provided by operations. This is very vividly illustrated in a recent funds statement published by City Investing Company where the sources of funds provided by operations are shown as follows:

	Year ended April 30,	
	19y0	19x9
	(in thousands)	
Source of funds:		
Operations:		
Net income	$ 68,040	$ 48,121
Noncash charges and (credits) to income:		
Depreciation and amortization	8,085	6,222
Equity in undisturbed income of unconsolidated subsidiaries	(54,823)	(32,896)
	$ 21,302	$ 21,447

Clearly, in the case of this enterprise the actual funds provided by operations are but a fraction of the reported net income. The increasing use of the equity method of accounting in taking up the earnings of investees under APB *Opinion No. 18* (see Chapter 7) will probably serve to increase further the disparity between reported income and funds provided by operations, a disparity to which the analyst must be ever alert.

The statement of changes in financial position is also of great value to the analyst who wants to project operating results on the basis of productive capacity acquired and planned to be acquired, and who wants to assess a company's future capacity to expand, its capital needs, and the sources from which they may be met. The statement is, thus, an essential bridge between the income statement and the balance sheet.

The funds statement probably owes its inception to a desire to learn more about the flow of liquid resources of a business. However, the statement of changes in financial position can provide more than information on the changes in liquid resources and their effect on a company's ability to meet current obligations. To the financial analyst the statement provides clues to important matters such as:

1. Feasibility of financing capital expenditures and possible sources of such financing.
2. Sources of funds to finance an expansion in the volume of business.
3. Future dividend policies.
4. Ability to meet future debt service requirements.

5. In general, an insight into the financial habits of management and resulting indications of future policies.

The statement of changes in financial position as a summary of overall investment and financing activities of an enterprise is, of course, far more reliable and credible evidence of a company's actions and intentions than are the statements and speeches of its management. This is why the statement is so important to the financial analyst and why, in the absence of a formal statement supplied as part of the financial report, many analysts did in the past construct one on an approximate basis using whatever information they could obtain. A thorough understanding of the techniques of preparation of the statement, covered earlier in the chapter, will help the analyst prepare such an approximate statement and enable him to understand the limitations to which incomplete information may subject it.

The analyst must be careful to examine the form in which the statement of source and application of funds is presented. Thus, some transactions are definitely related such as, for example, the purchase of certain assets and the issuance of debt or the payment of dividends out of specific earnings. The analyst must, however, be careful not to impute relationships among items merely on the basis of their presentation lest he reach misleading conclusions.

The significance of a change in liquidity, whether positive or negative, cannot be judged by means of the statement of sources and applications of funds alone. It must, of course, be related to other variables in a company's financial structure and operating results. Thus, for example, an increase of funds may have been gained by selling off various assets whose earning power will be missed in the future; or the increase may have been financed by means of incurrence of debt which is subject to high costs and/or onerous repayment terms.

The analyst must also be careful to note the scope of coverage of the funds statement he uses. Generally, the most revealing type of statement is the statement of changes in financial position as required by APB *Opinion No. 19*. The funds statement often contains details and information not available elsewhere in the financial report, and the analyst should be alert to the availability of this information.

Cash is the most liquid of assets and is not only the most ready and acceptable means of discharging obligations but is also the ultimate measure of realization of sales transactions. Thus, in certain types of business where liquidity and cash flows are of paramount importance, a statement of sources and applications of cash is often presented. Here the analyst will find the effect of all transactions on the company's cash (or cash plus marketable securities) balance. Although the statement is also referred to as a "statement of cash flow," this term is subject to considerable confusion and requires clarification.

CASH FLOW

The term "cash flow" was probably first coined by financial analysts. Its most common meaning is net income adjusted for charges not involving funds such as, for example, depreciation and depletion. In this sense, the term "cash flow" can be equated with "sources of funds from operations" found in the statement of changes in financial position, except that while the latter term includes adjustments of *all* nonfund items included in net income, the popular concept of "cash flow" is merely one of net income with depreciation expense added back, and hence a much cruder concept.

The most valid analytical use made of "cash flow" is when security analysts, in an attempt to eliminate distortions which arise from the variety of depreciation methods in use and the loose standards which govern the assumptions of useful lives of assets, try to compare the earnings of companies before depreciation.

The following example points up the distortions in net income comparisons which can occur due to the use of different depreciation methods. The use of different useful-life assumptions for the same kind of fixed assets can, of course, introduce additional distortions.

Assume that two companies (A and B) each invest $50,000 in a machine which generates $45,000 per year from operations before provision for depreciation. Thus, for the five-year assumed useful life of the machine, the results are as follows:

	Five-year period
Funds provided by operations ($45,000 × 5 years)	$225,000
Cost of the machine	50,000
Income from operations of the machine	$175,000
Average yearly net income	$ 35,000

However, the same $175,000 income over five years can be reported quite differently by using straight-line or sum-of-the-years'-digits depreciation. Thus (ignoring taxes) we have:

COMPANY A
Straight-Line Depreciation

Year	*Income before depreciation	Depreciation	Net income
1	$ 45,000	$10,000	$ 35,000
2	45,000	10,000	35,000
3	45,000	10,000	35,000
4	45,000	10,000	35,000
5	45,000	10,000	35,000
Total	$225,000	$50,000	$175,000

*Popularly termed "cash flow."

COMPANY B
Sum-of-the-Years'-Digits Depreciation

Year	Income before depreciation	Depreciation	Net income
1	$ 45,000	$16,667	$ 28,333
2	45,000	13,334	31,666
3	45,000	10,000	35,000
4	45,000	6,667	38,333
5	45,000	3,332	41,668
Total	$225,000	$50,000	$175,000

As the above example shows, while the pre-depreciation "cash flow" of the two companies is identical, indicating as it should, identical earning power, the after-depreciation income, while identical for the entire five-year period, can be quite different on a year-to-year basis, depending on the depreciation method in use.

The use of "cash flow" or more properly labeled "income before depreciation" is thus a valid analytical tool so long as the user knows specifically what its significance is and what its limitations are.

The limitations of the "cash flow" concept are entirely due to the widespread confusion of the term's meaning and to its misuse.

One source of confusion stems from a lack of definition of what "cash flow" really is. It is, of course, strictly speaking neither "cash" nor "flow." It is not cash because it is used within broader meaning of funds, that is, working capital. It is not "flow" because it represents net change and a very limited aspect of funds flow, that is, funds generated by operations. Moreover the "flow" focuses on an "inflow" and disregards mandatory or necessary outflows. Thus, there are many other flows, even among those identified with operations, which are found in a complete statement of changes in financial position.

The assertion often made that "cash flow" represents a discretionary fund which management can use as its sees fit is also misleading. There are mandatory "outflows" such as debt service, required dividends, preferred stock redemptions, essential capital asset replacements, which cannot be avoided or postponed and which can sharply reduce or even eliminate the discretionary "cash flow" pool generated by operations.

Another and even more serious confusion arises from the assertion of some, and particularly those managements which are dissatisfied by the level of their reported net income, that "cash flow" is a measure of performance superior to or more valid than "net income." This is like saying that depreciation, or other costs not involving the use of current funds, are not genuine expenses. This misconception is also discussed in the chapter dealing with depreciation costs. Only "net income" can be properly regarded as a measure of performance and can be validly related to the equity investment as an indicator of operating success. If we add back depreciation to net income and compute the resulting return on investment, we are, in effect, confusing the return *on* investment with an element of return *of* investment in fixed assets. Moreover, it should also be borne in mind that not only is depreciation a valid cost but that in times of inflation the depreciation funds recovered from sales may not be sufficient to replace the equipment because the charges are based on the lower historical costs.

Closely linked with the doubts of laymen and even of those who should know better, about the true nature of the depreciation cost is the confusion regarding whether or not depreciation is or is not a source of funds.

DEPRECIATION—A SOURCE OF FUNDS?

One major cause for the belief that depreciation is a source of funds is the manner in which it is presented in some statements of changes in financial position. Thus, the adding back of depreciation to net income is all too often not shown as an *adjustment* of net income in order to arrive at the desired figure of "funds provided by operations" but rather as if it is an independent source of funds similar to that stemming from borrowing of money or the sale of assets.

Illustration

Misleading Presentation		Proper Presentation	
Sources of funds:		*Sources of funds:*	
Net income	$75,000	Net income	$75,000
Depreciation	25,000	Add back* depreciation charge	25,000
Sale of bonds	60,000	Funds provided by operations	$100,000
Sale of machinery	40,000	Sale of bonds	60,000
		Sale of machinery	40,000
Total	$200,000	Total	$200,000

*Expense not requiring current outlay of funds.

It is not hard to understand why the misleading presentation could lead the laymen into believing that depreciation is a source of funds. Since it is shown in the same way as all sources of funds, it is a "source" like all others and would seem to suggest that the act of increasing the depreciation expense will increase the total sources of funds. This thinking overlooks, of course, the fact that depreciation acts to reduce net income and thus the act of increasing depreciation can have no effect on funds. On the other hand, the act of increasing permitted depreciation charges for tax return purposes may temporarily conserve funds by reducing the current tax liability.

The thinking regarding depreciation as a source of funds is encouraged by loose discussion in some of our best financial publications. Thus, *Fortune* of June 1970, in an article entitled "An Over Supply of Stocks" which discusses Whittaker Corporation's liquidity difficulties, states that even by utilization of various sources of funds the company would still not be able to cover debt payments due "unless there were a sizable increase in earnings and/or *depreciation* this year" (author's emphasis). To say that an increase in depreciation can supply funds to repay debt is like saying that the higher the costs the better.

The proper presentation brings out the essential fact that the reason depreciation (or similar charges or credits which do not affect current funds) is shown in the statement of sources and applications of funds is in order to show to the reader how the net income figure which is the result of operations is converted to a "funds provided by operations" figure needed in the funds statement.

The essential fact to be understood is that aside from miscellaneous sources of income the *basic* source of funds from operations in any enterprise is sales to customers. It is out of sales that all expenses are recovered and a profit, if any, is earned. If the sales price is sufficient to cover *all* costs, that is, those requiring and those not requiring current funds, then the process of sales will recover the depreciation costs in addition to other costs. If the sales price is not sufficiently high to cover all costs, depreciation will not be recovered or will not be fully recovered. Thus, the importance of revenues as *the* source of funds from operations should never be lost sight of.

Because of a lack of understanding of the factors discussed above, the confusion surrounding the concept of "cash flow" and the role of depreciation in the funds statement has been aggravated by statements found in widely respected financial periodicals. Thus, for example, the *Wall Street Journal* of August 4, 1969, contained the following statement by its economic columnist:

> Still another way of assessing the current price-earnings level is to observe "quality" of the earnings that go into the (price-earnings) ratio. Besides actual profits, companies also gain funds through depreciation. These depreciation funds represent sums deducted each year by corporations from pre-tax profits for the depreciation of such fixed assets as machine tools.
>
> While they don't show up as profits in company earnings reports, these depreciation funds are nearly as good as profits, in the view of many analysts. Cash from depreciation can be plowed into new facilities, and the more a company can finance such spending out of depreciation, the more its current earnings can be freed for dividend payments.

While we can surely assume that the columnist has a better than average understanding of the nature of depreciation, nevertheless, statements implying that "depreciation funds are nearly as good as profits" can only help increase the confusion surrounding this subject matter.

The above discussion clearly points out that the financial analyst must approach the funds statements as well as such concepts as "cash flow" and depreciation with understanding and with independence of viewpoint so as to avoid being trapped by the numerous cliches and useless generalizations which are all too often employed even by those who should know better.

QUESTIONS

1. What information can the user of financial statements obtain from the statement of changes in financial position?
2. Which are the two major concepts of liquidity commonly used in the preparation of the statement of changes in financial position?
3. While the "statement of changes in financial position" focuses normally on changes of working capital or cash, it also includes transactions which affect neither. Give three examples of such transactions.
4. In addition to depreciation, what are some other examples of costs and expenses not requiring the outlay of cash or working capital? What are examples of income items not bringing in cash or working capital?
5. Could the form in which revenues are received affect the statement of changes in financial position?
6. The book value of assets sold is often shown as a separate source of working capital or cash. What is the reason for this presentation?
7. APB *Opinion No. 19* states that stock dividends and split-ups are not required to be disclosed in the statement of changes in financial position. What is the reason for this exception? Would the conversion of preferred stock into common be shown in the statement of changes in financial position?
8. Under the abbreviated "T-account" method of preparing the funds statement which accounts would most likely require reconstruction?
9. What are some of the important clues which an analysis of the statement of changes in financial position can provide for the analyst?
10. What is meant by the term "cash flow"? Why is this term subject to confusion and misrepresentation?
11. A member of the board of directors of a company which faces shortage of funds in the coming year is told that none of the sources of funds available in the preceding year can be increased. He thereupon suggests increasing the amount shown as "depreciation" in the "sources" section of the funds statement. Comment on his suggestion.
12. A prominent academician wrote some years ago:

    ". . . just as in the first half of this century we saw the income statement displace the balance sheet in importance, so we may now be de-emphasising the income statement in favour of a statement of fund flows or cash flows . . . my own guess is that, so far as the history of accounting is concerned, the next 25 years may subsequently be seen to have been the twilight of income measurement."

    Comment on this prediction.

12

Effects of price level changes on financial statements

THE COMPARABILITY over time of accounting measurements expressed in dollars can be fully valid only if the purchasing power of the currency remains unchanged. This has only rarely been the case; indeed, the value of the dollar in terms of purchasing power has changed over any length of time. In recent experience, such change has invariably been a decline in purchasing power.

The distortive effect of price level changes on accounting measurements has long been recognized by leaders of industry and finance as well as by economists and accountants. However, as long as the annual rate of change was moderate, accountants, as those best situated to move towards change, elected to rely on education and disclosure rather than on an adjustment of the financial statements as the means of conveying such effects to the general reader.

In times of more severe price inflation, there is always clamor for a more formalized and systematic approach designed to adjust for the distortions arising from changes in the price level. There are businessmen who feel that depreciation based on original cost is not sufficient to provide for replacement of assets used up in production. They are, of course, except in cases of regulated utilities, not bound to historical cost depreciation in setting their prices, and thus their arguments are primarily directed towards the goal of having the tax authorities accept price level adjusted depreciation in computing taxable income. This quest has, so far, not born fruit.

Economists want price level adjusted statements so that financial data can be more validly compared and analyzed. Increasingly, in periods of significant inflation, accountants have recognized their responsibility to do something about the adjusting of accounts. Interestingly, financial analysts as a group have not been in the forefront of those demanding accounting change in this area.

While the endless debate surrounding the advisability of giving accounting recognition to price level changes continued, a few companies attempted to do something about the problem. Their attention focused on the income statement because they felt that there the mismatching of dollars of different purchasing power levels was greatest, and also because it was here that an appeal for tax relief was most likely to succeed. The items chosen for attention were those of relatively slower turnover that is, fixed assets and inventories. Most other items in the income statement are, because of more rapid turnover, expressed mainly in terms of current dollars.

Depreciation

The depreciation of fixed assets, occurring as it does over considerably long time periods, contains a significant amount of distortion in times of price level changes. Thus, some companies attempted to record depreciation on the basis of replacement cost, while others attempted to adjust the depreciation expense on the basis of index numbers reflecting the changing purchasing value of the dollar. Both attempts did not get very far because generally accepted accounting principles do not sanction a departure from unrestated historical cost and because the SEC upheld this position.

The objective of reflecting higher depreciation charges in the income statement was achieved in some measure by the adoption by some companies of accelerated forms of depreciation, that is, a method under which the bulk of an asset's cost is written off in the earlier years of its useful life. The acceptance by the tax authorities of such accelerated depreciation, as well as of other temporary acceleration methods such as under "Certificates of Necessity" in time of war, made up in some measure for the abandonment of "price level" or replacement depreciation.

It must be noted, however, that accelerated depreciation is no substitute for price level adjustments since it represents merely a shift in the timing of the write-offs in favor of the earlier years of an asset's life and a postponement of taxes. Thus, no significant advance towards recognition of price level changes is involved here. The chapters on income measurement contain further discussion on depreciation methods and their impact.

Inventories

Next to the allocation of costs of fixed assets to operations, inventories present a problem in times of price changes. Normally, if prices are constantly on the rise, the longer an inventory item is held the greater the divergence between its original cost and its replacement value is likely to be. Thus, many managements were eager to obtain recognition, particularly for tax purposes, of accounting methods which recognized current rather than historical costs as proper charges against income. As in the case of depreciation, here too attempts at abandoning unrestated historical costs have, so far, failed.

The method of inventory accounting which comes closest to meeting some of the objectives of those who wanted to recognize current replacement costs is the last-in, first-out (Lifo) method. Under this method, the cost of the latest acquisition of inventory items is charged to income first, thus leaving the oldest items in inventory. As was seen in the more extensive discussion of this subject under the heading of inventory accounting, all that this does is to inject current costs into the income statement at the expense of the balance sheet where the inventory is shown at unrealistically low cost. Moreover, if the year-to-year inventory levels decline, some inventory costs charged to income are likely to be old and therefore quite a bit lower than the desired replacement cost figures, thus producing unrealistically low costs which may lead to serious distortions of income. All this is, of course, due to the fact that like accelerated depreciation, Lifo inventory accounting does not represent a departure from historical-dollar accounting, and all that is achieved is the shift of costs to current periods from subsequent periods. The widespread adoption of Lifo inventory accounting is primarily due to its acceptability for income tax determination.

The need for comprehensive restatement of financial statements

The attempt to recognize price level changes in accounting for depreciation and inventories was not, as we have seen from the above discussion, soundly based or very successful. Aside from other shortcomings, one particular flaw in these approaches which was one of serious concern to the accounting profession was the selective restatement which they attempted. Thus, concentration on only depreciation or inventory ignored the effect of price level changes on all other items of the financial statements. As the discussion which follows will show, the cumulative effect of price level changes on various elements of the financial statements can be significant and substantial. Thus, a comprehensive restatement of the financial statements is needed in order to avoid distortion.

Research and professional pronouncements

In the early 1960s the accounting profession recognized that it could no longer ignore the effect of continuing inflation on the financial statements. Accordingly, it commissioned a research study which was published in 1963 as *Accounting Research Study No. 6*, "Reporting the Financial Effects of Price-Level Changes."

Following a period of further significant price inflation, the APB issued, in June 1969, its *Statement No. 3* entitled "Financial Statements Restated for General Price-Level Changes." While not carrying the weight of an "Opinion", which requires adherence by all members of the organized accounting profession, the Statement recommendations go further than prior pronouncements and, for the first time, spell out specific steps to be followed in the preparation of price level adjusted financial statements.

APB *Statement No. 3* in effect represents a stand-by tool to be used as and when the need arises. At the time of its issuance the rate of inflation was not considered serious enough to make publication of price level adjusted financial statements a mandatory requirement. Moreover, if presented such statements must always be considered as supplementary to the conventional historical financial statements with which they must always be associated.

PRINCIPLES UNDERLYING THE PREPARATION OF PRICE LEVEL ADJUSTED FINANCIAL STATEMENTS

The basic purpose of financial statements restated for general price level changes (more briefly referred to as "price level statements") is to present all elements of the financial statements in terms of dollars of the same purchasing power restated by means of a general price level index. General price level financial statements differ from historical-dollar statements only in the unit of measure used in them. Consequently they do not represent a departure from the historical cost principle. Moreover, they are subject to the same accounting principles as are used in the preparation of historical dollar financial statements with the only exception that gains or losses in the purchasing power of the dollar are recognized in general price level statements.

Not all items in the financial statements are affected equally by price level changes. As to effect of price level changes on accounting measurements, it is useful to distinguish between two major categories of items: monetary and nonmonetary.

Monetary items are those which represent a claim to a fixed number of dollars such as cash, accounts and notes receivable, and investments in bonds, or those representing an obligation to pay a fixed number of dollars such as accounts and notes payable, bonds payable, etc.

Since monetary items represent a claim to, or an obligation of, a fixed number of dollars, their value in terms of purchasing power varies with the general price level.

ILLUSTRATION 1. Assume that A invested $1,000 in a business at the beginning of 19x1 when the price level index stood at 100. The money was kept in a checking account throughout the year, and the balance at 12/31/x1 remained at $1,000 at which time the price index had advanced to 110. Conventional financial statements would show the financial condition of A at 12/31/x1, unchanged from the beginning of the year, as:

Cash in bank. . . . . $1,100   Capital $1,000

Price level statements, however, would recognize the loss in purchasing power suffered by the cash balance while the price level rose by 10 percent. The first step in such recognition is to restate the balance sheet to the price level prevailing at the end of the year 19x1. Thus:

Cash in bank. . . . . $1,000   Capital $1,100

What this interim restatement means is that if A is to have at the end of the year as much purchasing power at his command as he had at the beginning of the year, he *should* have $1,000 × 110/100 or $1,100. A glance at the above balance sheet reveals, however, that a further restatement is needed. A failed to preserve his purchasing power because cash as legal tender does not change from its nominal value and hence it can be stated only at its face value of $1,000. Thus, a write-down is required, resulting in a loss on monetary items of $100:

Loss on Monetary Items 100
    Cash in Bank   100

The final presentation of the price level financial statement of A at 12/31/x1 is then as follows:

Cash	$1,000	Capital (as restated). . . .		$1,100	
		Less: Loss on			
		monetary items	100	$1,000	
	$1,000			$1,000	

This financial statement, in effect, tells the reader that in order to preserve the original purchasing power invested, the capital should be $1,100; but owing to the loss in purchasing power of cash of $100, it is only $1,000.

In the same way that the holding of monetary assets during rising price levels results in losses of purchasing power, the owing of money during such periods results in gains of purchasing power because the liability may be satisfied by payment of currency having a lower purchasing power.

ILLUSTRATION 2. Assume that in addition to investing $1,000 on 1/1/x1, A also borrowed $1,000 from a friend. At inception his statement of financial condition was as follows:

Cash in bank.......	$2,000	Loan payable.......	$1,000
		Capital...........	1,000

Assuming that A engaged in no further transactions during 19x1, that the price level index rose from 100 on 1/1/x1 to 110 on 12/31/x1 and that interest can be ignored, the conventional financial statements will be unchanged as at 12/31/x1.

Price level financial statements, however, would reflect the changes in purchasing power of money as follows:

Holding of $2,000 cash resulted in a purchasing power *loss* of $2,000 × 10%........	$200
Owing $1,000 resulted in a purchasing power *gain* of $1,000 × 10%.............	100
Net purchasing power loss................	$100

The price level financial statement at 12/31/x1 would be as follows:

Cash............	$2,000	Loan payable.......		$1,000
		Capital...........	$1,100	
		Less: Net purchasing power loss........	100	
		Net capital.........		1,000
	$2,000			$2,000

From the above it can be observed that had the $2,000 kept in the bank been entirely financed by A's capital, he would have incurred a purchasing power loss of $200 (10 percent of $2,000). The fact that he borrowed $1,000 enabled him to pass on to his creditor the purchasing power loss arising from the holding of $1,000 in cash. Moreover, as we shall see below, had A invested the proceeds of the loan in a non-monetary item, he would have had a purchasing power gain of $100 (10 percent of $1,000).

Nonmonetary items are all items other than the monetary ones. Nonmonetary items are stated in terms of the purchasing power of the dollar at the time they were acquired. Thus, the holding of nonmonetary items does *not* give rise to general price level gains and losses. The basic assumption of price level statements is that the purchasing power of nonmonetary items is maintained unless the accounting principle of "the lower of cost or market" requires a write-down to market.

ILLUSTRATION 3. Assume the same facts as in Illustration 1 except that instead of keeping the money in the bank, A invests $1,000 in a plot of land. The conventional financial statements at both the beginning and the end of 19x1 would show:

Land............	$1,000	Capital...........	$1,000

The price level financial statement at 12/31/x1, at which time the price level index had risen from 100 to 110, would be as follows:

Land . . . . $1,100   Capital $1,100

This gives effect to the assumption that land, a nonmonetary asset, does not lose in purchasing power in times of rising prices, and thus it is restated to $1,100 ($1,000 × 110/100) which is at 12/31/x1 the equivalent in purchasing power that the $1,000 was as at 1/1/x1. This $1,100 for land is historical cost restated in terms of current purchasing power equivalent and has no further significance. Thus it does not represent, except by sheer coincidence, either current market value or replacement cost. However, if its market value is only $900 and it is, for instance, an inventory item rather than a long-term investment, it may have to be written down to this amount under the "lower-of-cost-or-market" principle.

If no write-down is called for the price level statement of A at 12/31/x1, it would remain as shown above indicating, in effect, that the purchasing power of the original $1,000 investment, now stated as $1,100, is assumed to have been maintained.

Two important conclusions arise from the above examples.

1. In times of price level changes the holding of monetary assets and liabilities gives rise to general price level gains and losses.
2. Nonmonetary assets and liabilities are assumed to maintain their purchasing power; and thus are restated, by means of the Gross National Product Implicit Price Deflator, to reflect the amount of dollars which represent the purchasing power equivalent to that prevailing at the time of their acquisition. The equity accounts reflect the net result of all changes in the equity including those due to price level changes.

EXTENDED ILLUSTRATION OF STATEMENT RESTATEMENT—ILLUSTRATION 4

We can now solidify our understanding of the process of restatement of price level financial statements by means of an extended illustration.

The Xtra Corporation was formed on January 1, 19x1, to perform commercial laundry services. On that date it acquired for $20,000 equipment having an estimated useful life of 10 years. The salvage value at the end of that period is estimated to equal removal costs, and the straight-line method of depreciation is to be used. The opening balance sheet of Xtra Corporation is shown in Exhibit 12–1.

Understanding corporate reports

EXHIBIT 12–1

XTRA CORPORATION
Balance Sheet, January 1, 19x1

Assets		Equity	
Cash	$20,000	Capital	$40,000
Equipment	20,000		
	$40,000		$40,000

During 19x1 the following results were achieved:

Sales		$50,000
Cost of services	$25,000	
Depreciation	2,000	
Other expenses (including taxes)	13,000	40,000
Net income		$10,000

The price level index at the beginning of operations was 100, and by the end of the year it increased to 120. We assume that the increase in the index was spread uniformly throughout the year and that all phases of the company's operations are also spread evenly throughout the period under consideration.

Price level index on January 1, 19x1	100
Price level index on December 31, 19x1	120
Average price level index during 19x1	110

The adjusted income statement shown in Exhibit 12–2 does not yet include the gain or loss arising from holding monetary items, and we

EXHIBIT 12–2
Restatement of income statement

	Conventional income statement year ended 12/31/x1		Conversion factor	Price level adjusted income statement in 12/31/x1 dollars	
Sales		$50,000	120/110 (1)		$54,545
Cost of services	$25,000		120/110 (1)	$27,275	
Depreciation of equipment	2,000		120/100 (2)	2,400	
Other expenses	13,000		120/110 (1)	14,180	
		40,000			43,855
Net income		$10,000			$10,690

(1) Since sales, cost of services, and other expenses are evenly spread over the year they were incurred, on average, at the average price level for 19x1 or at the index level of 110. To convert them to the price level existing at the end of 19x1, when the index stood at 120, we use the conversion factor of 120/110.

(2) The equipment, which is depreciated, was acquired at the beginning of 19x1 when the price level index was 100. At year-end, the index stood at 120 and the depreciation expense, which is recorded at year-end, is converted by means of a conversion factor of 120/100.

12. Effects of price level changes on financial statements

now proceed to determine this effect. The general price level gain or loss computation is best done within the framework of a statement accounting for changes in net monetary assets (in this example assumed to be only cash), a sort of statement of sources and uses of monetary items as shown in Exhibit 12–3.

EXHIBIT 12–3
General price level gain or loss computation

	Conventional statement	Conversion	Restated to 12/31/x1 dollars
Monetary items, 1/1/x1	$20,000	120/100 (1)	$24,000
Add: Sales	50,000	(2)	54,545
	$70,000		$78,545
Less: Cost of services and other expenses	38,000	(2)	41,455
Net monetary items at 12/31/x1	$32,000		
Net monetary items—restated (if there were no loss)			$37,090
Net monetary items at 12/31/x1 (as above)			32,000
Price level loss			$ 5,090

(1) In the absence of a change in purchasing power the monetary items (cash in this case) would have been restated to the price level at year-end—hence the 120/100 conversion.
(2) Sales and cost and expenses, with the exception of depreciation, represent inflows or outflows of monetary items. Thus they are converted on the same basis as in the income statement (see Exhibit 12–2).

Examination of the computation of price level gain or loss will reveal that it is based on a recognition of the fact that monetary assets lose purchasing power in times of rising price levels (and gain in times of deflation) and that the opposite is the case with monetary liabilities. Consequently, the difference between the restated total of monetary items and the nominal amount of these items represents the price level gain or loss. Thus the cash balance of $20,000, had it remained unchanged, should have gone up to $24,000 if the purchasing power residing in the $20,000 balance at the beginning of the year was to have been preserved. However, since cash as legal tender cannot change in face value, a $4,000 price level loss was incurred. Similarly, the proceeds from sales of $50,000 should have become $54,545 by year-end had the purchasing power of these proceeds been preserved. However, since the proceeds were in monetary items (usually cash or accounts receivable), a price level loss of $4,545 has been incurred in this area.

The price level adjusted income of	$10,690
Will now have to be reduced by a price level loss of	5,090
Bring the net income to	$ 5,600

If we assume for the sake of simplicity that the funds from operations merely increased Xtra Corporation's cash balance, we have in Exhibit 12–4 the conventional and price level adjusted balance sheets at December 31, 19x1.

EXHIBIT 12–4

	Conventional balance sheet as at 12/31/x1		Conversion factor		Balance sheet restated in 12/31/x1 dollars
Cash		$32,000	(1)		$32,000
Equipment.	$20,000		120/100	$24,000	
Less: Provision for depreciation. . . .	2,000	18,000	120/100	2,400	21,600
		$50,000			$53,600
Capital		$40,000	120/100 (2)		$48,000
Retained earnings . . .		10,000	(3)		5,600
		$50,000			$53,600

(1) Monetary items require no restatement because they represent a claim to, or obligation of, a fixed number of dollars.
(2) Capital is a nonmonetary item and thus is converted to the new price level equivalent.
(3) As determined by the restated income statement (see Exhibit 12–2 and price level adjusted net income computation above).

In the second year of its existence, the Xtra Corporation extended its activities somewhat so that it acquired an inventory of supplies for which it accounted on the first-in, first-out basis, borrowed $10,000 on 7/1/x2, and extended credit to customers. The financial statements at the end of 19x2 were as shown in Exhibits 12–5 and 12–6.

EXHIBIT 12–5

XTRA CORPORATION
Income Statement
For the Year Ending 19x2

Sales			$100,000
Cost of services:			
Inventory at 1/1/x2	. . .		
Purchases	$30,000		
Labor and other costs	40,000		
	$70,000		
Inventory at 12/31/x2	20,000	50,000	
			$ 50,000
Depreciation.	$ 2,000		
Other expenses (including taxes)	20,000	22,000	
Net income		$ 28,000	

EXHIBIT 12-6

XTRA CORPORATION
Balance Sheet
As at December 31, 19x2

Assets

Current Assets:		
Cash		$45,000
Accounts receivable		12,000
Inventories		20,000
Total Current Assets		$77,000
Equipment	$20,000	
Less: Accumulated depreciation	4,000	16,000
Total Assets		$93,000

Liabilities and Capital

Accounts payable			$ 5,000
Long-term debt			10,000
Capital		$40,000	
Retained earnings balance			
(1/1/x2)	$10,000		
Net income	28,000	38,000	78,000
Total Liabilities and Capital			$93,000

During 19x2, prices advanced; and by 12/31/x2 the price level index reached the level of 132. The average price level index for 19x2 was 126, and for the last quarter of the year it was 132. On the basis of this information, the restatement process of the Xtra Corporation's 19x2 financial statements, adjusted for price level changes, is shown in Exhibit 12-7.

Next we must roll forward the price level adjusted financial statements as at 12/31/x1 in order to express them in terms of dollars of 12/31/x2 purchasing power. This must be done in order to:

1. Have prior year financial statements restated in current dollars for comparative purposes.
2. Have the amount of retained earnings at the end of the prior year in current dollars for purposes of current (19x2) year restatement of retained earnings.
3. Utilize figures for purposes such as the computation of general price level gain or loss.

The final comparative price level adjusted financial statements are shown in Exhibits 12-11 and 12-12 (p. 310).

EXHIBIT 12–7
Restatement of income statement for the year ending 12/31/x2

	Conventional		Conversion factor	Price level adjusted	
Sales		$100,000	132/126		$104,762
Cost of services inventory (1/1/x2)	. . .			. . .	
Purchases	$30,000		132/126	$31,429	
Labor and other costs	40,000		132/126	41,905	
	$70,000			$73,334	
Inventory (12/31/x2)	20,000	50,000	132/132 (1)	20,000	53,334
		$ 50,000			$ 51,428
Depreciation	$ 2,000		132/100 (2)	$ 2,640	
Other expenses	20,000	22,000	132/126	20,952	23,592
Net income		$ 28,000			
					$ 27,836
General price level loss (see Exhibit 12-9)					3,676
Net income (adjusted)					$ 24,160

(1) Inventory restatement is based on the assumption that under Fifo the ending inventory is the one last purchased. Assuming that the inventory turnover is 4, the entire ending inventory was acquired in the last quarter of 19x2 which had an average price level of 132, that is, identical with that prevailing at year end. Hence the 132/132 conversion factor.
(2) Equipment was acquired when the price level index stood at 100.

EXHIBIT 12–8
Restatement ("roll forward") of 12/31/x1 price level statements to 12/31/x2 dollars

	Restated in 12/31/x1 dollars		Conversion factor (1)	Restated in 12/31/x2 dollars	
	Balance Sheet				
Cash		$32,000	132/120		$35,200
Equipment	$24,000		132/120	$26,400	
Less: Provision for depreciation	2,400	21,600	132/120	2,640	23,760
		$53,600			$58,960
Capital		$48,000	132/120		$52,800
Retained earnings		5,600	132/120		6,160
		$53,600			$58,960
	Income Statement				
Sales		$54,545	132/120		$60,000
Cost of services	$27,275		132/120	$30,003	
Depreciation	2,400		132/120	2,640	
Other expenses	14,180	43,855	132/120	15,598	48,241
		$10,690			$11,759
General price level loss		5,090	132/120		5,599
Net income		$ 5,600			$ 6,160

(1) Roll forward from 12/31/x1 when index stood at 120 to 12/31/x2 when index reached 132 level.

What the restated figures mean

The restated financial statements (Exhibits 12–11 and 12–12) eliminate the effects of price level changes by stating each item in terms of dollars (in this case 12/31/x2 dollars) of constant purchasing power. As restated, the relationships of these items among themselves as well as over time can be different from those prevailing among the unrestated items. Therein, of course, lies much of their significance as the following examples of selected relationships indicate:

	Conventional	Change	Adjusted	Change
Sales:				
19x1	$ 50,000		$ 60,000	
19x2	100,000		104,762	
Increase	$ 50,000	+100%	$ 44,762	+75%
Net income:				
19x1	$ 10,000		$ 6,160	
19x2	28,000		24,160	
Increase	$ 18,000	+180%	$ 18,000	+292%
Return on investment:				
19x1	22% (1)		11% (3)	
19x2	44% (2)		34% (4)	

(1) Income divided by average capital = $\dfrac{10{,}000}{(40{,}000 + 50{,}000) \div 2}$

(2) Income divided by average capital = $\dfrac{28{,}000}{(50{,}000 + 78{,}000) \div 2}$

(3) Income divided by average capital = $\dfrac{6{,}160}{(52{,}800 + 58{,}960) \div 2}$

(4) Income divided by average capital = $\dfrac{24{,}160}{(58{,}960 + 83{,}120) \div 2}$

The *sales* figure comparison indicates that expressed in unadjusted dollars, sales rose 100 percent from 19x1 to 19x2. On the basis of constant purchasing power dollars (here 12/31/x2 dollars), however, the increase was only 75 percent. Care is needed in interpreting these results. All that the above change means is that in terms of constant purchasing power dollars sales rose by 75 percent, and this is a more valid figure of percentage change than the 100 percent change, which compares sales levels expressed in dollars of different purchasing power. However, what cannot be inferred from the adjusted sales figures, for instance, is that the physical volume of sales rose by 75 percent. What the actual change in physical volume was depends on the change in the *specific* sales prices for the company's products or services. If they differ from changes in the *general* price level, no valid inferences regarding changes in physical volume can be drawn. Only if the company's sales price changes coincide exactly with price changes reflected in the general price level index can an adjusted sales change be deemed to reflect changes in the physical volume of sales.

EXHIBIT 12-9
General price level restatement—19x2 general price level gain or loss

	12/31/x1 Conventional	12/31/x1 Restated in 12/31/x2 dollars (1)	12/31/x2 Conventional restated in 12/31/x2 dollars
Net monetary items:			
Cash	$ 32,000	$35,200	$ 45,000
Receivables			12,000
Current liabilities			(5,000)
Long-term debt			(10,000)
Net monetary items	$ 32,000	$35,200	$ 42,000

	Conventional	Conversion factor	Restated to 12/31/x2 dollars
Net monetary items, 12/31/x1	$ 32,000	As above	$ 35,200
Add:			
Sales for 19x2	100,000	(2)	104,762
	$132,000		$139,962
Deduct:			
Purchases	$ 30,000	(2)	$ 31,429
Labor and other costs	40,000	(2)	41,905
Other expenses	20,000	(2)	20,952
	$ 90,000		$ 94,286
Net monetary items (conventional)	$ 42,000		
Net monetary items—restated, 12/31/x2 (if there were no loss)			$ 45,676
Net monetary items (conventional) as above			42,000
General price level loss			$ 3,676

(1) See Exhibit 12-8.
(2) See income statement conversion (Exhibit 12-7).

The greater rate of increase in price level adjusted *net income* as compared with the 180 percent increase in net income in the conventional financial statements can be explained as follows:

The general price level loss on monetary items in 19x1 (all in 12/31/x2 dollars) was $5,599 or 51 percent of the $11,759 income before that loss. This depressed considerably the base net income figure in the percentage comparison. By contrast, due in large measure to the monetary liabilities incurred in 19x2, the loss in purchasing power on monetary items in 19x2 was only $3,676 or 13 percent of the $27,836 income before such loss. This accounts for the much stronger year-to-year net profit increase in the restated net income figure as compared with the conventional net income figure.

Finally, the *return on investment* in both years is less on a price

EXHIBIT 12-10
Restatement of balance sheet as at December 31, 19x2

	Conventional		Conversion factor	Price level adjusted 12/31/x2	
Assets					
Current Assets:					
Cash		$45,000	(1)		$45,000
Accounts receivable		12,000	(1)		12,000
Inventories		20,000	(2)		20,000
Total Current Assets		$77,000			
Equipment	$20,000		132/100	$26,400	
Less: Provision for depreciation	4,000	16,000	(3)	5,280	21,120
Total Assets		$93,000			$98,120
Liabilities and Capital					
Accounts payable		$ 5,000	(1)		$ 5,000
Long-term debt		10,000	(1)		10,000
Capital	$ 4,000		132/100 (4)	$52,800	
Retained earnings balance (1/1/x2)	$10,000		(5)	$ 6,160	
Net income	28,000	38,000	78,000	see Exh. 12-7	24,160	30,320	83,120
Total Liabilities and Capital		$93,000			$98,120

(1) Monetary items—no restatement needed.
(2) See explanation in income statement conversion schedule (Exhibit 12-7).
(3) Balance of depreciation provision at 12/31/x1 in 12/31/x1 dollars—2,400 rolled forward to 12/31/x2 dollars (see "roll forward" Exhibit 12-8) $2,640
Depreciation provided in 19x2 (restated) (Exhibit 12-7) 2,640
  Total depreciation provision $5,280

(4) Capital was invested when price level index stood at 100. To preserve purchasing power, now that the index stands at 132, it must be 132/100 times original amount. This amount can also be taken from Exhibit 12-8.
(5) From statement showing "roll forward" of restated 12/31/x1 balance sheet to 12/31/x2 dollars (Exhibit 12-8).

level restated basis than on a conventional basis. This is due to the fact that in each year the price level restated net income is less than its conventional counterpart *and* because the capital base, on an restated basis, is larger after giving effect to the increase in the price level than it is in the conventional balance sheet. Thus these twin influences combine to reduce the price level restated return on investment as compared to the conventional figures.

IMPLICATIONS FOR ANALYSIS

There are a few basic facts about the effect of price level changes on the conventional financial statements which must be thoroughly understood by the financial analyst. One is that money, whether expressed in dollars or any other currency, is worth only what it will buy. Thus,

EXHIBIT 12-11

THE XTRA CORPORATION
Comparative Balance Sheet (Price Level Adjusted)
In 12/31/x2 Dollars

Assets		12/31/x2		12/31/x1 (1)
Current Assets:				
Cash		$45,000		$35,200
Accounts receivable		12,000		...
Inventories		20,000		...
Total Current Assets		$77,000		$35,200
Equipment	$26,400		$26,400	
Less: Provision for depreciation	5,280	21,120	2,640	23,760
Total Assets		$98,120		$58,960
Liabilities and Capital				
Accounts payable		$ 5,000		...
Long-term debt		10,000		...
Capital		$52,800		$52,800
Retained earnings balance				
1/1/x2	$ 6,160			
Add: Net income for				
19x2 (Exh. 14-12)	24,160	30,320	83,120	6,160
Total Liabilities and Capital		$98,120		$58,960

(1) See Exhibit 12-8.

EXHIBIT 12-12

THE XTRA CORPORATION
Comparative Statements of Income (Price Level Adjusted)
In 12/31/x2 Dollars

		Year ended 12/31/x2		Year ended 12/31/x1 (1)
Sales		$104,762		$60,000
Cost of services:				30,003
Inventory, 1/1/x2	...			
Purchases	$31,429			
Labor and other costs	41,905			
	$73,334			
Inventory, 12/31/x2	20,000	53,334		
		$ 51,428		$29,997
Depreciation	$ 2,640		$ 2,640	
Other expenses	20,952	23,592	15,598	18,238
Net income		$ 27,836		$11,759
General price level loss		3,676		5,599
Net income		$ 24,160		$ 6,160

(1) See Exhibit 12-8

if the price level changes, the value of money changes along with it; and hence a dollar received or spent in one period is not comparable with that received or spent in another period, the distortion being in proportion to the cumulative change in the general price level.

It is part of the "money illusion" to consider a dollar a dollar and to forget the obvious fact that the 1973 dollar represents a much smaller unit of general purchasing power than did, say, the 1950 dollar. Surely, the known difficulties and complexities of adjusting for the infusion into the financial statements of such disparate bundles of purchasing power, all under the common name of "dollar," and the simplifying assumptions needed in carrying out such restating process do not justify the attempts by many to ignore such effects. In times of changing price levels, the income statement, to single out one of the important measures of corporate performance, is composed of at least two distinct elements: (1) results of business activities expressed in terms of units of equal purchasing power and (2) changes resulting from price level changes. An intelligent assessment and analysis of these results require a separation and an understanding of these two disparate effects. By analogy, if we want to measure the speed of an automobile (business results) by reference to a moving train (price level changes), we must adjust for both the rate of speed and the direction of travel of the train before the true speed of the automobile can be determined.

ILLUSTRATION. A small-loan company whose assets are mostly of a monetary nature must, in times of significant price inflation, charge a rate of interest which will compensate it not only for the use of its capital funds but which will also compensate it for the loss of purchasing power of the funds lent. Thus, the proper interpretation of its income, which by conventional standards may seem unduly large, must include recognition of the offsetting general price level loss on monetary assets incurred by the company.

LIMITATIONS OF RESTATEMENT TECHNIQUE

The restatement method described earlier in the chapter represents a reasonable and feasible technique of restating for price level changes as well as a useful framework for visualizing the effects of price level changes on both monetary and nonmonetary assets, liabilities, and equities.

It is important for the analyst to understand what such restatements do and what they do not do. They do adjust historical costs to comparable dollars of uniform purchasing power. However, since we use an index of general purchasing power, such as the recommended Implicit Gross National Product Price Deflator, the restated figures do not represent, except by coincidence, either market values or replacement costs or any other measure of realizable values. To achieve a conversion to market values, we would have to apply *specific* price indexes to each class of assets; and this is, of course, not consistent with the purpose of *general* price level adjustments. Thus, whether or not we should use current market prices, replacement costs, etc., in lieu of historical costs is a question separate and apart from inflation and deflation. Even in times of stable prices, individual items display price instability, thus giving rise to a conflict between historical costs and current replacement costs. General price level adjustments are not designed to resolve this conflict.

INTERPRETATION OF EFFECTS OF PRICE LEVEL CHANGES

In times of changing price levels, the results shown by accounts prepared on the conventional basis are not a measure of increase or decrease of wealth in terms of purchasing power, and thus they do not reflect amounts which can prudently be regarded as available for the payment of dividends. Such earnings cannot be regarded as distributable earnings. Thus, for instance, some of the reported profit may merely represent recovery of unbooked price level depreciation or of inventory replacement cost achieved by means of realistic pricing policies. Moreover, the intelligent analyst knows that in times of rising price levels, replacement of productive facilities requires more dollars than are being "reserved" by conventional depreciation charges. An awareness on the part of analysts of these facts and the lack of any price level data disclosure so far is, in fact, responsible for the increasing importance attached to the "statement of changes in financial position." In this statement the analyst tries to trace the flow of funds and the corrosive effect of inflation on a company's liquidity and need for capital. He has to be particularly alert to the effect which inflation and the possible resulting overstatement of profits, relatively high taxes, dividends, and fixed asset replacement needs have on the company's financial resources, both present and future. The analyst is particularly on the lookout for evidence that management has recognized these problems and has allowed for them and their effects on the company's liquidity, profitability, and capital requirements.

The effect of price level changes on an entity's financial statements depends on both the rate of price level changes and the composition of assets, liabilities, and equities. A recent study[1] showed that even a moderate rate of inflation can, on a cumulative basis, cause very significant distortions of operating and financial results.

The composition of assets, liabilities, and equities are another important determinant of the effect of price level changes on an entity and on its financial statements.

The following are some useful generalizations regarding such effects in times of significant inflation:

[1] Paul Rosenfield, "Accounting for Inflation—A Field Test," *The Journal of Accountancy*, June 1969, pp. 45–50.

1. The larger the proportion of depreciable assets and the higher their age, the more unrestated income tends to be overstated. Thus, the income of capital intensive companies tends to be affected more than that of others by price level restatements.
2. The rate of inventory turnover has a bearing on price level effects. The slower the inventory turnover, the more income tends to be overstated. Thus, the Fifo inventory method is more likely to overstate income in times of rising price levels than is the Lifo method.
3. The mix of assets and liabilities as between monetary and nonmonetary is important. A net investment in monetary assets will, in times of rising price levels, lead to purchasing power losses, and purchasing power gains will result from a net monetary liability position.
4. The methods of financing also have an important bearing on results. The larger the amount of debt and the longer its maturities, the better the protection against purchasing power losses or the better the exposure to purchasing power gains.

Price level adjusted financial statements can, thus, contribute to a more intelligent analysis and, the stronger the rate of price change (say, inflation), the more necessary such analysis becomes. An article on the effects of severe inflation in Latin America[2] points out the danger of what the author refers to as "decapitalization." Thus, he states that "the true net worth is arrived at only when all assets and liabilities are expressed in present-day values," presumably, in the context of the article, meaning current purchasing power. Severe inflation can distort not only business results but also business practices. The author maintains that "inflation at any level will offset results of any corporation over a period of time. The effect must be recognized by managers of each operating unit." Thus, for example, in times of rampant inflation, such as recently occurred in South America, a manager may flee to the comparative safety of an investment in inventory (nonmonetary asset) that is larger than dictated by business needs, even though normal business judgment indicates a low inventory position and a high rate of inventory turnover.

As the discussion earlier in the chapter showed, only a comprehensive restatement of financial statements can convey a full and undistorted measure of the impact of general price level changes. Thus, for example, only such a restatement will enable the analyst to compute the real incidence of taxes, the dividend payment in relation to adjusted income, or the adjusted return on investment. With respect to the latter rate, for example, only a full restatement can show the adjusted capital as well as the adjusted income necessary for computation of the return on investment. If, for example, due to heavy investments in fixed assets,

---

[2] J. W. McKee, Jr., "Defending Profits against Inflation," *Financial Executive*, April 1968, pp. 74–80.

capital in the conventional statements is understated while income is overstated, the resulting return on the equity computation suffers from the impact of a double distortion.

While partial restatement of the financial statements for price level changes is not as valid a procedure as the comprehensive restatement, the outside analyst, in the absence of the considerable detail required for comprehensive restatement, will realize that recognition of the most important elements affected by price level changes in a superior procedure to no adjustment at all. Thus, in the absence of price level restated supplementary financial statements, the analyst will try to assess as best he can the effect of company's asset mix, its debt structure, and other factors which affect its posture and exposure to gain or loss in times of price level changes.

QUESTIONS

1. How do changing price levels affect the conventional (unrestated) financial statements of a company operating in an inflationary environment?
2. In what ways have businessmen attempted to meet some of the objectives of price level accounting? Evaluate these attempts briefly.
3. What is the basic purpose of "price level statements"?
4. In what respect do general price level statements differ from conventional financial statements?
5. Why is the distinction between monetary and nonmonetary items significant in accounting for the effects of price level changes?
6. On the basis of conventional financial statements, the year-to-year sales increase of Company X was 24 percent. Adjusted for price level changes, the increase was only 10 percent. Is it possible to infer from this that the physical volume of sales rose by 10 percent? Explain.
7. Why do general price level adjusted financial statements fail to meet the objectives of those who want to see fair market values or replacement values introduced to accounting?
8. What effect can the composition of the assets and liabilities of an enterprise have on the effect which price level changes can have on it? Elaborate by means of an example or two.
9. In the absence of supplementary financial statements restated for price level changes, how can the financial analyst assess the approximate effects of price level changes on the reported results?
10. *a)* How might it be maintained that a gain or a loss is incurred by holding a constant balance of cash through a period of price level change?
    b) Identify and give a justification for the typical accounting treatment accorded these gains or losses. (AICPA)

13

The auditor's opinion—meaning and significance

AN ENTITY's financial statements are the representations of its management. Management bears a primary responsibility for the fairness of presentation and the degree of informative disclosure in the financial statements it issues to interested parties, such as present and potential owners, creditors, and others. It has, however, become generally accepted that there is a need for an independent check on management's financial reporting.

The profession that has emerged to serve society's need in this respect by performing the attest function is the public accounting profession. It may be readily observed that the more developed a country's economy and the more diverse, free, and mobile its capital and money markets, the stronger and the more important its public accounting profession is likely to be. Surely, the United States experience supports this conclusion, for the public accounting profession here is perhaps the world's largest and most vital.

Some states recognize and license "Public Accountants" and "Licensed Accountants," and the requirements for practice under these titles vary from strict to feeble. However, there is another title which has the most consistent significance—that of "Certified Public Accountant." It can be acquired only by those who have passed the CPA examination, a rigorous series of tests which are uniform in all states and which are graded centrally under the auspices of the American Institute of Certified Public Accountants (AICPA). While no profession can insure uniformity of quality among its members, the successful completion of these examinations does insure that the candidate has demonstrated acceptable knowledge of accounting and auditing principles and practices.

Since the CPAs represent by far the most important segment of public accounting practice in the United States, our consideration of the auditor's opinion will be confined to that issued by the CPA and governed by the various pronouncements issued by his professional association, the AICPA.

In spite of the many real and imagined shortcomings of the auditor's work, and, as this work illustrates, there are many of both varieties, the auditor's function is of critical importance to the financial analyst. While improvements are needed in many areas of the auditor's work, his attestation to financial statements greatly increases their reliability to the analyst as well as the degree and quality of disclosure provided in them.

As in many areas of endeavor, so in the analysis of financial statements, partial or incomplete knowledge can be more damaging than a complete lack of it. This truth applies to the analyst's understanding and knowledge of the auditor's work and the significance of his opinion.

WHAT THE ANALYST NEEDS TO KNOW

In relying on the auditor's opinion, which covers the financial statements subject to review, the analyst must—

1. Learn as much as he can about the auditor upon whom he is relying.
2. Understand fully what the auditor's opinion means and the message it is designed to convey to the user.
3. Appreciate the limitations to which the opinion is subject, as well as implications which such limitations hold for the analysis of financial statements covered by the opinion.

Knowing the auditor

The possession by the auditor of the CPA certificate does assure the analyst that he has a reasonable qualification for practice as an auditor. However, as is the case in other professions, differences in ability, competence, and qualifications can be considerable.

The relationship between the auditor and those who rely on his opinion differs markedly from that existing in other professional relationships. While the auditor has both an obligation and a concurrent responsibility to users of his opinion, he is in most cases neither appointed nor compensated by them. He must look mostly to management for both recommendation for his appointment and the determination of his fee. When management's desires with respect to financial reporting are in conflict with the best interests of the outside users of financial statements, the auditor's integrity and independence are put to a stern test. Thus, one criterion of the auditor's reliability is his reputation for integrity and independence in the community at large and among respected members of the financial community. Whatever else the auditor must have, and his qualifications and skill must be considerable, without these attributes nothing else counts for very much. The reputation of an auditor for competence and for knowledge of his work can be established in a variety of ways. The auditor's professional credentials are one element, his membership and standing in state and national accounting associations another, and his participation in professional organizations yet another factor to be assessed by the analyst. An auditing firm's activities and past performance are usually well known in the community in which it operates.

Finally, the analyst, from his own experience is often able to form a judgment about the auditor's reputation for quality work. Since there exists considerable leeway in adherence to audit standards and in the application of accounting principles, an audit firm's "track record" of actual level of performances in these critical areas provides a firsthand guide to its reliability and integrity. The analyst would do well to note instances in which a CPA firm has accepted the least desirable acceptable accounting principle among the available alternatives, has equivocated unnecessarily in its opinion, or was found wanting in its application of auditing procedures.

What the auditor's opinion means

The auditor's opinion is the culmination of a lengthy and complicated process of auditing and investigation. It is here, and only here, that the auditor reports on the nature of his work and on the degree of responsibility he assumes. While his influence may be indirectly felt throughout the financial statements by the presentation, description, and footnote disclosure which he may have suggested or insisted upon, the opinion, and the opinion alone, remains his exclusive domain. Thus, the opinion and the references to the financial statements which it contains should always be carefully read. To ignore the auditor's opinion, or to assume that it does not mean what it says, or that it means more than it says, is foolhardy and unwarranted.

The auditor's responsibility to outsiders whom he does not know and who rely on his representations is considerable, and his exposure to liability arising therefrom is growing. Thus, the obligations which the standards of his profession impose on him, while extensive, are at the same time defined and limited. Consequently, no analyst is justified in assuming that the association of the auditor's name with the financial statements goes beyond what the auditor's opinion says, or is a form of insurance on which the analyst can rely to bail him out of bad decisions.

What exactly does the auditor's opinion say? The best starting point for us is an examination of an auditor's "clean opinion," that is, an opinion which is not qualified in any way. This will give us an idea of the greatest degree of responsibility the auditor is willing to assume. The "clean opinion," which covers two annual examinations, reads as follows:

To the Shareowners and Board of Directors
(Name of Company)

We have examined the balance sheet of (name of company) as of (date), and the related statement of income and retained earnings, and the statement of changes in financial position for the year then ended. Our examination was made in accordance with generally accepted auditing standards, and accordingly included such tests of the accounting records and such other auditing procedures as we considered necessary in the circumstances. We previously examined and reported upon the financial statements of the Company for the year ended (date).

In our opinion, the aforementioned financial statements present fairly the financial position of (name of company) at (date) and (date), and the results of its operations and changes in its financial position for the years then ended, in conformity with generally accepted accounting principles applied on a consistent basis.

(Name of accountants)

(City and date)

THE AUDITOR'S REPORT

The auditor's report is divided into two distinct parts: (1) the scope of the audit and (2) the auditor's opinion.

The scope of the audit

The scope paragraph of the auditor's report sets forth the financial statements examined, the period of time which they cover, and the scope of the audit to which they and the underlying records have been subjected.

The standard terminology refers to an examination made in accordance with "generally accepted auditing standards." This is "shorthand" for a very comprehensive meaning which is elaborated upon in the profession's literature and particularly in *Statement on Auditing Standards No. 1* issued by the Committee on Auditing Procedure of the AICPA in 1972. These auditing standards are broad generalizations classified under three headings: (1) general standards (2) standards of field work, and (3) standards of reporting.

General standards define the personal qualities required of the independent CPA. They are:

(a) The examination is to be performed by a person or persons having adequate technical training and proficiency as an auditor.
(b) In all matters relating to the assignment an independence in mental attitude is to be maintained by the auditor or auditors.
(c) Due professional care is to be exercised in the performance of the examination and the preparation of the report.

Standards of field work embrace the actual execution of the audit and cover the planning of the work, the evaluation of the client's system of internal control, and the quality and sufficiency of the evidence obtained. *Statement on Auditing Standards No. 1* enumerates them as follows:

1. The work is to be adequately planned and assistants, if any, are to be properly supervised.
2. There is to be a proper study and evaluation of the existing internal control as a basis for reliance thereon and for the determination of the resultant extent of the tests to which auditing procedures are to be restricted.
3. Sufficient competent evidential matter is to be obtained through inspection, observation, inquiries and confirmations to afford a reasonable basis for an opinion regarding the financial statements under examination.

Reporting standards govern the preparation and presentation of the auditor's report. They are intended to insure that the auditor's position is clearly and unequivocally stated and that the degree of responsibility he assumes is made clear to the reader. These standards are four in number:

1. The report shall state whether the financial statements are presented in accordance with generally accepted principles of accounting.
2. The report shall state whether such principles have been consistently observed in the current period in relation to the preceding period.
3. Informative disclosures in the financial statements are to be regarded as reasonably adequate unless otherwise stated in the report.
4. The report shall either contain an expression of opinion regarding the financial statements, taken as a whole, or an assertion to the effect that an opinion cannot be expressed. When an over-all opinion cannot be expressed, the reasons therefor should be stated. In all cases where an auditor's name is associated with financial statements the report should contain a clear-cut indication of the character of the auditor's examination, if any, and the degree of responsibility he is taking.

Audit standards are the yardsticks by which the quality of audit procedures are measured. The SEC in *Accounting Series Releases No. 21* stated:

... In referring to generally accepted auditing standards the Commission has in mind, in addition to the employment of generally recognized normal auditing procedures, their application with professional competence by properly trained persons.

Auditing procedures. The second phrase of the scope section states that the examination "included such tests of the accounting records and such other auditing procedures" as were considered necessary in the circumstances.

This statement encompasses the wide sweep of auditing theory brought to bear on the particular examination, as well as the professional discretion the auditor uses in the performance of his work.

The subject of auditing is, of course, a discipline in itself requiring for successful mastery a period of study and practical application. Thus, while we obviously cannot go with any degree of detail into what constitutes the process of auditing, it behooves all who use its end product to have a basic understanding of the process by which the auditor obtains assurance about the fair presentation of the financial statements as to which he expresses an opinion.

A basic objective of the financial audit is the detection of errors and irregularities, intentional or unintentional, which if undetected would materially affect the fairness of presentation of financial summarizations or their conformity with generally accepted accounting principles.

To be economically feasible and justifiable, auditing can aim only at a reasonable level of assurance in this respect about the data under review. This means that under a testing system, assurance can never be complete, and that the final audit conclusions are subject to this inherent probability of error.

Briefly stated, the auditor's basic approach is as follows: to gain assurance about financial summarizations the auditor must examine the accounting system of which they are a final product. If that system of internal control is well conceived, properly maintained, and implemented, it is assumed that it should result in valid financial records and summarizations.

Thus, the need for and the extent of the testing of the records is dependent on the degree of proper operation of the system of internal control.

The importance of internal control. The importance of the review of the system of internal control in the total audit framework can be gauged from a reading of the scope paragraph of the original standard opinion (used from about 1939 to 1948) which read in part as follows:

... have reviewed the system of internal control and the accounting procedures of the company, and, without making a detailed audit of the transactions, have examined or tested accounting records of the company and other supporting evidence by methods, and to the extent we deemed appropriate.

Even though these specific words have been deleted from the form of the present opinion, the phrase still accurately describes the auditor's work.

After ascertaining, by means of investigation and inquiry, what management's plan and design for a system of internal control is, if any, the auditor proceeds to test the system in order to ascertain whether it is in existence and is, in fact, being implemented as intended. This testing is called procedural testing.

If after application of procedural testing, the system of internal control is found to be well conceived and in proper operation, the amount of testing to which income statement items or individual assets and liabilities will be subjected will be very limited. The latter type of testing, which may be called "validation testing," will have to be increased significantly if procedural testing reveals the system of internal control to be deficient or not operational.

This method of checking out the system and then performing additional sample tests on the basis of its evaluation does, of course, leave room for a great deal of professional discretion, for "corner-cutting," and for a variety of qualities of judgment. Hence, it is subject to the risk of failure. Moreover, the usual audit, according to the accounting profession, is not primarily or specifically designed to disclose fraud, nor can it be relied on to disclose defalcations, although their discovery may result.

From the above discussion it should be clear that reliance on an audit must be based on an understanding of the nature of the audit process and the limitations to which it is subject.

The opinion section

The first paragraph of the auditor's report, which we discussed above, deals with the scope of his examination and the limitations or restrictions, if any, to which it was subject. The second paragraph (in practice the order of these paragraphs may be reversed) sets forth the auditor's opinion on:

1. The fairness of presentation of the financial statements;
2. Their conformity with generally accepted accounting principles; and
3. The consistent application of these principles in the financial statements.

The standard short-form report presented earlier in the chapter contained a "clean opinion," that is, the auditor had no qualifications to record as to any of the three criteria enumerated above. Any modifications of substance in the language of the auditor's opinion paragraph is, technically speaking, considered to be a qualification or a disclaimer. Not all qualifications are, of course, of equal significance to the user. Some deviations in language are explanatory in character and do not affect the auditor's opinion significantly. References to the work of other auditors is not regarded as a qualification but rather an indication of divided responsibility for the performance of the audit. Other explanatory comments may not carry over to affect the auditor's opinion and, at times, one may wonder why mention of them is necessary. On the other hand, certain qualifications or disclaimers are so significant as to cast doubt on the reliability of the financial statements or their usefulness for decision-making purposes.

Let us then examine the major categories of the auditor's qualifications and disclaimers, the occasions on which they are properly used, and the significance which they hold to the user of financial statements.

CONDITIONS GIVING RISE TO QUALIFICATIONS, DISCLAIMERS, OR ADVERSE OPINIONS

There are three main categories of conditions which require qualifications, disclaimers, or adverse opinions (collectively referred to as qualified opinions):

1. Limitations in the scope of the auditor's examination affected by (a) conditions which preclude the application of auditing procedures considered necessary in the circumstances or (b) restrictions imposed by the client.
2. The financial statements do not present fairly the financial position and/or results of operations because (a) they fail to conform with generally accepted accounting principles or (b) they do not contain adequate disclosure.
3. There exist uncertainties about the future resolution of material matters, the effect of which cannot presently be estimated or reasonably provided for.

CATEGORIES OF QUALIFIED OPINIONS[1]

Before a consideration of the variety of conditions which call for qualified opinions, let us consider the major types of qualifications which the auditor may express.

---
[1] As this book goes to press, the Auditing Standards Executive Committee of the AICPA has exposed a proposed statement on "Auditors' Reports." Since the changes proposed in the statement are very significant and the likelihood of their adoption

Qualification—"except-for" type

This qualification expresses an opinion on the financial statements except for repercussions stemming from conditions which must be disclosed in a middle paragraph(s) of the opinion. It may arise from limitations in the scope of the audit which, because of circumstances beyond the auditor's control or because of restrictions imposed by the audited company, result in a failure to obtain reasonably objective and verifiable evidence in support of events which have taken place. It may arise from a lack of conformity of the financial statements to generally accepted accounting principles. It may also arise in cases where there are uncertainties about future events which cannot be resolved or the effect of which cannot be estimated or reasonably provided for at the time the opinion is rendered. It is meant to be used in instances where the nature of the uncertainties is not so material as to require adverse opinion.

An uncertainty, such as due to operating losses or serious financial weakness which calls into question the fundamental assumption that an entity can continue to operate, also calls for qualified opinions rather than for a disclaimer of opinion.

DISCLAIMER OF OPINION

A disclaimer of opinion is a statement of inability to express an opinion. It must be rendered when insufficient competent evidential matter is available to the auditor to enable him to form an opinion on the financial statements. It arises mostly from limitations in the scope of the audit.

ADVERSE OPINIONS

An adverse opinion should be rendered in cases when the financial statements are not prepared in accordance with generally accepted ac-

---

good, it was deemed desirable to incorporate them in this work. The following summary of the major provisions of the proposed statement is intended to assist the reader in following developments after publication of this work and in identifying those changes which may not be adopted in the statement's final version:

1. An explanatory middle paragraph(s) would be required in the auditor's report whenever the auditor's opinion is other than unqualified.
2. An auditor's expression of a qualified opinion would always use the word "except" or "exception" in phrases such as "except for" or "with the exception of." The phrase "subject to," previously used in order to indicate that there is an uncertainty affecting the financial statements, no longer would be deemed appropriate.
3. The use of the disclaimer of opinion would be restricted to situations involving limitations on the scope of the auditor's examination. The disclaimer would no longer be used to express an auditor's reservations arising because there are uncertainties affecting the financial statements.
4. "Piecemeal" opinions would be prohibited.

counting principles, and this has a significant effect on the fair presentation of those statements. An adverse opinion results generally from a situation in which the auditor has been unable to convince his client to amend the financial statements so that they adhere to generally accepted accounting principles. The issuance of an adverse opinion must always be accompanied by a statement of the reasons for such an opinion.

Having covered the various types of opinions an auditor can express, let us now turn to the various conditions which call for qualifications in such opinions.

LIMITATIONS IN THE SCOPE OF THE AUDIT

A limitation in the scope of the auditor's examination, that is, an inability to perform certain audit steps which he considers necessary, will, if material, result in a qualification or disclaimer of his opinion.

Some limitations in the scope of the auditor's examination arise from an inability to perform certain audit steps because of conditions beyond the auditor's and the client's control, for example, an inability to observe the opening inventory where the audit appointment was not made until the close of the year. Other limitations may result from a client-imposed restriction on the auditor's work. Whatever the reason for an incomplete examination, the auditor must report the inadequacy of the examination and the conclusions which flow from such an inadequacy.

The accounting profession has approved "extended procedures" with respect to observation of inventories and the confirmation of accounts receivable. If these steps cannot be reasonably or practically performed, the auditor must, in order to issue an unqualified opinion, satisfy himself about the inventories and accounts receivable by alternative means. He must, however, no longer indicate such an omission of regular procedures in his opinion.

FAILURE OF FINANCIAL STATEMENTS TO CONFORM TO GENERALLY ACCEPTED ACCOUNTING PRINCIPLES

The auditor brings to bear his expertise in the application of auditing techniques and procedures to satisfy himself about the existence, ownership, and validity of presentation of the assets, the liabilities, and net worth as well as the statement of results. As an expert accountant, the auditor judges the fairness of presentation of financial statements and their conformity with generally accepted accounting principles. The latter is one of the most important functions of the auditor's opinion.

Fair presentation is, to an important extent, dependent on the degree of informative disclosure provided. Adherence to generally accepted accounting principles, which is another prerequisite of fairness of presentation, depends on the employment, in the financial statements, of principles having authoritative support. Opinions of the APB enjoy, by definition, authoritative support. If the accountant concurs in a company's use of an accounting principle which differs from that approved by the APB but which he believes enjoys the support of other authoritative sources, he need not qualify his opinion, but he must disclose that the principle used differs from those approved by the APB. This, of course, puts the onus on the auditor in justifying the departure from an APB approved principle.

If, because of lack of adequate disclosure or the use of accounting principles which do not enjoy authoritative support, the auditor concludes that the financial statements are not fairly presented, he must qualify his opinion or render an adverse opinion. The decision of whether to make his opinion an "except-for" type, which is a qualified opinion, or to render an adverse opinion, which states that the "financial statements do not present fairly . . ." hinges on the materiality of the effect of such a deficiency on the financial statements taken as a whole. The concept of materiality in accounting and auditing is, however, very vague and remains undefined by the accounting profession itself.

It is obvious that a qualification due to a lack of disclosure or a lack of adherence to generally accepted accounting principles is the result of the auditor's inability to persuade his client to modify the financial statements. Thus, an "except for" type of opinion is not proper, and an adverse opinion is called for together with a full description of the shortcomings in the financial statements as well as their total impact thereon.

The following are pertinent excerpts from an opinion qualified because of lack of adherence to generally accepted accounting principles:

> The company has provided for depreciation of plant and equipment on the straight-line basis in the accompanying financial statements; however, for federal income tax purposes the company has used the double-declining balance method in computing its depreciation. In computing the provision for federal income taxes for the year ended December 31, 19x5, the computation was based upon the higher depreciation used for tax return purposes and accordingly the provisions and the liability for federal income taxes are understated by $90,000, which represents the estimated amount which will be payable when depreciation for financial statement purposes exceeds that allowable on the income tax return.
>
> In our opinion, except that provision has not been made for the additional income taxes as described in the foregoing paragraph, the accompanying financial statements . . .

FINANCIAL STATEMENTS SUBJECT TO UNRESOLVED KNOWN UNCERTAINTIES

Whenever uncertainties about the future exist which cannot be resolved, or whose effect cannot be estimated or reasonably provided for at the time of the issuance of the auditor's opinion, a qualified opinion or a disclaimer of opinion may be required. Such uncertainties may relate to lawsuits, tax matters, or other contingencies, the outcome of which is dependent upon decisions of parties other than management. Or the uncertainties may relate to the recovery of the investment in certain assets through future operations or through their disposition.

The practical effect of an uncertainty qualification is to state the auditor's inability to assess the impact of the contingency, or the likelihood of its occurrence, and to pass on to the reader the burden of its evaluation.

One variety of "except for" qualification relates to the question of whether the going-concern assumption in accounting (see Chapter 19) is justified. This question arises when a company is incurring continued operating losses, deficits in the stockholder's equity, working capital insufficiencies, or defaults under loan agreements. In such cases the auditor expresses his doubt about the propriety of applying practices implicit in the going concern concept such as the valuation of fixed assets at cost.

The following are examples of pertinent portions of auditor reports relating to uncertainties:

As stated in Note 1 to the accompanying consolidated financial statements, the company had an investment of $1,800,000 at December 31, 19x1, in plant and other costs incurred in the development of commercial production of disk packs. Realization of this investment is dependent upon the successful development of the production process, adequate financing and subsequent sales at prices which will cover costs of production, including amortization of plant and development costs.

In our opinion, except for the effect of the matter referred to in the preceding paragraph. . . .

* * *

The accompanying financial statements of the Company have been prepared on the basis of a going concern although the ability of the Company to continue as a going concern is dependent upon future earnings. In this connection, it should be noted that in the period from commencement of operations through June 30, 19x8, the Company accumulated a net loss of $150,340.

Except for the appropriateness of the going concern concept and to the ability of the Company to realize its unamortized programming development costs through future profitable operations, in our opinion the accompanying financial statements present fairly . . .

EXCEPTIONS AS TO CONSISTENCY

The second standard of reporting requires that the auditor's report state whether the principles of accounting employed "have been consistently observed in the current period in relation to the preceding period."

The basic objective of the consistency standard is to assure the reader that comparability of financial statements as between periods has not been materially affected by changes in the accounting principles employed or in the method of their application. Thus, if a change has been made affecting the comparability of the financial statements, a statement of the nature of the changes and their effect on the financial statements is required.

There are three types of changes which must be considered here:

1. Changes in accounting principles employed, for example, a change in the method of depreciation.
2. Changes required by altered conditions, for example, a change in the estimated useful life of an asset.
3. Changed conditions unrelated to accounting which nevertheless have an effect on comparability, for example, the acquisition or disposition of a subsidiary.

Changes of type 1 involve the consistency standard and must be dealt with in the auditor's opinion. Changes of type 2 affect comparability but do not require comment in the auditor's report except in cases of SEC filings where that agency requires comment, in the auditor's opinion, of any change affecting comparability. Changes of type 3 require no comment in the auditor's opinion but where material require footnote disclosure.

LONG-FORM REPORT

Auditors are sometimes asked to prepare a report containing more extensive comment and additional details of the financial statements. Known as long-form reports, these reports ordinarily include details of individual items in the financial statements, explanatory comments, statistical data, and other informative material of both accounting and nonaccounting nature. In some cases such reports may also contain a more detailed description of audit steps performed.

In general, an auditor is not assuming more responsibility by providing additional detail and information, nor can the supplying of additional descriptive matter relieve him of his primary responsibility to give a clear-cut indication of the character of his examination and the responsibility he is taking.

SPECIAL REPORTS

There are circumstances where the standard short-form report of the auditor is not appropriate due to special circumstances or the limited scope of the examination which the auditor is requested to undertake. It is particularly important that the analyst read such reports carefully so that he is not misled into believing that the auditor is assuming here his ordinary measure of responsibility. The following are some types of special reports which the reader may encounter:

1. Reports by companies in the development stage where many uncertainties regarding development costs exist.
2. Reports by companies on a cash or incomplete basis of accounting.
3. Reports by nonprofit organizations.
4. Reports prepared for limited purposes. Such reports usually deal with certain aspects of the financial statements (such as computations of royalties, rentals, profit-sharing arrangements, or compliance with provisions of bond indentures, etc.).

UNAUDITED REPORTS

A certified public accountant may be engaged to prepare, or assist in the preparation of, unaudited financial statements. In such a capacity the auditor performs an accounting service and not an auditing service. Nevertheless, an auditor must disclose deficiencies in financial statements which are known to him, regardless of the capacity in which he is acting.

Unaudited financial statements with which an auditor is associated in any way must be clearly marked as "unaudited" and usually contain the following statement:

Mr. John Fry, President
Zero Manufacturing Company
Cresskill, New Jersey

The financial statements of Zero Manufacturing Company included in this report have been prepared from the books and records of the Company without audit and we express no opinion on them.

IMPLICATIONS FOR ANALYSIS

Auditing as a function and the auditor's opinion, as an instrument of assurance, are widely misunderstood. The responsibility for this lack of communication cannot be all laid at the auditor's door, for the profession has published a number of pamphlets in which it has endeavored to explain its function. Nor should the readers of financial statements bear the full responsibility for this state of affairs because the accounting profession's message in this area is often couched in technical and cautious language and requires a great deal of effort and background information for a full understanding.

A useful discussion of the implications of the current state of auditing to the user of audited financial statements may be presented in two parts:

1. Implications stemming from the nature of the audit process.
2. Implications arising from the professional standards which govern the auditor's opinion.

Implications inherent in the audit process

Auditing is based on a sampling approach to the data under audit. Statistical sampling is a relatively new concept in auditing, and while lending itself to many applications in theory, it is more limited in actual practice. Thus, most audit tests are based on "judgmental samples" of the data, that is, samples selected by the auditor's intuition, judgment, and evaluation of many factors. Often the size of the sample is necessarily limited by the economics of the accounting practice.

The reader must realize that the auditor does not aim at, nor can he ever achieve, complete certainty. Even a review of every single transaction—a process which would be economically unjustifiable—would not achieve such complete certainty.

Auditing is a developing art. Even its very basic theoretical underpinnings are far from fully understood or resolved. There is, for instance, no clear relationship between the auditor's evaluation of the effectiveness of the system of internal controls, which is a major factor on which the auditor relies, and the extent of audit testing and the nature of audit procedures employed. If we add to that the fact that the qualities of judgment among auditors may vary greatly, we should not be surprised to find that the history of auditing contains many examples of spectacular failures. On the other hand, as is the case with the risk of accidental death in commercial aviation, the percentage of failure to the total number of audits performed is very small indeed. Thus, the user of audited financial statements can, in general, be reassured about the overall results of the performance of the audit function, but he must remember that there is risk in reliance on its results in specific cases. Such risks are due to many factors, including the auditor's inability to detect fraud at the highest level and the application of proper audit tests to such an end (McKesson and Robbins case), the auditor's inability to grasp the extent of a deteriorating situation (the Yale Express case), the auditor's conception of the range of his responsibilities to probe and disclose (the Continental Vending case), and the quality of the audit (the Bar Chris Construction Company case and the Equity Funding Corporation of America case).

Thus, while the audit function will generally justify the reliance which financial analysts place on audited financial statements, such a reliance cannot be a blind one. The analyst must be aware that the entire audit process is a probabilistic one subject to many risks. Even its flawless application may not necessarily result in complete assurance, and most certainly cannot insure that the auditor has elicited all the facts, especially if there is high-level management collusion to withhold such facts from him. Finally, the heavy dependence of the auditing process on judgment will, of necessity, result in a wide range of quality of performance.

Thus, in short, when approaching audited financial statements, the analyst must be aware of the risks of failure inherent in an audit; he must pay attention to the identity of the auditors and to what their record has been; and armed with a knowledge of what auditors do and how they do it, he must himself assess the areas of possible vulnerability in the financial statements.

Implications stemming from the standards which govern the auditor's opinion

In relying on the auditor's opinion the analyst must be aware of the limitations to which the audit process is subject, and this was the subject of the preceding discussion. Moreover, he must understand what the auditor's opinion means and particularly what the auditor himself thinks he conveys to the reader by means of his opinion.

Let us first consider the unqualified opinion or the so-called "clean" opinion. The auditor maintains that he expresses an opinion on *management's* statements. He is very insistent on this point and attaches considerable importance to it. It means that normally he did not prepare the financial statements nor did he choose the accounting principles embodied in them. Instead, he reviews the financial statements presented to him by management and ascertains that they are in agreement with the books and records which he audited. He also determines that generally acceptable principles of accounting have been employed in the preparation of the financial statements but that does not mean that they are the *best* principles that could have been used. It is a well-known fact that management will often rely on the auditor, as an expert in accounting, to help them pick the principle which, while still acceptable, will come nearest to meeting their reporting objectives. Finally, the auditor will determine that the minimum standards of disclosure have been met so that all matters essential to a fair presentation of the financial statements are included in them.

One might well ask what difference it makes whether the auditor prepared the statements or not so long as he expresses an unqualified opinion on them. The accounting profession has never clearly explained what the implications of this really mean to the user of the financial statements. However, a number of such possible implications should be borne in mind by the analyst:

1. The auditor's knowledge about the financial statements is not as strong as that of the preparer who was in more intimate contact with all the factors which gave rise to the transactions. He knows only what he can see on the basis of a sampling process and may not know all that he should know.
2. Since many items in the financial statements are not capable of exact measurement, he merely reviews such measurements for reasonableness. His are not the original determinations, and unless he can successfully prove otherwise (as for example in the case of estimates of useful lives of property), management's determination will prevail. Thus, the auditor's opinion contains no reference to "present exactly" or "present correctly" but rather states that the statements "present fairly."
3. While the auditor may be consulted on the use of accounting principles he, as auditor rather than as preparer of such statements, does not select the principles to be used. Moreover, he cannot insist on the use of the *best* available principle any more than he is likely to *insist* on a degree of disclosure above the minimum considered as acceptable at the time.
4. The limitations to which the auditor's ability to audit are subject have never been spelled out by the accounting profession. Knowledgeable auditors do, of course, know about them; but there seems to be a tacit agreement, of doubtful value to the profession, not to discuss them. For example, is the auditor really equipped to audit the value of complex technical work in progress? Can he competently evaluate the adequacy of insurance reserves? Can he second-guess the client's estimate of the percentage of completion of a large contract? While such questions are rarely raised in public, let alone answered, they cannot be unequivocally answered in the affirmative.
5. While the preparer must, under the rules of double-entry bookkeeping, account for all items, large or small, the auditor is held to less exacting standards of accuracy in his work. Thus the error tolerances are wider. He leans on the doctrine of materiality which in its basic concept simply means that the auditor need not concern himself, in either the auditing or the reporting phases of his work, with trivial or unimportant matters. What is important or significant

is, of course, a matter of judgment and so far the profession has neither defined the concept nor set limits or established criteria to govern the application of the concept of materiality. This has given it an unwarranted degree of reporting latitude.[2]

Of course, auditors even as a profession, in contra-distinction to a business, must pay attention to the economics of their function and to the limits of the responsibilities they should assume. Thus, whether the foregoing limitations on the auditor's function and responsibility are justified or not, the analyst must recognize them as standards applied by auditors and evaluate his reliance on audited financial statements with a full understanding of them.

The auditor's reference to "generally accepted accounting principles" in his opinion should be well understood by the user of the financial statements. Such reference means that the auditor is satisfied that such principles have authoritative support and that they have been applied "in all material respects." Aside from understanding the operation of the concept of materiality, here the analyst must understand that the definition of what constitutes "generally accepted accounting principles" is often vague and subject to significant latitude in interpretation and application. Moreover, not all important areas of accounting are covered by authoritative pronouncements which define acceptable practice, for example, accounting for research and development costs.

Similarly indeterminate are present-day standards relating to disclosure. While minimum standards are increasingly established in pronouncements of the APB, accountants have not always adhered to them. The degree to which the lack of disclosure impairs the fair presentation of the financial statements remains subject to the auditor's judgment and discretion, and there are no definite standards which indicate at what point lack of disclosure is material enough to impair fairness of presentation and thus require a qualification in the auditor's report.

ILLUSTRATION. APB *Opinion No. 8* on Pensions requires disclosure regarding employee groups covered, a description of pension accounting and funding policies and other salient features of a company's pension plans and the accounting for it. Nevertheless, many companies fail to render a complete disclosure of such details without incurring qualifications in their audit reports.

When the auditor qualifies his opinion, the analyst is faced with an additional problem of interpretation, that is, what is the meaning and intent of the qualification and what effect should such qualifications have on his reliance on the financial statements? The usefulness of the

---

[2] See Leopold A. Bernstein, "The Concept of Materiality," *The Accounting Review*, January 1967; and Sam M. Woolsey, "Approach to Solving the Materiality Problem," *The Journal of Accountancy*, March 1973.

qualification to the analyst depends, of course, on its clarity, its lack of equivocation, and on the degree to which supplementary information and data enable an assessment of its effect. There are, however, some special problems in this area which deserve separate comment.

Qualification, disclaimers, and adverse opinions

As discussed in an earlier part of this chapter, generally when an auditor is not satisfied with the fairness of presentation of items in the financial statements, he issues an "except-for" type of qualification and when there are uncertainties which he cannot resolve, he issues a similar qualification. At some point the size and importance of items under qualification must result in *disclaimers of opinion* or *adverse opinions,* respectively. Where is this point? At what stage is a specific qualification no longer meaningful and an overall disclaimer of opinion necessary? Here again, the analyst won't find any guidelines by turning to the auditor's own professional pronouncements or literature. The boundaries are left entirely to the realm of judgment without the existence of even the broadest of criteria or guidelines.

ILLUSTRATION. United Park City Mines Company showed on its balance sheet as at December 31, 1972, $10.1 million of Mines and Mining Claims. The auditor's opinion stated in part:
"As set forth in Note 2, mines and mining claims, all of which are leased to Park City Ventures, are not fully developed and consequently the ultimate realization of these amounts and of related mining assets depends on circumstances which currently cannot be evaluated.
"In our opinion, based upon our examinations and the report of other independent accountants, subject to the realization of the carrying value of the equipment, mines and mining claims referred to in the preceding paragraph. . . ."
Question: In light of the fact that total assets on the company's balance sheet amounted to $17.6 million and total stockholder's equity to $16.1 million, are the $10.1 million of mining and mining claims not material enough to warrant a disclaimer of opinion rather than a qualification? Of what significance is the use of a qualification rather than a disclaimer of opinion in this case?

Uncertainty qualifications. When the auditor cannot assess the proper carrying value of an asset or determine the extent of a possible liability or find other uncertainties or contingencies which cannot be determined or measured, he will issue an "except for" opinion describing such uncertainties. The analyst using financial statements which contain such a qualification is, quite bluntly, faced with a situation where the auditor has passed on to him the uncertainty described and, consequently, the task of evaluating its possible impact. The analyst should recognize the situation for what it really is and not assume that he is dealing with a mere formality designed only for the auditor's self-protection.

In those cases where the "except for" opinion is given because of uncertainties which cannot be resolved, it is hard to blame the auditor for shifting the burden of evaluation on to the reader. At the same time, it must be remembered that as between the reader and the auditor, the latter, due to his firsthand knowledge of the company's affairs, is far better equipped to evaluate the nature of the contingencies as well as the probabilities of their occurrence. Thus, the analyst is entitled to expect, but will unfortunately not always get, a full explanation of all factors surrounding the uncertainty.

Lest the absence of an uncertainty qualification in the auditor's report lull the analyst into a false sense of security, it must be borne in mind that there are many contingencies and uncertainties which do not call for a qualification but which may nevertheless have very significant impact on the company's financial condition or results of operations. Examples of such contingencies or possibilities are:

1. Obsolescence of a major product line.
2. Loss of a significant customer.
3. Overextension of a business in terms of management capabilities.
4. Difficulty of getting large and complex production units on stream on time.

From the above discussion it should be obvious that the analyst must read with great care the auditor's opinion as well as the supplementary information to which it refers. The analyst can place reliance on the auditor, but regardless of the latter's standing and reputation, the analyst must maintain an independent and open-minded attitude. Auditors may differ on the conclusions which may be drawn from the same set of facts. The following case will illustrate this point:

ILLUSTRATION. During 1965 the Stanray Corporation added to its investment in a new boat manufacturing facility. The size of these investments as well as the adverse results which they brought to date caused the auditors to qualify their opinion as follows:

"The Company has made substantial investments in property, plant, and equipment in connection with its new boat manufacturing facility in Danville, Illinois. Material losses have been incurred in the production and distribution of boats, including costs related to the transfer of operations to the new plant in the early part of 1965, and losses are expected to continue into 1966.

"In our opinion, subject to the ability of the Company to recover its substantial investment in boat related assets, the accompanying financial statements referred to above present fairly the. . . ."

Possibly because of this qualification and possibly for other reasons the

13. The auditor's opinion—meaning and significance 335

company changed auditors,[3] and in 1966 the new auditors gave the company a "clean opinion" with the following footnote disclosure:

"(1) Investments in Danville, Illinois Facility: In 1964 and 1965, the company made substantial investments in property, plant, and equipment for a boat manufacturing facility in Danville, Illinois. The new facility consolidated all boat manufacturing previously performed in three small plants in a single location designed for mass production of small boats and other engineered reinforced fiber glass products. In 1965, production and distribution was started and extensive start-up costs and losses were incurred which continued in 1966. By the end of 1966, improvements in operating methods became evident and management believes that substantial improvements in performance will be reflected in 1967.

"(7) Prior Auditors' Report: The financial statements for 1965, which are presented for comparative purposes, were examined and reported on by public accountants other than (name of auditors.) The prior auditors' report on these statements was subject to the ability of the company to recover its substantial investment in boat related assets. Reference is made to Note 1 for an explanation of the investments in the Danville, Illinois boat facility."

In 1967, the management of Stanray wrote the venture off as a loss disclosing it as follows:

"(2) Discontinued U.S. Boat Operation: In June 1967, management decided to discontinue the Traveler Boat operations in the United States. The Traveler Boat plant and related assets have been sold at a loss of $3,738,238 after Federal Income tax credit, and that amount has been reflected in the accompanying Consolidated Statement of Earnings and Retained Earnings."

The $3.7 million loss was after a tax credit of $3 million and in addition to a current loss of $.5 million. Altogether it converted a $2 million gain from operations to a $2.2 million loss for the year.

The above case clearly illustrates the difference of opinion that can prevail regarding the seriousness and materiality of a situation and the consequent disclosure and need for qualification in the auditor's report. That may be natural, for different individuals exercise their judgment differently. However, this is also in no small measure due to an absence of standards of materiality or criteria governing the need for auditors' qualifications.

To the analyst the implication of the above should be clear. He must carefully consider the auditor's opinion in the light of attendant dis-

[3] In 1971 the SEC implemented a requirement requiring information regarding the circumstances surrounding the replacement of an entity's independent accountants by a new firm. It would require the entity to request the replaced firm to furnish to the Commission a letter setting forth the firm's understandings of the reasons for the change and indicating any problems encountered if the current year's audit had already begun by that firm. The disclosure made in answer to this item should be meaningful. If in any case it appears that the answer is unresponsive or inadequate, the Commission may call for a more explicit response.

closures and then form his own opinion on the possible impact of the conditions and developments which are disclosed.

QUESTIONS

1. In relying on an auditor's opinion what should the financial analyst know about the auditor and his work?
2. What are "generally accepted auditing standards"?
3. What are auditing procedures? What are some of the basic objectives of a financial audit?
4. What does the opinion section of the auditor's report usually cover?
5. Which are the three major categories of conditions which require the auditor to render qualifications, disclaimers, or adverse opinions?
6. What is an "except-for" type of audit report qualification?
7. What is a (a) disclaimer of opinion and (b) an adverse opinion? When are these properly rendered?
8. What is the practical effect of an uncertainty qualification in an auditor's report?
9. What types of changes may result in a consistency qualification in the auditor's report?
10. What are some of the implications to financial analysis which stem from the audit process itself?
11. The auditor does not prepare the financial statements on which he expresses an opinion but instead he samples the data and examines them in order to render a professional opinion on them. List some of the possible implications of this to those who rely on the financial statements.
12. What does the auditor's reference to "generally accepted accounting principles" mean to the analyst of financial statements?
13. Of what significance are "uncertainty qualifications" to the financial analyst? What type of contingencies may not even be considered by the auditor in his report?

part III

FINANCIAL STATEMENT ANALYSIS—THE MAIN AREAS OF EMPHASIS

14

Analysis of short-term liquidity

SIGNIFICANCE OF SHORT-TERM LIQUIDITY

THE DEGREE to which an enterprise can meet its current obligations is a measure of its short-term liquidity. Liquidity implies the ready ability to convert assets into cash or to obtain cash. The short term is conventionally viewed as a time span up to a year, although it is sometimes also identified with the normal operating cycle of a business, that is, the time span encompassing the buying-producing-selling and collecting cycle of an enterprise.

The importance of short-term liquidity can best be gauged by examining the repercussions which stem from a lack of ability to meet short-term obligations.

Liquidity is a matter of degree. A lack of liquidity may mean that the enterprise is unable to avail itself of favorable discounts and is unable to take advantage of profitable business opportunities as they arise. At this stage a lack of liquidity implies a lack of freedom of choice as well as constraints on management's freedom of movement.

A more serious lack of liquidity means that the enterprise is unable to pay its current debts and obligations. This can lead to the forced sale of long-term investments and assets and, in its most severe form, to insolvency and bankruptcy.

To the owners of an enterprise a lack of liquidity can mean reduced profitability and opportunity or it may mean loss of control and partial or total loss of the capital investment. In the case of owners with unlimited liability, the loss can extend beyond the original investment.

To creditors of the enterprise a lack of liquidity can mean delay in collection of interest and principal due them or it can mean the partial or total loss of the amounts due them.

Customers as well as suppliers of goods and services to an enterprise can also be affected by its short-term financial condition. Such effects may take the form of inability of the enterprise to perform under contracts and the loss of supplier relationships.

From the above description of the significance of short-term liquidity it can be readily appreciated why the measures of such liquidity have been accorded great importance. For, if an enterprise cannot meet its current obligations as they become due, its continued existence becomes in doubt and that relegates all other measures of performance to secondary importance if not to irrelevance.

While accounting determinations are made on the assumption of indefinite continuity of the enterprise, the financial analyst must always submit the validity of such assumption to the test of the enterprise's liquidity and solvency.

One of the most widely used measures of liquidity is working capital. In addition to its importance as a pool of liquid assets which provides a safety cushion to creditors, net working capital is also important because it provides a liquid reserve with which to meet contingencies and the ever present uncertainty regarding an enterprise's ability to balance the outflow of funds with an adequate inflow of funds.

WORKING CAPITAL

The basic concept of working capital is relatively simple. It is the excess of current assets over current liabilities. That excess is sometimes referred to as "net working capital" because some businessmen consider current assets as "working capital." A working capital deficiency exists when current liabilities exceed current assets.

The importance attached by credit grantors, investors, and others to working capital as a measure of liquidity and solvency has caused some enterprises, in the desire to present their current condition in the most favorable light, to stretch to the limit the definition of what constitutes a current asset and a current liability. For this reason the analyst must use his own judgment in evaluating the proper classification of items included in "working capital."

Current assets

Current assets include cash and other assets that are reasonably expected to be realized in cash or sold or consumed during the normal operating cycle of the business or within one year if the operating cycle is shorter than one year. Current liabilities include those expected to be satisfied by either the use of assets classified as current in the same balance sheet or the creation of other current liabilities, or those expected to be satisfied within a relatively short period of time, usually one year. (APB *Statement No. 4*, Par. 198.)

The general rule about the ability to convert current assets into cash within a year is subject to important qualifications. The most important qualification relates to the operating cycle. As more fully described in Chapter 3, the operating cycle comprises the average time span intervening between the acquisition of materials and services entering the production or trading process to the final realization in cash of the proceeds from the sale of the enterprise's products. This time span can be quite extended in industries which require a long inventory holding period (e.g., tobacco, distillery, and lumber) or those which sell on the installment plan. Whenever no clearly defined operating cycle is evident, the arbitrary one-year rule prevails.

The most common categories of current assets are:

1. Cash.
2. Cash equivalents (i.e., temporary investments).
3. Accounts and notes receivable.
4. Inventories.
5. Prepaid expenses.

Cash is, of course, the ultimate measure of a current asset since current liabilities are paid off in cash. However, earmarked cash held for specific purposes, such as plant expansion, should not be considered as current. Compensating balances under bank loan agreements cannot, in most cases, be regarded as "free" cash. SEC *Accounting Series Release No. 136* proposes that a company which has borrowed money from a bank segregate on its balance sheet any cash subject to withdrawal or usage restrictions under compensating balance arrangements with the lending bank.

Cash equivalents represent temporary investments of cash in excess of current requirements made for the purpose of earning a return on these funds.

The analyst must be alert to the valuation of such investments because they can be carried at cost when in the opinion of management, a drop in market value to below cost is of a "temporary" nature. Similarly, the "cash equivalent" nature of securities investments is sometimes stretched quite far.

The mere ability to convert an asset to cash is not the sole determinant of its current nature. It is the intention and normal practice that governs.

Intention is, however, not always enough. Thus, the cost of fixed assets which are intended for sale should be included in current assets only if the enterprise has a contractual commitment from a buyer to purchase the asset at a given price within the following year or the following operating cycle.

An example where the above principle was not followed is found in the 1970 annual report of International Industries. In this report the company carries as a current asset $37.8 million in "Real estate held for sale." A related footnote explains that "the company intends to sell this real estate during the ensuing operating cycle substantially at cost under sale and leaseback agreements, however, prevailing economic conditions may affect its ability to do so."

This is an obvious attempt to present a current position superior to the one the company can justifiably claim. Without the inclusion of real estate, the company's current ratio would have dropped to 1.1 (with working capital at about $3 million) as against a current ratio, based on reported figures, of 1.8 and a working capital of $40.3 million.

This reinforces the ever-recurring message in this text that the analyst cannot rely on adherence to rules or accepted principles of preparation of financial statements, but instead must exercise eternal vigilance in his use of ratios and all other analytical measures which are based on such statements.

Accounts receivable, net of provisions for uncollectible accounts, are current unless they represent receivables for sales, not in the ordinary course of business, which are due after one year. Installment receivables from customary sales usually fall within the operating cycle of the enterprise.

Receivables from affiliated companies or from officers and employees can be considered current only if they are collectible in the ordinary course of business within a year or, in the case of installment sales, within the operating cycle.

Inventories are considered current assets except in cases where they are in excess of current requirements. Such excess inventories, which should be shown as noncurrent, must be distinguished from inventories, such as tobacco, which require a long aging cycle. The variations in practice in this area are considerable, as the following illustrations will show, and should be carefully scrutinized by the analyst.

ILLUSTRATION 1. National Fuel Gas Company (prospectus dated 7/23/69) shows a current as well as a noncurrent portion of gas stored underground and explains this as follows:

"Included in property, plant, and equipment as gas stored underground—noncurrent is $18,825,232 at April 30, 1969, the cost of the volume of gas required to maintain pressure levels for normal operating purposes at the low point of the storage cycle. The portion of gas in underground storage included in current assets does not exceed estimated withdrawals during the succeeding two years."

ILLUSTRATION 2. Some trucking concerns include the tires on their trucks as current assets presumably on the theory that they will be used up during the normal operating cycle.

Prepaid expenses are considered current, not because they can be converted into cash but rather because they represent advance payments for services and supplies which would otherwise require the current outlay of cash.

Current liabilities

Current liabilities are obligations which would, generally, require the use of current assets for their discharge or, alternatively, the creation of other current liabilities. The following are current liabilities most commonly found in practice:

1. Accounts payable.
2. Notes payable.
3. Short-term bank and other loans.
4. Tax and other expense accruals.
5. Current portion of long-term debt.

The foregoing current liability categories are usually clear and do not require further elaboration. However, as is the case with current assets, the analyst cannot assume that they will always be properly classified for his purposes. Thus, for example, current practice sanctions the presentation as noncurrent of current obligations which are expected to be refunded. The degree of assurance of the subsequent refunding is mostly an open question which in the case of adverse developments may well be resolved negatively as far as the enterprise is concerned.

Another example which requires independent judgment and interpretation by the analyst is that of liabilities under "revolving loan agreements." Under such loan agreements the bank agrees to lend a company an amount up to a specified limit within a designated period of time which may extend to three years or even longer. Such borrowing may be evidenced by short-term (e.g., 90 days) notes and are renewable sometimes at the option of the borrower and often on the option of the bank. The fact that a bank agrees informally to renew such notes does not make them noncurrent, and yet this is how revolving credit liabilities are often presented. The following is an example of disclosure of such a liability:

Under the terms of a credit agreement with banks, as amended, the Company may borrow up to $30,000,000 on 90-day notes through March 31, 19x3.

The banks have the right under the agreement to request the Company to assign to them the moneys and claims for moneys due and to become due under each of its defense production contracts (other than those not legally assignable). In addition, the Company must maintain at all times an excess of current assets over current liabilities of at least $25,000,000.

The analyst must also be alert to the possibility of presentations designed to present the working capital in a better light than warranted by circumstances.

ILLUSTRATION 3. Penn Central Company excluded the current maturities of long-term debt from the current liability category and included it in the "long-term debt" section of the balance sheet. In 1969, this treatment resulted in an excess of current assets over current liabilities of $21 million, whereas the inclusion of current debt maturities among current liabilities would have resulted in a working capital *deficit* of $207 million. (The subsequent financial collapse of this enterprise is now a well-known event.)

The analyst must also ascertain whether all obligations, regarding which there is a reasonably good probability that they will have to be met, have been included as current liabilities in computing an effective working capital figure. Two examples of such obligations follow:

1. The obligation of an enterprise for notes discounted with a bank where the bank has full recourse in the event the note is not paid when due is generally considered a contingent liability. However, the likelihood of the contingency materializing must be considered in the computation of working capital. The same principle applies in case of loan guarantees.
2. A contract for the construction or acquisition of long-term assets may call for substantial progress payments. Such obligations for payments are, for accounting purposes, considered as commitments rather than liabilities, and hence are not found among the latter. Nevertheless, when computing the excess of liquid assets over short-term obligations such commitments must be recognized.

Other problem areas in definition of current assets and liabilities

An area which presented a problem of classification but which has now been settled in favor of consistency is that of deferred tax accounting (see Chapter 9). Thus, if an asset (e.g., installment accounts receivable) is classified as current, the related deferred tax arising from differences in treatment between book and tax return must be similarly classified.

Many concerns which have fixed assets as the main "working assets," such as, for example, trucking concerns and some leasing companies, carry as current prospective receipts from billings out of which their current equipment purchase obligations must be met. Such treatments, or the absence of any distinction between current and noncurrent on the balance sheet, as is the case with real estate companies, is an attempt by such concerns to convey to the reader their "special" financing and operating conditions which make the current versus noncurrent distinction inapplicable and which have no parallel in the regular trading or industrial concern.

Some of these "special" circumstances may indeed be present, but they do not necessarily change the relationship existing between current obligations and the liquid funds available, or reasonably expected to become available, to meet them. It is to this relationship that the analyst, faced with the task of evaluating liquidity, must train his attention.

Working capital as a measure of liquidity

The popularity of working capital as a measure of liquidity and of short-term financial health is so widespread that it hardly needs documentation. Credit grantors compute the relationship between current assets and current liabilities; financial analysts measure the size of the working capital of enterprises they analyze; government agencies compute aggregates of working capital of corporations; and most published balance sheets distinguish between current and noncurrent assets and liabilities. Moreover, loan agreements and bond indentures often contain stipulations regarding the maintenance of minimum working capital levels.

The absolute amount of working capital has significance only when related to other variables such as sales, total assets, etc. It is at best of limited value for comparison purposes and for judging the adequacy of working capital. This can be illustrated as follows:

	Company A	Company B
Current assets	$300,000	$1,200,000
Current liabilities	100,000	1,000,000
Working capital	$200,000	$ 200,000

While both companies have an equal amount of working capital, a cursory comparison of the relationship of current assets to current liabilities suggests that Company A's current condition is superior to that of Company B.

CURRENT RATIO

The above conclusion is based on the ratio of current assets to current liabilities. It is 3:1 (300,000/100,000) for Company A and 1.2:1 (1,200,000/1,000,000) for Company B. It is this ratio that is accorded substantial importance in the assessment of an enterprise's current liquidity.

Some of the basic reasons for the widespread use of the current ratio as a measure of liquidity are obvious:

1. It measures the degree to which current assets cover current liabilities. The higher the amount of current assets in relation to current liabilities the more assurance exists that these liabilities can be paid out of such assets.
2. The excess of current assets over current liabilities provides a buffer against losses which may be incurred in the disposition or liquidation of the current assets other than cash. The more substantial such a buffer is, the better for creditors. Thus, the current ratio measures the margin of safety available to cover any possible shrinkage in the value of current assets.
3. It measures the reserve of liquid funds in excess of current obligations which is available as a margin of safety against uncertainty and the random shocks to which the flows of funds in an enterprise are subject. Random shocks, such as strikes, extraordinary losses, and other uncertainties can temporarily and unexpectedly stop or reduce the inflow of funds.

What is not so obvious, however, is the fact that the current ratio, as a measure of liquidity and short-term solvency, is subject to serious theoretical as well as practical shortcomings and limitations. Consequently, before we embark on a discussion of the uses of the current ratio and related measures of liquidity, these limitations must be thoroughly understood.

Limitations of the current ratio

The first step in our examination of the current ratio as a tool of liquidity and short-term solvency analysis is to examine the components which are normally included in the ratio shown in Exhibit 14–1.

Disregarding, for purposes of this evaluation, prepaid expenses and similar unsubstantial items entering the computation of the current ratio,

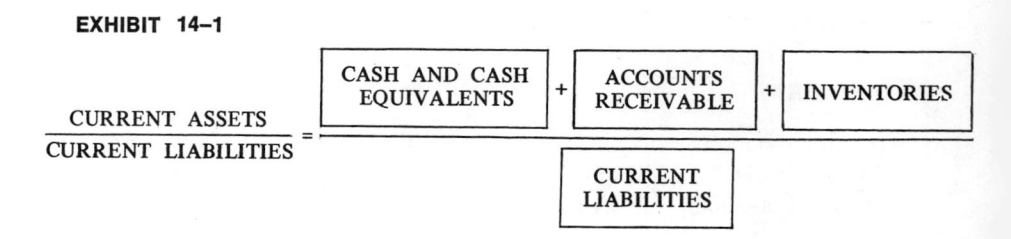

EXHIBIT 14–1

$$\frac{\text{CURRENT ASSETS}}{\text{CURRENT LIABILITIES}} = \frac{\text{CASH AND CASH EQUIVALENTS} + \text{ACCOUNTS RECEIVABLE} + \text{INVENTORIES}}{\text{CURRENT LIABILITIES}}$$

we are left with the above four major elements which comprise this ratio.

Now, if we define liquidity as the ability to balance required cash outflows with adequate inflows, including an allowance for unexpected interruptions of inflows or increases in outflows, we must ask: Does the relationship of these four elements at a given point in time—

1. Measure and predict the pattern of future fund flows?
2. Measure the adequacy of future fund inflows in relation to outflows.

Unfortunately, the answer to these questions is mostly negative. The current ratio is a static or "stock" concept of what resources are available at a given moment in time to meet the obligations at that moment. The existing reservoir of net funds does not have a logical or causative relationship to the future funds which will flow through it. And yet it is the future flows that are the subject of our greatest interest in the assessment of liquidity. These flows depend importantly on elements *not* included in the ratio itself, such as sales, profits, and changes in business conditions. To elaborate, let us examine more closely the four elements comprising the ratio.

Cash and cash equivalents The amount of cash held by a well-managed enterprise is in the nature of a precautionary reserve, intended to take care of short-term imbalances in cash flows. For example, in cases of a business downturn, sales may fall more rapidly than outlays for purchases and expenses. Since cash is a nonearning asset and cash equivalents are usually low-yielding securities, the investment in such assets is kept at a safe minimum. To conceive of this minimum balance as available for payment of current debts would require the dropping of the going-concern assumption underlying accounting statements. While the balance of cash has some relation to the existing level of activity, such a relationship is not very strong nor does it contain a predictive element regarding the future. In fact, some enterprises may use cash substitutes in the form of open lines of credit which, of course, do not enter at all into the computation of the current ratio.

The important link between cash and solvency in the minds of many is due to the well-known fact that a shortage of cash, more than any other factor, is the element which can clinch the insolvency of an enterprise.

Accounts receivable The major determinant of the level of accounts receivable is sales. The size of accounts receivable in relation to sales is governed by terms of trade and credit policy. Changes in receivables will correspond to changes in sales though not necessarily on a directly proportional basis.

When we look at accounts receivable as a source of cash we must, except in the case of liquidation, recognize the revolving nature of the asset with the collection of one account replaced by the extension of fresh credit. Thus, the level of receivables per se is not an index to future net inflows of cash.

Inventory As is the case with accounts receivable, the main determinant of the size of inventories is the level of sales, or expected sales, rather than the level of current liabilities. Given that the level of sales is a measure of the level of demand then, scientific methods of inventory management (economic order quantities, safe stock levels, and reorder points) generally establish that inventory increments vary not in proportion to demand but vary rather with the *square root* of demand.

The relationship of inventories to sales is further accented by the fact that it is sales that is the one essential element which starts the conversion of inventories to cash. Moreover, the determination of future cash inflows through the sale of inventories is dependent on the profit margin which can be realized because inventories are generally stated at the lower of *cost* or market. The current ratio, while including inventories, gives no recognition to the sales level or to profit margin, both of which are important elements entering into the determination of future cash inflows.

Current liabilities The level of current liabilities, the safety of which the current ratio is intended to measure, is also largely determined by the level of sales.

Current liabilities are a source of funds in the same sense that receivables and inventories tie up funds. Since purchases, which give rise to accounts payable, are a function of the level of activity (i.e., sales), these payables vary with sales. As long as sales remain constant or are rising, the payment of current liabilities is essentially a refunding operation. There again the components of the current ratio give little, if any, recognition to these elements and their effects on the future flow of funds. Nor do the current liabilities which enter into the computation of the current ratio include prospective outlays, such as commitments under construction contracts, loans, leases, or pensions, all of which affect the future outflow of funds.

Implications of the limitations to which the current ratio is subject

There are a number of conclusions which can be reached on the basis of the foregoing discussion:

1. Liquidity depends to some extent on cash or cash equivalents balances and to a much more significant extent on prospective cash flows.
2. There is no direct or established relationship between balances of working capital items and the pattern which future cash flows are likely to assume.
3. Managerial policies directed at optimizing the levels of receivables and inventories are oriented primarily towards efficient and profitable assets utilization and only secondarily at liquidity.

Given these conclusions, which obviously limit the value of the current ratio as an index of liquidity, and given the static nature of this ratio and the fact that it is composed of items which affect liquidity in different ways, we may ask why this ratio enjoys such widespread use and in what way, if any, it can be used intelligently by the analyst.

The most probable reasons for the popularity of the current ratio are evidently the simplicity of its basic concept, the ease with which it can be computed, and the readiness with which data for it can be obtained. It may also derive its popularity from the credit grantor's, and especially the banker's, propensity to view credit situations as conditions of last resort. They may ask themselves: "What if there were a complete cessation of funds inflow? Would the current assets then be adequate to pay off the current liabilities?" The assumption of such extreme conditions is, of course, not always a useful way of measuring liquidity.

To what use can the intelligent analyst put the current ratio?

Let it first be said that the analyst who wishes to measure short-term liquidity and solvency will find cash flow projections and pro forma financial statements to be the most relevant and reliable tools to use. This involves obtaining information which is not readily available to the external analyst and it also involves the need for a great deal of estimation. This area of analysis will be discussed in the next chapter.

The current ratio as a valid tool of analysis

Should the analyst want to use the current ratio as a static measure of the ability of current assets to satisfy the current liabilities, he will be employing a different concept of liquidity from the one discussed above. In this context liquidity means the readiness and speed with which current assets can be converted to cash and the degree to which such conversion will result in shrinkage in the stated value of current assets.

It is not our purpose here to discredit the current ratio as a valid tool of analysis but rather to suggest that its legitimate area of application is far less wide than popularly believed.

Defenders of this, the oldest and best known of financial ratios, may say that they are aware of the multitude of limitations and inconsistencies of concept outlined above but that they will "allow" for them in the evaluation of the ratio. A careful examination of these limitations suggests that such process of "allowing" for such limitations is well nigh impossible.

The better and most valid way to use this ratio is to recognize its limitations and to restrict its use to the analytical job it can do, that is, measuring the ability of *present* current assets to discharge *existing* current liabilities and considering the excess, if any, as a liquid surplus available to meet imbalances in the flow of funds and other contingencies. This should be done with an awareness of the fact that the test envisages a situation of enterprise liquidation whereas in the normal, going-concern situation current assets are of a revolving nature, for example, the collected receivable being replaced with a newly created one, while the current liabilities are essentially of a refunding nature, that is, the repayment of one is followed by the creation of another.

Given the analytical function of the current ratio, as outlined above, there are two basic elements which must be measured before the current ratio can form the basis for valid conclusions:

1. The quality of the current assets and the nature of the current liabilities which enter the determination of the ratio.
2. The rate of turnover of these assets and liabilities that is, the average time span needed to convert receivables and inventories into cash and the amount of time which can be taken for the payment of current liabilities.

To measure the above, a number of ratios and other tools have been devised, and these will be discussed in the section which follows.

Measures which supplement the current ratio

The most liquid of current assets is, of course, cash, which is the standard of liquidity itself. A close second to cash is "temporary investments" which are usually highly marketable and relatively safe temporary repositories of cash. These are, in effect, considered as "cash equivalents" and usually earn a modest return.

Cash ratios. The proportion which cash and cash equivalents constitute of the total current assets group is a measure of the degree of liquidity of this group of assets. It is measured by the cash ratio which is computed as follows:

$$\frac{\text{Cash} + \text{Cash equivalents}}{\text{Total current assets}}$$

Evaluation. The higher the ratio the more liquid is the current asset group. This, in turn, means that with respect to this cash and cash equivalents component there is a minimal danger of loss in value in case of liquidation and that there is practically no waiting period for conversion of these assets into usable cash.

With respect to the generally assumed freedom from risk of loss in value, the analyst should be alert to the possibility that the market value of the cash equivalents (securities) is lower than the cost at which the asset is shown on the balance sheet. In such cases, a meaningful computation of ratios should include the market value of the securities rather than the original cost which is of no relevance for this purpose.

ILLUSTRATION 1. E. F. MacDonald Company in 1970 showed in its current assets section $34.7 million of marketable securities. Also disclosed was the fact that the market value of the securities was only $28.8 million.

However, should the stated cost of marketable securities be below their market value, the latter should be used in computing liquidity ratios.

APB *Opinion No. 18* generally requires the carrying of investments, representing an interest of 20 percent or higher, at underlying equity. This is, of course, neither cost nor, necessarily, market value. While such substantial positions in the securities of another company are not usually considered cash equivalents, *should* they nevertheless be so considered, their market value would be the most appropriate figure to use in the computation of liquidity ratios. The equity method of accounting is discussed in Chapters 3 and 6.

As to the availability of cash, the analyst should bear in mind possible restrictions which may exist with respect to the use of cash balances. An example is the so-called "compensating balances" which banks, which extend credit, expect their customers to keep. While such balances can be used, the analyst must nevertheless assess the effect on a company's credit standing and credit availability, as well as on its banking connection, of a breach of the tacit agreement not to draw on the "compensating cash balance."

An additional ratio which measures cash adequacy should be mentioned. The cash to current liabilities ratio is computed as follows:

$$\frac{\text{Cash} + \text{Cash equivalents}}{\text{Current liabilities}}$$

It measures how much cash is available to pay current obligations. This is a severe test which ignores the refunding nature of current liabilities. It supplements the cash ratio discussed above in that it measures cash availability from a somewhat different point of view.

A tabulation appearing in *Fortune Magazine* of June 1972 indicates the significant variation in the holding of cash which exists among various companies:

Who has the cash . . .

Company	Cash	Percent of assets
Skyline	$ 30,220,000	50.2
Chicago Bridge & Iron	105,704,000	36.6
Texas Instruments	186,125,000	32.1
Polaroid	194,182,000	31.5
Loews	345,009,000	29.9
Avon Products	146,924,000	29.0
General Host	75,301,000	26.7
Schering-Plough	96,036,000	25.4
Zenith Radio	94,505,000	25.2
Tecumseh Products	40,953,000	25.2
Colgate-Palmolive	158,287,000	24.2
Searle (G.D.)	61,198,000	24.1
Becton, Dickinson	64,076,000	24.0
Briggs & Stratton	22,434,000	23.9
American Home Products	220,079,000	23.8
Pabst Brewing	61,154,000	23.7
Donnelley (R.R.) & Sons	70,218,000	23.2
Cannon Mills	60,446,000	22.7
Norton Simon	179,320,000	22.7
Ethyl	143,733,000	22.5

. . . And who hasn't

Mattel	$ 2,789,000	1.2
Ampex	4,900,000	1.2
Burlington Industries	16,080,000	1.2
Liggett & Myers	6,887,000	1.2
American Smelting & Refining	10,379,000	1.1
Coastal States Gas Producing	7,043,000	1.1
Riegel Paper	1,650,000	1.1
Gold Kist	1,858,000	1.0
American Beef Packers	247,000	0.8
Missouri Beef Packers	232,000	0.7
National Can	1,968,000	0.7
Monfort of Colorado	633,000	0.7

To view the cash ratio as a further extension of the acid test ratio (see below) would, except in extreme cases, constitute a test of short-term liquidity too severe to be meaningful. Nevertheless, the importance of cash as the ultimate form of liquidity should never be underestimated. The record of business failures provides many examples of insolvent companies, possessing sizable noncash assets, current and noncurrent, and no cash to pay debts or to operate with.

Measures of accounts receivable liquidity

In most enterprises which sell on credit, accounts and notes receivable are a significant part of working capital. In assessing the quality of working capital and of the current ratio, it is important to get some measure of the quality and the liquidity of the receivables.

Both the quality and liquidity of accounts receivable are affected by their rate of turnover. By quality is meant the likelihood of collection without loss. An indicator of this likelihood is the degree to which receivables are within the terms of payment set by the enterprise. Experience has shown that the longer receivables remain outstanding beyond the date on which they are due, the lower is the probability of their collection in full. Turnover is an indicator of the age of the receivables, particularly when it is compared with an expected turnover rate which is determined by credit terms granted.

The measure of liquidity is concerned with the speed with which accounts receivables will, on average, be converted into cash. Here again turnover is among the best measures to use.

AVERAGE ACCOUNTS RECEIVABLE TURNOVER RATIO

The receivable turnover ratio is computed as follows:

$$\frac{\text{Net sales on credit}}{\text{Average accounts receivable}}$$

The quickest way for an external analyst to determine the average accounts receivable is to take the beginning receivables of the period, add the ending receivables, and divide the sum by two. The use of monthly or quarterly sales figures can lead to an even more accurate result. The more widely sales fluctuate, the more subject to distortion this ratio is, unless the receivables are properly averaged.

Notes receivable arising from normal sales should be included in the accounts receivable figure in computing the turnover ratio. Discounted notes receivable which are still outstanding should also be included in the accounts receivable total.

The sales figure used in computing the ratio should be that of credit sales only, because cash sales obviously do not generate receivables. Since published financial statements rarely disclose the division between cash and credit sales, the external analyst may have to compute the ratio under the assumption that cash sales are relatively insignificant. If they are not insignificant, then a degree of distortion may occur in the ratio. However, if the proportion of cash sales to total sales remains relatively constant, the year-to-year comparison of changes in the receivables turnover ratio may nevertheless be validly based.

The average receivables turnover figure indicates how many *times*, on average, the receivables revolve, that is, are generated and collected during the year.

For example, if sales are $1,200,000 and beginning receivables are $150,000 while year-end receivables are $250,000, then receivable turnover is computed as follows:

$$\frac{1{,}200{,}000}{(150{,}000 + 250{,}000) \div 2} = \frac{1{,}200{,}000}{200{,}000} = 6 \text{ times}$$

While the turnover figure furnishes a sense of the speed of collections and is valuable for comparison purposes, it is not directly comparable to the terms of trade which the enterprise normally extends. Such comparison is best made by converting the turnover into days of sales tied up in receivables.

Collection period for accounts receivable

This measure, also known as *days sales in accounts receivable* measures the number of days it takes, on average, to collect accounts (and notes) receivable. The number of days can be obtained by dividing the average accounts receivable turnover ratio discussed above into 360, the approximate round number of days in the year. Thus

$$\text{Collection period} = \frac{360}{\text{Average accounts receivable turnover}}$$

Using the figures of the preceding example, the collection period is:

$$\frac{360}{6} = 60 \text{ days}$$

An alternative computation is to first obtain the average daily sale and then divide the *ending gross* receivable balance by it.

$$\text{Accounts receivable} \div \frac{\text{Sales}}{360}$$

The result will differ from the foregoing computation because the average accounts receivable turnover figure uses *average* accounts receivable, while this computation uses *ending* accounts receivable only; it thus focuses specifically on the latest accounts receivable balances. Using the figures from our example, the computation is as follows:

$$\text{Average daily sales} = \frac{\text{Sales}}{360} = \frac{1{,}200{,}000}{360} = \$3{,}333$$

$$\frac{\text{Accounts receivable}}{\text{Average daily sales}} = \frac{250{,}000}{3{,}333} = 75 \text{ days}$$

Note that if the collection period computation would have used ending receivables rather than *average* receivables turnover, the identical collection period, that is, 75 could have been obtained as follows:

$$\frac{\text{Sales}}{\text{Accounts receivable (ending)}} = \frac{\$1,200,000}{\$250,000} = 4.8 \text{ times}$$

$$\frac{360}{\text{Receivable turnover}} = \frac{360}{4.8} = 75 \text{ days}$$

The use of 360 days is arbitrary because while receivables are outstanding 360 days (used for computational convenience instead of 365), the sales days of the year usually number less than 300. However, consistent computation of the ratio will make for valid period to period comparisons.

An example of published collection periods is provided by Exhibit 14–2 as reported by the Credit Research Foundation, Inc., the research affiliate of the National Association of Credit Management.

Evaluation

When the collection period is compared with the terms of sale allowed by the enterprise, the degree to which customers are paying on time can be assessed. Thus, if the average terms of sale in the illustration used above are 40 days, then an average collection period of 75 days reflects either one or all of the following conditions:

1. A poor collection job.
2. Difficulty in obtaining prompt payment from customers in spite of diligent collection efforts.
3. Customers in financial difficulty.

The first conclusion calls for remedial managerial action, while the last two reflect particularly on both the quality and the liquidity of the accounts receivable.

It is always possible that an *average* figure is not representative of the receivables population it represents. Thus, it is possible that the 75-day average collection period does not represent an across-the-board payment tardiness on the part of customers but is rather caused by the excessive delinquency of one or two substantial customers.

The best way to investigate further an excessive collection period is to *age* the accounts receivable in such a way that the distribution of each account by the number of days past-due is clearly apparent. An aging schedule in a format such as given below will show whether the problem is widespread or concentrated:

Accounts receivable aging schedule:

	Days past due			
Accounts receivable	0–30	31–60	61–90	Over 90

The age distribution of the receivables will, of course, lead to better informed conclusions regarding the quality and the liquidity of the receivables as well as the kind of action which is necessary to remedy the situation.

Notes receivable deserve the particular scrutiny of the analyst because while they are normally regarded as more negotiable than open accounts, they may be of poorer quality than regular receivables if they originated as an extension device for an unpaid account rather than at the inception of the original sale.

In assessing the quality of receivables the analyst should remember that a significant conversion of receivables into cash, except for their use as collateral for borrowing, cannot be achieved without a cutback in sales volume. The sales policy aspect of the collection period evaluation must also be kept in mind. An enterprise may be willing to accept slow-paying customers who provide business which is, on an overall basis, profitable, that is, the profit on sale compensates for the extra use by the customer of the enterprise funds. This circumstance may modify the analyst's conclusions regarding the *quality* of the receivables but not those regarding their *liquidity*.

In addition to the consideration of profitability, an enterprise may extend more liberal credit in cases such as (1) the introduction of a new product, (2) a desire to make sales in order to utilize available excess capacity, or (3) special competitive conditions in the industry. Thus, the relationship between the level of receivables and that of sales and profits must always be borne in mind when evaluating the collection period. The trend of the collection period over time is always important in an assessment of the quality and the liquidity of the receivables.

Another trend which may be instructive to watch is that of the relation between the provision for doubtful accounts and gross accounts receivable. The ratio is computed as follows:

$$\frac{\text{Provision for doubtful accounts}}{\text{Gross accounts receivable}}$$

An increase in this ratio over time may indicate management's conclusion that the collectibility of receivables has deteriorated. Conversely, a decrease of this ratio over time may lead to the opposite conclusion or may cause the analyst to reevaluate the adequacy of the provision for doubtful accounts.

Measures of accounts receivable turnover are, as we have seen in

EXHIBIT 14-2
Manufacturers' summary medians and quartiles by industry groups, March 31, 1970

Industry group	No.	Days sales outstanding			Percent current			Percent over 90 days past due		
		Upper quartile	Median	Lower quartile	Upper quartile	Median	Lower quartile	Upper quartile	Median	Lower quartile
Total manufacturers	477	56.8	44.8	35.0	87.8	78.9	68.7	6.9	3.6	1.5
Apparel	20	66.7	51.2	44.2	90.0	81.6	64.1	9.0	4.7	2.2
Building materials	52	63.6	46.6	38.7	88.5	81.2	70.5	14.9	4.8	2.5
Chemicals	59	57.0	48.6	45.1	78.3	71.7	64.4	6.7	3.2	2.3
Containers	18	38.2	33.7	31.0	87.8	86.2	76.5	3.6	2.1	1.2
Drugs, cosmetics and soap	34	46.2	41.2	36.1	91.0	85.9	75.3	6.2	2.9	1.5
Electrical-electronics	42	63.6	49.8	43.9	85.6	75.1	59.6	10.2	4.4	2.2
Fabricated metal products	7	...	46.3	...	...	64.1	...	...	6.8	...
Farm machinery	8	170.6	108.7	51.9	94.7	92.3	52.9	8.7	4.8	.1
Food	46	28.2	22.8	18.4	94.8	89.7	78.2	2.1	1.1	.3
Home furnishings	26	55.5	53.4	38.3	83.8	77.8	70.3	6.3	3.1	.9
Industrial machinery	50	61.5	47.4	37.0	85.2	75.2	63.8	11.3	4.9	1.6
Industrial, professional, and scientific instruments	5	...	51.5	...	...	72.4	...	...	3.8	...
Leather and leather products	15	75.0	63.2	46.3	88.0	85.8	77.8	6.1	2.5	1.2
Leisure	16	95.7	57.4	50.2	94.3	86.3	65.6	11.0	2.5	.6
Nonferrous metals	19	52.5	46.5	40.2	84.3	77.8	68.0	4.9	3.5	2.0
Office equipment	15	83.9	67.2	53.3	72.0	53.0	44.7	24.4	16.8	6.0
Paper	28	38.9	35.5	31.9	88.7	83.9	79.9	3.7	1.9	1.0
Petroleum—wholesale	30	34.7	27.5	22.1	88.2	78.3	68.8	7.1	3.0	1.1
—credit cards	19	61.0	53.1	49.0	68.4	62.3	55.9	15.6	12.4	8.4
—heating fuel oil	4	...	33.9	...	...	60.3	...	...	3.5	...
Printing and publishing	8	114.7	89.5	48.6	85.2	56.9	30.4	38.1	21.4	5.6
Rubber products	4	...	62.3	...	...	89.1	...	...	2.0	...
Steel	12	40.5	37.3	28.1	83.7	79.1	66.9	4.6	1.9	.5
Textiles	6	...	61.3	...	...	84.8	...	...	2.0	...
Tobacco	4	...	18.7	...	...	85.9	...	...	.0	...
Transportation equipment	24	47.7	41.3	32.9	89.8	83.9	71.7	5.2	2.4	1.0
Watches and jewelry	3	...	59.2	...	...	...	...	...	...	...

this section, important in the evaluation of liquidity. They are also important as measures of asset utilization, a subject which will be covered in Chapter 17.

MEASURES OF INVENTORY TURNOVER

Inventories, in most enterprises, represent a very substantial proportion of the current asset group. This is so for reasons that have little to do with an enterprise's objective of maintaining adequate liquid funds. Reserves of liquid funds are seldom kept in the form of inventories. Inventories represent investments made for the purpose of obtaining a return. The return is derived from the expected profits which may result from sales. In most businesses a certain level of inventory must be kept in order to generate an adequate level of sales. If the inventory level is inadequate, the sales volume will fall to below the level otherwise attainable. Excessive inventories, on the other hand, expose the enterprise to expenses such as storage costs, insurance and taxes, as well as to risks of loss of value through obsolescence and physical deterioration. Moreover, excessive inventories tie up funds which can be used more profitably elsewhere.

Due to the risk involved in holding inventories as well as the fact that inventories are one step further removed from cash than receivables (they have to be sold before they are converted into receivables), inventories are normally considered the least liquid component of the current assets group. As is the case with most generalizations, this is not always true. Certain staple items, such as commodities, raw materials, standard sizes of structural steel, etc., enjoy broad and ready markets and can usually be sold with little effort, expense, or loss. On the other hand, fashion merchandise, specialized components, or perishable items can lose their value rapidly unless they are sold on a timely basis.

The evaluation of the current ratio, which includes inventories in its computation, must include a thorough evaluation of the quality as well as the liquidity of these assets. Here again, measures of turnover are the best overall tools available for such an evaluation.

Inventory turnover ratio

The inventory turnover ratio measures the average rate of speed with which inventories move through and out of the enterprise.

Computation. The computation of the average inventory turnover is as follows:

$$\frac{\text{Cost of goods sold}}{\text{Average inventory}}$$

Consistency of valuation requires that the cost of goods sold be used because, as is the case with inventories, it is stated principally at *cost*. Sales, on the other hand, normally include a profit. Although the cost of goods sold figure is now disclosed in most published income statements, the external analyst is still occasionally confronted with an unavailability of such a figure. In such a case the sales figure must be substituted. While this results in a theoretically less valid turnover ratio, it can still be used for comparison and trend development purposes, especially if used consistently and when sharp changes in profit margins are not present.

The average inventory figure is most readily obtained as follows:

$$\frac{\text{Opening inventory} + \text{Closing inventory}}{2}$$

Further refinement in the averaging process can be achieved, where possible and necessary, by adding up the monthly inventory figures and dividing the total by 12.

Days to sell inventory

A variation of the turnover figure is to express it in terms of the required number of *days to sell inventory*. Two methods of computation will be illustrated:

$$\frac{360 \text{ days}}{\text{Average inventory turnover}}$$

which measures the number of days it takes to sell the average inventory in a given year and,

$$\frac{\text{Ending inventory}}{\text{Cost of average day's sales}}$$

which measures the number of days which are required to sell the ending inventory, assuming the given rate of sales where the

$$\text{Cost of an average day's sales} = \frac{\text{Cost of goods sold}}{360}$$

Example of computations

Sales 1,800,000
Cost of goods sold 1,200,000
Beginning inventory 200,000
Ending inventory 400,000

$$\text{Inventory turnover} = \frac{1,200,000}{(200,000 + 400,000) \div 2} = \frac{1,200,000}{300,000} = 4 \text{ times}$$

Alternative computation when the cost of goods sold figure is not available

$$\text{Inventory turnover (based on sales)} = \frac{1{,}800{,}000}{300{,}000} = 6 \text{ times}$$

$$\text{Days to sell inventory} = \frac{360}{\text{Inventory turnover (based on cost of goods sold)}} = \frac{360}{4} = 90 \text{ days}$$

$$\text{Days to sell inventory (based as sales)} \frac{360}{6} = 60 \text{ days}$$

Alternative computation based on ending inventories

Step 1:

$$\frac{\text{Cost of goods sold}}{360} = \frac{1{,}200{,}000}{360} = 3{,}333 \text{ (cost of average day's sales)}$$

Step 2: $\dfrac{\text{Ending inventory}}{\text{Cost of average day's sales}} = \dfrac{400{,}000}{3{,}333} = 120 \text{ days}$

The difference between the three *days to sell inventory* figures is due to the fact that the last computation focuses on the ending inventory, being oriented towards the time it would take to sell it, while the first two use the average inventory figure.

Interpretation of inventory turnover ratios. The current ratio computation views its current asset components as sources of funds which can, as a means of last resort, be used to pay off the current liabilities. Viewed this way, the inventory turnover ratios give us a measure of the quality as well as of the liquidity of the inventory component of the current assets.

The quality of inventory is a measure of the enterprise's ability to use it and dispose of it without loss. When this is envisaged under conditions of forced liquidation, then recovery of cost is the objective. In the normal course of business the inventory will, of course, be sold at a profit. Viewed from this point of view, the normal profit margin realized by the enterprise assumes importance because the funds which will be obtained, and which would theoretically be available for payment of current liabilities, will include the profit in addition to the recovery of cost. In both cases costs of sale will reduce the net proceeds.

In practice a going concern cannot use its investment in inventory for the payment of current liabilities because any drastic reduction in normal inventory levels will surely cut into the sales volume.

A rate of turnover which is slower than that experienced historically, or which is below that normal in the industry, would lead to the preliminary conclusion that it includes items which are slow moving because they are obsolete, in weak demand, or otherwise unsaleable. Such conditions do, of course, cast doubt on the feasibility of recovering the cost of such items.

Further investigation may reveal that the slowdown in inventory turnover is due to a buildup of inventory in accordance with a future contractual commitment, in anticipation of a price rise, in anticipation of a strike or shortage, or for any number of other reasons which must be probed into further.

A better evaluation of inventory turnover can be obtained from the computation of separate turnover rates for the major components of inventory such as (1) raw materials, (2) work in process, and (3) finished goods. Departmental or divisional turnover rates can similarly lead to more useful conclusions regarding inventory quality. One should never lose sight of the fact that the total inventory turnover ratio is an aggregate of widely varying turnover rates of individual components.

The biggest problem facing the external analyst who tries to compute inventory turnover ratios by individual components is obtaining the necessary detailed data. This is, at present, rarely provided in published financial statements.

The turnover ratio is, of course, also a gauge of liquidity in that it conveys a measure of the speed with which inventory can be converted into cash. In this connection a useful additional measure is the conversion period of inventories.

Conversion period of inventories. This computation adds the collection period of receivables to the days needed to sell inventories in order to arrive at the time interval needed to convert inventories into cash.

Using figures developed in our examples of the respective ratios above, we get

Days to sell inventory	90
Days to collect receivables	60
Total conversion period of inventories...	150 days

It would thus normally take 150 days to sell inventory on credit and to collect the receivable. This is a period identical to the *operating cycle* which we discussed earlier in this chapter.

The effect of alternative methods of inventory measurement

In evaluating the inventory turnover ratio the analyst must be alert to the influence which alternative accounting principles have on the determination of the ratio's components. The basic discussion on alternative accounting principles of inventory measurement is found in Chapter 3. It is obvious that the use of the Lifo method of inventory valuation may render both the turnover ratios as well as the current ratio practically meaningless. Very little information is usually found in published financial statements which would enable the analyst to adjust the unrealistically low Lifo inventory valuation occurring in times of rising price levels so as to render it useful for inclusion in turnover ratio or the current ratio. Even if two companies employ Lifo cost methods for their inventory valuation computation of their ratios, using such inventory figures may nevertheless not be comparable because their respective Lifo inventory pools (bases) may have been acquired in years of significantly different price levels. The inventory figure enters the numerator of the current ratio and also the denominator because the inventory method utilized affects the income tax liability.

The analyst must also bear in mind that companies using the so-called "natural year" may have at their year-end an unrepresentatively low inventory level and that this may increase the turnover ratio to unrealistically high levels.

Prepaid expenses are expenditures made for benefits which are expected to be received in the future. Since most such benefits are receivable within a year or within an enterprise's operating cycle and thus will conserve the outlay of current funds, they are classified as current assets.

Usually, the amounts included in this category are relatively small compared to the size of the other current assets, and consequently no extensive discussion of their treatment is needed here. However, the analyst must be aware of the tendency of managements of enterprises with weak current positions to include in prepaid expenses deferred charges and other items of dubious liquidity. Such items must consequently be excluded from the computation of working capital and of the current ratio.

CURRENT LIABILITIES

In the computation of working capital and of the current ratio, current liabilities are important for two related reasons:

1. A basic objective of measuring the excess of current assets over current liabilities is to determine whether the latter are covered by current assets and what margin of safety is provided by the excess of such assets over current liabilities.
2. Current liabilities are deducted from current assets in arriving at the net working capital position.

In the computation of the current ratio, the point of view adopted towards current liabilities is *not* one of a continuing enterprise but rather of an enterprise in liquidation. This is so because in the normal course of operations, current liabilities are not paid off but are rather of a refunding nature. As long as the sales volume remains stable, purchases will also remain at a stable level, and that in turn will cause current liabilities to remain level. Increasing sales, in turn, will generally result in an increasing level of current liabilities. Thus, it can be generally stated that the trend and direction of sales is a good indication of the future level of current liabilities.

In assessing the quality of the current ratio, the nature of the current liabilities must be carefully examined.

Differences in the "nature" of current liabilities

Not all liabilities represent equally urgent and forceful calls for payment. At one extreme we find liabilities for taxes of all kinds which must be paid promptly regardless of current financial difficulties. The powers of collection of federal and local government authorities are as well known as they are powerful.

On the other hand, current liabilities to suppliers with whom the enterprise has a long standing relationship and who depend on, and value, the enterprise's business are of a very different degree of urgency. Postponement and renegotiation of such debts in times of financial stringency are both possible and are commonly found.

The "nature" of current liabilities in terms of our present discussion must be judged in the light of the degree of urgency of payment which attaches to them. It must also be remembered that if fund inflows from current revenues are also viewed as sources of funds available for the payment of current liabilities, then it should be borne in mind that labor costs and other current fund-requiring costs and expenses have a first call on sales revenues and that trade bills and other debts are paid only after such internal recurring charges have been met. This dynamic aspect of funds flow will be examined more closely in the chapter which follows.

The analyst must also be aware of unrecorded liabilities which may have a claim to current funds. Examples of these are purchase commitments and obligations under pensions and leases. Moreover, under long-term loan acceleration clauses, a failure to meet current installments of long-term debt may render the entire debt due and payable, that is, cause it to become current.

Days purchases in accounts payable ratio

A measure of the degree to which accounts payable represent current rather than overdue obligations can be obtained by calculating the *days purchases in accounts payable ratio.* This ratio is computed as follows:

$$\text{Accounts payable} \div \frac{\text{Purchases}}{360}$$

The difficulty which the external analyst will encounter here is that normally purchases are not separately disclosed in published financial statements. A very rough approximation of the amount of purchases can be obtained by adjusting the cost of goods sold figure for depreciation and other nonfund requiring charges as well as for changes in inventories. However, the cost of goods sold figure may contain significant cash charges, and this may reduce the validity of a computation which contains such an approximation of purchases.

INTERPRETATION OF THE CURRENT RATIO

In the foregoing sections we have examined the means by which the quality and the liquidity of the individual components of the current ratio is measured. This evaluation is, of course, essential to an overall interpretation of the current ratio as an indicator of short-term liquidity and financial strength.

The analyst must, however, exercise great care if he wants to carry the interpretation of the current ratio beyond the conclusion that it represents an excess of current resources over current obligations as of a given point in time.

Examination of trend

An examination of the trend of the current ratio over time can be very instructive. Two tools of analysis which were discussed in Chapter 2 are useful here. One is *trend analysis*, where the components of working capital as well as the current ratio would be converted into an index to be compared over time. The other is *common-size analysis*, by means of which the *composition* of the current asset group is examined over time. A historical trend and common-size comparison over time, as well as an intra-industry comparison of such trends can also be instructive.

Interpretation of changes over time

Changes in the current ratio over time must, however, be interpreted with great care. They do not automatically imply changes in liquidity or operating results. Thus, for example, in a prosperous year an increased liability for taxes may result in a lowering of the current ratio. Conversely, during a business contraction, current liabilities may be paid off while there may be a concurrent involuntary accumulation of inventories and uncollected receivables causing the ratio to rise.

In times of business expansion, which may reflect operating successes, the enterprise may suffer from an expansion in working capital requirements, otherwise known as a "prosperity squeeze" with a resulting contraction of the current ratio. This can be seen in the following example:

	Year 1	Year 2
Current assets	$300,000	$600,000
Current liabilities	100,000	400,000
Working capital	$200,000	$200,000
Current ratio	3:1	1.5:1

As can be seen from the above example, a doubling of current assets, accompanied by a quadrupling of current liabilities and an unchanged amount of working capital will lead to a halving of the current ratio. This is the effect of business expansion unaccompanied by an added capital investment. Inflation can have a similar effect on a business enterprise.

Possibilities of manipulation

The analyst must also be aware of the possibilities of year-end manipulation of the current ratio, otherwise known as "window dressing."

For example, towards the close of the fiscal year the collection of receivables may be pressed more vigorously, advances to officers may be called in for temporary repayment, and inventory may be reduced to below normal levels. Proceeds from these steps can then be used to pay off current liabilities. The effect on the current ratio of the reduction of current liabilities through the use of current assets can be seen in the following example:

Payoff of $50,000 in liabilities

	Before	After
Current assets	$200,000	$150,000
Current liabilities	100,000	50,000
Current ratio	2:1	3:1

The accounting profession, sensing the propensity of managements to offset liabilities against assets, has strengthened its prohibitions against offsets by restricting them strictly to situations where the legal right to offset exists.

To the extent possible, the analyst should go beyond year-end measures and should try to obtain as many interim readings of the current ratio as possible, not only in order to guard against the practice of "window dressing" described above but also in order to gauge the seasonal changes to which the ratio is exposed. The effect of a strong current ratio in December on an assessment of current financial condition may be considerably tempered if it is discovered that at its seasonal peak in July the enterprise is dangerously close to a serious credit squeeze.

The use of "rules of thumb" standards

A popular belief that has gained considerable currency is that the current ratio can be evaluated by means of "rules of thumb." Thus, it is believed that if the current ratio is 2:1 (or 200 percent), it is sound and anything below that norm is bad while the higher above that figure the current ratio is, the better.

This rule of thumb may reflect the lender's, and particularly the banker's, conservatism. The fact that it is down from the norm of 2.5:1 prevailing at the turn of the century may mean that improved financial reporting has reduced this size of the "cushion" which the banker and other creditors would consider as the minimum protection they need.

What the 2:1 standard means is that there are $2 of current assets available for each dollar of current liabilities or that the value of current assets can, on liquidation, shrink by 50 percent before it will be inadequate to cover the current liabilities. Of course, a current ratio much higher than 2:1, while implying a superior coverage of current liabilities, may also mean a wasteful accumulation of liquid resources which do not "carry their weight" by earning an appropriate return for the enterprise.

It should be evident by now that the evaluation of the current ratio in terms of rules of thumb is a technique of dubious validity. This is so for two major reasons:

1. As we have learned in the preceding sections, the quality of the current assets, as well as the composition of the current liabilities which make up this ratio, are the most important determinants in an evaluation of the quality of the current ratio. Thus, two companies which have identical current ratios may nevertheless be in quite different current financial condition due to variations in the quality of the working capital components.
2. The need of an enterprise for working capital varies with industry conditions as well as with the length of its own particular *net trade cycle*.

The net trade cycle

An enterprise's need for working capital depends importantly on the relative size of its required inventory investment as well as on the relationship between the credit terms it receives from it suppliers as against those it must extend to its customers.

Illustration. Assume a company shows the following data at the end of 19x1:

Sales for 19x1	$360,000
Receivables	40,000
Inventories	50,000
Accounts payable	20,000

The following tabulation measures the company's cash cycle in terms of days:

$$\text{Sales per day} \frac{\$360,000}{360} = \underline{\underline{\$1,000}}$$

Number of days sales in:	
Accounts receivable	40 days
Inventories	50
Total trade cycle	90 days
Less: Accounts payable	20
Net trade cycle	70 days

From the above we can see that the company is keeping 50 days of sales in inventory and that it receives only 20 sales days of trade credit while it must extend 40 sales days of credit to its customers. Obviously the higher the *net trade cycle* a company has the larger its investment in working capital is likely to be. Thus, in our above example, if the company could lower its investment in inventories by 10 sales days, it could lower its investment in working capital by $10,000. A similar result can be achieved by increasing the number of days sales in accounts payable by 10.

The working capital requirements of a supermarket with its high inventory turnover and low outstanding receivables are obviously lower than those of a tobacco company with its slow inventory turnover.

Valid working capital standards

Comparison with industry current ratios as well as analyses of working capital requirements such as the net trade cycle analysis described above can lead to far more valid conclusions regarding the adequacy of an enterprise's working capital than can a mechanical comparison of its current ratio to the 2:1 "rule of thumb" standard.

The importance of sales

In an assessment of the overall liquidity of current assets, the trend of sales is an important factor. Since it takes sales to convert inventory into receivables or cash, an uptrend in sales indicates that the conversion of inventories into more liquid assets will be easier to achieve than when sales remain constant. Declining sales, on the other hand, will retard the conversion of inventories into cash.

Common-size analysis of current assets composition

The composition of the current asset group, which can be analyzed by means of common-size statements, is another good indicator of relative working capital liquidity.

Consider, for example, the following comparative working capital composition:

	Year 1 $	Year 1 %	Year 2 $	Year 2 %
Current Assets:				
Cash	30,000	30	20,000	20
Accounts receivable	40,000	40	30,000	30
Inventories	30,000	30	50,000	50
Total Current Assets	100,000	100	100,000	100

From the simple illustration above it can be seen, even without the computation of common-size percentages, that the liquidity of the current asset group has deteriorated in year 2 by comparison with year 1. However, the use of common-size percentage comparisons will greatly facilitate the evaluation of comparative liquidity, regardless of the size and complexity of the dollar amounts involved.

The liquidity index

The measurement of the comparative liquidity of current assets can be further refined through the use of a *liquidity index*. The construction of this index (first suggested by A. H. Finney) can be illustrated as follows:

Using the working capital figures from the common-size computation above, and assuming that the conversion of inventories into accounts receivable takes 50 days on average and that the conversion of receivables into cash takes an average of 40 days, the index is computed as follows:

Year 1

	Amount	×	Days removed from cash	=	Product dollar-days
Cash	30,000		...		...
Accounts receivable	40,000		40		1,600,000
Inventories	30,000		90		2,700,000
Total	100,000 (a)				4,300,000 (b)

$$\text{Liquidity index} = \frac{b}{a} = \frac{4,300,000}{100,000} = \underline{\underline{43}}$$

Year 2

	Amount	×	Days removed from cash	=	Product dollar-days
Cash	20,000		...		...
Accounts receivable	30,000		40		1,200,000
Inventories	50,000		90		4,500,000
Total	100,000				5,700,000

$$\text{Liquidity index} \frac{5,700,000}{100,000} = \underline{\underline{57}}$$

The computation of the respective liquidity indices for the years 1 and 2 tells what we already knew instinctively in the case of this simple example, that is, that the liquidity has deteriorated in year 2 as compared to year 1.

The liquidity index must be interpreted with care. The index is in itself a figure without significance. It gains its significance only from a comparison between one index number and another as a gauge of the period to period change in liquidity or as a company to company comparison of relative liquidity. Increases in the index signify a deterioration in liquidity while decreases signify changes in the direction of improved liquidity. The index is a weighing mechanism and its validity depends on the validity of the assumptions implicit in the weighing process.

An additional popular technique of current ratio interpretation is to submit it to a somewhat sterner test.

ACID-TEST RATIO

This test is the acid-test ratio, also known as the "quick ratio" because it is assumed to include the assets most quickly convertible into cash.

The acid-test ratio is computed as shown in Exhibit 14–3.

The omission of inventories from the acid-test ratio is based on the belief that they are the least liquid component of the current asset group. While this is generally so, we have seen in an earlier discussion in this chapter that this is not always true and that certain types of

EXHIBIT 14–3

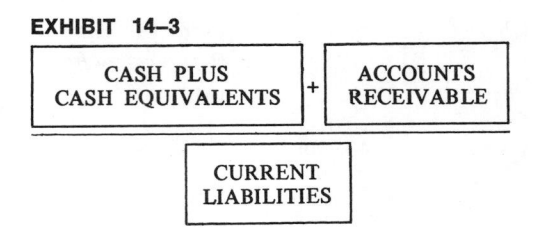

```
┌─────────────────┐   ┌─────────────┐
│   CASH PLUS     │ + │  ACCOUNTS   │
│ CASH EQUIVALENTS│   │ RECEIVABLE  │
└─────────────────┘   └─────────────┘
        ┌──────────────────┐
        │     CURRENT      │
        │   LIABILITIES    │
        └──────────────────┘
```

inventory can be more liquid than are slow-paying receivables. Another reason for the exclusion of inventories is the belief, quite often warranted, that the valuation of inventories normally requires a greater degree of judgment than is required for the valuation of the other current assets.

Since prepaid expenses are usually insignificant in relation to the other current assets, the acid test ratio is sometimes computed simply by omitting the inventories from the current asset figure.

The interpretation of the acid-test ratio is subject to most of the same considerations which were discussed regarding the interpretation of the current ratio. Moreover, the acid-test ratio represents an even sterner test of an enterprise's liquidity than does the current ratio, and the analyst must judge by himself what significance to his conclusions the total omission of inventories, as a source of current funds, is.

OTHER MEASURES OF SHORT-TERM LIQUIDITY

The static nature of the current ratio which measures the relationship of current assets to current liabilities, at a given moment in time, as well as the fact that this measure of liquidity fails to accord recognition to the great importance which cash flows play in an enterprise's ability to meet its maturing obligations has lead to a search for more dynamic measures of liquidity.

Cash flow ratios

Such measures utilize net cash flow as an index of liquidity.

Cash flow, a term whose weakness was discussed in Chapter 11, basically represents net income adjusted for nonfund (working capital) charges and credits. Many analysts superficially identify this with net income plus depreciation, and this in turn can lead to the omission of other very significant nonfund charges or credits.

Liquidity ratios which use cash flow as a component nevertheless have the advantage of recognizing the importance of cash flow in the measurement of liquidity.

One such ratio relates current liabilities to the cash flow for the year:

$$\frac{\text{Current liabilities}}{\text{Cash flow for the year}}$$

This measure relates the current liabilities as at the end of a period to the cash flow occurring during the year ended on the same date. It measures how many times current liabilities are covered by the cash flow of the year just elapsed. It is, of course, backward looking while current liabilities as of a certain date must be paid out of *future*, rather than past, cash flow. Nevertheless, in the absence of drastic changes in conditions, the latest yearly cash flow represents at least a good basis for an estimate of the next period's cash flow.

Importance of nonfund items in net income. Since the conversion of income into cash flow depends on the size of the net *nonfund* items included in it, a useful comparison measure is the relationship between the net nonfund items in income and net income. The computation of this ratio is as follows:

$$\frac{\text{Net nonfund items in income}}{\text{Net income}}$$

The higher the relationship of net nonfund requiring items to net income the greater the cash flow is in relation to reported net income and, thus, the higher the cash flow will be in relation to a given net income figure. An example of the computation of the *net nonfund items* follows:

Depreciation	$3,500,000
Depletion	1,200,000
Patent amortization	400,000
Deferred income taxes	2,800,000
Total nonfund charges	$7,900,000
Less: Unremitted earnings of foreign subsidiaries	2,100,000
Net nonfund requiring items	$5,800,000

If net income is $58,000,000, the net nonfund items ratio is as follows:

$$\frac{5,800,000}{58,000,000} = .1 \text{ or } 10 \text{ percent}$$

This means that cash flow will normally be expected to approximate 110 percent of net income.

A variation of the cash flow ratio, which focuses on cash expenses of the year, measures how many days of expenses the most liquid current assets could finance assuming that all other cash inflows were to suddenly dry up. This is computed as follows:

$$\frac{\text{Cash} + \text{cash equivalents} + \text{receivables}}{\text{Year's cash expenses}}$$

The external analyst may not find the figure of year's cash expenses easily available. Moreover, like the acid test ratio, the sternness of this test is such that its usefulness must be carefully weighed by the analyst.

The above measures recognize, of course, the importance of net cash flows, and especially the importance of prospective net cash flows to the assessment of short-term liquidity. Cash flow projections are the subject of the chapter which follows.

QUESTIONS

1. Why is short-term liquidity so significant? Explain from the viewpoint of various parties concerned.
2. The concept of working capital is simple, that is, the excess of current assets over current liabilities. What are some of the factors that make this simple computation complicated in practice?
3. What are "cash equivalents"? How should an analyst value them in his analysis?
4. Can fixed assets be included in current assets? If so, explain the situation under which the inclusion may be allowed.
5. Some installment receivables are not collectible within one year. Why are they included in current assets?
6. Are all inventories included in current assets? Why or why not?
7. What is the theoretical justification for including prepaid expenses in current assets?
8. The company under analysis has a very small amount of current liabilities but the long-term liabilities section shows a significant balance. In the footnote to the audited statements, it is disclosed that the company has a "revolving loan agreement" with a local bank. Does this disclosure have any significance to you?
9. Some industries are subject to peculiar financing and operating conditions which call for special consideration in drawing the distinction between what is "current" and what is "noncurrent." How should the analyst recognize this in his evaluation of working capital?
10. Your careful computation of the working capitals of Companies A and B reveals that both have the same amount of working capital. Are you ready to conclude that the liquidity position of both is the same?
11. What is the current ratio? What does it measure? What are the reasons for its widespread use?
12. The holding of cash generally does not yield a return. Why does an enterprise hold cash at all?

13. Is there a relationship between the level of inventories and that of sales? Are inventories a function of sales? If there is a functional relationship between the two, is it proportional?
14. What are the major objectives of management in determining the size of inventory and receivables investment?
15. What are the theoretical limitations of the current ratio as a measure of liquidity?
16. If there are significant limitations attached to the current ratio as a measure of liquidity, what is the proper use of this tool?
17. What are cash ratios? What do they measure?
18. How do we measure the "quality" of various current assets?
19. What does the average accounts receivable turnover measure?
20. What is the collection period for accounts receivable? What does it measure?
21. A company's collection period is 60 days this year as compared to 40 days of last year. Give three or more possible reasons for this change.
22. What is an accounts receivable aging schedule? What is its use in the analysis of financial statements?
23. What are the repercussions to an enterprise of (*a*) overinvestment or (*b*) underinvestment in inventories?
24. What problems would you expect to encounter in an analysis of a company using the Lifo inventory method in an inflationary economy? What effects do the price changes have (*a*) on the inventory turnover ratio and (*b*) on the current ratio?
25. Why does the "nature" of the current liabilities have to be analyzed in assessing the quality of the current ratio?
26. An apparently successful company shows a poor current ratio. Explain the possible reasons for this.
27. What is "window dressing"? Is there any way to find out whether the financial statements are "window dressed" or not?
28. What is the "rule of thumb" governing the expected size of the current ratio? What dangers are there in using this rule of thumb mechanically?
29. Describe the importance which the sales level plays in the overall current financial condition and liquidity of the current assets of an enterprise.
30. What is a liquidity index? What significance do the liquidity index numbers have?
31. What do cash flow ratios attempt to measure?

15

Funds flow analysis and financial forecasts

THE PRECEDING CHAPTER examined the various measures which are derived from past financial statement data and which are useful in the assessment of short-term liquidity. The chapter which follows will focus on the use of similar data in an evaluation of longer term solvency. The limitations to which these approaches are subject are due mainly to their static nature, that is, to their reliance on status reports, as of a given moment, of claims against an enterprise and the resources available to meet these claims.

An important and, in many cases, superior alternative to such static measures of conditions prevailing at a given point in time is the analysis and projection of more dynamic models of cash and funds flow. Such models use the present only as a starting point, and while building on reliable patterns of past experience, they utilize the best available estimates of future plans and conditions in order to forecast the future availability and disposition of cash or working capital.

OVERVIEW OF CASH FLOW AND FUNDS FLOW PATTERNS

Before we examine the methods by means of which funds flow projections are made, it would be useful to get a thorough understanding of the nature of funds flow. Exhibit 15–1 presents a diagram of the flow of funds through an enterprise. This diagram parallels the accounting cycle diagram presented in Chapter 1 (Exhibit 1–1).

The flow of funds diagram focuses on two concepts of funds: cash

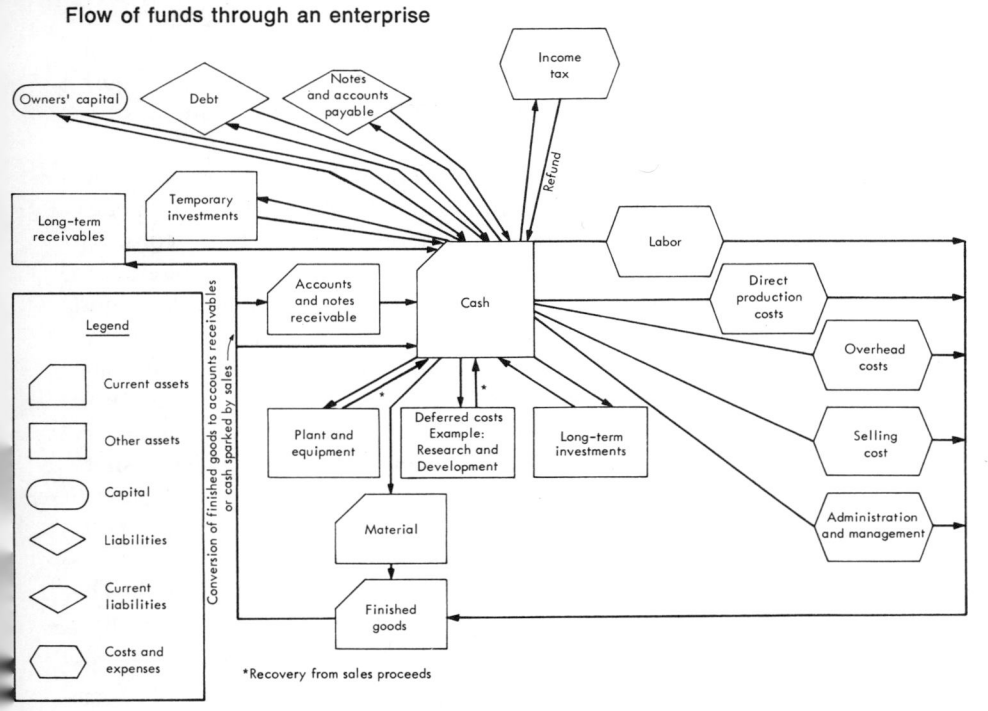

EXHIBIT 15–1
Flow of funds through an enterprise

and working capital. It was pointed out in Chapter 11 that in the context of funds flow analysis, the term "funds" is synonymous with "working capital."

Cash (including cash equivalents) is the ultimate liquid asset. Almost all decisions to invest in assets or to incur costs require the immediate or eventual use of cash. This is why managements focus, from an operational point of view, on *cash* rather than on working capital. The focus on the latter represents mainly the point of view of creditors who consider as part of the liquid assets pool other assets, such as receivables and inventories, which are normally converted into cash within a relatively short time span.

Careful examination of the flows depicted in Exhibit 15–1 should contribute greatly to the reader's understanding of the importance of liquid funds in an enterprise as well as the factors which cause them to be converted into assets and costs. The following factors and relationship are worthy of particular note:

♦ Since the diagram focuses on cash and funds flows only, assets, liabilities, and other items which are not directly involved, such as

prepayments and accruals, as well as the income account are not included in it. Some flows are presented in simplified fashion for an easier understanding of relationships. For example, accounts payable are presented as direct sources of cash, whereas in reality they represent a temporary postponement of cash payment for the acquisition of goods and services.
- It is recognized that the holding of cash provides no return or a very low return and that in times of rising price levels, cash as a monetary asset is exposed to purchasing power loss. However, these considerations aside, the holding of this most liquid of assets represents, in a business sense, the lowest exposure to risk. Management must make the decision to invest cash in assets or costs, and such a conversion increases risk because the certainty of ultimate reconversion into cash is less than 100 percent. There are, of course, a variety of risks. Thus, the risk involved in a conversion of cash into temporary investments is lower than the risk involved in committing cash to long-term, long-payout assets such as plant, machinery, or research costs. Similarly, the investment of cash in a variety of assets and costs for the creation and marketing of a new product involves serious risk regarding the recovery in cash of amounts so committed. The short-term liquidity as well as the long-term solvency of an enterprise depends on the recovery and realizability of such outlays.
- The inflow and outflow of cash (or funds) are highly interrelated. A failure of any part of the system to circulate can affect the entire system. A cessation of sales affects the vital conversion of finished goods into receivables or cash and leads, in turn, to a drop in the cash reservoir. Inability to replenish this reservoir from sources such as owners' capital, debt, or accounts payable (upper left-hand corner of diagram) can lead to a cessation of production activities which will result in a loss of future sales. Conversely, the cutting off of expenses, such as for advertising and marketing, will slow down the conversion of finished goods into receivables and cash. Longer term blockages in the flows may lead to insolvency.
- The diagram clarifies the interrelationship between profitability, income, and cash flow. The only real source of funds from operations is sales. When finished goods, which for the sake of simplicity represent the accumulation of *all* costs and expenses in the diagram, are sold, the profit margin will enhance the inflow of liquid funds in the form of receivables and cash. The higher the profit margin the greater the accretion of these funds.

Income, which is the difference between the cash and credit sales and the cost of goods sold, can have a wide variety of effects on cash flow. For example, the costs which flow from the utilization of plant and equipment or from deferred charges generally do not involve the use of current funds. Similarly, as in the case of land sales on long-term installment terms, the creation of long-term receivables through sales reduces the impact of net income on cash flow. It can be readily seen that adding back depreciation to net income creates a very crude measure of cash flow.

♦ The limitation of the cash flow concept can be more clearly seen. As cash flows into its reservoir management has a *degree* of discretion as to where to direct it. This discretion depends on the amount of cash already committed to such outlays as dividends, inventory accumulation, capital expenditures, or debt repayment. The total cash inflow also depends on management's ability to tap sources such as equity capital and debt. With respect to noncommitted cash, management has, at the point of return of the cash to the reservoir, the discretion of directing it to any purpose it deems most important. It is this noncommitted cash flow segment that is of particular interest and importance to financial analysts.

♦ Under present accounting conventions certain cash outlays, such as those for training or sales promotion, are considered as business (period) costs and are not shown as assets. These costs can, nevertheless, be of significant future value in either the increasing of sales or in the reduction of costs.

SHORT-TERM CASH FORECASTS

In the measurement of short-term liquidity the short-term cash forecast is one of the most thorough and reliable tools available to the analyst.

Short-term liquidity analysis is of particular interest to management in the financial operations of an enterprise and to short-term credit grantors who are interested in an enterprise's ability to repay short-term loans. The security analyst will pay particular attention to the short-term cash forecast when an enterprise's ability to meet its current obligations is subject to substantial doubt.

Realistic cash forecasts can be made only for relatively short time spans. This is so because the factors influencing the inflows and outflows of cash are many and complex and cannot be reliably estimated beyond the short term.

Importance of sales estimates

The reliability of any cash forecast depends very importantly on the forecast of sales. In fact, a cash forecast can never reach a higher degree of reliability than the sales forecast on which it is based. Except for transactions involving the raising of money from external sources or the investment of money in long-term assets, almost all cash flows relate to and depend on sales.

The sales forecast involves considerations such as:

1. The past direction and trend of sales volume.
2. Enterprise share of the market.
3. Industry and general economic conditions.
4. Productive and financial capacity.
5. Competitive factors.

These factors must generally be assessed in terms of individual product lines which may be influenced by forces peculiar to their own markets.

Pro forma financial statements as an aid to forecasting

The reasonableness and feasibility of short-term cash forecasts can be checked by means of pro forma financial statements. This is done by utilizing the assumptions underlying the cash forecast and constructing, on this basis, a pro forma statement of income covering the period of the forecast and a pro forma balance sheet as at the end of that period. The ratios and other relationships derived from the pro forma financial statements should then be checked for feasibility against historical relationships which have prevailed in the past. Such relationships must be adjusted for factors which it is estimated will affect them during the period of the cash forecast.

Illustration of techniques of short-term cash forecasting

The Prudent Corporation has recently introduced an improved product which has enjoyed excellent market acceptance. As a result, management has budgeted sales for the six months ending June 30, 19x1 as follows:

	Estimated sales
January	$100,000
February	125,000
March	150,000
April	175,000
May	200,000
June	250,000

The cash balance at January 1, 19x1 is $15,000, and the treasurer foresees a need for additional funds necessary to finance the sales expansion. He has obtained a commitment from an insurance company for the sale to them of long-term bonds as follows:

| April | $50,000 (less $2,500 debt costs) |
| May | 60,000 |

He also expects to sell real estate at cost: $8,000 in May and $50,000 in June. In addition, equipment with an original cost of $25,000 and a book value of zero was to be sold for $25,000 cash in June.

The treasurer considers that in the light of the expanded sales volume the following minimum cash balances will be desirable:

January	$20,000
February	25,000
March	27,000
April, May, and June	30,000

He knows that during the next six months he will not be able to meet his cash requirements without resort to short-term financing. Consequently he approaches his bank and finds it ready to consider his company's needs. The loan officer suggests that in order to determine the cash needs and the sources of funds for loan repayment, the treasurer prepare a cash forecast for the six months ending June 30, 19x1 and pro forma financial statements for that period.

The treasurer, recognizing the importance of such a forecast, proceeded to assemble the data necessary to prepare it.

The pattern of receivables collections based on experience was as follows:

Collections	Percent of total receivable
In month of sale	40
In the second month	30
In the third month	20
In the fourth month	5
Write-off of bad debts	5
	100

On the basis of this pattern and the expected sales the treasurer constructed Schedule A shown in Exhibit 15–2.

An analysis of past cost patterns resulted in the estimates of cost and expense relationships for the purpose of the cash forecast (Schedule B) shown in Exhibit 15–3.

It was estimated that all costs in Schedule B (exclusive of the $1,000 monthly depreciation charge) will be paid for in cash in the month incurred, except for material purchases which are to be paid 50 percent in the month of purchase and 50 percent in the following month. Since the product is manufactured to specific order, no finished goods inventories are expected to accumulate.

Schedule C (Exhibit 15–4) shows the pattern of payments of accounts payable (for materials).

EXHIBIT 15-2

SCHEDULE A
Estimates of Cash Collections
For the Months January–June, 19x1

	January	February	March	April	May	June
Sales	$100,000	$125,000	$150,000	$175,000	$200,000	$250,000
Collections:						
1st month—40%	$ 40,000	$ 50,000	$ 60,000	$ 70,000	$ 80,000	$100,000
2nd month—30%		30,000	37,500	45,000	52,500	60,000
3rd month—20%			20,000	25,000	30,000	35,000
4th month—5%				5,000	6,250	7,500
Total cash collections	$ 40,000	$ 80,000	$117,500	$145,000	$168,750	$202,500
Write-offs—5%				$5,000	$6,250	$7,500

EXHIBIT 15-3

SCHEDULE B
Cost and Expense Estimates for Six Months
Ending June 30, 19x1

Materials . . . . 30% of sales
Labor . . . . 25% of sales
Manufacturing overhead:
   Variable . . . . 10% of sales
   Fixed . . . . $48,000 for six months (including $1,000
                                  of depreciation per month)
Selling expenses . . . . 10% of sales
General and administrative expenses:
   Variable . . . . 8% of sales
   Fixed . . . . $7,000 per month

EXHIBIT 15-4

SCHEDULE C
Pro Forma Schedule of Cash Payments for Materials Purchases
For the Months January–June 19x1

	January	February	March	April	May	June
Materials purchased during month	$40,000	$38,000	$43,000	$56,000	$58,000	$79,000
Payments:						
1st month—50%	$20,000	$19,000	$21,500	$28,000	$29,000	$39,500
2nd month—50%		20,000	19,000	21,500	28,000	29,000
Total payments	$20,000	$39,000	$40,500	$49,500	$57,000	$68,500

Equipment costing $20,000 will be bought in February for notes payable which will be paid off, starting that month, at the rate of $1,000 per month. The new equipment will not be fully installed until sometime in August 19x1.

Exhibit 15-5 presents the cash forecast for the six months ending June 30, 19x1 based on the data given above. Exhibit 15-6 presents the pro forma income statement for the six months ending June 30, 19x1. Exhibit 15-7 presents the actual balance sheet of The Prudent Corporation as at January 1, 19x1 and the pro forma balance sheet as at June 30, 19x1.

The financial analyst should examine the pro forma statements critically and submit to feasibility tests the estimates on which the forecasts are based. The ratios and relationships revealed by the pro forma financial statements should be analyzed and compared to similar ratios of the past in order to determine whether they are reasonable and feasible of attainment. For example, the current ratio of The Prudent Corporation increased from 2.6 on 1/1/x1 to 3.2 in the pro forma balance sheet as of 6/30/x1. During the six months ended 6/30/x1 a pro forma return on average equity of almost 16 percent was projected. Many other significant measures of turnover, common-size statements, and trends can be computed. The reasonableness of these comparisons and results must be assessed. They can help reveal serious errors and inconsistencies in the assumptions which underly the projections and thus help strengthen confidence in their reliability.

Differences between short-term and long-term forecasts

The short-term cash forecast is, as we have seen, a very useful and reliable aid in projecting the state of short-term liquidity. Such a detailed approach is, however, only feasible for the short term, that is, up to about 12 months. Beyond this time horizon the uncertainties become so great as to preclude detailed and accurate cash forecasts. Instead of focusing on collections of receivables and on payments for labor and materials, the longer term estimates focus on projections of net income and on other sources and uses of funds. Over the longer term the emphasis on cash becomes less important, and the estimation process centers on funds, that is, working capital. Over the short term the difference between cash and other working capital assets is significant. Over the longer term, however, the distinction between cash, receivables, and inventories becomes less significant because such longer periods include the operating cycles over which inventories and receivables are normally converted into cash. In other words, if the trade cycle is 90 days long, such a period is not as significant in a 3-year forecast as it is in relation to a 6 or 12 months span. The further we peer into the future, the

EXHIBIT 15–5

THE PRUDENT CORPORATION
Cash Forecast
For the Months January–June 19x1

	January	February	March
Cash balance—beginning	$15,000	$20,000	$ 25,750
Add: Cash receipts:			
Collections of accounts receivable (Schedule A)	40,000	80,000	117,500
Proceeds from sale of real estate			
Proceeds from additional long-term debt			
Proceeds from sale of equipment			
Total cash available	$ 55,000	$100,000	$143,250
Less: Disbursements:			
Payments for:			
Materials purchases (Schedule C)	$20,000	$39,000	$ 40,500
Labor	25,000	31,250	37,500
Fixed factory overhead	7,000	7,000	7,000
Variable factory overhead	10,000	12,500	15,000
Selling expenses	10,000	12,500	15,000
General and administrative	15,000	17,000	19,000
Taxes			
Purchase of fixed asset		1,000	1,000
Total disbursements	87,000	120,250	135,000
Tentative cash balance (negative)	$ (32,000)	$ (20,250)	$ 8,250
Minimum cash balance required	20,000	25,000	27,000
Additional borrowing required	$ 52,000	$ 46,000	$ 19,000
Repayment of bank loan			
Interest paid on balance outstanding at rate of ½ per month (1)			
Ending cash balance	$ 20,000	$ 25,750	$ 27,250
Loan balance	$ 52,000	$ 98,000	$117,000

(1) Interest is computed at the rate of ½% per month and paid on date of repayment which occurs at month end. Loan is taken out at beginning of month.

broader are the financial statement categories which we must estimate and the less detailed are the data behind the estimates.

The projection of future statements of changes in financial position is best begun with an analysis of prior year funds statements. To this data can then be added all available information and estimates about the future needs for funds and the most likely sources of funds needed to cover such requirements.

ANALYSIS OF STATEMENTS OF CHANGES IN FINANCIAL POSITION

In Chapter 11 we examined the principles underlying the preparation of the statement of changes in financial position (funds statement) as

April	May	June	Six-month totals
$ 27,250	$ 30,580	$ 30,895	$ 15,000
145,000	168,750	202,500	753,750
	8,000	50,000	58,000
47,500	60,000		107,500
		25,000	25,000
$219,750	$267,330	$308,395	$959,250
$ 49,500	$ 57,000	$ 68,500	$274,500
43,750	50,000	62,500	250,000
7,000	7,000	7,000	42,000
17,500	20,000	25,000	100,000
17,500	20,000	25,000	100,000
21,000	23,000	27,000	122,000
		19,000	19,000
1,000	1,000	1,000	5,000
157,250	178,000	235,000	912,500
$ 62,500	$ 89,330	$ 73,395	$ 46,750
30,000	30,000	30,000	
...	...	...	$117,000
$ 30,000	$ 58,000	$ 29,000	(117,000)
1,920	435	145	2,500
$ 30,580	$ 30,895	$ 44,250	$ 44,250
$ 87,000	$ 29,000	...	...

well as the uses to which the statement may be put by the analyst. We shall now focus on the analysis of the statement of changes in financial position paying particular attention to the value of such an analysis to a projection of future funds flows.

In any analysis of financial statements the most recent years are the most important because they represent the most recent experience. Since there is an inherent continuity in business events, it is this latest experience that is likely to have the greatest relevance to the projection of future results. So it is with the statement of changes in financial position.

It is important that the analyst obtain statements of changes in financial position for as many years as possible. This is particularly important in the case of an analysis of this statement since the planning and execution of plant expansions, of modernization schemes, of working capital

EXHIBIT 15-6

THE PRUDENT CORPORATION
Pro Forma Income Statement
For the Six Months Ending June 30, 19x1

		Source of estimate
Sales	$1,000,000	Based on sales budget (page 378)
Cost of sales:		
Materials	$ 300,000	Schedule B
Labor	250,000	Schedule B
Overhead	148,000	Schedule B
	$ 698,000	
Gross profit	$ 302,000	
Selling expense	$ 100,000	Schedule B
Bad debts expense	18,750	Schedule A
General and administrative expense	122,000	Schedule B
Total	$ 240,750	
Operating income	$ 61,250	
Gain on sale of equipment	25,000	
Interest expense	(2,500)	Exhibit 15-5, footnote 1
Income before taxes	83,750	
Income taxes	38,055	30% of first $25,000; 52% of balance. Pay ½ in June and accrue balance
Net income	$ 45,695	

increases as well as the financing of such activities by means of short-term and long-term debt and by means of equity funds is an activity which is likely to encompass many years. Thus, in order for the analyst to be able to assess management's plans and their execution, statements of changes in financial position covering a number of years must be analyzed. In this way a more comprehensive picture of management's financial habits can be obtained and an assessment of them made.

First illustration of statement of changes in financial position analysis

The five-year statement of changes in financial position of the Modern Inns Company is as shown in Exhibit 15-8. One of the most important factors revealed by these statements is that during the five years ending in 19x5 the fixed assets additions have significantly exceeded the provisions of depreciation for the respective five years. Thus, even allowing for the effects of price level changes, that is, for the fact that the depreciation is based on the lower acquisition costs of many years ago and

EXHIBIT 15-7

THE PRUDENT CORPORATION
Balance Sheets

	Actual January 1, 19x1		Pro forma June 30, 19x1	
Assets				
Current Assets:				
Cash	$ 15,000		$ 44,250	
Accounts receivable (net)	6,500		234,000	
Inventories—raw materials	57,000		71,000	
Total Current Assets		$ 78,500		$349,250
Real estate	$ 58,000		...	
Fixed assets	206,400		$201,400	
Accumulated depreciation	(36,400)		(17,400)	
Net Fixed Assets		228,000		184,000
Other assets		3,000		3,000
Deferred debt expenses				2,500
Total Assets		$309,500		$538,750
Liabilities and Equity				
Current Liabilities:				
Accounts payable	$ 2,000		$ 41,500	
Notes payable	28,500		43,500	
Accrued taxes	...		19,055	
Total Current Liabilities		$ 30,500		$104,055
Long-term debt	$ 15,000		$125,000	
Common stock	168,000		168,000	
Retained earnings	96,000		141,695	
		279,000		434,695
Total Liabilities and Equity		$309,500		$538,750

that the present purchases are made on the basis of current, higher level prices, it is clear that the company is going through a period of significant investments in fixed assets. This is also evident from the fact that only in 19x3 did deferred taxes, presumably due to differences between book and tax depreciation, start to become a material and increasing source of funds. This is an often important source of funds which arises from the postponement of taxes due to timing differences permitted by the tax law. As long as the accelerated methods of depreciation are availed of and the total assets account is growing, deferred taxes, as a source of funds, (or postponement of tax payments), are also likely to grow.

The company has been able to finance the fixed assets expansion mostly with funds derived from operations and at the same time increased its cash dividends year after year. In 19x4, the year of peak investments in fixed assets, the working capital dropped by $8.1 million,

EXHIBIT 15–8

MODERN INNS COMPANY
Statement of Changes in Financial Position
Years ended December

	19x5	19x4	19x3	19x2	19x1
Sources of funds:					
Net income before extraordinary gain	$11,416,000	$ 9,029,000	$ 9,581,000	$ 8,587,000	$ 9,285,000
Depreciation	9,635,000	9,053,000	8,602,000	8,285,000	7,210,000
Deferred income taxes	864,000	576,000	173,000		
Total from operations	$21,915,000	$18,658,000	$18,356,000	$16,872,000	$16,495,000
Increase in noncurrent notes payable	6,393,000			210,000	3,607,000
Extraordinary gain	707,000		1,814,000		
Deferred income taxes on extraordinary gain			582,000		
Disposals of fixed assets	1,295,000	780,000	1,251,000	2,493,000	301,000
Proceeds from exercise of stock options		468,000	899,000	535,000	705,000
Decrease in other assets	2,402,000				
Decrease in working capital		8,148,000	1,017,000		
	$32,712,000	$28,054,000	$23,919,000	$20,110,000	$21,108,000
Applications of funds:					
Fixed asset additions	$16,630,000	$23,197,000	$13,858,000	$12,831,000	$18,587,000
Decrease in noncurrent notes payable		2,037,000	5,394,000		
Cash dividends declared	2,403,000	2,307,000	1,994,000	743,000	
Increase in other assets		513,000	2,673,000	103,000	21,000
Increase in working capital	13,679,000			6,433,000	2,500,000
	$32,712,000	$28,054,000	$23,919,000	$20,110,000	$21,108,000

and this was more than made up in the following year. While in 19x5 notes payable (long-term) increased by $6.4 million, this merely reinstated the decrease in notes payable of 7.4 million which occurred in 19x3 and 19x4.

A *forecast* of future statements of changes in financial position would take into consideration the increasing earnings trend, the larger depreciation stemming from fixed assets additions, as well as a possible continuation in the growth of deferred taxes, which constitute a source of funds.

Second illustration of statement of changes in financial position analysis

Exhibits 15–9 and 15–10 present the statement of changes in financial position of the Migdal Corporation and the same data expressed in common-size percentages. The common-size statement of changes in financial position is a useful tool of analysts in that it enables the analysis to compare readily the changes which occurred over time in the relative contributions of various categories of sources and uses of funds.

The statements in Exhibits 15–9 and 15–10 reveal that net income has been steadily growing since 19x1 and contributed increasingly, on an absolute basis, to funds from operations. As a percentage of total funds generated, funds from operations fluctuated from a low of 33.5 percent in 19x1 to a high of 97.4 percent in 19x4. This is due to substantial inflows from borrowings in 19x1 and an absence of external financing in 19x4. To finance its significant additions to equipment and to working capital, the company resorted mostly to substantial equity financing in 19x3 and in 19x6. More modest additions to debt occurred in 19x1 to 19x3. The relationship of depreciation to income as a percentage of total funds has held steady over the years thus facilitating the projection of these elements.

Third illustration of statement of changes in financial position analysis

The Exeter Chemical Company presents the five-year statement of changes in financial position shown in Exhibit 15–11. This statement has a column for totals encompassing the period covered by the statement. This is a useful feature since it affords a view of the cumulative totals of sources and uses of funds over the longer term. Since cash and cash equivalents are the most liquid portions of the current assets group, the changes in working capital are separated to indicate changes in working capital exclusive of these liquid items and changes in the cash items.

An analysis of the statement in Exhibit 15–11 reveals that the sources

EXHIBIT 15-9

MIGDAL CORPORATION
Statement of Changes in Financial Position
For the Years Ended 19x1–x6

	19x6	19x5	19x4	19x3	19x2	19x1
Funds were provided from:						
Current operations:						
Net income	$1,641,889	$1,385,021	$1,140,113	$ 822,362	$ 532,872	$ 422,065
Depreciation	596,207	436,102	335,019	275,331	193,827	114,096
Amortization of preoperating expenses	152,525	135,156	184,726	73,394	52,885	36,036
Deferred taxes	38,000	(80,000)	43,500	(7,053)	(22,447)	18,881
Funds from operations	$2,428,621	$1,876,279	$1,703,358	$1,164,034	$ 779,584	$ 591,078
Net proceeds from sale of stock	2,526,871			1,340,375		424,982
Exercise of stock options	94,458	7,445	44,663	2,922		
Transfer of deferred taxes to current assets		86,000				
Long-term borrowing				500,000	300,000	750,000
Total	$5,049,950	$1,969,724	$1,748,021	$3,007,331	$1,057,137	$1,766,060
Funds were used for:						
Additions to equipment	$2,256,821	$1,326,761	$ 678,101	$ 535,708	$1,000,593	$ 610,406
Additions to other assets	331,397	188,205	170,063	147,291	127,250	89,017
Reduction in long-term debt	175,000	175,000	100,000	25,000	69,174	32,863
Other		18,975	3,721			30,349
Total	$2,763,218	$1,708,941	$ 951,885	$ 707,999	$1,197,017	$ 162,635
Increase (decrease) in working capital	$2,286,732	$ 260,783	$ 796,136	$2,299,332	$ (139,880)	$1,003,425
Increases (decreases) to working capital:						
Cash and U.S. Treasuries	$ 103,288	$ (60,252)	$ 340,304	$2,124,704	$ (97,370)	$ 263,161
Receivables	279,010	(72,138)	122,950	(79,788)	77,086	30,741
Inventories	2,244,180	1,848,771	737,350	1,184,078	1,416,723	645,078
Prepaid expenses	253,689	149,772	28,075	(4,739)	98,623	62,461
Current portion of long-term debt		(75,000)	(75,000)	500,000	(453,642)	164,515
Accounts payable	(458,504)	(1,394,811)	(87,807)	(809,927)	(897,663)	(681)
Income taxes payable	302,593	217,493	(143,122)	(389,473)	(128,063)	(41,195)
Other payables	(437,524)	(353,052)	(126,614)	(155,523)	(155,574)	(120,655)
Total	$2,286,732	$ 260,783	$ 796,136	$2,299,332	$ (139,880)	$1,003,425

EXHIBIT 15-10

MIGDAL CORPORATION
Statement of Changes in Financial Position
Common Size
For the Years Ended 19x1-x6

	19x6	19x5	19x4	19x3	19x2	19x1
Funds were provided from:						
Current operations:						
Net income	32.5%	70.3%	65.2%	27.3%	50.4%	23.9%
Depreciation	11.8	22.1	19.2	9.2	18.3	6.5
Amortization of preoperating expenses	3.0	6.7	10.6	2.4	5.0	2.0
Deferred taxes	.8	(4.1)	2.5	(.2)	(2.0)	1.1
Funds from operations	48.1%	95.3%	97.4%	38.7%	73.7%	33.5%
Net proceeds from sale of stock	50.0			44.6		24.0
Exercise of stock options	1.9	.4		.1		
Transfer of deferred taxes to current assets		4.4	2.6			
Long-term borrowing				16.6	28.4	42.5
Total	100.0%	100.0%	100.0%	100.0%	100.0%	100.0%
Funds were used for:						
Additions to equipment	44.7%	67.4%	38.8%	17.8%	94.6%	34.6%
Additions to other assets	6.6	9.6	9.7	4.9	12.0	5.0
Reduction in long-term debt	3.5	8.9	5.7	.8	6.5	1.9
Other		1.0	.2			1.7
Total	54.8%	86.8%	54.5%	23.5%	113.2%	43.2%
Increase (decrease) in working capital	45.2%	13.2%	45.5%	76.5%	(13.2)%	56.8%
Increases (decreases) in working capital:						
Cash and U.S. Treasuries	4.5%	(23.1)%	42.7%	92.4%	(69.6)%	26.2%
Receivables	12.2	(27.7)	15.4	(3.5)	55.1	3.1
Inventories	98.1	708.9	92.6	51.5	1012.8	64.3
Prepaid expenses	11.1	57.4	3.5	(.2)	70.5	6.2
Current portion of long-term debt		(28.7)	(9.4)	21.7	(324.3)	16.4
Accounts payable	(20.1)	(534.8)	(11.0)	(35.2)	(641.7)	(.1)
Income taxes payable	13.2	83.4	(18.0)	(16.9)	(91.5)	(4.1)
Other payables	(19.0)	(135.4)	(15.8)	(9.8)	(111.1)	(12.0)
Total	100.0%	100.0%	100.0%	100.0%	100.0%	100.0%

EXHIBIT 15-11

EXETER CHEMICAL COMPANY
Statement of Changes in Financial Position
(in thousands)

	Total	19x4	19x3	19x2	19x1	19x0
Source of funds:						
Net income	$ 412,712	$114,891	$ 82,990	$ 78,368	$ 68,656	$ 67,807
Provisions for:						
Depreciation, depletion, etc.	498,427	120,268	114,606	97,639	86,876	79,038
Deferred income taxes	35,804	11,980	12,373	11,451		
Insurance reserve	2,000	2,000				
Outside financing:						
5¾% promissory notes	99,593			99,593		
Other	4,945	3,276	1,669			
Common shares issued under options	40,245	12,108	14,532	2,639	9,926	1,040
Other—net	(13,622)	(429)	(5,368)	2,366	(7,918)	(2,273)
	$1,080,104	$264,094	$220,802	$292,056	$157,540	$145,612
Disposition of funds:						
Dividends on common shares	$ 155,029	$ 37,606	$ 34,978	$ 29,470	$ 27,316	$ 25,659
Plant additions and replacements	776,511	218,105	114,502	168,833	153,818	121,253
Investment in affiliated companies	60,913	13,340	18,443	9,597	9,810	9,723
Retirement of debt	73,590	10,418	13,452	17,877	21,928	9,915
Increase in working capital[1]	95,001	29,845	18,042	14,614	5,021	27,479
Increase—(decrease) in cash and securities	(80,940)	(45,220)	21,385	51,665	(60,353)	(48,417)
	$1,080,104	$264,094	$220,802	$292,056	$157,540	$145,612

(1) Exclusive of cash and securities.

of funds from operations over the five-year period were as follows:

	Millions	
Net income.		$413
Nonfund requiring charges:		
Depreciation, depletion, etc.	$498	
Deferred income taxes	36	
Insurance reserves.	2	536
Total.		$949

Deducting dividends of $155 million from funds provided by operations, there remain funds totaling $794 million or an amount slightly in excess of the sum spent on plant additions and replacements. Thus, investments in affiliated companies, the retirement of debt, and the increase in net working capital over the period were financed by means of promissory notes and the issuance of common stock under options. It is also interesting to note that while working capital increased by $95 million over the five years ending 19x4, cash and marketable securities decreased by almost $81 million. Undoubtedly the substantial increase in activity, as evidenced by a near doubling of net income over the five-year period, necessitated an expansion of funds invested in receivables and inventories.

EVALUATION OF THE STATEMENT OF CHANGES IN FINANCIAL POSITION

The foregoing examples of analyses of the statement of changes in financial position illustrate the variety of information and insights which can be derived from them. Of course, the analysis of statements of changes in financial position is to be performed within the framework of an analysis of all the financial statements, and thus the conclusion reached from an analysis of one statement may be strengthened and corroborated by an analysis of the other financial statements.

There are some useful generalizations that can be made regarding the value of the analysis of the statement of changes in financial position to the financial analyst.

This statement enables the analyst to appraise the quality of management decisions over time, as well as their impact on the results of operations and financial condition of the enterprise. When the analysis encompasses a longer period of time, the analyst can evaluate management's response to the changing economic conditions as well as to the opportunities and the adversities which invariably present themselves.

Evaluation of the statement of changes in financial position analysis will indicate the purposes to which management chose to commit funds, where it reduced investment, the source from which it derived additional funds, and to what extent it reduced claims against the enterprise. Such an analysis will also show the disposition of earnings over the years, as well as how management has reinvested the internal fund inflow over which it had discretion.

As depicted in Exhibit 15–1 earlier in this chapter, the circulation of funds in an enterprise involves a constant flow of funds and their periodic reinvestment. Thus, funds are invested in labor, material, and overhead costs as well as in long-term assets, such as inventories and plant and equipment, which join the product-cost stream at a slower rate. Eventually, by the process of sales, these costs are converted back into accounts receivable and into cash. If operations are profitable the funds recovered will exceed the amounts invested, thus augmenting the funds inflow or cash flow. Losses have, of course, the opposite effect.

What constitutes funds inflow, or cash flow, as it is often more crudely referred to, is the subject of considerable confusion. Generally the funds provided by operations, that is, net income adjusted for nonfund requiring or supplying items, is an index of management's ability to redirect funds away from areas of unfavorable profit opportunity into areas of greater profit potential. However, not all the funds provided by operations may be so available because of existing commitments for debt retirement, stock redemption, equipment replacement, and dividend payments. Nor are funds provided by operations the only potential cash inflows, since management can avail itself of external sources of capital in order to bolster its funds inflow. The components of the "sources of funds from operations" figure hold important clues to the stability of that source of funds. Thus, for example, depreciation is a more stable element in the total than net income itself in that it represents a recovery by the enterprise of the investment in fixed assets out of selling prices even before a profit is earned.

In evaluating the statement of changes in financial position, the analyst will judge a company's quality of earnings by the impact which changes in economic and industry conditions have on its flow of funds. If in his estimates of future earnings potential he foresees a need for additional capital, his analysis of the funds statement will be directed towards a projection of the source from which these funds will be obtained, and what dilution of earnings per share, if any, this will involve.

The analysis and evaluation of the statement of changes in financial position is, as the foregoing discussion suggests, an important early step in the projection of future statements of changes in financial position.

PROJECTION OF STATEMENTS OF CHANGES IN FINANCIAL POSITION

No thorough model of an enterprise's future results is complete without a concurrent forecast of the size of funds needed for the realization of the projections in the model as well as an assessment of the possible sources from which such funds can be derived.

If a future expansion of sales and profits is forecast, the analyst must know whether the enterprise has the "financial horsepower" to see such an expansion through by means of internally generated funds and, if not, where the required future funds are going to come from.

The projection of the statement of changes in financial position will start with a careful estimate of the expected changes in each individual category of assets and the funds which will be derived from or required by such changes. Some of the more important factors to be taken into consideration follow:

1. The net income expected to be generated by future results will be adjusted for nonfund items, such as depreciation, depletion, deferred income taxes, and nonremitted earnings of subsidiaries and investees, in order to arrive at estimates of funds provided by operations.
2. Sources of funds from disposals of assets, sale of investments, and the sale of stocks and bonds will be estimated.
3. The needs for working capital will be arrived at by estimating the required level of the individual working capital items such as cash, receivables, and inventories and reducing this by the expected levels of payables.
4. Expected capital expenditures will be based on the present level of operations as compared with productive capacity, as well as on an estimate of the future level of activity implied by the profit projections.
5. Mandatory debt retirement and desirable minimum levels of dividend payments will also be estimated.

The impact of adversity

The projected statement of changes in financial position is useful not only in estimating the funds implications of future expansion and opportunity but also in assessing the impact on the enterprise of sudden adversity.

A sudden adversity, from the point of view of its impact on the flow of funds, will usually manifest itself in a serious interruption in the inflow of funds. This can be brought about by such events as recessions, strikes, or the loss of a major customer or market. In this context a projection of the statement of changes in financial position would be a first step in the assessment of the defensive posture of an enterprise. The basic question to which such an analysis is directed is this: what can the enterprise do; and what resources, both internal and external, can it marshal to cope with a sudden and serious reduction in the inflow of funds?

The strategies and alternatives available to an enterprise faced with such adversities are ably examined and discussed in a work by Professor Donaldson.[1] Dr. Donaldson defines financial mobility as the capacity to redirect the use of financial resources in response to new information about the company and its environment.

The projected "sources and uses of funds" statement is an important tool in the assessment of the resources available to meet such "new information" as well as in planning the changes in financial strategy which this may require.

To the prospective credit grantor such an approach represents an excellent tool in the assessment of risk. In estimating the effects of, for example, a recession, on the future flow of funds he can trace through not only the potential shrinkage in cash inflows from operations but also the effects of such shrinkage on the uses of funds and on the sources from which they can be derived.

Inclusion of "funds flow" and earnings forecasts in prospectuses

In 1973 the Securities and Exchange Commission took the first steps towards an integration of projections into the disclosure system. While not requiring disclosure of projections, the SEC established first and experimental standards which determine who can issue a forecast and which are aimed to assure that published projections are reasonably based and are reliable. Many problems, including those related to legal liability for companies, their accountants, and others, on the forecasts remain to be resolved.

The reader of this chapter should appreciate that funds flow forecasts depend on a projection of income and that all forecasts are highly interrelated. Moreover, no forecast can be better than the assumptions on which it is based. The analyst should, consequently, train most of his attention on the validity of these assumptions rather than merely on the mechanics of the forecasting process.

CONCLUSION

In the assessment of future liquidity, the use of cash forecasts for the short term and of projected statements of changes in financial position for the longer term represent some of the most useful tools available to the financial analyst. In contrast to ratio measures of liquidity, these tools involve a detailed examination of sources and uses of funds. Such

---

[1] Gordon Donaldson, *Strategy for Financial Mobility* (Boston: Graduate School of Business Administration, Harvard University, 1969).

examination and estimation processes can be subjected to feasibility tests by means of pro forma statements and to the discipline inherent in the double-entry accounting system.

QUESTIONS

1. What is the primary difference between funds flow analysis and ratio analysis? Which is superior and why?
2. "From an operational point of view, management focuses on cash rather than working capital." Do you agree with the statement? Why or why not?
3. What is the relationship between inflows and outflows of cash?
4. Why is the short-term cash forecast important to the financial analyst?
5. What is the first step to be taken in preparing a cash forecast, and what considerations are required in such a step?
6. What are pro forma financial statements? How are they utilized in conjunction with funds flow projections?
7. What are the limitations of short-term cash forecasts?
8. If the usefulness of a short-term cash forecast is limited, what analytical approach is available to the financial analyst who wants to analyze future flows of working capital?
9. What useful information do you, as a financial analyst, expect to get from the analysis of past statements of changes in financial position (funds statement)?
10. What are the differences between short-term and long-term financial forecasts?
11. What analytical function does the common-size statement of changes in financial position serve?
12. Why is a projected statement of changes in financial position necessary when you have historical data which are based on actual performance?
13. If actual operations are seriously affected by unforeseen adversities, would a projected statement of changes in financial position still be useful?
14. "Cash flow per share" is sometimes used in common stock analysis in the same fashion as *earnings per share*. In financial analysis, shouldn't the former be used more often than the latter? Explain. (C.F.A.)

16

Analysis of capital structure and long-term solvency

IMPORTANCE OF CAPITAL STRUCTURE

THE CAPITAL structure of an enterprise consists basically of equity funds and debt. It is measured in terms of the relative magnitude of the various sources of funds of the enterprise. The inherent financial stability of an enterprise and the risk of insolvency to which it is exposed are importantly dependent on the sources of its funds as well as on the type of assets it holds and the relative magnitude of such asset categories. Exhibit 16–1 presents an example of the distribution of assets of an enterprise and the sources of funds used to finance their acquisition. It is evident from the diagram in Exhibit 16–1 that within the framework of equality prevailing between assets and liabilities plus capital, a large variety of combinations of assets and sources of funds used to finance them is possible.

ACCOUNTING PRINCIPLES

The amounts at which liabilities and equity accounts are shown on the financial statements are governed by the application of generally accepted accounting principles. The principles governing the measurement of liabilities are discussed in Chapter 5, and those governing the accounting for equities are covered in Chapter 6. The analyst must keep these principles in mind when analyzing the capital structure and its effect on long-term solvency. While it can be stated, as a broad

EXHIBIT 16–1
Asset distribution and capital structure of an enterprise

Assets	Liabilities and capital
Current assets	Current liabilities
Long-term investments	Long-term notes and bonds
Property, plant and equipment (net)	
	Subordinated notes and debentures
	Deferred credits
	Provisions and reserves
	Minority interests in consolidated subsidiaries
	Preferred stock
Intangible assets	Common stock equity (including retained earnings)
Deferred charges	

generalization, that the accounting principles governing the measurement of liabilities and equities do not affect the analysis of financial statements as importantly as do those governing the measurement of assets, a study of the above-mentioned chapters will reveal aspects of real importance to the analyst.

Certain aspects of these accounting principles are so important to the measurement of capital structure that their effect on such measurements will be reviewed here.

The nature of many items on the right-hand side of the balance sheet is quite clear-cut. Thus, current liabilities and most kinds of long-term debt clearly belong in the debt category of the capital structure. On the other hand, the common stock equity, comprised of the Common Stock, Paid-In Surplus, and Retained Earnings accounts, represents the capital category which is that segment of the capital structure exposed to the greatest amount of risk. As such, it represents the equity segment of the total capital structure.

There are, however, accounts whose classification as between debt or equity is not so clear-cut. The proper decision of how to classify them depends on a thorough understanding of their nature and/or the particular conditions of issue to which they are subject.

Deferred credits

Most deferred credits, such as premiums on bonds, represent allocation accounts designed primarily to aid in the measurement of income. They do not present an important problem of analysis because they are relatively insignificant in size. Deferred income items, such as subscription income received in advance, represent an obligation for future service and are, as such, clearly liabilities.

One type of deferred credit which is much more sizable, and consequently much more important, is *deferred income taxes*. As already pointed out in Chapter 9, this account is not a liability in the usual sense because the government does not have a definite short-term or even longer term claim against the enterprise. Nevertheless, this account does represent the aggregate exhaustion in tax deductibility of assets and other items, over and above that recorded for book purposes, and this means that at some time in the future it, that is, the deferred tax account, will be used to reduce the increased income taxes which will become payable. Even if the likelihood of the deferred tax account "reversing" in the foreseeable future is quite good, there still remains the question of whether the time-adjusted present value of such future "reversals" should not be used instead of the nominal face value amount of the deferred credit.

To the analyst the important question here is whether to treat the deferred tax account as a liability, as an equity item, or as part debt and part equity. The decision here depends on the nature of the deferral, the past experience with the account (e.g., has it been constantly growing?), and the likelihood of future "reversal." To the extent that such future "reversal" is only a remote possibility, the deferred credit can be viewed as a source of funds of such long-term nature as to be classifiable as equity. On the other hand, if the possibility of a "drawing down" of the deferred tax account in the foreseeable future is quite strong, then the account is more in the nature of a long-term liability. In classifying the deferred tax account as between debt and equity, the analyst must be guided by considerations such as the ones discussed above.

Long-term leases

According to APB *Opinion No. 5*, a situation in which the lease payments build up a material equity in the property, calls for capitalization of the lease and the inclusion of the long-term lease obligation among liabilities.

Should the disclosed terms of a lease which is not capitalized in the financial statements indicate to the analyst that it is nevertheless the equivalent of a purchase, he should make, as best he can, an estimate of the amount to be included among liabilities. In this the analyst will be aided by the disclosure requirements with respect to leases which are not capitalized in accordance with APB *Opinion No. 5*. These disclosures, required by APB *Opinion No. 31*, are discussed in Chapter 5.

Provisions and reserves

Provisions such as for guarantees and warranties represent obligations to offer future service and should be classified as such. Reserves for self-insurance are not clear-cut liabilities but reflect rather contingencies which can become future liabilities. Generally speaking, reserves created by charges to income may also be considered as liabilities. However, general contingency reserves or reserves for very indeterminate purposes should not be considered as genuine liabilities.

Minority interests in consolidated financial statements represent a liability of the consolidated group to minority shareholders of the subsidiaries included therein. The analyst should recognize, however, that these are not liabilities similar in nature to debt because they have neither mandatory dividend payment nor principal repayment requirements. Capital structure measurements concentrate on the mandatory payments aspects of liabilities. From this point of view, minority interests are more in the nature of outsider's claim to equity or an offset representing their proportionate ownership of assets.

Commitments and contingent liabilities

The analyst must make a judgment regarding the probability of commitments or contingencies becoming actual liabilities and should then treat these items accordingly.

Convertible debt is generally classified among liabilities. However, if the conversion terms are such that the only reasonable assumption that can be made is that the debt will be converted into common stock, then it may be classified as equity for purposes of capital structure analysis.

Preferred stock has mostly the fixed payment (dividend) characteristics of debt. However, since there is no absolute obligation for payment of dividends or repayment of principal, preferred stock has more of an equity quality than a debt characteristic for purposes of determining the risk inherent in the capital structure of an enterprise.

Effect of intangible assets

Intangible assets and deferred items of dubious value which are included on the asset side of the balance sheet have an effect on the computation of the total equity of an enterprise. To the extent that the analyst cannot evaluate or form an opinion on the present value or future utility of such assets, he may exclude them from consideration and thus reduce the amount of equity capital by an equal amount. However, the arbitrary exclusion of all intangible assets from the capital base is an unjustified exercise in overconservatism.

The foregoing discussion related to the classification of balance sheet items as between debt and equity. Let us now turn to an examination of the significance of capital structure in financial analysis.

The significance of capital structure

The significance of capital structure is derived, first and foremost, from the essential difference between debt and equity.

The equity is the basic risk capital of an enterprise. Every enterprise must have some equity capital which bears the risk to which it is inevitably exposed. The outstanding characteristic of equity capital is that it has no guaranteed or mandatory return which must be paid out in any event and no definite timetable for repayment of the capital investment. Thus, capital which can be withdrawn at the contributor's option is not really equity capital and has, instead, the characteristics of debt. From the point of view of an enterprise's stability and exposure to the risk of insolvency, the outstanding characteristic of equity capital is that it is permanent, can be counted on to remain invested in times of adversity, and has no mandatory requirement for dividends. It is such funds that an enterprise can most confidently invest in long-term assets and expose to the greatest risks. Their loss, for whatever reason, will not necessarily jeopardize the firm's ability to pay the fixed claims against it.

Both short-term and long-term debt, in contrast to equity capital, must be repaid. The longer the term of the debt and the less onerous its repayment provisions, the easier it will be for the enterprise to service it. Nevertheless, it must be repaid at certain specified times regardless of the enterprise's financial condition; and so must interest be paid in the case of most debt instruments. Generally, the failure to pay principal or interest will result in proceedings under which the common stockholders may lose control of the enterprise as well as part or all of their investment. Should the entire equity capital of the enterprise be wiped out by losses, the creditors may also stand to lose part or all of their principal and interest due.

It can be readily appreciated that the larger the proportion of debt in the total capital structure of an enterprise, the greater is the likelihood of a chain of events leading to an inability to pay interest and principal when due.

To the investor in the common stock of an enterprise, the existence of debt represents a risk of loss of his investment, and this is balanced by the potential of high profits arising from financial leverage. Excessive debt may also mean that management's initiative and flexibility for profitable action will be stifled and inhibited.

The creditor needs as large a capital base as possible as a cushion which will shield him against losses which can result from adversity. The smaller the relative capital base, or conversely, the larger the proportionate contribution of funds by creditors, the smaller is the creditors' cushion against loss and consequently the greater their risk of loss.

While there has been a considerable debate, particularly in academic circles, over whether the *cost of capital* of an enterprise varies with different capital structures, that is, with various mixes of debt and equity, the issue seems significantly clearer from the point of view of outsiders to the enterprise, such as creditors or investors, who must make decisions on the basis of conditions as they are. In the case of otherwise identical entities the creditor exposes himself to greater risk if he lends to the company with 60 percent of its funds provided by debt (and 40 percent by equity capital) than if he lends to a similar company which derives, say, only 20 percent of its funds from debt.

Under the Modigliani-Miller[1] thesis the cost of capital of an enterprise in a perfect market is, except for the tax deductibility of interest, not affected by the debt-equity relationship. This is so, they assert, because each individual stockholder can inject, by use of personally created leverage, his own blend of risk into the total investment position. Thus, under this theory, the advantage of debt will be offset by a markdown in a company's price-earnings ratio.

---

[1] F. Modigliani and M. Miller, "The Cost of Capital, Corporation Finance and the Theory of Investment," *American Economic Review*, June 1958, pp. 261–97.

The degree of risk in an enterprise, as judged by the outside prospective investor is, however, a given; and our point of view, as well as our task here, is to measure the degree of risk residing in the capital structure of an enterprise.

REASONS FOR EMPLOYMENT OF DEBT

The primary reason for the employment of debt by an enterprise is that up to a certain point, debt is, from the point of view of the ownership, a less expensive source of funds than equity capital. This is so for two main reasons:

1. The interest cost of debt is fixed, and thus, as long as it is lower than the return which can be earned on the funds supplied by creditors, this excess return accrues to the benefit of the equity (ownership).
2. Unlike dividends, which are considered a distribution of profits, interest is considered an expense and is, consequently, tax deductible.

A further discussion of these two main reasons follows.

The concept of financial leverage

Financial leverage means the use in the capital structure of an enterprise of debt which pays a fixed return. Since no creditor or lender would be willing to put up loan funds without the cushion and safety provided by the owners' equity capital, this borrowing process is also referred to as "trading on the equity," that is, utilizing the existence of a given amount of equity capital as a borrowing base.

In Exhibit 16–2, a comparison is made of the returns achieved by two companies having identical assets and earnings before interest expense. Tax considerations are ignored for purposes of this illustration because the tax advantage of debt will be separately illustrated in an example that will follow. Company X derives 40 percent of its funds from debt while Company Y has no debt. In year 1, when the average return on total assets is 15 percent, the return on the stockholders' equity of Company X is 21 percent. This higher return is due to the fact that the stockholders benefited from the excess return on total assets over the cost of debt. For Company Y the return on equity always equals the return on total assets. In year 2 the return on total assets of Company X was equal to the interest cost of debt and, consequently, the effects of leverage were neutralized. The results of year 3 show that leverage is a double-edged sword. Thus, when the return on total assets falls below the cost of debt, Company X's return on the equity is lower than that of debt-free Company Y.

EXHIBIT 16–2
Trading on the equity—results under different earning assumptions (in thousands of dollars)

	Assets	Debt payable	Stock-holders' equity	Income before interest	6% debt interest	Income after interest	Return* on— Total assets	Return* on— Stock-holders' equity
Year 1:								
Co. X.........	$1,000,000	$400,000	$ 600,000	$150,000	$24,000	$126,000	15%	21%
Co. Y.........	1,000,000	...	1,000,000	150,000	...	150,000	15	15
Year 2:								
Co. X.........	1,000,000	400,000	600,000	60,000	24,000	36,000	6	6
Co. Y.........	1,000,000	...	1,000,000	60,000	...	60,000	6	6
Year 3:								
Co. X.........	1,000,000	400,000	600,000	25,000	24,000	1,000	2.5	.2
Co. Y.........	1,000,000	...	1,000,000	25,000	...	25,000	2.5	2.5

*On total assets = $\dfrac{\text{Income before interest}}{\text{Total assets}}$

On stockholders' equity = $\dfrac{\text{Income after interest}}{\text{Stockholders' equity}}$

The effect of tax deductibility of interest

The second reason given for the advantageous position of debt is the tax deductibility of interest as opposed to the distribution of dividends. This can be illustrated as follows:

Assume Companies A and B have identical assets and operating earnings. The latter, amounting to $10,000, are of equal quality.[2] Company A has no debt, while Company B has $20,000 in bonds outstanding, paying an interest coupon of 6 percent. Assuming an average tax rate of 50 percent, the results of the two companies can be summarized as follows:

	Company A	Company B
Operating earnings	$10,000	$10,000
Interest (6% of $20,000)	...	1,200
Income before taxes	$10,000	$ 8,800
Taxes (50%)	5,000	4,400
Net income	$ 5,000	$ 4,400
Add back interest paid to bondholder	...	1,200
Total return to security holders	$ 5,000	$ 5,600

Disregarding the leverage effects obtainable when the rate of return on assets is higher than the interest rate, as illustrated in the preceding example, even if the return on assets is equal to the interest rate, the total amount available for distribution to the bondholders and stockholders of Company B is $600 higher than the amount available for the stockholders of Company A. This is due to the lower total tax liability to which the security holders of Company B are subject.

It should be borne in mind that the value of the tax deductibility of interest is dependent on the existence of sufficient earnings. However, uncovered interest charges can be carried back and carried forward as part of tax loss carry-overs permitted by law.

Other advantages of leverage

In addition to the advantages accruing to equity stockholders from the successful employment of financial leverage and the tax deductibility of interest expenses, a sound longer term debt position can result in other advantages to the equity owner. A rapidly growing company can avoid earnings dilution through the issuance of debt. Moreover, if interest rates are headed higher, all other things being equal, a leveraged company will be more profitable than its nonleveraged competitor. Finally, there is a financial benefit from advantageously placed debt be-

---

[2] The concept of the quality of earnings is discussed in Chapter 20.

cause debt capital is not always available to an enterprise and the capacity to borrow may disappear should adverse operating results occur.

Measuring the effect of financial leverage

The effect of leverage on operating results is positive when the return on the equity capital exceeds the return on total assets. This difference in return isolates the effect which the return on borrowed money has on the return on the owner's capital. As was seen in the example in Exhibit 16–2, leverage is positive when the return on assets is higher than the cost of debt. It is negative when the opposite conditions prevail. The terms "positive" and "negative" are not used here in the strict algebraic sense.

The effect of financial leverage can be measured by the following formula:

$$\text{Financial leverage index} = \frac{\text{Return on equity capital}}{\text{Return on total assets}}$$

Using the data in Exhibit 16–2 we compute the financial leverage indices of Company X for years 1, 2, and 3 as follows:

Financial leverage index

$$\text{Year 1:} \quad \frac{.21}{.15} = 1.4$$

$$\text{Year 2:} \quad \frac{.06}{.06} = 1$$

$$\text{Year 3:} \quad \frac{.002}{.025} = .08$$

In year 1 when the return on equity exceeded that on total assets, the index at 1.4 was positive. In year 2 when the return on equity equaled that on total assets, the index stood at 1 reflecting a neutralization of financial leverage. In year 3 the index, at .08, was way below 1.0, thus indicating the very negative effect of financial leverage in that year. The subject of return on investment is discussed in Chapter 17.

Measuring the effect of capital structure on long-term solvency

From the foregoing discussion it is clear that the basic risk involved in a leveraged capital structure is the risk of running out of cash under conditions of adversity.

Debt involves a commitment to pay fixed charges in the form of interest and principal repayments. While certain fixed charges can be postponed in times of cash shortage, those associated with debt cannot be postponed without adverse repercussion to the ownership and also to the creditor groups.

Long-term projections—usefulness and limitations

If a shortage of cash required to service the debt is the most adverse possibility envisaged, then the most direct and most relevant measure of risk inherent in the leveraged capital structure of an enterprise would be a projection of future cash resources and flows which would be available to meet these cash requirements. These projections must assume the worst set of economic conditions which are likely to occur, since this is the most realistic and useful test of safety from the debtor's point of view. If only prosperous and normal times are to be assumed, then the debtor would not need his preferred position and would be better off with an equity position where the potential rewards are higher.

In Chapter 15 we concluded that detailed cash flow projections can be reliably made only for the short term. Consequently they are useful only in the measurement of short-term liquidity.

The statement of changes in financial position can be projected over a relatively longer term because such a projection is far less detailed than a projection of cash flows. However, as we saw in the discussion of such projections in the preceding chapter, this lack of detail as well as the longer time horizon reduces the reliability of such projections.

The short term is understood to encompass, generally, a period of up to one year. The longer term, however, is a much wider ranging period. Thus, it may include a solvency analysis with respect to a three-year term loan, or it may encompass the evaluation of risk associated with a 30-year bond issue. Meaningful projections covering the period over which the interest and principal of the term loan will be paid can still reasonably be made. However, a 30-year projection of funds flow covering the bond issue would be an unrealistic exercise. For this reason longer term debt instruments often contain sinking fund provisions which act to reduce the uncertain time horizon, and stipulations of additional security in the form of specific assets pledged as collateral. Moreover, they contain provisions such as for the maintenance of minimum working capital levels or restrictions on the payment of dividends, all of which are designed to insure against a deterioration in the financial ratios prevailing at the time the bonds are issued.

Desirable as funds flow projections may be, their use for the extended longer term is severely limited. For this reason a number of measures of long-term solvency have evolved which are more static in nature and are based on asset and earnings coverage tests. These measures will be considered below.

CAPITAL STRUCTURE ANALYSIS—COMMON-SIZE STATEMENTS

A simple measure of financial risk in an enterprise is the composition of its capital structure. This can be done best by constructing a common-size statement of the liabilities and equity section of the balance sheet as shown in Exhibit 16–3.

EXHIBIT 16–3
Liabilities and equity section—with common-size percents

Current liabilities	$ 428,000	19.0%
Long-term debt	$ 500,000	22.2%
Equity capital:		
Preferred stock	$ 400,000	17.8%
Common stock	800,000	35.6
Paid-in capital	20,000	.9
Retained earnings	102,000	4.5
Total Equity	$1,322,000	58.8%
Total Liabilities and Equity	$2,250,000	100.0%

An alternative way of analyzing capital structure with common-size percentages would be to focus only on the longer term capital funds by excluding the current liabilities from total funds.

The advantage of a common-size analysis of capital structure is that it presents clearly the relative magnitude of the sources of funds of the enterprise, a presentation which lends itself readily to a comparison with similar data of other enterprises.

A variation of the approach of analyzing capital structure by means of common-size percentages is to analyze it by means of ratios.

CAPITAL STRUCTURE RATIOS

The basic ratio measurements of capital structure relate the various components of the capital structure to each other or to their total. Some of these ratios in common use are as follows:

Equity capital/total liabilities

This ratio measures the relationship of the equity capital, inclusive of preferred stock, to total liabilities, that is, both current and long-term liabilities. A ratio in excess of 1 to 1 indicates that the owners of the enterprise have a greater financial stake in it than do the creditors. Additionally, assuming that the assets are presented at close to realizable values, a ratio of 1 to 1 would mean that creditors have $2 in assets as security for each $1 of credit they extended to the enterprise. This generalization would have to be modified, of course, if some creditors have a prior claim on specific assets or all assets. To the extent that senior creditors have prior claims, the relative security of junior debt is diminished.

Equity capital/long-term debt

This ratio measures the relative contributions of equity capital and of long-term debt to the total capitalization of an enterprise. A ratio in excess of 1:1 indicates a higher equity capital participation as compared to long-term debt. The complement of this ratio is the familiar debt/equity ratio which is computed as follows:

$$\frac{\text{Long-term debt}}{\text{Equity capital}}$$

Ratios measuring the proportion which equity capital represents of the total funds invested in the enterprise are a variation the common-size analysis approach. The following are among the ratios which accomplish this purpose:

$$\frac{\text{Equity capital}}{\text{Equity capital plus all liabilities}}$$

is a ratio which expresses the relationship between equity capital and the total funds available to the entity.

$$\frac{\text{Long-term debt}}{\text{Equity capital plus all liabilities}}$$

measures the relative contribution of long-term debt to the total funds available to the enterprise.

Equity capital at market value

Accounting principles in current use place their primary emphasis on historical costs rather than on current values. Since the shareholder's capital is the residual of assets minus liabilities, this accounting can result in equity capital book value figures which are far removed from realistic market values.

One method of correcting this flaw in the stated equity capital amounts, particularly when they enter importantly into the computation of many of the ratios which we have considered above, is to restate them by converting the assets from historical cost to current market values. Presently financial statements provide only meager and spotty data on current values, and as a consequence the analyst generally has no reliable alternative sources from which to obtain them.

One way of overcoming the problem of giving recognition to market values is to compute the equity capital at current (or some kind of average) market value of the stock issues which comprise it. On the assumption that the market value of the common capitalization will give recognition to current asset values, which are based on their earning power, this amount would then be used in the computation of the various debt-equity ratios.

A serious objection to this method is that stock prices fluctuate widely and may, particularly in times of overspeculation, not be representative of "true" values at a given moment. However, this argument can be countered with considerable evidence that the judgment of the marketplace is most of the time superior to that of other judgmental processes and that use of average market prices would solve the problem of temporary aberrations. Thus, the use of equity capital figures computed at current, or at average, market values has much to commend it. Being more realistic they can improve the ratio measurements in which they are used.

One important advantage of earnings-coverage ratios, as will be seen in the subsequent discussion of this subject, is that they are based on the earning power of assets rather than on the amount at which they are carried in the financial statements. Market values do, of course, give recognition to such earning power of an entity's assets. Thus, ratio measures, such as debt-equity ratios, which use equity capital amounts at market value, are more consistent with earnings-coverage ratios than are ratios using historical book values.

Interpretation of capital structure measures

The common-size and ratio analyses of capital structure, which have been examined above, are all measures of risk inherent in the capital structure of an enterprise. The higher the proportion of debt, the larger the fixed charges of interest and debt repayment, and the greater the likelihood of insolvency during protracted periods of earnings decline or other adversities.

One obvious value of these measures is that they serve as screening devices. Thus, when the ratio of debt to equity capital is relatively small, say 10 percent or less, there is normally no need to be concerned with this aspect of an enterprise's financial condition; and the analyst may well conclude that he can spend his time better by directing his attention to the more critical areas revealed by his analysis.

Should an examination of the debt-equity ratios reveal that debt is indeed a significant factor in the total capitalization, then further analysis is necessary.

Such an analysis will encompass many aspects of an enterprise's financial condition, results of operations, and future prospects.

An analysis of short-term liquidity is always important because before the analyst starts to assess long-term solvency he has to be satisfied about the short-term financial survival of the enterprise. Chapter 14 examines the analysis of short-term liquidity, and the analyst will use the tools discussed there to assess the situation and also to relate the size of working capital to the size of long-term debt. Loan and bond indenture covenants requiring the maintenance of minimum working capital ratios attest to the importance attached to current liquidity in insuring the long-term solvency of an enterprise.

Additional analytical steps of importance will include an examination of debt maturities (as to size and spacing over time), interest costs, and other factors which have a bearing on the risk. Among those, the earnings stability of the enterprise and its industry as well as the kind of assets its resources are invested in are important factors.

MEASURES OF ASSETS DISTRIBUTION

The type of assets an enterprise employs in its operations should determine to some extent the sources of funds used to finance them. Thus, for example, it is customarily held that fixed and other long-term assets should not be financed by means of short-term loans. In fact, the most appropriate source of funds for investment in such assets is equity capital. On the other hand, working capital, and particularly seasonal working capital needs, can be appropriately financed by means of short-term credit.

In judging the risk exposure of a given capital structure, the asset composition is one of the important factors to consider. This asset composition is best measured by means of common-size statements of the

EXHIBIT 16–4
Assets section—with common-size percents

Current Assets:		
Cash	$ 376,000	16.7%
Accounts receivable (net)	425,000	18.9
Merchandise inventory	574,000	25.5
Total Current Assets	$1,375,000	61.1%
Investments	268,000	11.9
Land, property, and equipment (net)	368,000	16.4
Intangibles	239,000	10.6
Total Assets	$2,250,000	100.0%

asset side of the balance sheet. For example, Exhibit 16–4 shows the common-size asset section of the balance sheet whose liabilities and equity section was presented in Exhibit 16–3.

Judging *only* by the distribution of assets and the related capital structure, it would appear that since a relatively high proportion of assets is current (61 percent), a 41 percent debt and current liabilities position (see Exhibit 16–3) is not excessive. Other considerations and measurements may, however, change this conclusion.

Asset coverage is an important element in the evaluation of long-term solvency. Assets of value provide protection to holders of debt obligations both because of their earning power and because of their liquidation value. Additionally, they represent the bases on which an enterprise can obtain the short-term financing which may be required to tie it over a period of financial stringency.

The relationship between asset groups and selected items of capital structure can also be expressed in terms of ratios.

Fixed assets/equity capital is a ratio which measures the relationship between long-term assets and equity capital. A ratio in excess of 1:1 means that some of the fixed assets are financed by means of debt.

If the financial structure ratios are such that they require further analysis, one of the best areas for further investigation calls for tests which measure an enterprise's ability to service its debt requirements out of earnings. This is the area we shall turn to next.

MEASURES OF EARNINGS COVERAGE

One conclusion of our discussion of debt-equity ratios was that a major usefulness of these measurements lies in their function as a screening device, that is, a means of deciding whether the apparent risk inherent in the capital structure of an enterprise requires further investigation and analysis. An important limitation of the measurements of debt-equity relationships is that they do not focus on the availability of funds, or cash, flows which are necessary to service the enterprise's debt. In fact, as a debt obligation is repaid the debt-equity ratio tends to improve whereas the yearly amount of cash needed to pay interest and sinking fund requirements may remain the same or may even increase, as for example, in the case of level payment debt or loans with "balloon" repayment provisions.

Earnings-coverage ratios measure directly the relationship between debt related fixed charges and the earnings available to meet these charges. While the concept behind this measurement is simple and straightforward, its practical implementation is complicated by the problem of defining what should be included in "earnings" and in "fixed charges."

EARNINGS AVAILABLE TO MEET FIXED CHARGES

As was seen in Chapter 11, dealing with the statement of changes in financial position, net income determined under the principles of accrual accounting is not the same thing as sources of funds provided by operations. Specifically, certain items of income, such as undistributed earnings of subsidiaries and controlled companies or sales on extended credit terms, do not create funds, that is, working capital. Similarly, certain expenses such as depreciation, amortization, depletion, and deferred income tax charges do not require the outlay of current funds. On the other hand, it should be borne in mind that a parent company can determine the dividend policy of a controlled subsidiary.

Fixed-debt charges are paid out of current funds rather than out of net income. Thus, the analyst must realize that an unadjusted net income figure may not be a correct measure of funds available to meet fixed charges.

Since fixed charges are paid off with cash, a clarification is needed as to why we accept here working capital as the equivalent of cash. The reason is that over the longer term the conversion period of current assets into cash becomes relatively insignificant. Thus, even if the conversion period of inventories into receivables, and ultimately into cash, is 120 days this period is not significant compared with the longer term period over which the fixed charges of debt must be paid.

The use of net income as an approximation of funds provided by operations may, in some instances, be warranted while in others it may significantly overstate or understate the amount actually available for the servicing of debt. Thus, the soundest approach to this problem lies not in generalizations but rather in a careful analysis of the nonfund generating items included in income as well as the nonfund requiring expenses charged to that income. In considering depreciation as a nonfund requiring expense, the analyst must realize that over the long run an enterprise must replace its plant and equipment.

The problem of determining the amount of income to be included in fixed-charge-coverage ratios requires consideration of a number of additional factors:

1. *The treatment of extraordinary gains and losses.* As pointed out in the more comprehensive discussion of this subject in Chapters 9 and 20, extraordinary gains and losses enter into the determination of longer term average earnings power. As such they must be recognized as a factor which may, over the longer term, contribute to or reduce the funds available to pay fixed charges. Any computation of earnings-coverage ratios utilizing average earnings figures must recognize the existence of extraordinary gains and losses over the years. This is particu-

larly true of earnings-coverage ratios where what we measure is the risk of loss of sources of funds for payment of fixed charges.

2. *Preferred dividends* need not be deducted from net income because the payment of such dividends is not mandatory. However, in consolidated financial statements, preferred dividends of a subsidiary whose income is consolidated must be deducted because they represent a charge which has priority over the distribution of earnings to the parent.

3. Earnings which are attributed to *minority interests* should be deducted from net income available for fixed charges. An exception arises where preferred stock dividend requirements of a consolidated subsidiary are considered fixed charges and where they also represent a significant portion of the total minority interest. In such instances, the coverage ratio should be computed on the basis of earnings before deducting minority interests.

If a subsidiary with a minority interest has a loss, the credit in the income statement which results from the minority's share in the loss should be excluded from consolidated earnings for purposes of the coverage ratio computation. The parent would, in most cases, meet fixed-charge obligations of its subsidiary to protect its own credit standing, whether or not legally obligated to do so.

4. *The impact of income taxes* on the computation of earnings-coverage ratios should always be carefully assessed. Since interest is a tax-deductible expense, it is met out of pretax income. Thus, the income out of which interest payments are met is pretax income. On the other hand, preferred dividends or sinking fund payments are not tax deductible and must be paid out of after-tax earnings.

5. The *level of income* used in the computation of earnings-coverage ratios deserves serious consideration. The most important consideration here is: what level of income will be most representative of the amount that will actually be available in the *future* for the payment of debt-related fixed charges. An average earnings figure encompassing the entire range of the business cycle, and adjusted for any known factors which may change it in the future, is most likely to be the best approximation of the average source of funds from future operations which can be expected to become available for the payment of fixed charges. Moreover, if the objective of the earnings-coverage ratio is to measure the creditor's maximum exposure to risk, then the proper earnings figure to use is that achieved at the low point of the enterprise's business cycle.

FIXED CHARGES TO BE INCLUDED

Having considered the amount of earnings which should be included in the earnings coverage, we shall now turn to an examination of the types of fixed charges properly includable in the computation of this ratio.

1. Interest on long-term debt

Interest on long-term debt is the most direct and most obvious fixed charge which arises from the incurrence of long-term debt. Interest expense includes the amortization of deferred bond discount and premium. The bond discount and issue expenses represent the amount by which the par value of the bond indebtedness exceeded the proceeds from the bond issue. As such, the discount amortization represents an addition to the stated interest expense. The amortization of bond issue premium represents the reverse situation, and thus results in a reduction of interest expense over the period of amortization.

If low coupon bonds have only a short period to run before maturity and it is likely that they will have to be refinanced with higher coupon bonds, it may be appropriate to incorporate in fixed charges the expected higher interest costs.

Interest on income bonds must, at best, be paid only as earned. Consequently, it is not a fixed charge from the point of view of the holder of fixed interest securities. It must, however, be regarded as a fixed charge from the point of view of the income bond issuer.

In public utilities, interest on funds tied up in construction projects which earn, as yet, no return, are usually excluded from interest costs and capitalized as costs of construction. For purposes of earnings-coverage calculations the exclusion of this interest factor from fixed charges results in a failure to measure the total burden of servicing long-term debt. Consequently, a more realistic measure of coverage can be arrived at by adding the "interest during construction" credit back to the income figure used in the coverage calculation. At the same time the total interest amount, without benefit of a credit for interest charged during construction, is used in the coverage computation.

The SEC has been paying increasing attention to the computation of the ratio of earnings to fixed charges in prospectuses and has clarified the point that the amount of interest added back to income must not necessarily equal the interest amount included in the "fixed charges" part of the ratio computation.

In determining the earnings side of the ratio of earnings to fixed charges, interest is to be added back to pretax net earnings. The amount of interest to be added back should include the amount shown as interest expense plus the amount of interest which has found its way into other captions of the income statement such as, for example, capitalized interest expense now being written off to cost of sales as a part of the cost of land, construction, or other items sold. The add-back should not include the amounts of interest expense capitalized which are still carried in the balance sheet as, for instance, inventory, since such interest charges have already been removed from the income statement. The reason for this is to remove from the amount considered to be earnings of the enterprise, all amounts which have been paid out or accrued as interest and which have not been otherwise excluded from the income statement.

For the purpose of determining fixed charges, however, interest expense should include all interest applicable to the period which has been paid or accrued by the company on its total debt structure which existed during the period, including the amounts capitalized, even though some of the capitalized amount will remain in inventory or other balance sheet accounts.

Exhibit 16–5 presents an example of the computation of the ratio of earnings to fixed charges illustrating the principles discussed above:

EXHIBIT 16–5
Computation of actual and pro forma ratio of earnings to fixed charges

	19x1	19x2
Earnings:		
Income before provision for income taxes.	$225,700	$370,200
Interest and debt expense included in cost of sales	279,400	523,100
Interest charged direct to income.	1,800	9,600
Lease rentals (1/3)	1,700	5,100
Total.	$508,600	$908,000
Fixed charges:		
Interest and debt expenses capitalized in real estate	$583,700	$727,300
Interest charged direct to income.	1,800	9,600
Lease rentals (1/3)	1,700	5,100
Total.	$587,200	$742,000
Interest on debentures at assumed rate of 7½%.		187,500
Interest on debt to be retired		(5,400)
Pro forma.		$924,100
Ratio of earnings to fixed charges:		
Historical	.87	1.22
Pro forma		.98

2. Interest implicit in lease obligations

Chapter 5 on the analysis of liabilities discussed the present status of accounting recognition of leases as financing devices. The more recent professional pronouncements on this subject have had the effect of causing the most obvious financing leases to be capitalized and included both among assets and long-term liabilities in the balance sheet. These pronouncements have also led to a greater degree of footnote disclosure on all types of leases.

When a lease is capitalized, the interest portion of the lease payment is designated as such on the income statement while most of the balance is usually considered as repayment of the principal obligation. A problem arises, however, when the analyst feels that certain leases which should have been capitalized are not so treated in the financial statements. The issue here actually goes beyond the pure accounting question of whether capitalization is, or is not, appropriate. It stems rather from the fact that a long-term lease represents a fixed obligation which must be given recognition in the computation of the earnings coverage ratio. Thus, even long-term leases which, from an accounting theory point of view, need not be capitalized must be considered as including fixed charges which have to be included in the coverage ratio computation.

The problem of extracting the interest portion of long-term lease payments is not a simple one. The external analysts can only guess at the rate of interest implicit in a lease agreement; and, moreover, the information provided regarding other features of the leases is often inadequate for reasonably accurate determinations regarding the interest component. Consequently, in the absence of such data, a more arbitrary method of determining the interest component becomes necessary and is far better than no allowance at all for this factor.

It is interesting to note that the SEC regulations, basing themselves on a rule of thumb developed by Graham & Dodd,[3] provide that in the absence of evidence to the contrary, one third of rentals on such items as machinery, equipment, computers, and other personal property as well as real property will be assumed to represent the interest factor included in lease payments. Such interest factor, which is considered as a fixed charge, presumably includes the profit of the lessor. "Delay rentals" in the extractive industries represent payment for the privilege of deferring the development of properties and, being in the nature of not regularly recurring compensation to owners, are not considered as rentals includable in the earnings-coverage ratio.

As with the offsetting of interest income against interest expense, the general rule is that rental income should not be offset against rental expense when determining fixed charges. An exception is made, however, where the rental income represents a direct reduction in rental expense.

In the absence of information which would lead to a more accurate estimate of the interest component of lease payments, the analyst can accept the estimation process suggested by the SEC, not only because it is frequently available but also because it represents a reasonable estimate. Conceptually, the most valid method of determining the interest portion of rentals is by means of present-value analysis. Such analysis

---

[3] B. Graham, D. L. Dodd, and S. Cottle. *Security Analysis* (4th ed.; New York: McGraw-Hill Book Co., Inc., 1962), p. 344. (This rule was developed in a previous edition of this work.)

determines the rate of discount which equates the present value of a stream of lease payments and the residual value of the property at the end of the lease, if any, to the cost of the property. This rate of interest (discount) can then be used in computing the interest portion of the lease. Expense factors, such as for property taxes, maintenance, and insurance, should be excluded from the lease payments for purposes of such a calculation. The necessary information for an exact computation of this kind is, unfortunately, rarely available to the external analyst.

3. Capitalized interest

The interest cost reflected in the income statement (wherever found, e.g., as financial cost or as part of cost of sales) is not the only one to be considered in arriving at the amount of interest to be included in fixed charges. Thus, interest that is not currently expensed but which is capitalized during the period must also be considered as a fixed charge. Capitalization occurs, for example, in the case of real estate development companies where interest costs are added to the cost of land held for sale and expensed as part of the cost of land only when it is sold.

4. Other elements to be included in fixed charges

The foregoing discussions concerned the determination of fixed financing charges, that is, interest and the interest portion of lease rentals. These are the most widely used measures of "fixed charges" included in earnings-coverage ratios. However, if the purpose of this ratio is to measure an enterprise's ability to meet fixed commitments which if unpaid could result in repercussions ranging all the way from financial embarrassment to insolvency, there are other fixed charges to be considered. Thus, when consolidated financial statements are presented, preferred stock dividend requirements of consolidated subsidiaries must be included as part of fixed charges. The most important category to be considered here, however, are principal repayment obligations such as sinking fund requirements, serial repayment provisions, and the principal repayment component of lease rentals.

PRINCIPAL REPAYMENT REQUIREMENTS

Principal repayment obligations are, from a cash-drain point of view, just as onerous as obligations to pay interest. In the case of rentals, the obligations to pay principal and interest must be met simultaneously.

A number of reasons have been advanced to indicate why the requirements for principal repayments are not given recognition in earnings-coverage ratio calculations:

1. It is claimed that sinking fund payment requirements do not have the same degree of urgency as do interest payments and that, consequently, they should be excluded. This is based on the assumption that creditors would be willing to agree to a temporary suspension of such payments even though this generally constitutes an act of bankruptcy. This is an assumption of doubtful validity. Moreover, if the coverage ratio is designed to measure safety, then a situation where an enterprise must renegotiate or forego adhering to debt repayment provisions is in itself symptomatic of a rather unsafe condition.
2. Another objection to the inclusion of sinking fund or other periodic principal repayment provisions in the calculation of the earnings-coverage ratio is that this may result in double counting, that is, the funds recovered by depreciation already provide for debt repayment. Thus, if earnings reflect a deduction for depreciation, then fixed charges should not include provisions for principal repayments.

    There is some merit in this argument if the debt was used to acquire depreciable fixed assets and if there is some correspondence between the pattern of depreciation charges and that of principal repayments. It must, moreover, be borne in mind that depreciation funds are recovered generally only out of profitable operations, and consequently this argument is valid only under an assumption of such operations.

    Our discussion of the definition of "earnings" to be included in the coverage-ratio calculations emphasized the importance of funds provided by operations as the measure of resources available to meet fixed charges. The use of this concept would, of course, eliminate the double counting problem since nonfund-requiring charges such as depreciation would be added back to net income for the purpose of the coverage computations.

A more serious problem regarding the inclusion of debt repayment provisions among "fixed charges" arises from the fact that not all debt agreements provide for sinking fund payments or similar repayment obligations. Any arbitrary allocation of indebtedness over time would be an unrealistic theoretical exercise and would ignore the fact that to the extent that such payments are not required in earlier years, the immediate pressure on the cash resources of the enterprise is reduced. In the longer run, however, larger maturities as well as "balloon" payments will have to be met.

The most useful solution to this problem lies in a careful analysis and assessment of the yearly debt repayment requirements which will serve as the basis on which to judge the effect of these obligations on the long-term solvency of the enterprise. The assumption that debt can always be refinanced, rolled over, or otherwise paid off from current operations is not the most useful approach to the problem of risk evaluation. On the contrary, the existence of debt repayment obligations as well as the timing of their maturity must be recognized and included in an overall assessment of the long-term ability of the enterprise to meet its fixed obligations. The inclusion of sinking fund or other early repayment requirements in fixed charges is one way of recognizing the impact of such requirements on fund adequacy.

The recognition of the effect of long-term debt repayment requirements on longer term liquidity is exemplified in the following quotation from a report by the management of Indian Head, Inc. included in the 1970 annual report:

> *Corporate liquidity.* In planning and executing our program of diversification and internal improvement over the years, we have used long-term debt to achieve a better-than-average return on our stockholders' equity. But we have arranged and structured this debt with a prudent regard for the importance of maintaining a strong position of corporate liquidity. In view of widespread current concern about this vitally important matter, we call your attention to the following facts:
>
> 1. Our current cash balances (and cash equivalents) stand at $15.5 million, about as strong as they were at year-end and substantially greater than a year ago.
> 2. Mid-year is historically our cash lowpoint, and we expect our cash position to grow significantly during the balance of the year.
> 3. Indian Head has no bank or other short-term borrowings outstanding.
> 4. We have substantial firm lines of credit available.
> 5. Our total long-term debt repayment requirements over the next five years are as follows: (in millions)
>
> | 1970 | 1971 | 1972 | 1973 | 1974 |
> |------|------|------|------|------|
> | $1.4 | $1.4 | $3.7 | $3.7 | $3.8 |
>
> 6. In 1969, our cash flow was $24 million—17 times the debt amortization requirements in each of the years 1970 and 1971.
> 7. The average rate of interest on our debt is 6.4%.
> 8. With this healthy cash situation, Indian Head is in a strong position to weather the current economic storm and to consider any attractive opportunities that may develop.

5. Other fixed charges

While interest payments and debt repayment requirements are the fixed charges most directly related to the incurrence of debt, there is no logical justification to restrict the evaluation of long-term solvency only to these charges and commitments. Thus, a complete analysis of fixed charges which an enterprise is obliged to meet must include all long-term rental payment obligations (not only the interest portion thereof) and particularly those rentals which must be met under any and all circumstances, under noncancellable leases, otherwise known as "hell-and-high-water" leases.

The reason why short-term leases can be excluded from consideration as fixed charges is that they represent an obligation of limited duration, usually less than three years, and can consequently be discontinued in a period of severe financial stringency. Here, the analyst must, however, evaluate how essential the rented items are to the continuation of the enterprise as a going concern.

Other charges which are not directly related to debt, but which must nevertheless be considered as long-term commitments of a fixed nature, are long-term purchase contracts not subject to cancellation and other similar obligations.

6. Guarantees to pay fixed charges

Guarantees to pay fixed charges of unconsolidated subsidiaries should result in additions to fixed charges if the requirement to honor the guarantee appears imminent.

ILLUSTRATION OF EARNINGS-COVERAGE RATIO CALCULATIONS

Having discussed the various considerations which enter into the decision of what factors to include in the earnings-coverage ratio computation, we will address ourselves now to the simpler question of how the ratio is computed. The computation of the various coverage ratios will be based on the illustration in Exhibit 16–6.

TIMES-INTEREST-EARNED RATIO

This is the simplest and one of the most widely used coverage ratios. The ratio is computed as follows:

$$\frac{\text{Income before taxes} + \text{Interest expense}}{\text{Interest expense}}$$

Using the data in Exhibit 16–6 the computation of the times-interest-earned ratio is as follows:

$$\frac{2{,}200{,}000 + 700{,}000}{700{,}000} = 4.1 \text{ times}$$

EXHIBIT 16-6

THE LEVERED CORPORATION
Abbreviated Income Statement

Net sales		$13,400,000
Undistributed earnings of subsidiaries		600,000
		$14,000,000
Cost of goods sold	$7,400,000	
Selling, general, and administrative expenses	1,800,000	
Depreciation (excluded from above costs)	800,000	
Interest expense (inclusive of interest portion of rents)	700,000	
Rental expense	900,000	
Share of minority interests in consolidated income	200,000	11,800,000
Income before taxes		$ 2,200,000
Income taxes:		
Current $800,000		
Deferred 300,000		1,100,000
Income before extraordinary items		$ 1,100,000
Gain on sale of investment in land (net of $67,000 tax)		200,000
Net income		$ 1,300,000
Dividends:		
On common stock	$ 400,000	
On preferred stock	200,000	600,000
Earnings retained for the year		$ 700,000

Selected notes to the financial statements

1. The interest expense is composed of the following charges:

a) Interest on $6 million 6% senior notes due 19x0	$360,000
b) Interest on $4 million 7% subordinated convertible debentures	280,000
c) Interest portion of $160,000 in rents which have been capitalized	50,000
d) Other interest costs	10,000
	$700,000

   Sinking fund requirements on the 6 percent senior notes are $500,000 annually.
2. The company has a 10-year noncancellable raw material purchase commitment amounting to $100,000 annually.

As was pointed out in our discussion earlier in this chapter, since interest is a tax-deductible expense it is met out of pretax income. Interest is added back to pretax income because it was deducted in arriving at such income.

Computation of coverage ratio for an individual bond issue

There is a serious question regarding the validity of an interest coverage ratio which does not take into account all interest charges or, as we shall see later, all fixed charges. As regards interest charges, while payment of senior bond interest takes precedence over the subordinated or junior bond interest, the fact remains that default in the payment of any contractual obligation may set in motion a chain of events which could prove detrimental to, and perhaps even result in loss, to senior bondholders.

422 Understanding corporate reports

If we compute the coverage ratio for a senior bond only, we omit from interest charges the interest due to holders of junior issues. Using the data in Exhibit 16-6 we compute the interest coverage ratio for the 6 percent senior notes as follows:

$$\frac{\text{Income before taxes} + \text{Interest expense}}{\text{Interest on senior issue}}$$

$$\frac{2{,}200{,}000 + 700{,}000}{360{,}000} = 8.1 \text{ times}$$

The analyst should be careful to avoid the error, now rarely made, of computing the interest coverage on a junior bond issue by omitting the senior bond interest from it. In terms of the data in Exhibit 16-6, this erroneous computation would be:

$$\frac{2{,}200{,}000 + 700{,}000}{280{,}000} = 10 \text{ times}$$

This is obviously a wrong earnings coverage measure because it suggests that the junior bond is better covered than the senior one.

It should be noted that this is strictly a computation of interest coverage. The more correct and comprehensive coverage of fixed charges would also include the interest portion of long term rentals ($\frac{1}{3}$ of $900,000) in both numerator and denominator of the senior bond coverage computation resulting in a coverage ratio of 4.9.

RATIOS OF EARNINGS TO FIXED CHARGES

Our discussion earlier in this chapter examined the various concepts of what should be included in "fixed charges" for purposes of computing the ratio of earnings to fixed charges. We shall illustrate below the application of these various concepts by using the data contained in Exhibit 16-6.

Fixed-charges-coverage ratio—the SEC standard

According to the SEC's definition, fixed charges include, in addition to (A) interest costs (inclusive of amortization of debt discount, expense and premium), (B) a portion (usually one third) of rentals. Earnings in our example would exclude undistributed income of unconsolidated subsidiaries (C).

$$\frac{\text{Income before taxes} - (C) + (A) + (B)}{(A) + (B)}$$

$$= \frac{2{,}200{,}000 - 600{,}000 + 700{,}000 + \frac{1}{3}(900{,}000)}{700{,}000 + \frac{1}{3}(900{,}000)} = 2.6 \text{ times}$$

Fixed-charges-coverage ratios—expanded concept of fixed charges

If we adopt the point of view that failure to meet any fixed obligations could lead to trouble and even to insolvency, then we want to establish how well such fixed obligations are covered by earnings. Thus, in addition to the fixed charges included in the computation in the preceding example, the following must now be considered for inclusion:

Annual sinking fund requirements on 6 percent senior note ($500,000). This represents an obligation which if not met may result in financial embarrassment or even insolvency. This fixed charge differs from the others considered so far in that it is not tax deductible. In order to bring it to a basis comparable to that of the tax-deductible fixed charges, we must convert it into the pretax amount which is needed to yield an after-tax outlay equal to the fixed charge. This is done by multiplying the fixed charge by a step-up factor computed as follows:

$$\frac{1}{1 - \text{Tax rate}}$$

Assuming a tax rate of 50 percent in this case we get:

$$\$500{,}000 \times \left(\frac{1}{1 - .50}\right) = \$1{,}000{,}000$$

The converted sinking fund fixed charge of $1,000,000 will be used in the computation of the coverage ratio.

Long-term rental ($900,000). The earnings coverage computation, defined by the SEC, included as fixed charges only that portion of rentals which is attributable to the interest factor. This approach views as fixed charges only those fixed obligations which are in the nature of interest. Under the expanded concept of fixed charges, any obligation to pay fixed amounts over the longer term is considered a fixed charge because a failure to make such payments can set in motion a chain of events whose end result may be similar to that flowing out of a failure to pay interest.

The data in Exhibit 16–6 indicate that the leases represent long-term obligations. In the case of these lease rentals the interest portion is, from a contractual point of view, indistinguishable from the principal repayment portion ($600,000). Consequently, under the expanded concept of fixed charges the entire amount of rentals ($900,000), rather than only the interest portion, is viewed as a fixed charge whose degree of coverage by earnings it is important to establish.

Noncancellable raw material purchase commitments. According to Exhibit 16–6 the annual noncancellable long-term purchase commitment amounts to $100,000. The reason why this payment is considered a fixed charge under the "expanded" concept is that it represents a noncancellable obligation to pay out a fixed annual sum of money over a 10-year period.

From the point of view of the income tax impact, this item is akin to interest or rental payments in that it ultimately becomes a tax-deductible charge. The raw materials acquired under the purchase contracts enter ultimately into the cost of goods sold. If we assume that raw material inventory levels at the end of the year are not significantly higher than they were at the beginning of the year, then the fixed charge remains unadjusted at $100,000.

Recognition of benefits stemming from fixed charges

Consideration must be given to the question whether the benefits derived by an enterprise from the incurrence of fixed charges are given recognition in the earnings included in the coverage ratio. In the case of interest the benefits stem from the use of the funds derived from the loan. Similarly, rental payments benefit revenues through the productive use of the items leased. The benefits derived from the raw material commitments are reflected in sales revenues. Since outlays for raw materials represent a variable cost, they would ordinarily not be included in fixed charges because they represent an expense that can be varied in accordance with the volume of business transacted. In our example the fixed nature of the charge for raw materials stems from a noncancellable commitment to buy. This reduces discretion and variability. If, in the judgment of the analyst, such commitments represent rock-bottom requirements which will exist even under the most pessimistic estimates of product demand, then he may decide not to consider the purchase commitment as a fixed charge.

Computation of coverage ratio—expanded concept of fixed charges

In accordance with the preceding discussion the earnings-coverage ratio would, based on the data in Exhibit 16–6, be computed as follows:

$$\frac{\text{Income before taxes} + \text{Interest} + \text{Rental expense}}{\text{Interest} + \text{Rental expense} + \text{Purchase commitment} + \text{Sinking fund}\left(\frac{1}{1-.50}\right)}$$

$$= \frac{2{,}200{,}000 + 700{,}000 + 900{,}000}{700{,}000 + 900{,}000 + 100{,}000 + 1{,}000{,}000} = 1.4 \text{ times}$$

Pro forma computations of coverage ratios

In cases where fixed charges yet to be incurred are to be recognized in the computation of the coverage ratio, for example, interest costs under a prospective incurrence of debt, it is quite proper to estimate the benefits which will ensue from such future inflows of funds and to include these estimated benefits in the pro forma income. Benefits to be derived from a prospective loan can be measured in terms of interest savings obtainable from a planned refunding operation, income from short-term investments in which the proceeds may be invested, or similarly reasonable estimates of future benefits.

The SEC will usually insist on the presentation of pro forma computation of the ratio of earnings to fixed charges which reflects changes to be effected under prospective financing plans. Exhibit 16-5 presented an example of such a computation and is not based on data presented in Exhibit 16-6.

Cash flow coverage of fixed charges

The discussion earlier in this chapter pointed out that net income is generally not a reliable measure of funds provided by operations which are available to meet fixed charges. The reason is, of course, that fixed charges are paid with cash or, from the longer term point of view, with funds (working capital) while net income includes items of revenue which do not generate funds as well as expense items which do not require the current use of funds. Thus, a better measure of fixed charges coverage may be obtained by using as numerator funds obtained by operations rather than net income. This figure can be obtained from the statement of changes in financial condition which, under APB *Opinion No. 19*, is now a required financial statement and should, consequently, be generally available.

Under this concept the coverage ratio would be computed as follows:

$$\frac{\text{Funds provided by operations} + \text{Fixed charges}}{\text{Fixed charges}}$$

Using the data in Exhibit 16-6 and the broadest definition of "fixed charges," we compute the coverage ratio as follows:

Funds provided by operations (pretax)

Income before extraordinary items*	$1,100,000
Add back—income taxes	1,100,000
Pretax income	$2,200,000
Less: Nonfund generating income:	
Undistributed earnings of subsidiaries	600,000
	$1,600,000
Add: Expenses not requiring funds:	
Depreciation	800,000
Funds provided by operations (before taxes)	$2,400,000

*Assuming that a one-year calculation can properly omit extraordinary items.

Using the fixed charges we discussed under the "expanded concept" in the previous example, that is,

Interest	$ 700,000
Rental expense	900,000
Purchase commitments	100,000
Sinking fund requirement $\left(\frac{1}{1-.50}\right)$	1,000,000
Total	$2,700,000

We compute the times fixed charges covered by funds provided by operations as follows:

$$\frac{\$2,400,000 + 700,000 + 900,000 + 100,000}{2,700,000} = 1.5 \text{ times}$$

It is interesting to note that the SEC definition of "income to be included in the coverage calculation" recognizes only one type of non fund generating revenue, that is, undistributed earnings of subsidiaries. It seems rather arbitrary to insist on only one type of "nonfund" adjustment when it can be assumed that in times of financial stress a parent can direct a subsidiary to distribute dividends. Perhaps it is a measure of conservatism that the SEC coverage-ratio formula ignores nonfund-requiring charges such as depreciation. However, it must be recognized that over the long run, and coverage ratios are concerned with the longer term, asset replacement needs may well equal, if not exceed, the amounts charged as depreciation. Thus, while such needs cannot be exactly anticipated and scheduled by external analysts, they must be taken into account, and one way of doing this is to omit depreciation from consideration as a charge not requiring the outlay of funds.

If depreciation is added back to net income, then there is little justification for not including principal repayment requirements, such as sinking fund requirements, among the fixed charges. In this case, the "double counting" problem discussed earlier is clearly eliminated.

A case, similar to that involved in the consideration of depreciation, can be made, under certain circumstances, against considering deferred income taxes as a non fund requiring charge in the computation of the coverage ratio of a long-term bond. Here we must recognize that over the long term, the higher charges of expenses for tax purposes which may have given rise to the tax deferral will result in lower future expense charges for tax purposes, thus causing the tax deferral to "reverse" and requiring higher taxes in the future. The treatment of deferred taxes in the coverage ratio computation will then depend on the analyst's judgment as to the expected future behavior of the deferred tax account, that is, whether it is likely to grow, stabilize, or decline.

Stability of "flow of funds from operations"

Since the relationship between the "flow of funds from operations" to the fixed charges of an enterprise is so important to an evaluation of long-term solvency, it is important to assess the stability of that flow. This is done by a careful evaluation of the elements which comprise the sources of funds from operations. For example, depreciation is usually a stable component which does not change drastically from year to year. Thus, one measure of the stability of the funds flow from operations is the percentage which the depreciation add-back to net income is of the total funds provided by operations. The higher this percentage the more stable the sources of funds from operations can normally be assumed to be.

EARNINGS COVERAGE OF PREFERRED DIVIDENDS

In the evaluation of preferred stock issues, it is often instructive to calculate the earnings coverage of preferred dividends, much in the same way the interest or fixed charges coverage of debt issues is computed.

In our discussion of coverage ratios for individual bond issues, earlier in this chapter, we pointed out the misleading results which can result from a class by class coverage computation where junior and senior bonds are outstanding. Thus, we concluded that the computation of a coverage ratio on an overall basis is a more meaningful approach. The same principle applies to the computation of the coverage of preferred dividends, that is, the computation must include as charges to be covered by earnings all fixed charges which take precedence over the payment of preferred dividends.

As in the case of the interest or fixed charge coverage computations, the final ratio depends on a definition of "fixed charges."

Since preferred dividends are not tax deductible, after-tax income must be used to cover them. Consequently the basic formula for computing preferred dividend coverage is:

$$\frac{\text{Income before tax} + \text{Fixed charges}^*}{\text{Fixed charges} + \text{Preferred dividends}\left(\frac{1}{1 - \text{Tax rate}}\right)}$$

*Which *are* tax deductible.

If, for example, we adopt the SEC definition of fixed charges and assume a tax rate of 50 percent, then, based on the data in Exhibit 16–5, we compute the preferred dividend coverage ratio as follows:

Fixed charges:
　Interest costs . . . . $ 700,000
　One third of rentals   300,000
　　　Total. $1,000,000

$$\frac{2{,}200{,}000 + 1{,}000{,}000}{1{,}000{,}000 + 200{,}000\left(\dfrac{1}{1-.50}\right)} = 2.3 \text{ times}$$

The above method of computation is superior to the one, suggested by some authorities, which uses after-tax income in the coverage calculation in order to recognize the nondeductibility, for tax purposes, of the preferred dividends.

If there are two or more preferred issues outstanding, a by-class coverage computation can be made by omitting from it the dividend requirements of the junior issue but always including all prior fixed charges and preferred dividends.

A refinement of the above computation is achieved by substituting for the assumed tax rate the actual composite average tax rate incurred by the entity for the period. This actual tax rate is computed by relating the actual tax provision for the period to income before such taxes.

EVALUATION OF EARNINGS-COVERAGE RATIOS

The earnings-coverage ratio test is a test of the ability of an enterprise to meet its fixed charges out of current earnings. The orientation towards earnings is a logical one because the bondholder or other long-term creditor is not as much interested in asset coverage or what he can salvage in times of trouble, as he is interested in the ability of the enterprise to stay out of trouble by meeting its obligations currently and as a going concern. Given the limited returns obtainable from debt instruments, an increase in the interest rate cannot compensate the creditor for a serious risk of loss of principal. Thus, if the probability of the enterprise meeting its obligations as a going concern is not strong, then a creditor relationship can hardly be advantageous.

Importance of earnings variability

One very important factor in the evaluation of the coverage ratio is the pattern of behavior of cash flows over time, or the behavior of its surrogate—earnings. The more stable the earnings pattern of an enterprise or industry the lower the relative earnings coverage ratio that will be acceptable. Thus, a utility, which in times of economic downturn is likely to experience only a mild falloff in demand, can justify a lower earnings coverage ratio than can a cyclical company such as a machinery manufacturer which may experience a sharp drop in sales in times of recession. Variability of earnings is, then, an important factor in the determination of the coverage standard. In addition, the trend of earnings is an important factor which must be considered apart from their variability.

Importance of method of computation and of underlying assumptions

The coverage standard will also depend on the method of computation of the coverage ratio. As we saw above, varying methods of computing the coverage ratio assume different definitions of "income" and of "fixed charges." It is reasonable to expect lower standards of coverage for the ratios which employ the most demanding and stringent definitions of these terms. For example, based on data in Exhibit 16–6, the earnings-coverage ratio of interest was 4.1 times, while the coverage ratio under an expanded concept of fixed charges worked out to only 1.4 times.

The standards will also vary with the kind of earnings which are utilized in the coverage computation, that is, average earnings, the earnings of the poorest year, etc. Moreover, the quality of earnings is an important factor. The concept of earnings quality is discussed in Chapter 20.

It is not advisable to compute earnings-coverage ratios under methods which are not theoretically sound and whose only merit is that they are conservative. Thus, using after-tax income in the computation of the coverage ratio of fixed charges which are properly deductible for tax purposes is not logical and introduces conservatism in the wrong place. Any standard of coverage adequacy must, in the final analysis, be related to the willingness and ability of the lender to incur risk.

Example of minimum standard of coverage

A standard suggested by a well-known work on security analysis[4] lists the following minimum coverage ratios of fixed charges:

1. *By 7- to 10-year average earnings:*

	Coverage	
	Before taxes	After taxes
Public utilities.	4x	2.4x
Railroads.	5x	2.9x
Industrials.	7x	3.8x

2. *By earnings of the poorest year:*

Public utilities.	3x	1.9x
Railroads.	4x	2.4x
Industrials.	5x	2.9x

---
[4] Graham, Dodd and Cottle, *op. cit.* p. 348.

KEY ELEMENTS IN THE EVALUATION OF LONG-TERM SOLVENCY

The process of evaluation of long-term solvency of an enterprise differs markedly from that of the assessment of short-term liquidity. In the latter the time horizon is short and it is often possible to make a reasonable projection of funds flows. It is not possible to do this for the longer term, and thus the measures used in the evaluation of longer term solvency consist of coverage ratios, that is, coverage of debt by assets and other resources, such as the ability to borrow at short notice and the coverage of fixed charges by earnings. Here earnings are used as the surrogate of liquid funds generated by operations. Earnings are, of course, a most desirable and reliable source of funds for the repayment of debt and the payment of interest. Moreover, a reliable trend of high-level earnings is one of the best assurances of an enterprise's ability to borrow in times of a shortage of funds and its consequent ability to extricate itself from the very conditions which lead to insolvency.

These then are the indicia of financial strength on which the analysis of long-term solvency must rely. Moreover, he must continually monitor them so that changes in conditions which underlie a given assessment of the situation do not go undetected.

RATIOS AS PREDICTORS OF FAILURE

The most common use to which financial statement ratios are put is to use them as pointers in the direction of further investigation and analysis. Some investigation and experimentation has been undertaken to determine to what extent ratios can be used as predictors of failure. As such they could provide valuable additional tools in the analysis of long-term solvency.

The basic idea behind bankruptcy prediction models is that through observation of the trend and behavior of certain ratios of various firms before failure, those characteristics in ratios which predominate in failing firms can be identified and used for prediction purposes. The expectation is that signs of deterioration detected by means of ratio behavior can be observed early enough and clearly enough so that action can be taken to avoid substantial risk of default and failure.

Empirical studies

Among the earliest studies to focus on the behavior of ratios prior to the failure of firms were those of Winakor and Smith[5] who studied

---

[5] Arthur Winakor and Raymond F. Smith, *Changes in Financial Structure of Unsuccessful Firms*, Bureau of Business Research (Urbana, Ill.: University of Illinois Press, 1935).

16. Analysis of capital structure and long-term solvency

a sample of 183 firms which experienced financial difficulties for as long as 10 years prior to 1931, the year when they failed. Analyzing the 10-year trend of 21 ratios they concluded that the ratio of net working capital to total assets was among the most accurate and reliable indicator of failure.

Fitzpatrick[6] analyzed the three- to five-year trends of 13 ratios of 20 firms that had failed in the 1920–29 period. By comparing them to the experience of a control group of 19 successful firms, he concluded that all of his ratios predicted failure to some extent. However, the best predictors were found to be the return on net worth and the net worth to total debt ratio.

Merwin[7] studied the experience of a sample of 939 firms during the 1926–36 period. Analyzing an unspecified number of ratios he found that three ratios were most sensitive in predicting "discontinuance" of a firm as early as four to five years before such discontinuance. The three ratios were the current ratio, net working capital to total assets, and net worth to total debt. They all exhibited declining trends before "discontinuance" and were at all times below estimated normal ratios.

Focusing on the experience of companies which experienced defaults on debt and bank credit difficulties, Hickman[8] studied the experience of corporate bond issues during 1900–1943 and reached the conclusion that the times-interest-earned ratio and the net-profit-to-sales ratio were useful predictors of bond issue defaults.

In a study using more powerful statistical techniques than used in its predecessors, Beaver[9] found that financial ratios proved useful in the prediction of bankruptcy and bond default at least five years prior to such failure. He determined that ratios could be used to distinguish correctly between failed and nonfailed firms to a much greater extent than would be possible by random prediction.

Among his conclusions were that both in the short-term and the long-term cash-flow-to-total-debt ratios were the best predictors, capital structure ratios ranked second, liquidity ratios third, while turnover ratios were the worst predictors.

In an investigation of the ability of ratios to predict bond rating

---

[6] Paul J. Fitzpatrick, *Symptoms of Industrial Failures* (Washington: Catholic University of America Press, 1931); and Paul J. Fitzpatrick, *A Comparison of the Ratios of Successful Industrial Enterprises with Those of Failed Companies* (Washington: The Accountants Publishing Co., 1932).

[7] Charles L. Merwin, *Financing Small Corporations: In Five Manufacturing Industries, 1926–36* (New York: National Bureau of Economic Research, 1942).

[8] W. Braddock Hickman, *Corporate Bond Quality and Investor Experience* (Princeton, N.J.: Princeton University Press, 1958), pp. 395–431.

[9] William H. Beaver, "Financial Ratios as Predictors of Failure," *Empirical Research in Accounting, Selected Studies, 1966*, Supplement to Vol. 4, (*Journal of Accounting Research*, pp. 71–127.

changes and bond ratings of new issues, Horrigan[10] found that the rating changes could be correctly predicted to a much greater extent by the use of ratios than would be possible through random prediction.

Conclusions

The above research efforts, while pointing out the significant potential which ratios have as predictors of failure as well as other variables of interest to decision makers, nevertheless indicate that these tools and concepts are in an early stage of development.

The studies focused on experience with failed firms *after the fact.* While they presented evidence that firms which did not fail enjoyed stronger ratios than those which ultimately failed, the ability of ratios to predict failure has not been conclusively proved. Another important question yet to be resolved is whether the observation of certain types of behavior by certain ratios can be accepted as a better means of the analysis of long-term solvency than is the current use of the various tools described earlier in this chapter. Further research may show that the use of ratios as predictors of failure will best complement rather than supplement the rigorous financial analysis suggested in this chapter. However, as monitoring and attention-directing tools they hold considerable promise.

QUESTIONS

1. Why is the analysis of capital structure important?
2. How should deferred income taxes be treated in the analysis of capital structure?
3. In the analysis of capital structure how should lease obligations which have not been capitalized be treated? Under what conditions should they be considered the equivalent of debt?
4. How would you classify (i.e., equity or liability) the following items. State your assumptions and reasons:
   a) Minority interest in consolidated financial statement.
   b) General contingency reserve for indefinite purpose.
   c) Reserve for self-insurance.
   d) Guarantee for product performance on sale.
   e) Convertible debt.
   f) Preferred stock.
5. What is meant by "financial leverage," and in what case(s) is such leverage most advantageous?
6. In the evaluation of long-term solvency why are long-term projections

---

[10] James O. Horrigan, "The Determination of Long-term Credit Standing with Financial Ratios," *Empirical Research in Accounting, Selected Studies, 1966,* Supplement to Vol. 4, *Journal of Accounting Research,* pp. 44–62.

necessary in addition to a short-term analysis? What are some of the limitations of long-term projections?

7. What is the difference between common-size analysis and capital structure ratio analysis? Why is the latter useful?

8. The amount of equity capital shown on the balance sheets, which is based on historical cost, at times differs considerably from realizable market value. How should a financial analyst allow for this in the analysis of capital structure?

9. Why is the analysis of assets distribution necessary?

10. What does the earnings coverage ratio measure and in what respects is it more useful than other tools of analysis?

11. Your analysis of additional information leads you to conclude that the rental payment under a long-term lease should have been capitalized. If it was not capitalized on the financial statement, what approaches would you take?

12. For the purpose of earnings-coverage ratio computation, what are your criteria for inclusion of an item in "fixed charges"?

13. The company under analysis has a purchase commitment of raw materials under a noncancellable contract which is substantial in amount. Under what conditions would you include the purchase commitment in the computation of fixed charges?

14. Is net income generally a reliable measure of funds available to meet fixed charges? Why or why not?

15. Company B is a wholly owned subsidiary of Company A. The latter is also Company B's principal customer. As potential lender to Company B, what particular facets of this relationship would concern you most? What safeguards, if any, would you require?

16. Comment on the statement: "debt is a supplement to, not a substitute for, equity capital."

17. A company in need of additional equity capital decides to sell convertible debt thus postponing equity dilution and ultimately selling its shares at an effectively higher price. What are the advantages and disadvantages of such a course of action?

18. a) What is the basic function of restrictive covenants in long-term debt indentures (agreements)?
    b) What is the function of provisions regarding:
       (1) Maintenance of minimum working capital (or current ratio).
       (2) Maintenance of minimum net worth.
       (3) Restrictions on the payment of dividends.
       (4) Ability of creditors to elect a majority of the board of directors of the debtor company in the event of default under the terms of the loan agreement.

19. What is your opinion on the use of ratios as predictors of failure? Your answer should recognize the empirical research which has been recently done in this area.

17

Analysis of return on investment and of asset utilization

DIVERSE VIEWS OF PERFORMANCE

IN THIS AGE of increasing social consciousness there exist many views of what the basic objectives of business enterprises are or should be. There are those who will argue that the main objective of a business enterprise should be to make the maximum contribution to the welfare of society of which it is capable. That includes, aside from the profitable production of goods and services, consideration of such immeasurables as absence of environmental pollution and a contribution to the solution of social problems. Others, who adhere to the more traditional *laissez faire* school, maintain that the major objective of a business enterprise organized for profit is to increase the wealth of its owners and that this is possible only by delivering to society (consumers) that which it wants. Thus, the good of society will be served.

An extended discussion of these differing points of view on performance is beyond the purpose of this text. Since the analysis of financial statements is concerned with the application of analytical tools to that which can be measured, we shall concentrate here on those measures of performance which meet the objectives of financial analysis.

CRITERIA OF PERFORMANCE EVALUATION

There are many criteria by which performance can be measured. Changes in sales, in profits, or in various measures of output are among the criteria frequently utilized.

17. Analysis of return on investment and of asset utilization

No one of these measurements, standing by itself, is useful as a comprehensive measure of enterprise performance. The reasons for this are easy to grasp. Increases in sales are desirable only if they result in increased profits. The same is true of increases in volume of production. Increases in profits, on the other hand, must be related to the capital that is invested in order to attain these profits.

IMPORTANCE OF RETURN ON INVESTMENT (ROI)

The relationship between net income and the capital invested in the generation of that income is one of the most valid and most widely recognized measures of enterprise performance. In relating income to invested capital the ROI measure allows the analyst to compare it to alternative uses of capital as well as to the return realized by enterprises subject to similar degrees of risk. The investment of capital can always yield some return. If capital is invested in government bonds, the return will be relatively low because of the small risk involved. Riskier investments require higher returns in order to make them worthwhile. The ROI measure relates income (reward) to the size of the capital that was needed to generate it.

MAJOR OBJECTIVES IN THE USE OF ROI

Economic performance is the first and foremost purpose of business enterprise. It is, indeed, the reason for its existence. The effectiveness of operating performance determines the ability of the enterprise to survive financially, to attract suppliers of funds, and to reward them adequately. ROI is the prime measure of economic performance. The analyst uses it as a tool in two areas of great importance:

1. An indicator of managerial effectiveness.
2. A method of projecting earnings.

An indicator of managerial effectiveness

The earning of an adequate or superior return on funds invested in an enterprise depends first and foremost on the resourcefulness, skill, ingenuity, and motivation of management. Thus, the longer term ROI is of great interest and importance to the financial analyst because it offers a prime means of evaluating this indispensible criterion of business success: the quality of management.

A method of projecting earnings

A second important function served by the ROI measure is that of a means of earnings projection. The advantage of this method of earnings projection is that it links the amount of earnings which it is estimated an enterprise will earn to the total invested capital. This adds discipline and realism to the projection process, which applies to the present and expected capital investment the return which is expected to be realized on it. The latter will usually be based on the historical and incremental rates of return actually earned by the enterprise, and adjusted by projected changes, as well as on expected returns on new projects.

The rate of ROI method of earning projection can be used by the analyst as either the primary method of earnings projection or as a supplementary check on estimates derived from other projection methods.

Internal decision and control tool

While our focus here is on the work of the external financial analyst, mention should be made of the very important role which ROI measures play in the individual investment decisions of an enterprise as well as in the planning, budgeting, coordination, evaluation, and control of business operations and results.

It is obvious that the final return achieved in any one period on the total investment of an enterprise is composed of the returns (and losses) realized by the various segments and divisions of which it is composed. In turn, these returns are made up of the results achieved by individual product lines, projects, etc.

The well-managed enterprise exercises rigorous control over the returns achieved by each of its "profit centers" and rewards its managers on the basis of such results. Moreover, in evaluating the advisability of new investments of funds in assets or projects, management will compute the estimated returns it expects to achieve from them and use these estimates as a basis for its decision.

BASIC ELEMENTS OF ROI

The basic concept of ROI is relatively simple to understand. However, care must be used in determining the elements entering its computation because there exist a variety of views, which reflect different objectives, of how these elements should be defined.

The basic formula for computing ROI is as follows:

$$\frac{\text{Income}}{\text{Investment}}$$

We shall now examine the various definitions of "investment" and of the related "income."

Defining the investment base

There is no one generally accepted measure of capital investment on which the rate of return is computed. The different concepts of investment reflect different objectives. Since the term "return on investment (ROI)" covers a multitude of concepts of investment base and income, there is need for more specific terms to describe the actual investment base used.

Total assets. Return on total assets is perhaps the best measure of the *operating efficiency* of an enterprise. It measures the return obtained on *all* the assets entrusted to management. By removing from this computation the effect of the method used in financing the assets, the analyst can concentrate on the evaluation or projection of operating performance.

Modified asset bases. For a variety of reasons some ROI computations are based not on total assets but rather on an adjusted amount.

One important category of adjustments relates to "unproductive" assets. In this category assets omitted from the investment base include idle plant, facilities under construction, surplus plant, surplus inventories and surplus cash, intangible assets, and deferred charges. The basic idea behind these exclusions is not to hold management responsible for earning a return on assets which apparently do not earn a return. While this theory may have validity in the use of ROI as an internal management and control tool, it lacks merit when applied as a tool designed to evaluate management effectiveness on an overall basis. Management is entrusted with funds by owners and creditors, and it has discretion as to where it wants to invest them. There is no reason for management to hold on to assets which bring no return. If there are reasons for keeping funds invested in such assets, then there is no reason to exclude them from the investment base. If the long-run profitability of an enterprise is benefited by keeping funds invested in assets which have no return or a low return in the interim, then the longer term ROI should reflect such benefits. In conclusion, it can be said that from the point of view of an enterprise evaluation by the external analyst there is rarely any justification to omit assets from the investment base merely because they are not productively employed or do not earn a current return.

The exclusion of intangible assets from the investment base is often due to skepticism regarding their value or their contribution to the earning power of the enterprise. Under generally accepted accounting principles intangibles are carried at cost. However, if the cost exceeds their future utility, they must be written down or else the analyst will at least find an uncertainty exception regarding their carrying value included in the auditor's opinion. Accounting for intangible assets is discussed in Chapter 4. The exclusion of intangible assets from the asset (investment) base must be justified on more substantial evidence than a mere lack of understanding of what these assets represent or an unsupported suspicion regarding their value.

Depreciable assets in the investment base. An important difference of opinion prevails with respect to the question of whether depreciable assets should be included in the investment base at original cost or at an amount net of the accumulated allowances for depreciation.

One of the most prominent advocates of the inclusion of fixed assets at gross amount in the investment base, for purposes of computing the return on investment, is the management of E. I. duPont de Nemours and Company which pioneered the use of ROI as an internal management tool.

In a pamphlet describing the company's use of the ROI method in the appraisal of operating performance, this point of view is expressed as follows:[1]

> *Calculation of return on investment.* Return on investment as presented in the chart series is based upon *gross* operating investment and earnings *net* of depreciation.
>
> Gross operating investment represents all the plant, tools, equipment and working capital made available to operating management for its use; no deduction is made for current or other liabilities or for the reserve for depreciation. Since plant facilities are maintained in virtually top productive order during their working life, the depreciation reserve being considered primarily to provide for obsolescence, it would be inappropriate to consider that operating management was responsible for earning a return on only the net operating investment. Furthermore, if depreciable assets were stated at net depreciated values, earnings in each succeeding period would be related to an ever-decreasing investment; even with stable earnings, Return on Investment would continually rise, so that comparative Return on Investment ratios would fail to reveal the extent or trend of management performance. Relating earnings to investment that is stable and uniformly compiled provides a sound basis for comparing the "profitability of assets employed" as between years and between investments.
>
> In the case of any commitment of capital—e.g., an investment in a security—it is the expectation that in addition to producing earnings while committed, the principal will eventually be recovered. Likewise, in the case of funds invested in a project, it is expected that in addition to the return earned while invested, the working capital will be recovered through liquidation at the end of the project's useful life and the plant investment will be recovered through depreciation accruals. Since earnings must allow for this recovery of plant investment, they are stated net of depreciation.

It is not difficult to take issue with the above reasoning. It must, however, be borne in mind that the duPont system is designed for use in the internal control of separate productive units as well as for the control of operating management. Our point of view here is, however,

---

[1] American Management Association, *Executive Committee Control Charts,* AMA Management Bulletin No. 6, 1960, p. 22.

that of evaluating the operating performance of an enterprise taken as a whole. While the recovery of capital out of sales and revenues (via depreciation), by an enterprise operating at a profit, can be disregarded in the evaluation of a *single* division or segment, it cannot be disregarded for an enterprise taken as a whole because such recovery is reinvested somewhere within that enterprise even if it is not reinvested in the particular segment which gave rise to the depreciation and which is evaluated for internal purposes. Thus, for an enterprise taken as a whole, the "net of depreciation" asset base is a more valid measure of investment on which a return is computed. This is so for the reasons given above and also because the income which is usually related to the investment base is net of the depreciation expense.

The tendency of the rate of return to rise as assets are depreciated (see also Chapter 8) is offset by the retention of capital recovered by means of depreciation, on which capital a return must also be earned. Moreover, maintenance and repair costs rise as equipment gets older, thus tending to offset the reduction, if any, in the asset base.

Among other reasons advanced in support of the use of fixed assets at their gross amount is the argument that the higher amounts are designed to compensate for the effects of inflation on assets expressed in terms of historical cost. In the discussion of the price level problem in Chapter 12 it was pointed out that price level adjustments can validly be made only within the framework of a complete restatement of all elements of the financial statements. Crude "adjustments," such as using the gross asset amount, are apt to be misleading and are generally worse than no adjustments at all.

Long-term liabilities plus equity capital. The use of long-term liabilities plus equity capital as the investment base differs from the "total assets" base only in that current liabilities are excluded as suppliers of funds on which the return is computed. The focus here is on the two major suppliers of longer term funds, that is, long-term creditors and equity shareholders.

Shareholders' equity. The computation of return on shareholders' equity measures the return accruing to the owners' capital. As was seen in the discussion of financial leverage in Chapter 16, this return reflects the effect of the employment of debt capital on the owners' return. Since preferred stock, while in the equity category, is usually nevertheless entitled only to a fixed return, it is also omitted from the calculation of the final return on equity computation.

Difference between investor's cost and enterprise investment base

For purposes of computing the ROI, a distinction must be drawn between the investment base of an enterprise and that of an investor.

440   Understanding corporate reports

The investor's investment base is, of course, the price he paid for his equity securities. Except for those cases in which he acquired such securities at book value, his investment base is going to differ from that of the company in which he has invested. In general, the focus in ROI computations is on the return realized by the enterprise rather than the return realized on the investment cost of any one shareholder.

Averaging the investment base

Regardless of the method used in arriving at the investment base, the return achieved over a period of time is always associated with the investment base that was, on average, actually available to the enterprise over that period of time. Thus, unless the investment base did not change significantly during the period, it will be necessary to average it. The most common method of averaging for the external analyst is that of adding the investment base at the beginning of the year to that at the end of the year and dividing their total by two. A more accurate method of averaging, where the data is available, is to average by month-end balances, that is, adding the month-end investment bases and dividing the total by 12.

Relating income to the investment base

In the computation of ROI, the definition of return (income) is dependent on the definition of the investment base.

If the investment base is defined as comprising total assets, then income *before* interest expense is used. The exclusion of interest from income deductions is due to its being regarded as a payment for the use of money to the suppliers of debt capital in the same way that dividends are regarded as a reward to suppliers of equity capital. Income, before deductions for interest or dividends, is used when it is related to total assets or to long-term debt plus equity capital.

When the return on the equity capital is computed, net income after deductions for interest and preferred dividends is used. If the preferred dividends are cumulative, they are deducted in arriving at the balance of earnings accruing to the common stock, whether these dividends were declared or not.

The final ROI must always reflect all applicable costs and expenses and that includes income taxes. Some computations of ROI nevertheless omit deductions of income taxes. One reason for this practice is the desire to isolate the effects of tax management from those of operating performance. Another reason is that changes in tax rates affect comparability over the years. Moreover, companies which have tax loss

17. Analysis of return on investment and of asset utilization 441

carry-forwards find that the deduction of taxes from income adds confusion and complications to the ROI computations.

It must, however, be borne in mind that income taxes reduce the final return and that they must be taken into consideration particularly when the return on shareholders' equity is computed.

Illustration of ROI computations

The computation of ROI under the various concepts of "investment base" discussed above will now be illustrated by means of the data contained in Exhibits 17–1 and 17–2. The computations are for the year 19x9 and based on figures rounded to the nearest million dollars.

EXHIBIT 17–1

AMERICAN CAN COMPANY
Statement of Income
For Years Ended December 31, 19x8 and 19x9
(in thousands of dollars)

	19x8	19x9
Net sales	1,636,298	1,723,729
Costs and expenses	1,473,293	1,579,401
Operating income	163,005	144,328
Other income net	2,971	1,784
	165,976	146,112
Interest expense	16,310	20,382
Provision for federal and other taxes on income	71,770	61,161
Net income	77,896	64,569
Less dividends:		
Preferred stock	2,908	2,908
Common stock	39,209	38,898
	42,117	41,806
Net income reinvested in the business	35,779	22,763

Return on total assets

$$\frac{\text{Net income} + \text{Interest}}{\text{Total assets}}$$

$$\frac{65 + 20}{1,372} = 6.2\%$$

Two refinements are possible in this computation and become necessary if their use would make a significant difference in the result.

One refinement recognizes that the year-end total asset figure may be different from the average amount of assets employed during the

EXHIBIT 17-2

AMERICAN CAN COMPANY
Statements of Financial Position
As at December 31, 19x8 and 19x9
(in thousands of dollars)

	19x8	19x9
Assets		
Current Assets:		
Cash	25,425	25,580
Eurodollar time deposits and temporary cash investments	38,008	28,910
Accounts and notes receivable—net	163,870	176,911
Inventories	264,882	277,795
Total Current Assets	492,185	509,196
Investments in and receivables from nonconsolidated subsidiaries	33,728	41,652
Miscellaneous investments and receivables	5,931	6,997
Funds held by trustee for construction		6,110
Land, buildings, equipment, and timberlands—net	773,361	790,774
Deferred charges to future operations	16,117	16,452
Goodwill and other intangible assets	6,550	6,550
Total Assets	1,333,982	1,371,621
Liabilities		
Current Liabilities:		
Notes payable to banks—principally Eurodollar	7,850	13,734
Accounts payable and accrued expenses	128,258	144,999
Dividends payable	10,404	10,483
Federal and other taxes on income	24,370	13,256
Long-term indebtedness payable within one year	9,853	11,606
Total Current Liabilities	180,735	194,078
Long-term indebtedness	350,565	335,945
Deferred taxes on income	86,781	101,143
Total Liabilities	618,081	631,166
Capital		
Preferred, 7% cumulative and noncallable, par value $25 per share; authorized 1,760,000 shares	41,538	41,538
Common, par value $12.50 per share; authorized 30,000,000 shares	222,245	222,796
Capital in excess of par value	19,208	20,448
Earnings reinvested in the business	436,752	459,515
Less: Common treasury stock	(3,842)	(3,842)
Total Capital	715,901	740,455
Total Liabilities and Capital	1,333,982	1,371,621

year. This calls for adding the total assets at the beginning and end of the year and dividing by two.

The second refinement recognizes that interest is a tax-deductible expense and that if the interest cost is excluded the related tax benefit must also be excluded from income. If we assume the average tax rate to be 50 percent that means that we add back only *half* the interest cost.

Reflecting these two refinements the formula becomes:

$$\frac{\text{Net income} + \text{Interest expense} \times (1 - \text{Tax rate})}{(\text{Beginning total assets} + \text{Ending total assets}) \div 2}$$

Using the data in Exhibits 17–1 and 17–2,

$$\frac{65 + 20(1 - .5)}{(1{,}334 + 1{,}372) \div 2} = 5.5\%$$

Since the return on total assets shown by the refined method differs significantly from the uncorrected method, the use of the refined method, which is the theoretically correct one, is indicated.

Return on modified asset bases. Since our discussion earlier in the chapter came to the conclusion that in normal circumstances most of the modifications in the amount of total assets are not logically warranted, no illustrations of such computation will be given here.

Return on long-term liabilities plus equity capital

$$\frac{\text{Net income} + \text{Interest expense} \times (1 - \text{tax rate})}{\text{Average long-term liabilities plus equity capital}}$$

Using the data in Exhibits 17–1 and 17–2:

$$\frac{65 + (20 \times .5)}{(437 + 716 + 437 + 740) \div 2} = 6.4\%$$

It should be noted that deferred taxes on income are included among the long-term liabilities. In the computation of return on long-term liabilities and equity capital, the question of how to classify deferred taxes does not really present a problem because after careful consideration of the circumstances giving rise to the deferrals, the analyst will decide whether they are to be considered as either debt or equity. In this computation both debt and equity are aggregated anyway. The problem of classification becomes more real in computing the return on shareholders' equity. In the examples which follow we assume circumstances where deferred taxes are considered to be more in the nature of a long-term liability than of an equity nature.

Return on stockholders' equity. The basic computation of return on the equity excludes from the investment base all but the common stockholders' equity.

$$\frac{\text{Net income} - \text{Preferred dividends}}{\text{Average common stockholders' equity}}$$

Using data in Exhibits 17–1 and 17–2:

$$\frac{65 - 3}{(674 + 699) \div 2} = 9 \text{ percent}$$

The higher return on shareholders' equity as compared to the return on total assets reflects the positive workings of financial leverage.

Should it be desired, for whatever reason, to compute the return on total stockholders' equity, the investment base would include the preferred shareholders' equity, while net income would not reflect a deduction for preferred dividends. The formula would then be:

$$\frac{\text{Net income}}{\text{Average total shareholders' equity (common and preferred)}}$$

Where convertible debt sells at a substantial premium above par and is clearly held by investors for its conversion feature, there is justification for treating it as the equivalent of equity capital. This is particularly true when the company can choose at any time to force conversion of the debt by calling it.

Analysis and interpretation of ROI

Earlier in the chapter we mentioned that ROI analysis is particularly useful to the analyst in the areas of evaluation of managerial effectiveness, enterprise profitability, and as an important tool of earnings projection.

Both the evaluation of management and the projection of earnings by means of ROI analysis are complex processes requiring thorough analysis. The reason for this is that the ROI computation usually includes components of considerable complexity.

Components of the ROI ratio. If we focus first on return on total assets we know that the primary formula for computing this return is:

$$\frac{\text{Net income} + \text{interest } (1 - \text{Tax rate})}{\text{Average total assets}}$$

For purposes of our discussion and analysis let us look at this computation in a simplified form:

$$\frac{\text{Net income}}{\text{Total assets}}$$

Since sales are a most important yardstick in relation to which profitability is measured and are, as well, a major index of activity, we can recast the above formula as follows:

$$\frac{\text{Net income}}{\text{Sales}} \times \frac{\text{Sales}}{\text{Total assets}}$$

The relationship of net income to sales measures operating performance and profitability. The relationship of sales to total assets is a

17. Analysis of return on investment and of asset utilization

measure of asset utilization or turnover, a means of determining how effectively (in terms of sales generation) the assets are utilized. It can be readily seen that both factors, profitability as well as asset utilization, determine the return realized on a given investment in assets.

Profitability and asset utilization are, in turn, complex ratios which normally require thorough and detailed analysis before they can be used to reach conclusions regarding the reasons for changes in the return on total assets.

Exhibit 17–3 presents the major factors which influence the final return

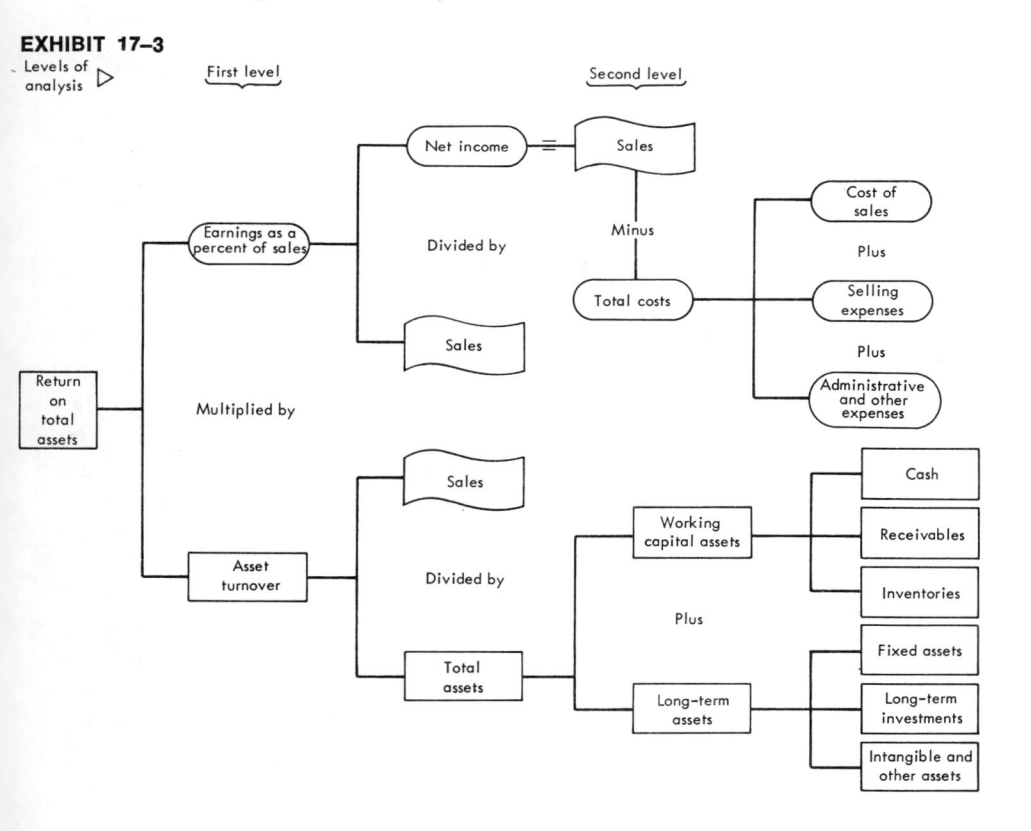

EXHIBIT 17–3
Levels of analysis ▷

First level / Second level

Return on total assets =
- Earnings as a percent of sales = Net income ÷ Sales
  - Net income
  - Sales = Total costs + ...
    - Total costs = Cost of sales Plus Selling expenses Plus Administrative and other expenses
- Multiplied by
- Asset turnover = Sales ÷ Total assets
  - Total assets = Working capital assets Plus Long-term assets
    - Working capital assets: Cash, Receivables, Inventories
    - Long-term assets: Fixed assets, Long-term investments, Intangible and other assets

on total assets. In the next section we shall be concerned with the interaction of profitability (net income/sales) and of asset utilization or turnover (sales/total assets) which, in Exhibit 17–3 is regarded as the first level of analysis of the return on total assets. As can be seen from Exhibit 17–3, the many important and complex factors which, in turn, determine profitability and asset utilization represent a second level of analysis of the return on total assets. Chapters 18 and 19 will take up the analysis of results of operations, and Chapter 20 will deal with the evaluation and projection of earnings. The analysis of asset utilization will be discussed in subsequent sections of this chapter.

Relationship between profitability and asset turnover. The relationship between return on total assets, profitability, and capital turnover (utilization) is illustrated in Exhibit 17–4, which indicates that when we

EXHIBIT 17–4
Analysis of return on total assets

	Company X	Company Y	Company Z
1. Sales	$5,000,000	$10,000,000	$10,000,000
2. Net income	500,000	500,000	100,000
3. Total assets	5,000,000	5,000,000	1,000,000
4. Profit as % of sales $\left(\frac{2}{1}\right)$	10%	5%	1%
5. Asset turnover $\left(\frac{1}{3}\right)$	1	2	10
Return on total assets (4 × 5)	10%	10%	10%

multiply profitability (expressed as a percentage) by asset utilization (expressed as a turnover) we obtain the return on total assets (expressed as a percentage relationship).

Company X realizes its 10 percent return on total assets by means of a relatively high profit margin and a low turnover of assets. The opposite is true of Company Z, while Company Y achieves its 10 percent return by means of a profit margin half that of Company X and an asset turnover rate twice that of Company X. It is obvious from Exhibit 17–4 that there are many combinations of profit margins and turnover rates which can yield a return on assets of 10 percent.

In fact, as can be seen from Exhibit 17–5, there exist an infinite variety of combinations of profit margin and asset turnover rates which yield a 10 percent return on assets. The chart in the exhibit graphically relates asset turnover (vertical axis) to profitability (horizontal axis).

The curve, sloping from the upper left area of low profit margins and high asset turnover rates, traces out the endless combinations of profitability and asset turnover rates which yield a 10 percent return on total assets. The data of Companies X and Y (from Exhibit 17–4) are represented by dots on the graph, while the data of Company Z cannot be fitted on it since the full curve has not been shown. The other lettered dots represent the profit-turnover combination of other companies within a particular industry. This clustering of the results of various companies around the 10 percent return on assets slope is a useful way of comparing the returns of many enterprises within an industry and the major two elements which comprise them.

The chart in Exhibit 17–5 is also useful in assessing the relative courses

EXHIBIT 17–5

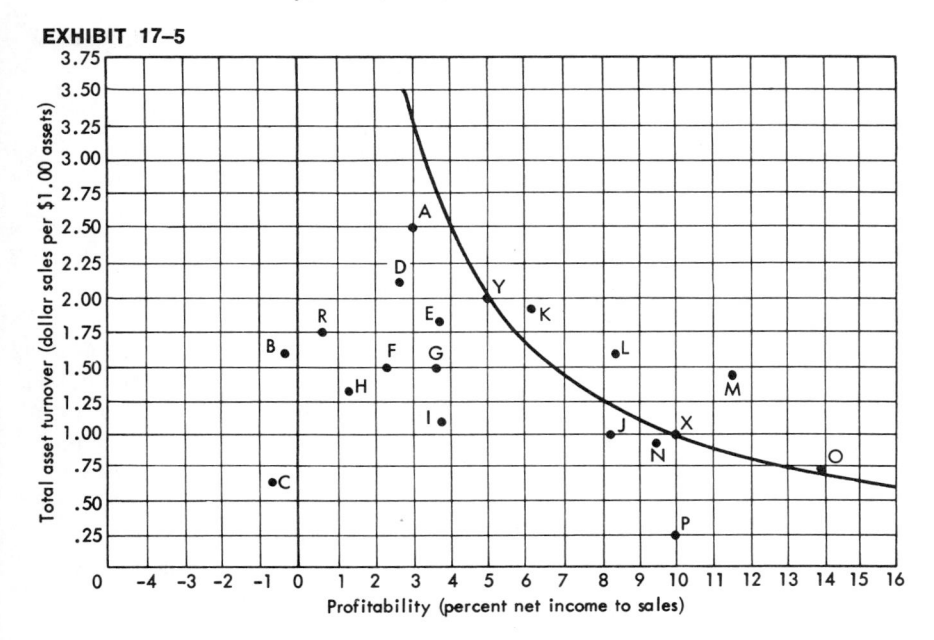

[Chart: X-axis "Profitability (percent net income to sales)" from -4 to 16; Y-axis "Total asset turnover (dollar sales per $1.00 assets)" from 0 to 3.75. A hyperbolic iso-ROI curve is plotted. Company points: A (≈4, 2.55), B (≈1, 1.55), C (≈-1, 0.65), D (≈3, 2.25), E (≈4, 1.80), F (≈4, 1.55), G (≈5, 1.55), H (≈2.5, 1.40), I (≈4.5, 1.10), J (≈8, 1.00), K (≈7, 1.80), L (≈9, 1.55), M (≈11, 1.40), N (≈9, 0.85), O (≈13, 0.75), P (≈9, 0.30), R (≈2, 1.85), X (≈11, 1.05), Y (≈6, 2.10).]

of action open to different enterprises which want to improve their respective returns on investments.

Companies B and C must, of course, restore profitability before the turnover rate becomes a factor of importance. Assuming that all the companies represented in Exhibit 17–5 belong to the same industry and that there is an average representative level of profitability and turnover in it, Company P will be best advised to pay first and particular attention to improvement in its turnover ratio, while Company R should pay foremost attention to the improvement of its profit margin. Other companies, such as Company I, would best concentrate on both the turnover and the profit margin aspects of ROI improvement.

While the above analysis treats profitability and turnover as two independent variables, they are, in fact, interdependent. As will be seen from the discussion of break-even analysis in Chapter 19, a higher level of activity (turnover), when fixed expenses are substantial, will tend to increase the profit margin because, within a certain range of activity, costs increase proportionally less than sales. In comparing two companies within an industry the analyst, in evaluating the one having the lower asset turnover, will make allowance for the potential increase in profitability that can be associated with a projected increase in turnover that is based primarily on an expansion of sales.

Analysis of return on total assets can reveal the weaknesses as well as the potential strengths of an enterprise. Assume that two companies in the same industry have returns on total assets as follows:

	Company A	Company B
1. Sales	$ 1,000,000	$20,000,000
2. Net income	100,000	100,000
3. Total assets	10,000,000	10,000,000
4. Profitability $\left(\frac{2}{1}\right)$	10%	.5%
5. Turnover of assets $\left(\frac{1}{3}\right)$	.1 times	2 times
Return on investment (4 × 5)	1%	1%

Both companies have poor returns on total assets. However, remedial action for them lies in different areas and the analyst will concentrate on the evaluation of the feasibility of success of such improvement.

Company A has a 10 percent profit on sales which, let us assume, is about average for the industry. However, each dollar invested in assets supports only 10 cents in sales whereas Company B gets $2 of sales for each dollar invested in its assets. The analyst's attention will naturally be focused on Company A's investment in assets. Why is its turnover so low? Are there excess assets which yield little or no return or are there idle assets which should be disposed of? Or, as often is the case, are the assets inefficiently or uneconomically utilized? Quite obviously, Company A can achieve more immediate and significant improvements by concentrating on improving turnover (by increasing sales, reducing investment, or both) than by striving to increase the profit margin beyond the industry average.

The opposite situation prevails with respect to Company B where attention should first be focused on the reasons for the low profit margin and to the improvement of it as the most likely avenue of success in increasing ROI. The reasons for low profitability can be many, including inefficient equipment and production methods, unprofitable product lines, excess capacity with attendant high fixed costs, excessive selling or administrative costs, etc.

The company with the low profitability may discover that changes in tastes and in technology have resulted in an increased investment in assets being needed to finance a dollar of sales. This means that in order to maintain its return on assets the company must increase its profit margin or else production of the product is no longer worthwhile.

There is a tendency to regard a high profit margin as a sign of high earnings quality. This view was rebutted by W. M. Bennett[2] who pointed out the importance of return on capital as the ultimate test of profitability. He presented the following table comparing during a given year

---

[2] William M. Bennett, "Capital Turnover vs. Profit Margins," *Financial Analysts Journal*, March–April 1966, pp. 88–95.

the similar profit margins of five companies with their respective returns on capital:

	Profit margin as % of sales	Profit as % of capital
Whirlpool	5.3%	17.1%
Corn Products	5.9	12.0
Goodyear	5.5	9.6
U.S. Plywood	5.5	8.0
Distillers Seagram	5.0	6.7

It is evident that in the case of these five companies, which have similar profit margins, the rate of capital turnover made the difference in the return on capital performance, and this must be taken into account by the analyst. Thus, a supermarket chain will be content with a net profit margin of 1 percent or less because it has a high rate of turnover due to a relatively low investment in assets, and a high proportion of leased assets (such as stores and fixtures). Similarly, a discount store will accept a low profit margin in order to obtain a high rate of asset turnover (primarily of inventories). On the other hand, capital intensive industries such as steels, chemicals, and autos, which have heavy investments in assets and resulting low asset turnover rates, must achieve high net profit margins in order to offer investors a reasonable return on capital.

ANALYSIS OF ASSET UTILIZATION

As is graphically illustrated in Exhibit 17-3, the return on total assets depends on (1) getting the largest profit out of each dollar of sales and (2) obtaining the highest possible amount of sales per dollar of invested capital (net assets).

The intensity with which assets are utilized is measured by means of asset turnover ratios. That utilization has as its ultimate measure the amount of sales generated since sales are in most enterprises the first and essential step to profits. In certain special cases, such as with enterprises in developmental stages, the meaning of turnover may have to be modified in recognition of the fact that most assets are committed to the development of future potential. Similarly, abnormal supply problems and strikes are conditions which will affect the state of capital utilization and, as such, will require separate evaluation and interpretation.

Evaluation of individual turnover ratios

Changes in the basic turnover ratio which enters the determination of the ROI calculation, that is,

$$\frac{\text{Sales}}{\text{Total assets}}$$

can be evaluated meaningfully only by an analysis of changes in the turnover rates of individual asset categories and groups which comprise the total assets.

Sales to cash. As was seen in the discussion in Chapter 14, cash and cash equivalents are held primarily for purposes of meeting the needs of day-to-day transactions as well as a liquidity reserve designed to prevent the shortages which may arise from an imbalance in cash inflows and outflows. In any type of business there is a certain logical relationship between sales and the cash level that must be maintained to support it.

Too high a rate of turnover of cash may be due to a cash shortage which can ultimately result in a liquidity crisis if the enterprise has no other ready sources of funds available to it.

Too low a rate of turnover may be due to the holding of idle and unnecessary cash balances. Cash accumulated for specific purposes or known contingencies may result in temporary decreases in the rate of turnover.

The basic trade-off here is between liquidity and the tying up of funds which yield no return or a very modest return.

Sales to receivables. Any organization which sells on credit will find that the level of its receivables is a function of sales. A relatively low rate of turnover here is, among other reasons, likely to be due to an overextension of credit, to an inability of customers to pay, or to a poor collection job.

A relatively high rate of turnover may indicate a strict credit extension policy or a reluctance or inability to extend credit. Determining the rate of turnover here is the trade-off between sales and the tying up of funds in receivables.

Sales to inventories. The maintenance of a given level of sales generally requires a given level of inventories. This relationship will vary from industry to industry depending on the variety of types, models, colors, sizes, and other classes of varieties of items which must be kept in order to attract and keep customers. The length of the production cycle as well as the type of item (e.g., luxury versus necessity; perishable versus durable) has a bearing on the rate of turnover.

A slow rate of turnover indicates the existence of problems such as overstocking, slow-moving or obsolete inventories, overestimating of sales or a lack of balance in the inventory. Temporary problems such as strikes at important customers may also be responsible for this.

A higher than normal rate of turnover may mean an underinvestment in inventory which can result in lack of proper customer service and in loss of sales.

In this case the trade-off is between tying up funds in inventory, on one hand, and sacrificing customer service and sales on the other.

Sales to fixed assets. While the relationship between property, plant, and equipment and sales is a logical one on a long-term basis, there are many short-term and temporary factors which may upset this relationship. Among these factors are conditions of excess capacity, inefficient or obsolete equipment, multishift operations, temporary changes in demand, and interruptions in the supply of raw materials and parts.

It must also be remembered that increases in plant capacity are not gradual but occur, instead, in lumps. This too can create temporary and medium-term changes in the turnover rates. Often, leased facilities and equipment, which do not appear on the balance sheet, will distort the relationship between sales and fixed assets.

The trade-off here is between investment in fixed assets with a correspondingly higher break-even point on one hand, and efficiency, productive capacity, and sales potential on the other.

Sales to other assets. In this category we find, among others, such assets as patents and deferred research and development costs. While the direct relationship between these individual categories of assets and current sales levels may not be evident, no assets are held or should be held by an enterprise unless they contribute to sales or to the generation of income. In the case of deferred research and development costs, the investment may represent the potential of future sales. The analyst, must, in his evaluation of rates of asset utilization, allow for such factors.

Sales to short-term liabilities. The relationship between sales and short-term trade liabilities is a predictable one. The amount of short-term credit which an enterprise is able to obtain from suppliers depends on its needs for goods and services, that is, on the level of activity (e.g., sales). Thus, the degree to which it can obtain short-term credit depends also importantly on the level of sales. This short-term credit is relatively cost-free and, in turn, reduces the investment of enterprise funds in working capital.

Use of averages

Whenever the level of a given asset category changes significantly during the period for which the turnover is computed, it is necessary to use averages of asset levels in the computation. The computation then becomes

$$\frac{\text{Sales}}{(\text{Asset at beginning of period} + \text{Asset at end of period}) \div 2}$$

To the extent that data is available and the variation in asset levels during the period warrants it, the average can be computed on a monthly or quarterly basis.

Other factors to be considered in return on asset evaluation

The evaluation of the return on assets involves many factors of great complexity. As will be seen from the discussion in Chapter 20, the inclusion of extraordinary gains and losses in single period and average net income must be evaluated. Chapter 12 has examined the effects of price level changes on ROI calculations, and these, too, must be taken into account by the analyst.

The analyst must bear in mind that return on asset calculations are most commonly based on book values appearing in the financial statements rather than on market values which, in most cases, may be more relevant and economically more significant. Also, quite often, a return is earned by enterprises on assets which either do not appear in the financial statements or are significantly understated therein. Examples of such assets are intangibles such as patents, trademarks, expensed research and development costs, advertising and training costs, etc. Other excluded assets may include leaseholds and the value of natural resources discovered.

In analyzing the trend of return on assets over the years, the effect of acquisitions accounted for as poolings of interest (see Chapter 7) must be isolated and their chance of recurrence evaluated.

The external analyst will not usually be able to obtain data on ROI by segments, product lines, or divisions of an enterprise. However, where his bargaining power or position allows him to obtain such data, they can make a significant contribution to the accuracy and reliability of his analysis.

A consistently high return on assets is the earmark of an effective management and can distinguish a growth company from one experiencing merely a cyclical or seasonal pickup in business.

An examination of the factors which comprise the return on assets will usually reveal the limitations to which their expansion is subject. Neither the profit margin nor the asset turnover rate can expand indefinitely. Thus, an expanding asset base via external financing and/or internal earnings retention will be necessary for further earnings growth.

Equity growth rate

The equity growth rate by means of earnings retention can be calculated as follows:

$$\frac{\text{Net income} - \text{Payout}}{\text{Common shareholders' equity}} = \text{Percent increase in common equity}$$

This is the growth rate due to the retention of earnings. It indicates the possibilities of earnings growth without resort to external financing. These increased funds, in turn, will earn the rate of return which the enterprise can obtain on its assets and thus contribute to growth in earnings.

Return on shareholders' equity

Up to now we have examined the factors affecting the return on total assets. However, of great interest to the owner group of an enterprise is the return on the stockholders' equity. The rate of return on total assets and that on the stockholders' equity differs because a portion of the capital with which the assets are financed is usually supplied by creditors who receive a fixed return on their capital or, in some cases, no return at all. Similarly, the preferred stock usually receives a fixed dividend. These fixed returns differ from the rate earned on the assets (funds) which they provide, and this accounts for the difference in returns on assets and those of stockholders' equity. This is the concept of financial leverage which was already discussed at length in Chapter 16.

Equity turnover

The computation of the return on shareholders' equity is composed of the following two major elements:

$$\frac{\text{Net income}}{\text{Sales}} \times \frac{\text{Sales}}{\text{Average shareholders' equity}}$$

The equity turnover (sales/average shareholder's equity) can be further analyzed by breaking it down into two elements:

$$\frac{\text{Sales}}{\text{Net operating assets}} \times \frac{\text{Net operating assets}}{\text{Average shareholders' equity}}$$

The first factor measures asset utilization which we have discussed earlier in the chapter. The second factor is a measure of the use of financial leverage by the enterprise. The more an enterprise uses borrowed funds to finance its assets the higher this ratio will be.

Measuring the financial leverage index

The financial leverage index, as we already saw in Chapter 16, can be measured as follows:

$$\frac{\text{Return on equity}}{\text{Return on total assets}} = \frac{\text{Assets}}{\text{Equity}} \times \frac{\text{Net income}}{\text{Net income} + \text{Interest } (1 - \text{Tax rate})}$$

454   Understanding corporate reports

The formula for return on total assets

$$\frac{\text{Net income} + \text{Interest } (1 - \text{Tax rate})}{\text{Total assets}}$$

can be converted to a return on stockholders' equity formula by multiplying it by the financial leverage index.

$$\frac{\text{Net income} + \text{Interest } (1 - \text{Tax rate})}{\text{Total assets}} \times (\text{Financial leverage index})$$

In the discussion that follows, the leverage index for American Can Company, based on the data of Exhibits 17–1 and 17–2 in this chapter, is as follows:

$$\frac{\text{Return on stockholders' equity}}{\text{Return on total assets}} = \frac{8.8\%}{5.47\%} = 1.61$$

A financial leverage index greater than 1 is positive, that is, it indicates that the use of borrowed and other noncommon equity funds increases the common stockholders' return. A leverage index below 1 has the opposite effect.

Analysis of financial leverage effects

The effect which each noncommon equity capital source has on the return on the common equity can be analysed in detail. Using the data of American Can Company which was included in Exhibits 17–1 and 17–2, earlier in this chapter we can undertake such an analysis as follows:

An analysis of the American Can Company balance sheet as at 12/31/x9 discloses the following major sources of funds (in thousands):

Current liabilities (exclusive of current portion of long-term debt)		$ 182,472
Long-term debt	$335,945	
Current portion	11,606	347,551
Deferred taxes		101,143
Preferred stock		41,538
Common stockholders' equity		698,917
Total Investment or Total Assets		$1,371,621

The income statement for 19x9 includes (in thousands):

Income before taxes		$ 125,730
Income (and other) taxes		61,161*
Net income	$	64,569
Preferred dividends		2,908
Income accruing to common shareholders	$	61,661
Total interest expense	$	20,382
Assumed interest on short-term notes (5%)		687
Balance of interest on long-term debt	$	19,695

*Average tax rate of 49%.

17. Analysis of return on investment and of asset utilization

The return on total assets is computed as follows:

$$\frac{\text{Net income} + \text{Interest} (1 - \text{Tax rate})}{\text{Total assets}}$$

$$= \frac{64{,}569 + 20{,}382\,(1 - .49)}{1{,}371{,}621} = 5.47\%$$

The 5.47 percent return represents the average return on all assets employed by the company. To the extent that suppliers of capital other than the common stockholders get a lower reward than an average of 5.47 percent the common equity benefits by the difference. The opposite is true when the suppliers of capital receive more than a 5.47 percent reward in 19x9.

Exhibit 17–6 presents an analysis showing the relative contribution and reward of each of the major suppliers of nonequity funds and their effect on the returns earned by the common stockholders.

EXHIBIT 17–6
Analysis of composition of return on shareholders' equity (slide rule accuracy computations in thousands of dollars)

Category of fund supplier	Fund supplied	Earnings on fund supplied at rate of 5.47%	Payment to suppliers of funds	Accruing to (detracting from) return on common stock
Current liabilities	182,472	9,981	350 (1)	9,631
Long-term debt	347,551	19,011	10,044 (2)	8,967
Deferred taxes	101,143	5,533	None	5,533
Preferred stock	41,538	2,272	2,908 (3)	(636)
Earnings in excess of compensation to suppliers of funds 23,495
Add: Common stockholder's equity	698,917	38,231	...	38,231
Totals	1,371,621	75,028 (4)	13,302	
Total income (return) on stockholders' equity 61,726 (4)

(1) Interest cost of $686 less 49% tax.
(2) Interest cost of $19,695 less 49% tax.
(3) Preferred dividends—not tax deductible.
(4) Slight differences with statement figures are due to rounding.

As can be seen from Exhibit 17–6 the $9,631,000 accruing to the common equity from use of current liabilities is largely due to its being free of interest costs. The advantage of $8,967,000 accruing from the use of long-term debt is substantially due to the tax deductability of interest. Since the preferred dividends are not tax deductible, the unimpressive return on total assets of 5.45 percent resulted in a disadvantage to the common equity of $636,000. The value of tax deferrals can be clearly seen in this case where the use of cost-free funds amounted to an annual advantage of $5,533,000.

We can now carry this analysis further (all dollar amounts in thousands):

The return on the common stockholder equity is as follows:

$$\frac{\text{Net income less preferred dividends}}{\text{Common stockholders' equity}} = \frac{61,661^3}{698,917} = 8.8 \text{ percent}$$

The net advantage which the common equity reaped from the working of financial leverage (Exhibit 17-6) is $23,495.

As a percentage of the common stockholders' equity, this advantage is computed as follows:

$$\frac{\text{Earnings in excess of compensation to outside suppliers of funds}}{\text{Common stockholders' equity}} = \frac{\$23,495}{\$698,917} = 3.36 \text{ percent}$$

The return on common stockholders' equity can now be viewed as being composed as follows:

Return on assets	5.47%
Leverage advantage accruing to common equity.	3.36
Return on common equity.	8.8%

QUESTIONS

1. Why is "return on investment (ROI)" one of the most valid measures of enterprise performance? How is this measure used by the financial analyst?
2. How is ROI used as an internal management tool?
3. Discuss the validity of excluding "nonproductive" assets from the asset base used in the computation of ROI. Under what circumstances is the exclusion of intangible assets from the asset base warranted?
4. Why is interest added back to net income when the ROI is computed on total assets?
5. Under what circumstances may it be proper to consider convertible debt as equity capital in the computation of ROI?
6. Why must the net income figure used in the computation of ROI be adjusted to reflect the asset base (denominator) used in the computation?
7. What is the relationship between ROI and sales?
8. Company A acquired Company B because the latter had a record of profitability (net income to sales ratio) exceeding that of its industry. After the acquisition took place a major stockholder complained that the acquisition resulted in a low return on investment. Discuss the possible reasons for his complaint.

---

[3] Ties in (except for rounding difference) with total income accruing to common stockholders in Exhibit 17-6.

9. Company X's profitability is 2 percent of sales. Company Y has a turnover of assets of 12. Both companies have ROIs of 6 percent which is considered unsatisfactory by industry standards. What is the asset turnover of Company X and what is the profitability ratio of Company Y? What action would you advise to the managements of the respective companies?
10. What is the purpose of measuring the asset utilization of different asset categories?
11. What factors enter into the evaluation of the ROI measures?
12. How is the equity growth rate computed? What does it signify?
13. How is the "financial leverage index" computed? What is the significance of a financial leverage index reading of 1?
14. a) What is "equity turnover" and how is it related to the rate of return on equity?
    b) "Growth in per share earnings generated from an increase in equity turnover probably cannot be expected to continue indefinitely." Do you agree or disagree? Explain briefly, bringing out in your answer the alternative causes of an increase in equity turnover. (C.F.A.)

18

Analysis of results of operations—I

THE SIGNIFICANCE OF INCOME STATEMENT ANALYSIS

THE INCOME STATEMENT presents in summarized fashion the results of operations of an enterprise. These results, in turn, represent the major reason for the existence of a profit-seeking entity, and they are important determinants of its value and solvency.

Some of the most important decisions in security analysis and credit evaluation are based on an evaluation of the income statements. To the security analyst income is often the single most important determinant of security values, and hence the measurement and the projection of income are among his most important analytical objectives. Similarly, to the credit grantor income is the most natural as well as the most desirable source of interest and principal repayment. In almost all other aspects of financial analysis the evaluation and projection of operating results assume great importance.

THE MAJOR OBJECTIVES OF INCOME ANALYSIS

In the evaluation of the income of an enterprise the analyst is particularly interested in an answer to the following questions:

1. What is the net income of the enterprise?
2. What elements in the income statement can be used and relied upon for purposes of earnings forecasting?
3. What is the trend of income over the years?

What is the income of the enterprise?

Based on the simple proposition that net income is the excess of revenues over costs and expenses during an accounting period, many people, including astute professional analysts, are exasperated at the difficulties they encounter in their search for the "true earnings" or the "real earnings" of an enterprise.

Why, they ask, should it be possible for so many different "acceptable" figures of "net income" to flow out of one set of circumstances? Given the economic events which the enterprise experienced during a given period, is there not only *one* "true" result, and is it not the function of accountancy to identify and measure such result?

Those who have studied Part II of this text will know why the answer to the last question must be "no". In this chapter, dealing with the analysis of income, it is appropriate to summarize *why* this is so.

"Net income" is not a specific quantity. Net income is not a specific flow awaiting the perfection of a flawless meter with which it can be precisely measured. There are a number of reasons for this:

1. The determination of income is dependent on estimates regarding the outcome of future events. This peering into the future is basically a matter of judgment involving the assessment of probabilities based on facts and estimates.

While the judgment of skilled and experienced professionals, working on the basis of identical data and information, can be expected to fall within a narrow range, it will nevertheless *vary* within such a range. The estimates involve the allocation of revenues and costs as between the present and the future. Put another way, they involve the determination of the future utility and usefulness of many categories of unexpired costs and of assets as well as the estimation of future liabilities and obligations.

2. The accounting principles governing the determination and measurement of income at any given time are the result of the cumulative experience of the accounting profession, of regulatory agencies, of businessmen, and others. They reflect a momentary equilibrium which is based partly on knowledge and experience and partly on the compromise of widely differing views on methods of measurement. Chapter 8 indicates the great variety of these views. While the accounting profession has moved to narrow the range of acceptable alternative measurement principles, the alternatives nevertheless remain; and their complete elimination in the near future is unlikely.

3. Beyond the problem of honest differences in estimation and other judgments, as well as in the variety of alternative acceptable principles, is the problem arising from the diverse ways in which the judgments and principles are applied.

Theoretically, the independent professional accountant should be concerned first and foremost with the fair presentation of the financial statements. He should make accounting a "neutral" science which gives expression and effect to economic events but does not itself affect the results presented. To this end he should choose from among alternative principles those most applicable to the circumstances and should disclose all facts, favorable and adverse, which may affect the user's decision.

In fact, the accounting profession as a whole has not yet reached such a level of independence and detachment of judgment. It is subject to the powerful pressures on the part of managements who have, or at least feel that they have, a vital interest in the way in which results of operations are presented. The auditors are most vulnerable to pressures in those areas of accounting where widely differing alternatives are equally acceptable and where accounting theory is still unsettled. Thus, they may choose the lowest level of acceptable practice rather than that most which is appropriate and fair in the circumstances. Although relatively less frequent, cases of malpractice and collusion in outright deception by independent accountants nevertheless still surface from time to time.

The analyst cannot ignore this possibility, and must be aware of it and ever alert to it. It calls for constant vigilance in the analysis of audited data, particularly when he has reason to suspect a lack of independence and objectivity in the application of accounting principles.

In addition to the above reasons which are inherent in the accounting process, there exists another reason why there cannot be such a thing as an absolute measure of "real earnings." It is that financial statements are general-purpose presentations designed to serve the diverse needs of many users. Consequently, a single figure of "net income" cannot be relevant to all users, and that means that the analyst must use this figure and the additional information disclosed in the financial statements and elsewhere as a starting point and adjust it so as to arrive at a "net income" figure which meets his particular interests and objectives.

ILLUSTRATION 1. To the buyer of an income-producing property, the depreciation expense figure which is based on the seller's cost is not relevant. In order to estimate the net income he can derive from such property, depreciation based on the expected purchase price of the property must be substituted.

ILLUSTRATION 2. To the analyst who exercises independent judgment and uses knowledge of the company he is analyzing and the industry of which it is a part, the reported "net income" marks the start of his analysis. He adjusts the "net income" figure for changes in income and expense items which he judges to be warranted. These may include, for example, estimates of bad debts, of depreciation, and of research costs as well as the treatment of extraordinary gains and losses. Comparisons with other companies may call for similar adjustments so that the data can be rendered comparable.

From the above discussion it should be clear that the search for a figure of "real income" represents an emphasis that is misplaced and which should instead be directed to a determination of *relevant* net income.

Obstacles in the determination of "relevant income." The discussion so far has centered on the analyst's proper focus in his attempts to arrive at an income figure which is relevant to his purposes. In addition to the basic considerations which stem from the nature of the accounting process itself, there are other obstacles which mean that the analyst must bring to bear on his work of analysis, not only an understanding of the processes of income measurement but also an understanding of the many pitfalls and obstacles which lie in his way. The following are some of the most important of these considerations and obstacles:

1. *Fraud, misrepresentation, and lack of disclosure.* Over the years, and especially since the enactment of the Securities Acts of 1933 and 1934, and with improvement in the audit function in this country, the incidence of outright fraud and deliberate misrepresentation in financial statements has diminished markedly. But they have not been completely eliminated and probably never will. Nor can the analyst ever rule out the possibility of spectacular failures in the audit function. While each major audit failure tends to contribute to the improvement of regulation and of auditing, they have not prevented the recurrence of such failures as the security holders of McKesson & Robbins, of Seabord Commercial Corporation, of H. L. Green, of Miami Window, of Yale Express, of BarChris Construction Company, of Continental Vending Company, of Mill Factors Corporation, and Equity Funding Company, well know.

The analyst must always assess the vulnerability to failure and to irregularities of the company he is analyzing and the character and the propensities of its management, as a means of establishing the degree of risk that it will prove to be the relatively rare exception to the general rule.

2. *Factors affecting the "quality of earnings."* The analyst must realize that not only is it impossible to arrive at a single figure of "net income" but that identical earnings figures may possess different degrees of quality. While the elements which make up the quality of earnings will be examined in more detail in Chapter 20, we can identify here three major categories of such elements.

a) One type of factor that affects the quality of earnings is the accounting and computational discretion of management and that of the attesting accountants in choosing from among accepted alternative accounting principles. These choices can be liberal, that is, assuming the most optimistic view of the future, or they can be conservative. Generally, the quality of conservatively determined earnings is higher because they are less likely to prove overstated in the light of future developments than those determined in a "liberal" fashion. Unwarranted or excessive conservatism, while contributing to the temporary "quality" of earnings, actually results in a lack of reporting integrity over the long run and cannot be considered as a desirable factor.

b) The second type of factor affecting the quality of earnings is related to managerial discretion over the size of income streams and particularly over the reported amount of costs and expenses. Discretionary types of expenses, such as repairs and maintenance, advertising, and research and development costs can be varied for the sole purpose of managing the level of reported net income (or loss) rather than for legitimate operating or business reasons. Here, too, the analyst's task is to identify management's actions and its real motivation.

c) The third factor affecting the quality of earnings is not primarily a result of discretionary actions of managements, although skillful management can modify its effects. It is the effect of cyclical and other economic forces on earnings and particularly on their variability. Variability of earnings is generally an undesirable factor and, consequently, the higher the variability the lower the quality of these earnings.

Having examined the question of what the earnings of an enterprise are, we shall now turn to the question of earnings forecasting.

What elements in the income statement can be used in forecasts?

For decision-making purposes by external analysts the importance of determining the level of enterprise earnings or "earnings power" lies primarily in its use in forecasting future results. Security, credit, and most other types of financial analysis are oriented towards the future so that past and present results derive most of their value from their use as a basis for earnings projection.

Granted that the decision maker is interested primarily in future prospects, his approach to assessing them must be based primarily on the present as well as on the past. While expected future changes in conditions must be given recognition, the experience of the present and the past form the base to which such adjustments are applied. In doing this the analyst relies on the degree of continuity and perseverance of momentum which is the common experience of the enterprise and the industry of which it is part. Random shocks and sudden changes are always possible, but they are the exception rather than the rule.

The importance to the analyst of the underlying continuity of business affairs should not be overemphasized. One should not confuse the basis for the projection of future results, which the past record represents, with the forecast which is the end product. As a final objective the analyst is interested in a projection of net income. Net income is the result of the offset of two big streams: (1) total revenues and (2) total costs.

Considering that net income represents most frequently but a relatively small portion of either stream, one can see how a relatively minor change in either of these large streams can cause a very significant change in net income.

The analyst will concentrate on identifying those elements in the income and cost streams which show stability, proven relationships, and predictability, and will separate them from those elements which are random, erratic, or nonrecurring and which, consequently, do not possess the elements of stability required for a reasonably reliable forecast. To the intelligent analyst the most desirable income statement is the one containing a maximum of meaningful disclosure which will allow him to do this, rather than one containing built-in interpretations which channel him to specific conclusions.

The analyst must be on his guard against the well-known tendency of managements to practice income smoothing, thus trying to give to the income and expense streams a semblance of stability which they do not possess. This is usually done in the name of "removing distortions" from the results of operations, whereas what is really achieved is the masking of the natural and cyclical irregularities which are part of the reality of the enterprise's experience and with which reality it is the analyst's primary task to come to grips.

Need to identify erratic elements. In his analysis of the income statement the analyst will strive to identify erratic and unstable factors which he will separate from what may be called the enterprise's stable or basic "earning power." These factors include temporary demand (as was the case with the temporary shortage of color-TV tubes which in the 1960s temporarily increased the fortunes of National Video Company), unusual costs, such as those due to strikes, and genuine items of extraordinary gain and loss.

"Earning power"—a complex quantum always subject to change. Those earnings from which the unstable and nonrecurring elements have been removed, cannot, of course, be relied upon conclusively to represent the core "earning power" of the enterprise. That "earning power," as was seen in Chapter 17, is the result of the complex interaction of profitability and asset turnover. These factors are complex and

are subject to a multitude of influences which result in change. In the final analysis, their stability is also dependent on two key factors which account for profitability: men and money. Translated into our analytical terms they mean (1) management and (2) assets.

1. *Management.* That it takes resourceful management to "breathe life" into assets by employing them profitably and causing their optimum utilization is well known. The assumption of stability of relationships and trends implies that there has been no major change in the skill, depth, and the continuity of the management group or a radical change in the type of business in which their skill has been proven by a record of successful performance.

2. *Assets.* The second essential ingredient to profitable operations is funds or resources with which the assets essential to the successful conduct of business are acquired. No management, no matter how ingenious, can expand operations and have an enterprise grow without an adequate asset base. Thus, continuity of success and the extrapolation of growth must be based on an investigation of the sources of additional funds which the enterprise will need and the effect of the method of financing on net income and earnings per share.

The financial condition of the enterprise, as was seen in Chapters 14 and 16, can have a bearing on the results of operations. A lack of liquidity may inhibit an otherwise skillful management, and a precarious or too risky capital structure may lead to limitations by others on its freedom of action.

The above factors, as well as other economic, industry, and competitive factors, must be taken into account by the analyst when projecting the earnings of an enterprise. Ideally, in projecting earnings, the analyst should add a lot of knowledge about the future to some knowledge of the past. Realistically the analyst must settle for a lot of knowledge about the past and present and only a limited knowledge of the future.

Determining the trend of income over the years

Having determined the size of a company's basic earnings as well as the factors which require adjustment before those earnings can be used as a basis for forecasts, it remains for the analyst to determine the variability of these earnings, that is, changes in their size over the business cycle and over the longer term.

Evaluation of earnings variability. Earnings which fluctuate up and down with the business cycle are less desirable than earnings which display stability over such cycle. The basic reason for this is that fluctuating earnings cause fluctuations in market prices. Earnings which display a steady growth trend are of the most desirable type. In his evaluation of earnings, the intelligent analyst realizes the limitations to which the earnings figure of any one year is subject. Therefore, depending on his specific purposes, he will consider the following earnings figures as improvements over the single year figure:

1. *Average earnings* over periods, such as 5 to 10 years, smooth out erratic and even extraordinary factors as well as cyclical influences, thus presenting a better and more reliable measure of "earning power" of an enterprise.
2. *Minimum earnings* are useful in decisions, such as those bearing on credit extension, which are particularly sensitive to risk factors. They indicate the worst that could happen based on recent experience.

The importance of earnings trends. In addition to the use of single, average, or minimum earnings figures, the analyst must be alert to earnings trends. These are best evaluated by means of trend statements such as those presented in Exhibit 7 of Chapter 2. The earnings trend contains important clues to the nature of the enterprise (i.e., cyclical, growth, defensive) and the quality of its management.

Distortions of trends. Analysts must be alert to accounting distortions designed to affect trends. Some of the most common and most pervasive manipulative practices in accounting are designed to affect the presentation of earnings trends. These manipulations are based on the assumptions, generally true, that the trend of income is more important than its absolute size; that retroactive revisions of income already reported in prior periods have little, if any, market effect on security prices[1]; and that once a company has incurred a loss, the size of the loss is not as significant as the fact that the loss has been incurred.

These assumptions and the propensities of some managements to use accounting as a means of improving the appearance of the earnings trend has led to techniques which can be broadly described as income smoothing.

Income smoothing. A number of requirements must be met by the income-smoothing process so as to distinguish it from outright falsehoods and distortions.

The income-smoothing process is a rather sophisticated and insidious device. It does not rely on outright or patent falsehoods and distortions but rather uses the wide leeway existing in accounting principles and their interpretation in order to achieve its ends. Thus, income smoothing is performed within the framework of "generally accepted accounting principles." It is a matter of form rather than one of substance. Consequently, it does not involve a real transaction (e.g., postponing an actual

---

[1] This was recognized by APB *Opinion No. 20* which, with but three exceptions, forbids the retroactive restatement of prior year financial statements. For a discussion of this Opinion see Chapter 9.

sale to another accounting period in order to shift revenue) but only a redistribution of credits or charges among periods. The general objective is to moderate income variability over the years by shifting income from good years to bad years, by shifting future income to the present (in most cases presently reported earnings are more valuable than those reported at some future date), or vice versa. Similarly, income variability can be moderated or modified by the shifting of costs, expenses, or losses from one period to another.

Income smoothing may take many forms. Hereunder are listed some forms of smoothing to which the analyst should be particularly alert:

1. The retroactive revision of results already reported, generally with the objective of relieving future income of charges which would have otherwise been made against it. The accounting profession has moved to limit the abuses in this area. (See discussion in Chapter 9.)
2. Misstatements, by various methods, of inventories as a means of redistributing income among the years. The Londontown Manufacturing Company case[2] provides a classic example of such practices.
3. The offsetting of extraordinary credits by identical or nearly identical extraordinary charges as a means of removing an unusual or sudden injection of income which may interfere with the display of a growing earnings trend. (For examples and further discussion see Chapter 9.)
4. The provision of reserves for future costs and losses as a means of increasing the adverse results of what is already a poor year and utilizing such reserves to relieve future years of charges against income which would otherwise be properly chargeable against it. (For examples and further discussion see Chapter 9.)
5. The substantial write-downs of operating assets (such as plant and equipment) or of intangibles (such as research and development or goodwill) in times of economic slowdown when operating results are already poor. The reason usually given for such write-downs is that carrying the properties at book value cannot be economically justified. (For example, Cudahy Packing Company has effected such a write-down of plant but had to reverse it in a subsequent year.) Particularly unwarranted is the practice of writing down operating assets to the point at which a target return on investment (which management thinks it *should* earn) is realized.
6. Timing the inclusion of revenues and costs in periodic income in such a way as to influence the overall trend of income (or loss) over the years. (Examples are the timing of sales or other disposition

---

[2] Details can be found in an SEC decision issued October 31, 1963 (41SEC676-688).

of property, incurring and expensing of discretionary costs such as research and development, advertising, maintenance, etc.) This category, unlike most others, entails more than accounting choice in that it may involve the timing of actual business transactions.

Having discussed the major objectives of income statement analysis and the considerations entering into the analyst's work, we shall now proceed to examine the specific tools of analysis which are useful in analyzing the various components of the income statement.

ANALYSIS OF COMPONENTS OF THE INCOME STATEMENT

The analysis of the income statements of an enterprise can be conceived of as encompassing two levels: (1) the accounting principles used and their implication and (2) the tools of income statement analysis.

Accounting principles used and their implication

The analyst must have a thorough understanding of the principles of income, cost, and expense accounting and measurement employed by the enterprise. Moreover, since most assets, with the exception of cash and receivables actually collectible, represent costs deferred to the future, the analyst must have a good understanding of the principles of asset measurement employed by the enterprise so that he can relate them to the income accounting of the enterprise as a means of checking the validity of that accounting. Finally, he must understand and assess the implications which the use of one accounting principle, as opposed to another, has on the measurement of the income of an enterprise and its comparison to that of other enterprises.

Most chapters in Part II of this work deal with this phase or level of financial statement analysis.

Tools of income statement analysis

The second level of analysis consists of applying the appropriate tools of analysis to the components of the income statement and the interpretation of the results shown by these analytical measures. The application of these tools is aimed at achieving the objectives of the analysis of results of operations mentioned earlier, such as the projection of income and the assessment of its stability and quality.

The remainder of this chapter will be devoted to an examination of these tools and to the interpretation of the results achieved through their use.

THE ANALYSIS OF SALES AND REVENUES

The analysis of sales and revenues is centered on answers to the basic questions:

1. What are the major sources of revenue?
2. How stable are these sources and what is their trend?
3. How is the earning of revenue determined and how is it measured?

Major sources of revenue

Knowledge of major sources of revenues (sales) is important in the analysis of the income statement particularly if the analysis is that of a multimarket enterprise. Each major market or product line may have its own separate and distinct growth pattern, profitability, and future potential.

The best way to analyze the composition of revenues is by means of a common-size statement which shows the percentage of each major class of revenue to the total. This information can also be portrayed graphically on an absolute dollar basis as shown in Exhibit 18–1. With inclusion of an increasing amount of product line information in published financial statements, and particularly in prospectuses, the external analyst will be able to obtain more readily the data necessary for this analysis. Exhibit 18–2 shows an example of such disclosure taken from a prospectus filed by the MITE Corporation. In addition to sources of sales it gives income contribution and inventories by product line.

FINANCIAL REPORTING BY DIVERSIFIED ENTERPRISES

The user of the financial statements of diversified enterprises faces, in addition to the usual problems and pitfalls of financial analysis, the problem of sorting out and understanding the impact which the different individual segments of the business have on the sum total of reported results of operations and financial condition. The author of an important study in the reporting by diversified companies has defined a conglomerate company as follows:[3]

> . . . one which is so managerially decentralized, so lacks operational integration, or has such diversified markets that it may experience rates of profitability, degrees of risk, and opportunities for growth which vary within the company to such an extent that an investor requires information about these variations in order to make informed decisions.

---

[3] R. K. Mautz, "Identification of the Conglomerate Company," *Financial Executive,* July 1967, p. 26.

EXHIBIT 18–1
Analysis of sales by product line over time

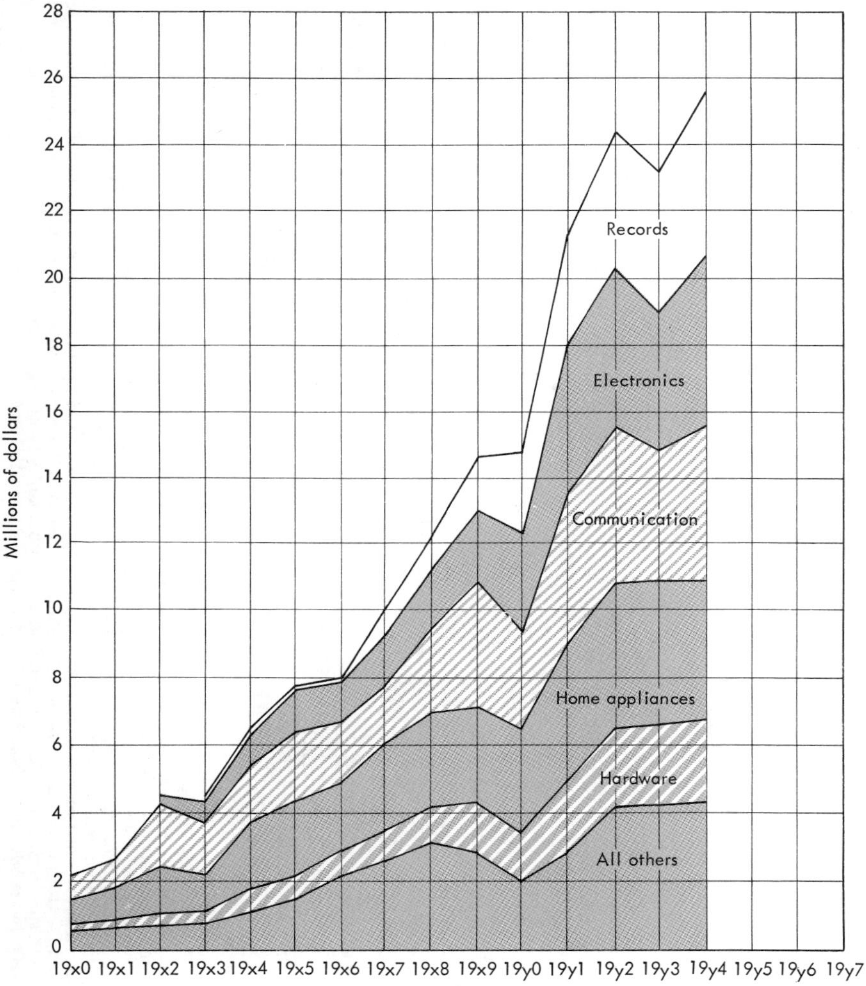
Millions of dollars
28
26
24
22
20
18
16
14
12
10
8
6
4
2
0
19x0 19x1 19x2 19x3 19x4 19x5 19x6 19x7 19x8 19x9 19y0 19y1 19y2 19y3 19y4 19y5 19y6 19y7
Records
Electronics
Communication
Home appliances
Hardware
All others

Reasons for the need for data by significant enterprise segments

The above definition suggests some of the most significant reasons why financial analysts require as much information and detailed data as possible about the various segments of an enterprise. The analysis, evaluation, projection, and valuation of earnings requires that these be broken down into categories which share similar characteristics of variability, growth potential, and risk. Similarly, the asset structure and the financing requirements of various segments of an enterprise can vary significantly and thus require separate analysis and evaluation.

EXHIBIT 18-2

MITE CORPORATION
Information as to Production Lines

	Year ended February 28, 19x7	Year ended February 29, 19x8	Year ended February 28, 19x9	12 weeks ended May 23, 19x9
Data communications equipment:				
Net sales	$4,616,000 (47%)	$5,625,000 (49%)	$4,847,000 (38%)	$1,589,000 (46%)
Income contribution	578,000 (47%)	876,000 (62%)	996,000 (49%)	350,000 (44%)
Inventory	2,615,000 (64%)	2,469,000 (47%)	2,103,000 (36%)	1,897,000 (33%)
Time recording devices:				
Net sales	3,394,000 (35%)	4,205,000 (37%)	4,376,000 (35%)	948,000 (27%)
Income contribution	441,000 (36%)	311,000 (22%)	34,000 (2%)	95,000 (12%)
Inventory	1,193,000 (29%)	2,234,000 (42%)	2,574,000 (44%)	2,728,000 (48%)
Hardware for electronics industry: (4)				
Net sales			1,564,000 (12%)	427,000 (12%)
Income contribution			771,000 (38%)	212,000 (27%)
Inventory			311,000 (5%)	287,000 (5%)
Home sewing products:				
Net sales	1,505,000 (15%)	1,436,000 (13%)	1,408,000 (11%)	292,000 (8%)
Income contribution	291,000 (24%)	289,000 (20%)	276,000 (13%)	79,000 (10%)
Inventory	398,000 (10%)	534,000 (10%)	449,000 (8%)	526,000 (9%)
Corporate totals:				
Net sales	$9,718,000	$11,382,000	$12,634,000	$3,486,000
Income contribution	$1,218,000	$1,424,000	$2,051,000	$ 792,000
General and administrative expenses	$ 468,000	$ 490,000	$ 1,020,000	$ 373,000
Other expenses	(20,000)	76,000	68,000	3,000
Income before federal income taxes	$ 770,000	$ 858,000	$ 963,000	$ 416,000
Inventory	$4,087,000	$ 5,305,000	$ 5,785,000	$5,742,000

(1) The allocation of overhead in computing cost of goods sold for the purposes of the above table reflects the application of departmental overhead rates, product line overhead rates, and material handling rates.

(2) MITE does not maintain records of its general and administrative expenses on a product line basis and does not believe that such expenses are incurred in proportion to the net sales, cost of goods sold, or selling expenses of the product lines. For this reason, MITE's aggregate general and administrative expenses cannot be allocated in a precise manner among MITE's product lines.

(3) The inventory figures shown are net of progress payments. The inventory figures for product lines do not include allocations of raw materials, material handling, reserves against inventory adjustment, unrecorded liabilities, and purchase price variance. The aggregate net amount of these unallocated items at the end of each period shown were ($162,000), $20,000, $288,000, and $246,000, respectively.

(4) The Amatom Electronic Hardware Division was acquired by MITE as at March 1, 19x8.

Thus, the credit grantor may be interested in knowing which segments of an enterprise provide funds and which are net users of funds.

The composition of an enterprise, the relative size and profitability of its various segments, the ability of management to make profitable acquisitions, and the overall performance of management represents additional important information which the analyst seeks from its segmented data. As will be seen from the discussion in Chapter 20, among the best ways to construct an earnings forecast is to build the projections, to the extent possible, segment by segment.

Disclosure of "line of business" data

The degree of informative disclosure about the results of operations and the asset base of segments of a business can vary widely. Full disclosure would call for providing detailed income statements, statements of financial position, and statements of changes in financial position for each significant segment. This is rarely found in practice because of the difficulty of obtaining such breakdowns internally, and also because of management's reluctance to divulge information which could harm the enterprise's competitive position. Short of the disclosure of complete financial statements by business segment, a great variety of partial detail has been suggested.

Income statement data

Revenues only. In most enterprises this should not present great difficulties.

Gross profit. This involves complex problems of interdivisional transfer pricing as well as allocation of indirect overhead costs.

Contribution margin. Contribution margin reporting (see also Chapter 19) is based on assigning to each segment the revenues, costs, and expenses for which that segment is solely responsible. It is a very useful concept in management accounting, but for purposes of public reporting of segment data it presents problems because there are no generally accepted methods of cost allocation and, consequently, they can vary significantly from company to company and even within one enterprise. Disclosure of allocation methods, while helpful, will not remove all the problems facing the user of such data.

Net income (after full cost allocation). The further down the income statement we report by segment, the more pervasive and the more complex the allocation procedures become. Reporting segment net income would require allocating all joint expenses to each specific business activity on some rational basis, even though they may not be directly related to any particular one.

Balance sheet data

A breakdown by segments of assets employed would be needed in an assessment of the efficiency of operations by segment, in the evaluation of segmental management, as well as in the computation of divisional return on investment.

In most companies only certain assets, such as, for example, plant and equipment, inventories, and certain intangibles, are identified directly with a specific segment. An allocation of all assets would have to be arbitrary since in many enterprises cash, temporary investments, and even receivables are centralized at the group or corporate headquarters level.

Ratios, trend indices, and other measures of activity

Disclosure of ratios such as gross profit ratios, or return on investment, or percentage of income or assets to total income or assets would leave open to even more serious question the methods by which these measurements have been arrived at. Thus, such information can be only of very limited use to the serious user of financial statements.

Recommendations by the APB

In recognition of the importance of segmented information to users of financial statements, the APB issued in 1967 a Statement entitled "Disclosure of Supplemental Financial Information by Diversified Companies." This Statement is not a formal Opinion but is significant in that it encourages companies to disclose voluntarily supplemental financial information as to industry segments of a business. The Statement also indicated that the APB would issue a formal Opinion on the subject after examining the results of studies then in progress and after conducting any further research it deemed necessary.

Recommendations of research studies

Interest in the subject of reporting by diversified companies has sparked research efforts into the types of disclosures which are necessary and feasible and the problems related thereto.[4] The most extensive re-

---

[4] See Morton Backer and Walter B. McFarland, *External Reporting for Segments of a Business* (New York: National Association of Accountants, 1968). Also see Robert T. Sprouse, "Diversified Views about Diversified Companies," *Journal of Accounting Research*, Vol. 7, No. 1 (Spring 1969), pp. 137–59; and A. Rappaport and E. H. Lerner, *A Framework for Financial Reporting by Diversified Companies* (New York: National Association of Accountants, 1969).

search effort was that undertaken by Professor R. K. Mautz[5] and whose recommendations were, briefly, as follows:

1. Diversified companies with certain characteristics should report sales and the relative contribution to profits of each major broad industry group.
2. Management, working within recommended guidelines, should determine the information and group breakdowns which would be meaningful to investors.
3. Companies which are unitary in nature, that is, which operate almost completely within a single broadly defined industry, or which are highly integrated, should not be expected to fractionalize themselves for reporting purposes.
4. Companies which to a material degree (15 percent or more of a company's gross revenues) are active in more than one broadly defined industry should meet the extended disclosure requirements.
5. Disclosures may be included in parts of the annual report other than the formal financial statements and should carry a clear indication of the limitation of their usefulness.

SEC reporting requirements

In 1969 the SEC announced amendments to three of its registration forms: Forms S-1 and S-7 under the 1933 Act, and Form 10 under the 1934 Act. The amendments related to sections which require a brief description of the business done and intended to be done by the registrant and its subsidiaries. The effect of the amendment was to include a requirement for comprehensive lines of business information to be disclosed by registrants who, with their subsidiaries, are engaged in more than one line of business.

In 1970 the Commission revised its annual report form (Form 10-K) to include a requirement of annual reporting of line of business information identical with the requirements in the three registration statements referred to above.

The new provisions are intended to elicit information with respect to those lines of business that contributed, during either of the last two fiscal years, a certain proportion of (1) the total of sales and revenues, or (2) income before income taxes and extraordinary items and without deduction of loss resulting from operations of any line of business. For companies with total sales and revenues of more than $50 million, the proportion is 10 percent; for smaller companies, 15 percent. Similar disclosure is also required with respect to any line of business

---

[5] *Financial Reporting by Diversified Companies* (New York: Financial Executives Research Foundation, 1968).

which resulted in a loss of 10 percent or more (15 percent or more for smaller companies) of income before income taxes, extraordinary items, and loss operations. The period to be covered by the information is each of a maximum of the last five fiscal years subsequent to December 31, 1966.

The requirements are spelled out as follows:

If it is impracticable to state the contribution to income (or loss) before income taxes and extraordinary items for any line of business, state the contribution thereof to the results of operations most closely approaching such income, together with a brief explanation of the reasons why it is not practicable to state the contribution to such income or loss.

Instructions. 1. If the number of lines of business for which information is required exceeds ten, the registrant may, at its option, furnish the required information only for the ten lines of business deemed most important to an understanding of the business. In such event, a statement to that effect shall be set forth.

2. In grouping products or services as lines of business, appropriate consideration shall be given to all relevant factors, including rates of profitability of operations, degrees of risk and opportunity for growth. The basis for grouping such products or services and any material changes between periods in such groupings shall be briefly described.

3. Where material amounts of products or services are transferred from one line of business to another, the receiving and transferring lines may be considered a single line of business for the purpose of reporting the operating results thereof.

4. If the method of pricing intra-company transfers of products or services or the method of allocation of common or corporate costs materially affects the reported contribution to income of a line of business, such methods and any material changes between periods in such methods and the effect thereof shall be described briefly.

5. Information regarding sales or revenues or income (or loss) from different classes of products or services in operations regulated by Federal, State or municipal authorities may be limited to those classes of products or services required by any uniform system of accounts prescribed by such authorities.

It should be noted that the information as to lines of business does not presently have to be attested to be independent public accountants.

Implications for analysis

The increasing complexity of diversified business entities and the loss of identity which acquired companies suffer in the published financial statements of conglomerates have created serious problems for the financial analyst.

As the foregoing discussion indicated, increasing attention has been given to the problems of reporting segmented financial data, and the SEC reporting requirements are a first step in the direction of enforcing the disclosure of a minimum amount of information. And minimal it is, because, it is hardly sufficient to enable the analyst to achieve such analytical objectives as the building of reasonable earnings forecasts on a segment by segment basis. Moreover, since the SEC requirements do not include disclosure of assets committed by segment, no assessment of relative return on investment or of funds requirements by segment is possible on the basis of the data required to be furnished.

Yet, even if the analyst wants to use such data as is provided for purposes of assessing the relative profitability of segments, their exposure to risk or the opportunities for growth which they afford, he must be very careful in his assessment of the reliability of the data on which he bases his conclusions.

The more specific and detailed the information provided is the more likely it is to be based on extensive allocations of costs and expenses. Allocation of common costs, as practiced for internal accounting purposes, are often based on such concepts as "equity," "reasonableness," and "acceptability to managers." These concepts have often little relevance to the objectives of financial analysis.

Bases of allocating joint expenses are largely arbitrary and subject to differences of opinions as to their validity and precision. Some specific types of joint expenses which fall into this category are general and administrative expenses of central headquarters, research and development costs, certain selling costs, advertising, interest, pension costs, and federal and state income taxes.

There are, at present, no generally accepted principles of cost and expense allocation or any general agreement on the methods by which the costs of one segment should be transferred to another segment in the same enterprise. Moreover, the process of formulating such principles or of reaching such agreement has not even begun. The analyst who uses segmented data must bear these limitations firmly in mind.

Stability and trend of revenues

The relative trend of sales of various product lines or revenues from services can best be measured by means of trend percentages as illustrated in Table 18–1.

TABLE 18–1
Trend percentage of sales by product line
(19x1 = 100)

	19x1	19x2	19x3	19x4	19x5
Product A	100	110	114	107	121
Product B	100	120	135	160	174
Product C	100	98	94	86	74
Service A	100	101	92	98	105

Sales indices of various products lines can be correlated and compared to composite industry figures or to product sales trends of specific competitors.

Important considerations bearing on the quality and stability of the sales and revenues trend include:

1. The sensitivity of demand for the various products to general business conditions.
2. The ability of the enterprise to anticipate trends in demand by the introduction of new products and services as a means of furthering sales growth and as replacement of products for which demand is falling.
3. Degree of customer concentration, dependence on major customers, as well as demand stability of major customer groups.
4. Degree of product concentration and dependence on a single industry.
5. Degree of dependence on relatively few star salesmen.
6. Degree of geographical diversification of markets.

Methods of revenue determination and measurement

Chapter 8 contains a discussion of the variety of methods of revenue recognition and measurement which coexist in various industries. Some of these methods are more conservative than others. The analyst must be familiar with the income recognition methods used by the enterprise he is analyzing as well as the methods used by companies with which the enterprise's results of operations are being compared.

QUESTIONS

1. What are the major objectives of income analysis?
2. Why can "net income" not be a single specific quantity?
3. What are some of the most important pitfalls and obstacles which lie in the way of the determination of "relevant income"?
4. Name some elements which affect the "quality of earnings."
5. Why is a forecast of income so significantly vulnerable to change?
6. To what limitations is the earnings figure of any one year subject? What type of earnings figure represents an improvement over that of a single period?
7. What is income smoothing? How can it be distinguished from outright falsehoods?
8. Name three forms of income smoothing.
9. Two levels can be identified in the analysis of the income statement. Name them.

18. Analysis of results of operations—I

10. Why is knowledge of major sources of revenue (sales) of an enterprise important in the analysis of the income statement?
11. Why are information and detailed data about the segments of diversified enterprises important to financial analysts?
12. Disclosure of various types of information by "line of business" has been proposed. Comment on the value of such information and the feasibility of providing it in published financial statements.
13. Which important considerations have a bearing on the quality and the stability of a sales and revenue trend?

19

Analysis of results of operations—II

THIS CHAPTER continues and concludes the discussion of the analysis of results of operations begun in the preceding chapter.

ANALYSIS OF COST OF SALES

In most enterprises[1] the cost of goods or services sold is, as a percentage of sales, the single most significant cost category. As the discussion in Chapter 8 shows, the methods of determining cost of sales encompass a wide variety of alternatives. Moreover, there is, particularly in unregulated industries, no agreed-to uniform cost classification method which would result in a clear and generally accepted distinction among such basic cost and expense categories as cost of sales, administrative, general, sales, and financial expenses. This is particularly true in the classification of general and administrative expenses. Thus, in undertaking cost comparisons the analyst must be ever alert to methods of classification and the effect they can have on the validity of comparisons within an enterprise or among enterprises.

GROSS PROFIT

The excess of sales over the cost of sales is the gross profit or gross margin. It is commonly expressed as a percentage:

---
[1] Exceptions can be found, for example, in some land sales companies where selling and other costs may actually exceed the cost of land sold.

Sales	$10,000,000	100%
Cost of sales	7,200,000	72
Gross profit	$ 2,800,000	28%

The gross profit percentage is a very important operating ratio. In the above example the gross profit is $2,800,000 or 28 percent of sales. From this amount all other costs and expenses must be recovered and any net income that is earned is the balance remaining after all expenses. Unless an enterprise has an adequate gross profit, it can be neither profitable nor does it have an adequate margin with which to finance such essential future-directed discretionary expenditures as research and development and advertising. Gross profit margins vary from industry to industry depending on such factors as competition, capital investment, the level of costs other than direct costs of sales which must be covered by the gross profit, etc.

Factors in the analysis of gross profit

In the analysis of gross profit the analyst will pay particular attention to—

1. The factors which account for the variation in sales and costs of sales.
2. The relationship between sales and costs of sales and management's ability to control this relationship.

ANALYSIS OF CHANGES IN GROSS MARGIN[2]

A detailed analysis of changes in gross margin can usually be performed only by an internal analyst because it requires access to data such as the number of physical units sold, unit sales prices, as well as unit costs. Such data are usually not provided in published financial statements. Moreover, unless the enterprise sells a single product, this analysis requires detailed data by product line. The external analyst, unless he has special influence on the company analyzed, will usually not have access to the data required for the analysis of gross margin.

Despite the above limitations to which gross margin analysis is subject, it is instructive to examine its process so that the elements accounting for variations in gross margin can be more fully understood.

---

[2] In this discussion the terms "gross profit" and "gross margin" are used interchangeably. Some writers reserve the term "gross margin" for situations where the cost of goods sold excludes overhead costs, that is, direct costing. This is not the intention here.

EXAMPLE OF ANALYSIS OF CHANGE IN GROSS MARGIN

Company A shows the following data for two years:

		Unit of measure	Year ended December 31, 19x1	Year ended December 31, 19x2	Increase	Decrease
1.	Net sales	Thousands of dollars	657.6	687.5	29.9	
2.	Cost of sales	Thousands of dollars	237.3	245.3	8.0	
3.	Gross margin	Thousands of dollars	420.3	442.2	21.9	
4.	Units of product sold	Thousands	215.6	231.5	15.9	
5.	Selling price per unit (1 ÷ 4)	Dollars	3.05	2.97		.08
6.	Cost per unit (2 ÷ 4)	Dollars	1.10	1.06		.04

Based on the above data, Exhibit 19–1 presents an analysis of the change in gross margin of $21,900 from 19x1 to 19x2. This analysis is based on the principle of focusing on one element of change at a time. Thus, in Exhibit –1 the analysis of variation in sales involves the following steps:

Step 1: We focus on the year-to-year change in volume while *assuming* that the unit selling price remained unchanged at the former, 19x1, level. Since both the volume change (15.9) and the unit selling price ($3.05) are positive, the resulting product ($48.5) is positive.

Step 2: We focus now on the change in selling price which represents a year to year decrease (—$.08) and *assume* the volume (215.6) to be unchanged from the prior year level so as to single out the change due to price change. Algebraically here the multiplication of a negative (price change) by a positive (volume) results in a negative product (—$17.2).

Step 3: We must now recognize that the *assumptions* used in steps 1 and 2 above, that is, that the volume remained unchanged while the unit price changed and vice versa, are temporary expedients used to single out major causes for change. To complete the computation we must recognize that by making these assumptions we left out the *combined* change in volume and unit price. The change in volume of 15.9 represents an *increase* and, consequently, is *positive*. The unit selling price change represents a *decrease* (—$.08) and hence is *negative*. As a result the product is negative (—$1.3).

EXHIBIT 19-1
COMPANY A
Statement Accounting for Variation in Gross Margin between Years 19x1 and 19x2

Thousands of dollars

I. *Analysis of variation in sales*
  (1) Variation due to change in volume of products sold
     Change in volume (15.9) × 19x1 unit selling price (3.05)................................ $48.5
  (2) Variation due to change in selling price
     Change in selling price (−$.08) × 19x1 sales volume (215.6) .... −17.2
                                                                $31.3
  (3) Variation due to combined change in sales volume (15.9) and unit sales price (−$.08)................. − 1.3
  Increase in net sales $30.0*

II. *Analysis of variation in cost of sales*
  (1) Variation due to change in volume of products sold:
     Change in volume (15.9) × 19x1 cost per unit ($1.10) $17.5
  (2) Variation due to change in cost per unit sold: change in cost per unit (−$.04) × 19x1 sales volume (215.6) .... − 8.6
                                                                $ 8.9
  (3) Variation due to combined change in volume (15.9) and cost per unit (−$.04)................... − .6
  Increase in cost of sales .... $ 8.3*
       Net variation in gross margin $21.7*

*Differences are due to rounding.

Step 4: Adding up the—

Variation due to volume change $48.5
Variation due to price change..................... −17.2
Combined change of volume and unit price .... − 1.3
We account for the causes behind the sales increase $30.0

The analysis of variation in the cost of sales follows the same principles.

Interpretation of changes in gross margin

The analysis of variation in gross margin is useful in identifying major causes of change in the gross margin. These changes can consist of one or a combination of the following factors:

1. Increase in sales volume.
2. Decrease in sales volume.

3. Increase in unit sales price.
4. Decrease in unit sales price.
5. Increase in cost per unit.
6. Decrease in cost per unit.

The presence of the "combined change of volume and unit sales price" and the "combined volume and unit cost" in the analysis presents no problem in interpretation since their amount is always minor in relation to the main causative factors of change.

The interpretation of the results of the analysis of gross margin involves the identification of the major factors responsible for change in the gross margin and an evaluation of the reasons for change in the factors. Such an analysis can also focus on the most feasible areas of improvement (i.e., volume, price, or cost) and the likelihood of realizing such improvements. For example, if it is determined that the major reason for a decline in gross margin is a decline in unit sales prices and that it reflects a situation of overcapacity in the enterprise's industry with attendant price cutting, then the situation is a serious one because of the limited control management has on such a development. If, on the other hand, the deterioration in the gross margin is found to be due to increases in unit costs, then this may be a situation over which management can exercise a larger measure of control and, given its ability to do so, an improvement is a more likely possibility.

BREAK-EVEN ANALYSIS

The second level of cost analysis is importantly concerned with the relationship between sales and the cost of sales but goes beyond that segment of the income statement. This level encompasses break-even analysis and is concerned with the relationship of sales to most costs, including, but not limited to, the cost of sales.

Concepts underlying break-even analysis

The basic principle underlying break-even analysis is the behavior of costs. Some costs vary directly with sales while others remain essentially constant over a considerable range of sales. The first category of costs is classified as *variable* while the latter are known as *fixed* costs.

The distinction among costs according to their behavior can be best understood within the framework of an example. In order to focus first on the basic data involved and on the technique of break-even analysis, we shall examine it by means of a simple illustration:

An enterprising graduate student saw an opportunity to sell slide rules at a financial analysts convention due to take place in his hometown. Upon inquiry he learned that he would have to get a vendor's license from the convention organizing committee at a cost of $10 and that the rental of a room in which to sell will amount to $140. The cost of slide rules was to be 30 cents each with the right to return any that were not sold. The student decided that 80 cents was the proper sales price per slide rule and wondered whether the undertaking will be worthwhile. As a first step he decided to compute the number of slide rules he will have to sell in order to break even.

Equation approach

We start from the elementary proposition that

Sales = Variable cost + Fixed costs + Profit (or − Loss)

Since at break even there is neither gain nor loss the equation is

Sales = Variable cost + Fixed costs

If we designate the number of slide rules which must be sold to break even as X, we have

$$.80X = .30X + 150$$

where

Sales = Unit sales price (.80) × X
Variable costs = Variable cost per unit (.30) × X
Fixed costs = License fee ($10) + Rental ($140)

These costs are fixed because they will be incurred regardless of the number of slide rules sold.

Solving the equation we get

$$.50X = 150$$
$$X = 300 \text{ units or slide rules}$$
to be sold to break even

In this example the number of slide rules to be sold is important information because the student needs to assess the likelihood of obtaining the size of demand which will make his venture profitable. This approach is, however, limited to a single product enterprise.

If, as is common in business, an enterprise sells a mix of goods, the unit sales break-even computation becomes impracticable and the focus is on dollar sales. This would be the situation if our student sold in addition to slide rules, stationery and books.

This more prevalent break-even computation can be illustrated with the data already given.

If we designate the dollar sales at break even as Y, we get:

$$Y = \text{Variable cost percentage } Y + \text{Fixed costs}$$
$$= .375Y + 150$$
$$.625Y = 150$$
$$Y = \$240 \text{ (sales at break even)}$$

In this computation the variable cost percentage is the ratio of variable costs (.30) to sales price (.80). This means that each dollar of sales entails an incurrence of $.375 for variable costs or 37.5 percent of the sales price.

Graphic presentation

Exhibit 19–2 portrays the results attained above in graphic form. A graph drawn to scale will yield a solution approximating in accuracy that obtained by the formula method. Moreover it portrays under one set of assumptions not only the break-even point but also a whole range

EXHIBIT 19–2
Slide rule illustration—break-even chart

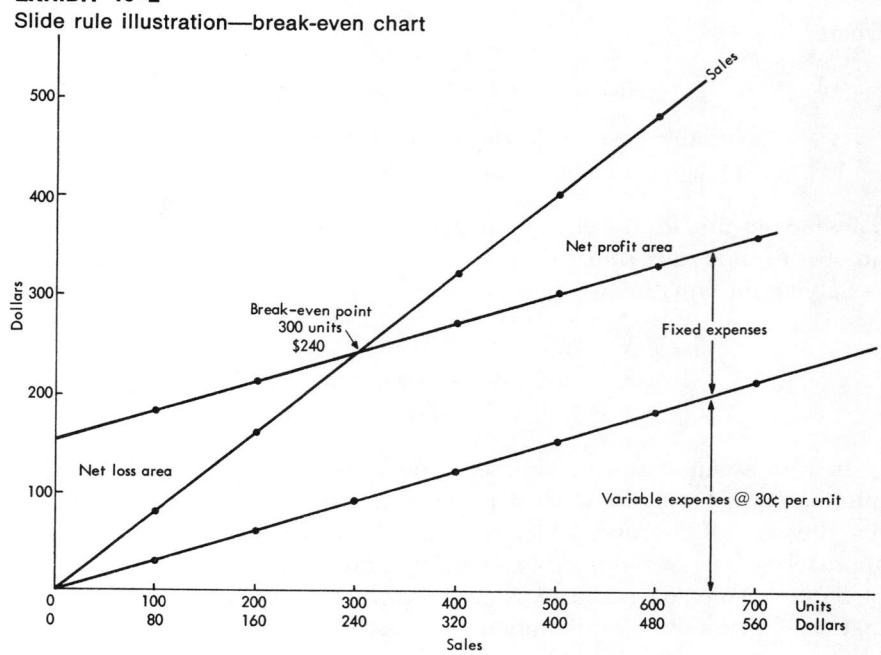

of profitable operations above that point as well as the losses below it.

Steps in preparation

1. In Exhibit 19-2 the horizontal scale shows the slide rule sales in both units and dollars. The vertical scale presents costs in dollars only. Variable costs are drawn as a linear function, that is, the costs increase in direct proportion with sales. This is shown in Exhibit 19-3.

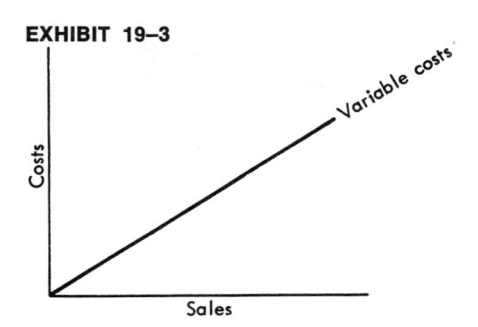

EXHIBIT 19-3

2. Fixed costs have a different behavior pattern. Over a given range of sales they do not change. Graphically we portray this as in either Exhibit 19-4 or 19-5.

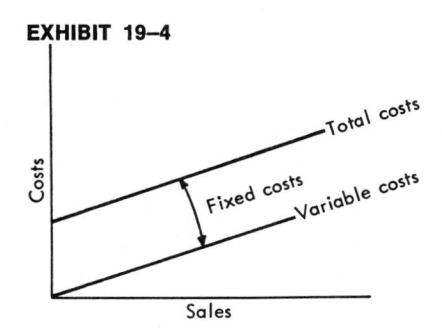

EXHIBIT 19-4

This straight line relationship of fixed costs is not, however, ever-present. It prevails only over a given level of sales which we in this context can refer to as the "relevant range of sales."

Referring to our slide rule example, there is a maximum number of slide rules which can be sold over a given period of time in one room. Should the demand exceed that number, another room would have to be added. That in turn may necessitate another salesman. That

EXHIBIT 19–5

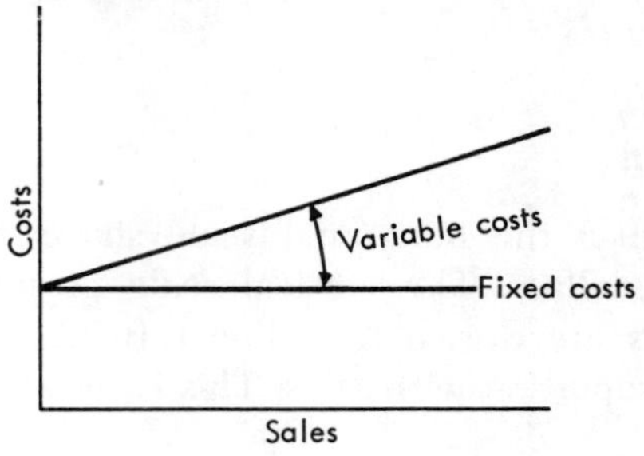
Costs
Variable costs
Fixed costs
Sales

will result in a substantial "step-up" in fixed costs because an increase of 10 percent over the maximum selling capacity of one room cannot be met by renting $\frac{1}{10}$ of another room. These incremental steps in fixed costs are graphically portrayed in Exhibit 19–6.

EXHIBIT 19–6

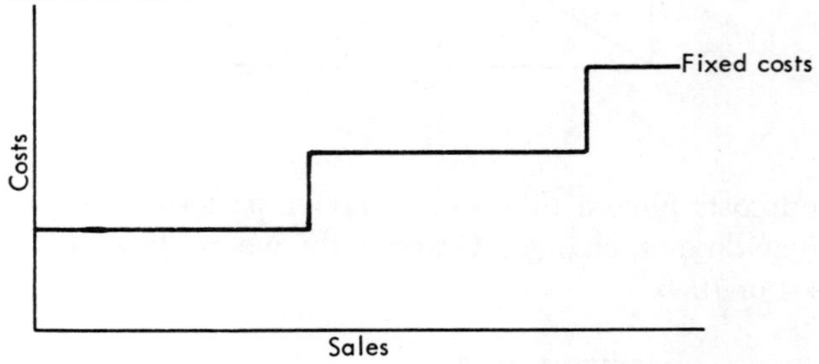
Fixed costs
Costs
Sales

3. The plotting of sales on the break-even chart is relatively simple. It represents a linear function plotted at a 45° angle as shown in Exhibit 19–7. The 45° angle for the sales line obtains whenever the X and the Y axes use the same scale.

EXHIBIT 19–7

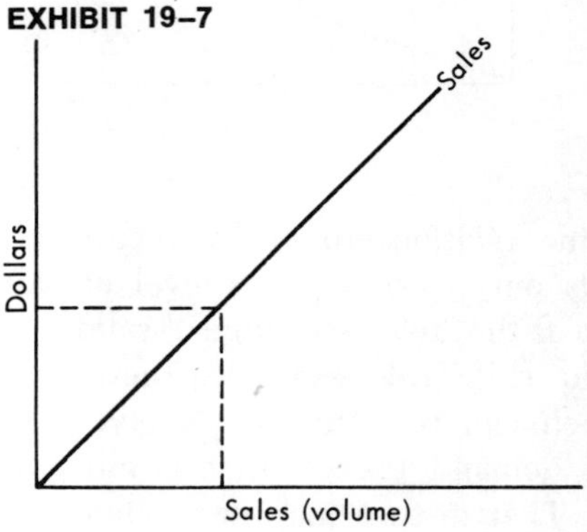
Sales
Dollars
Sales (volume)

This means that from any point on the sales line a point on the sales (volume) axis is equidistant to a corresponding point on the cost axis.

4. The superimposition of variable cost, fixed costs, and sales lines in one graph results in the break-even chart, and the point of intersection of the "sales line" and the "total cost line" represents the break-even point as illustrated in Exhibit 19–2.

Contribution margin approach

Another technique of break-even analysis which can produce additional insights into the relationship of sales, costs, and profits is the contribution margin approach. It will be illustrated here by means of the foregoing slide rule example.

The contribution margin is what is left of the net sales price after deduction of the variable costs. It is from this margin that fixed costs must first be met and after that a profit earned.

Sales price per slide rule	$.80
Variable costs per slide rule	.30
Unit contribution margin	$.50

Since each unit (slide rule) sold contributes $.50 to overhead and for profit, the break-even point in units is

$$\frac{\text{Fixed costs}}{\text{Unit contribution margin}} = \frac{\$150}{\$.50} = 300 \text{ units}$$

Thus, after 300 units are sold the fixed costs are covered and each additional unit sale yields a profit equal to the unit contribution margin, that is, $.50.

If, as is more usual, the break-even point is to be expressed in dollars of sales, the formula involves use of the contribution margin ratio rather than the unit contribution margin. The contribution margin ratio is a percentage relationship computed as follows:

$$\frac{\text{Unit contribution margin}}{\text{Unit sales price}} = \frac{.50}{.80} = .625 \text{ or } 62.5 \text{ percent}$$

The slide rule problem dollar break-even point can now be calculated as follows:

$$\frac{\text{Fixed costs}}{\text{Contribution margin ratio}} = \frac{150}{.625} = \$240$$

488   Understanding corporate reports

The contribution margin is an important tool in break-even analysis, and its significance will be the subject of further discussion later in this section.

Slide rule problem—additional considerations

The break-even technique illustrated above lends itself to a variety of assumptions and requirements. The following are additional illustrations, all using the original data of our examples, unless changed assumptions are introduced:

Case 1: Assume that our student decided that in order to make the venture worthwhile he requires a net profit of $400. How many slide rules must be sold to achieve this objective?

$$\text{Sales} = (\text{Variable cost \%})(\text{sales}) + \text{Fixed costs} + \text{Profit}$$

$$S = .375S + \$150 + \$400$$
$$.625S = 550$$
$$S = \$880$$

$$\frac{880}{.80} = 1{,}100 \text{ units}$$

Case 2: Assume that the financial analysts convention committee offered to provide the student with a room free of charge if he agreed to imprint on the slide rules the Financial Analysts Society's seal. However, this would increase the cost of slide rules from 30 cents to 40 cents per unit. Under the original assumptions the break-even point was 300 slide rules. What should it be if the student accepts the committee's proposal?

Here we have a reduction of fixed costs by $140 and an increase in variable costs of 10 cents per unit.

If X be the number of slide rules sold at break-even point, then:

$$\text{Sales} = \text{Variable costs} + \text{Fixed costs}$$
$$.80X = .40X + \$10$$
$$.40X = 10$$
$$X = 25 \text{ slide rules}$$

This proposal obviously involves a much lower break-even point and hence reduced risk. However, the lower contribution margin will at higher sales levels reduce total profitability. We can determine at what level of unit sales the original assumption of a 30 cents per unit variable cost and $150 fixed cost will equal the results of the 40 cents per unit variable cost and $10 fixed costs.

Let X be the number of units (slide rules) sold, then:

$$.40X + \$10 = .30X + \$150$$
$$.10X = 140$$
$$X = 1{,}400 \text{ slide rules}$$

Thus, if more than 1,400 slide rules are sold, the alternative which includes the 30 cents variable cost will be more profitable.

Having examined the break-even analysis technique and some types of decisions for which it is useful, we will now turn to a discussion of the practical difficulties and the theoretical limitations to which this approach is subject.

Break-even technique—problem areas and limitations

The intelligent use of the break-even technique and the drawing of reasonably valid conclusions therefrom depends on a resolution of practical difficulties and on an understanding of the limitations to which the techniques are subject.

Fixed, variable, and semivariable costs. In the foregoing simple examples of break-even analysis, costs were clearly either fixed or variable. In the more complex reality found in practice, many costs are not so clearly separable into fixed and variable categories. That is, they do not either stay constant over a considerable change in sales volume or respond in exact proportion to changes in sales.

We can illustrate this problem by reference to the costs of a food supermarket. As was discussed above, some costs will remain fixed within a certain range of sales. Rent, depreciation, certain forms of maintenance, utilities, and supervisory labor are examples of such fixed costs. The level of fixed costs can, of course, be increased by simple management decision unrelated to the level of sales, for example, the plant superintendent's salary may be increased.

Other costs, such as the cost of merchandise, trading stamps, supplies, and certain labor will vary closely with sales. These costs are truly variable. Certain other costs may, however, contain both fixed and variable elements in them. Examples of such "semivariable" costs are repairs, some materials, indirect labor, fuel, utilities, payroll taxes, and rents which contain a minimum payment provision and are also related to the level of sales. Break-even analysis requires that the variable component of such expenses be separated from the fixed component. This is often a difficult task for the management accountant and an almost impossible task for the outside analyst to perform without the availability of considerable internal data.

Simplifying assumptions in break-even analysis. The estimation of a variety of possible results by means of break-even calculations or charts requires the use of simplifying assumptions. In most cases these simplifying assumptions do not destroy the validity of the conclusions reached. Nevertheless, in reaching such conclusions the analyst must be fully aware of these assumptions and of their possible effect.

The following are some of the more important assumptions implicit in break-even computations:

1. The factors comprising the model, implicit in any given break-even situation, actually behave as assumed, that is,
   a) That the costs have been reasonably subdivided into their fixed and variable components;
   b) That variable costs fluctuate proportionally with volume;
   c) That fixed costs remain fixed over the range relevant to the situation examined; and
   d) That unit selling prices will remain unchanged over the range encompassed by the analysis.
2. In addition, there are certain operating and environmental assumptions which emphasize the static nature of any one break-even computation. It is assumed:
   a) That the mix of sales will remain unchanged,
   b) That efficiency of operations will remain constant,
   c) That prices of costs factors will not change,
   d) That the only factor affecting costs is volume,
   e) That beginning and end of period inventory levels will remain substantially unchanged, and
   f) That there is no substantial change in the general price level during the period.

The formidable array of assumptions enumerated above points out the susceptibility of break-even computations to significant error. Not all the assumptions are, however, equally important, or, if not justified, will have an equal impact on the validity of conclusions. For example, the assumption that the selling price will not change with volume is contrary to economic theory and often is contrary to reality. Thus, the sales line is a curved rather than a linear function. However, the degree of error will depend on the actual degree of deviation from a strict linear relationship. Another basic assumption is that volume is *the* major, if not the only, factor affecting costs. We know, however, that strikes, political developments, legislation, and competition, to name a few other important factors, have a decided influence on costs. The analyst must, consequently, keep these simplifying assumptions firmly in mind and be aware of the dynamic factors which may require modifications in his conclusions.

Break-even analysis—uses and their implications

The break-even approach can be a useful tool of analysis if its limitations are recognized and its applications are kept in proper perspective.

The emphasis on the break-even, that is, zero profit, point is an unfortunate distortion of the objective of this type of analysis. Instead, the break-even situation represents but one point in a flexible set of projections of revenues and of the costs which will be associated with them under a given set of future conditions.

The managerial applications of break-even analysis are many. It is useful, among others, in price determination, expense control, and in the projection of profits. Along with standard cost systems it gives management a basis for pricing decisions under differing levels of activity. In conjunction with flexible budgets it represents a powerful tool of expense control. The break-even chart is also a useful device with which to measure the impact of specific managerial decisions, such as plant expansion and new product introduction or of external influences, on the profitability of operations over various levels of activity.

To financial analysts the function of profit projections is one of vital importance. Moreover, the ability to estimate the impact on profitability of various economic conditions or managerial courses of action is also an extremely important one. Both of these are importantly aided by break-even analysis. The intelligent use of this technique and a thorough understanding of its operation are the factors which account for its importance to the external financial analyst.

Illustration of break-even technique application. Exhibit 19–8 presents the break-even chart of the Multi-Products Company as at a given point in time. It is subject to the various assumptions which were discussed above including that relating to the ability to separate costs into their fixed and variable components.

At break even a very condensed income statement of Multi-Products Company will be as follows:

Sales		$1,387,000
Costs:		
Variable	$887,000	
Fixed.	500,000	1,387,000
Net income		0

The variable cost percentage is 887/1387 or about 64 percent. The contribution margin ratio is 36 percent (100 − Variable cost percentage of 64). The variable cost percentage means that on average, out of every dollar of sales 64 cents go to meet variable costs, that is, costs which would not be incurred if the sale did not occur. The contribution margin ratio is basically the complement of the variable cost percentage.

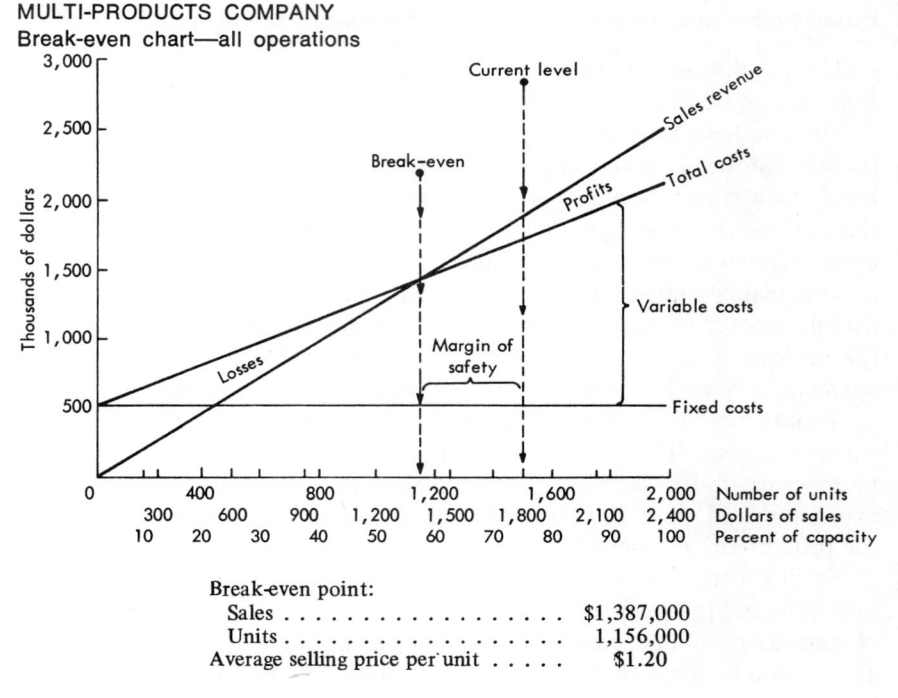

EXHIBIT 19-8
MULTI-PRODUCTS COMPANY
Break-even chart—all operations

[Break-even chart showing Sales revenue, Total costs, Variable costs, and Fixed costs lines. Chart displays Current level, Break-even point, Profits, Losses, and Margin of safety. X-axis shows Number of units (0 to 2,000), Dollars of sales (300 to 2,400), and Percent of capacity (10 to 100). Y-axis shows Thousands of dollars from 0 to 3,000.]

Break-even point:
Sales $1,387,000
Units 1,156,000
Average selling price per unit $1.20

It indicates that each dollar of sales generates a contribution of 36 cents towards meeting fixed expenses and the earning of a profit beyond the break-even point. The contribution margin earned on sales of $1,387,000 is just sufficient to cover the $500,000 in fixed costs. Quite obviously, the lower the fixed costs, the less sales it would take to cover them and the lower the resulting break-even point. In the most unlikely event that the Multi-Products Company would have no fixed costs, that is, all costs varied directly with sales, the company would have no break-even point, that is, it would start making a profit on the very first dollar of sales.

The break-even chart reflects the sale of a given mix of products. Since each product has different cost patterns and profit margins, any significant change in the product mix will result in a change in the break-even point and consequently in a change in the relationship between revenues, costs, and results. Although Exhibit 19-8 shows the number of units on the sales (volume) axis, this figure and the average selling price per unit are of limited significance because they represent averages prevailing as a result of a given mix of products.

The importance of a relatively stable sales mix to the successful application of break-even analysis suggests that this technique cannot be usefully employed in cases where the product mix varies greatly over the short term. Nor, for that matter, can break-even analysis be usefully applied in cases where there are sharp and frequent fluctuations in sales prices or in costs of production, such as raw materials.

Exhibit 19–8 indicates that given the existing mix of products, the present level of fixed costs of $500,000 can be expected to prevail up to a sales level of approximately $2,400,000. This is the point at which 100 percent of theoretical capacity will be reached. The break-even point is at 60 percent of capacity while the current level of sales is at about 75 percent of capacity. This means that when the 100 percent capacity level is reached, the fixed costs may have to undergo an upward revision. If Multi-Products is reluctant to expand its capacity and thus increase its fixed costs and break-even point, assuming that variable costs do not decrease, it may have to consider other alternatives such as:

1. Foregoing an increase in sales.
2. Increasing the number of shifts, which could increase variable costs significantly.
3. Subcontracting some of its work to outsiders, thus foregoing some of the profit of increased activity.

Exhibit 19–8 also presents to the analyst at a glance the company's present position relative to the break-even point. The current level of sales of $1,800,000 is about $413,000 above the break-even point. This is also known as the "safety margin," that is, the margin that separates the company from a no-profit condition. This concept can be expanded to indicate on the chart at what point the company will earn a desired return on investment, at what point the common dividend may be in jeopardy, and at what point the preferred dividend may no longer be covered by current earnings.

It is obvious that the data revealed by a reliably constructed break-even chart or by the application of break-even computations is valuable in profit projection, in the assessment of operating risk, as well as in an evaluation of profit levels under various assumptions regarding future conditions and managerial policies.

Analytical implications of break-even analysis

From the above discussion of a specific situation, such as that illustrated in Exhibit 19–8, we will now turn to a more general review of conclusions which can be derived from break-even analysis.

The concept of operating leverage. Leverage and fixed costs go together. As we have seen in Chapter 16, financial leverage is based on fixed costs of funds for a portion of the resources used by the enterprise. Thus, earnings above that fixed cost magnify the return on the residual funds and vice versa.

The fixed costs of a business enterprise, in the sense in which we have discussed them so far in this chapter, form the basis of the concept of operating leverage. Until an enterprise develops a volume of sales which is sufficient to cover its fixed costs, it will incur a loss. Once it has covered the fixed costs, further increments in volume will result in more than proportionate increases in profitability. The following will illustrate the nature of operating leverage:

Illustration of the working of operating leverage. In a given enterprise the cost structure is as follows:

$$\text{Fixed costs} = \$100,000$$
$$\text{Variable cost percentage} = 60 \text{ percent}$$

The following tabulation presents the profit or loss at successively higher levels of sales and a comparison of relative percentage changes in sales volume and in profitability:

Sales	Variable costs	Fixed costs	Profit (loss)	Percentage increase over preceding step Sales	Profit
$100,000	$ 60,000	$100,000	$(60,000)	...	...
200,000	120,000	100,000	(20,000)	100%	...
250,000	150,000	100,000	...	25	...
300,000	180,000	100,000	20,000	20	Infinite
360,000	216,000	100,000	44,000	20	120%
432,000	259,200	100,000	72,800	20	65%

The working of operating leverage is evident in the above tabulation. Starting at break even, the first 20 percent sales increase resulted in an infinite increase in profits because they started from a zero base. The next 20 percent increase in sales resulted in a 120 percent profit increase over the preceding level while the sales increase that followed resulted in a 65% profit increase over the preceding level. The effects of leverage diminish as the sales increase above the break-even level because the bases to which increases in profits are compared get progressively larger.

Leverage, of course, works both ways. It will be noted that a drop in sales from $200,000 to $100,000, representing 50 percent decrease, resulted in a tripling of the loss.

One important conclusion from this to the analyst is that enterprises operating near their break-even point will have relatively larger percentage changes of profits or losses for a given change in volume. On the upside the volatility will, of course, be desirable. On the downside, however, it can result in adverse results which are significantly worse than those indicated by changes in sales volume alone.

Another aspect is operating *potential,* sometimes erroneously referred to as leverage, which derives from a high level of sales accompanied by very low profit margins. The potential here, of course, is the room for improvements in profit margins. Even relatively slight improvements in profit margins, applied on a large sales level, can result in dramatic changes in profits. Thus, the popular reference to a semblance of leverage for what is really a potential for improvement.

Another aspect of the same *potential* occurs when the sales volume *per share* is large. Obviously an improvement in profitability will be translated into larger earnings per share improvements.

The significance of the variable cost percentage

The volatility of profits is also dependent on the variable cost percentage. The low variable cost enterprise will achieve higher profits for a given increment in volume once break-even operations are reached than will the high variable-cost enterprise.

ILLUSTRATION. Company A has fixed costs of $700,000 and a variable cost equal to 30 percent of sales. Company B has fixed costs of $300,000 and variable costs equal to 70 percent of the sales. Assume that both companies have now reached sales of $1,000,000 and are, consequently, at break even. A $100,000 increment in sales will result in a profit of $70,000 for Company A and only in a profit of $30,000 for Company B. Company A has not only greater operating leverage but can, as a result, afford to incur greater risks in going after the extra $100,000 in sales than can Company B.

From the above example it is evident that the *level* of the break-even point is not the only criterion of risk assessment but that the analyst must also pay attention to the variable cost ratio.

The significance of the fixed cost level

Given a certain variable cost percentage, the higher the fixed costs, the higher the break-even point of an enterprise. In the absence of change in other factors, a given percentage change in fixed costs will result in an equal percentage change in the break-even point. This can be illustrated as follows:

First break-even situation

Sales		$100,000
Variable expenses	$60,000	
Fixed costs	40,000	100,000
Profit		–0–

Second break-even situation—20% increase in fixed costs

Sales (increase of 20%)		120,000
Variable expenses (60%)	72,000	
Fixed cost (40,000 + 20%)	48,000	120,000
		-0-

Thus a fixed cost increase of 20 percent, with the variable cost ratio remaining unchanged, resulted in a 20 percent increase in the break-even point.

An increase in the break-even point of an enterprise generally increases operational risk. It means that the enterprise is dependent on a higher volume of sales in order to break even. Looked at another way, it means that the enterprise is more vulnerable to economic downturns as compared to its situation with a lower break-even point. The substantial acquisition of the large capacity Boeing 747 aircraft by the airlines provides an example of the effects of high break-even points. While these large aircraft lowered the variable cost per passenger, they relied also on a projected increase in the number of passengers. When this failed to materialize, the airlines' profit margins deteriorated swiftly with many of them going into the red. There are other repercussions to high levels of fixed costs. Thus, for example, a higher break-even point may mean that the enterprise has less freedom of action in fields such as labor relations. A high level of fixed costs makes strikes more expensive and subjects the enterprise to added pressure to submit to higher wage demands.

Often, added fixed costs in the form of automatic machinery are incurred in order to save variable costs, such as labor, and to improve efficiency. That can be very profitable in times of reasonably good demand. In times of low demand, however, the higher level of fixed costs sets in motion the process of reverse operational leverage discussed above, with attendant rapidly shrinking profits or even growing losses. High fixed costs reduce an enterprise's ability to protect its profits in the face of shrinking sales volume.

Investments in fixed assets, particularly in sophisticated machinery, can bring about increases in fixed costs far beyond the cost of maintaining and replacing the equipment. The skills required to operate such equipment are quite specialized and require skilled personnel which the enterprise may be reluctant to dismiss for fear of not being able to replace them when business turns up again. This converts what should be variable costs into de facto fixed costs.

While fixed costs are incurred in order to increase capacity or to decrease variable costs, it is often advisable to cut fixed costs in order to reduce the risks associated with a high break-even point. Thus, a company may reduce fixed costs by switching from a salaried sales force to one compensated by commissions based on sales. It can avoid added fixed costs by adding work shifts, buying ready-made parts, subcontracting work, or discontinuing the least profitable product lines.

In evaluating profit performance, past and future, of an enterprise, the analyst must always keep in mind the effect that the level of fixed costs can have on operating results under a variety of business conditions. Moreover, in projecting future results the analyst must bear in mind that any given level of fixed costs is valid only up to the limits of practical capacity within a range of product mixes. Beyond such a point a profit projection must take into consideration not only the increased levels of fixed costs required but also the financial resources which an expansion will require as well as the cost and sources of the funds which will be needed.

The importance of the contribution margin

The analyst must be alert to the absolute size of an enterprise's contribution margin because operating leverage is importantly dependent on it. He must, moreover, be aware of the factors which can change this margin, that is, changes in variable costs as well as changes in selling prices.

While we have focused on the individual factors which affect costs, revenues, and profitability, in practice changes result from a combination of factors. Projected increases in sales volume will increase profits only if costs, both fixed and variable, are controlled and kept within projected limits. Break-even analysis assumes that efficiency remains constant. However, experience teaches us that cost controls are more lax in times of prosperity than they are in times of recession. Thus, the analyst cannot assume constant efficiency any more than he can assume a constant product mix. The latter is also an important variable which must be watched by the analyst. Questions of why an enterprise realized lower profits on a higher volume of sales can often be explained, at least in part, by reference to changes in sales mix.

In spite of its important limitations, the break-even approach is an important tool of analysis to the financial analyst.

Its ability to aid the external analyst in performance evaluation and in profit projection makes its use worthwhile to him in spite of the laborious work which it often entails and the fragmentary and scarce amounts of information on which, of necessity, it must be based.

ADDITIONAL CONSIDERATIONS IN THE ANALYSIS OF COST OF SALES

Gross margin analysis focuses on changes in costs, prices, and volume. Break-even analysis, in turn, focuses on the behavior of costs in relation to sales volume and on management's ability to control costs in the face of rising and falling revenues. The effectiveness of these and other methods of cost analysis depends on the degree of data availability as well as on an understanding of the accounting principles which have been applied.

The ability of the analyst to make the rough approximations which are necessary to separate costs into fixed and variable components depends on the amount of detail available. Disclosure of major cost components such as materials, labor, and various overhead cost categories can be helpful. The more detailed the breakdowns of expense categories the more likely is the analyst to be able to construct meaningful break-even estimates.

In the evaluation of the cost of sales and the gross margin, and particularly in its comparison with those of other enterprises, the analyst must pay close attention to distortions which may arise from the utilization of a variety of accounting principles. While this is true of all items of cost, attention must be directed particularly to inventories and to depreciation accounting. These two areas, considered in detail in Chapters 4 and 8, merit special attention not only because they represent costs which are usually substantial in amount but also because of the proliferation of alternative principles which may be employed in accounting for them.

DEPRECIATION

Depreciation is an important cost element particularly in manufacturing and service enterprises. It is mostly fixed in nature because it is computed on the basis of elapsed time. However, if its computation is based on production activity the result is a variable cost.

Because depreciation is computed in most cases on the basis of time elapsed, the ratio of depreciation expense to income is not a particularly meaningful or instructive relationship. In the evaluation of depreciation expense the ratio of depreciation to gross plant and equipment is more meaningful. The ratio is computed as follows:

$$\frac{\text{Depreciation expense}}{\text{Assets subject to depreciation}}$$

This ratio can, of course, be computed by major categories of assets. The basic purpose is to enable the analyst to detect changes in the composite rate of depreciation used by an enterprise as a means of evaluating its adequacy and of detecting attempts at income smoothing.

AMORTIZATION OF SPECIAL TOOLS AND SIMILAR COSTS

The importance of the cost of special tools, dies, jigs, patterns, and molds costs varies from industry to industry. It is of considerable importance, for example, in the auto industry where special tool costs are associated with frequent style and design changes. The rate of amortization of such costs can have an important effect on reported income and is important to the analyst in an assessment of that income as well as in its comparison with that of other entities within an industry. The ratios that can be used to analyze charges in the deferral and amortization policies of such costs are varied and focus on their relationship to sales and other classes of assets.

The yearly expenditure for special tools can be related to and expressed as a percentage or (1) sales and (2) net property and equipment.

The yearly amortization of special tools can be related to (1) sales, (2) unamortized special tools, and (3) net property and equipment.

A comparison of the yearly trend in these relationships can be very helpful in an analysis of the consistency of income reporting of a single enterprise. The comparison can be extended further to an evaluation of the earnings of two or more enterprises within the same industry. This approach is indicative of the type of analysis which various elements of costs lend themselves to.

MAINTENANCE AND REPAIRS COSTS

Maintenance and repairs costs vary in significance with the amount invested in plant and equipment as well as with the level of productive activity. They have an effect on the cost of goods sold as well as on other elements of cost. Since maintenance and repairs contain elements of both fixed and variable costs, they cannot vary directly with sales. Thus, the ratio of repairs and maintenance costs to sales, while instructive to compare from year to year or among enterprises, must be interpreted with care. To the extent that the analyst can determine the fixed and the variable portions of maintenance and repairs costs, his interpretation of their relationship to periodic sales will be more valid.

Repairs and maintenance are, to a significant extent, discretionary costs. That is, the level of expense can, within limits, be regulated by management for a variety of reasons including those aimed at the improvement of reported income or to the preservation of liquid resources. Certain types of repairs cannot, of course, be postponed without resulting breakdowns in productive equipment. But many types of preventive repairs and particularly maintenance can be postponed or skimped on with results whose effects lie mainly in the future. Thus, the level of repair and maintenance costs both in relation to sales and to plant and equipment is of interest to the analyst. It has, of course, a bearing on the quality of income, a subject which we shall consider in the next chapter.

The level of repair and maintenance costs is also important in the evaluation of depreciation expense. Useful lives of assets are estimated by the use of many assumptions including those relating to the upkeep and maintenance of the assets. If, for instance, there is a deterioration in the usual or assumed level of repairs and maintenance, the useful life of the asset will, in all probability, be shortened. That may, in turn, require an upward revision in the depreciation expense or else income will be overstated.

OTHER COSTS AND EXPENSES—GENERAL

Most, although not all, cost and expense items found in the income statement have some identifiable or measurable relationship to sales. This is so because sales are the major measure of activity in an enterprise except in instances when production and sales are significantly out of phase.

Two analytical tools whose usefulness is based, in part, on the relationship that exists between sales and most costs and expenses should be noted here:

1. The *common-size income statement* expresses each cost and expense item in terms of its percentage relationship to net sales. This relationship of costs and expenses to sales can then be traced over a number of periods or compared with the experience of other enterprises in the same industry. Exhibit 2-2 of Chapter 2 illustrates a common-size income statement covering a number of years.

2. The *index number analysis of the income statement* expresses each item in the income statement in terms of an index number related to a base year. In this manner relative changes of income statement items over time can be traced and their significance assessed. Expense item changes can thus be compared to changes in sales and to changes in related expense items. Moreover, by use of common-size balance sheets, percentage changes in income statement items can be related to changes in assets and liabilities. For example, a given change in sales would normally justify a commensurate change in inventories and in accounts receivable. Exhibit 2–8 in Chapter 2 illustrates an index number analysis of a condensed income statement.

Selling expenses

The analysis of selling costs has two main objectives:

1. The evaluation over time of the relationship between sales and the costs needed to bring them about.
2. An evaluation of the trend and the productivity of future-directed selling costs.

The importance of selling costs in relation to sales varies from industry to industry and from enterprise to enterprise. In some enterprises selling costs take the form of commissions and are, consequently, highly variable in nature, while in others they contain important elements of fixed costs.

After allowing for the fixed and variable components of the selling expenses, the best way to analyze them is to relate them to sales. The more detailed the breakdown of the selling expense components is the more meaningful and penetrating can such analysis be. Exhibit 19-9 presents an example of such an analysis.

EXHIBIT 19-9

TRYON CORPORATION
Comparative Statement of Selling Expenses
(dollar amounts in thousands)

	19x3 $	19x3 %	19x2 $	19x2 %	19x1 $	19x1 %	19x0 $	19x0 %
Sales	1,269		935		833		791	
Trend percentage		160		118		105		100
Selling expenses (% are of sales):								
Advertising	84	6.6	34	3.6	28	3.4	24	3.0
District branch expenses*	80	6.3	41	4.4	38	4.6	32	4.1
Delivery expense (own trucks)	20	1.6	15	1.6	19	2.3	22	2.8
Freight-out	21	1.7	9	1.0	11	1.3	8	1.0
Salesmen's salary expense	111	8.7	76	8.1	68	8.1	61	7.7
Salesmen's travel expense	35	2.8	20	2.1	18	2.2	26	3.3
Miscellaneous selling expense	9	.7	9	1.0	8	.9	7	.9
Total	360	28.4	204	21.8	190	22.8	180	22.8

*Includes rent, regional advertising, etc.

Analysis of Exhibit 19-9 indicates that for the entire period selling costs have been rising faster than sales and that in 19x3 they took 5.6 percent more of the sales dollar than they did in 19x0. In this period salesmen's salaries increased by 1.0 percent of sales, advertising by 3.6 percent of sales, and branch expenses by 2.2 percent of sales. The drop in delivery expense may possibly be accounted for by the offsetting increase in freight costs.

A careful analysis should be made of advertising costs in order to determine to what extent the increase is due to the promotion of new products or the development of new territories which will benefit the future.

When selling expenses as a percentage of sales show an increase, it is instructive to focus on the selling expense increase which accompanies a given increase in sales. It can be expected that beyond a certain level greater sales resistance is encountered in effecting additional sales. That sales resistance or the development of more remote territories may involve additional cost. Thus, it is important to know what the percentage of selling expense to sales is or to new sales as opposed to old ones. This may have, of course, implications on the projection of future profitability. If an enterprise can make additional sales only by spending increasing amounts of selling expenses, its profitability may suffer. Offsetting factors, such as those related to break-even operations or to economies of scale must also be considered.

Future directed marketing costs

Certain categories of sales promotion costs, particularly advertising, result in benefits which extend beyond the period in which they were incurred. The measurement of such benefits is difficult if not impossible, but it is a reasonable assumption that there is a relationship between the level of expenditures for advertising and promotion and the sales level, present and future.

Since expenditures for advertising and other forms of promotion are discretionary in nature, the analyst must carefully follow the year to year trend in these expenditures. Not only does the level of such expenditures have a bearing on future sales estimates, but it also indicates whether management is attempting to "manage" reported earnings. The effect of discretionary costs on the "quality" of earnings reported will be the subject of further discussion in the chapter that follows.

GENERAL, ADMINISTRATION, FINANCIAL, AND OTHER EXPENSES

Most costs in this category tend to be fixed in nature. This is largely true of administrative costs because such costs include significant amounts of salaries and occupancy expenditures. However, there may be some "creep" or tendency for increases in this category, and this is particularly true in prosperous times. Thus, in analyzing this category of expense the analyst should pay attention to both the trend of administrative costs as well as to the percentage of total sales which they consume.

Financial costs

Financial costs are, except for interest on short-term indebtedness, fixed in nature. Moreover, unless replaced by equity capital, most borrowed funds are usually refinanced. This is because of the long-term nature of most interest-bearing obligations. Included in these costs are the amortization of bond premium and discount as well as of debt issue expenses. A good check on an enterprise's cost of borrowed money as well as credit standing is the calculation of the average effective interest rate paid. This rate is computed as follows:

$$\frac{\text{Total interest cost}}{\text{Total indebtedness subject to interest}}$$

The average effective interest rate paid can be compared over the years or compared to that of other enterprises. It is also significant in that it sheds light on the credit standing of the enterprise.

"Other" expenses

"Other" expenses are, of course, a nondescript category. The total amount in this category should normally be rather immaterial in relation to other costs. Otherwise, it can obscure substantial costs which, if revealed, may provide significant information about the enterprise's current and future operations. Nonrecurring elements may also be included in the "other expense" category, and this may add to the significance of this category to the analyst.

The analyst must also be alert to the tendency to offset "other" expenses against "other" income. Here too the major problem is one of concealment of important information and data. Here it is important that details of the major items comprising the offset amount be given.

OTHER INCOME

Miscellaneous income items which are small in amount are usually of no significance to the analyst. However, since "other income" may include returns from various investments, it may contain information about new ventures and data regarding investments which is not available elsewhere. Such investments may, of course, have future implications, positive or negative, which exceed in significance the amounts of current income which are involved.

INCOME TAXES

Income taxes represent basically a sharing of profits between an enterprise and the governmental authority by which they are imposed. Since most enterprises with which this text is concerned are organized in corporate form, we shall focus primarily on corporate income taxes.

Income taxes are almost always significant in amount and normally can take about half of a corporation's income before taxes. For this reason the analyst must pay careful attention to the impact which income taxes have on net income.

Except for the rate on the first $25,000 of income, which is lower, corporate income is normally taxed at the rate of about 50 percent. Differences in the timing of recognition of income or expense items as between taxable income and book income should not influence the effective tax rate because of the practice of interperiod income tax allocation which aims to match the tax expense with the book income regardless of when the tax is paid. Income tax allocation was discussed in Chapter 9.

The relationship between the tax accrual and the pretax income, otherwise known as the effective tax rate or tax ratio, will, however, be influenced by permanent tax differences. These are differences which arise from provisions in the tax law which:

1. Do not tax certain revenues (e.g., interest on municipal obligations and proceeds from life insurance).
2. Do not allow certain expenses as deductions in arriving at taxable income (e.g., goodwill amortization, fines, premiums on officers' life insurance).
3. Tax certain income at reduced rates (e.g., dividend income, capital gains).
4. Allow certain costs beyond the amount taken for book purposes (e.g., excess of statutory depletion over book depletion).

The effective tax rate or tax ratio is computed as follows:

$$\frac{\text{Income tax expense for period}}{\text{Income before income taxes}}$$

This ratio may also deviate from the normal or expected rate because of the following additional reasons:

1. The basis of carrying property for accounting purposes may differ from that for tax purposes as a result of reorganizations, business combinations, etc.
2. Nonqualified as well as qualified stock-option plans may result in book-tax differences.
3. Certain industries, such as savings and loan associations, shipping lines, and insurance companies enjoy special tax privileges.
4. Tax-loss carryforwards, while benefiting current income because of past losses, are now shown as extraordinary items, unless previously recognized because they were thought to be assured "beyond measurable doubt."

The important thing is that both for income evaluation as well as for net income projection the analyst must know the reasons why the tax ratio deviates from the normal or the expected. Income taxes are such an important element of cost that even relatively small changes in the effective tax rate can explain important changes in net income. Moreover, without an understanding of the factors which cause changes in the effective tax rate of a company, the analyst is missing an important ingredient necessary in the forecasting of future net income. Thus, it is unfortunate that APB *Opinion No. 11* merely recommends, rather than requires, that "the nature of significant differences between pretax income and taxable income be disclosed." However, the SEC has moved to require an explanation of why an entity's tax differs from the normal incidence of tax to which it can be expected to be subject.

In spite of the importance of an understanding of the factors which influence income taxes, to the analysis of the income statement there are instances when the explanations of reasons for changes in the ratio of taxes to pretax income contained in the financial statements are either lacking altogether or are so vague as to be meaningless. This has led some analysts to concentrate on an analysis of pretax income. While this approach avoids the tax analysis problem it omits from the analysis an important element entering into the determination of net income.

On the other hand, certain companies which have important tax-book differences disclose in detail the makeup of their taxable income. An example of such a presentation is shown in Exhibit 19–10.

Information such as given in Exhibit 19–10 is useful in the analysis of the income tax accrual but may have to be supplemented by additional data on changes resulting from permanent tax differences.

The reason why some analysts are particularly interested in the way income is reported for tax purposes, as is, for example, shown in Exhibit 19–10 is that they use it as a check on the validity of reported income. That the income declared for tax purposes in a given period is a more valid or accurate portrayal of results than that arrived at under generally accepted accounting principles is highly doubtful. At any rate it is a superficial way of searching for the adjusted income figure the analyst is after. Most of the time the income for tax purposes is more conservatively arrived at than that for book purposes. For example, sales may be recognized on the installment basis rather than on an accrual basis. Similarly, conservatism is achieved when a more accelerated method of depreciation is used for tax than for book purposes, or if research and development costs which should be deferred are expensed instead. All this leads to understated income rather than to a more accurate or valid income determination. Thus, in seeking a "safe" or conservative income in the enterprise's tax return, the analyst may actually deceive himself. While the tax return may provide a check on income reporting, it cannot take the place of the income statement, prepared in accordance with generally accepted accounting principles, and properly adjusted by the analyst. The purpose of tax accounting is to facilitate the rising of revenues in accordance with the fiscal and economic objectives of

EXHIBIT 19-10
Summary of amounts shown on various income tax returns

	19x5	19x6	19x7	19x8	19x9
Income:					
Realized profit on installment sales	$ 46,313	$ 173,385	$ 153,830	$ 86,345	$ 310,795
Sales of homes and homesites	3,833,158	2,363,048	3,083,877	3,733,864	3,976,660
Service fees and participation		17,175	137,477	169,297	164,972
Interest income and other	31,697	92,083	186,282	710,565	576,475
Total income	$3,911,168	$2,645,691	$3,561,466	$4,700,071	$5,028,902
Costs and expenses:					
Cost of sales	$3,425,484	$2,102,977	$2,609,420	$2,947,386	$3,090,198
Selling, general, and administrative expenses	236,096	263,806	413,271	518,281	727,468
Interest	117,955	73,803	321,146	480,890	360,888
Total costs and expenses	$3,779,535	$2,440,586	$3,343,837	$3,946,557	$4,178,454
Taxable income	$ 131,633	$ 205,105	$ 217,629	$ 753,514	$ 850,448
Taxes on income	48,666	84,525	58,746	243,326	383,891
Net income, tax basis	$ 82,967	$ 120,580	$ 158,883	$ 510,188	$ 466,557
Per share	$ .30	$ .12	$ .16	$ .51	$ .47

the government. The purpose of a statement of income prepared in accordance with generally accepted accounting principles is to present fairly the results of operations of an entity. The fact that there are many obstacles in the full achievement of the latter objective requires caution on the part of the analyst rather than a flight to the tax return. All things considered, the income statement is in general still a better starting point from which to adjust income than is the tax return.

While the focus on net income and on earnings per share requires a thorough analysis of changes in the effective tax rate, it must be borne in mind that many, if not most, analysts attach relatively greater importance to pretax earnings. This is due to the greater importance which is assigned to pretax operating results, which require management skills of a high order, as compared with changes due to variations in the effective tax rate over which, it is assumed, management has comparatively limited control.

THE OPERATING RATIO

The operating ratio is yet another intermediate measure in the analysis of the income statement. It measures the relationship between all operating costs and net sales and is computed as follows:

$$\frac{\text{Cost of goods sold} + \text{Other Operating expenses}}{\text{Net sales}}$$

The ratio is designed to enable a comparison within an enterprise or with enterprises of the proportion of the sales dollar absorbed by all operating costs. Only other income and expense items as well as income taxes are excluded from the computation of this ratio.

In effect this ratio represents but an intermediate step in the common-size analysis of the income statement. It is, in and of itself, not of great analytical significance because it is a composite of many factors which require separate analysis. These factors comprise the analysis of gross margin and of other major expense categories discussed earlier. Thus, the operating ratio cannot be properly interpreted without a thorough analysis of the reasons accounting for variations in gross margin and for changes in selling, general, administrative, and other costs.

NET INCOME RATIO

The net income ratio is the relationship between net income and total revenues and is computed as follows:

$$\frac{\text{Net income}}{\text{Total revenues}}$$

It represents the percentage of total revenue brought down to net income. In addition to its usefulness as an index of profitability, the net profit ratio represents, as was seen in Chapter 17, a main component of the computation of the return on investment.

Statement accounting for variation in net income

In the analysis of year-to-year changes in net income it is useful to separate the elements which contributed to an increase in net income from those which contributed to a decrease. A statement which does that and which also indicates the percentage increase or decrease in these factors is the "statement accounting for the variations in net income."

Exhibit 19–11 presents comparative statements of income of the Alliance Company. Based on the data in these income statements, Ex-

EXHIBIT 19–11

ALLIANCE COMPANY
Income Statements
For Years Ended March 31, 19x1, 19x2
(amounts in thousands)

	19x1	19x2	Dollar increase (decrease) 19x2	Percentage increase (decrease) 19x2
Net sales	$94,313	$102,888	$8,575	9%
Cost of sales	71,516	77,922	6,406	9
Gross profit	$22,797	$ 24,966	$2,169	10
Selling, general, and administrative and other expenses:				
Selling expenses	$ 3,300	$ 4,298	$ 998	30
General and administrative expenses	2,610	3,191	581	22
Financing expenses	4,627	4,916	289	6
Total Operating Expenses	$10,537	$ 12,405	$1,868	18
Operating profit	$12,260	$ 12,561	$ 301	2
Other income and expenses (Net)	1,447	1,752	305	21
Profit before taxes on income	$13,707	$ 14,313	$ 606	4.
Taxes on income	4,500	4,604	104	2
Net income	$ 9,207	$ 9,709	$ 502	5

hibit 19–12 presents a "statement accounting for variations in net income." This statement is simple to prepare and allows the analyst to single out for further analysis those elements of income and expense which had the greatest impact on the change in net income from one period to another.

EXHIBIT 19-12

ALLIANCE COMPANY
Statement Accounting for Variation in Net Income
For the Year Ended December 31, 19x2
(amounts in thousands)

			Percentage increase
Items tending to increase net income:			
Increase in gross margin on sales:			
Increase in net sales:			
Net sales, 19x2	102,888		
Net sales, 19x1	94,313	8,575	9
Deduct: Increase in cost of goods sold:			
Cost of goods sold, 19x2	77,922		
Cost of goods sold, 19x1	71,516	6,406	9
Net increase in gross margin:			
Gross margin, 19x2	24,966		
Gross margin, 19x1	22,797	2,169	10
Increase in other revenue and expense (net)			
Net 19x2	1,752		
Net 19x1	1,447	305	21
Total of items tending to increase net income		2,474	
Items tending to decrease net income:			
Increase in selling expenses:			
Selling expenses, 19x2	4,298		
Selling expenses, 19x1	3,300	998	30
Increase in general and administrative expenses:			
General and administrative expenses, 19x2	3,191		
General and administrative expenses, 19x1	2,610	581	22
Increase in financing expenses:			
Financing expenses, 19x2	4,916		
Financing expenses, 19x1	4,627	289	6
Increase in estimated federal income taxes:			
Estimated federal income taxes, 19x2	4,604		
Estimated federal income taxes, 19x1	4,500	104	2
Total of items tending to decrease net income		1,972	
Net increase in net income:			
Net income, 19x2	9,709		
Net income, 19x1	9,207	502	5

QUESTIONS

1. What are the most important elements in the analysis of gross profit?
2. What is the basic principle underlying break-even analysis? What are fixed costs? Variable costs? Semivariable costs?
3. Certain assumptions which underlie break-even computations are often

referred to as simplifying assumptions. Name as many of these as you can.
4. In break-even computation what is the "variable cost percentage"? What is its relationship to "contribution margin ratio"?
5. What alternatives to an increase in fixed costs can an enterprise consider when it approaches 100 percent of theoretical capacity?
6. What is operating leverage? Why do leverage and fixed costs go together? What are the analytical implications of operating leverage?
7. Of what analytical significance are (*a*) the break-even point and (*b*) the variable cost ratio?
8. What is a useful measure of the adequacy of current provisions for depreciation?
9. To what factors can maintenance and repair costs be meaningfully related?
10. What are the main objectives of an analysis of selling expenses?
11. List some of the reasons why the effective tax rate of one enterprise may vary from that of another enterprise?

20

The evaluation and projection of earnings

OBJECTIVES OF EARNINGS EVALUATION

IN THE preceding chapters we have examined the steps which have to be taken and the understanding which must be brought to bear on the analysis of the operating performance of an enterprise. This chapter will examine the additional considerations involved in the achievement of two major and closely interrelated objectives of income statement analysis:

1. The evaluation of the earnings level and its quality.
2. The projection of future earnings.

Evaluation of earnings level

The discussions through Part II of this work have pointed out that much of the accounting process of income determination involves a high degree of estimation. Chapters 8 and 9 on the analysis of the income statement have explained that the income of an enterprise, as measured by the accounting process, is not a specific amount but can vary depending on the assumptions used and the various principles applied. Complicating these measurements still further is the fact that numerous accounting periods can receive benefits from a single cash outlay and that it may take a number of periods before a transaction results in the collection of all amounts due. For that reason, creditors, in particular, are greatly interested in the cash equivalent of reported earnings.

This distinction between income and the related cash flows has led some of those uninitiated in the income determination process to doubt the validity of all accounting measurements. This, however, is an extreme and unwarranted position because, as any student of accounting should know, the concept of income is the result of a series of complex assumptions and conventions, and exists only as the creation and the approximation of this system of measurements. This system is always subject to reexamination and is, despite its shortcomings, still the most widely accepted method of income determination.

In examining the level of reported income of an enterprise, the analyst must determine the effect of the various assumptions and accounting principles used on that reported income. In addition the analyst tries to assess the quality of the earnings so as to render them comparable and in order to determine the valuation which should be placed on these earnings. The quality of earnings depends, among other factors, on:

1. The degree of conservatism with which the estimates of present and future conditions are arrived at. That is, the degree of risk that estimates or assumptions may prove overoptimistic or downright unwarranted and misleading.
2. The degree to which adequate provision has been made for the maintenance of assets and for the maintenance and enhancement of present and future earning power. This requires the analysis of discretionary and future directed costs.
3. The stability and the growth trend of earnings as well as the predictability of factors which may influence their future levels. This requires, among other steps, the identification and analysis of nonrecurring and extraordinary elements in the income statement.

The evaluation of the earnings level and of the earnings trend is intimately tied in with the evaluation of management. The evaluation of the management group cannot be separated from the results which they have actually achieved. Whatever other factors may have to be considered, results over a period of time are the acid test of management's ability, and that ability is perhaps the most important intangible (i.e., unquantifiable) factor in the prediction of future results. The analyst must be alert to changes in the management group and must assess its depth, stability, and possible dependence on the talents of one or a few individuals.

The evaluation of the growth potential of earnings requires that as much information as possible be obtained about the different product lines or segments which make up the aggregate earnings. Rappaport and Lerner[1] have illustrated the use of a segmented earnings contribution matrix which may prove useful in an assessment of earnings quality and growth potential, as well as in the valuation of aggregate earnings. These are shown in Tables 20–1 and 20–2.

TABLE 20–1
Earnings contribution and growth rates by industry segments

Industry	Earnings contributions (in $000)	Growth rate of earnings contribution over the past 3 years (in %)
Leisure time:		
1. Camp equipment	100	11
2. Fishing equipment	50	2
3. Boats	72	15
4. Sporting goods	12	3
	234	
Agribusiness:		
1. Milk processing	85	2
2. Canning	72	8
3. Chicken farming	12	15
	169	
Education:		
1. Text publishing	40	3
2. Papers and supplies	17	6
	57	
Total	460	

TABLE 20–2
Segmented earnings contribution matrix

	Growth rate (in %)			
Industry	0–5	5–10	10–15	Total
Leisure time	$ 62	$ 0	$172	$234
Agribusiness	85	72	12	169
Education	40	17	0	57
Total	$187	$89	$184	$460

The projection of earnings

The second major objective of income analysis is the projection of income. The evaluation of the level of earnings is, from an analytical point of view, closely related to their projection. This is so because

---

[1] A. Rappaport and E. M. Lerner, *A Framework for Financial Reporting by Diversified Companies* (New York: National Association of Accountants, 1969), pp. 18–19.

a valid projection of earnings involves an analysis of each major component of income and a considered estimate of its probable future size. Thus, some of the factors discussed in the preceding section are also applicable to earnings projection.

Projection must be differentiated from extrapolation. The latter is based on an assumption of the continuation of an existing trend and involves, more or less, a mechanical extension of that trend into the uncharted territory of the future.

Projection, on the other hand, is based on a careful analysis of as many individual components of income and expense as is possible and a considered estimate of their future size taking into consideration interrelationships among the components as well as probable future conditions. Thus, forecasting requires as much detail as is possible to obtain. In addition the "stability" of the individual components must be assessed in terms of the likelihood of their future recurrence. This lends particular importance to the analysis of nonrecurring factors and of extraordinary items.

Projection requires the use of an earnings record covering a number of periods. Repeated or recurring performance can be projected with a better degree of confidence than can random events.

Projection also requires use of enterprise data by product line or segment wherever different segments of an enterprise are subject to different degrees of risk, possess different degrees of profitability, or have differing growth potentials.

For example, the following tabulation of divisional earnings results indicates the degree to which the results of a component of an enterprise can be masked by the aggregate results:

	Earnings in million dollars			
	19x1	19x2	19x3	19x4
Segment A	1,800	1,300	900	400
Segment B	100	200	400	800
Total net income	1,900	1,500	1,300	1,200

Judgment on the earnings potential of the enterprise depends, of course, importantly on the relative importance of, as well as the future prospects of, segment B. The subject of product line reporting is discussed in Chapter 18.

Let us now consider in further detail some of the important factors which enter into the evaluation of the earnings level of an enterprise and the projection of its earnings. The mechanics of earnings forecasting were considered in Chapter 15 as part of the process of projecting short-term fund flows.

EVALUATION OF DISCRETIONARY AND FUTURE-DIRECTED COSTS

Discretionary costs are outlays which managements can vary to some extent from period to period in order to conserve resources and/or to influence reported income. For this reason they deserve the special attention of analysts who are particularly interested in knowing whether the level of expenses is in keeping with past trends and with present and future requirements.

Two important categories of discretionary costs are repairs and maintenance and advertising.

Maintenance and repairs

As was already discussed in the preceding chapter, management has considerable leeway in performing maintenance work and some discretion with respect to repairs. The analyst can relate these costs to the level of activity because they do logically vary with it. Two ratios are particularly useful in comparing the repair and maintenance levels from year to year:

$$\frac{\text{Repairs and maintenance}}{\text{Sales}}$$

This ratio relates the costs of repairs and maintenance to this most available measure of activity. In the absence of sharp inventory changes, sales are a good indicator of activity. If year-to-year inventory levels change appreciably, an adjustment may be needed whereby ending inventories at approximate selling prices are added to sales and beginning inventories, similarly adjusted, are deducted from them.

The other ratio is:

$$\frac{\text{Repairs and maintenance}}{\text{Property, plant, and equipment (exclusive of land) and net of accumulated depreciation}}$$

It measures repair and maintenance costs in relation to the assets for which these costs are incurred. Depending on the amount of information available to the analyst, the ratio of repair and maintenance costs to specific categories of assets can be developed. It should be noted that substandard repairs and maintenance on assets may require revisions in the assumptions of useful lives for depreciation purposes.

The absolute trend in repair and maintenance costs from year to year can be expressed in terms of index numbers and compared to those of related accounts. The basic purpose of all these measurements is to determine whether the repair and maintenance programs of the enterprise have been kept at normal and necessary levels or whether they have been changed in a way that affects the quality of income and its projection into the future.

Advertising

Since a significant portion of advertising outlays has effects beyond the period in which it is incurred, the relationship between advertising outlays and short-term results is a tenuous one. This also means that managements can, in certain cases, cut advertising costs with no commensurate immediate effects on sales, although it can be assumed that over the longer term sales will suffer. Here again, year-to-year variations in the level of advertising expenses must be examined by the analyst with the objective of assessing their impact on the quality of reported earnings as well as their impact on future sales.

There are a number of ways of assessing the trend in advertising outlays. One is to convert them into trend percentages using a "normal" year as a base. These trend percentages can then be compared to the trend of sales and of gross and net profits. An alternative measure would be the ratio of

$$\frac{\text{Advertising expenses}}{\text{Sales}}$$

which, when compared over the years, would also indicate shifts in management policy. The ratio of

$$\frac{\text{Advertising}}{\text{Total selling costs}}$$

must also be examined so as to detect shifts to and from advertising to other methods of sales promotion.

Research and development costs

The significance and the potential value of research and development costs are among the most difficult elements of the financial statements to analyze and interpret. Yet they are important, not only because of their relative size, but even more so because of their significance for the projection of future results.

Research and development costs have gained in aura of glowing potential in security analysis far beyond that warranted by actual experience. Mentioned most frequently are some of the undeniably spectacular and successful commercial applications of industrial research in the post-World War II era in such fields as chemistry, electronics, and photography. Not mentioned are the vast sums spent for endeavors labeled "research" which are expensed or written off while benefits from these fall far short of the original costs.

The analyst must pay careful attention to research and development costs and to the absence of such costs. In many enterprises they represent substantial costs, much of them fixed in nature, and they can represent the key to future success or failure. We must first make a careful distinction between what can be quantified in this area and, consequently, analyzed in the sense in which we consider analysis in this work, and what cannot be quantified and must consequently be evaluated in qualitative terms.

In the area of research and development costs the qualitative element looms large and important. The definition of what constitutes "research" is subject to wide-ranging interpretations as well as to outright distortion. The label "research" is placed on activities ranging from those of a first-class scientific organization engaged in sophisticated pure and applied research down to superficial and routine product and market testing activities.

Among the many factors to be considered in the evaluation of the quality of the research effort are the caliber of the research staff and organization, the eminence of its leadership, as well as the commercial results of their research efforts. This qualitative evaluation must accompany any other kinds of analysis. Finally, a distinction must be drawn between government or outsider sponsored research and company directed research which is most closely identified with its own objectives. From the foregoing discussion it is clear that research cannot be evaluated on the basis of the amounts spent alone. Research outlays represent an expense or an investment depending on how they are applied. Far from guaranteeing results, they represent highly speculative ventures which depend on the application of extraordinary scientific as well as managerial skills for their success. Thus, spending on research cannot guarantee results and should not be equated with them.

Having considered the all-important qualitative factors on which an evaluation of research and development outlays depends, the analyst should obtain at least an estimate or approximate answer to two important questions related to the accounting for such costs:

1. Approximately how much of the current research and development outlays which have been expensed have future utility and potential?
2. How much of the research and development costs which have been deferred or capitalized should have been expensed because they have no future value or a future value subject to significant doubt?

The "future potential" of research and development costs is, from the point of view of the analyst, a most important consideration. Research cost productivity can be measured by relating research and development outlays to:

1. Sales Growth
2. New product introductions
3. Acquisition of plant and equipment (to exploit the results of research)
4. Profitability

It must be recognized, however, that often the analyst will not have the adequate information which is necessary for him to check on the judgment of management and their independent accountants in their treatment of research and development outlays.

Another important aspect of research and development outlays is their discretionary nature. It is true that those enterprises which have established research and development departments impart a fixed nature to a segment of these costs. Nevertheless they can be increased or curtailed at the discretion of managements, often with no immediate adverse effects on sales. Thus, from the point of view of assessing the quality of reported income, the analyst must evaluate year-to-year changes in research and development outlays. This he can do by means of trend percentage analysis as well as by years of analysis of ratios such as the ratio of

$$\frac{\text{Research and development outlays}}{\text{Sales}}$$

Research and development *outlays* must be differentiated from research and development *costs*. The former represent funds expended for research and development activities during a period regardless of whether they were expensed or deferred. It is usually possible to convert research and development costs into outlays by adjusting the cost figure for the net changes, from one period to the next, in the Deferred Research and Development account. For example:

Research and development costs, 19x1	$150,000
Deferred research and development, 12/31/x0	620,000
Deferred research and development, 12/31/x1	760,000

Outlays for research and development during 19x1:

Research and development costs	$150,000
Add: Net increase in the deferred research and development account	140,000
Total outlays for 19x1	$290,000

A careful comparison of outlays for research and development over the years will indicate to the analyst whether the effort is a sustained one or one which varies with the ups and downs of operating results.

Other future-directed costs

In addition to advertising and research and development, there are other types of future-directed outlays. An example of such outlays are the costs of training operating, sales, and managerial talent. Although these outlays for the development of human resources are usually expensed in the year in which they are incurred, they may have future utility, and the analyst may want to recognize this in his evaluation of current earnings and of future prospects.

EXTRAORDINARY GAINS AND LOSSES

Both the evaluation of current earnings levels and the projection of future earnings rely importantly on the separation of the stable elements of income and expense from those which are random, nonrecurring, and erratic in nature.

Stability and regularity are important characteristics affecting the quality of earnings. Moreover, in making earnings projections the forecaster relies, in addition, on repetitiveness of occurrence. Thus, in order to separate the relatively stable elements of income and expense of an enterprise from those which are random or erratic in nature, it is important, as a first step, to identify those gains and losses which are nonrecurring and unusual as well as those which are truly extraordinary.

This separation is a first step which is mostly preparatory in nature. Following it is a process of judgment and analysis which aims at determining how such nonrecurring, unusual, or truly extraordinary items should be treated in the evaluation of present income, and of management performance as well as in the projection of future results.

Significance of accounting treatment and presentation

The validity of any accounting treatment and presentation is largely dependent on its usefulness to those who make decisions on the basis of financial statements. Unfortunately, particularly in the area of the accounting for, and the presentation of, extraordinary gains and losses, the usefulness of this accounting has been impaired because of the great importance attached to it by those who report the results of operations and who are judged by them.

The accounting for, and the presentation of, extraordinary gains and losses has always been subject to controversy. Whatever the merits of the theoretical debate surrounding this issue, the fact remains that one of the basic reasons for the controversial nature of this topic is reporting management's great interest in it. Managements are almost always concerned with the amount of net results of the enterprise as well as with the manner in which these periodic results are reported. This concern is reinforced by a widespread belief that most investors and traders accept the reported net income figures, as well as the modifying explanations which accompany them, as true indices of performance. Thus, extraordinary gains and losses often become the means by which managements attempt to modify the reported operating results and the means by which they try to explain these results. Quite often these explanations are subjective and are slanted in a way designed to achieve the impact and impression desired by management.

The accounting profession has tacitly, if not openly, recognized the role which the foregoing considerations play in the actual practice of reporting extraordinary gains and losses. Its latest pronouncements on this subject, which has been discussed in Chapter 9, have at least insured a fuller measure of disclosure of extraordinary gains and losses and their inclusion in the income statement. This represents an improvement over prior pronouncements which, in an attempt to arrive at a "true" index of operating performance, sanctioned the exclusion of certain extraordinary gains and losses from the income statement.

In present *practice,* however, the definition of what is "extraordinary" or "unusual" has undergone constant expansion and liberalization. Thus, often extraordinary gains and losses are presented in ways designed to convey to the reader the particular impressions and message desired by managements. Although no generalizations are possible, or necessary for our purpose, it can be stated that all too often the message which is conveyed to the reader by means of the presentation and/or description of extraordinary items is:

1. That certain losses are of such an unusual and nonrecurring nature that they can be omitted from a consideration of enterprise results and from the projection of future results. (Newspapers and even financial services have been alarmingly prone to convey such impressions.)
2. That certain losses occurred due to causes beyond the control of management and consequently they should not be considered in an evaluation of management's performance record.

Whenever such an impression is conveyed, the analyst must guard against being influenced by it in his own evaluation of enterprise results. He must, instead, use his own analysis and evaluation in arriving at a judgment of whether such conclusions are warranted. Because, as we have seen, the accounting treatment and presentation of extraordinary items and that of other nonrecurring gains and losses is not always governed by, or directly responsive to, the needs of analysts and other decision makers, it is not a reliable guide to their analysis and evaluaticn. All the analyst can and should expect to find in the income statement is full disclosure with respect to all unusual, nonrecurring, and extraordinary items so that he may use them in his own analysis and evaluation of that statement.

Analysis and evaluation

The basic objectives in the identification and evaluation of extraordinary items by the analyst are:

1. To determine whether a particular item is to be considered "extraordinary" for purposes of analysis, that is, whether it is so unusual, nonoperating, and nonrecurring in nature that it requires special adjustment in the evaluation of current earnings levels and of future earning possibilities.
2. To decide what form the adjustment for items which are considered as "extraordinary" in nature should take.

Determining whether an item of gain or loss is extraordinary. The infirmities and shortcomings of present practice as well as the considerations which motivate it lead to the inescapable conclusion that the analyst must arrive at his own evaluation of whether a gain or loss should be considered as extraordinary and, if so, how to adjust for it.

In arriving at this decision it is useful to subdivide items, commonly classified as unusual or extraordinary, into three basic categories:

a. Nonrecurring operating gains or losses. By "operating" we usually identify items connected with the normal and usual operations of the business. The concept of normal operations is more widely used than understood and is far from clear and well defined. Thus, in a company operating a machine shop, operating expenses would be considered as those associated with the work of the machine shop. The proceeds from a sale above cost of marketable securities held by the company as an investment of excess cash would be considered a nonoperating gain. So would the gain (or loss) on the sale of a lathe, even if it were disposed of in order to make room for one that would increase the productivity of the shop.

The concept of recurrence is one of frequency. There are no predetermined generally accepted boundaries dividing the recurring event from the nonrecurring. An event (which in this context embraces a gain or loss) occurring once a year can be definitely classified as "recurring." An event, the occurrence of which is unpredictable and which in the past has either not occurred or occurred very infrequently, may be classified as nonrecurring. On the other hand, an event that occurs infrequently but whose occurrence is predictable raises some question as to its designation. An example of the latter would be the relining of blast furnaces. They last for many years; while their replacement is infrequent, the need for it is predictable. Some companies provide for their replacement by means of a reserve. Casualties do not, however, accrue in similar fashion.

Nonrecurring operating gains or losses are, then, gains or losses connected with or related to operations that recur infrequently and/or unpredictably. Examples follow:

1. Foreign operations give rise to exchange adjustments because of currency fluctuations or devaluations.
2. An unusually severe decline in market prices requires a large writedown of inventory from cost to market.
3. Strikes or other conditions limiting the supply of a commodity result in the realization of profits from the liquidation of low-cost Lifo inventories.
4. A move of a plant from one location to another results in substantial moving, rearrangement, and start-up expenses.
5. A decision to liquidate an unprofitable product line results in abandonment, liquidation, and closing expenses as well as the liquidation of inventories at substantial losses.
6. Research and development costs that have been capitalized in the past must be written off as nonproductive of the anticipated revenues. They become operating charges of a nonrecurring nature, presumably because conditions in the current period proved their lack of value.
7. Extraordinary production and subcontracting costs are incurred because of a strike (either at the company's plant or at that of a supplier).
8. Failure of a major customer results in a substantial bad-debt provision.
9. Plant, equipment, or other operating assets are sold at a gain or a loss.

Often, the nature of the business and the frequency of occurrence of events determine the classification of an item in practice. Thus, gains and losses on the sale of rental cars are considered operating and recurring in a car-rental company, even though the cars are revenue-earning equipment. However, the sale at a gain or loss of a machine tool, which is also revenue earning, may sometimes be classified as extraordinary. The frequency of disposal of aircraft should result in gains or losses being considered as "ordinary" in the airline industry. However, some airlines consider them as "extraordinary."

The degree of recurrence or "repetitiveness" of certain items of income or expense can vary greatly from one type of business to another as well as from one kind of item to another. The lack of annual recurrence does not necessarily mean that an item is unusual, because there is no law requiring events to fall neatly into the short fiscal periods for which business chooses to account. In the world of business there is a random distribution of events that must be recognized. Thus, depending on the type of business and other factors, a degree of variability and abnormality must be expected. In fact, this is the essence of business risk.

In considering how to treat nonrecurring, operating gains and losses, the analyst would do best to recognize the fact of inherent abnormality and the lack of a recurring annual pattern in business and treat them as belonging to the results of the period in which they are reported.

We must also address ourselves to the question of what should be considered as "normal operations." Thus, it is a bakery's purpose to bake bread, rolls, and cakes, but it is presumably outside its normal purpose to buy and sell marketable securities for gain or loss, or even to sell baking machinery that is to be replaced for the purpose of more efficient baking.

This narrow interpretation of the objectives of a business has undergone considerable revision in modern financial theory. Thus, rather than the "baking bread" or any other specific objective, the main objective and task of management is viewed as that of increasing the capital of the owners, or expressed differently, the enhancing of the value of the common stock. This, according to modern financial theory, can be accomplished by means of the judicious combination of an optimal financing plan and any mix of operations opportunities that may be available to achieve the desired purpose.

The analyst should not be bound by the accountant's concept of "normal operations," and thus he can usefully treat a much wider range of gains and losses as being derived from "operations." This approach reinforces our conclusion that most nonrecurring, *operating* gains and losses should, from the point of view of analysis, be considered part of the operating results of the year in which they occur.

This approach is offered as a general guideline rather than as a mechanical rule. The analyst may, after examination of all attendant circumstance, conclude that some such items require separation from the results of a single year. The relative size of an item could conceivably be a factor requiring such treatment. In this case the best approach is to emphasize *average earnings* experience over, say, five years rather than the result of a single year. This approach of emphasizing average earnings becomes almost imperative in the case of enterprises which have widely fluctuating amounts of nonrecurring and other extraordinary items included in their results. After all, a single year is too short and too arbitrary a period on the basis of which to evaluate the earnings power of an enterprise or the prospects for future results. Moreover, we are all familiar with enterprises which defer expenses and postpone losses and come up periodically with a loss year which cancels out much of the income reported in preceding years.

b) *Recurring, nonoperating gains or losses.* This category includes items of a nonoperating nature that recur with some frequency. An example would be the recurring amortization of a "bargain purchase credit." Other possible examples are interest income and the rental received from employees who rent company-owned houses.

While items in this category may be classified as "extraordinary" in published financial statements, the narrow definition of "nonoperating" which they involve as well as their recurrent nature are good reasons why they should not be excluded from current results by the analyst. They are, after all, mostly the result of the conscious employment of capital by the enterprise, and their recurrence requires inclusion of these gains or losses in estimates designed to project future results.

c) *Nonrecurring, nonoperating gains or losses.* Of the three categories, this one possesses the greatest degree of "abnormality." Not only are the events here nonrepetitive and unpredictable, but they do not fall within the sphere of normal operations. In most cases these events are extraneous, unintended, and unplanned. However, they can rarely be said to be totally unexpected. Business is ever subject to the risk of sudden adverse events and to random shocks, be they natural or man-made. In the same manner, business transactions are also subject to unexpected windfalls. One good example in this category is the loss from damage done by the crash of an aircraft on a plant not located in the vicinity of an airport. Other, but less clear-cut, examples in this category may also include:

1. Substantial uninsured casualty losses which are not within the categories of risk to which the enterprise can reasonably be deemed to be subject.
2. The expropriation by a foreign government of an entire operation owned by the enterprise.
3. The seizure or destruction of property as a result of an act of war, insurrection, or civil disorders, in areas where this is totally unexpected.

It can be seen readily that while the above occurrences are, in most cases, of a nonrecurring nature, their relation to the operations of a business varies. All are occurrences in the regular course of business. Even the assets destroyed by acts of God were acquired for operating purposes and thus were subject to all possible risks.

Of the three categories this one comes closest to meeting the criterion of being "extraordinary." Nevertheless, truly unique events are very rare. What looks at the time as unique may, in the light of experience turn out to be the symptom of new sets of circumstances which affect and may continue to affect the earning power as well as the degree of risk to which an enterprise is subject.

The analyst must bear in mind such possibilities, but barring evidence to the contrary, he can regard items in this category as extraordinary in nature and thus omit them from the results of operations of a *single* year. They are, nevertheless, part of the longer term record of results of the enterprise. Thus, they enter the computation of *average earnings,* and the propensity of the enterprise to incur such gains or losses must be considered in the projection of future average earnings.

The foregoing discussion has tried to point out that the intelligent classification of extraordinary items provides a workable solution to their treatment by the analyst. There are, however, other aspects of the evaluation of extraordinary items which must be considered here. One is the effect of extraordinary items on the resources of an enterprise; the other is their effect on the evaluation of management performance.

Effect of extraordinary items on enterprise resources. Every extraordinary gain or loss has a dual aspect. In addition to recording a gain (whether extraordinary or not) a business records an increase in resources. Similarly, a loss results in a reduction of resources. Since return on investment measures the relationship of net income to resources, the incurrence of extraordinary gains and losses will affect this important measure of profitability. The more material the extraordinary item, the more significant that influence will be. In other words, if earnings and events are to be used to make estimates about the future, then extraordinary items convey something more than past performance. Thus, if an extraordinary loss results in the destruction of capital on which a certain return is expected, that return may be lost to the future. Conversely, an extraordinary gain will result in an addition of resources on which a future return can be expected.

This means that in projecting profitability and return on investment, the analyst must take into account the effect of recorded "extraordinary" items as well as the likelihood of the occurrence of future events which may cause extraordinary items.

Effect on evaluation of management. One implication frequently associated with the reporting of extraordinary gains and losses is that they have not resulted from a "normal" or "planned" activity of management and that, consequently, they should not be used in the evaluation of management performance. The analyst should seriously question such a conclusion.

What is "normal activity" in relation to management's deliberate actions? Whether we talk about the purchase or sale of securities, of other assets not used in operations, or of divisions and subsidiaries that definitely relate to operations, we talk about actions deliberately taken by management with specific purposes in mind. Such actions require, if anything, more consideration or deliberation than do ordinary everyday operating decisions because they are most often unusual in nature and involve substantial amounts of money. They are true tests of management ability. The results of such activities always qualify or enhance the results of "normal" operations, thus yielding the final net results.

Similarly, management must be aware of the risk of natural or manmade disasters or impediments in the course of business. The decision to engage in foreign operations is made with the knowledge of the special risks which this involves and the decision to insure or not is a normal operating decision. Nothing can really be termed completely unexpected or unforeseeable. Management does not engage, or is at least not supposed to engage, in any activity unconsciously; hence, whatever it does is clearly within the expected activity of a business. Being engaged in foreign operations carries with it the risk of currency fluctuations and even of expropriations, and the returns expected from such ventures must compensate for such risks. Every type of enterprise is subject to specific risks which are inherent in it, and managements do not enter such ventures blindly.

It does not require much elaboration to show that the borderline between what is extraordinary and what is "normal" is thin and shifting. One example will suffice. The current expensing of research and development outlays places them clearly into the "normal" expense category. But, under the presently acceptable alternative of deferring research and development costs, future lump-sum write-offs, particularly as part of abandonment of a product line, may occur in a year in which an operating loss has already occurred or one where in there is a sizable gain to offset its effect. The analyst must realize that managements have considerable discretion in deciding on the timing and even the amount of extraordinary items.

When it comes to the assessment of results that count and results that build or destroy value, the distinction of what is normal and what is not fades almost into insignificance. Management's beliefs about the quality of its decisions are nearly always related to the normalcy, or lack thereof, of surrounding circumstances. This can be clearly seen in the management report section of many annual reports. Of course, management has to take more time to explain failure or shortcomings than to explain success. Success hardly needs an explanation, unless it involves circumstances not likely to be repeated. Failure often evokes long explanations, and more often than not, unusual or unforeseeable circumstances are blamed for it. If only normal conditions had prevailed, everything would have been much better. But in a competitive economy, normal conditions hardly ever prevail for any length of time. Management is paid to anticipate and expect the unusual. No alibis are permitted. Explanations are never a substitute for performance.

BALANCE SHEET ANALYSIS AS A CHECK ON THE VALIDITY AND QUALITY OF REPORTED EARNINGS

The amounts at which the assets and liabilities of an enterprise are stated hold important clues to an assessment of both the validity as well as the quality of its earnings. Thus, the analysis of the balance sheet is an important complement to the other approaches of income analysis discussed in this chapter, and elsewhere in this work.

Importance of carrying amounts of assets

The importance which we attach to the amounts at which assets are carried on the balance sheet is due to the fact that, with few exceptions such as cash, investments, and land, the cost of most assets enters ultimately the cost stream of the income statement. Thus, we can state the following as a general proposition: Whenever assets are overstated the income, both present and cumulative, is overstated because it has been relieved of charges needed to bring such assets down to realizable values.

It would appear that the converse of this proposition should also hold true, that is, that to the extent to which assets are understated, the income, current and cumulative, is also understated. Two accounting conventions qualify this statement importantly. One is the convention of conservatism, which calls for the recognition of gains only as they are actually realized. Although there has been some movement away from a strict interpretation of this convention, in general most assets are carried at original cost even though their current market or realizable value is far in excess of that cost.

The other qualifying convention is that governing the accounting for business combinations. As was seen in the discussions in Chapter 7, the "pooling of interests" principle allows an acquiring company to carry forward the old book values of the assets of the acquired company even though such values may be far less than current market values or the consideration given for them. Thus, the analyst must be aware of the fact that such an accounting will allow the recording of profits, when the values of such understated assets are realized, which represents nothing more than the surfacing of such hitherto understated assets. Since such profits have, in effect, previously been bought and paid for, they cannot be considered as representing either the earning power of the enterprise or an index of the operating performance of existing management.

Importance of provisions and liabilities

Continuing our analysis of the effect of balance sheet amounts on the measurement of income, we can enunciate the further proposition that an understatement of provisions and liabilities will result in an overstatement of income because the latter is relieved of charges required to bring the provision or the liabilities up to their proper amounts. Thus, for example, an understatement of the provision for taxes, for product warranties, or for pension costs means that income, current and cumulative, is overstated.

Conversely, an overprovision for present and future liabilities or losses results in the understatement of income or in the overstatement of losses. As was seen in the discussion in Chapter 9, provisions for future costs and losses which are excessive in amount represent attempts to shift the burden of costs and expenses from future income statements to that of the present.

Bearing in mind the general propositions regarding the effect on income of the amounts at which assets and liabilities are carried in the balance sheet, the critical analysis and evaluation of such amounts represents an important check on the validity of reported income.

Balance sheet analysis and the quality of earnings

There is, however, a further dimension to this kind of analysis in that it also has a bearing on an evaluation of the quality of earnings. This approach is based on the fact that various degrees of risk attach to the probability of the future realization of different types of assets.

Thus, for example, the future realization of accounts receivable has generally a higher degree of probability than has the realization of deferred research and development costs. Moreover, the future realization of inventory costs can, generally, be predicted with greater certainty than can the future realization of goodwill or of deferred start-up costs. The analysis of the assets carried in the balance sheet by risk class or risk category holds clues to and is an important measure of the quality of reported income. Stated another way, if the income determination process results in the deferral of outlays and costs which carry a high degree of risk that they may not prove realizable in the future, then that income is of a lower quality than income which does not involve the recording of such high-risk assets.

Effect of valuation of specific assets on the validity and quality of reported income

In order to illustrate the importance of balance sheet analysis to an evaluation of reported income, let us now examine the effect of the valuation of specific assets on the validity and quality of that income.

Accounts receivable. The validity of the sales figure depends on the proper valuation of the accounts receivable which result from it. This valuation must recognize the risk of default in payment as well as the time value of money. On the latter score, APB *Opinion No. 21* provides that if the receivable does not arise from transactions with customers or suppliers in the normal course of business under terms not exceeding a year, then, except for some other stated exceptions, it must be valued using the interest rate applicable to similar debt instruments. Thus, if the receivable bears an interest rate of 5 percent while similar receivables would, at the time, be expected to bear an interest rate of 7 percent, both the receivable and the sale from which it arose would be restated at the lower discounted amount.

Inventories. Overstated inventories lead to overstated profits. Overstatements can occur due to errors in quantities, errors in costing and pricing, or errors in the valuation of work in process. The more technical the product and the more dependent the valuation is on internally developed cost records, the more vulnerable are the cost estimates to error and misstatement. The basic problem here arises when costs which should have been written off to expense are retained in the inventory accounts.

An understatement of inventories results from a charge-off to income of costs which possess future utility and which should be inventoried. Such an understatement of inventories results in the understatement of current income and the overstatement of future income.

Deferred charges. Deferred charges such as research and development costs, start-up and preoperating costs must be scrutinized carefully because their value depends, perhaps more than that of other assets, on estimates of future probabilities and developments. Experience has shown that often such estimates have proven overoptimistic or that they did not contain sufficient provisions for future contingencies. Thus, the risk of failure to attain expectations is relatively higher here than in the case of other assets. However, as was pointed out in the discussion of research and development costs earlier in this chapter, a full evaluation involves many intangible factors which the analyst must recognize and evaluate.

MONITORING EARNINGS TREND

In our discussion of the analysis and the prediction of earnings, we recognize that a year represents too short and too arbitrary a time period for purposes of income measurement and evaluation. Because of the length of time required to assess the ultimate workout and the results of many investments and outlays and because of the presence of numerous nonrecurring and extraordinary factors, the determination of the normal or actual earnings level of an enterprise is best measured by means of average earnings realized over a number of years.

The period of time over which an earnings average should be calculated will vary with the industry of which the enterprise is part and with other special circumstances. However, in general, a from 5- to 10-year earnings average will smooth out many of the distortions and the irregularities which impair the significance of a single year's results.

Methods of earnings averaging and trend determination

There are a number of methods available for determining and comparing an earnings trend. We will discuss three of these:
1. Moving average.
   a) Simple.
   b) Weighted.
2. Weighted average.
3. Compounded annual growth rate.

For purposes of illustration we shall use the following hypothetical earnings for Companies A and B for the period of 19x1 through 19x5.

Years	Company A	Company B
19x1	$1,000	$ 300
19x2	300	500
19x3	1,000	700
19x4	200	900
19x5	1,500	1,100
Total	$4,000	$3,500

If we compute a simple arithmetic average, we get $800 (4,000 ÷ 5) for Company A and $700 ($3,500 ÷ 5) for Company B. However, these figures do not provide very useful information on trends; in fact, the simple arithmetic average completely ignores trend.

1. Moving average

a) Simple moving average. The moving average is a good smoothing device and it becomes useful when the original data varies from year to year to such a degree that it becomes difficult to sense its trend. When data is subject to cyclical variations, the moving average has the advantage of always encompassing a time span covering an entire cycle. A moving average based on a 5- to 10-year span will be appropriate in most circumstances.

Three-year simple moving averages are computed in Table 20–3, and the corresponding graph is shown in Exhibit 20–1(b).

TABLE 20-3
Simple moving average

Years	Company A		Company B	
19x3	$\frac{1{,}000 + 300 + 1{,}000}{3}$	= 767	$\frac{300 + 500 + 700}{3}$	= 500
19x4	$\frac{300 + 1{,}000 + 200}{3}$	= 500	$\frac{500 + 700 + 900}{3}$	= 700
19x5	$\frac{1{,}000 + 200 + 1{,}500}{3}$	= 900	$\frac{700 + 900 + 1{,}100}{3}$	= 900

By 19x5, the simple moving averages of the two companies are the same: $900.

b) Weighted moving average. In earnings comparisons, as well as in the evaluation of earnings trends, the most recent year carries the greatest relative weight because it reflects the latest or most up-to-date experience. Emphasis on the most recent years can be expressed by assigning relative weights to the earnings of different years which, while somewhat arbitrary, are, nevertheless, consistent.

Table 20–4 shows a three-year moving average. A weight of 1 is assigned to the first year, a weight of 2 to the second year, and a weight of 3 to the third year in order to recognize the increasing degree of importance attached to the income of the more recent year. For example, had it been a five-year moving average, a weight of 1 would have been given to the first year and a weight of 5 to the fifth year. Denominator is the sum of weights; in this case 6 (1 + 2 + 3).

The graph is shown in Exhibit 20–1(c). Graphs (b) and (c) look almost identical; however, graph (c) shows that Company A is slightly higher than Company B due to the fact that Company A's earnings in 19x5 were substantially higher than Company B and a relative weight of 3 was given to that year.

2. Weighted average

Some time it may be useful to have a single average figure for earnings of the past with due weights given to the most recent years. The

EXHIBIT 20-1

a) Raw data

b) Simple moving average

c) Weighted moving average

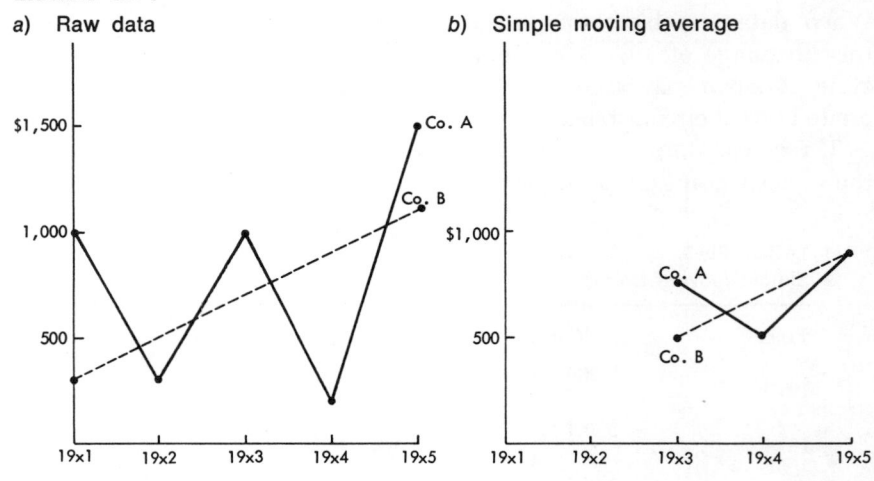

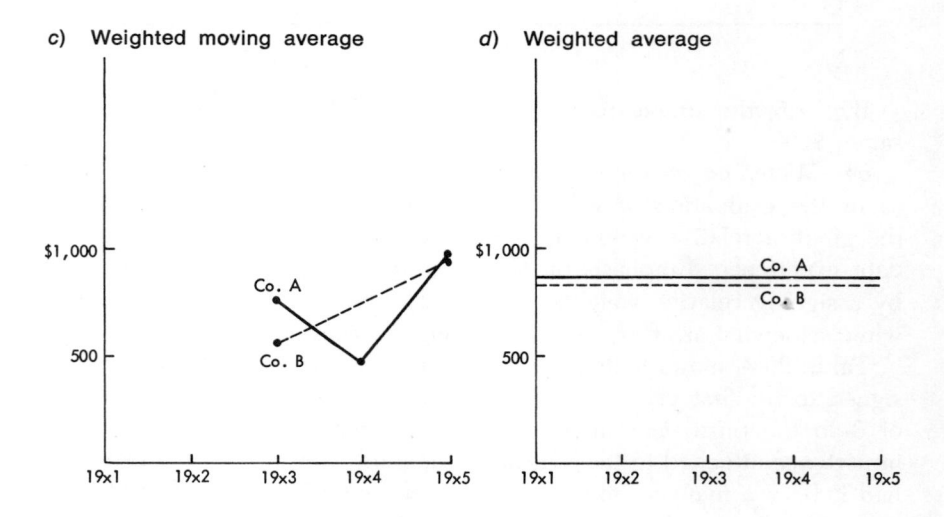

d) Weighted average

weighted average provides such information. Table 20–5 shows that the weighted average is $860 for Company A and $833 for Company B. Although the weighted average represents for some purposes a significant improvement over the simple arithmetic average, it nevertheless does not provide any clue about earnings trend or their variability.

The graph in Exhibit 20–1 (*d*) shows that Company A's earnings average is superior to that of Company B, yet Company B's earnings trend is superior to that of Company A. In order to compensate for this weakness of the weighted average, it is advisable to compute the variability ratio as supplementary information.

TABLE 20-4
Weighted moving average

COMPANY A

Year	19x1	19x2	19x3	19x4	19x5
Earnings	$1,000	$ 300	$1,000	$ 200	$1,500
Weight					
1	1,000	300	1,000	200	1,500
2	2,000	600	2,000	400	3,000
3	3,000	900	3,000	600	4,500
Total			4,600	2,900	5,900
			÷ 6	÷ 6	÷ 6
			= 767	= 483	= 983

COMPANY B

Earnings	$300	$500	$700	$900	$1,100
Weight					
1	300	500	700	900	1,100
2	600	1,000	1,400	1,800	2,200
3	900	1,500	2,100	2,700	3,300
Total			3,400	4,600	5,800
			÷ 6	÷ 6	÷ 6
			= 567	= 767	= 967

TABLE 20-5
Weighted average earnings

		Company A		Company B	
Years	Weight	Yearly earnings	Weighted earnings	Yearly earnings	Weighted earnings
19x1	1	$1,000	$ 1,000	$ 300	$ 300
19x2	2	300	600	500	1,000
19x3	3	1,000	3,000	700	2,100
19x4	4	200	800	900	3,600
19x5	5	1,500	7,500	1,100	5,500
Total	15		$12,900		$12,500
Weighted five-year average		$\frac{\$12,900}{15} = \$860$		$\frac{\$12,500}{15} = \$833$	

The variability ratio. The variability ratio measures the magnitude of the percentage difference between the peak year and the lowest year in a time series. Since we divide the peak year (numerator) by the lowest year (denominator), the latter automatically becomes the base year, and the magnitude of variation percentage in the peak year is explained with reference to the base year.

Variability ratios:

$$\text{Company A: } \frac{1{,}500}{200} = 7.5 \qquad \text{Company B: } \frac{1{,}100}{300} = 3.7$$

Company	Weighted average	Variability ratio
A.	$860	7.5
B.	$833	3.7

Now we can conclude that although the two companies' earnings are approximately equal, the quality of Company B's earnings is higher than that of Company A because Company B's earnings present a less erratic pattern over time.

3. *Compounded annual growth rate*

Sometimes we are interested in knowing the annual growth rate of earnings as well as the absolute amount of the earnings.

If a given trend has been that of continuous growth and the first year is the lowest year (or close to the lowest year) while the peak year is the last year in the time series, we can obtain the approximate compounded annual growth rate by simply looking at a table for "Amount of $1 at Compounded Interest Rate."

For example, the net income of an enterprise grew from $218,000 in 19x1 to $331,000 in 19x5, a growth of 52 percent $(331/218 - 1)$ over the four years. We want to find the approximate annual growth rate over the previous year which would increase $1 to $1.52 after four years. Look at the table for a figure nearest 1.52 in the row of 4 years and read up that column to find the interest (growth) rate in the "Amount of $1" table. In this case, the rate is 11 percent. Of course, this expediency sometimes will not give the exact growth rate, but it will be sufficient for most analysis purposes.

Growth at 11 percent

Year 1	Year 2	Year 3	Year 4	Year 5
$218,000	$241,980	$268,598	$298,144	$330,940
100%	111%	123%	137%	152%

When the table does not provide growth rates which we are interested in due to extremely rapid growth rates (as in our present example of Companies A and B), we have to compute the growth rate by using the formula:

$$S = P(1 + r)^n$$

where,

S = Earnings of nth year,
P = Earnings of base year,
r = Growth rate, and
n = Number of years in the time series, excluding base year.

The computation can be simplified by the following transformation:

$S' = \dfrac{S}{P}$: Earnings of the nth year as multiples (or percent) of that of the base year

Then, the formula will be:

$$S' = (1 + r)^n \text{ and we solve for } r$$

In applying these methods the analyst should of course realize that the significance of the resultant compounded annual growth rate depends on the "appropriateness" of the base year amount and the last year amount.

For example, for Company A, if we pick 19x1 as base year, annual growth rate has been about 11 percent annually over the four years by consulting the table (more precisely, it is 10.7 percent). On the other hand, had we picked 19x2 as a base figure, we would compute:

$$S' = \dfrac{1{,}500}{300} = 5 \quad \text{and} \quad (1+r)^3 = 5$$

By using logarithm, we solve for r:

$$\log(1+r)^3 = \log 5$$
$$3\log(1+r) = .69897$$
$$\log(1+r) = \dfrac{.69897}{3} = .23299$$

Looking at logarithm table, we find that approximately,

$$\log 1.71 = .23299,$$

therefore,

$$r = 1.71 - 1 = 71 \text{ percent}$$

Growth at 71 percent

Years	Growth rate	Amount
19x2	...	$ 300.00
19x3	71%	513.00
19x4	71	877.23
19x5	71	1,500.06

By choosing a different base year when the year-to-year earnings variation is significant (such as in the case of Company A), the growth rate is either 11 percent or 71 percent, a difference of 60 percent!

For Company B, if we pick 19x1 as base year, then

$$S' = \frac{1,100}{300} = 3.667$$

and

$$\log(1+r)^4 = \log 3.667$$
$$4\log(1+r) = .56431$$
$$\log(1+r) = \frac{.56431}{4} = .141078$$

and

$$\log 1.384 = .141078,$$

therefore, $1 + r = 1.384$, and the growth rate is about 38.4 percent. Had we picked 19x2 as the base year, then

$$S' = \frac{1,100}{500} = 2.2,$$
$$\log(1+r)^3 = \log 2.2$$
$$3\log(1+r) = .34242$$
$$\log(1+r) = \frac{.34242}{3} = .11414$$
$$\log 1.301 = .11414$$

therefore, the growth rate is 30.1 percent.

THE EVALUATION OF EARNINGS TRENDS

In evaluating earnings trends the analyst relies also on such indicators of future conditions as capital expenditures, order backlogs, as well as demand trends in individual product lines.

It is important to realize that no degree of sophistication in the techniques used in earnings projections can eliminate the inevitable uncertainty to which all forecasts are subject. Even the best and most soundly based projections retain a significant probability of proving widely off the mark because of events and circumstances which cannot be foreseen.

The most effective means by which the analyst and decision maker can counter this irreducible uncertainty is to keep close and constant watch over how closely actual results conform to his projections. This requires a constant monitoring of results and the adjustment and updating of projections in the light of such results.

INTERIM EARNINGS

The need to follow closely the results achieved by an enterprise requires frequent updatings of such results. Interim financial statements, most frequently issued on a quarterly basis, are designed to fill this need. They are used by decision makers as means of updating current results as well as in the prediction of future results.

If, as we have seen, a year is a relatively short period of time in which to account for results of operations, then trying to confine the measurement of results to a three-month period involves all the more problems and imperfections. For this and other reasons the reporting of interim earnings is subject to serious limitations and distortions. The intelligent use of reported interim results requires that we have a full understanding of these possible problem areas and limitations. The following is a review of some of the basic reasons for these problems and limitations, as well as their effect on the determination of reported interim results.

Year-end adjustments

The determination of the results of operations for a year requires a great many estimates, as well as procedures, such as accruals and the determination of inventory quantities and carrying values. These procedures can be complex, time-consuming, and costly. Examples of procedures requiring a great deal of data collection and estimation include estimation of the percentage of completion of contracts, determination of cost of work in process, the allocation of under- or overabsorbed overhead for the period, and the determination of inventory under the Lifo method. The complex, time-consuming, and expensive nature of these procedures can mean that they are performed much more crudely during interim periods and are often based on records which are less complete than are their year-end counterparts. The result inevitably is a less accurate process of income determination which, in turn, may require year-end adjustments which can modify substantially the interim results already reported.

Seasonality

Many enterprises experience at least some degree of seasonality in their activities. Sales may be unevenly distributed over the year, and so it may be with production and other activities. This tends to distort comparisons among the quarterly results of a single year. It also presents problems in the allocation of many budgeted costs, such as advertising, research and development, and repairs and maintenance. If expenses vary with sales, they should be accrued on the basis of expected sales for the full year. Obviously, the preparer of yearly financial statements has the benefit of hindsight which the preparer of interim statements does not. There are also problems with the allocation of fixed costs among quarters.

Two excerpts from interim financial statements illustrate the problems encountered in these areas:

Because of a seasonal production cycle, and in accordance with practices followed by the Company in reporting interim financial statements prior to 19x4, $435,000 of unabsorbed factory overhead has been deferred at July 4, 19x5. Due to uncertainties as to production and sales in 19x4, $487,000 of such unabsorbed overhead was expensed during the first 6 months of 19x4.

....

Raytheon's third quarter results, even after leveling of certain expenses, reflect the seasonally high third quarter operating levels of D. C. Heath. Like other school and college textbook publishers, D. C. Heath realizes a large portion of its annual sales and earnings in the third quarter, which includes the start if the academic year.

APB *Opinion No. 28*

In 1973 the APB moved to establish some guidelines on Interim Financial Reporting. In its *Opinion No. 28* it concluded that interim reports should be prepared in accordance with generally accepted accounting principles used in the preparation of the latest financial statements. Adopting the point of view that a quarterly report is an integral part of a full year rather than a distinct unit, it calls for the accrual of revenues and for the spreading of certain costs among the quarters of a year. For example, it sanctions the accrual of such year-end adjustments as inventory shrinkages, quantity discounts, and uncollectible accounts; but it prohibits the accrual of advertising costs on the ground that benefits of such costs cannot be anticipated. Losses cannot, generally, be deferred beyond the interim period in which they occur. Moreover, the Opinion calls for the inclusion of extraordinary items in the interim period in which they occur. Income taxes should be accrued on the basis of the effective tax rate expected to apply to the full year.

Revised SEC reporting requirements

In April 1972 the SEC issued a *Release No. 9559* (under the 1934 Securities Act) entitled "Financial Reporting—Quarterly and Other Interim Reports of Operations." In this Release, the SEC urges greater diligence in preparing news releases on fiscal or interim results, including specific suggestions for improvement in some cases.

The salient points made by this release are as follows:

1. Disclosures in news releases should be prepared using the Form 10-Q (for quarterly reports) and Form 8-K (for current reports) instructions as guidelines.
2. Comparative figures presented should be accompanied by sufficient disclosure of unusual events and transactions and their effect to permit a proper understanding.
3. Results of operations for the fourth quarter of the fiscal year should be published separately.
4. Adequate information with respect to year-end adjustments or unusual transactions which occurred in the fourth quarter should be furnished.

Implications for analysis

We have examined the problems of the reliability of interim results arising from the short periods which they cover, from the difficulties of estimation, and from the relative lack of care with which such statements are often prepared. In most cases interim income statements are too abbreviated to form a basis for thorough analysis. In addition they are, in most cases, not accompanied by balance sheets; and thus an important check on the validity and the quality of reported income is missing and an evaluation of concurrent changes in financial position is not possible.

The analyst must exercise great care in the interpretation and use of interim financial statements. Most interim financial statements are unaudited, and the new APB Opinion on this subject will not change this. Thus, there is no assurance that the principles which it includes will be adhered to in such statements. The practice of minimal disclosure in interim statements may continue to handicap the financial analyst. Moreover, not all principles promulgated by the APB on the subject of interim financial statements are useful to the analyst. For example, the inclusion of extraordinary items in the results of the quarter in which they occur will require careful adjustment to render them meaningful for purposes of analysis.

Some problems of seasonality in interim results of operations can be overcome by considering in the analysis not merely the results of a single quarter, but also the year-to-date cumulative results which incorporate the results of the latest available quarter. This is the most effective way of monitoring the results of an enterprise and bringing to bear on its analysis the latest data on operations that are available.

QUESTIONS

1. Distinguish between income and cash flow. Why is there a distinction between the two?
2. *a)* What is meant by "quality of earnings"? Why do analysts assess it?
   b) On what major elements does the quality of earnings depend?
3. What is the difference between projection and extrapolation of earnings?
4. *a)* What are discretionary costs?
   b) Of what significance are discretionary costs to an analysis of the quality of earnings?
5. *a)* Why is the evaluation of research and development costs important to the analysis and projection of income?
   b) What are some of the precautions required in analyzing research and development expenses?
6. Why does the analyst wish to identify nonrecurring as well as extraordinary items in the income statement?
7. Why are managements so greatly interested in the reporting of extraordinary gains and losses?
8. What are the basic objectives of the analyst in the identification and the evaluation of extraordinary items?
9. *a)* Into what categories can items which are described as unusual or extraordinary in the financial statements be usefully subdivided into for purposes of analysis?
   b) Give examples of each such category.
   c) How should the analyst treat items in each category? Is such a treatment indicated under all circumstances? Explain.
10. What are the effects of extraordinary items on—
    a) Enterprise resources?
    b) The evaluation of managements?
11. Comment on the following statement:
    "Extraordinary gains or losses have not resulted from a 'normal' or 'planned' activity of management and, consequently, they should not be used in the evaluation of managerial performance."
    Do you agree?
12. *a)* What is the relationship between the carrying amounts of various assets and earnings reported?
    b) What is the relationship between the amounts at which liabilities, including provisions, are carried and earnings reported?
13. Explain briefly the relationship between the quality of earnings and the following balance sheet items:
    a) Accounts receivable.
    b) Inventories.
    c) Deferred charges.

20. The evaluation and projection of earnings

14. In what way is balance sheet analysis a check on the validity as well as the quality of earnings?
15. Comment on the effect which the "risk category" of an asset has on the quality of reported earnings.
16. Describe a number of methods used to determine and compare earnings trends.
17. What is the variability ratio? What does it measure?
18. *a)* What are interim financial statements used for?
    b) What accounting problems which are peculiar to interim statements must the analyst be aware of?
19. Why are interim earnings reports particularly useful in the monitoring of earnings trends?
20. Interim financial reporting can be subject to serious limitations and distortions. Discuss some of the reasons for this.
21. What factors (*a*) within the company, and (*b*) within the economy, have and are likely to affect the degree of variability in the earnings per share, dividends per share, and market price per share, of common stock? (C.F.A.)

21

Comprehensive analysis of financial statements

THE METHODOLOGY OF FINANCIAL STATEMENT ANALYSIS

THE MARSHALLING, arrangement, and presentation of data for purposes of financial statement analysis can be standardized to some extent in the interest of consistency and organizational efficiency. However, the actual process of analysis must be left to the judgment of the analyst so that he may allow for the great diversity of situations and circumstances which he is likely to encounter in practice, and thus give full reign to his own initiative, originality, and ingenuity. Nevertheless, there are some useful generalizations and guidelines which may be stated as to a general approach to the task of financial statement analysis.

To begin with, financial statement analysis is oriented towards the achievement of definite objectives. In order that the analysis best accomplish these objectives, the first step is to define them carefully. The thinking and clarification leading up to such a definition of objectives is a very important part of the analytical process, for it insures a clear understanding of objectives, that is, of what is pertinent and relevant and what is not, and thus also leads to avoidance of unnecessary work. This clarification of objectives is indispensable to an *effective* as well as to an *efficient* analysis: *effective*, in that, given the specifications, it focuses on the most important and most relevant elements of the financial statements; *efficient*, in that it leads to an analysis with maximum economy of time and effort.

21. Comprehensive analysis of financial statements

SITUATION 1. The bank's loan officer, dealing with a request for a short-term loan to finance inventory, may define his objective as assessing the intention and the ability of the borrower to repay the loan on time. Thus, the analyst can concentrate on what is needed to achieve this objective and need not, for instance, address himself to industry conditions which can affect the borrowing entity only over the longer term.

Once the objective of the analysis has been defined, the next step is the formulation of specific questions the answers to which are needed in the achievement of such objectives.

SITUATION 2. The loan officer in Situation 1 now needs to define the critical criteria which will affect his decision. For instance, the question of the lender's *willingness* to repay the short-term loan bears in his character, and financial statement analysis can reveal only the history of past loans granted it. Thus, tools other than financial statement analysis will have to be employed to get complete information on the lender's character.

Among the other questions on which the loan officer will need information are the following:

1. What is the enterprise's short-term liquidity?
2. What will its sources and uses of funds be during the duration of the loan agreement?

Financial statement analysis can go far towards providing answers to such questions.

Having defined the objective and having translated it into specific questions and criteria which must be resolved, the analyst is ready for the third step in the analysis process. This is to decide which tools and techniques of analysis are the most appropriate, effective, and efficient ones to use in working on the particular decision problem at hand.

SITUATION 3. Following the sequence developed in the above Situations 1 and 2, the loan officer will now decide which financial statement analysis tools are most appropriate to use in this case. He may choose one or more of the following:

1. Short-term liquidity ratios.
2. Inventory turnover measures.
3. Cash flow projections.
4. Analyses of changes in financial position.

These analyses will have to include estimates and projections of future conditions toward which most, if not all, financial analysis is oriented.

The fourth and final step in analysis is the interpretation of the data and measures assembled as a basis for decision and action. This is the most critical and difficult of the steps, and the one requiring the application of a great deal of judgment, skill, and effort. Interpretation is a process of investigation and evaluation, and of envisaging the reality which lies behind the figures examined. There is, of course, no mechanical substitute for this process of judgment. However, the proper definition of the problem and of the critical questions which must be answered, as well as the skillful selection of the most appropriate tools of analysis available in the circumstances, will go a long way towards a meaningful interpretation of the results of analysis.

SITUATION 4. Following the sequence of the first three examples above, the collection, by the loan officer, of the data described in Situation 3 is, of course, not the end result of his analysis. These data must be integrated, evaluated, and interpreted for the purposes of reaching the basic decision of whether to make the loan and, if so, in what amount.

By way of analogy, the weather forecasting function provides an example of the difference between the availability of analytical data and its successful interpretation. Thus, the average listener to weather information does not know how to interpret barometric pressure, relative humidity, or wind velocity. What he needs to know is the weather forecast which results from an interpretation of these data.

The intelligent analyst and interpreter of financial statement data must always bear in mind that a financial statement is at best an abstraction of an underlying reality. Further mathematical manipulation of financial data can result in second, third, and even further levels of abstractions; and the analyst must always keep in mind the business reality behind the figures. No map of the Rocky Mountains can fully convey the grandeur of the terrain. One has to see them in order to appreciate them because maps, like financial statements, are, at best abstractions. That is why security analysts must, at some point, leave the financial statements and visit the companies which they analyze in order to get a full understanding of the phenomena revealed by their analysis. This is particularly true because the static reality portrayed by the abstractions found in the financial statements cannot remain static for very long. Reality is ever changing.

A recognition of the inherent limitations of financial data is needed for intelligent analysis. This does not detract from their importance because financial statements and data are the only means by which the financial realities of an enterprise can be reduced to a common denominator which is quantified and which can be mathematically manipulated and projected in a rational and disciplined way.

SIGNIFICANCE OF THE "BUILDING BLOCK" APPROACH TO FINANCIAL ANALYSIS

The six major "building blocks" of financial analysis which we have examined in this text are:

1. Short-term liquidity.
2. Funds flow.
3. Capital structure and long-term solvency.
4. Return on investment.
5. Asset utilization.
6. Operating performance.

The "building block" approach to financial statement analysis involves:

1. The determination of the major objectives which a particular financial analysis is to achieve.
2. Arriving at a judgment about which of the six major areas of analysis (i.e., our "building blocks") must be evaluated with what degree of emphasis and in what order of priority.

For example, the security analyst, in his evaluation of the investment merit of a particular issue of equity securities, may attach primary importance to the earning capacity and potential of the enterprise. Thus, the first "building block" of his analysis will be the evaluation of "operating performance" and the next, perhaps, "return on investment." A thorough analysis will, of course, require that attention be paid to the other four major areas of analysis, although with perhaps lesser degrees of emphasis, that is, depth. This attention to the other major areas of analysis is necessary in order to detect possible problem areas, that is, areas of potential risk. Thus, further analysis may reveal a liquidity problem arising from a "thin" working capital condition, or it may reveal a situation of inadequate capital funds which may stifle growth and flexibility. It is conceivable that these problem areas may reveal themselves to be so important as to overshadow the question of earning power, thus leading to a change in the relative emphasis which the analyst will accord to the main areas of his particular analysis.

While the subdivision of the analysis into six distinct aspects of a company's financial condition and performance is a useful approach, it must be borne in mind that these areas of analysis are highly interrelated. For example, the operating performance of an enterprise can be affected by the lack of adequate capital funds or by problems of short-term liquidity. Similarly, a credit evaluation cannot stop at the point where a satisfactory short-term liquidity position has been determined because existing or incipient problems in the "operating performance" area may result in serious drains of funds due to losses. Such drains can quickly reverse the satisfactory liquidity position which may prevail at a given point in time.

At the start of his analysis the analyst will tentatively determine the relative importance of the areas which he will examine and the order in which they will be examined. This order of emphasis and priority may subsequently change in the light of his findings and as the analysis progresses.

THE EARMARKS OF GOOD FINANCIAL ANALYSIS

As we have noted, the foundation of any good analysis is a thorough understanding of the objectives to be achieved and the uses to which it is going to be put. Such understanding leads to economy of effort as well as to a useful and most relevant focus on the points that need to be clarified and the estimates and projections that are required.

In practice, rarely can all the facts surrounding a particular analysis be obtained, so that most analyses are undertaken on the basis of incomplete and inadequate facts and data. The process of financial analysis is basically one of reducing the areas of uncertainty—which can, however, never be completely eliminated.

A good analysis separates clearly for the reader the interpretations and conclusions of the analysis from the facts and data upon which they are based. This not only separates fact from opinion and estimate, but also enables the reader to follow the rationale of the analyst's conclusions and allows him to modify them as his judgment dictates. To this end the analysis should contain distinct sections devoted to:

1. General background material on the enterprise analyzed, the industry of which it is a part, and the economic environment in which it operates.
2. Financial and other data used in the analysis as well as ratios, trends, and other analytical measures which have been developed from them.
3. Assumptions as to the general economic environment and as to other conditions on which estimates and projections are based.
4. A listing of positive and negative factors, quantitative and qualitative, by important areas of analysis.
5. Projections, estimates, interpretations, and conclusions based on the aforementioned data. (Some analyses list only the positive and negative factors developed by the analysis and leave further interpretations to the reader.)

A good analysis should start with a brief "Summary and Conclusion" section as well as a table of contents to help the busy reader decide how much of the report he wants to read and on which parts of it to concentrate.

The writer of an analytical report must guard against the all-too-common tendency to include irrelevant matter in it. For example, the reader need not know the century-old details of the humble beginnings of the enterprise under analysis nor should he be taken on a "journey" along all the fruitless byways and missteps which the analyst inevitably encountered in his process of ferreting out and separating the important from the insignificant. Irrelevant bulk or "roughage" can only serve to confuse and distract the reader of a report.

Ambiguities and equivocations which are employed to avoid responsibility or to hedge conclusions do not belong in a good analytical report. Finally, the writers of such reports must recognize that we are all judged on the basis of small details. Consequently, the presence of mistakes in grammar or of obvious errors of fact in a report can plant doubt in the reader's mind as to the competence of the author and the validity of his analysis.

SPECIAL INDUSTRY OR ENVIRONMENTAL CHARACTERISTICS

In this text, the analysis of the various segments of financial statements was treated from the point of view of the regular commercial or industrial enterprise. The financial analyst must, however, recognize that there are industries with distinct accounting treatments which arise either from their specialized nature or from the special conditions, such as governmental regulation, to which they are subject. The analysis of the financial statements of such enterprise requires a thorough understanding of the accounting peculiarities to which they are subject, and the analyst must, accordingly, prepare himself for his task by the study and the understanding of the specialized areas of accounting which affect his particular analysis.

Thus, for example, the analysis of a company in the Oil and Gas Industry requires a thorough knowledge of such accounting concepts peculiar to that industry such as the determination of "cost centers," prediscovery costs, discovery costs, and the disposition of capitalized costs. There are particular problems in the treatment of exploratory, development, and other expenditures as well as in amortization and depletion practices.

Life insurance accounting, to cite another example, also requires specialized knowledge which arises from the peculiarities of this industry and from the regulation to which it is subject. There are special problems in the area of recognition of premium revenues, the accounting for acquisition costs of new business, and the determination of policy reserves.

Public utility regulation has resulted in specialized accounting concepts and problems of which every utility analyst must be aware. There are tax allocation problems resulting in differences among companies which "normalize" taxes versus those which "flow" them through. Then there are problems related to the adequacy of provisions for depreciation, and problems concerning the utility's "rate base" and the method by which it is computed.

As in any field of endeavor specialized areas of inquiry require that specialized knowledge be brought to bear upon them. Financial analysis is, of course, no exception.

ILLUSTRATION OF A COMPREHENSIVE ANALYSIS OF FINANCIAL STATEMENTS—MARINE SUPPLY CORPORATION

The following analysis of the financial statements and other data of the Marine Supply Corporation will serve as an illustration of this process.

Introduction

The Marine Supply Corporation, a leader in the outboard motor industry, was incorporated some 40 years ago. While outboard motor engines and related marine products still account for the bulk of the company's sales, other products are gaining in importance and growing at a rate much faster than the primary products (see Exhibit 21–1, sales breakdown).

EXHIBIT 21–1

MARINE SUPPLY CORPORATION
Sales Breakdown
(in millions of dollars)

Product	19x5 Sales	%	19y0 Sales	%	Sales increase 19x5–19y0 %	Annual growth rates* %
Marine products	135.0	74.5	217.3	71.0	+ 61	10
Lawn care equipment	16.2	9.0	30.5	10.0	+ 88	13
Vehicles	14.1	7.8	19.6	6.4	+ 39	7
Chain saws	9.4	5.2	9.5	3.1	+ 1	0
Snow vehicles	5.1	2.8	23.4	7.7	+359	36
Miscellaneous	.9	.7	4.2	1.8	+367	36
Total	180.7	100.0	304.5	100.0	+ 69	11.2

*Five-year period, compounded annually.

Snow vehicle production was launched in fiscal year 19x4. Its growth rate looks dramatic because it starts from an extremely low base. Outboard motors can be regarded as the primary base of the company's growth, and outboard engines contribute an even larger portion of corporate profits.

While most of Marine Supply Corporation's products have some commerical applications, they are sold primarily for recreation or leisure-time purposes. Being generally big-ticket items, the company's sales are greatly subject to swings in consumer buying cycles.

The use of outboard motors and the majority of the company's other products is largely confined to the warmer months of late spring, summer, and early fall. This means peak retail demand for these items is seasonal; dealer buying tends to be concentrated in this period as well. As a result, the first quarter of the company's fiscal year (ending December) frequently produces a nominal deficit while the June quarter generates 40 percent or more of annual profits.

Marine Supply is one of the world's largest manufacturers of outboard motors; its twin lines command something more than one half the U.S.–Canadian market (by far the most important), and the company estimates a similar proportion overseas. Competition in the industry is keen but is generally centered on performance (racing) results rather than price. Marine Supply's principal advantages are:

1. A highly efficient sales-distribution-repair network (currently about 8,000 dealers) in North America.
2. Exceptional brand loyalty.
3. Almost total domination of the lower horsepower ranges where the vast majority of engines are still sold.

Marine Supply's position in golf carts is also dominant, but its degree of domination is less pronounced. While an important factor in snow vehicles, lawn care, and chain saws, these are highly fragmented markets with many competitors. Still, the company's marketing strategy is the same as in outboards: build a quality product with a strong dealer organization, use intensive advertising, and maintain a premium price structure. This approach has been successful in lawn mowers where Lawn King is a strong competitor despite tremendous product similarity among all brands. In snow vehicles—a comparatively new product to which Marine Supply was a comparative late comer—the company has not yet been totally successful in building its market share.

Financial statements

The financial statements of Marine Supply Corporation are presented in Exhibits 21–2, 21–3, and 21–4 below.

The auditor's opinion on the financial statements has been unqualified for the past six years.

Additional information

Marine Supply has a good, if very cyclical, historic operating performance record. In 19w4, for example, sales were only $73 million as

EXHIBIT 21-2

MARINE SUPPLY CORPORATION
Balance Sheets
As of September 30 for Years 19x5-y0
(in millions of dollars)

	19x5	19x6	19x7	19x8	19x9	19y0
Assets						
Current Assets:						
Cash and equivalents	15.00	24.30	12.10	17.40	19.50	17.48
Receivables	22.50	25.50	31.40	35.60	46.50	53.70
Inventories	49.50	57.60	64.70	78.90	100.80	97.32
Other current assets	...	.00	.0	.10	.0	.00
Total Current Assets	87.00	106.40	108.20	131.80	166.80	168.50
Gross plant	85.20	88.60	98.70	114.70	129.70	137.90
Accumulated depreciation	(45.20)	(48.70)	(52.50)	(56.10)	(60.80)	(65.88)
Net plant	40.00	39.90	46.20	58.60	68.90	72.02
Intangibles	.20	.0	.0	.0	.0	.0
Other assets	6.80	6.40	10.70	11.90	12.70	15.44
Total Assets	134.00	152.70	165.10	202.30	248.40	255.97
Liabilities and Capital						
Current Liabilities:						
Accounts payable	1.10	1.10	7.00	15.20	24.60	24.53
Other current liabilities	15.80	24.90	23.50	26.90	35.00	36.75
Total Current Liabilities	16.90	26.00	30.50	42.10	59.60	61.28
Long-term debt	14.50	13.50	12.40	28.70	45.70	46.04
Deferred taxes and investment credits	1.94	2.19	2.57	4.58	5.38	7.14
Other liabilities	2.39	2.57	2.03	1.52	2.57	1.05
Total Liabilities	35.73	44.26	47.50	76.90	113.25	115.51
Net worth	98.27	108.44	117.60	125.40	135.15	140.46
Total Liabilities and Capital	134.00	152.70	165.10	202.30	248.40	255.97

against $304.5 million in 19y0, more than 300 percent increase. Over the same span net income grew from $5.5 million to $13.4 million, an increase of 144 percent. The slower gain in net income, reflecting sharply reduced operating margins due largely to Federal Trade Commission action in the mid 19w0s, has meant erosion of the company's return on investment from an exceptional 25 percent (on net worth) in the 19w4–w6 period to just over 11 percent for the last three years.

Exhibit 21–5, fifteen-year growth rates—annually compounded, compares various growth rates, first using single years, then a three-year span.

Note that with the exception of sales per share, the growth rates are still higher for the single year comparisons. This is attributable to the very low 19w4 base and the tremendous gains from 19w4 through 19x6—a three-year span in which sales, net income, dividends, and book value each increased from 75 percent to 133 percent.

EXHIBIT 21-3

MARINE SUPPLY CORPORATION
Income Statement
For Years Ending September 30
(in millions of dollars)

	19x5	19x6	19x7	19x8	19x9	19y0
Net sales	180.70	212.50	233.40	280.20	327.10	304.48
Other income	...	...	...	...	...	.19
Total revenue	180.70	212.50	233.40	280.20	327.10	304.67
Cost of goods sold* (excluding depreciation)	113.35	130.95	145.03	180.16	209.52	190.58
Depreciation	4.28	4.26	4.40	4.75	5.59	6.25
Gross profit	63.07	77.29	83.97	95.29	111.99	107.84
Selling, general, and administrative expenses	41.98	47.04	54.04	61.99	71.44	72.99
Operating income	21.09	30.25	29.93	33.30	40.55	34.85
Fixed interest charges	.70	1.05	1.23	2.10	4.73	6.60
Other expenses	.62	.54	.62	1.05	1.54	...
Net income before tax	19.77	28.66	28.08	30.15	34.28	28.25
Income taxes:						
Deferred	.47	.26	.38	.37	.80	1.75
Current	8.66	12.73	12.47	14.12	16.40	13.11
Net income	10.64	15.67	15.23	15.66	17.08	13.39
Common dividends	5.13	6.35	6.37	7.98	8.06	8.08
Retained earnings	5.51	9.32	8.86	7.68	9.02	5.31
*Includes:						
Research and development costs	11.8	11.2	13.4	12.1	12.4	12.8
Maintenance and repairs	10.3	10.4	11.6	12.4	12.7	11.5

Exhibit 21-6, five-year growth rates—annually compounded, indicates the most recent five-year performance, first on a single-year basis, then using three-year "smoothed" base. On either basis, the company's record looks better in recent years than over the long pull.

Two noteworthy points should be made about this record:

1. The gains represent almost solely internal growth. Acquisitions have been few, their relative size quite small, and their profit contributions have often been negative,
2. No adjustments need be made for dilution. The company has no convertible securities outstanding; stock options are also insignificant.

Exhibits 21-7 through 21-10 are based on the financial statements of Marine Supply Corporation.

While the economy in general was slow in 19y0, 19x8 and 19x9 were good years for boat sales; and responses at boat shows across the country were strong in those years. Compared to automobiles, revolutionary model changes are rare in the boating industry.

The company's contract with the union expired at the end of 19y0,

EXHIBIT 21-4

MARINE SUPPLY CORPORATION
Statement of Changes in Financial Position
For Years Ending September 30
(in thousands of dollars)

	19x5	19x6	19x7	19x8	19x9	19y0	Total %	Total Amount
Source:								
From operations:								
Net earnings	10,642	15,666	15,375	15,662	17,078	13,390	46.5	87,813
Depreciation	4,284	4,264	4,448	4,747	5,587	6,254	15.7	29,584
Amortization of tooling	…	3,360	2,755	4,595	6,484	6,637	12.6	23,831
Other—principally provision for deferred income taxes	755	527	493	372	800	1,753	2.5	4,700
Total from operations	15,681	23,817	23,071	25,376	29,949	28,034	77.3	145,928
Proceeds from sale of:								
Long-term borrowings	…	…	…	17,030	18,202	1,391	19.4	36,623
Plant and equipment (net)	174	662	326	146	347	112	.9	1,767
Common stock	52	859	294	317	732	…	1.2	2,254
Other items, net	…	…	45	1,808	413	…	1.2	2,266
Total sources	15,907	25,338	23,736	44,677	49,643	29,537	100.0	188,838
Application:								
Additions to plant and equipment	2,964	4,739	11,177	16,639	16,109	9,461	32.3	61,089
Tooling expenditures	…	2,565	7,635	6,430	6,825	7,398	16.3	30,853
Long-term debt maturing currently	1,136	1,073	1,126	1,035	1,142	1,073	3.6	6,585
Dividends paid	5,128	6,351	6,369	7,981	8,060	8,080	22.2	41,969
Other items, net	408	355	…	1,199	…	3,526	2.9	5,488
Total applications	9,636	15,083	26,307	33,284	32,136	29,538	77.3	145,984
Working capital increase (decrease)	6,271	10,255	(2,571)	11,393	17,507	(1)	22.7	42,854

EXHIBIT 21–5
MARINE SUPPLY CORPORATION
Fifteen-Year Growth Rates
(annually compounded)

Per share	19w4-y0	19w4-w6 to 19x8-y0
Sales	8.0%	8.0%
Net income	4.6	3.3
Dividends	10.0	7.4
Book value	11.0	7.4

EXHIBIT 21–6
MARINE SUPPLY CORPORATION
Five-Year Growth Rates
(annually compounded)

Per share	19x5-y0	19x4-x6 to 19x8-y0
Sales	10.5%	9.7%
Net income	4.2	5.7
Dividends	9.0	9.6
Book value	7.0	5.7

EXHIBIT 21–7
MARINE SUPPLY CORPORATION
Common-Size Balance Sheets

	19x5	19x6	19x7	19x8	19x9	19y0
Assets						
Current Assets:						
Cash and equivalents	11	16	7	9	8	7
Receivables	17	16	19	18	18	21
Inventories	37	38	39	39	41	38
Total current assets	65	70	65	65	67	66
Land, plant, and equipment, net	30	26	28	29	28	28
Other assets	5	4	7	6	5	6
Total Assets	100	100	100	100	100	100
Liabilities and Equity						
Current liabilities	13	17	18	21	24	24
Long-term debt	11	9	8	14	18	18
Deferred taxes and investment credits	1	1	2	2	2	3
Other liabilities	2	2	1	1	1	...
Total Liabilities	27	29	29	38	45	45
Net worth	73	71	71	62	55	55
Total Liabilities and Equity	100	100	100	100	100	100

EXHIBIT 21-8

MARINE SUPPLY CORPORATION
Common-Size Income Statements

Item	19x5	19x6	19x7	19x8	19x9	19y0	Industry composite 19y0
Net sales	100.0%	100.0%	100.0%	100.0%	100.0%	100.0%	100.0%
Cost of goods sold* (excluding depreciation)	62.7	61.6	62.1	64.3	64.1	62.6	64.6
Depreciation	2.4	2.0	1.9	1.7	1.7	2.1	2.8
Gross profit	34.9	36.4	36.0	34.0	34.2	35.3	32.6
Selling, general, and administrative expenses	23.2	22.2	23.2	22.1	21.8	24.0	21.0
Operating income	11.7	14.2	12.8	11.9	12.4	11.4	11.6
Interest expense	.4	.5	.5	.7	1.4	2.2	0.8
Other income (expense)	(.3)	(.2)	(.3)	(.4)	(.5)	(.1)	0.2
Net income before tax	10.9	13.5	12.0	10.8	10.5	9.3	11.0
Deferred taxes	.2	.1	.2	.1	.2	.6	.3
Income taxes	4.8	6.0	5.3	5.0	5.0	4.3	4.9
Net income	5.9	7.4	6.5	5.6	5.2	4.4	5.8
*Including: Research and development	6.5	5.2	5.7	4.3	3.8	4.2	5.4
Maintenance and repairs	5.7	4.9	5.0	4.4	3.9	3.8	6.2

EXHIBIT 21-9

MARINE SUPPLY CORPORATION
Trend Index of Selected Accounts
(19x5 = 100)

Account	19x6	19x7	19x8	19x9	19y0
Cash	162	81	116	130	117
Accounts receivable	109	140	158	207	239
Inventory	116	131	159	204	197
Total current assets	122	124	151	192	194
Total current liabilities	154	180	249	353	363
Working capital	115	111	128	153	153
Fixed assets	100	116	147	172	180
Other assets	94	157	175	187	227
Long-term debt	93	86	198	315	318
Total liabilities	124	133	215	317	323
Equity capital	110	120	128	138	143
Net sales	118	129	155	181	169
Cost of goods sold	116	128	159	185	168
Gross profit	123	133	151	178	171
Selling, general, and administrative expenses	112	132	148	170	174
Interest expense	150	176	300	676	945
Total expenses	114	128	155	182	172
Operating income	143	142	158	192	165
Profit before taxes	145	142	153	173	143
Net income	147	143	147	161	126

EXHIBIT 21–10

MARINE SUPPLY CORPORATION
Selected per Share Results

Item	19x5	19x6	19x7	19x8	19x9	19y0
Sales	$22.90	$26.71	$29.28	$34.85	$40.48	$37.68
Net income	1.35	1.97	1.91	1.95	2.11	1.66
Dividends	.65	.80	.80	1.00	1.00	1.00
Book value	12.43	13.63	14.76	15.60	16.73	17.38

and the company was not sure during 19y0 whether it could avoid a strike.

After careful analysis, we conclude that about one half of deferred taxes and investment credits account balances will be reversed in the future; however, the possibility of reversal in the foreseeable future for the remaining one half is very remote. "Other liabilities" represent various debts having the characteristic of long-term debt. "Other current liabilities" represent amounts owing to various banks under revolving credit agreement.

The company is nearing its production capacity limits, necessitating new construction. For example, in 19x8 and 19x9, the company was forced to utilize some aging facilities on a multishift basis. "Other assets" consisted almost entirely of deferred research and development expenses. The company amortizes research and development over five years.

The period 19x5–y0 has been by far the most prosperous in Marine Supply's history. Sales and earnings have each reached peak levels, although the last six years have not been as profitable as mid 19w0's.

Based on the foregoing data and information we are to analyze the financial statements of Marine Supply Corporation with the following alternative points of view (objectives) in mind:

1. That of a bank to extend to the company a short-term loan of $15 million.
2. That of an insurance company to whom the company wants to sell privately $30 million of 25-year bonds.
3. That of an investor considering a substantial investment in the company.

These diverse and broad points of view require that we analyze all major aspects of the company's financial condition and results of operations, that is:

1. Short-term liquidity.
2. Funds flow.
3. Capital structure and long-term solvency.
4. Return on investment.

5. Asset utilization.
6. Operating performance.

The following assumptions will be used in the projection of operating results and of fund flows for 19y1:

It is expected that the annual growth rate by product line will continue except that snow vehicles and miscellaneous are expected to grow at a rate of 29 percent and 30 percent respectively. Improvements in production facilities will lower the cost of goods (exclusive of depreciation) to 60 percent of sales. The composite depreciation rate (depreciation expense as a percent of ending net plant) is expected to be 10 percent. Amortization of tooling costs included in cost of goods sold will be 10 percent higher than in 19y0. Selling expenses, which amount to one fourth of the selling, general, and administrative group of expenses are expected to go up by 10 percent in 19y1. The other three fourths of this category will remain unchanged. Taxes will average 53 percent of income before taxes, and the amount of deferred taxes will amount to the same proportion of the total tax accrual as in 19y0. Dividend payout is expected to amount to 50 percent of net income.

In order to retire $15 million in revolving credit notes (shown under current liabilities) and to finance a major plant expansion and modernization program just starting, the company expects to sell at par, early in 19y1, $30 million in 30-year 7 percent sinking fund bonds. That will leave $20 million in revolving credit notes outstanding. Interest expenses in 19y1 are estimated at $5,810,000. The maturities and sinking fund requirements of long-term debt are as follows:

(million $)

19y1	1.0
19y2	2.3
19y3	4.4
19y4	8.6
19y5	12.2

Research and development outlays are expected to amount to $3 million in 19y1, and outlays for tooling are planned at $13 million.

The company plans to spend $30 million in 19y1 on plant and equipment. Sales of equipment are expected to bring in $200,000 after tax. The chain-saw division which has a book value of $5 million is expected to be disposed of for $2 million, net of tax.

The problem of obtaining a meaningful and valid standard of external comparison for this analysis has been a difficult one. Two major sources of such data are industry statistics, such as those compiled by Robert Morris Associates, Standard & Poor's, or Dun & Bradstreet, or comparative data derived from companies of similar size and in similar lines of business. In this case comparative data was developed from the published reports of companies in lines of business similar to those of Marine Supply Company.

Analysis of short-term liquidity

Exhibit 21–11 presents some important liquidity measures of Marine Supply Corporation over the last six years. Both the current ratio and the acid test ratio have been declining over this period. However, they are still at sound levels in 19y0 on an absolute basis and also when compared to industry averages. The downward trend in these measures must be interpreted in the light of management's possible policy and intent. It is quite conceivable, particularly in view of the lower levels of the comparable industry ratios, that the current position in earlier years was unnecessarily strong and represented a wasteful tying up of resources which did not earn an acceptable return for the company. A glance at the common-size analysis in Exhibit 21–7 reveals the changes which have occurred in the composition of working capital elements over the past six years; the proportion of cash and cash equivalents among the current assets has dropped by almost half even though the absolute amount of cash and equivalents has not diminished on average. There has been a significant increase in current liabilities; they now represent almost a quarter of the funds invested in the enterprise whereas in 19x5 they represented by 13 percent of the total. This is confirmed in the trend index analysis (Exhibit 21–9) which shows that since 19x5 current liabilities have increased 3.63 times while cash increased 1.17 times, receivables 2.39 times, and inventories only 1.97 times. That the increase in current liabilities was out of proportion to that of sales is seen by the fact that during the same period sales increased only 1.69 times. That means that Marine Supply Corporation was somehow able to secure short-term credit from suppliers and banks at a rate twice as fast as that warranted by growth in sales. This, in turn, is importantly responsible for the steady decline in the current and the acid-test ratios.

A more serious problem area is the quality of the two important elements of current assets: accounts receivable and inventories. The accounts receivable turnover has undergone constant decline over the past six years, reaching a low point of 5.67 in 19y0. In that year it compared unfavorably as to 8.2 turnover in the industry. The alternative measure of "days' sales in accounts receivable" presents a similar picture with an increasing number of "days' sales" tied up in receivables. The 19y0 figure of 63.5 days compares to an industry experience of 44.0 days. It also compares unfavorably to the company's most common terms of sales of net 30 days. Thus, it is possible that the collectibility and the liquidity of accounts receivable have deteriorated.

EXHIBIT 21-11

MARINE SUPPLY CORPORATION
Short-Term Liquidity Analysis

Units		19x5	19x6	19x7	19x8	19x9	19y0	Industry composite 19y0
Ratio	Current ratio................	5.15	4.09	3.55	3.13	2.80	2.75	2.40
Ratio	Acid-test ratio...............	2.22	1.88	1.43	1.26	1.11	1.16	.90
Times	Accounts receivable turnover.....	8.03	8.67	7.43	7.87	7.03	5.67	8.20
Times	Inventory turnover............	2.29	2.27	2.24	2.28	2.08	1.96	2.30
Days	Days sales in receivables........	44.8	41.5	48.5	45.7	51.2	63.5	44.0
Days	Days to sell inventory..........	157.2	158.6	160.7	157.9	173.1	183.7	156.2
Days	Conversion period.............	202.0	200.1	209.2	203.6	224.3	247.2	200.2
%	Cash to current assets..........	17.24	22.84	11.18	13.20	11.69	10.37	9.80
%	Cash to current liabilities.......	88.76	93.46	39.67	41.33	32.72	28.52	29.60
$(MM)	Working capital...............	70.10	80.40	77.70	89.70	107.20	107.22	...
#	Liquidity index...............	127	118	139	134	150	163	...

Inventory turnover has also decreased over the past six years, although the deterioration has not been as marked as has been the case with receivables. A number of factors could account for this, including a larger number and variety of outboard motors, lawn mowers, and snow vehicles models which must be stocked, the larger variety of spare parts that these require, as well as a possible accumulation of raw materials in anticipation of a strike at suppliers. It is also possible that Marine Supply Corporation overestimated sales for 19y0, while sales dropped 7 percent from the 19x9 level, inventories dropped by only 3 percent, thus contributing to the turnover slowdown. The 19y0 turnover of Marine Supply Corporation of 1.96 compares unfavorably with the 2.3 industry average. In 19y0 it took 183.7 days to sell the average inventory compared to an industry average of 156.2 days. The comparable figure for the company in 19x5 was 157.2 days.

The deterioration in the liquidity of the principal operating assets of the current asset group, accounts receivable, and inventories is also seen in the period of days it takes to convert inventories into cash. It grew from 202 days in 19x5 to 247.2 days in 19y0 and compares to an industry average of only 200.2 days in the latter year.

The liquidity index at 163 in 19y0 up from 127 in 19x5, also corroborates the deterioration in the liquidity of the current assets which we have already determined in the analysis of individual components of working capita.

It is conceivable that further analysis and inquiry from management will reveal that the slowdown in the turnover of accounts receivable and inventories does not affect their ultimate realization even if that would take a longer time. In that case the repercussions of such a slowdown lie in the area liquidity and funds flow as well as in the area of asset utilization which will be examined later in this analysis.

Analysis of funds flow

This analysis has two main objectives:

1. To supplement the static measures used to assess short-term liquidity by means of a short-term funds flow forecast.
2. To analyze the statement of changes in financial position in order to assess its implications on the longer term flow of funds (i.e., long-term solvency).

Our first step will be to build a funds flow forecast for Marine Supply Corporation in 19y1. Since sources of funds from operations are an important element of funds and a projection of earnings will be necessary anyway, we start with such a projection for 19y1, using the data and the supplementary information provided (see Exhibit 21–12).

Having established the estimated net income for 19y1 we can now proceed, using the data and the additional information we now have, to construct an estimated statements of sources and uses of working capital (funds) for 19y1.

Exhibit 21–13 projects an increase in working capital of about $16 million. If this forecast proves reasonably accurate, the current ratio should improve to about 3:1. As is true of all forecasts, their reliability depends on the validity of the assumptions on which they are based.

EXHIBIT 21–12

MARINE SUPPLY CORPORATION
Projected Income Statement for 19y1
(millions of dollars)

	19y0 sales level	Increment factor	19y1 estimated amount	Total	%
Net sales:					
Marine products	217.3 ×	1.10	239.03		
Lawn care equipment	30.5 ×	1.13	34.47		
Vehicles	19.6 ×	1.07	20.97		
Snow vehicles	23.4 ×	1.29	30.19		
Miscellaneous	4.2 ×	1.30	5.46	330.12	100.0
Cost of goods sold (exclusive of depreciation)			198.07		60.0
Depreciation (1)			8.70		2.6
				206.77	62.6
Gross profit				123.35	37.4
Selling, general, and administrative expenses:					
General and administrative (2)			54.74		
Selling (3)			20.08		
Amortization of research and development costs			1.00	75.82	23.0
				47.53	14.4
Interest expenses				5.81	1.8
Income before taxes				41.72	12.6
Income taxes:					
Current			19.24		
Deferred (4)			2.88	22.12	6.7
				19.60	5.9
Loss on disposal of chain-saw division (net of tax)				3.00	.9
Net income				16.60	5.0

(1) Beginning net plant plus half of 19y1 additions times 10%: (72.2 + 15.0) × 10%. It is assumed that the plant additions were in use, on average, half of the year.
(2) Three fourths of 72.99 (last year selling, general, and administrative).
(3) Selling expenses at 10% above the 19y0 level (72.99 − 54.74) × 1.10.
(4) Deferred taxes at 13% of the total provision for the year which amounts to 53% of pretax income.

EXHIBIT 21-13
MARINE SUPPLY CORPORATION
Projected Statement of Sources and Uses of Funds for 19y1
(in millions of dollars)

Sources of funds:		
From operations:		
Net income	16.60	
Add: Items not requiring current funds:		
Depreciation	8.70	
Amortization of tooling costs	7.30	
Deferred income taxes	2.88	
Amortization of research and development	1.00	
Loss on sale of chain-saw division	3.00	
Total from operations		39.48
Proceeds from sale of 7% sinking fund bonds		30.00
Sale of chain-saw division		2.00
Sale of equipment		.20
Total sources		71.68
Uses of funds:		
Additions to plant and equipment	30.00	
Outlays for tooling	13.00	
Outlays for research and development	3.00	
Long-term debt maturities	1.00	
Dividends declared	8.30	
Total uses		55.30
Increase in working capital		16.38

The assumption that Marine Supply Corporation can sell $30 million in 7 percent sinking fund bonds appears reasonable in the light of the company's present capital structure. Its failure to do so would require either the abandonment or deferral of expansion and modernization plans or it will result in a deterioration of the current ratio to about 2.5.

The projected net income of $16.6 million for 19y1 appears reasonable because it is based on the assumption of a continuation of present sales trends and a reduction in the growth rate of two product line categories. However, it is more vulnerable on the expense side. The increase in the gross margin is predicated on increases in productivity which are envisaged but which are yet to be realized. Moreover, any program of expansion and modernization is subject to the risk of delays, misjudgments, and short falls which may delay, postpone, or completely undermine the realization of improvements and economies. On the other hand, the increases in fixed costs which such a program entails are a reality with which the enterprise must live for a long time.

Any degree of failure to realize savings and improvements will also affect the short-term flow of funds. Thus, for example, continuing the assumption that 50 percent of the net income will be distributed as dividends, a 5 percent increase in cost of goods sold (exclusive of depreciation) will lower the inflow of funds as follows:

	Millions of dollars (approximately)
Increase in cost of goods sold (exclusive of depreciation)—5% of $198 million	9.90
Less tax effect at 53%	5.25
	4.65
Less: Dividend reduction (50%)	2.32
	2.33
Less: Deferred taxes (13% of 8.75)	.68
Reduction in funds available from operations	1.65

A similar computation can, of course, be made for any other change in assumptions. The likelihood of any of the above assumptions materializing and the probability attached to them is, ultimately, a matter of judgment.

The longer range funds flow picture is subject to a great many uncertainties. Examination of the company's historical pattern of fund flows over the 19x5 to 19y0 period (see Exhibit 21-4) is revealing. Funds from operations provided 77 percent of all funds inflows while long-term borrowing provided most of the rest. Such borrowing occurred mostly in 19x8 and 19x9. Equity financing was negligible.

Additions to plant and equipment used about 32 percent of all funds available. These outlays were, however, twice as high as the provision for depreciation. With the company bumping against the ceiling of its practical capacity in many lines this trend is likely to continue. Already in 19y1 capital expenditures are planned at three times the 19y0 level and long-term debt will be incurred to finance this as well as the working capital needs of an expanding business. As will be discussed further under "capital structure" there is, of course, a limit to the company's debt capacity, and equity financing will be required. This may explain the company's relatively generous dividend policy over the recent years.

In spite of relatively heavy long-term borrowing in 19x8 and 19x9 long-term debt maturities and sinking fund requirements are low. These will, however, increase sharply from $1 million in 19y1 to $12 million in 19y5. The proposed $30 million bond issue in 19y1 will undoubtedly add to these maturities.

The longer term fund flow outlook of Marine Supply Corporation is one of increasing demand for funds due to accelerating outlays for plant equipment and tooling as well as sharply rising debt service outlays. While funds from operations have been significant and are growing, they will have to continue to do so to meet increasing demands. Since funds from operations represented 77 percent of all sources of funds in the past six years, the company's fund flow is particularly vulnerable to any reduction in net income. Working capital needs will also increase along with the expected increase in sales volume.

It should be borne in mind that focusing on *net* working capital does not tell the whole story of Marine Supply Corporation's borrowing. Included in current liabilities are $35 million in revolving credit notes. The company may well want to convert this short-term interest sensitive debt into a longer term type of obligation. A beginning towards this goal is expected to be made in 19y1. That too will require using up some of the company's shrinking capacity to finance by means of long-term debt.

Analysis of capital structure and long-term solvency

Having just examined the funds aspect of Marine Supply Corporation's long-term solvency we now turn to an examination of its capital structure and the risk inherent in it. The change in the company's capital structure can be gauged by means of a number of measurements and comparisons.

Looking at Exhibit 21-7 we see that the contribution of equity capital to the total funds invested in the enterprise has shrunk from 73 percent in 19x5 to 55 percent in 19y0. With the expected issuance of $30 million on additional bonds, this proportion can be expected to dip below 50 percent. The long-term debt portion of the total funds invested in the enterprise increased from 11 percent in 19x5 to 18 percent in 19y0 and is headed considerably higher in 19y1.

In Exhibit 21-9 we can see the relative change in debt, equity, and other related elements in the financial statements. On a basis of 19x5 = 100 long-term debt rose to 318 while equity capital increased only to 143. In the same period net sales rose only to 169, net income to 126, while interest costs soared to 945. Quite clearly the company decided to finance its needs by means of debt, both short and long term. Reasons for this could be an unwillingness to dilute the equity or a desire to incur monetary liabilities in times of inflation. Whatever the reason, the leverage and hence the risk in the capital structure increased substantially. This is particularly true because Marine Supply Corporation is in a relatively cyclical industry and relies on a share of the consumer's discretionary dollar.

The capital structure and long-term solvency ratios in Exhibit 21-14 bear out these conclusions. Equity to total debt stands at 1.29 in 19y0 compared to 2.86 in 19x5, and compares to an industry composite of 1.4. Similarly, equity to long-term debt stands at 2.84 in 19y0 compared to an industry composite of 3.1. The times interest earned ratio plummeted from 29.24 in 19x5 to 5.28 in 19y0 and compares with an industry composite of 8.6. The income projections as well as the borrowing plans

EXHIBIT 21-14

MARINE SUPPLY CORPORATION
Capital Structure and Long-Term Solvency Ratios

	19x5	19x6	19x7	19x8	19x9	19y0	19y0 industry composite
Equity to total debt	99.24* / 34.76 = 2.86	109.54 / 43.16 = 2.54	118.89 / 46.21 = 2.57	127.69 / 74.61 = 1.71	137.84 / 110.56 = 1.25	144.03 / 111.94 = 1.29	1.4
Equity to long-term debt	39.24 / 17.86* = 5.56	109.54 / 17.16 = 6.38	118.89 / 15.71 = 7.57	127.69 / 32.51 = 3.93	137.84 / 50.96 = 2.70	144.03 / 50.66 = 2.84	3.1
Equity to net fixed assets	2.48	2.75	2.57	2.18	2.00	2.00	2.2
Times interest earned	29.24	28.30	23.83	15.36	8.25	5.28	8.6

*Computed as following:
```
One half of deferred income taxes . . . . . . . . . . . . . . .   .97
Net worth shown . . . . . . . . . . . . . . . . . . . . . . . . 98.27
Adjusted net worth . . . . . . . . . . . . . . . . . . . . . . 99.24

Total liabilities shown . . . . . . . . . . . . . . . . . . . . 35.73
Less: One half of deferred income taxes . . . . . . . . . . . .   .97
Adjusted total liabilities . . . . . . . . . . . . . . . . . . 34.76
Less: Total current liabilities . . . . . . . . . . . . . . . . 16.90
Adjusted long-term debt . . . . . . . . . . . . . . . . . . . . 17.86
```

for 19y1 would result in an improved interest coverage ratio of 8.2 as a consequence of the refinancing of high-interest short-term debt and also because the 7 percent bonds will be outstanding for only part of the year. This improvement in the coverage ratio may, however, prove to be only temporary in nature.

As we saw from the longer term funds flow analysis, the company is now entering a period of increasing capital investment needs and of increasingly heavy debt service schedules. It does this at a time when its debt is high in relation to its equity capital and when shrinking interest coverage ratios exert downward pressure on its credit rating. Moreover, the increasing fixed charges which stem from recent substantial additions to plant and equipment make operating results more vulnerable to cyclical downturn with the result that sources of funds from operations are similarly vulnerable.

Analysis of return on investment

The return which the company realizes on total assets, Exhibit 21-15, has been on the decline in recent years, having declined from 10.6 percent in 19x6 (which was the best year in this respect) to 6.4 percent in 19y0. Even if we regard 19x6 as an unusually good year, the decline

EXHIBIT 21-15

MARINE SUPPLY CORPORATION
Return on Investment Ratios

	19x5	19x6	19x7	19x8	19x9	19y0	19y0 industry composite
Return on total assets . . .	8.2% (1)	10.6%	9.6%	8.3%	7.8%	6.4%	9.3%
Return on equity capital . .	10.8% (2)	14.5%	13.0%	12.5%	12.6%	9.5%	12.8%
Return on long-term liabilities and equity	9.4% (3)	12.8%	11.8%	10.5%	10.3%	8.5%	10.6%
Financial leverage index . .	1.32 (4)	1.37	1.23	1.27	1.32	1.33	. . .
Equity growth rate	5.6 (5)	8.6	7.5	6.1	6.7	3.8	. . .

Notes

(1) $\dfrac{\text{Net income} + \text{Interest expense}(1-\text{Tax rate})}{\text{Total assets}} = \dfrac{10.64 + .7(1-.46)}{134}$

(2) $\dfrac{\text{Net income}}{\text{Net worth}} = \dfrac{10.64}{98.27}$

(3) $\dfrac{\text{Net income} + \text{Interest expense}(1-\text{Tax rate})}{\text{Long-term liabilities} + \text{Equity}} = \dfrac{11.018}{134.0 - 16.90}$

(4) $\dfrac{\text{Return on equity capital}}{\text{Return on total assets}} = \dfrac{10.8}{8.2}$

(5) $\dfrac{\text{Net income} - \text{Payout}}{\text{Common shareholders' equity}} = \dfrac{\text{Amount retained}}{\text{Common shareholders' equity}} = \dfrac{5.51}{98.27}$

from the prior year return levels is quite significant. In comparison with an industry return on total assets in 19y0 of 9.3 percent, the company's 6.4 percent return is also significantly worse. This negative trend over the past six years is reason for concern and requires further investigation. The two major elements which make up the return on total assets, that is, net profit margin and asset turnover, will be examined later in this analysis.

In comparison with the return on total assets, the decline in the return on equity has not been quite as significant. This is mainly due to the relatively advantageous use of short-term and long-term credit. The financial leverage index (Exhibit 21-15) which in 19y0 stands at 1.33 is practically unchanged from its 19x5 level. It must be noted, however, that the company cannot expand its debt much more from the present level since over the past six years debt has expanded very significantly. Thus, in the immediate future an adequate return on equity will be dependent primarily on improvements in profitability and in asset utilization. As can be seen from Exhibit 21-15, the equity growth rate from earnings retention has shrunk in 19y0 to 3.8 percent from over 6 percent in the two years before that and from 8.6 percent in 19x6. This is largely due to the maintenance of a generous dividend policy in the face of shrinking earnings. This shrinkage in the internal equity growth rate comes at a time when the company is increasingly in need of additional equity capital. Conceivably, however, a liberal dividend record can facilitate in the future the raising of equity capital.

Analysis of asset utilization

Exhibit 21–16 indicates that in most categories the asset utilization ratios have been declining over the past six years. The sales to total assets ratio is down to 1.2 in 19y0 from the 1.4 level in 19x8 and compares

EXHIBIT 21–16

MARINE SUPPLY CORPORATION
Asset Utilization Ratios

	19x5	19x6	19x7	19x8	19x9	19y0	19y0 industry composite
Sales to cash and equivalents..	12.0	8.7	19.3	16.1	16.8	17.4	9.1
Sales to receivables	8.0	8.7	7.4	7.9	7.0	5.7	10.6
Sales to inventories	3.7	3.7	3.6	3.6	3.2	3.1	4.1
Sales to working capital	2.6	2.6	3.0	3.1	3.1	2.8	4.0
Sales to fixed assets.	4.5	5.3	5.1	4.8	4.7	4.2	6.4
Sales to other assets.	26.6	33.2	21.8	23.5	25.8	19.7	22.3
Sales to total assets	1.3	1.4	1.4	1.4	1.3	1.2	1.5
Sales to short-term liabilities. .	10.7	8.2	7.7	6.7	5.5	5.0	...

to an industry average 1.5 times. The impact of this change can be assessed as follows:

Given the company's net income to sales ratio in 19y0 of 4.4 percent and a net of tax interest expense of about 1.1 percent (Exhibit 21–8) a total asset turnover of 1.4 (the 19x8 rate) would have yielded a return on total assets of 7.7 percent $[(4.4 + 1.1) \times 1.4]$ rather than the 6.4 percent return actually realized in 19y0. At a rate of turnover of 1.5 (industry average) the present profit rate would yield a return on investment of about 8.2 percent $[(4.4 + 1.1) \times 1.5]$.

The asset categories where the turnover rate has dropped most sharply over the six years are "other assets" and "receivables." Only cash showed an increase in turnover (utilization). Judging by the fact that there were significant fixed asset additions in 19x8 and 19x9 (see Exhibit 21–9), the drop in the fixed asset turnover rate was moderate. It must be borne in mind that it takes time before fixed asset additions become sufficiently productive to generate an expected volume of sales. In addition, certain types of fixed asset outlays represent improvements in production facilities which lead to efficiencies and savings rather than to expansion of productive capacity. Such outlays, consequently, do not lead to greater sales but rather to savings in variable costs and result in improvements in profit margins. Exhibit 21–8 indicates that while profit margins are below the 19x6–x7 levels, they have been in an improving trend in the last three years. The drop over the six-year span in the turnover of the "other assets" group reflects growth in deferred charges, particularly tooling.

Analysis of operating performance

Exhibit 21-8 presents common-size income statements of the company for the six years, 19x5–y0.

The gross profit of Marine Supply Corporation has held within a relatively narrow range over the last six years. In 19y0 at 35.3 percent the gross profit margin is higher than in the preceding two years but is below the levels reached in 19x6 and 19x7. It does compare favorably to the industry gross margin of 32.6 percent. However, the research and development costs as well as the repair and maintenance costs included in the cost of goods sold figure are lower, as a percentage of sales than the industry composite. This aspect of the quality of earnings will be further discussed below.

In 19y0 the percentage relationship between depreciation expense and sales was 2.1 percent up from 1.7 percent the year before. The disparity between this percentage and the industry composite of 2.8 percent is noteworthy because it may affect the quality of Marine Supply Corporation's earnings. It would appear that an inadequate amount of depreciation is recorded by Marine Supply Corporation. Before a definite judgment can be made, additional information would be required. The company is now approaching the limit of practical capacity in many of its product lines. Competitors may have more reserve capacity available and that may express itself in a relatively higher composite depreciation rate. It is also possible that Marine Supply Corporation's equipment is, on average, of an older vintage, and hence lower cost, than its competitors'. On the other hand, a lower composite depreciation rate than necessary is a factor which lowers the quality of the company's earnings.

We have two more measures available to judge the size of the yearly depreciation charge:

	19x5	19x6	19x7	19x8	19x9	19y0
Accumulated depreciation as a percentage of gross plant.	53	55	53	49	47	48
Annual depreciation expense as a percentage of gross plant.	5.0	4.8	4.4	4.2	4.3	4.5

The decline in the percentage of accumulated depreciation in relation to gross plant most likely reflects the substantial additions of new equipment in recent years. The decline of depreciation expense as a percentage of gross plant is, however, indicative of a less conservative depreciation policy in the more recent years.

Selling, general, and administrative expenses as a percentage of sales have, generally, been on the rise. In 19y0 they stood at 24 percent which compares to an industry composite figure of only 21 percent. Thus, by the time we reach operating income, the advantage which the company held over the industry because of larger gross margin has now been neutralized. Operating income for Marine Supply Corporation represents 11.4 percent of sales, and that compares with 11.6 percent for the industry. Further inquiries should be made to determine whether the selling expense component or the general and administrative part are responsible for the increase in this category.

Interest expenses have shown by far the steepest increase over the past six years. On the basis of 19x5 = 100 they have grown to 945 (almost tenfold) by 19y0 (Exhibit 21–9). This is due, of course, primarily to the sharp expansion of debt. Moreover, the short-term revolving debt is interest sensitive and thus introduces a measure of uncertainty in the forecasting of future interest charges.

Two other aspects of the quality of Marine Supply Corporation's earnings should be noted.

Research and development costs as a percentage of sales have been in a declining trend having reached 4.2 percent in 19y0 down from 6.5 percent in 19x5 (Exhibit 21–3). This raises a question about the effect on future sales and profits of the decline in the research and development cost outlays in relation to sales. Similarly, the percentage of sales devoted to repairs and maintenance has declined from 5.7 percent in 19x5 to 3.8 percent in 19y0, a matter of concern particularly in the light of the fact that Marine Supply Corporation's facilities are, on average, older now than in 19x5. In the latter year the percentage of repair and maintenance expense in relation to gross plant was 12.1 percent. In 19y0 that relationship dropped to 8.3 percent. This *prima facie* evidence of a deterioration in the quality of Marine Supply Corporation's earnings merits further investigation.

The total effective tax rate of Marine Supply Corporation in 19y0 is 52 percent which compare to industry composite effective rate of 47 percent. The net income to sales of Marine Supply Corporation is 4.4 percent for 19y0 significantly below the industry composite of 5.8 percent for that year. However, since 19y0 was a year of labor trouble and recession for the company, the percentages of net income to sales prevailing in the prior years, which are closer to the industry average, may be taken as more representative of the company's earning power.

Exhibit 21–17 analyzes the change occurring in net income between the 19x5–x7 period and the 19x8–y0 period. Sales increased by 46 percent, but due largely to greater increases in the cost of good sold (49 percent) and interest expenses (353 percent) the increase in net income was held to only 11 percent.

EXHIBIT 21–17

MARINE SUPPLY CORPORATION
Statement Accounting for Variations in Net Income
Three-Year Period 19x5–x7 (Average) Compared to Three-Year Period 19x8–y0 (Average)
(in millions of dollars)

Items tending to increase net income:				
Increase in net sales:				
Net sales, 19x8–y0	303.93			
Net sales, 19x5–x7	208.87	95.06		46%
Deduct increase in cost of goods sold:				
Cost of goods sold, 19x8–y0	193.42			
Cost of goods sold, 19x5–x7	129.78	63.64		49
Net increase in gross margin			31.42	
Items tending to decrease net income:				
Increase in depreciation:				
Depreciation, 19x8–y0	5.53			
Depreciation, 19x5–x7	4.31	1.22		28
Increase in selling, general, and administrative expenses:				
S.G.A., 19x8–y0	68.81			
S.G.A., 19x5–x7	47.69	21.12		44
Increase in interest expense:				
Interest expense, 19x8–y0	4.48			
Interest expense, 19x5–x7	.99	3.49		353
Increase in other income and expense:				
Other income and expense, 19x8–y0	.80			
Other income and expense, 19x5–x7	.59	.21		36
Net increase in expenses			26.04	
Net increase in profit before taxes			5.38	21
Increase in income taxes:				
Income taxes, 19x8–y0	15.52			
Income taxes, 19x5–x7	11.66		3.86	33
Net increase in net income			1.52	11

Summary and conclusions

This analysis has examined all facets of Marine Supply Corporation's record of results of operations and financial position and has estimated the projected results and fund flows for one year. An analysis such as this is an indispensable step in arriving at a decision on the three questions posed. Nevertheless, essential as the data and information developed by this analysis is, it is not sufficient in most cases to arrive at a final conclusion. This is so because qualitative and other factors can have an important bearing on the final conclusion. Only when all the factors, those developed by the analysis as well as the others, have been assembled can a decision be reached by the application of judgment.

For example, the *bank* which is asked to extend short-term credit must take into consideration the character of the management, past loan experience, as well as the on-going relationship with the loan applicant.

In addition to the foregoing intangibles, the long-term lender will focus on such matters as security arrangements and provisions which safeguard the solvency of the recipient of the loan.

The *equity investor* is, of course, interested in earning power and in earnings per share, but many considerations and judgments must be joined with these data before an investment decision is made. Thus, for instance, what earnings are, and what they are likely to be, is the product of financial analysis. At what price-earnings ratio they should be capitalized is a question for investment judgment. Similarly, the risk inherent in an enterprise, the volatility of its earnings, and the breadth and quality of the market for its securities are factors which must also be considered. They determine whether an investment fits into the investor's portfolio and whether it is compatible with his investment objectives.

Since the ultimate conclusions regarding problems, such as the lending and investing decision which we consider in this case, is based on more than the data and facts brought out by financial analysis alone, it follows that the most useful way to present the results of financial analysis is to summarize them by listing the most relevant and salient points which were developed by the analysis and which the decision maker should consider. This we shall do in this case.

The following are the main points which have been developed by our analysis of Marine Supply Corporation.

Short-term liquidity. The current ratio is in a downtrend but still stands at a relatively sound level. The downtrend may, in part, represent a correction of former excessive levels in the ratio.

The current assets are, as a whole, less liquid than in former years. The slower turnover in accounts receivable indicates a possible deterioration in collectibility. The decline in inventory turnover may be due to diversity of product line rather than to unsaleable or obsolete items in stock.

Current liabilities have risen sharply in recent years, and they now represent one fourth of all funds available to the enterprise.

The decline in liquidity is evidenced by a rise in the liquidity index.

Fund projections for 19y1 indicate a projected increase in working capital of $16 million by the end of that year. This assumes, however, the successful sale of $30 million in bonds and that expense projections which incorporate benefits of efficiencies will be realized. There is a moderate amount of risk that these projections may not be realized.

Capital structure and long-term solvency. In 19y0 equity capital represented 55 percent of total funds invested in the enterprise down from 73 percent in 19x5. In recent years (see Exhibit 21–9) long-term debt increased drastically (3.18 times), out of proportion to such measures as growth in sales (1.69 times) or in equity (1.43 times).

The reduction of equity capital relative to debt and all funds invested in the company is not a favorable development in view of the fact that Marine Supply Corporation is in a cyclical industry. The company may be nearing the limit of its debt capacity.

Times interest earned is down to 5.29 in 19y0 (from 29.24 in 19x5). If a portion of rentals would be included as fixed charges, the coverage ratio would drop lower still. Next year, assuming the $30 million in long-term bonds are sold, this ratio is slated to improve to 8.2 times.

Over the last six years 77 percent of all funds inflows were funds generated by operations. Thus, a very substantial source of funds is vulnerable to changes in operating results. Over the longer term, demand for funds is expected to increase significantly. Long-term debt maturities are slated to increase sharply even excluding those from the $30 million bond issue which is expected to be sold in 19y1. There will be a growing need of funds for plant and equipment. Provisions for depreciation were consistently below fixed asset additions in recent years.

Return on investment and asset utilization. The return on investment is in a declining trend. In 19y0 the return on total assets was 6.4 percent compared with an industry composite of 9.3 percent. Due to the advantageous use of debt the return on equity was 9.5 percent in 19y0 where the disparity with the industry composite of 12.8 percent is less marked.

The decline in the return on total assets is due to the twin effects of declining asset utilization rates as well as a decline in profitability per dollar of sales.

Operating performance. The company's gross profit percentage has held relatively steady over the past six years. Other costs have neutralized Marine Supply Corporation's higher gross margin compared to the industry. Interest expenses have risen sharply over recent years. Both research and development expenses and repair and maintenance outlays have declined as a percentage of sales in recent years.

The significant decline in net income as a percentage of sales to 4.4 percent in 19y0 (industry composite 5.8 percent) is due to the particularly adverse labor and economic conditions of that year. In prior years the company's net as a percentage of sales, compared more favorably to industry experience.

Projected income for 19y1, based on the assumptions stated in the analysis, is $16.6 million after a loss of $3 million on disposal of the chain-saw division. On a per share basis the net income per share is expected to be $2.06 per share compared to earnings per share in 19y0 of $1.66 and in 19x9 of $2.11. In 19y0 income per share before the loss on the chain-saw division is projected at $2.43.

USES OF THE FINANCIAL STATEMENT ANALYSIS

The foregoing analysis of the financial statements of Marine Supply Corporation consists of two major parts: (1) the detailed analysis and (2) the summary and conclusions. As was mentioned earlier, in a formal analytical report the summary and conclusions section may precede the detailed analysis so that the reader is presented with material in the order of its importance to him.

The *bank* loan officer who has to decide on the short-term loan application by the company will normally give primary attention to short-term liquidity analysis and to the funds flow projection and secondarily to capital structure and operating results.

The investment committee of the *insurance company* may, in taking a longer term point of view, pay attention first to capital structure and long-term solvency and then to operating performance, return on investment, asset utilization, and short-term liquidity, and in that order of emphasis.

The *potential investor* in Marine Supply Corporation's shares will, of course, be interested in all the aspects of our analysis. His emphasis may, however, be different again and take the following order of priority: results of operations, return on investment, capital structure, and long-term solvency and short-term liquidity.

An adequate financial statement analysis will, as the Marine Supply Corporation analysis illustrates, contain in addition to the analysis of the data, enough information and detail so as to allow the decision maker to follow the rationale behind the analyst's conclusions as well as allow him to expand it into areas not covered by the analysis.

COMPUTER ASSISTED FINANCIAL ANALYSIS

Throughout this text the emphasis has been on the application of thoughtful and logical analysis upon carefully evaluated and verified data. Financial statement analysis does, however, involve a significant amount of work of a computational nature as well as numerous logical steps which can be preplanned and programmed. It is in these areas that the financial analyst can utilize computers to great advantage.

The modern electronic computer has a remarkable facility for performing complex computations with great speed. Moreover, it can perform these computations, comparisons, and other logical steps for long periods of time without exhaustion and, once properly programmed, will do them without error. In today's environment, when business complexity has outstripped our ability to grasp it and when our ability to generate information has outrun our ability to utilize it, the computer can render vital assistance.

The intelligent use of the computer's formidable capabilities in financial analysis depends, however, on thorough understanding of the limitations to which this powerful tool is subject. Thus, the computer lacks the ability to make intuitive judgments or to gain insights, capabilities which are essential to a competent and imaginative financial analysis. Moreover, the stored data bases on which computer assisted security analysis often relies do not include information which, as was seen in Part II of this text, is needed to adjust accounting data in order to render it comparable or in order to make it conform to the analyst's specific needs. This is particularly true for the following reasons:

1. The data bank lacks information on accounting policies and principles employed by a given enterprise. This information is essential to an interpretation of the data and to its comparison to other data.
2. Footnotes and other explanatory or restrictive information usually found in individual enterprise reports containing the financial statements are also generally not available.
3. Lack of retroactive adjustments, because the necessary data are often not available.
4. Errors and omissions may occur when large masses of financial data are processed on a uniform basis for purposes of inclusion in the data base.
5. The aggregation of dissimilar or noncomparable data results in a loss of vital distinctions and thus reduces its meaning and its value for analysis. In summary, the outputs depend on the quality of the inputs.

Given an understanding of the limitations to which the computer is subject, the following are the more significant uses which can be made of this tool in the broad area of financial analysis:

1. Data storage and retrieval

A machine-accessible comprehensive data base is essential to the use of the computer in most phases of security and credit analysis. The ability of the computer to store vast amounts of data and to afford access to them is one of its important capabilities. Another is the ability to sift these data, to manipulate them mathematically and to select from among them in accordance with set criteria, as well as to constantly update and modify them.

A large commercially available data base comprising financial information on many hundreds of corporations covering twenty or more years is available from COMPUSTAT, a service of Standard and Poor's Corporation.

2. Specialized financial analysis

   A. *Financial analysis in credit extension*

      a) Storage of facts for comparison and decision making.
      b) Projection of enterprise cash requirements under a variety of assumptions.
      c) Projection of financial statements under a variety of assumptions showing the impact of changes on key variables. Known as *sensitivity analysis,* this technique allows the user to explore the effect of systematically changing a given variable repeatedly by a predetermined amount.
      d) The introduction of probabilistic inputs. The data can be inserted as probability distributions, either normally shaped or skewed, or random probability distributions otherwise known as "Monte Carlo trials."

   B. *Security analysis*

      a) Calculations based on past data.
      b) Trend computations.
        —Simple
        —Regression analysis
      c) Predictive models.
      d) Projections and forecasts.
      e) Sensitivity analysis.
      f) Complex probabilistic analysis.

Given an understanding of the capabilities of the modern electronic computer, as well as the limitations to which it is subject, the financial analyst will find in it an important tool which promises to grow in importance as new applications to which it can be put are perfected in the future.

QUESTIONS

1. What kind of processes should normally precede an analysis of financial statements?
2. What are the analytical implications of the fact that financial statements are, at best, an abstraction of underlying reality?
3. Name the six major "building blocks" of financial analysis. What does the "building block" approach involve?

4. What are some of the earmarks of a good analysis? Into what distinct sections should a well-organized analysis be divided?
5. What additional knowledge and analytical skills must an analyst bring to bear upon the analysis of enterprises in specialized or regulated industries?
6. What are some of the principal uses of computers in investment analysis? (C.F.A.)
7. What are the most important limitations or disadvantages to the application of computers to security analysis? (C.F.A.)

INDEX

Index

A

Accelerated depreciation, 197
  price level changes, 296
Accountant
  Certified, 315
  Licensed, 315
  Public, 315
Accounting
  cycle, 9, 49
  framework, simplifications and rigidities of, 5
  function of, 7
  inconsistency, 84
  interrelationships, among accounts, 10
  postulates, 8
  purposes of, 8
  risk, 53
  specialized industry, 547
  uniformity, 75
Accounting changes, 240
  in accounting estimate, 242
  in accounting principle, 242
  catch-up adjustment, 242
  correction of an error, 243
  historical summaries of financial information, 244
  implications for analysis, 244
  materiality, 243
  in reporting entity, 243

Accounting conventions, 66-67
  consistency, 67
  full disclosure, 67
Accounting data, 3
  importance of, 4
  interim nature of, 6
  limitations of, 5
  monetary expression, 5
  simplification and rigidities of, 5
Accounting principles
  alternatives, 65
  analytical review of, 41
  change of; *see* APB *Opinion No. 20*
  changes in the application of, 67
  having authoritative support, 357
  in measurement of capital structure, 398
  used in income statement, 467
Accounting Principles Board (APB)
  opinions
    No. 5, 103
    No. 6, 169
    No. 7, 183
    No. 8, 117, 207
    No. 9, 125, 230
    No. 10, 104, 123, 179
    No. 11, 114, 217, 223
    No. 12, 211
    No. 14, 222
    No. 15, 247, 265

Accounting Principles Board
  (APB)—*Cont.*
  opinions—*Cont.*
    No. 16, 150, 164
    No. 17, 84, 140, 164, 221
    No. 18, 73, 139, 168, 187
    No. 19, 270, 286
    No. 20, 203, 240
    No. 21, 54, 529
    No. 23, 75, 144
    No. 25, 212
    No. 27, 106
    No. 28, 538
    No. 30, 233
    No. 31, 105
  Statement No. 3, 298
Accounting Research Bulletin
  No. 43, 169
  No. 50, 111
Accounting Research Studies
  No. 1, 8
  No. 4, 103
  No. 6, 298
  No. 11, 218
Accounts receivable, 342, 347
  aging schedule, 356
  average turnover ratio, 353
  collection period for, 354
  effect on quality of earnings, 529
  evaluation of collection period for, 355
  items to be included in turnover ratio computation, 353
  measure of liquidity, 352
  quality of, 353
  turnover ratio, meaning of, 353
  valuation, effect on reported income of, 529
Accruals
  cost and expense, 192
  of interest, 182
  of revenue, 177
Acid test ratio, 369
Acquisition, 72
  for equity securities, 166
  expenses, 91
  method, 81
  of property rights, 103
Actuarial cost method, 208
Advance
  payments, 88
  royalties, 91
Adverse opinion, 323, 333
Advertising
  costs (expenses), 91
  evaluation of, 516
  ratios, 516
Affiliate, income of, 187
Affiliation, 72

Aging cycle, 65
AICPA; *see* Accounting Principles Board (APB) Opinions
Allan Wood Steel Company, 222
Allis Chalmers Mfg. Co., 237
Allocation, 60
  assumption of activity, 61
  overhead, 61, 78
Alternatives, acceptable, 92
Amerada Hess Corporation, 236
American Bakeries Co., 104
American Can Company, 441, 454
American Express Co., 192
American Financial Corporation, 184
American Machine & Foundry, 189
American Management Association, 438
American Saint Gobain Corporation, 123
Amortization
  of bond discount or premium, 76
  of gain or loss from sale of properties, 104
  as intangibles, 85
  rate of, 87
  of special tools and similar costs, 498
Analysis of financial statements; *see* Financial statements analysis
Analyst
  credit, 3
  external, 3
  internal, 3
  merger and acquisition, 3
  security, 3
Arthur Andersen & Co., 79
Asset(s)
  carrying values of, 133
  composition, 410
  distribution, measures of, 410
  effect of valuation of specific assets on the validity and quality of reported income, 528
  essential ingredient for earnings, 464
  idle, 78
  importance of carrying amounts of, 527
  intangible, 83
  long-lived, 78
  measurement, 94
  method of acquisition, 81
  "redeployed," 80
  return on modified, 437
  return on total, 437
  tangible, 84
  unproductive, 437
  valuation, 57, 77, 152
  wasting, 81
Asset turnover
  ratio, 449
  relationship between profitability and, 446

Index

Asset utilization, 434
  analysis of, 449, 558
    an illustration, 566
  ratios, 449
    an example of, 566
Atcoa, 107
Audit procedures, 320
  committee on, 318
  confirmation of accounts receivable, 324
  implications inherent in the audit process, 329
  inventory, 66
  limitations, 321
  observation of inventories, 324
  procedural testing, 321
  relationship between internal control and extent of audit testing and nature of, 330
  sampling approach, 329
  validation testing, 321
Auditing standards
  foreign, 167
  general standards, 319
  implications stemming from standards which govern auditor's opinion, 330
  reporting standards, 319
  standards of field work, 319
  Statement on, No. 1, 318
Auditor, 316
  confirmation of liabilities, 100
  independence, 317
  integrity, 317
  liability, 317
  responsibility, 317
Auditor's opinion, 93, 315
  adverse opinion, 323
  "clean" opinion, 318
  conditions giving rise to qualifications, disclaimers or adverse opinions, 322
  disclaimer of opinion, 323
  failure of financial statements to conform to generally accepted accounting principles, 324
  fairness of financial statements, 42
  implications for analysis, 328
  limitations in the scope of the audit, 324
  meaning, 317
  qualified opinion, 322
  what the analyst needs to know, 316
Auditor's report
  disclaimer, 322
  level of assurance, 320
  long-form report, 327
  opinion section, 321

Auditor's report—*Cont.*
  qualification, 322
  scope paragraph, 318
  special reports, 328
  standard short-form report, 322
  unaudited reports, 328
  work of other auditors, 502
Average
  cost, 63
    an example of, 69
  use of, 451

B

Backer, Morton, 472
Balance sheet, 12
  analysis as a check on the validity and quality of reporting earnings, 527
  analysis, index numbers, 30
  analysis and the quality of earnings, 528
  comparative, an example, 20
  diagram, 13
Banker, 16
Bankruptcy, 106
Bar Chris Construction Company case, 330
Bargain purchase credit, 86, 113
Base year, 27
Beaver, William H., 431
Bennett, William M., 448
Berry Petroleum Company, 101
"beyond any reasonable doubt," 94
Billings on uncompleted contracts, 112
Bond, 98
  below par, 98
  discount, 51, 88, 98
  par, 98
  premium, 76
Book value, 128
  adjustments for, 133
  net, 79
  per share, 128
    an example of, 129
  significance of, 132
  uses of, 132
Borrower, 98
Breach in loan provision, 102
Break-even analysis, 482
  analytical implications, 493
  applications, an illustration, 491
  assumptions in, 490
  concepts underlying, 482
  contribution margin approach, 487
  equation approach, 483
  graphic presentation, 484
  illustration of, 482

582　Index

Break-even analysis—*Cont.*
　problem areas and limitations, 489
　steps in preparation of, 485
　uses and their implications, 491
Break-even chart
　example of, 492
　interpretation of, 492
Briloff, Abraham J., 149
Brunswick Corporation, 53, 189
Business Combinations, 136
　accounting for, 145
　　APB *Opinion Nos. 16* and *17,* 149
　accounting methods for, 147
　initiated before November 1, 1970, 87

C

Call provision, 123
Capital, 120, 400
　additional paid-in, 124
　changes arising from business combinations, 124
　cost of, 401
　　Modigliani-Miller thesis, 401
　distribution, 125
　donations, 124
　in excess of par or stated value, 124
　gains, 75
　losses, 75
　paid-in, 124
　surplus, 124
　　accounts, 124
Capital stock
　classification, 121
　disclosure, 121
　outstanding, 121
Capital structure
　analysis, common-size statements, 407
　complex, 250
　diagram of, 397
　effect of, on long-term solvency, 406
　importance of, 396
　measures, interpretation of, 409
　ratios, 407
　significance of, 400
　simple, 247
Capital structure and long-term solvency, 396
　accounting principles, 396
　analysis of, 396
　　an illustration of, 563
　ratios, 564
Capitalization of
　costs, 83
　earnings, 41
　lease, 104
Carrying amount of assets, 87

Cash, 49, 341, 347, 375
　compensating balances, 49
　to current liabilities ratio, 351
　equivalents, 341, 347
　flow, 290
　　coverage of fixed charges, 425
　　limitations of the concept, 291
　　overview of, patterns, 374
　　ratios, 370
　forecasts, 40
　　difference between short-term and long-term, 381
　　illustration of short-term, 378
　　short-term, 377
　　ratios, 350
　restriction on, 49, 341
　statement of sources and applications of cash, 285–86
Celanese Corporation, 59, 194
Cenco Instruments Corporation, 110
City Investing Company, 164, 264, 288
Claim, 97
"Clean" opinion, 93
Collateral, pledged, 98
Collectibility
　implications for analysis, 188
　of receivables, 113
Collection period, 354
Commitment(s), 110, 399
　disclosure, 110
　to issue stock, 122
Common-size
　balance sheets, an example of, 33, 553
　comparison, 34
　financial statements, 32
　income statements, an example of, 554
　intercompany comparison, 36
Common-size analysis
　of balance sheet, 34
　of current assets composition, 368
　of current ratio, 364
　of income statement, 34, 500
　of revenue, 468
Common stock, 121
　equivalents, 250
　par value, 121
　residual rights of, 132
　two-class, as common stock equivalents, 251
　warrants, 131
Common stockholders, 121
Comparability of inventory, 67
Comparative financial statements, 19, 27
　balance sheets, 24
　　an example of, 20
　　price-level adjusted, 310
　changes in financial position, 29

Comparative financial statements—*Cont.*
  condensed operating statements, an example of, 28
  income statements
    an example of, 26
    price-level adjusted, 310
    year-to-year comparison, 19
Comparison with external data, 18
Compensating (cash) balances, 50, 351
Completed contract method, 64, 182
Compounded annual growth rate, 534
Computation of ratios
  asset-utilization, 38
  capital structure and long-term solvency, 38
  operating performance, 38
  return on investment, 38
  short-term liquidity, 38
Computer assisted
  credit extension analysis, 573
  financial analysis, 572
  security analysis, 574
Computer Sciences Corporation, 92
Conglomerate company, definition of, 468
Consideration given for goodwill, 83
Consistency, 67, 327
Consolidated
  balance sheet, 80
  financial statements, 137
  income, 80
Consolidating financial statements, 137
Consolidation
  basic technique of, 137
  cost method, 141
  equity method, 139
  examples of, 137
  implications for analysis, 143
  of leasing subsidiaries, 139
  principles governing, 138
  validity of taking up earnings, 143
Construction, 77
Continental Vending case, 330
Contingency, 111
Contingent
  assets, unrecorded, 94
  liabilities, 111, 401
    disclosure, 111
    examples of, 112
    unrecorded, 133
  shares, as common stock equivalents, 251
Continuity of business affairs, 463
Contract, 91
  accounting, 181
  implications for analysis, 189
Contribution margin
  approach of break-even analysis, 487
  importance of, 497

Contribution margin—*Cont.*
  ratio, 487
  unit, 487
Control
  incomplete or temporary, in consolidation, 139
  internal, return on investment as a tool of, 436
  of the lessor, 104
Control Data Corporation, 112
Convalariums of America, Inc., 189
Conversion, 132
  feature, 98
  period of inventories, 361
  rights, 122
Convertibility, 98
Convertible
  debentures, 131
  debt, 222, 250, 400
  preferred stock, 73, 250
  securities, 246
Copyright, 86
Corporate joint venture, 73
Cost
  accounting, 60
  accrual, 192
  balances, 6
  behavior of, 482
  capitalized, 84
  current expensing of, 59
  definition of, 58
  in depletion, 194
  developing and testing, 61
  of development, 81
  of discovery, 81
  estimated and actual, 61
  of exploration, 81
  flow, 62
  general and administrative, 61
  of goods sold
    analysis of, 478
    cost classification method, 478
  includible, 58
  intangible assets, 83
  inventoriable, 58
  method, 141
    investment in subsidiary, 187
  objectivity of, 7
  plus-fixed-fee contract, 52
  of sales, 478
    analysis of, additional consideration in, 499
    analysis of variation in, 481
  unamortized, 86
Coupon rate, 89, 98
Convenants
  debt, 98
  restrictive, 132

584 Index

Conversion privilege, 98
Credit analyst, 3, 66
  importance of income analysis to, 458
Credit Research Foundation, Inc., 357
Creditor, 144, 401
Cudahy Packing Company, 79, 466
Current
  costs, 297
  expenditure, 77
  expensing of cost, 59
  market value, 78
  operating cycle, 97; see also Normal operating cycle
  replacement cost, 64
  value, 77
Current assets, 49, 65, 340
  common-size analysis of, 368
  general rule of classification, exceptions to, 341
  inclusion of fixed assets in, 342
  problem areas in definition, 344
Current liabilities, 97, 343, 348, 362
  contingent liabilities, 344
  contract for the construction or acquisition of long-term assets, 344
  differences in the nature of, 363
  loan guarantees, 344
  problem areas in definition, 344
Current ratio, 347
  changes over time, 364
  common-size analysis, 364
  implications of the limitations, 348
  interpretation of, 364
  limitations of, 346
  measures which supplement, 350
  possibilities of manipulation, 365
  rules of thumb standards, 366
  trend analysis, 364
  valid standards, 367
  as a valid tool of analysis, 349
Customer accounts, purchased, 91

D

Data storage and retrieval, 573
Days
  purchases in accounts payable, 363
  sales in accounts receivable, 354
  to sell inventory, 359
    alternative computation, 360
Debentures, 98
Debt, 401
  in consolidated financial statements, 144
  discount and expenses, 91
  equity ratio, 408
  instrument, 72
  long-term lease as, 106

Debt—Cont.
  reasons for employment of, 402
  with warrants, 222
Decision making
  by external analysts, 462
  internal, return on investment as tool of, 436
  process in financial analysis, 17
Deere & Company, 235
Default, 98
Deferred
  charges, 88
    effect on reported income, 529
    implications for analysis, 91
    reasons for, 88
  compensation contracts, 211
  costs, reasons for, 88
  credits, 112, 398
    implications for analysis, 115
  expenses, 91
  gains, 113
  income, 112
    examples of, 113
    taxes, reversal of, 398
  investment tax credit, 114
    amortization, 114
  profit, 113
  reserves, 115
  taxes, 113, 398
    credit, 114
    liability, 114
Deficit, 125
Delay rentals, 416
Depletion, 81, 194
Deposits, 112
Depreciation, 43, 194
  accelerated, 197
  annuity method, 205
  as bookkeeping expense, 202
  changing price levels, 204
  compound interest method, 199
  cost of sales, as an element of, 498
  declining balance, 197
  decreasing charge method, 197
  definition, 79
  difference between book and tax, 201
  double-declining balance method, 198
  evaluation of, 43
  to gross plant and equipment ratio, 498
  guidelines and rules, 195
  implications for analysis, 200
  method of allocation, 196
  obsolescence, 79, 195
  physical deterioration, 195
  price level changes and, 296
  rate, factors influencing, 195
  rate of return, illustration of, 205

Depreciation—*Cont.*
  in real estate, 203
  as source of funds, 292
  straight-line method, 196
  sum-of-the-years'-digits method, 198
  technical innovation, 79
  unit of production method, 199
  useful life, 195
Development costs, 90, 214
  implications for analysis, 219
Dilution
  anti-dilution, 253
  of the equity, 250
Direct measurement, 17
Disclaimer of opinion, 323, 333
Disclosure, 67
  capital stock, regarding, 121
  of commitments, 110
  of contingent liabilities, 111
  extraordinary items, 231
  lack of, 461
  on leasing, 105
  standards of, 232
Discount
  on bonds, 51, 88, 98
  on notes, 55
Discretionary costs, 499
  evaluation of, 515
Distortion, 78
Diversified enterprise
  data by significant enterprise segments, 469
  disclosure of "line of business" data, 471
  financial reporting by, 468
  implications for analysis, 474
  income statement data, 471
  recommendations by APB on disclosure, 472
  recommendations of research studies on disclosure, 472
  SEC reporting requirements, 473
Dividend, 125
  arrearage of, 121
  cumulative, 121
  in kind, 125
  on preferred stock, 121
  stock, 125
  in stock of another corporation, 125
Dollar, size of, 78
Donaldson, Gordon, 394
Donaldson, Lufkin & Jenrette, Inc., 50
Double-entry bookkeeping, 8
  basic equation of, 9
E. I. duPont de Nemours and Company, 438
Dynamic models, 374

E

Earning(s)
  available to meet fixed charges, 412
  average, 465, 523
  averaging and trend determination, methods, 530
  balance sheet analysis and the quality of, 528
  contribution and growth rates by industry segments, 513
  contribution matrix, segmented, 513
  coverage, measures of, 411; *see also* Fixed coverage ratio
  coverage, minimum standard, 429
  coverage of preferred dividends, 427
  coverage ratio
    evaluation of, 428
    an illustration of calculation, 420
  extrapolation of, 514
  factors affecting the quality of, 461
  to fixed charges; *see* Fixed charges, coverage ratios
  growth, 146
  interim, 537
  level, evaluation of, 511
  minimum, 465
  overstatement in prior years, 88
  power, 75, 469
  projection of, 513
  quality of, 512
  trends
    evaluation of, 536
    importance of, 465
    monitoring, 530
  unremitted, 76
  variability
    evaluation of, 464, 536
    importance of, 428
Earnings per share, 246
  APB *Opinion No. 15*, 247
  common stock equivalents, 250
  complex capital structure, 250
  comprehensive illustration of computation of, 257
  disclosures, 256
  elections as of May 31, 1969, 256
  fully diluted, 254; *see also* Fully diluted earnings per share
  implications for analysis, 265
  pooling of interest, an example of, 248
  primary, 250; *see also* Primary earnings per share
  purchase, an example of, 248
  requirements for additional disclosures, 256
  retroactive adjustment for stock dividend and stock option, 248

586   Index

Earnings per share—*Cont.*
  simple capital structure, 247
  statement accounting for changes in, 267
  weighted average of common shares outstanding, 247
Eckmar Corporation, 59
Economic life, 86
Effective interest rate, 98
E. F. MacDonald Company, 351
Employee
  benefits, 211
  compensation, 117
  stock purchase plan, 122
EPS, 246; *see also* Earnings per share
Equity, 400
  common stock, 398
  versus cost method, an example of, 142
  growth rate, 452
  implications for analysis, 132
  investor, 16; *see also* Security analyst
  in leased property, 104
  method, 139
    corporate joint venture, 73
    an example of, 73
    investment in subsidiary, 187
    procedures followed in applying, 140
    validity of taking up earnings, 143
  securities, 50
  trading on the, 402
    an example of, 404
  turnover, 453
Equity capital, 92
  composition of, 132
  to equity capital plus all liabilities ratio, 408
  to long-term debt ratio, 408
  at market value, 408
  to total liabilities ratio, 407
Equity Funding Corporation of America case, the, 330
Evidence, indirect, 17
Excess of cost as unidentifiable intangibles, 84
Excess of par, 98
Exeter Chemical Company, 390
Expected life, 77
Expense accrual, 192
Exploration and development in extractive industries, 216
Exploration rights, 83
Exploratory expenditures, 214
  accounting treatment of, 218
  implications for analysis, 218
External
  analyst, decision-making by, 482

External—*Cont.*
  business expansion, 145
  data, 18
    advantages of, 18
    care in use of, 18
Extraordinary charge, 80
Extraordinary gains and losses, 126, 229, 519
  all-inclusive concept, 230
  analysis and evaluation, 521
  current-operating-performance concept, 230
  determining criteria of, 521
  disclosure, 231
  effect of, on enterprise resources, 525
  effect of, on evaluation of management, 525
  foreign currency translation, 170
  implications for analysis, 231
  implicit message of, 520
  infrequency of occurrence, 231
  items affecting results of prior years, 229
  materiality, 233
  position of accounting profession, 232
  significance of accounting treatment and presentation, 519
  technique of offset, 234
  unusual nature, 231

F

Fair
  market value, 83
  presentation of financial statements, 325
  rental value in lease, 103
  value, 41, 54, 153
    in lease, 104
    in purchase accounting, 148
Farrington Manufacturing Company, 89
FASB; *see* Financial Accounting Standards Board
Feasibility tests, 481
Fedders Corporation, 127
Fifo, 62
  an example of, 69
Finance charge, unearned, 182
  methods of recognition of, 182
Finance company accounting, 182
Financial
  accounting
    data, 4
    reports, 4
  analysts and auditing, 316
  condition, statement of, 12
  costs, 502
  forecasts, 374

Financial—*Cont.*
  leverage
    concept of, 402
    effects, analysis of, 454
    index, 405, 453
    measuring the effects of, 405
    other advantages of, 404
    stability of an enterprise, 396
Financial Accounting Standards Board, 105
Financial analysis
  approach to, 544
  computer assisted, 572
  in credit extension, 574
  earmarks of a good analysis, 546
  security analysis, 574
  significance of the "building block" approach, 544
  special industry or environmental characteristics, 547
  specialized, 574
  summary and conclusion, an illustration, 569
Financial Executives Research Foundation, 473
Financial position, statement of changes in, 40, 269
  abbreviated method of preparation, 284
  analysis of, 382
  analysis of fixed assets accounts, 273
  basis of preparation, 270
  broad concept of, 270
  common-size, 385
  comparative, 29
  conclusion, 394
  current items, 270
  evaluation of, 391
  example of, 284
  funds provided by operations, 276
  implications for analysis, 287
  inclusion of "funds flow" and earnings forecasts in prospectuses, 394
  noncurrent items, 270
  nonfund requiring charges, 276
  operations summary account, 279
  preparation, an example of, 271, 276
  projection of, 392, 561
    for evaluation of the impact of adversity, 393
  relationship between income statement and balance sheet, 275
  significance and purpose, 269
  sources of funds from operations, 274
  sources and uses of funds summary account, 279

Financial position, statement of changes in—*Cont.*
  "T-account" technique, 276
  uses of, 270, 288
Financial statement(s), 12
  audited, 67
  common-size, 32
  comparative, 19
  historical-dollar, 298
  interim nature of, 6
  price-level changes and, 7
  property, plant and equipment, 81
  responsibility for, 315
  restated for general price-level changes, 298; *see also* Price-level statements
  uncertainty of, 6
Financial statement analysis
  approaches to, 3, 17
  banker's interest, 16
  "building blocks" of, 40, 544
  comparison, 17
  comprehensive, 542
    an illustration, 548
  equity investor interest, 16
  function of, 3
  as indirect evidence, 17
  methodology, 542
  raw material of, 4
  steps in, 542
  tools and techniques of, 16
  uses of, 572
Financing method of lease, 109
Finney, A. H., 368
First-in-first-out; *see* Fifo
Fitzpatrick, Paul J., 431
Fixed
  assets, 77
    equity capital ratio to, 411
    loss of utility, 78
    tangible, 77
  costs, 61, 192, 489
    level, the significance of, 495
  overhead, 62; *see also* Overhead costs
Fixed charges, 412
  adjustment for nontax deductibility, 423
  cash flow coverage of, 425
  coverage, 108
  coverage ratios, 412, 422
    determining the amount of income to be included in computation of, 412
    evaluation of, 428
    example of computation, 232, 415
    example of minimum standard, 429
    expanded concept of fixed charges, 423

Fixed charges—*Cont.*
  coverage ratios —*Cont.*
    fixed charges to be included in computation of, 413
    illustration of calculation, 420
    importance of method of computation and of underlying assumptions, 429
    pro forma computations of, 424
    SEC standard, 422
    SEC on treatment of interest, 414
    guarantees to pay, 420
    recognition of benefits stemming from, 424
Flow
  of costs, 62
  of goods, 62
Forecasts
  differences between short-term and long-term, 381
  forecasting, 514
  income elements to be used, 462
Foreign
  accounting practices, 166
  auditing standards, 166
  currencies
    current/noncurrent approach, 169
    devaluation gains or losses, 170
    monetary/nonmonetary approach, 170
    translation of, 168
    translation gains and losses, 170
    translation process, 168
  investment, political climate, 143
  operations, 136
    accounting for, 166
    implications for analysis, 171
Form 10k, 118
Formulae as intangible assets, 83
Fortune, 292, 351
Franchise(s)
  accounting, 181
  cost of, 86
  as identifiable tangibles, 84
  as intangible assets, 83
Fraud, 461
Freight-in, 58, 77
Fully diluted earnings per share, 254
  anti-dilution, 253
  computation of, 254
  example of computation, 255
  treasury stock method, 254
Funds
  flow
    analysis, 374
      illustration of, 559
    diagram, 376
    overview of, patterns, 374

Funds—*Cont.*
  provided by operations, 276, 392
  stability of flow of, 427
  sources of, 276
  statement, 269; *see also* Statement of changes in financial position
  statement of sources and applications (uses) of funds, 276; *see also* Statement of changes in financial position
  uses of, 276
Future
  contingent benefits, 83
  costs, 117, 164
  expected benefits, 83, 89
  income tax benefits, 91
  losses, 117, 164
  obligations, 83
  operations, 88
  period, 88
  recoverability, 89
  services as liability, 97
Future directed costs, 502
  evaluation of, 515
  others, 519

G

Gain or loss
  material, from the sale of properties, 104
  from sale of treasury stock, 124
Garlock, Inc., 94
General and administrative costs (expenses), 61, 502
General Aniline & Film Corporation, 123
General Development Corporation, 180, 257, 285
General Foods Corporation, 109
General Leisure Products Corporation, 165
General Motors, 86
General price-level, gains and losses, 250
  auditor's reference to, meaning of, 332
Generally accepted auditing standards, 318
Georgia Pacific Corporation, 99
Glen Alden Corporation, 130
Going concern
  convention, 66
Goodwill, 83, 94, 219
  accounting for, 87
  acquisition of, 88
  arising from investment, 141, 147
  effect of amortization of, 166
  excess of cost over book value of assets acquired, 221
  expiration of, 221

Index   589

Goodwill—*Cont.*
 fair market value, 220
 forty-year maximum life, 88
 implications for analysis, 220
 intangible, 86
 in purchase method, 148, 154
 tax effect, 221
 treatment of, 155
 write-off as extraordinary item, 221
Gould Inc., 148
Government contracts, 52
Government securities, 97
Graham, Dodd and Cottle, 416
The Grand Union Company, 127
Graniteville Company, 67
Gross margin
 changes in
  analysis of, 479
  interpretation of, 481
  variation in, statement accounting for, 481
Gross National Product Implicit Price Deflator, 301
Gross profit, 478
 analysis of change in, an example of, 479
 factors in the analysis of, 479
 margin, 478
 method, 64
 percentage, 479
Guarantees, 117

H

"Hell-and-high-water" leases, 420
Hickman, W. Braddock, 431
Historical cost, 77, 297
 usefulness, 82
Historical summaries of financial information, 244
Holdren, George C., 68
Home Insurance Company, 165
Homogeneity, lack of, in consolidation, 139
Horizontal analysis, 32; *see also* Trend analysis
Horrigan, James O., 432

I

Identifiable assets, 84
Idle capacity, 78
Import duty, 58
Imputed interest, 54, 91
Incentives for sale, 98
Income
 analysis, the major objectives of, 458

Income—*Cont.*
 concepts of, 176
 definition of, 436, 459
 before depreciation, 202
 determining trend of, 464
 equalization, 116
 implications for analysis, 188
 manipulation, 143, 203
 meaning of, 175, 459
 recognition problems, 185
 smoothing, 116, 465
  forms of, 466
 of subsidiaries and affiliates, 187
Income statement, 14
 accounting principles used and their implications, 467
 analysis, 175, 207
  components of, 467
  significance of, 458
  tools of, 467
 common-size analysis, 34, 500
 diagram, 14
 distortions, 239
 effect of the variety of accounting principles on reported income, 241
 erratic elements in, 463
 ideal income figure, 239
 implications for analysis, 238
 index number analysis of, 500
 projected, an example of, 560
 tax loss carry-backs and carry-forwards, 223
 uncertainties, 239
 value of assets, 83
Income tax, 223, 503
 adjustments, 126
 in computation of return on investment, 440
 difference between tax and book accounting, 224
 disclosure on, 506
 federal, 94
 implications for analysis, 228
 permanent tax differences, 504
 tax allocation, 224
 tax loss carry-backs and carry-forwards, 223
Inconsistency, accounting, 84
Indebtedness, evaluation of the terms of, 101
Indefinite life, 91
Indenture, 98
Indeterminate life, 84
Index number, 27
 balance sheet analysis, an example of, 30
 comparison, 29
 computation, 29

Index number—*Cont.*
  condensed operating statement analysis, an example of, 32
  trend series, 27
Indian Head, Inc., 419
Industry conditions and practices, 101, 547
Inflation, effects of, on financial statements, 312
Insolvency, risk of, 396
Installation, 77
Installment
  purchase
    APB *Opinion No. 5*, 103
    by lease, 103
  receivables, 342
  sales
    deferred profit on, 113
    revenue recognition, 179
Insurance, 43
Intangible(s)
  acquired, 84
  amortization of, 85
  assets, 83, 400
    unrecorded, 94, 133
  costs, 84, 91
  costs of developing, maintaining or restoring, 84
  drilling and development costs, 91
  exchange for property, 83
  identifiable, 84
  implications for analysis, 87
  method of acquisition, 84
  as most valuable asset, 87
  other considerations regarding the accounting for, 85
  purchased, 83
  recording of, 84
  unidentifiable, 84
  valuation, 84
Intercompany
  comparison, 35
  profits and losses, 140
  transactions, 137
Intercorporate investments, 136
  accounting methods for, 136
  implications for analysis, 143
  less than majority ownership, 143
  reasons for, 136
Interest
  capitalized, 417
  costs (expenses), 222
    during construction, 77, 222
    implications for analysis, 222
    imputation of, 99, 222
  effect of tax deductibility of, 404
  implicit in lease obligations, 415
    position of SEC, 416

Interest—*Cont.*
  method, 55
    an example of, 55
    as specified in APB *Opinion No. 21*, 54
  rate
    average effective, paid, 503
    effective, 98
    imputed, 54
  in return on investment computation, 442
Interim reports
  APB *Opinion No. 28*, 538
  earnings, 537
  implications for analysis, 539
  SEC reporting requirements, 538
Interim statements, 537
Internal control, 320
International Industries, 342
Inventory, 51, 342, 348
  accounting, 62
  audit procedures, 66
  book figure, 68
  classification, 65
  comparability, 67
  conversion period of, 361
  cost flows, 62
  current requirement, 65
  days to sell, 359
  effect of alternative methods of inventory methods, 361
  in excess of current requirements, 342
  financial analysis on, 66
  implications for financial analysis, 65
  includible costs, 58
  liquidity of, 358
  under long-term contracts, 64
  method(s), 69
    effect on ratios, 70, 361
    example of, 69
    interim statements, 64
  price level changes and, 297
  reserves, 167
  significance to financial analysts, 57
  tobacco and liquor industries, 65
  turnover, measure of, 358
  turnover ratio, 358
    interpretation of, 360
  valuation, 58
    effect on reported income, 529
    example of, 63
    implications for analysis, 65
    "at market," 64
    objective of, 63
    price level, 63
Investee, 73
Investment(s), 51
  account, 137

Investment(s)—*Cont.*
  accounting for, 74, 187
  base
    averaging, 440
    for computation of return on investment, 437
    depreciable assets in, 438
    difference between investor's cost and enterprise, 439
    relating income to, 440
  carrying amount of, 75, 351
  in common stock, 72, 140
    20 percent, 72, 74
    20 percent – 50 percent, 73–74
    over 50 percent, 74
  corporate joint venture, 73
  decision, illustration of, 41
  definitions of, 436
  implications for anaysis, 74
  intercorporate, 136
  long-term, 72, 76
  loss in value, 75
  losses on, in subsidiaries and affiliates, 190
  market value, 107
  overvaluation, 76
  in research, 89
  size of, 74
  in suppliers, 72
  tax credit, 94, 227; *see also* Deferred investment tax credit
    flow-through method, 227
  undervaluation, 74
  valuation of, 51
Investor, 74
  in common stock, 401
  cost of, 439
Issuance of bond, 98

J–K

Johnson & Johnson, 170
Joint venture(s), 76
  corporate, 73
  earnings, 76, 188
Kinney National Service Co., 131

L

Labor, 60
Last-in-first-out; *see* Lifo
LCM; *see* Lower of cost or market
Lease
  breakdown of rentals, 108
  capitalization, 108
  contract, 86
  disclosure requirement of SEC, 105
  equity build up, 104
  finance, 183

Lease—*Cont.*
  as financing method, 103
  implications for analysis, 106
  income, accounting for, 183
  information useful for analysis, 107
  initial term, 103
  long-term, 106
  methods of accounting, 109, 183
  noncancellable, 105
  obligations under, 102
  operating, 183
  purchase, 81
  similarity to debt, 102
  terms, 102
Leasehold, improvements, 86
Leasing
  costs, 91
  as methods of acquisition, 81, 102
  sales of subsidiaries, 185
  short-term, 81
Legal life, 86
Lerner, E. H., 472
Lessee, 103
  operating method, 110
Louis Lesser Enterprises, Inc., 204
Lessor, 104
  financing method, 109
Liabilities, 97
  analysis of, 97
  carrying amount of, importance of, 528
  on consolidated financial statements, 144
  current, 97
  evaluation of terms of indebtedness, 101
  implications for analysis, 100
  long-term, 98
  short-term; *see* Short-term liabilities
License(s)
  cost of, 86
  as intangible assets, 83
Lifo, 62, 68
  example of, 69
  price-level changes, 68, 297
  tax, 63
Line of business, information about, 471
Lionel Corporation, 102
Liquidation
  involuntary, 131
  preference, 131
  premium, 131
  rights of preferred stock, 123
  value of preferred stock, 130
Liquidity, 339
  concepts of, 270
  index, 368
  short-term, 339
  working capital as a measure of, 345

Litigation, contingency, 112
Litton Industries, 235
Long-term report, 329
Long-term
  contract, 64
  debt (liabilities), 98
    current portion, 97
    plus equity capital as the investment base, 439
    to equity capital plus all liabilities ratio, 408
  installment receivables, 52
  investments, 72
  liabilities, 98
  objectives, 72
  projections, usefulness and limitations, 406
  receivables, 54
  solvency
    key elements in the evaluation of, 430
    measuring the effect of capital structure on, 405
Loss
  ascertainable, 65
  deferred, 92
Lower of cost or market, 56, 68

M

McFarland, Walter B., 472
McKee, J. W. Jr., 313
McKesson & Robbins, Inc. case, 66, 329
Maintenance and repairs costs, 499
  evaluation of, 515
  level of, 499
  ratios, 515
Management, 76
  commentary in annual report, 101
  flexibility in reporting, 65
  role of, in earnings, 464
Managerial effectiveness, return on investment as an indicator, of, 435
Margin of safety, 493
  for creditor, 102, 144
Market value
  lower limit, 64
  upper limit, 64
Marketable securities, 50, 76
  accounting treatment of changes in value of, 50
  implications for analysis, 50
  standards of valuation, 76
  write-down, 76
Marketing costs, future directed, 502
Masonite Corporation, 95

Matching
  of cost and revenue, 58, 88
  tax with income, 113
Materiality, implications for analysis, 192
Maturity, 98
Mautz, R. K., 468, 473
May, Marvin M., 146
Mayer, Fred, Inc., 221
Medco, Inc., 66
Membership, as intangible assets, 83
Memorex Corporation, 185
Merger, 246
  distortions in accounting for, 146
  effect on EPS, an example of, 247
  expenses, 91
  growth companies with others, 146
  illustration of, 146
  reasons for, 145
Merwin, Charles L., 431
Miller, M., 401
Mineral deposits, 72
Mining companies, 81
Minority interests, 399
Misrepresentation, 461
Mite Corporation, 468
Modigliani, F., 401
Molybdenum Corporation of America, 65
Monetary
  expression, 5
  items, 298
  unit, unstable, 7
Moonitz, Maurice, 8
Mortgage interest, 43
Moving
  average
    cost, 63
    simple, 530
    weighted, 531
  expenses, 90
Muller, Gerlard G., 168

N

National Association of Credit Management, 357
National Can Corp., 85
National Fuel Gas Co., 342
National General Corp., 76
Natural resources, 81
  cost of development, 83
Natural Video Co., 463
Negative goodwill, 154
Nelson, A. Tom, 109
Net asset value, 128
Net income
  not a specific quantity, 459
  projection of, 463
  ratio, 507

Net income—*Cont.*
  statement accounting for variation in, 508
  specific purpose, examples of, 460
Net realizable value, 86
Net trade cycle, 367
Net working capital, 340
Net worth
  to fixed assets, 38
  to long-term debt, 38
  to total debt, 38
Newmont Mining Corporation, 187
Noncurrent assets, 72
Nonfund items, importance of, in net income, 371
Noninterest bearing debt, 99
Nonmonetary items, 300
Nonoperating gains and losses
  nonrecurring, 524
  recurring, 524
Nonrecurring
  litigation, 126
  nonoperating gains or losses, 524
  operating gains and losses, 521
Normal
  accrual cost, 208
  operating cycle, 52, 65
  operations, 523
  profit margin, 64
North American Rockwell Corporation, 213
Notes, 98
  APB *Opinion No. 21*, 54
  discounted, 344
  market value, 54
  receivable, 52, 356

O

Objectives
  of accounting, for stockholders' equity, 120
  of business enterprise, 434
  of earnings evaluation, 511
  of financial analyst, 316
  of financial audit, 320
  of financial statement analysis, 542
    examples of, 543
  of funds flow analysis, 559
  of income analysis, 458
Objectivity, 81
Observation of physical inventory, 66
Obsolescence, 79
Offset
  assets against liabilities, 97
  debt against assets, 99
  to manipulate current ratio, 365
"One line consolidation," 140

Operating
  cycle, 98
  efficiency, return on investment as a measure of, 437
  income, 79
  gains and losses, nonrecurring, 521
  leverage
    concept of, 493
    illustration of the working of, 494
  losses
    current, 75
    of subsidiary, 90
  method of lease, 109
  performance, analysis of, an illustration, 567
  potential, 495
  ratio, 507
  results, overstated, 89
Operations
  analysis of results of, 458, 478
  results of, 14, 458
Opportunity cost, 82
Option
  capital stock, regarding, 121
  purchases of property by lease, 104
  renewal of lease by lessee, 103
Ordinary course of business, 76
Organization costs, 77, 81, 91
Original cost(s), 101
Other expense, 503
Other income, 503
Overhead costs, 60
  fixed, 62, 78
  overapplied (absorbed), 61
  underapplied (absorbed), 61
  variable, 78
Overstatement
  earnings of prior years, 88
  of income, 162
  of return on investment, 163
Owens Illinois Company, 341

P

Paper profits, 51
Parent company, 75, 137, 143
  discretion of, 143
Part-pooling-part-purchase, 148
Participating securities, as common stock equivalents, 251
Patent, 84, 86
Penn Central Company, 344
Pension
  costs, 91, 207
    actuarial gains or losses, 209
    disclosures required, 210
    illustration of minimum-maximum provision, 209

Pension—*Cont.*
  costs—*Cont.*
    implications for analysis, 212
    materiality of, 212
    maximum provision, 208
    minimum provision, 208
    normal pension costs, 209
    past service cost, 208
    vested benefits, 208
  other supplementary employee benefits, 211
  plan, 117
Percentage-of-completion method, 64, 182
Performance
  diverse views of, 434
  evaluation, criteria of, 434
Period cost(s), 60, 193
  interest expense as, 222
  research expenses as, 89
Plant rearrangement costs, 91
Pooling of interest, 147
  arguments for, 160
  compared to purchase accounting, 149
  conditions for, 150
  illustration of, 156
  implications for analysis, 160
  important features of, 162
  versus purchase accounting, 160
  voting securities, 148
Predictive functions of financial statement analysis, 17
Preferred
  dividends, earnings coverage of, 427
  shareholder, 121
  stock, 121, 400
    convertible, 73
    liquidation value, 130
Premium on
  bond, 98
  notes, 55
  preferred stock, 121
Preoperating costs (expenses), 90
Prepaid
  expenses, 88, 243, 362
    implications for analysis, 91, 360
  insurance, 88
Present value, 54, 81
  capitalization of lease at, 103
  of lease payments, 110
Price changes and inventory methods, 64
Price-earnings ratio, 146
Price level, 78
  adjusted depreciation, 295
  adjusted financial statements, principles underlying the preparation of, 298

Price level—*Cont.*
  changes, 295
    depreciation, 247
    economists, accountants and financial analysts, 295
    effects of, on financial statements, 295
    implications for analysis, 309
    interpretation of effects of, 312
    inventory methods and, 68, 297
    need for comprehensive restatement for financial statements, 297
    research and professional pronouncements, 298
  index
    general, 250
    specific, 311
  statements, 298
    blance sheet, 309
    general price level gain or loss computation, 303
    illustration of restatement, 301
    income statement, 302
    limitations of restatement technique, 311
    meaning of restated figures, 307
    rolling forward, 304
Price Waterhouse & Company, 114
  study on deferred tax 227
Primary earnings per share, 250
  computation of, 251
  exceptions to treasury stock method, 252
  an example of, 253
  treasury stock method, 251
Prime rate, 55
Principal repayment requirements, 417
Prior period adjustments, 125
Process(es), as intangible assets, 83
Product
  costs, 193
    direct, 193
    indirect, 193
    joint, 193
  lines
    analysis of, 470
    trend percentage of sales by, 475
  new, 89
  research and development costs, 90
Production level, 61
Profitability, relationship between asset turnover and, 449
Pro forma
  financial statements
    balance sheet, an example of, 381
    forecasting, as an aid to, 378
    income statement, an example of, 384
    ratios and other relationships derived from, 378

Pro forma—*Cont.*
　supplementary disclosure under the purchase method, 155
Progress billings, 64, 182
Projections, of earnings, return on investment as a method for, 435
Promoter stock, 88
Promotional expenses, 91
Property
　losses and conversions, 91
　material equity in, 103
　right(s), 81, 103
　taxes, 91
Property, plant, and equipment, 77
　acquisition and disposition of, 11
　flows to and from, 11
　implications for analysis, 81
　recovery of, 12
　self-constructed, 77
　use of, 12
Prospectuses, inclusion of funds flow and earnings forecasts in, 394
Prosperity squeeze, 365
Provision, 116, 399
　carrying amount of, importance of, 528
　for doubtful accounts, 113, 356
　for future costs and losses, 164
　implications for analysis, 118
　for possible losses, 53
　for taxes, 75, 144
　for uncollectible accounts, 56
Public accounting profession, 315
Public utilities, 77
Purchase
　by leasing, 81, 104
　of on-going business, 85
Purchase method of accounting, 163
　allocation of total cost, 154
　application of, 152
　of business combination, 148
　compared to pooling of interest, 149
　contingent additional consideration, 153
　goodwill, treatment of, 155
　guidelines for valuation of assets and liabilities, 154
　illustration of, 158
　implications for analysis, 160
　in investment, 147
　price level and, 166
　pro forma supplementary disclosure, 155
Purchase versus pooling of interest, 160
　illustration of accounting mechanics, 156
　implications for analysis, 160
Purchasing power, 295

Q

Qualified opinion, 101, 333
　categories of, 322
　due to contingency, 101
　due to uncertainty, 333
　example of, due to lack of adherence to generally accepted accounting principles, 325
　"except-for" type, 323
　exception as to consistency, 327
　financial statements subject to unresolved known uncertainties, 326
　uncertainties which do not call for, 334
Quality of earnings, 512
　balance sheet analysis, 528
　evaluation of specific assets, 528
Quick ratio, 369

R

Rappaport, A., 472
Ratio(s)
　analysis, 35
　　empirical studies, 430
　computation of various, 38
　definition of, 35
　distortion in, 81
　interpretation of, 35
　maintenance of, required, 102
　methods of computation, 38
　as predictors of failure, 430
Raw materials, 66
Real estate
　accounting, 179
　company, 99, 104
　taxes, 43, 72
Receivables, 51
　from affiliated companies, 52, 342
　collectibility, 53, 179
　implications for analysis, 56
　installment, 342
　long-term, 54
　　installment, 52
　noninterest bearing, 54
　from officers and employees, 52, 342
Recording function, 8
Recurring
　costs, 117
　nonoperating gains and losses, 524
Redemption of preferred stock, 121
Reinstallation costs, 91
Relevant income, obstacles in the determination of, 461
Rental
　costs, 91
　income, 43
　payments, 81

596 Index

Repairs and maintenance, 43
Replacement costs, 77, 264
Reported income
    effect of valuation of specific assets on the validity and quality of, 529
    manipulation of, 76
Reporting standards, 67
Research and development costs, 89, 214
    accounting problems, 215
    applied, 214
    basic or pure, 214
    current accounting alternatives, 215
    evaluation of, 516
    future potential of, 517
    implications for analysis, 218
    ratio, 518
    types of, 214
    uncertainty, 215
Reserve, 116, 399
    for future costs and losses, 80, 236
    for future losses, 79, 118
    implications for analysis, 118
    wasting assets, 81
Residual claims, 120
Restriction
    indenture, 98
    on retained earnings, 127
Results of operations, analysis of, 458, 478
Retail method, 34
Retained earnings, 125
    appropriation of, 126
    consolidated, 145
    restrictions on, 127
Retirement plan, 90
Return on asset evaluation, other factors to be considered in, 452
Return on investment, 434
    analysis, an illustration of, 537
    analysis and interpretation of, 444
    basic elements of, 436
    computation, illustration of, 441
    importance of, 435
    investment base, 437
    major objectives in the use of, 435
    ratio
        components of, 444
        an example of, 441, 465
Return on stockholders' (shareholders') equity; see Stockholders' equity
Return on total assets
    computation, 441
    curve, a diagram, 447
    example of analysis, 447
    factors affecting, a diagram, 445
Revenue
    accrual of, 177

Revenue—*Cont.*
    analysis of, 468
    implications for analysis, 188
    major sources of, 468
    recognition
        conditions for, 178
        examples of, 185
        implications for analysis, 190
        timing of, 181, 189
    reserve, 186
    stability and trend of, 475
Revolving
    credit, 98
    loan agreement, 343
Riegel Paper Corporation, 80
ROI; *see* Return on investment
Rolling forward of price level adjusted financial statements, 306
Rosenfield, Paul, 312
Royalties, unearned, 112

S

Sale and leaseback, 104
Sales
    analysis of, 468
    by product line, a diagram, 469
    effect of liquidity, 370
    estimate, importance of, 377
    relationship between short-term liquidity and, 451
    as source of funds, 293
Sales to
    accounts receivable ratio, 450
    cash ratio, 450
    fixed assets ratio, 451
    inventories ratio, 450
    other assets ratio, 451
Salvage value, 79
Saunders Leasing System, 184
Schenley Industries, Inc., 186
Scott, O. M., and Sons Co., 88, 218
Seasonal growing and packing expenses, 91
Seasonality, 537
Secret reserves, 167
Securities Exchange Commission, 66
    accounting principles and, 66
    Accounting Series Release
        No. 21, 320
        No. 95, 180
        No. 136, 341
        No. 138, 238
    filings with, 67
    inclusion of "funds flow" and earnings forecasts in prospectuses, 394
    on lease, 105
    on price level adjustment, 296

Index 597

Securities Exchange Commission—*Cont.*
    Release No. 9559 (under 1934 Securities Act), 538
Security analyst, importance of income analysis to, 458
Self-insurance, 117
    reserve for, 117
Selling
    expenses, 500
        comparative statement of, 501
    price of intangibles, 86
Selling, general and administrative expenses, 91
Semivariable costs, 192, 489
Senior claim (securities), 146
    rights and priorities of, 148
Set-up costs, 77
Short-term cash forecasts, 377
Short-term liquidity, 339
    an illustration of analysis, 557
    other measures of, 370
Signal Companies, Inc., 89
Sinking fund, 98
    payment to, 418
Sources of funds, 276
    from operations, 274, 289
Specialized financial analysis, 39
Sprouse, Robert T., 472
Standard & Poor's Corporation, 220
Standard cost, 61
Stanray Corporation, 334
Start-up costs, 90
Stated value, 121
Statement of changes in financial position; *see* Financial position, statement of changes in
Statement of sources and applications of cash, 285
    an example of, 285
    technique of preparation, 286
Statement of variation in gross margin, 40
Statutory merger, 157
Stock
    dividend, 124
    purchase contracts, 251
    split, 125
    warrants, as common stock equivalents, 251
Stock options, 212
    as common stock equivalents, 251
    implications for analysis, 213
    valuation of, 213
Stockholders' equity, 120
    analysis of, 120
    implications for analysis, 134
    return on, 443, 453
        analysis of composition of, 455

Stockholders' equity—*Cont.*
    in return on investment computation, 439
Stover Broadcasting Company, 110
Straight-line depreciation method, 196
Structural analysis of common-size financial statements, 32
Struther Wells Corporation, 94
Sublease, noncancellable, 105
Subscription income, 113
Subsidiary, 74, 137
    debt of, 136
    earnings, 76
    in foreign country, 143
    income of, 187
    provision for taxes on undistributed earnings of, 144
    securities of, as common stock equivalents, 251
    unconsolidated, 104, 139
Sun Oil Company, 217

T

"T-account" technique, 276
    an illustration of, 278
    statement of changes in financial position, 276
Tangible fixed asset, 77
    implications for analysis, 81
Tax
    allocation, 113, 224
        deferred tax, 226
        interperiod, 225
        intraperiod, 227
        permanent difference between tax and financial accounting, 224
        timing difference between tax and financial accounting, 224
    benefits, 116
    carryovers, 94
    deferred, 114
    deductibility of interest, the effect of, 404
    Lifo, 63
    loss carry-forwards and carry-backs, 223
        in computation of return on investment, 440
    postponement of, 116
    provision for, 75
    rate, effective, 504
    ratio, 504
    refunds, 52
Term-loan, 98
Time, Inc., 185

598   Index

Times interest earned
 coverage ratio for an individual bond issue, 421
 ratio, 421
Tishman Realty and Construction Company, 141
Tooling costs, 90
Trademark(s), 84
Training costs, 84
Treasury stock, 124
Trend analysis, 19
 current ratio, 364
 index number, 19
 using comparative financial statements, 19
Trend index, an example of, 554
Trends
 distortion, 465
 earnings, 464

U

Unaudited reports, 328
Uncertainty, 89
 assessing, in regard to liabilities, 101
 collection of receivables, 179
 in consolidation, 139
 in income measurement, 177
  qualified opinion, 326, 333
 in research and development, 215
 use of cost method under, 141
Undepreciated balance, 83
Understatement of assets, 162
Undistributed earnings of subsidiary, 144
Unearned
 finance charge, 113
 rental income, 113
United States Leasing International, 146
Unrealized profit, 113
Useful life, 77, 81
 depreciation, 195
 identifiable intangibles, 84
 leased property, 103
 limited, 86
 unidentifiable intangibles, 85
Uses of funds, 276
U.S. Steel Corporation, 212
Utilities, 43
Utilities & Industries Corp., 82

V

Vacation pay, 91
Validity of deferral, 91
Valuation
 in business combination, 152
 guidelines for, 154

Value
 appraised, 78
 permanent impairment of, 76
 potential, 81
Variability ratio, 533
Variable cost(s), 192, 482, 489
 percentage, the significance of, 495
 ratio, 495
Variance, 61
Variation, overhead, 61
Vatter, W. J., 277
Vertical analysis, 32; *see also* Common-size analysis
Voting rights, 123

W

Wall Street Journal, 92, 293
Stewart Warner Corporation, 190
Warrants, 98, 122
Warranty, 117
Wasting assets, 81
Weighted average, 531
Whittaker Corporation, 292
Willcox & Gibbs, Inc., 90
Winakor & Smith, 430
Window dressing, 365
Woolsey, Sam M., 332
Working capital, 269, 340
 absolute amount of, 345
 analysis of changes in each element of, 283
 classification of items, 271
 as a measure of liquidity, 345
 valid standards, 367
Write-down
 of assets, 78
 of intangibles, 84, 92
 of investments, 141
 of marketable securities, 76
Write-off
 of intangibles, 84, 92
 lump-sum, 88
 rate of, 203
Write-up of assets, 78

Y

Yale Express case, the, 329
Year-end adjustments, 537
Yearly loan payment requirement, 99
 an example of schedule, 99
Year-to-year
 change, 19
 comparison, 19
Youngstown Sheet and Tube Co., 212